Dictionary of Finance and Investment Terms

Fifth Edition

John Downes

Editor, *Beating the Dow*
Former Vice President, AVCO Financial Services, Inc.
Office for Economic Development, City of New York

Jordan Elliot Goodman

Financial Analyst, *NBC News at Sunrise*
Author, *Everyone's Money Book*
Creator, *The Money Answers Program*
Former Wall Street Correspondent,
MONEY Magazine, Time Warner Incorporated
Former Business News Commentator,
Mutual Broadcasting System

BARRON'S

All inquiries should be addressed to:
Barron's Educational Series, Inc.
250 Wireless Boulevard
Hauppauge, NY 11788
http://www.barronseduc.com

Library of Congress Catalog Card No. 98-38302

International Standard Book No. 0-7641-0790-9

Library of Congress Cataloging-in-Publication Data
Downes, John, 1936–
    Dictionary of finance and investment terms / John Downes, Jordan
Elliot Goodman. — 5th ed.
        p.   cm.
    ISBN 0-7641-0790-9
    1. Finance — Dictionaries. 2. Investments—Dictionaries.
I. Goodman, Jordan Elliot. II. Title.
HG151.D69   1998
332′.03—dc21   98-38302
                                                                            CIP

PRINTED IN THE UNITED STATES OF AMERICA

19 18 17 16 15 14 13

CONTENTS

PREFACE TO THE FIFTH EDITION

People retiring in the early years of the 21st century, the baby boom generation, have witnessed a revolution in the world of finance and investment. The forces of globalization assure that their children, face a future just as dynamic.

Deregulation of the securities, banking, and savings industries, starting in the 1970s, made a vast range of financial and investment products and services available to people at all economic levels. It also led to abuses and financial losses that required government intervention and a modernization of investor safeguards.

Merger mania in the "roaring 1980s" saw many of America's best-known corporations embroiled in hostile takeovers or leveraged buyouts financed by junk bonds, giving rise to defensive tactics known by such colorful names as the "poison pill," the "Pac-Man strategy," or the "white knight." Insider trading scandals were one result, but another was the innovation of investment techniques designed to capitalize on the profit opportunities created by corporate takeovers.

The 1990s brought corporate downsizing and restructuring, massive stock buybacks, strategic mergers on a global scale, and a prolonged bull market fueled by corporate profitability, low inflation, and sustained economic growth.

With globalization, the world's economies, more free of trade and economic barriers, have become more interdependent and in some ways more vulnerable. On the eve of the new millennium, floundering Asian economies and a recession in Japan threatened markets in the United States and challenged the confidence of a new European Monetary Union with its common currency, the Euro, and its promise of expanded financial markets.

Advanced communications systems have created both greater simplicity and greater complexity in the more unified world of finance and investment. By linking markets and processing massive information, these systems have given rise to investment vehicles, transactions, and methods of managing risk not previously imaginable.

The generation produced by the baby boomers must plan its personal finances in an economy offering less assurance of future financial security. The restructurings of the 1990s made corporations more efficient but took their human toll, just as the demographics that earlier created surpluses in the Social Security system became less favorable for future recipients. The enormous growth of 401(k) and individual retirement accounts, addresses this problem but also points to its gravity.

The introduction of Roth IRAs, the lowering of long-term capital gains tax rates, and other provisions of the Taxpayer Relief Act of 1997 and the IRS Restructuring and Reform Act of 1998, also recognize the increasing importance of self-reliance in personal financial planning.

This thoroughly revised *Dictionary of Finance and Investment Terms* covers the 20th century's major developments in investments, taxation, economics, consumer and corporate finance, and related fields. Adding a more comprehensive global dimension, it defines and clarifies the language that will be used in financial decision-making in the new millennium.

We wish especially to acknowledge Roberta Yafie, whose fact-checking and research went well beyond the call of duty; Mary Falcon, Barron's editor, who ably and patiently coordinated an immense amount of detail; and our original Barron's editor, Tom Hirsch. Suzanne and Jason Goodman, Katie and Annie Downes, and Nancy Weinberg all sacrificed unselfishly at different stages of the project and we thank them.

We also thank *Accounting Today*, American Association of Individual Investors, American Bankers Association, American Council of Life Insurance, American Express Company, American Institute of Certified Public Accountants, American Society of CLU & ChFC (Chartered Life Underwriters), American Stock Exchange, Associated Credit Bureaus, Bankers Trust Company, A.M. Best & Company, The Bond Buyer, Bond Market Association, Boston Stock Exchange, Chase Manhattan Bank NA, Chicago Board of Trade, Chicago Board Options Exchange, Chicago Mercantile Exchange, Cincinnati Stock Exchange, Coffee, Sugar & Cocoa Exchange, COMEX, Commodity Futures Trading Commission, Dow Jones & Company, Employee Benefit Research Institute, The European Commission, Fannie Mae, Federal Energy Regulatory Commission, Federal Reserve Bank of New York, Federal Trade Commission, FINEX, Frank Russell Company, Futures Industry Association, Goldman Sachs & Company, Health Insurance Institute of America, Hulbert Financial Digest, IBC Organization, I/B/E/S Incorporated, Insurance Information Institute, Intermarket Management Incorporated, Internal Revenue Service, International Petroleum Exchange, International Swaps and Derivatives Association, Investment Management Consultants Association, Investment Program Association, J.P. Morgan, Kansas City Board of Trade, Richard J. Kittrell, Esq/ Kittrell & Kittrell P.C., Liquidity Financial Corporation, Mercer and Company, Merrill Lynch, Minneapolis Grain Exchange, Montreal Exchange/Bourse de Montreal, Morgan Stanley Dean Witter, Morningstar, Mortgage Bankers Association, Municipal Bond Investors Assurance Corporation, National Association of Investors Corporation, National Association of Real Estate Investment Trusts, National Association of Realtors, National Association of Securities Dealers, National Association of Variable Annuities, National Credit Union Administration, New York Cotton Exchange, New York Futures Exchange, New York Life Insurance Company, New York Mercantile Exchange, New York Stock Exchange, Office of Thrift Supervision, Options Clearing Corporation, Options Institute, Pacific Exchange, Pension Benefit Guaranty Corporation, Philadelphia Stock Exchange, Prudential Securities, Salomon Smith Barney, Securities and Exchange Commission, Securities Industry Association, Standard & Poor's, Toronto Stock Exchange, Trimedia Incorporated, U.S. Department of Commerce, U.S. Department of Labor, Value Line Investment Survey, Vancouver Stock Exchange, Visa International, The Weiser Group, Wheat First Butcher Singer Incorporated, Wilshire Associates, Winnipeg Commodity Exchange, World Gold Council, Wrap Industry Association, and Zacks Investment Research.

John Downes
Jordan Elliot Goodman

HOW TO USE THIS BOOK EFFECTIVELY

Alphabetization: All entries are alphabetized by letter rather than by word so that multiple-word terms are treated as single words. For example, **NET ASSET VALUE** follows **NET ASSETS** as though it were spelled **NETASSETVALUE,** without spacing. Similarly, **ACCOUNT EXECUTIVE** follows **ACCOUNTANT'S OPINION.** In unusual cases, abbreviations or acronyms appear as entries in the main text, in addition to appearing in the back of the book in the separate listing of Abbreviations and Acronyms. This is when the short form, rather than the formal name, predominates in common business usage. For example, NASDAQ is more commonly used in speaking of the National Association of Securities Dealers Automated Quotations system than the name itself, so the entry is at **NASDAQ.** Numbers in entry titles are alphabetized as if they were spelled out.

Abbreviations and Acronyms: A separate list of abbreviations and acronyms follows the Dictionary. It contains shortened versions of terms defined in the book, plus several hundred related business terms.

Cross references: In order to gain a fuller understanding of a term, it will sometimes help to refer to the definition of another term. In these cases the additional term is printed in SMALL CAPITALS. Such cross references appear in the body of the definition or at the end of the entry (or subentry). Cross references at the end of an entry (or sub-entry) may refer to related or contrasting concepts rather than give more information about the concept under discussion. As a rule, a term is printed in small capitals only the first time it appears in an entry. Where an entry is fully defined at another entry, a reference rather than a definition is provided; for example, **EITHER-OR ORDER** *see* ALTERNATIVE ORDER.

Italics: Italic type is generally used to indicate that another term has a meaning identical or very closely related to that of the entry. Occasionally, italic type is also used to highlight the fact that a word used is a business term and not just a descriptive phrase. Italics are also used for the titles of publications.

Parentheses: Parentheses are used in entry titles for two reasons. The first is to indicate that an entry's opposite is such an integral part of the concept that only one discussion is necessary; for example, **REALIZED PROFIT (OR LOSS).** The second and more common reason is to indicate that an abbreviation is used with about the same frequency as the term itself; for example, **OVER THE COUNTER (OTC).**

Examples, Illustrations, and Tables: The numerous examples in this Dictionary are designed to help readers gain understanding and to help them relate abstract concepts to the real world of finance and investment. Line drawings are provided in addition to text to clarify concepts best understood visually; for example, technical chart patterns used by securities analysts and graphic concepts used in financial analysis.

A

ABANDONMENT voluntarily giving up all rights, title, or claims to property that rightfully belongs to the owner. An example of abandoned property would be stocks, bonds, or mutual funds held in a brokerage account for which the firm is unable to locate the listed owner over a specified period of time, usually a few years. If ruled to be abandoned, the property may revert to the state under the laws of ESCHEAT. In addition to financial assets, other kinds of property that are subject to abandonment include patents, inventions, leases, trademarks, contracts, and copyrights.

ABC AGREEMENT agreement between a brokerage firm and one of its employees spelling out the firm's rights when it purchases a New York Stock Exchange membership for the employee. Only individuals can be members of the NYSE, and it is common practice for a firm to finance the purchase of a membership, or SEAT, by one of its employees. The NYSE-approved ABC Agreement contains the following provisions regarding the future disposition of the seat: (1) The employee may retain the membership and buy another seat for an individual designated by the firm. (2) The employee may sell the seat and give the proceeds to the firm. (3) The employee may transfer the seat to another employee of the firm.

ABILITY TO PAY

Finance: borrower's ability to meet principal and interest payments on long-term obligations out of earnings. Also called *ability to service.* *See also* FIXED CHARGE COVERAGE.

Industrial relations: ability of an employer, especially a financial organization to meet a union's financial demands from operating income.

Municipal bonds: issuer's present and future ability to generate enough tax revenue to meet its contractual obligations, taking into account all factors concerned with municipal income and property values.

Taxation: the concept that tax rates should vary with levels of wealth or income; for example, the progressive income tax.

ABOVE PAR *see* PAR VALUE.

ABS *see* AUTOMATED BOND SYSTEM.

ABSOLUTE PRIORITY RULE *see* BANKRUPTCY.

ABSORBED

Business: a cost that is treated as an expense rather than passed on to a customer.

Also, a firm merged into an acquiring company.

Cost accounting: indirect manufacturing costs (such as property taxes and insurance) are called absorbed costs. They are differentiated from variable costs (such as direct labor and materials). *See also* DIRECT OVERHEAD.

Finance: an account that has been combined with related accounts in preparing a financial statement and has lost its separate identity. Also called *absorption account* or *adjunct account*.

Securities: issue that an underwriter has completely sold to the public.

Also, in market trading, securities are absorbed as long as there are corresponding orders to buy and sell. The market has reached the *absorption point* when further assimilation is impossible without an adjustment in price. *See also* UNDIGESTED SECURITIES.

ABUSIVE TAX SHELTER LIMITED PARTNERSHIP the Internal Revenue Service deems to be claiming illegal tax deductions—typically, one that inflates the value of acquired property beyond its fair market value. If these writeoffs are denied by the IRS, investors must pay severe penalties and interest charges, on top of back taxes.

ACCELERATED COST RECOVERY SYSTEM (ACRS) provision instituted by the ECONOMIC RECOVERY TAX ACT OF 1981 (ERTA) and modified by the TAX REFORM ACT OF 1986, which established rules for the DEPRECIATION (the recovery of cost through tax deductions) of qualifying assets within a shorter period than the asset's expected useful (economic) life. With certain exceptions, ACRS rules provided for greater acceleration over longer periods of time than ERTA rules, and were effective for property placed in service between 1980 and 1987. *See also* MODIFIED ACCELERATED COST RECOVERY SYSTEM.

ACCELERATED DEPRECIATION Internal Revenue Service-approved methods used in the DEPRECIATION of fixed assets placed in service prior to 1980 when the ACCELERATED COST RECOVERY SYSTEM (ACRS) became mandatory. Such methods provided for faster recovery of cost and earlier tax advantages than traditional STRAIGHT LINE DEPRECIATION and included such methods as DOUBLE-DECLINING BALANCE METHOD (now used in some ACRS classes) and SUM-OF-THE-YEARS' DIGITS METHOD.

ACCELERATION CLAUSE provision, normally present in an INDENTURE agreement, mortgage, or other contract, that the unpaid balance is to become due and payable if specified events of default should occur. Such events include failure to meet interest, principal, or sinking fund payments; insolvency; and nonpayment of taxes on mortgaged property.

ACCEPTANCE

In general: agreement created when the drawee of a TIME DRAFT (bill of exchange) writes the word "accepted" above the signature and designates a date of payment. The drawee becomes the acceptor, responsible for payment at maturity.

Also, paper issued and sold by sales finance companies, such as General Motors Acceptance Corporation.

Banker's acceptance: time draft drawn on and accepted by a bank, the customary means of effecting payment for merchandise sold in import-export transactions and a source of financing used extensively in international trade. With the credit strength of a bank behind it, the banker's acceptance usually qualifies as a MONEY MARKET instrument. The liability assumed by the bank is called its acceptance liability. *See also* LETTER OF CREDIT.

Trade acceptance: time draft drawn by the seller of goods on the buyer, who becomes the acceptor, and which is therefore only as good as the buyer's credit.

ACCOMMODATIVE MONETARY POLICY Federal Reserve policy to increase the amount of money available for lending by banks. When the Fed implements an accommodative policy, it is known as easing the money supply. During a period of easing, interest rates fall, making it more attractive for borrowers to borrow, thereby stimulating the economy. The Fed will initiate an accommodative policy when interest rates are high, the economy is weak, and there is little fear of an outbreak of inflation. Once interest rates have been lowered enough to stimulate the economy, the Fed may become concerned about inflation again and switch to a TIGHT MONEY policy. *See also* MONETARY POLICY.

ACCOUNT
In general: contractual relationship between a buyer and seller under which payment is made at a later time. The term *open account* or *charge account* is used, depending on whether the relationship is commercial or personal.

Also, the historical record of transactions under the contract, as periodically shown on the *statement of account.*

Banking: relationship under a particular name, usually evidenced by a deposit against which withdrawals can be made. Among them are demand, time, custodial, joint, trustee, corporate, special, and regular accounts. Administrative responsibility is handled by an *account officer.*

Bookkeeping: assets, liabilities, income, and expenses as represented by individual ledger pages to which debit and credit entries are chronologically posted to record changes in value. Examples are cash, accounts receivable, accrued interest, sales, and officers' salaries. The system of recording, verifying, and reporting such information is called accounting. Practitioners of accounting are called *accountants.*

Investment banking: financial and contractual relationship between parties to an underwriting syndicate, or the status of securities owned and sold.

Securities: relationship between a broker-dealer firm and its client wherein the firm, through its registered representatives, acts as agent in buying and selling securities and sees to related administrative matters. *See also* ACCOUNT EXECUTIVE; ACCOUNT STATEMENT.

ACCOUNTANT'S OPINION statement signed by an independent public accountant describing the scope of the examination of an organization's books and records. Because financial reporting involves considerable discretion, the accountant's opinion is an important assurance to a lender or investor. Depending on the scope of an audit and the auditor's confidence in the veracity of the information, the opinion can be unqualified or, to some degree, qualified. Qualified opinions, though not necessarily negative, warrant investigation. Also called *auditor's certificate.*

ACCOUNT BALANCE net of debits and credits at the end of a reporting period. Term applies to a variety of account relationships, such as with banks, credit card companies, brokerage firms, and stores, and to classifications of transactions in a bookkeeping system. The same account may be an asset account balance or a liability account balance, depending on which side of the transaction you are on. For example, your bank balance is an asset account to you and a liability account to the bank. Your credit card (debit) balance is a liability account to you and an asset account (account receivable) to the credit card company.

ACCOUNT EXECUTIVE brokerage firm employee who advises and handles orders for clients and has the legal powers of an AGENT. Every account executive must pass certain tests and be registered with the NATIONAL ASSOCIATION OF SECURITIES DEALERS (NASD) before soliciting orders from customers. Also called *registered representative. See also* BROKER.

ACCOUNTING PRINCIPLES BOARD (APB) board of the American Institute of Certified Public Accountants (AICPA) that issued (1959–73) a series of ACCOUNTANT'S OPINIONS constituting much of what is known as GENERALLY ACCEPTED ACCOUNTING PRINCIPLES. *See also* FINANCIAL ACCOUNTING STANDARDS BOARD (FASB).

ACCOUNT RECONCILIATION the process of adjusting the balance in your checkbook to match your bank statement. Your checkbook balance, plus outstanding checks, less bank charges, plus interest (if any), should equal the balance shown on your bank statement.

ACCOUNTS PAYABLE amounts owing on open account to creditors for goods and services. Analysts look at the relationship of accounts payable to purchases for indications of sound day-to-day financial management. *See also* TRADE CREDIT.

ACCOUNTS RECEIVABLE money owed to a business for merchandise or services sold on open account, a key factor in analyzing a company's LIQUIDITY—its ability to meet current obligations without additional revenues. *See also* ACCOUNTS RECEIVABLE TURNOVER; AGING SCHEDULE; COLLECTION RATIO.

ACCOUNTS RECEIVABLE FINANCING short-term financing whereby accounts receivable serve as collateral for working capital advances. *See also* FACTORING.

ACCOUNTS RECEIVABLE TURNOVER ratio obtained by dividing total credit sales by accounts receivable. The ratio indicates how many times the receivables portfolio has been collected during the accounting period. *See also* ACCOUNTS RECEIVABLE; AGING SCHEDULE; COLLECTION RATIO.

ACCOUNT STATEMENT

In general: any record of transactions and their effect on charge or open-account balances during a specified period.

Banking: summary of all checks paid, deposits recorded, and resulting balances during a defined period. Also called a *bank statement.*

Securities: statement summarizing all transactions and showing the status of an account with a broker-dealer firm, including long and short positions. Such statements must be issued quarterly, but are generally provided monthly when accounts are active. Also, the OPTION AGREEMENT required when an option account is opened.

ACCREDITED INVESTOR under Securities and Exchange Commission Regulation D, a wealthy investor who does not count as one of the maximum of 35 people allowed to put money into a PRIVATE LIMITED PARTNERSHIP. To be accredited, such an investor must have a net worth of at least $1 million or an annual income of at least $200,000, or must put at least $150,000 into the deal, and the investment must not account for more than 20% of the investor's worth. Private limited partnerships use accredited investors to raise a larger amount of capital than would be possible if only 35 less-wealthy people could contribute.

ACCRETION

1. asset growth through internal expansion, acquisition, or such causes as aging of whisky or growth of timber.
2. adjustment of the difference between the price of a bond bought at an original discount and the par value of the bond.

ACCRUAL BASIS accounting method whereby income and expense items are recognized as they are earned or incurred, even though they may not have been received or actually paid in cash. The alternative is CASH BASIS accounting.

ACCRUAL BONDS bonds that do not make periodic interest payments, but instead accrue interest until the bond matures. Also known as *zero-coupon bonds. See also* ZERO-COUPON SECURITIES.

ACCRUED BENEFITS pension benefits that an employee has earned based on his or her years of service at a company. *See also* VESTING.

ACCRUED INTEREST interest that has accumulated between the most recent payment and the sale of a bond or other fixed-income security. At the time of sale, the buyer pays the seller the bond's price plus accrued interest, calculated by multiplying the coupon rate by the number of days that have elapsed since the last payment.

Accrued interest is also used in a real estate LIMITED PARTNERSHIP when the seller of a building takes a lump sum in cash at the time of sale and gives a second mortgage for the remainder. If the rental income from the building does not cover the mortgage payments, the seller agrees to let the interest accrue until the building is sold to someone else. Accrued interest deals were curtailed by the 1984 tax act.

ACCRUED MARKET DISCOUNT increase in market value of a DIS-COUNT BOND that occurs because of its approaching MATURITY DATE (when it is redeemable at PAR) and not because of declining market interest rates.

ACCUMULATED DIVIDEND dividend due, usually to holders of cumulative preferred stock, but not paid. It is carried on the books as a liability until paid. *See also* CUMULATIVE PREFERRED.

ACCUMULATED PROFITS TAX surtax on earnings retained in a business to avoid the higher personal income taxes they would be subject to if paid out as dividends to the owners.

Accumulations above the specified limit, which is set fairly high to benefit small firms, must be justified by the reasonable needs of the business or be subject to the surtax. Because determining the reasonable needs of a business involves considerable judgment, companies have been known to pay excessive dividends or even to make merger decisions out of fear of the accumulated profits tax. Also called *accumulated earnings tax.*

ACCUMULATION
Corporate finance: profits that are not paid out as dividends but are instead added to the company's capital base. *See also* ACCUMULATED PROFITS TAX.
Investments: purchase of a large number of shares in a controlled way so as to avoid driving the price up. An institution's accumulation program, for instance, may take weeks or months to complete.
Mutual funds: investment of a fixed dollar amount regularly and reinvestment of dividends and capital gains.

ACCUMULATION AREA price range within which buyers accumulate shares of a stock. Technical analysts spot accumulation areas when a stock does not drop below a particular price. Technicians who use the ON-BAL-ANCE VOLUME method of analysis advise buying stocks that have hit their accumulation area, because the stocks can be expected to attract more buying interest. *See* chart on next page. *See also* DISTRIBUTION AREA.

ACES acronym for *Advanced Computerized Execution System,* run by the NASDAQ stock market. ACES automates trades between order-entry and market-maker firms that have established trading relationships with each other, designating securities at specified quantities for automatic execution. Once trading parameters are set, ACES facilitates order entry, best-price order execution and limited-order maintenance, as well as a variety of inventory control capabilities. Trades are then automatically reported for public dissemination and sent for comparison and clearing.

ACCUMULATION AREA

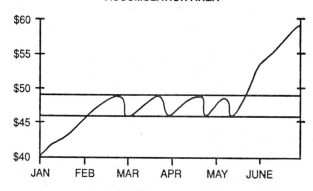

ACID-TEST RATIO *See* QUICK RATIO.

ACKNOWLEDGMENT verification that a signature on a banking or brokerage document is legitimate and has been certified by an authorized person. Acknowledgment is needed when transferring an account from one broker to another, for instance. In banking, an acknowledgment verifies that an item has been received by the paying bank and is or is not available for immediate payment.

ACQUIRED SURPLUS uncapitalized portion of the net worth of a successor company in a POOLING OF INTERESTS combination. In other words, the part of the combined net worth not classified as CAPITAL STOCK.

In a more general sense, the surplus acquired when a company is purchased.

ACQUISITION one company taking over controlling interest in another company. Investors are always looking out for companies that are likely to be acquired, because those who want to acquire such companies are often willing to pay more than the market price for the shares they need to complete the acquisition. *See also* MERGER; POOLING OF INTERESTS; TAKEOVER.

ACQUISITION COST
Finance: price plus CLOSING COSTS to buy a company, real estate or other property.
Investments: SALES CHARGE incurred to buy a LOAD FUND or the original price, plus brokerage commissions, of a security. *See also* TAX BASIS.

ACROSS THE BOARD movement in the stock market that affects almost all stocks in the same direction. When the market moves up across the board, almost every stock gains in price.

An across-the-board pay increase in a company is a raise of a fixed percent or amount for all employees.

ACTING IN CONCERT two or more investors working together to achieve the same investment goal—for example, all buying stock in a company they want to take over. Such investors must inform the Securities and Exchange Commission if they intend to oust the company's top management or acquire control. It is illegal for those acting in concert to manipulate a stock's price for their own gain.

ACTIVE ACCOUNT account at a bank or brokerage firm in which there are many transactions. An active banking account may generate more fees for each check written or ATM transaction completed. An active brokerage account will generate more commission revenue for the brokerage firm than an inactive account. Banks usually impose minimum charges for maintaining a checking and savings account. Many brokerage firms levy a fee if an account does not generate a high enough level of activity. If there is no activity in an account for five years or more, the account may be subject to ESCHEAT procedures in which the account's assets revert to the state.

ACTIVE BOND CROWD members of the bond department of the New York Stock Exchange responsible for the heaviest volume of bond trading. The opposite of the active crowd is the CABINET CROWD, which deals in bonds that are infrequently traded. Investors who buy and sell bonds in the active crowd will tend to get better prices for their securities than in the inactive market, where spreads between bid and asked prices are wider.

ACTIVE BOX collateral available for securing brokers' loans or customers' margin positions in the place—or *box*—where securities are held in safekeeping for clients of a broker-dealer or for the broker-dealer itself. Securities used as collateral must be owned by the firm or hypothecated—that is, pledged or assigned—by the customer to the firm, then by the broker to the lending bank. For margin loans, securities must be hypothecated by the customer to the broker.

ACTIVE MARKET heavy volume of trading in a particular stock, bond, or commodity. The spread between bid and asked prices is usually narrower in an active market than when trading is quiet.

Also, a heavy volume of trading on the exchange as a whole. Institutional money managers prefer such a market because their trades of large blocks of stock tend to have less impact on the movement of prices when trading is generally active.

ACTUALS any physical commodity, such as gold, soybeans, or pork bellies. Trading in actuals ultimately results in delivery of the commodity to the buyer when the contract expires. This contrasts with trading in commodities of, for example, index options, where the contract is settled in cash, and no physical commodity is delivered upon expiration. However, even when trading is in actuals most futures and options contracts are closed out before the contract expires, and so these transactions do not end in delivery.

ACTUARY mathematician employed by an insurance company to calculate premiums, reserves, dividends, and insurance, pension, and annuity rates, using risk factors obtained from experience tables. These tables are based on both the company's history of insurance claims and other industry and general statistical data.

ADDITIONAL BONDS TEST test limiting the amount of new bonds that can be issued. Since bonds are secured by assets or revenues of a corporate or governmental entity, the underwriters of the bond must insure that the bond issuer can meet the debt service requirements of any additional bonds. The test usually sets specific financial benchmarks, such as what portion of an issuer's revenues or cash flow can be devoted to paying interest.

ADDITIONAL PAID-IN CAPITAL *see* PAID-IN CAPITAL.

ADDITIONAL VOLUNTARY CONTRIBUTIONS contributions made by an employee into a tax-deferred savings account, such as a 401(k) or 403(b), beyond the level at which an employer will match the investment. Depending on the level of contributions, these may be made on a pretax or aftertax basis. Tax law limits the total amount of money that can be contributed to such a tax-deferred account. In any case, all funds so contributed accumulate without taxation until withdrawn at retirement. The employee chooses the investment vehicles in which the money is invested.

ADEQUACY OF COVERAGE test of the extent to which the value of an asset, such as real property, securities, or a contract subject to currency exchange rates, is protected from potential loss either through INSURANCE or HEDGING.

ADJUSTABLE RATE MORTGAGE (ARM) mortgage agreement between a financial institution and a real estate buyer stipulating predetermined adjustments of the interest rate at specified intervals. Mortgage payments are tied to some index outside the control of the bank or savings and loan institution, such as the interest rates on U.S. Treasury bills or the average national mortgage rate. Adjustments are made regularly, usually at intervals of one, three, or five years. In return for taking some of the risk of a rise in interest rates, borrowers get lower rates at the beginning of the ARM than they would if they took out a fixed rate mortgage covering the same term. A homeowner who is worried about sharply rising interest rates should probably choose a fixed rate mortgage, whereas one who thinks rates will rise modestly, stay stable, or fall should choose an adjustable rate mortgage. Critics of ARMs charge that these mortgages entice young homeowners to undertake potentially onerous commitments.

Also called a Variable Rate Mortgage (VRM), the ARM should not be confused with the GRADUATED PAYMENT MORTGAGE, which is issued at a fixed rate with monthly payments designed to increase as the borrower's income grows. *See also* CAP; COST OF FUNDS; GROWING EQUITY MORTGAGE; MORTGAGE INTEREST DEDUCTION; SELF-AMORTIZING MORTGAGE; SHARED APPRECIATION MORTGAGE; TEASER RATE.

ADJUSTABLE RATE PREFERRED STOCK (ARPS) PREFERRED STOCK, whose dividend instead of being fixed is adjusted, usually quarterly, based on changes in the Treasury bill rate or other money market rate. The prices of adjustable rate preferreds are less volatile than fixed rate preferreds. Also called *floating rate* or *variable rate* preferred. *See also* CAPS; DUTCH AUCTION PREFERRED STOCK; MANDATORY CONVERTIBLES.

ADJUSTED BALANCE METHOD formula for calculating finance charges based on ACCOUNT BALANCE remaining after adjusting for payments and credits posted during the billing period. Interest charges under this method are lower than those under the AVERAGE DAILY, PREVIOUS BALANCE, and PAST DUE BALANCE METHODS.

ADJUSTED BASIS base price from which to judge capital gains or losses upon sale of an asset like a stock or bond. The cost of commissions in effect is deducted at the time of sale when net proceeds are used for tax purposes. The price must be adjusted to account for any stock splits that have occurred since the initial purchase before arriving at the adjusted basis.

ADJUSTED DEBIT BALANCE (ADB) formula for determining the position of a margin account, as required under Regulation T of the Federal Reserve Board. The ADB is calculated by netting the balance owing the broker with any balance in the SPECIAL MISCELLANEOUS ACCOUNT (SMA), and any paper profits on short accounts. Although changes made in Regulation T in 1982 diminished the significance of ADBs, the formula is still useful in determining whether withdrawals of cash or securities are permissible based on SMA entries.

ADJUSTED EXERCISE PRICE term used in put and call options on Government National Mortgage Association (Ginnie Mae) contracts. To make sure that all contracts trade fairly, the final exercise price of the option is adjusted to take into account the coupon rates carried on all GNMA mortgages. If the standard GNMA mortgage carries an 8% yield, for instance, the price of GNMA pools with 12% mortgages in them are adjusted so that both instruments have the same yield to the investor.

ADJUSTED GROSS INCOME (AGI) income on which an individual or couple computes federal income tax. AGI is determined by subtracting from gross income any unreimbursed business expenses and other allowable adjustments—for example, INDIVIDUAL RETIREMENT

ACCOUNTS, SEP and Keogh payments, and alimony payments. Other adjustments include: forfeiture of interest penalties because of premature withdrawals from a certificate of deposit; capital loss deductions up to $3,000; rent and royalty expenses; 50% of self-employed tax liability; health insurance deductions for the self-employed and net operating losses. AGI is the individual's or couple's income before itemized deductions such as medical expenses, state and local income taxes, and real estate taxes. Once AGI exceeds certain income thresholds detailed in the tax code, some itemized deductions are disallowed. For example, for those married couples filing jointly in 1997 with adjusted gross incomes over $121,200, itemized deductions are reduced by 3% of the excess of AGI, over $121,200. These thresholds are adjusted upwards annually.

ADJUSTMENT BOND bond issued in exchange for outstanding bonds when recapitalizing a corporation that faces bankruptcy. Authorization for the exchange comes from the bondholders, who consider adjustment bonds a lesser evil. These bonds promise to pay interest only to the extent earned by the corporation. This gives them one of the characteristics of income bonds, which trade flat—that is, without accrued interest.

ADMINISTRATOR court-appointed individual or bank charged with carrying out the court's decisions with respect to a decedent's estate until it is fully distributed to all claimants. Administrators are appointed when a person dies without having made a will or without having named an executor, or when the named executor cannot or will not serve. The term *administratrix* is sometimes used if the individual appointed is a woman.

In a general sense, an administrator is a person who carries out an organization's policies.

AD VALOREM Latin term meaning "according to value" and referring to a way of assessing duties or taxes on goods or property. As one example, ad valorem DUTY assessment is based on value of the imported item rather than on its weight or quantity. As another example, the city of Englewood, New Jersey, levies an ad valorem property tax based on the assessed value of property rather than its size.

ADVANCE
Employee benefits: cash given to an employee before it is needed or earned. A travel advance is supplied so that an employee has cash to use on an upcoming business trip. A salary advance is provided to help the employee cover emergency expenses.
Securities: increase in the price of stocks, bonds, commodities, or other assets. Often heard when referring to the movement of broad indexes, e.g., "The Dow Jones Industrials advanced 15 points today."
Trade: advance payment for goods or services that will be delivered in the near future. For example, home contractors require an advance from homeowners to pay for building materials.

ADVANCE-DECLINE (A-D) measurement of the number of stocks that have advanced and the number that have declined over a particular period. It is the ratio of one to the other and shows the general direction of the market. It is considered bullish if more stocks advance than decline on any trading day. It is bearish if declines outnumber advances. The steepness of the A-D line graphically shows whether a strong bull or bear market is underway.

ADVANCE-DECLINE LINE

ADVANCED FUNDED PENSION PLAN pension plan under which assets are set aside in amounts and at times approximately coincident with the accruing of benefit rights. In this way, funds are set aside in advance of the date of retirement.

ADVANCE REFUNDING
Government securities: exchange of maturing government securities prior to their due date for issues with a later maturity. It is through advance refunding that the national debt is extended as an alternative to the economic disruptions that would result from eliminating the debt all at once.

Municipal bonds: sale of new bonds (the refunding issue) in advance, usually by some years, of the first call date of the old bonds (the issue to be refunded). The refunding issue would normally have a lower rate than the issue to be refunded, and the proceeds would be invested, usually in government securities, until the higher-rate bonds become callable. This practice, also called *prefunding*, has been curtailed by several tax acts. *See also* REFUNDING ESCROW DEPOSITS (REDs).

ADVERSE OPINION opinion expressed by a company's independent auditors that the firm's financial statements do not accurately reflect the company's current financial position or operating results. An adverse opinion is a far more serious finding than a QUALIFIED OPINION, in which only some issues are of concern to the auditor. Investors should be extremely cautious about investing in any company with an adverse opinion from its auditors.

ADVERSE SELECTION tendency of people with significant potential to file claims wanting to obtain insurance coverage. For example, those with severe health problems want to buy health insurance, and people going to a dangerous place such as a war zone want to buy more life insurance. Companies employing workers in dangerous occupations want to buy more worker's compensation coverage. In order to combat the problem of adverse selection, insurance companies try to reduce their exposure to large claims by either raising premiums or limiting the availability of coverage to such applicants.

ADVISORY LETTER newsletter aiming to offer financial advice to subscribers. The letter may offer a broad economic and market outlook, or it may focus on a particular sector of the stock, bond, or commodity markets. Some advisory letters specialize in recommending only mutual funds. Some letters also advise their subscribers of new recommendations through a toll-free hotline, which can be updated much more quickly than a printed letter. If the advisory letter recommends specific securities, the author usually is registered with the Securities and Exchange Commission as a REGISTERED INVESTMENT ADVISOR. *See also* HULBERT RATING.

AFFIDAVIT written statement made under oath before an authorized person, such as a notary public.

AFFIDAVIT OF DOMICILE AFFIDAVIT made by the executor of an estate that certifies the decedent's place of residence at the time of death. Before securities can be transferred from an estate, it must be verified that no liens exist against them in the home state of the decedent.

AFFILIATE

In general: two companies are affiliated when one owns less than a majority of the voting stock of the other, or when both are subsidiaries of a third company. A SUBSIDIARY is a company of which more than 50% of the voting shares are owned by another corporation, termed the PARENT COMPANY. A subsidiary is always, by definition, an affiliate, but subsidiary is the preferred term when majority control exists. In everyday use, affiliate is the correct word for intercompany relationships, however indirect, where the parent-subsidiary relationship does not apply.

Banking Act of 1933: any organization that a bank owns or controls by stock holdings, or which the bank's shareholders own, or whose officers are also directors of the bank.

Internal Revenue Service: for purposes of consolidated tax returns an affiliated group is composed of companies whose parent or other inclusive corporation owns at least 80% of voting stock.

Interstate Commerce Commission, Account 706: 1. Controlled by the accounting company alone or with others under a joint agreement.

2. Controlling the accounting company alone or with others under a joint agreement.

Investment Company Act: company in which there is any direct or indirect ownership of 5% or more of the outstanding voting securities.

AFFILIATED CORPORATION corporation that is an AFFILIATE.

AFFILIATED PERSON individual in a position to exert direct influence on the actions of a corporation. Among such persons are owners of 10% or more of the voting shares, directors, and senior elected officers and any persons in a position to exert influence through them—such as members of their immediate family and other close associates. Sometimes called a *control person.*

AFFORDABILITY INDEX standard established by the National Association of Realtors (NAR) to gauge the financial ability of consumers to buy a home. A reading of 100 means a family earning the national median family income (reported by the Census Bureau) can qualify for a mortgage on a typical median-priced existing single-family home. An index above 100 signifies that a family earning the median income more than qualifies for a mortgage loan on a median-priced home, assuming a 20% downpayment. Therefore, an increase in the Affordability Index shows that a family is more able to afford the median priced home. The prevailing mortgage interest rate is the effective rate on loans closed on existing homes from the Federal Housing Finance Board (for the U.S.) and HSH Associates of Butler, NJ (for various regions). The mortgage is based on an 80% loan (20% down payment) and a qualifying ratio of 25%, meaning that 25% of the borrower's gross monthly income will be needed to cover housing costs, including the mortgage. The 25% qualifying ratio covers expected principal and interest payments, but does not cover taxes and insurance.

There are 3 different types of indices calculated by NAR. The Fixed Rate Index is based on the current effective interest rate on 30-year fixed rate mortgages. The Adjustable Rate Index is calculated using the prevailing effective interest rate on adjustable-rate mortgages. The Composite Index uses a weighted average of the interest rates on fixed and adjustable rate mortgages, weighted by the relative proportion of fixed and adjustable rate loans closed on existing homes.

NAR also calculates a first-time homebuyer Affordability Index, which recognizes the special characteristics of first-time home buyers and the homes they purchase. The group most likely to purchase a first home consists of a young renter family with a head of household aged 25 to 44 and a lower median income than the overall population. This index assumes a 10% downpayment, and adds one quarter of a percentage point to the mortgage rate for the required private mortgage insurance. The first-time home is calculated at 85% of the median price of all existing homes purchased. Some economists maintain that every one-point increase in the home mortgage interest rate results in 300,000 fewer home sales.

AFTER ACQUIRED CLAUSE clause in a mortgage agreement providing that any additional mortgageable property acquired by the borrower after the mortgage is signed will be additional security for the obligation.

   While such provisions can help give mortgage bonds a good rating and enable issuing corporations to borrow at favorable rates, by precluding additional first mortgages, they make it difficult to finance growth through new borrowings. This gives rise to various maneuvers to remove after acquired clauses, such as redemption or exchange of bonds or changes in indenture agreements.

AFTER-HOURS DEALING OR TRADING trading of stocks and bonds after regular trading hours on organized exchanges. This may occur when there is a major announcement about positive or negative earnings or a takeover at a particular company. The stock price may therefore soar or plummet from the level at which it closed during regular trading hours. Some brokerage firms specialize in making over-the-counter markets around the clock to accommodate after-hours dealing. *See* MAKE A MARKET.

AFTERMARKET *see* SECONDARY MARKET.

AFTERTAX BASIS basis for comparing the returns on a corporate taxable bond and a municipal tax-free bond. For example, a corporate bond paying 10% would have an aftertax return of 6.4% for someone in the 36% tax bracket. So any municipal bond paying higher than 6.4% would yield a higher aftertax return.

AFTERTAX REAL RATE OF RETURN amount of money, adjusted for inflation, that an investor can keep, out of the income and capital gains earned from investments. Every dollar loses value to inflation, so investors have to keep an eye on the aftertax real rate of return whenever they commit their capital. By and large, investors seek a rate of return that will match if not exceed the rate of inflation.

AGAINST THE BOX SHORT SALE by the holder of a LONG POSITION in the same stock. BOX refers to the physical location of securities held in safekeeping. When a stock is sold against the box, it is sold short, but only in effect. A short sale is usually defined as one where the seller does not own the shares. Here the seller *does* own the shares (holds a long position) but does not wish to disclose ownership; or perhaps the long shares are too inaccessible to deliver in the time required; or, prior to the TAXPAYER RELIEF ACT OF 1997, he may have been holding his existing position to get the benefit of long-term capital gains tax treatment. In any event, when the sale is made against the box, the shares needed to cover are borrowed, probably from a broker. This technique was eliminated as a way to reduce tax liabilities in the TAXPAYER RELIEF ACT OF 1997. *See also* SELLING SHORT AGAINST THE BOX.

AGED FAIL contract between two broker-dealers that is still not settled 30 days after the settlement date. At that point the open balance no longer counts as an asset, and the receiving firm must adjust its capital accordingly.

AGENCY

In general: relationship between two parties, one a principal and the other an AGENT who represents the principal in transactions with a third party.

Finance: certain types of accounts in trust institutions where individuals, usually trust officers, act on behalf of customers. Agency services to corporations are related to stock purchases and sales. Banks also act as agents for individuals.

Government: securities issued by government-sponsored entities and federally related institutions. Agency securities are exempt from Securities and Exchange Commission (SEC) registration requirements. *See also* AGENCY SECURITIES.

Investment: act of buying or selling for the account and risk of a client. Generally, an agent, or broker, acts as intermediary between buyer and seller, taking no financial risk personally or as a firm, and charging a commission for the service.

AGENCY SECURITIES securities issued by U.S. government-sponsored entities (GSEs) and federally related institutions.

GSEs currently issuing securities comprise eight privately owned, publicly chartered entities created to reduce borrowing costs for certain sectors of the economy, such as farmers, homeowners, and students. They include the Federal Farm Credit Bank System, Farm Credit Financial Assistance Corporation, Federal Home Loan Bank, FEDERAL HOME LOAN MORTGAGE CORPORATION, FEDERAL NATIONAL MORTGAGE ASSOCIATION (FNMA), STUDENT LOAN MARKETING ASSOCIATION (SLMA), FINANCING CORPORATION (FICO). GSEs issue discount notes (with maturities ranging from overnight to 360 days) and bonds. With the exception of the Farm Credit Financial Assistance Corporation, GSE securities are not backed by the full faith and credit of the U.S. government. Other GSEs that formerly issued directly now borrow from the FEDERAL FINANCING BANK.

Federally related institutions are arms of the U.S. government and generally have not issued securities directly into the marketplace since the Federal Financing Bank was established to meet their consolidated borrowing needs in 1973. They include the EXPORT-IMPORT BANK (EXIMBANK) of the United States, the Commodity Credit Corporation, the Farmers Housing Administration, the General Services Administration, the GOVERNMENT NATIONAL MORTGAGE ASSOCIATION (GNMA), the Maritime Administration, the Private Export Funding Corporation, the Rural Electrification Administration, the Rural Telephone Bank, the SMALL BUSINESS ADMINISTRATION (SBA), the Tennessee Valley Authority (TVA), and the Washington Metropolitan Area Transit Authority. Except for the Private Export Funding Corporation and the TVA, federally related institution obligations are backed by the full faith and credit of the U.S. government.

Agency securities are exempt from SEC registration and from state and local income taxes.

See also FEDERAL FARM CREDIT SYSTEM; FEDERAL HOME LOAN BANK SYSTEM.

AGENT individual authorized by another person, called the principal, to act in the latter's behalf in transactions involving a third party. Banks are frequently appointed by individuals to be their agents, and so authorize their employees to act on behalf of principals. Agents have three basic characteristics:
1. They act on behalf of and are subject to the control of the principal.
2. They do not have title to the principal's property.
3. They owe the duty of obedience to the principal's orders.

See also ACCOUNT EXECUTIVE; BROKER; TRANSFER AGENT.

AGGREGATE EXERCISE PRICE in stock options trading, the number of shares in a put or call CONTRACT (normally 100) multiplied by the EXERCISE PRICE. The price of the option, called the PREMIUM, is a separate figure not included in the aggregate exercise price. A July call option on 100 XYZ at 70 would, for example, have an aggregate exercise price of 100 (number of shares) times $70 (price per share), or $7000, if exercised on or before the July expiration date.

In options traded on debt instruments, which include GOVERNMENT NATIONAL MORTGAGE ASSOCIATION (GNMA) pass-throughs, Treasury bills, Treasury notes, Treasury bonds, and certain municipal bonds, the aggregate exercise price is determined by multiplying the FACE VALUE of the underlying security by the exercise price. For example, the aggregate exercise price of put option Treasury bond December 90 would be $90,000 if exercised on or before its December expiration date, the calculation being 90% times the $100,000 face value of the underlying bond.

AGGREGATE SUPPLY in MACROECONOMICS, the total amount of goods and services supplied to the market at alternative price levels in a given period of time; also called *total output.* The central concept in SUPPLY-SIDE ECONOMICS, it corresponds with aggregate demand, defined as the total amount of goods and services demanded in the economy at alternative income levels in a given period, including both consumer and producers' goods; aggregate demand is also called *total spending.* The aggregate supply curve describes the relationship between price levels and the quantity of output that firms are willing to provide.

AGGRESSIVE GROWTH MUTUAL FUND mutual fund holding stocks of rapidly growing companies. While these companies may be large or small, they all share histories of and prospects for above-average profit growth. Aggressive growth funds are designed solely for capital appreciation, since they produce little or no income from dividends. This type of mutual fund is typically more volatile than the overall stock market, meaning its shares will rise far more than the average stock during bull markets and will fall much farther than the typical stock in a bear market. Investors in aggressive growth funds must realize that the value of their shares will fluctuate sharply over time. Aggressive growth funds are also called *maximum capital gains funds* or *capital appreciation funds.*

AGING SCHEDULE classification of trade ACCOUNTS RECEIVABLE by date of sale. Usually prepared by a company's auditor, the *aging,* as the schedule is called, is a vital tool in analyzing the quality of a company's receivables investment. It is frequently required by grantors of credit.

The schedule is most often seen as: (1) a list of the amount of receivables by the month in which they were created; (2) a list of receivables by maturity, classified as current or as being in various stages of delinquency. The following is a typical aging schedule.

	dollars (in thousands)	
Current (under 30 days)	$14,065	61%
1–30 days past due	3,725	16
31–60 days past due	2,900	12
61–90 days past due	1,800	8
Over 90 days past due	750	3
	$23,240	100%

The aging schedule reveals patterns of delinquency and shows where collection efforts should be concentrated. It helps in evaluating the adequacy of the reserve for BAD DEBTS, because the longer accounts stretch out the more likely they are to become uncollectible. Using the schedule can help prevent the loss of future sales, since old customers who fall too far behind tend to seek out new sources of supply.

AGREEMENT AMONG UNDERWRITERS contract between participating members of an investment banking SYNDICATE; sometimes called *syndicate contract* or *purchase group agreement.* It is distinguished from the *underwriting agreement,* which is signed by the company issuing the securities and the SYNDICATE MANAGER, acting as agent for the underwriting group.

The agreement among underwriters, (1) appoints the originating investment banker as syndicate manager and agent; (2) appoints additional managers, if considered advisable; (3) defines the members' proportionate liability (usually limited to the amount of their participation) and agrees to pay each member's share on settlement date; (4) authorizes the manager to form and allocate units to a SELLING GROUP, and agrees to abide by the rules of the selling group agreement; (5) states the life of the syndicate, usually running until 30 days after termination of the selling group, or ending earlier by mutual consent.

AIR POCKET STOCK stock that falls sharply, usually in the wake of such negative news as unexpected poor earnings. As shareholders rush to sell, and few buyers can be found, the price plunges dramatically, like an airplane hitting an air pocket.

AIRPORT REVENUE BOND tax-exempt bond issued by a city, county, state, or airport authority to support the expansion and operations of an airport. The repayment of principal and interest is backed by either the general revenues of airport authority or lease payments generated by one or more airlines using the facilities. In some cases, airport revenue bonds are backed directly by the financial strength of the major airline using the airport, which makes the bonds more risky, because airlines are particularly sensitive to economic cycles and could go out of business in a down cycle.

ALIEN CORPORATION company incorporated under the laws of a foreign country regardless of where it operates. "Alien corporation" can be used as a synonym for the term *foreign corporation.* However, "foreign corporation" also is used in U.S. state law to mean a corporation formed in a state other than that in which it does business.

ALIMONY PAYMENT money paid to a separated or divorced spouse as required by a divorce decree or a legal separation agreement. The IRS allows qualifying payments as DEDUCTIONS by the payor and they are taxable income to the payee.

ALLIED MEMBER general partner or voting stockholder of a member firm of the New York Stock Exchange who is not personally a member. Allied members cannot do business on the trading floor. A member firm need have no more than one partner or voting stockholder who owns a membership, so even the chairman of the board of a member firm may be no more than an allied member.

ALLIGATOR SPREAD spread in the options market that "eats the investor alive" with high commission costs. The term is used when a broker arranges a combination of puts and calls that generates so much commission the client is unlikely to turn a profit even if the markets move as anticipated.

ALL IN underwriting shorthand for *all included,* referring to an issuer's interest rate after giving effect to commissions and miscellaneous related expenses.

ALL OR NONE (AON)
   Investment banking: an offering giving the issuer the right to cancel the whole issue if the underwriting is not fully subscribed.
   Securities: buy or sell order marked to signify that no partial transaction is to be executed. The order will not automatically be canceled, however, if a complete transaction is not executed; to accomplish that, the order entry must be marked FOK, meaning FILL OR KILL.

ALL ORDINARIES INDEX the major index of Australian stocks, representing 330 of the most active listed companies, or the majority of the equity capitalization (excluding foreign companies) listed on the AUSTRALIA STOCK EXCHANGE (ASX). The index is made up of 23 sub-indices representing various industry categories, and it summarizes market price movements by following changes in the aggregate market values of the companies listed.

ALLOTMENT amount of securities assigned to each of the participants in an investment banking SYNDICATE formed to underwrite and distribute a new issue, called *subscribers* or *allottees.* The financial responsibilities of the subscribers are set forth in an allotment notice, which is prepared by the SYNDICATE MANAGER.

ALLOWANCE deduction from the value of an invoice, permitted by a seller of goods to cover damages or shortages. *See also* RESERVE.

ALL-SAVERS CERTIFICATE *see* ECONOMIC RECOVERY TAX ACT OF 1981 (ERTA).

ALPHA
1. coefficient measuring the portion of an investment's RETURN arising from specific (nonmarket) risk. In other words, alpha is a mathematical estimate of the amount of return expected from an investment's inherent values, such as the rate of growth in earnings per share. It is distinct from the amount of return caused by VOLATILITY, which is measured by the BETA coefficient. For example, an alpha of 1.25 indicates that a stock is projected to rise 25% in price in a year when the return on the market and the stock's beta are both zero. An investment whose price is low relative to its alpha is undervalued and considered a good selection.
   In the case of a MUTUAL FUND, alpha measures the relationship between the fund's performance and its beta over a three-year period.
2. on the London Stock Exchange, now called the International Stock Exchange of the United Kingdom and Republic of Ireland (ISE), the designation *alpha stocks* is applied to the largest and most actively traded companies in a classification system that was adopted after the BIG BANG in October 1986 and was replaced in January 1991 with the NORMAL MARKET SIZE (NMS) classification system.

ALPHABET STOCK categories of common stock associated with particular subsidiaries created by acquisitions and restructuring. Examples would be General Motors "E" stock, issued to acquire Electronic Data Systems (EDS), and "H" stock, which was originally issued in the mid-1980s, when GM acquired Hughes Aircraft and combined it with existing electronics operations to form GM Hughes Electronics Corporation. Subsequent to these acquisitions, GM spun off its holdings in EDS so that EDS now trades as a separate company again. General Motors H was recapitalized when Hughes' defense operations were spun off to Raytheon in 1997. The reissued General Motors H (GMH) now tracks the Hughes telecommunications and space businesses that GM retained. The significance of alphabetical categories is that they have different voting rights and pay dividends tied to the operating performance of the particular divisions. Alphabet stock differs from CLASSIFIED STOCK, which is typically designated Class A and Class B, in that classified stock implies a hierarchy of powers and privileges, whereas alphabet stock simply separates differences. *See also* TRACKING STOCKS.

ALTERNATIVE MINIMUM TAX (AMT) federal tax aimed at ensuring that wealthy individuals, trusts, estates, and corporations pay at least some income tax. For individuals, the AMT is computed by adding TAX PREFERENCE ITEMS such as passive losses from tax shelters, accelerated depreciation of property acquired before 1987, and tax-exempt interest on private-purpose bonds issued after August 7, 1986, to adjusted gross income. From this amount, a $45,000 exemption must be subtracted for a married couple filing jointly, $33,750 for a single filer, and $22,500 for a married couple filing separately, or for trusts and estates. (These exemptions are phased out when AMT taxable income exceeds $150,000 for a married couple filing jointly, $112,500 for single filers, and $75,000 for a married couple filing separately.) The remaining amount, up to $175,000 for a married couple filing jointly ($87,500 for a married couple filing separately), is subject to a 26% tax rate. Any amount over $175,000 ($87,500 for couple filing separately) is subject to a 28% tax rate.

The corporate AMT has the same exemptions but a tax rate of 20%. It is imposed on the amount of money in excess of the alternative minimum taxable income (AMTI) over the exemption amount. In determining the corporate AMT, an adjustment called the adjusted current earnings (ACE) must be made. The ACE adjustment increases a corporation's AMTI by 75% of the amount by which its ACE exceeds its AMTI. This adjustment is designed to eliminate some of the tax savings generated by corporations that have high income for accounting purposes but pay little or no tax as a result of tax benefits. Calculating the correct individual or corporate AMT can be extremely complex and is best left to a professional accountant.

ALTERNATIVE ORDER order giving a broker a choice between two courses of action; also called an *either-or order* or a *one cancels the other order.* Such orders are either to buy or to sell, never both. Execution of one course automatically makes the other course inoperative. An example is a combination buy limit/buy stop order, wherein the buy limit is below the current market and the buy stop is above.

AMBAC Indemnity Corporation *see* MUNICIPAL BOND INSURANCE.

AMENDED TAX RETURN Internal Revenue Service tax return filed on Form 1040X to correct mistakes made on the original return. Amended returns must be filed within three years of the original filing.

AMENDMENT addition to, or change, in a legal document. When properly signed, it has the full legal effect of the original document.

AMERICAN ASSOCIATION OF INDIVIDUAL INVESTORS (AAII) nonprofit organization, based in Chicago, designed to educate individual investors about stocks, bonds, mutual funds, and other financial alternatives through seminars, conferences, and publications. The AAII also evaluates investment-oriented software in a publication called *Computerized Investing.* The AAII web site (www.aaii.org) provides extensive information on the basics of investing, as well as a reference section on a wide variety of topics such as annuities, mutual funds, dividend reinvestment plans and discount brokers. The AAII regularly polls its members for their outlook on the stock market, and the AAII Index of Bullish, Bearish and Neutral Outlook is published weekly in *Barron's* under Investor Sentiment Readings.

AMERICAN DEPOSITARY RECEIPT (ADR) receipt for the shares of a foreign-based corporation held in the vault of a U.S. bank and entitling the shareholder to all dividends and capital gains. Instead of buying shares of foreign-based companies in overseas markets, Americans can buy shares in the U.S. in the form of an ADR. ADRs are available for hundreds of stocks from numerous countries.

AMERICAN DEPOSITARY SHARE (ADS) share issued under a deposit agreement representing the underlying ordinary share which trades in the issuer's home market. The terms ADS and ADR tend to be used interchangeably. Technically, the ADS is the instrument that actually is traded, while the ADR is the certificate that represents a number of ADSs.

AMERICAN STOCK EXCHANGE (AMEX) primary marketplace in the U.S. for equities, bonds, options and derivative securities. Located at 86 Trinity Place in lower Manhattan, AMEX was known as the *Curb Exchange* until 1921. AMEX trades more than 900 issues on its primary list. The two main indices tracking AMEX stocks are the AMEX Composite Index and the AMEX Major Market Index. In the options market, AMEX trades options on 30 broad-based and sector indices and more than 900 stocks and 109 LONG-TERM EQUITY ANTICIPATION SECURITIES (LEAPS). AMEX is a leader in listing warrants on foreign currencies and indices as well as hybrid instruments and other structured products. AMEX trades such derivatives as DIAMONDS (which track the Dow Jones Industrial Average); STANDARD & POOR'S DEPOSITORY RECEIPTS (SPDRS), which track the S&P 500 and are usually called Spiders and WORLD EQUITY BENCHMARK SHARES (WEBS), which track the performance of various countries stock indices.

In 1998, AMEX agreed to merge with the NATIONAL ASSOCIATION OF SECURITIES DEALERS (NASD), making it a subsidiary of NASD. Under terms of the merger, AMEX equity and options markets continue to operate separately from the NASDAQ Stock Market and NASDAQ International, both operated by NASD. The AMEX equity market continues as a centralized, specialist-based auction market with manual and enhanced electronic access. The options structure remains unchanged. Trading hours: 9:30 A.M.–4:00 P.M., Monday through Friday. *See also* EMERGING COMPANY MARKETPLACE (ECM); SECURITIES AND COMMODITIES EXCHANGES; SPDR; STOCK INDICES AND AVERAGES.

AMORTIZATION accounting procedure that gradually reduces the cost value of a limited life or intangible asset through periodic charges to income. For fixed assets the term used is DEPRECIATION, and for wasting assets (natural resources) it is depletion, both terms meaning essentially the same thing as amortization. Most companies follow the conservative practice of writing off, through amortization, INTANGIBLE ASSETS such as goodwill. It is also common practice to amortize any premium over par value paid in the purchase of preferred stock or bond investments. The purpose of amortization is to reflect resale or redemption value.

Amortization also refers to the reduction of debt by regular payments of interest and principal sufficient to pay off a loan by maturity.

Discount and expense on funded debt are amortized by making applicable charges to income in accordance with a predetermined schedule. While this is normally done systematically, charges to profit and loss are permissible at any time in any amount of the remaining discount and expense. Such accounting is detailed in a company's annual report.

AMPS acronym for *Auction Market Preferred Stock,* Merrill Lynch's answer to Salomon Brothers' DARTS and First Boston's STARS. These and other proprietary products are types of DUTCH AUCTION PREFERRED STOCK. Since the auctions take place every 49 days, the shares meet the 46-day holding period required for the 70% dividend exclusion allowed corporations under the tax code.

AMSTERDAM EXCHANGES (AEX) formed by the 1997 merger of the Amsterdam Stock Exchange (ASE), the European Options Exchange (EOE), and Necigef (the Dutch Central Institution for Girosecurities transactions). AEX is a private limited company with shareholders and the central Dutch securities exchanges for stocks, bonds, options and agricultural futures. It is responsible for regulation and control in trading, listing, settlements and safe custody for the exchanges and systems it operates. The stock exchange, founded in 1602, is the oldest in the world. The NEW YORK STOCK EXCHANGE is based on the Dutch system. The majority of domestic shares are bearer shares, while foreign equities generally are in registered form. In February 1997, a market was launched for high-growth, small-cap companies. Trading System Amsterdam (TSA) consists of a wholesale and retail segment; the distinction between the two is determined by the transaction size. The wholesale segment can be traded directly on the screen-based Automatic Interprofessional Dealing System (AIDA). The retail sector has a central market, a floor with specialists. The wholesale sector also may utilize the central market. The Netherlands Central Bureau of Statistics (CBS) All Share Index and the Total Return Index include all ordinary shares of Dutch companies listed on the AEX, except shares of property funds, investment funds, and holding companies. The AEX Index is composed of a weighted average of the 25 most actively-traded Dutch stocks, selected annually. The Amsterdam Midcap Index (AMX) focuses on medium-sized companies.

The AEX-Optiebeurs trades financial futures, stock options, and index options by open outcry and electronically. Futures and options are traded on its EOE Index, as well as the Eurotop 100 Index, the Dutch Top 5 Index and the U.S. dollar. Futures are traded on the *notional bond.* Options are traded on the Jumbo dollar, gold and silver. The AEX-Agrarische Termijnmarket trades futures on live hogs, piglets, potatoes and wheat by open outcry. Trading hours for all AEX divisions are 9:30 A.M. to 4:30 P.M., Monday through Friday.

ANALYSIS *see* FUNDAMENTAL ANALYSIS; TECHNICAL ANALYSIS.

ANALYST person in a brokerage house, bank trust department, or mutual fund group who studies a number of companies and makes buy or sell recommendations on the securities of particular companies and industry groups. Most analysts specialize in a particular industry, but some investigate any company that interests them, regardless of its line of business. Some analysts have considerable influence, and can therefore affect the price of a company's stock when they issue a buy or sell recommendation. *See also* CREDIT ANALYST.

AND INTEREST phrase used in quoting bond prices to indicate that, in addition to the price quoted, the buyer will receive ACCRUED INTEREST.

ANGEL INVESTMENT GRADE bond, as distinguished from FALLEN ANGEL.

ANKLE BITER stock issue having a MARKET CAPITALIZATION of less than $500 million. Generally speaking, such small-capitalization stocks are more speculative than "high-cap" issues, but their greater growth potential gives them more RELATIVE STRENGTH in recessions. *See also* SMALL FIRM EFFECT.

ANNUAL BASIS statistical technique whereby figures covering a period of less than a year are extended to cover a 12-month period. The procedure, called *annualizing,* must take seasonal variations (if any) into account to be accurate.

ANNUAL EXCLUSION tax rule allowing a taxpayer to exclude certain kinds of income from taxation on a tax return. For example, interest earned from municipal bonds must be reported, even though it is not taxed by the federal government. Proceeds from life insurance policies paid by reason of the death of the insured are not taxable. Gifts received of $10,000 or less are also not taxable, and are therefore subject to the annual exclusion rule. This $10,000 gift tax exclusion limit is subject to upward revision in $1,000 increments tied to the rate of inflation based on the TAXPAYER RELIEF ACT OF 1997.

ANNUALIZE to convert to an annual basis. For example, if a mutual fund earns 1% in a month, it would earn 12% on an annualized basis, by multiplying the monthly return by 12. Many economists annualize a monthly number such as auto sales or housing starts to make it easier to compare to prior years.

ANNUAL MEETING once-a-year meeting when the managers of a company report to stockholders on the year's results, and the board of directors stands for election for the next year. The chief executive officer usually comments on the outlook for the coming year and, with other senior officers, answers questions from shareholders. Stockholders can also request that resolutions on corporate policy be voted on by all those owning stock in the company. Stockholders unable to attend the annual meeting may vote for directors and pass on resolutions through the use of PROXY material, which must legally be mailed to all shareholders of record.

ANNUAL PERCENTAGE RATE (APR) cost of credit that consumers pay, expressed as a simple annual percentage. According to the federal Truth in Lending Act, every consumer loan agreement must disclose the APR in large bold type. *See also* CONSUMER CREDIT PROTECTION ACT OF 1968.

ANNUAL RENEWABLE TERM INSURANCE *see* TERM INSURANCE.

ANNUAL REPORT yearly record of a corporation's financial condition that must be distributed to shareholders under SECURITIES AND EXCHANGE COMMISSION regulations. Included in the report is a description of the company's operations as well as its balance sheet and income statement. The long version of the annual report with more detailed financial information—called the 10-K—is available upon request from the corporate secretary.

ANNUAL RETURN TOTAL RETURN per year from an investment, including dividends or interest and capital gains or losses but excluding commissions and other transactions costs and taxes. A *compound annual return* represents the annual rate at which money would have to compound to reach the cumulative figure resulting from annual total returns. It is a discount rate and different from *average annual return,* which is simply an arithmetic mean of annual returns.

ANNUITANT individual receiving benefits from an annuity. The annuity owner can choose to annuitize the policy, meaning that he or she begins to receive regular payments from the annuity.

ANNUITIZE to begin a series of payments from the capital that has built up in an ANNUITY. The payments may be a fixed amount, or for a fixed period of time, or for the lifetimes of one or two *annuitants,* thus guaranteeing income payments that cannot be outlived. *See also* DEFERRED PAYMENT ANNUITY; FIXED ANNUITY; IMMEDIATE PAYMENT ANNUITY; VARIABLE ANNUITY.

ANNUITY form of contract sold by life insurance companies that guarantees a fixed or variable payment to the annuitant at some future time, usually retirement. In a FIXED ANNUITY the amount will ultimately be paid out in regular installments varying only with the payout method elected. In a VARIABLE ANNUITY, the payout is based on a guaranteed number of units; unit values and payments depend on the value of the underlying investments. All capital in the annuity grows TAX-DEFERRED. Key considerations when buying an annuity are the financial soundness of the insurance company *(see* BEST'S RATING), the returns it has paid in the past, and the level of fees and commissions paid to salesmen.

ANNUITY CERTAIN annuity that pays a specified monthly level of income for a predetermined time period, frequently ten years. The annuitant is guaranteed by the insurance company to receive those payments for the agreed upon time period without exception or contingency. If the annuitant dies before the time period expires, the annuity payments are then made to the annuitant's designated beneficiaries. The level of payment in an annuity certain will be higher than for a LIFE ANNUITY because the insurance company knows exactly what its liability will be, whereas with a life annuity, payments depend on how long the annuitant lives.

ANNUITY STARTING DATE date on which an ANNUITANT begins receiving payments from an annuity. Generally, any distributions before age 59½ are subject to a 10% penalty from the IRS, so most annuities start paying after the annuitant has attained that age. The later an annuitant waits to start receiving payments, the higher his or her monthly payments will be under a life annuity, because the insurance company has had more time to invest the money, and the annuitant's remaining life expectancy is shorter.

ANTICIPATED HOLDING PERIOD time during which a limited partnership expects to hold onto an asset. In the prospectus for a real estate limited partnership, for instance, a sponsor will typically say that the anticipated holding period for a particular property is five to seven years. At the end of that time the property is sold, and, usually, the capital received is returned to the limited partners in one distribution.

ANTICIPATION
In general: paying an obligation before it falls due.
Finance: repayment of debt obligations before maturity, usually to save interest. If a formalized discount or rebate is involved, the term used is *anticipation rate.*
Mortgage instrument: when a provision allows prepayment without penalty, the mortgagee is said to have the *right of anticipation.*
Trade payments: bill that is paid before it is due, not discounted.

ANTITRUST LAWS federal legislation designed to prevent monopolies and restraint of trade. Landmark statutes include:

1. the Sherman Anti-Trust Act of 1890, which prohibited acts or contracts tending to create monopoly and initiated an era of trustbusting.
2. the Clayton Anti-Trust Act of 1914, which was passed as an amendment to the Sherman Act and dealt with local price discrimination as well as with the INTERLOCKING DIRECTORATES. It went further in the areas of the HOLDING COMPANY and restraint of trade.
3. the Federal Trade Commission Act of 1914, which created the Federal Trade Commission or FTC, with power to conduct investigations and issue orders preventing unfair practices in interstate commerce.

ANY-AND-ALL BID offer to pay an equal price for all shares tendered by a deadline; contrasts with TWO-TIER BID. *See also* TAKEOVER.

ANY-INTEREST-DATE CALL provision found in some municipal bond indentures that gives the issuer the right to redeem on any interest payment due date, with or without a premium (depending on the indenture).

APPRAISAL FEE fee charged by an expert to estimate, but not determine, the market value of property. An appraisal is an opinion of value, and is usually required when real property is sold, financed, condemned, taxed, insured, or partitioned. For example, the appraisal of a work of art done to establish value for the IRS when the art is to be donated to a charity may differ from the appraisal if the piece of art is about to be sold at auction. Similarly, the appraisal of a piece of real estate for insurance purposes may differ from an appraisal for determining property taxes. The appraisal fee is usually a set dollar amount, though in some cases may be calculated as a percentage of the value of the property appraised.

APPRECIATION increase in the value of an asset such as a stock, bond, commodity, or real estate.

APPROVED LIST list of investments that a mutual fund or other financial institution is authorized to make. The approved list may be statutory where a fiduciary responsibility exists. *See also* LEGAL LIST.

APS acronym for *Auction Preferred Stock,* Goldman Sach's DUTCH AUCTION PREFERRED STOCK product.

ARBITRAGE profiting from differences in price when the same security, currency, or commodity is traded on two or more markets. For example, an *arbitrageur* simultaneously buys one contract of gold in the New York market and sells one contract of gold in the Chicago market, locking in a profit because at that moment the price on the two markets is different. (The arbitrageur's selling price is higher than the buying price.) *Index arbitrage* exploits price differences between STOCK INDEX FUTURES and underlying stocks. By taking advantage of momentary disparities in prices between markets, arbitrageurs perform the economic function of making those markets trade more efficiently. *See also* GAR-BATRAGE; RISK ARBITRAGE.

ARBITRAGE BONDS bonds issued by a municipality in order to gain an interest rate advantage by refunding higher-rate bonds in advance of their call date. Proceeds from the lower-rate refunding issue are invested in treasuries until the first call date of the higher-rate issue being refunded. Arbitrage bonds, which always raised a question of tax exemption, were further curtailed by the TAX REFORM ACT OF 1986.

ARBITRAGEUR person or firm engaged in ARBITRAGE. Arbitrageurs attempt to profit when the same security or commodity is trading at different prices in two or more markets. Those engaged in RISK ARBI-TRAGE attempt to profit from buying stocks of announced or potential TAKEOVER targets.

ARBITRATION dispute resolution mechanism designed to help aggrieved parties recover damages. In arbitration, an impartial person or panel hears all sides of the issues as presented by the parties, evaluates the evidence, and decides how the matter should be resolved. Arbitration is final and binding, and is subject to review by a court only on a very limited basis. *See also* ARBITRATION PANEL.

ARBITRATION PANEL each sponsoring organization maintains a roster of individuals whose professional experience qualifies them for service as arbitrators. The arbitrators are not employees of the sponsoring organization and they, not the sponsoring organization, determine the outcome of the dispute. The arbitrators receive an honorarium from the SELF-REGULATORY ORGANIZATIONS.

ARITHMETIC MEAN simple average obtained by dividing the sum of two or more items by the number of items.

ARMS' INDEX better known as TRIN; technical indicator named for *Barron's* writer Richard Arms.

ARM'S LENGTH TRANSACTION transaction that is conducted as though the parties were unrelated, thus avoiding any semblance of conflict of interest. For example, under current law parents may rent real estate to their children and still claim business deductions such as depreciation as long as the parents charge their children what they would charge if someone who is not a relative were to rent the same property.

ARREARAGE
In general: amount of any past-due obligation.
Investments: amount by which interest on bonds or dividends on CUMULATIVE PREFERRED stock is due and unpaid. In the case of cumulative preferred stock, common dividends cannot be paid by a company as long as preferred dividends are in arrears.

ARTICLES OF INCORPORATION document filed with a U.S. state by the founders of a corporation. After approving the articles, the state issues a certificate of incorporation; the two documents together become the CHARTER that gives the corporation its legal existence. The charter embodies such information as the corporation's name, purpose, amount of authorized shares, and number and identity of directors. The corporation's powers thus derive from the laws of the state and from the provisions of the charter. Rules governing its internal management are set forth in the corporation's BYLAWS, which are drawn up by the founders.

ARTIFICIAL CURRENCY *currency substitute,* such as SPECIAL DRAWING RIGHTS (SDRs) and EUROPEAN CURRENCY UNITS (ECUs).

ASCENDING TOPS chart pattern tracing a security's price over a period of time and showing that each peak in a security's price is higher than the preceding peak. This upward movement is considered bullish, meaning that the upward trend is likely to continue. *See also* DESCENDING TOPS.

ASCENDING TOPS

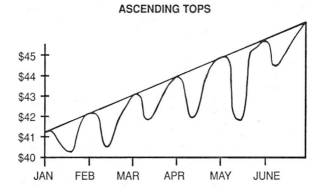

ASKED PRICE
1. price at which a security or commodity is offered for sale on an exchange or in the over-the-counter market. Generally, it is the lowest round lot price at which a dealer will sell. Also called the *ask price, asking price, ask,* or OFFERING PRICE.
2. per-share price at which mutual fund shares are offered to the public, usually the NET ASSET VALUE per share plus a sales charge, if any.

ASPIRIN acronym for *Australian Stock Price Riskless Indexed Notes.* Zero-coupon, four-year bonds guaranteed by the Treasury of New South Wales repayable at face value plus the percentage increase by which the Australian Stock Index of All Ordinaries (common stocks) rises above 1372 points during the period. *See also* ALL ORDINARIES INDEX.

ASSAY test of a metal's purity to verify that it meets the standards for trading on a commodities exchange. For instance, a 100 troy-ounce bar of refined gold must be assayed at a fineness of not less than 995 before the Comex will allow it to be used in settlement of a gold contract.

ASSESSED VALUATION dollar value assigned to property by a municipality for purposes of assessing taxes, which are based on the number of mills per dollar of assessed valuation. If a house is assessed at $100,000 and the tax rate is 50 mills, the tax is $5000. Assessed valuation is important not only to homeowners but also to investors in municipal bonds that are backed by property taxes.

ASSET anything having commercial or exchange value that is owned by a business, institution, or individual. *See also* CAPITAL ASSET; CURRENT ASSETS; DEFERRED CHARGE; FIXED ASSET; INTANGIBLE ASSET; NONCURRENT ASSET.

ASSET ALLOCATION apportioning of investment funds among categories of assets, such as CASH EQUIVALENTS, STOCK, FIXED-INCOME INVESTMENTS, and such tangible assets as real estate, precious metals, and collectibles. Also applies to subcategories such as government, municipal, and corporate bonds, and industry groupings of common stocks. Asset allocation affects both risk and return and is a central concept in personal financial planning and investment management.

ASSET ALLOCATION MUTUAL FUND mutual fund that switches between stocks, bonds, and money market securities to maximize shareholders' returns while minimizing risk. Such funds, which have become extremely popular in recent years, relieve individual shareholders of the responsibility of timing their entry or exit into different markets, since the fund manager is making those decisions. Theoretically, asset allocation funds provide a built-in buffer against declining stock and bond prices because the manager can move all the fund's assets into safe money market instruments. On the other hand, the manager has flexibility to invest aggressively in international and domestic stocks and bonds if he or she sees bull markets ahead for those securities.

ASSET-BACKED SECURITIES bonds or notes backed by loan paper or accounts receivable originated by banks, credit card companies, or other providers of credit and often "enhanced" by a bank LETTER OF CREDIT or by insurance coverage provided by an institution other than the issuer. Typically, the originator of the loan or accounts receivable paper sells it to a specially created trust, which repackages it as securities with a minimum denomination of $1000 and a term of five years or less. The securities are then underwritten by brokerage firms who reoffer them to the public. Examples are CERTIFICATES FOR AUTOMOBILE RECEIVABLES (CARs) and so-called *plastic bonds,* backed by credit card receivables. Because the institution that originated the underlying loans or receivables is neither the obligor nor the guarantor, investors should evaluate the quality of the original paper, the worth of the guarantor or insurer, and the extent of the protection. *See also* PASS-THROUGH SECURITY.

ASSET COVERAGE extent to which a company's net assets cover a particular debt obligation, class of preferred stock, or equity position.

Asset coverage is calculated as follows: from assets at their total book value or liquidation value, subtract intangible assets, current liabilities, and all obligations prior in claim to the issue in question. Divide the result by the dollar amount of the subject issue (or loan) to arrive at the asset coverage ratio. The same information can be expressed as a percentage or, by using units as the divisor, as a dollar figure of coverage per unit. The variation to determine preferred stock coverage treats all liabilities as paid; the variation to arrive at common stock coverage considers both preferred stock and liabilities paid. The term most often used for the common stock calculation is *net book value per share of common stock.*

These calculations reveal *direct* asset coverage. *Overall* asset coverage is obtained by including the subject issue with the total of prior obligations and dividing the aggregate into total tangible assets at liquidating value.

Asset coverage is important as a cushion against losses in the event of liquidation.

ASSET DEPRECIATION RANGE SYSTEM (ADR) range of depreciable lives allowed by the Internal Revenue Service for particular classes of depreciable assets. The ADR system was replaced when the ECONOMIC RECOVERY TAX ACT OF 1981 (ERTA) introduced the ACCELERATED COST RECOVERY SYSTEM (ACRS) but was revived with modifications of ACRS under the TAX REFORM ACT OF 1986. The ADR system assigns an upper and lower limit to the estimated useful lives of asset classes. ACRS classes are based on the mid-points of these ranges. Under the alternative depreciation system, taxpayers may elect STRAIGHT LINE DEPRECIATION over the applicable ADR-class life.

ASSET FINANCING financing that seeks to convert particular assets into working cash in exchange for a security interest in those assets. The term is replacing *commercial financing* as major banks join commercial finance companies in addressing the financing needs of companies that do not fit the traditional seasonal borrower profile. Although the prevalent form of asset financing continues to be loans against accounts receivable, *inventory loans* are common and *second mortgage loans,* predicated as they usually are on market values containing a high inflation factor, seem to gain popularity by the day. *See also* ACCOUNTS RECEIVABLE FINANCING.

ASSET-LIABILITY MANAGEMENT matching an individual's level of debt and amount of assets. Someone who is planning to buy a new car, for instance, would have to decide whether to pay cash, thus lowering assets, or to take out a loan, thereby increasing debts (or liabilities). Such decisions should be based on interest rates, on earning power, and on the comfort level with debt. Financial institutions carry out asset-liability management when they match the maturity of their deposits with the length of their loan commitments to keep from being adversely affected by rapid changes in interest rates.

ASSET MANAGEMENT ACCOUNT account at a brokerage house, bank, or savings institution that combines banking services like check writing, credit cards, and debit cards; brokerage features like buying securities and making loans on margin; and the convenience of having all financial transactions listed on one monthly statement. Such accounts are also termed *central asset accounts* and are known by such proprietary names as the Cash Management Account (Merrill Lynch), Active Assets Account (Morgan Stanley Dean Witter), or Schwab One Account (Charles Schwab).

ASSET PLAY stock market term for a stock that is attractive because the current price does not reflect the value of the company's assets. For example, an analyst could recommend a hotel chain, not because its hotels are run well but because its real estate is worth far more than is recognized in the stock's current price. Asset play stocks are tempting targets for takeovers because they provide an inexpensive way to buy assets.

ASSET STRIPPER corporate raider who takes over a company planning to sell large assets in order to repay debt. The raider calculates that after selling the assets and paying off the debt, he or she will be left with valuable assets that are worth more than his or her purchase price.

ASSET VALUE net market value of a company's assets on a per-share basis as opposed to the market value of the shares. A company is under-valued by the stock market when asset value exceeds share value.

ASSIGN sign a document transferring ownership from one party to another. Ownership can be in a number of forms, including tangible property, rights (usually arising out of contracts), or the right to transfer ownership at some later time. The party who assigns is called the *assignor* and the party who receives the transfer of title—the assignment—is the *assignee.*

Stocks and registered bonds can be assigned by completing and signing a form printed on the back of the certificate—or, as is sometimes preferred for safety reasons, by executing a separate form, called an *assignment separate from certificate* or *stock/bond power.*

When the OPTIONS CLEARING CORPORATION learns of the exercise of an option, it prepares an assignment form notifying a broker-dealer that an option written by one of its clients has been exercised. The firm in turn assigns the exercise in accordance with its internal procedures.

An assignment for the benefit of creditors, sometimes called simply an *assignment,* is an alternative to bankruptcy, whereby the assets of a company are assigned to the creditors and liquidated for their benefit by a trustee.

ASSIGNED RISK PLANS facilities available in all 50 states in which drivers can obtain auto insurance if they are unable to buy it in the regular or "voluntary" market. Every insurer licensed in the state must participate in these facilities, which are also known as *joint underwriting facilities*. When premiums are too low to cover losses, insurers are usually assessed to make up the difference, and these costs are passed on to all of their customers.

ASSIMILATION absorption of a new issue of stock by the investing public after all shares have been sold by the issue's underwriters. *See also* ABSORBED.

ASSUMED INTEREST RATE rate of interest that an insurance company uses to determine the payout on an ANNUITY contract. The higher the assumed interest rate, the higher the monthly payout will be.

ASSUMPTION act of taking on responsibility for the liabilities of another party, usually documented by an *assumption agreement.* In the case of a MORTGAGE assumption, the seller remains secondarily liable unless released from the obligations by the lender.

ASX DERIVATIVES AND OPTIONS MARKET (ASXD) the world's sixth-largest options market, trading options on more than 50 of Australia's and New Zealand's leading companies. Cash-settled options are traded on three indices—the ALL-ORDINARIES INDEX, Twenty Leaders Index, and Gold Index. Formerly known as the Australian Options Market, ASXD was established in 1976 to trade put and call options in the securities of 38 leading Australian companies. Trading is quote driven with liquidity provided by market makers, through open outcry on the Sydney floor of the Australia Stock Exchange, and remote access via the Derivatives Automated Trading System (DATS).

ATP acronym for *arbitrage trading program,* better known as PROGRAM TRADING. Program traders simultaneously place orders for stock index futures and the underlying stocks in an attempt to exploit price variations. Their activity is often blamed for excessive VOLATILITY.

AT PAR at a price equal to the face, or nominal, value of a security. *See also* PAR VALUE.

AT RISK exposed to the danger of loss. Investors in a limited partnership can claim tax deductions only if they can prove that there's a chance of never realizing any profit and of losing their investment as well. Deductions will be disallowed if the limited partners are not exposed to economic risk—if, for example, the general partner guarantees to return all capital to limited partners even if the business venture should lose money.

ATHENS STOCK EXCHANGE (ASE) principal stock exchange in Greece. There are no restrictions on foreign membership on the exchange. Most investors are domestic, private, and institutional; the role of foreign institutional investors is gaining. The ASE General Index represents 75 companies, about 76% of equity market capitalization and turnover. Listings on the Parallel Market Index of companies in northern Greece are promoted by the Thessaloniki Stock Exchange, opened in 1996. The exchange uses an automated trading system, XTS, for all listed companies. Only bonds are traded by open outcry. Equities are traded on account or for cash. Settlement of all transactions is within three days. Trading hours are 10:45 A.M. to 1:30 P.M., Monday through Friday, with a half-hour pre-trading session from 10:15 A.M. to 10:45 A.M.

ATTAINED AGE age at which a person is eligible to receive certain benefits. For example, someone may be eligible to receive the proceeds from a trust when they reach age 21. Or someone who has attained the age of 65 may be eligible for certain pension or other retirement benefits. In some cases, the person may have to take some action when they reach the attained age, such as retire from a company.

AT THE CLOSE ORDER

Securities: market order that is to be executed in its entirety at the closing price on the exchange of the stock named in the order. If it is not so executed, the order is to be treated as canceled.

Futures/Options: in futures and options, a MARKET ON CLOSE ORDER, which is a contract to be executed on some exchanges during the closing period, during which there is a range of prices.

AT THE MARKET *see* MARKET ORDER.

AT THE MONEY at the current price, as an option with an exercise price equal to or near the current price of the stock or underlying futures contract. *See also* DEEP IN/OUT OF THE MONEY; IN THE MONEY; OUT OF THE MONEY.

AT THE OPENING ORDER

Securities: market or limited price order to be executed on the opening trade of the stock on the exchange. If the order, or any portion of it, is not executed in this manner, it is to be treated as canceled.

Futures/Options: in futures and options, a MARKET ON OPEN ORDER, during which there is a range of prices at the opening.

AUCTION MARKET system by which securities are bought and sold through brokers on the securities exchanges, as distinguished from the over-the-counter market, where trades are negotiated. Best exemplified by the NEW YORK STOCK EXCHANGE, it is a double auction system or TWO-SIDED MARKET. That is because, unlike the conventional auction with one auctioneer and many buyers, here we have many sellers and many buyers. As in any auction, a price is established by competitive bidding between brokers acting as agents for buyers and sellers. That the system functions in an orderly way is the result of several trading rules: (1) The first bid or offer at a given price has priority over any other bid or offer at the same price. (2) The high bid and low offer "have the floor." (3) A new auction begins whenever all the offers or bids at a given price are exhausted. (4) Secret transactions are prohibited. (5) Bids and offers must be made in an audible voice.

Also, the competitive bidding by which Treasury bills are sold. *See also* BILL; DUTCH AUCTION.

AUCTION-RATE PREFERRED STOCK *see* DUTCH AUCTION PRE-FERRED STOCK.

AUDIT professional examination and verification of a company's accounting documents and supporting data for the purpose of rendering an opinion as to their fairness, consistency, and conformity with GENERALLY ACCEPTED ACCOUNTING PRINCIPLES. *See also* ACCOUNTANT'S OPINION.

AUDITOR'S CERTIFICATE *see* ACCOUNTANT'S OPINION.

AUDITOR'S REPORT public accountant's declaration following the completion of an examination of corporate financial statements. Also called *accountant's opinion.*

AUDIT TRAIL step-by-step record by which accounting data can be traced to their source. Questions as to the validity or accuracy of an accounting figure can be resolved by reviewing the sequence of events from which the figure resulted.

AUNT MILLIE derogatory term for an unsophisticated investor. Wall Street professionals may say that "This investment will interest Aunt Millie," meaning that it is simple to understand. It may also imply that such small investors will not be able to appreciate the amount of risk posed by the investment relative to the opportunity for profit. Brokers and financial advisors, using the KNOW YOUR CUSTOMER rule, should not recommend complex and risky investments to Aunt Millie investors.

AUSTRALIA STOCK EXCHANGE (ASX) six trading floors, formerly independent entities in Adelaide, Brisbane, Hobart (Tasmania), Melbourne, Perth, and Sydney, are wholly owned subsidiaries of the ASX, linked through the Stock Exchange Automated Trading System (SEATS). Administrative headquarters is in Sydney. The resources sector—mining and energy businesses—accounts for one-third of total market capitalization; industrials—including banks, retail, media, transportation—comprise the balance. The most important Australian stocks are tracked by the ALL-ORDINARIES INDEX, which consists of 330 of the most active shares and represents the vast majority of equity capitalization, excluding foreign companies. Settlement is three business days after a transaction through the Clearing House Electronic Sub-register System (CHESS). SEATS trading hours are

10 A.M. to 4 P.M. (EST) Monday through Friday; dealings are permitted outside these hours according to the exchange's after-hours trading rules.

AUTEX SYSTEM electronic system for alerting brokers that other brokers want to buy or sell large blocks of stock. Once a match is made, the actual transaction takes place over the counter or on the floor of an exchange.

AUTHENTICATION identification of a bond certificate as having been issued under a specific indenture, thus validating the bond. Also, legal verification of the genuineness of a document, as by the certification and seal of an authorized public official.

AUTHORITY BOND bond issued by and payable from the revenue of a government agency or a corporation formed to administer a revenue producing public enterprise. One such corporation is the Port Authority of New York and New Jersey, which operates bridges and tunnels in the New York City area. Because an authority usually has no source of revenue other than charges for the facilities it operates, its bonds have the characteristics of revenue bonds. The difference is that bondholder protections may be incorporated in the authority bond contract as well as in the legislation that created the authority.

AUTHORIZED SHARES maximum number of shares of any class a company may legally create under the terms of its ARTICLES OF INCORPORATION. Normally, a corporation provides for future increases in authorized stock by vote of the stockholders. The corporation is not required to issue all the shares authorized and may initially keep issued shares at a minimum to hold down taxes and expenses. Also called *authorized stock.*

AUTOMATED BOND SYSTEM (ABS) New York Stock Exchange computerized system that records bids and offers for inactively traded bonds until they are cancelled or executed. Before the ABS, such limit orders were kept in steel cabinets, giving rise to the terms CABINET SECURITY and CABINET CROWD (traders in inactive bonds).

AUTOMATED ORDER ENTRY SYSTEM electronic system that expedites the execution of smaller orders by channeling them directly to the specialist on the exchange floor, bypassing the FLOOR BROKER. The New York Stock Exchange calls its system DOT (Designated Order Turnaround). Other systems include Auto Ex, OSS, PACE, SOES, and SOREX.

AUTOMATIC EXTENSION granting of more time for a taxpayer to file a tax return. By filing an IRS Form 4868 by the original due date of the tax return, a taxpayer can automatically extend his or her filing date by four months, though the tax payment (based on the taxpayer's best estimate) is still due on the original filing date.

AUTOMATIC FUNDS TRANSFER fast and accurate transfer of funds, often internationally, from one account or investment vehicle to another without direct management, using modern electronic and telecommunications technology. A broker's instant transfer of stock sale proceeds to a money market fund is one example.

AUTOMATIC INVESTMENT PROGRAM any program in which an investor can accumulate or withdraw funds automatically. Some of the most popular automatic investment programs include:
- mutual fund debit programs, in which a mutual fund will automatically debit a preset amount from a bank savings or checking account to buy fund shares on a weekly, monthly, quarterly, or annual basis.
- mutual fund reinvestment programs, in which all dividends and capital gains are automatically reinvested in more shares of the fund.
- stock dividend reinvestment plans, in which companies offer their shareholders the opportunity to reinvest their dividends in more shares of the company, and in some cases, buy additional shares at a discount with little or no brokerage commissions.
- defined contribution plans, offered by employers to their employees, which allow automatic investment in several funds through payroll deduction. Corporate plans are called 401(k), nonprofit and educational plans are called 403(b), and federal and municipal government plans are called 457s. To entice employees to participate in these plans, many employers match employee contributions.
- savings bond payroll savings plans, which allow employees to purchase savings bonds through payroll deduction.

In addition to allowing automatic purchases of shares, automatic investment programs also permit participants to withdraw a set amount of money on a regular basis. These are known as AUTOMATIC WITHDRAWAL plans. For example, a retiree may request that a mutual fund automatically sell a fixed dollar amount of shares every month and send him or her a check.

AUTOMATIC REINVESTMENT *see* CONSTANT DOLLAR PLAN; DIVIDEND REINVESTMENT PLAN.

AUTOMATIC WITHDRAWAL mutual fund program that entitles shareholders to a fixed payment each month or each quarter. The payment comes from dividends, including realized capital gains and income on securities held by the fund.

AVERAGE appropriately weighted and adjusted ARITHMETIC MEAN of selected securities designed to represent market behavior generally or important segments of the market. Among the most familiar averages are the Dow Jones industrial and transportation averages.

Because the evaluation of individual securities involves measuring price trends of securities in general or within an industry group, the various averages are important analytical tools.

See also STOCK INDEXES AND AVERAGES.

AVERAGE COST
   Investing: average cost of shares of stock or in a fund bought at different prices. *See also* AVERAGE DOWN; AVERAGE UP; CONSTANT DOLLAR PLAN.
   Manufacturing: total of fixed and variable costs divided by units of production. Companies with relatively low average costs are better able to withstand price-cutting pressures from competition. Term also describes INVENTORY valuation method whereby the cost of goods available for sale is divided by the number of units available for sale.

AVERAGE DAILY BALANCE method for computing interest or finance charges on bank deposit accounts, credit cards, and charge accounts. Deposit accounts use the daily closing balance divided by the number of days in the period and apply the interest rate to that. Credit and charge cards divide the balances owed each day by the number of days and apply the finance charge. The average daily balance method, widely used by department stores, is less favorable to the consumer than the ADJUSTED BALANCE METHOD used for interest earned on bank deposit accounts but more favorable than the PREVIOUS BALANCE METHOD used by most credit cards.

AVERAGE DOWN strategy to lower the average price paid for a company's shares. An investor who wants to buy 1000 shares, for example, could buy 400 at the current market price and three blocks of 200 each as the price fell. The average cost would then be lower than it would have been if all 1000 shares had been bought at once. Investors also average down in order to realize tax losses. Say someone buys shares at $20, then watches them fall to $10. Instead of doing nothing, the investor can buy at $10, then sell the $20 shares at a capital loss, which can be used at tax time to offset other gains. However, the WASH SALE rule says that in order to claim the capital loss, the investor must not sell the $20 stock until at least 30 days after buying the stock at $10. *See also* CONSTANT DOLLAR PLAN.

AVERAGE EQUITY average daily balance in a trading account. Brokerage firms calculate customer equity daily as part of their procedure for keeping track of gains and losses on uncompleted transactions, called MARK TO THE MARKET. When transactions are completed, profits and losses are booked to each customer's account together with brokerage commissions. Even though daily fluctuations in equity are routine, average equity is a useful guide in making trading decisions and ensuring sufficient equity to meet MARGIN REQUIREMENTS.

AVERAGE LIFE average length of time before the principal of a debt issue is scheduled to be repaid through AMORTIZATION or SINKING FUND payments. *See also* HALF-LIFE.

AVERAGE UP buy on a rising market so as to lower the overall cost. Buying an equal number of shares at $50, $52, $54, and $58, for instance, will make the average cost $53.50. This is a mathematical reality, but it does not determine whether the stock is worth buying at any or all of these prices.

AVERAGING *see* CONSTANT DOLLAR PLAN.

AWAY FROM THE MARKET expression used when the bid on a LIMIT ORDER is lower or the offer price is higher than the current market price for the security. Away from the market limit orders are held by the specialist for later execution unless FILL OR KILL (FOK) is stipulated on the order entry.

B

BABY BELLS the seven regional telephone companies created when AT&T was broken up in 1984. The original consent decree creating the Baby Bells gave them a monopoly over local phone service but banned them from participating in the long-distance or equipment manufacturing business. AT&T was excluded from the local phone business in return. Over time, these distinctions eroded. According to the Telecommunications Act of 1996, the Baby Bells can offer long-distance service, AT&T and other long-distance providers like WorldCom-MCI and Sprint can offer local service. The original seven Baby Bells were: NYNEX in the Northeast; Bell Atlantic in the Mid-Atlantic states; BELLSOUTH in the South; SBC (Southwestern Bell Corp.) in the Southwest; Ameritech in the Midwest; U.S. West in the Rocky Mountain States; and Pacific Telesis in the West. Subsequently, Bell Atlantic acquired NYNEX and SBC acquired Pacific Telesis and Ameritech.

BABY BOND convertible or straight debt bond having a par value of less than $1000, usually $500 to $25. Baby bonds bring the bond market within reach of small investors and, by the same token, open a source of funds to corporations that lack entree to the large institutional market. On the negative side, they entail higher administrative costs (relative to the total money raised) for distribution and processing and lack the large and active market that ensures the liquidity of conventional bonds.

BACKDATING
   In general: dating any statement, document, check or other instrument earlier than the date drawn.
   Mutual funds: feature permitting fundholders to use an earlier date on a promise to invest a specified sum over a specified period in exchange for a reduced sales charge. Backdating, which usually accompanies a large transaction, gives retroactive value to purchases from the earlier date in order to meet the requirements of the promise, or LETTER OF INTENT.

BACK-END LOAD redemption charge an investor pays when withdrawing money from an investment. Most common in mutual funds and annuities, the back-end load is designed to discourage withdrawals. Back-end loads typically decline for each year that a shareholder remains in a fund. For example, if the shareholder sells shares in the first year, a 5% sales charge is levied. The charge is 4% in the second year, 3% in the third year, 2% in the fourth year, 1% in the fifth year, and no fee is charged if shares are sold after the fifth year. Also called *contingent deferred sales load, deferred sales charge, exit fee, redemption charge.*

BACKING AWAY broker-dealer's failure, as market maker in a given security, to make good on a bid for the minimum quantity. This practice is considered unethical under the RULES OF FAIR PRACTICE of the NATIONAL ASSOCIATION OF SECURITIES DEALERS.

BACKLOG value of unfilled orders placed with a manufacturing company. Whether the firm's backlog is rising or falling is a clue to its future sales and earnings.

BACK MONTHS in futures and options trading, the months with the expiration dates furthest out in time. *See also* FURTHEST MONTH.

BACK OFFICE bank or brokerage house departments not directly involved in selling or trading. The back office sees to accounting records, compliance with government regulations, and communication between branches. When stock-market trading is particularly heavy, order processing can be slowed by massive volume; this is called a back office crunch.

BACK TAXES taxes that have not been paid when due. Taxpayers may owe back taxes if they underreported income or overstated deductions, either accidentally, or by design. The Internal Revenue Service and state and local taxing authorities have the right to audit past tax returns and demand payment of back taxes, plus interest and penalties.

BACK-TESTING applying current stock selection criteria to prior periods to create hypothetical PORTFOLIO performance history. A major limitation of back-testing is that it ignores the effect of an investment strategy's popularity on portfolio total returns.

BACK UP turn around; reverse a stock market trend. When prices are moving in one direction, traders would say of a sudden reversal that the market backed up.

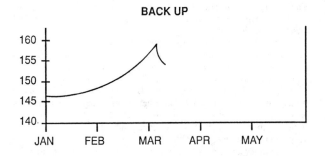

BACK UP

BACKUP LINE BANK LINE of credit in the name of an issuer of commercial paper, covering maturing notes in the event that new notes cannot be marketed to replace them. Ideally, the unused line should always equal the commercial paper outstanding. In practice, something less than total coverage is commonplace, particularly because the compensating balances normally required in support of the line are also available to meet maturing paper.

BACKUP WITHHOLDING system used by the Internal Revenue Service to ensure that taxpayers without Social Security numbers have taxes withheld on earnings. In an instance where a Form 1099 can not be filed by a payor, such as a bank or brokerage, 20% of the interest or dividends is withheld and remitted to the IRS. To avoid backup withholding, you must fill out a federal W-9 form for the financial institution, verifying that your Social Security number is correct.

BACKWARDATION
1. pricing structure in commodities or foreign-exchange trading in which deliveries in the near future have a higher price than those made later on. Backwardation occurs when demand is greater in the near future. *See also* CONTANGO.
2. London Stock Exchange term for the fees and interest due on short sales of stock with delayed delivery.

BAD DEBT
Banks and Corporations: open account balance or loan receivable that has proven uncollectible and is written off. Traditionally, companies and financial institutions have maintained a RESERVE for uncollectible accounts, charging the reserve for actual bad debts and making annual, tax deductible charges to income to replenish or increase the reserve. Companies and large banks ($500 million or more in assets) must generally use the direct charge-off method for tax purposes, although bad debt reserves continue to appear on balance sheets for reporting purposes. Small banks and thrift institutions continue using the reserve method for tax purposes, although with strict limitations. The relationship of bad debt WRITE-OFFS and recoveries to accounts receivable can reveal how liberal or conservative a firm's credit and charge-off policies are.

Individuals: Individuals lending money may deduct bad debts on their tax return when the debtor does not repay the loan. Bad business debts are fully deductible from gross income on Schedule C for self-employed individuals. Nonbusiness bad debts can be deducted as short-term capital losses on Schedule D. These short-term losses can offset capital gains plus $3,000 of other income. Any excess bad debt losses can be carried forward into future tax years. In order to determine whether a bad debt deduction is legitimate:
1. the debt must be legally valid
2. A debtor-creditor relationship must be formalized at the time the debt arose
3. the funds providing the loan must have previously been reported as income or part of the individual's capital and
4. the individual must prove that the debt became worthless in that tax year.

BAD DELIVERY opposite of GOOD DELIVERY.

BAD TITLE title to property that does not clearly confer ownership. Most frequently applied to real estate, a bad title may prevent a homeowner from selling the property. Title may be clouded by unpaid taxes or other unsatisfied liens, a faulty or incomplete certificate of occupancy, an incorrect survey, or uncorrected building violations, among other causes. Steps must be taken to rectify these problems before title to a property can be legally transferred. Also called *cloud on title.*

BAILING OUT selling a security or commodity quickly without regard to the price received. An investor bails out of a position if losses are mounting quickly and he or she is no longer able to sustain further losses. For example, someone who has sold a stock short may bail out by covering his or her position at a loss if the stock rises sharply.

     The term is also used to describe the act of rescuing a person or corporate or government entity in financial distress. For example, the federal government bailed out the Federal Deposit Insurance Corporation with hundreds of billions of dollars when it had to pay for closing down hundreds of bankrupt savings and loans through the Resolution Trust Corporation. When the Chrysler Corporation was teetering near bankruptcy in the early 1980s, the federal government bailed it out by providing loan guarantees.

BAILOUT BOND bond issued by RESOLUTION FUNDING CORPORATION (REFCORP) to finance the rescue or disposition of SAVINGS AND LOAN ASSOCIATIONS that were failing in the 1980s and 1990s. The principal of REFCORP securities is backed by zero-coupon Treasury bonds and the U.S. Treasury guarantees interest payments. Because this is stronger backing than that enjoyed by other GOVERNMENT SECURITIES issued by agencies, bailout bonds yield only slightly more than TREASURIES of comparable maturity. Once the savings and loan crisis ended in the mid-1990s, no more bailout bonds were issued, though existing issues continued to trade in the bond market. *See also* OFFICE OF THRIFT SUPERVISION (OTS).

BALANCED BUDGET *see* BUDGET.

BALANCED MUTUAL FUND fund that buys common stock, preferred stock, and bonds in an effort to obtain the highest return consistent with a low-risk strategy. A balanced fund typically offers a higher yield than a pure stock fund and performs better than such a fund when stocks are falling. In a rising market, however, a balanced mutual fund usually will not keep pace with all-equity funds.

BALANCE OF PAYMENTS system of recording all of a country's economic transactions with the rest of the world during a particular time period. Double-entry bookkeeping is used, and there can be no surplus or deficit on the overall balance of payments. The balance of payments is typically divided into three accounts—current, capital, and gold—

and these can show a surplus or deficit. The current account covers imports and exports of goods and services; the capital account covers movements of investments; and the gold account covers gold movements. The balance of payments helps a country evaluate its competitive strengths and weaknesses and forecast the strength of its currency. From the standpoint of a national economy, a surplus on a part of the balance of payments is not necessarily good, nor is a deficit necessarily bad; the state of the national economy and the manner of financing the deficit are important considerations. *See also* BALANCE OF TRADE.

BALANCE OF TRADE net difference over a period of time between the value of a country's imports and exports of merchandise. Movable goods such as automobiles, foodstuffs, and apparel are included in the balance of trade; payments abroad for services and for tourism are not. When a country exports more than it imports, it is said to have a favorable balance of trade; when imports predominate the balance is called unfavorable. The balance of trade should be viewed in the context of the country's entire international economic position, however. For example, a country may consistently have an unfavorable balance of trade that is offset by considerable exports of services; this country would be judged to have a good international economic position. *See also* BALANCE OF PAYMENTS.

BALANCE SHEET financial report, also called *statement of condition* or *statement of financial position,* showing the status of a company's assets, liabilities, and owners' equity on a given date, usually the close of a month. One way of looking at a business enterprise is as a mass of capital (ASSETS) arrayed against the sources of that capital (LIABILITIES and EQUITY). Assets are equal to liabilities and equity, and the balance sheet is a listing of the items making up the two sides of the equation. Unlike a PROFIT AND LOSS STATEMENT, which shows the results of operations over a period of time, a balance sheet shows the state of affairs at one point in time. It is a snapshot, not a motion picture, and must be analyzed with reference to comparative prior balance sheets and other operating statements.

BALLOON final payment on a debt that is substantially larger than the preceding payments. Loans or mortgages are structured with balloon payments when some projected event is expected to provide extra cash flow or when refinancing is anticipated. Balloon loans are sometimes called *partially amortized loans.*

BALLOON INTEREST in serial bond issues, the higher COUPON rate on bonds with later maturities.

BALLOON MATURITY bond issue or long-term loan with larger dollar amounts of bonds or payments falling due in the later years of the obligation.

BAN *see* BOND ANTICIPATION NOTE.

BANKER'S ACCEPTANCE *see* ACCEPTANCE.

BANK DISCOUNT BASIS *see* DISCOUNT YIELD.

BANK HOLDING COMPANY company that owns or controls two or more banks or other bank holding companies. As defined in the Bank Holding Company Act of 1956, such companies must register with the BOARD OF GOVERNORS of the FEDERAL RESERVE SYSTEM and hence are called registered bank holding companies. Amendments to the 1956 act set standards for acquisitions (1966) and ended the exemption enjoyed by one-bank holding companies (1970), thus restricting bank holding companies to activities related to banking.

BANK INSURANCE FUND (BIF) FEDERAL DEPOSIT INSURANCE CORPORATION (FDIC) unit providing deposit insurance for banks other than thrifts. BIF was formed as part of the 1989 savings and loan association bailout bill to keep separate the administration of the bank and thrift insurance programs. There are thus two distinct insurance entities under FDIC: BIF and SAVINGS ASSOCIATION INSURANCE FUND (SAIF). Deposit insurance coverage remains unaffected. *See also* OFFICE OF THRIFT SUPERVISION (OTS).

BANK INVESTMENT CONTRACT (BIC) bank-guaranteed interest in a portfolio providing a specified yield over a specified period. For insurance company equivalent, *see* GUARANTEED INVESTMENT CONTRACT (GIC).

BANK LINE bank's moral commitment, as opposed to its contractual commitment, to make loans to a particular borrower up to a specified maximum during a specified period, usually one year. Because a bank line—also called a *line of credit*—is not a legal commitment, it is not customary to charge a commitment fee. It is common, however, to require that compensating balances be kept on deposit—typically 10% of the line, with an additional 10% of any borrowings under the line. A line about which a customer is officially notified is called an *advised line* or *confirmed line.* A line that is an internal policy guide about which the customer is not informed is termed a *guidance line.*

BANKMAIL bank's agreement with a company involved in a TAKEOVER not to finance another acquirer's bid.

BANK QUALITY *see* INVESTMENT GRADE.

BANKRUPTCY state of insolvency of an individual or an organization—in other words, an inability to pay debts. There are two kinds of legal bankruptcy under U.S. law: involuntary, when one or more creditors petition to have a debtor judged insolvent by a court; and voluntary, when the debtor brings the petition. In both cases, the objective is an orderly and equitable settlement of obligations.

The 1978 Bankruptcy Reform Act removed some of the rigidities of the old law and permitted more flexibility in procedures. The

Bankruptcy Reform Act of 1984 curtailed some of the more liberal provisions (mainly affecting consumer bankruptcy) of the 1978 act.

Chapter 7 of the 1978 act, dealing with LIQUIDATION, provides for a court-appointed interim trustee with broad powers and discretion to make management changes, arrange unsecured financing, and generally operate the debtor business in such a way as to prevent loss. Only by filing an appropriate bond is the debtor able to regain possession from the trustee.

Chapter 11, which deals with REORGANIZATION of businesses, provides that, unless the court rules otherwise, the debtor remains in possession of the business and in control of its operation. Debtor and creditors are allowed considerable flexibility in working together.

Chapter 13, which deals with debt adjustment or reorganization for individuals, allows people to put forward a plan to repay creditors over time, usually from future income. Most consumer reorganizations take place under Chapter 13 of the bankruptcy law. A Chapter 13 bankruptcy normally requires monthly payments to the bankruptcy trustee for a period of three to five years. Once payments have been completed under the plan, the debtors are entitled to a discharge. Chapter 13 reorganizations also allow debtors to keep more property than in a Chapter 7 liquidation.

BANK TRUST DEPARTMENT part of a bank engaged in settling estates, administering trusts and guardianships, and performing AGENCY services. As part of its personal trust and ESTATE PLANNING services, it manages investments for large accounts—typically those with at least $50,000 in assets. People who cannot or do not want to make investment decisions are commonly bank trust department clients. Known for their conservative investment philosophy, such departments have custody over billions of dollars, making them a major factor in the movement of stock and bond prices.

Among other things, the departments also act as trustee for corporate bonds, administer pension and profit-sharing plans, and function as TRANSFER AGENTS.

BANK WIRE computerized message system owned and administered by about 250 participating banks in about 75 U.S. cities. Like the FED WIRE, the bank wire transmits large dollar credit transfer information. It also provides information about loan participations, securities transactions, Federal Reserve System funds borrowings, credit history, the payment or nonpayment of "wire fate" items, and other essential matters requiring prompt communication.

BARBELL PORTFOLIO portfolio of bonds distributed like the shape of a barbell, with most of the portfolio in short-term and long-term bonds, but few bonds in intermediate maturities. This portfolio can be adjusted to emphasize short- or long-term bonds, depending on whether the investor thinks interest rates are rising or falling. A portfolio with a higher concentration in medium-term bonds than short- or long-term bonds is called a *bell-shaped curve portfolio.*

BAREFOOT PILGRIM unsophisticated investor who has lost his or her shirt and shoes in securities trading.

BAROMETER selective compilation of economic and market data designed to represent larger trends. Consumer spending, housing starts, and interest rates are barometers used in economic forecasting. The Dow Jones Industrial Average and the Standard & Poor's 500 Stock Index are prominent stock market barometers. The Dow Jones Utility Average is a barometer of market trends in the utility industry.

A *barometer stock* has a price movement pattern that reflects the market as a whole, thus serving as a market indicator. General Motors, for example, is considered a barometer stock.

BARRON'S CONFIDENCE INDEX weekly index of corporate bond yields published by *Barron's,* a Dow Jones financial newspaper. The index shows the ratio of the average yield on 10 top-grade bonds to the average yield on 10 intermediate-grade bonds. People who are worried about the economic outlook tend to seek safety in a FLIGHT TO QUALITY, whereas investors who feel secure about the economy are more likely to buy lower-rated bonds. The spread between high- and low-grade bonds thus reflects investor confidence about the economy. *Barron's* also publishes other confidence indicators, such as the TED SPREAD (the difference between Treasury Bill Futures and Eurodollar Futures contract prices); the Lehman Brothers Treasury Bond Index; the Lehman Brothers Corporate Bond Index; the Ryan Labs Treasury Index; the Bond Buyer 20 Bond Index; the Bond Buyer Municipal Bond Index and the Stock/Bond Yield Gap, which is the difference between the yield on the highest-grade corporate bonds and the yield on the stocks in the Dow Jones Industrial Average.

BARTER trade of goods or services without use of money. When money is involved, whether in such forms as wampum, checks, or bills or coins, a transaction is called a SALE. Although barter is usually associated with undeveloped economies, it occurs in modern complex societies. In conditions of extreme inflation, it can be a preferred mode of commerce. Where a population lacks confidence in its currency or banking system, barter becomes commonplace. In international trade, barter can provide a way of doing business with countries whose soft currencies would otherwise make them unattractive trading partners.

BASE in TECHNICAL ANALYSIS, a chart pattern in which the SUPPORT LEVEL and the RESTRICTED LEVEL come together. During a *basing* period, supply and demand are in relative equilibrium and the stock trades in a narrow range. A positive or negative BREAKOUT from a basing period can be a powerful buy or sell signal.

BASE MARKET VALUE average market price of a group of securities at a given time. It is used as a basis of comparison in plotting dollar or percentage changes for purposes of market INDEXING.

BASE PERIOD particular time in the past used as a yardstick when measuring economic data. A base period is usually a year or an average of years; it can also be a month or other time period. The U.S. rate of INFLATION is determined by measuring current prices against those of a base period; for instance, the CONSUMER PRICE INDEX is determined by comparing current prices with prices in the base reference years of 1982–1984 and the PRODUCER PRICE INDEX is determined by comparing current prices with prices in the base reference year of 1987.

BASE RATE interest rate charged by banks to their best corporate customers in Great Britain. It is the British equivalent of the PRIME RATE in the United States. Many other consumer loan rates are pegged to the base rate in Britain.

BASIC EARNINGS PER SHARE *see* EARNINGS PER SHARE.

BASIS
In general: original cost plus out-of-pocket expenses that must be reported to the Internal Revenue Service when an investment is sold and must be used in calculating capital gains or losses. If a stock was bought for $1000 two years ago and is sold today for $2000, the basis is $1000 and the profit is a capital gain.
Bonds: an investor's YIELD TO MATURITY at a given bond price. A 10% bond selling at 100 has a 10% basis.
Commodities: the difference between the cash price of a hedged money market instrument and a FUTURES CONTRACT.

BASIS POINT smallest measure used in quoting yields on bills, notes, and bonds. One basis point is .01%, or one one-hundredth of a percent of yield. Thus, 100 basis points equal 1%. A bond's yield that increased from 8.00% to 8.50% would be said to have risen 50 basis points.

BASIS PRICE
In general: price an investor uses to calculate capital gains when selling a stock or bond. *See also* BASIS.
Odd-lot trading: the price arbitrarily established by an exchange floor official at the end of a trading session for a buyer or seller of an odd lot when the market bid and asked prices are more than $2 apart, or if no round-lot transactions have occurred that day. The customer gets the basis price plus or minus the odd-lot differential, if any. This procedure for determining prices is rare, since most odd lots are transacted at the market bid (if a sale) or asked (if a buy) or at prices based on the next round-lot trade.

BASKET
1. unit of 15 or more stocks used in PROGRAM TRADING.
2. program trading vehicles offered by the NEW YORK STOCK EXCHANGE (called *Exchange Stock Portfolio* or *ESP*) and the CHICAGO BOARD OPTIONS EXCHANGE (called *Market Basket*) to institutional investors and index arbitrageurs. Both baskets permit the

purchase in one trade of all the stocks making up the STANDARD & POOR'S 500 COMPOSITE INDEX. ESP's design requires a minimum trade of approximately $5 million, and Market Basket's, around $1.7 million. The baskets were introduced in late 1989 to solve problems revealed when institutions tried to negotiate large block trades on BLACK MONDAY and to head off an exodus of program trading business to overseas exchanges. Subsequently, trading in these instruments ceased due to lack of trading volume.

3. informal name for *index participations* (also called *cash index participations* or *CIPS),* a controversial financial instrument introduced and then withdrawn by the American and Philadelphia stock exchanges in 1989. The product allowed small investors to buy a portfolio position (in the Standard & Poor's index of 500 stocks and in a 25-stock index that has historically correlated with the Dow Jones Industrial Average) without buying individual stocks. It retained advantages of stock ownership by having no expiration date (like a future or an option) and providing for quarterly dividend payments. Originally approved by the SECURITIES AND EXCHANGE COMMISSION as a security, the instrument was challenged by the COMMODITIES FUTURES TRADING COMMISSION, which claimed it was a futures contract. When a federal court ruled against the SEC, the exchanges stopped trading the product.

See also DIAMONDS, SPDR.

BD FORM document that brokerage house must file and keep current with the Securities and Exchange Commission, detailing the firm's finances and officers.

BEACON acronym for the *Boston Exchange Automated Communication Order-routing Network.* This electronic system allows the automatic execution of trades based on the prevailing stock prices on the consolidated market, any of the seven U.S. securities exchanges.

BEAR person with a pessimistic market outlook. Contrast with BULL.

BEARER BOND *see* COUPON BOND.

BEARER FORM security not registered on the books of the issuing corporation and thus payable to the one possessing it. A bearer bond has coupons attached, which the bondholder sends in or presents on the interest date for payment, hence the alternative name COUPON BONDS. Bearer stock certificates are negotiable without endorsement and are transferred by delivery. Dividends are payable by presentation of dividend coupons, which are dated or numbered. Most securities issued today, with the exception of foreign stocks, are in registered form, including municipal bonds issued since 1983.

BEAR HUG TAKEOVER bid so attractive in terms of price and other features that TARGET COMPANY directors, who might be opposed for other reasons, must approve it or risk shareholder protest.

BEAR MARKET prolonged period of falling prices. A bear market in stocks is usually brought on by the anticipation of declining economic activity, and a bear market in bonds is caused by rising interest rates.

BEAR RAID attempt by investors to manipulate the price of a stock by selling large numbers of shares short. The manipulators pocket the difference between the initial price and the new, lower price after this maneuver. Bear raids are illegal under Securities and Exchange Commission rules, which stipulate that every SHORT SALE be executed on an UPTICK (the last price was higher than the price before it) or a ZERO PLUS TICK (the last price was unchanged but higher than the last preceding different price).

BEARS acronym for *Bonds Enabling Annual Retirement Savings* and the flip side of *CUBS*, acronym for *Calls Underwritten By Swanbrook.* Holders of BEARS receive the face value of bonds underlying call options but exercised by CUBS holders. If the calls are exercised, BEARS holders receive the aggregate of the exercise prices.

BEAR SPREAD strategy in the options market designed to take advantage of a fall in the price of a security or commodity. Someone executing a bear spread could buy a combination of calls and puts on the same security at different *strike prices* in order to profit as the security's price fell. Or the investor could buy a put of short maturity and a put of long maturity in order to profit from the difference between the two puts as prices fell. *See also* BULL SPREAD.

BEAR TRAP situation confronting short sellers when a bear market reverses itself and turns bullish. Anticipating further declines, the bears continue to sell, and then are forced to buy at higher prices to cover. *See also* SELLING SHORT.

BELL signal that opens and closes trading on major exchanges—sometimes actually a bell but sometimes a buzzer sound.

BELLWETHER security seen as an indicator of a market's direction. In stocks, 3M Company (MMM) is considered both an economic and a market bellwether because it sells to a diverse range of other producers and because so much of its stock is owned by institutional investors who have much control over supply and demand on the stock market. Institutional trading actions tend to influence smaller investors and therefore the market generally. There are bellwethers in specific industries, for example, Microsoft and Intel act as bellwethers for the technology stocks. In bonds, the 30-year U.S. Treasury bond is considered the bellwether, denoting the direction in which all other bonds are likely to move.

BELOW PAR *see* PAR VALUE.

BENEFICIAL OWNER person who enjoys the benefits of ownership even though title is in another name. When shares of a mutual fund are held by a custodian bank or when securities are held by a broker in STREET NAME, the real owner is the beneficial owner, even though, for safety or convenience, the bank or broker holds title.

BENEFICIARY

1. person to whom an inheritance passes as the result of being named in a will.
2. recipient of the proceeds of a life insurance policy.
3. party in whose favor a LETTER OF CREDIT is issued.
4. one to whom the amount of an ANNUITY is payable.
5. party for whose benefit a TRUST exists.

BEQUEST giving of assets, such as stocks, bonds, mutual funds, real estate, and personal property, to beneficiaries through the provisions of a will.

BEST EFFORT arrangement whereby investment bankers, acting as agents, agree to do their best to sell an issue to the public. Instead of buying the securities outright, these agents have an option to buy and an authority to sell the securities. Depending on the contract, the agents exercise their option and buy enough shares to cover their sales to clients, or they cancel the incompletely sold issue altogether and forgo the fee. Best efforts deals, which were common prior to 1900, entailed risks and delays from the issuer's standpoint. What is more, the broadening of the securities markets has made marketing new issues easier, and the practice of outright purchase by investment bankers, called FIRM COMMITMENT underwriting, has become commonplace. For the most part, the best efforts deals we occasionally see today are handled by firms specializing in the more speculative securities of new and unseasoned companies. *See also* BOUGHT DEAL.

BEST'S RATING rating assigned to insurance companies by A.M. Best Co. A Best's Rating is important to buyers of insurance or annuities because it provides an opinion of a company's ability to meet its obligations to policyholders. Best's Ratings are also important to investors in insurance stocks. The top rating is A++. Other companies providing ratings of insurance companies include Duff & Phelps in Chicago, MOODY'S INVESTORS SERVICES in New York, STANDARD & POOR'S in New York and Weiss Research in Palm Beach Gardens, Florida.

BETA

1. coefficient measuring a stock's relative VOLATILITY. The beta is the covariance of a stock in relation to the rest of the stock market. The Standard & Poor's 500 Stock Index has a beta coefficient of 1. Any stock with a higher beta is more volatile than the market, and any with a lower beta can be expected to rise and fall more slowly than the market. A conservative investor whose main concern is preservation of capital should focus on stocks with low betas, whereas one willing to take high risks in an effort to earn high rewards should look for high-beta stocks. *See also* ALPHA.

2. on the London Stock Exchange, the designation *beta stocks* applies to the second tier in a four-level hierarchy introduced with BIG BANG in October 1986 and replaced in January, 1991 with the NORMAL MARKET SIZE (NMS) classification system. With ALPHA stocks representing the equivalent of American BLUE CHIP issues, beta stocks represented smaller issues that were less actively traded. *See also* DELTA (2); GAMMA STOCKS.

BID

  1. price a prospective buyer is ready to pay. Term is used by traders who MAKE A MARKET (maintain firm bid and OFFER prices) in a given security by standing ready to buy or sell round lots at publicly quoted prices and by the SPECIALIST in a stock, who performs a similar function on an exchange.

  2. TENDER OFFER in a TAKEOVER attempt.

  3. any offer to buy at a specified price.

  See also ANY-AND-ALL BID; COMPETITIVE BID; TREASURIES.

BID AND ASKED bid is the highest price a prospective buyer is prepared to pay at a particular time for a trading unit of a given security; asked is the lowest price acceptable to a prospective seller of the same security. Together, the two prices constitute a QUOTATION; the difference between the two prices is the SPREAD. Although the bid and asked dynamic is common to all securities trading, "bid and asked" usually refers to UNLISTED SECURITIES traded OVER THE COUNTER.

BID-ASKED SPREAD difference between BID and offer prices. The term *asked* is usually used in OVER-THE COUNTER trading; *offered* is used in exchange trading. The bid and asked (or offered) prices together comprise a QUOTATION (or *quote*).

BIDDER party that is ready to buy at a specified price in a TWO-SIDED MARKET or DUTCH AUCTION.

BIDDING UP practice whereby the price bid for a security is successively moved higher lest an upswing in prices leaves orders unexecuted. An example would be an investor wanting to purchase a sizable quantity of shares in a rising market, using buy limit orders (orders to buy at a specified price or lower) to ensure the most favorable price. Since offer prices are moving up with the market, the investor must move his limit buy price upward to continue accumulating shares. To some extent the buyer is contributing to the upward price pressure on the stock, but most of the price rise is out of his control.

BID-TO-COVER RATIO number of bids received in a Treasury security auction compared to the number of bids accepted. A high ratio (over 2.0) is an indication that bidding was aggressive and the auction successful. A low ratio, indicating the government had difficulty selling its securities, is usually accompanied by a long TAIL, a wide spread between the average and high yield (the average and lowest accepted bid).

BID WANTED (BW) announcement that a holder of securities wants to sell and will entertain bids. Because the final price is subject to negotiation, the bid submitted in response to a BW need not be specific. A BW is frequently seen on published market quotation sheets.

BIG BANG deregulation on October 27, 1986, of London-based securities markets, an event comparable to MAY DAY in the United States and marking a major step toward a single world financial market.

BIG BLUE popular name for International Business Machines Corporation (IBM), taken from the color of its logotype.

BIG BOARD popular term for the NEW YORK STOCK EXCHANGE.

BIG FIVE largest U.S. accounting firms as measured by revenue. They do the accounting and auditing for most major corporations, signing the AUDITOR'S REPORT that appears in every annual report. They also offer various consulting services. Over time, there have been several mergers among the top accounting firms, which formerly were called the Big Eight, and until 1998, the Big Six. In alphabetical order they are: Andersen Worldwide; PricewaterhouseCoopers; Deloitte & Touche; Ernst & Young; and KPMG Peat Marwick.

BIG PRODUCER broker who is very successful, and thereby produces a large volume of commission dollars for the brokerage firm he or she represents. Big producers typically will bring in $1 million or more per year in commissions for their firms. In order to retain big producers, many brokerage firms try to tie them to the firm with GOLDEN HANDCUFFS.

BIG THREE the three large automobile companies in America, which are, alphabetically, Chrysler, Ford, and General Motors. Since the automobile business has such a major influence on the direction of the economy, the Big Three's fortunes are closely followed by investors, analysts, and economists. Because auto company profits rise and fall with the economy, they are considered to be CYCLICAL STOCKS. In 1998, Chrysler merged with Daimler-Benz to create DaimlerChrysler AG.

BIG UGLIES stocks that are out of favor with the investing public. These usually are large industrial companies such as steel or chemical firms that are not in glamorous businesses. Because they are unpopular, Big Uglies typically sell at low price/earnings and price/book value ratios.

BILL

In general: (1) short for *bill of exchange,* an order by one person directing a second to pay a third. (2) document evidencing a debtor's obligation to a creditor, the kind of bill we are all familiar with. (3) paper currency, like the $5 bill. (4) *bill of sale,* a document used to transfer the title to certain goods from seller to buyer in the same way a deed to real property passes.

Investments: short for *due bill,* a statement of money owed. Commonly used to adjust a securities transaction when dividends, interest, and other distributions are reflected in a price but have not yet been disbursed. For example, when a stock is sold ex-dividend, but the dividend has not yet been paid, the buyer would sign a due bill stating that the amount of the dividend is payable to the seller.

A due bill may accompany delivered securities to give title to the buyer's broker in exchange for shares or money.

U.S. Treasury bill: commonly called bill or T-bill by money market people, a Treasury bill is a short-term (maturities up to a year), discounted government security sold through competitive bidding at weekly and monthly auctions in denominations from $10,000 to $1 million.

The auction at which bills are sold differs from the two-sided auction used by exchanges. Here, in what is sometimes termed a *Dutch auction,* the Treasury invites anyone interested to submit a bid, called a TENDER, then awards units to the highest bidders going down a list. Three-and six-month bills are auctioned weekly, nine-month and one-year bills monthly. Although the yield on bills may barely top the inflation rate, the high degree of safety together with the liquidity provided by an active SECONDARY MARKET make bills popular with corporate money managers as well as with banks and other government entities.

Individuals may also purchase bills directly, in amounts under $500,000, at no transaction charge, from a Federal Reserve bank, the Bureau of Federal Debt, or certain commercial banks. Bills bought on this basis are priced by noncompetitive bidding, with subscribers paying an average of the accepted bids.

Treasury bills are the most widely used of all government debt securities and are a primary instrument of Federal Reserve monetary policy. *See also* TAX ANTICIPATION BILL; TREASURY DIRECT.

BILLING CYCLE interval between periodic billings for goods sold or services rendered, normally one month, or a system whereby bills or statements are mailed at periodic intervals in the course of a month in order to distribute the clerical workload.

BILL OF EXCHANGE *see* DRAFT.

BINDER sum of money paid to evidence good faith until a transaction is finalized. In insurance, the binder is an agreement executed by an insurer (or sometimes an agent) that puts insurance coverage into force before the contract is signed and the premium paid. In real estate, the binder holds the sale until the closing and is refundable.

BI-WEEKLY MORTGAGE LOAN mortgage loan on which the borrower makes 26 half-month payments a year, resulting in earlier loan retirement and lower total interest costs than with a fully amortized loan with regular monthly payments. For example, a 30-year mortgage may be retired in 20 years if paid bi-weekly. Many bi-weekly plans offer automatic electronic debiting of the borrower's bank account.

BLACK FRIDAY sharp drop in a financial market. The original Black Friday was September 24, 1869, when a group of financiers tried to corner the gold market and precipitated a business panic followed by a depression. The panic of 1873 also began on Friday, and Black Friday has come to apply to any debacle affecting the financial markets.

BLACK MONDAY October 19, 1987, when the Dow Jones Industrial Average plunged a record 508 points following sharp drops the previous week, reflecting investor anxiety about inflated stock price levels, federal budget and trade deficits, and foreign market activity. On Monday, October 27, 1997, the Dow dropped 554 points, precipitated by economic and currency upheaval in Southeast Asia. While the point drop set a new record, the percentage decline based on a higher Dow was far less than in 1987. That 1997 day is also called *Bloody Monday*. Many blamed PROGRAM TRADING for the extreme VOLATILITY.

BLACK-SCHOLES OPTION PRICING MODEL model developed by Fischer Black and Myron Scholes to gauge whether options contracts are fairly valued. The model incorporates such factors as the volatility of a security's return, the level of interest rates, the relationship of the underlying stock's price to the *strike price* of the option, and the time remaining until the option expires. Current valuations using this model are developed by the Options Monitor Service and are available from Standard & Poor's Trading Systems, 11 Broadway, New York, NY 10004.

BLANK CHECK check drawn on a bank account and signed by the maker, but with the amount of the check to be supplied by the drawee. Term is used as a metaphor for any situation where inordinate trust is placed in another person.

BLANK CHECK OFFERING INITIAL PUBLIC OFFERING (IPO) by a company whose business activities have yet to be determined and which is therefore speculative. Similar to the BLIND POOL concept of limited partnerships.

BLANKET CERTIFICATION FORM *see* NASD FORM FR-1.

BLANKET FIDELITY BOND insurance coverage against losses due to employee dishonesty. Brokerage firms are required to carry such protection in proportion to their net capital as defined by the Securities and Exchange Commission. Contingencies covered include securities loss, forgery, and fraudulent trading. Also called *blanket bond.*

BLANKET RECOMMENDATION communication sent to all customers of a brokerage firm recommending that they buy or sell a particular stock or stocks in a particular industry regardless of investment objectives or portfolio size.

BLENDED RATE mortgage financing term used when a lender, to avoid assuming an old mortgage at an obsoletely low rate, offers the incentive to refinance at a rate somewhere between the old rate and the rate on a new loan.

BLIND POOL limited partnership that does not specify the properties the general partner plans to acquire. If, for example, a real estate partnership is offered in the form of a blind pool, investors can evaluate the project only by looking at the general partner's track record. In a *specified pool,* on the other hand, investors can look at the prices paid for property and the amount of rental income the buildings generate, then evaluate the partnership's potential. In general, blind pool partnerships do not perform better or worse than specified pool partnerships.

BLIND TRUST trust in which a fiduciary third party, such as a bank or money management firm, is given complete discretion to make investments on behalf of the trust beneficiaries. The trust is called blind because the beneficiary is not informed about the holdings of the trust. Blind trusts often are set up when there is a potential conflict of interest involving the beneficiary and the investments held in the trust. For example, a politician may be required to place his assets in a blind trust so that his votes are not influenced by his trust's portfolio holdings.

BLITZKREIG TENDER OFFER TAKEOVER jargon for a tender offer that is completed quickly, usually because it was priced attractively. *Blitzkreig* translates from the German as "lightning-like war" and was used to describe World War II bombing raids. Legislation passed in the 1960s was aimed at curtailing surprise takeovers, so the term is relative. *See also* SATURDAY NIGHT SPECIAL.

BLOCK large quantity of stock or large dollar amount of bonds held or traded. As a general guide, 10,000 shares or more of stock and $200,000 or more worth of bonds would be described as a block.

BLOCK POSITIONER dealer who, to accommodate the seller of a block of securities, will take a position in the securities, hoping to gain from a rise in the market price. Block positioners must register with the Securities and Exchange Commission and the New York Stock Exchange (if member firms). Typically they engage in ARBITRAGE, HEDGING, and SELLING SHORT to protect their risk and liquidate their position.

BLOCK TRADE *see* BLOCK.

BLOODY MONDAY *see* BLACK MONDAY.

BLOWOUT quick sale of all shares in a new offering of securities. Corporations like to sell securities in such environments, because they get a high price for their stock. Investors are likely to have a hard time getting the number of shares they want during a blowout. Also called *going away* or *hot issue.*

BLUE CHIP common stock of a nationally known company that has a long record of profit growth and dividend payment and a reputation for quality management, products, and services. Some examples of blue chip stocks: International Business Machines, General Electric, and Du Pont. Blue chip stocks typically are relatively high priced and have moderate dividend yields.

BLUE LIST daily financial publication listing bonds offered for sale by several hundred dealers and banks and representing billions of dollars in par value. The *Blue List,* published by a Standard & Poor's subsidiary, mainly contains data on municipal bonds. With its pertinent price, yield, and other data, the *Blue List* is the most comprehensive source of information on activity and volume in the secondary market for tax-exempt securities. Some corporate bonds offered by the same dealers are also included. Full name, *Blue List of Current Municipal Offerings.* The *Blue List* is also available through an on-line database on the Internet at www.bluelist.com.

BLUE-SKY LAW law of a kind passed by various states to protect investors against securities fraud. These laws require sellers of new stock issues or mutual funds to register their offerings and provide financial details on each issue so that investors can base their judgments on relevant data. The term is said to have originated with a judge who asserted that a particular stock offering had as much value as a patch of blue sky.

BOARD BROKER employee of the CHICAGO BOARD OPTIONS EXCHANGE who handles AWAY FROM THE MARKET orders, which cannot immediately be executed. If board brokers act as agents in executing such orders, they notify the exchange members who entered the orders.

BOARD OF DIRECTORS group of individuals elected, usually at an annual meeting, by the shareholders of a corporation and empowered to carry out certain tasks as spelled out in the corporation's charter. Among such powers are appointing senior management, naming members of executive and finance committees (if any), issuing additional shares, and declaring dividends. Boards normally include the top corporate executives, termed *inside directors,* as well as OUTSIDE DIRECTORS chosen from business and from the community at large to advise on matters of broad policy. Directors meet several times a year and are paid for their services. They are considered control persons under the securities laws, meaning that their shares are restricted. As insiders, they cannot (1) buy and sell the company's stock within a 6-month period; (2) sell short in the company's stock, and if they sell owned shares must deliver in 20 days and/or place certificates in mail within 5 days; (3) effect any foreign or arbitrage transaction in the company's stock; (4) trade on material information not available to the public.

BOARD OF GOVERNORS OF THE FEDERAL RESERVE SYSTEM seven-member managing body of the FEDERAL RESERVE SYSTEM, commonly called the Federal Reserve Board. The board sets policy on issues relating to banking regulations as well as to the MONEY SUPPLY.

BOARD ROOM
 Brokerage house: room where customers can watch an electronic board that displays stock prices and transactions.
 Corporation: room where the board of directors holds its meetings.

BO DEREK STOCK perfect stock with an exemplary record of earnings growth, product quality, and stock price appreciation. These stocks are named after the movie "10" in which Bo Derek was depicted as the perfect woman.

BOGEY target for purchasing or selling a security or achieving some other objective. An investor's bogey may be a 10% rate of return from a particular stock. Or it may be locking in an 8% yield on a bond. A money manager's bogey may be to beat the Standard & Poor's 500 index.

BOILERPLATE standard legal language, often in fine print, used in most contracts, wills, indentures, prospectuses, and other legal documents. Although what the boilerplate says is important, it rarely is subject to change by the parties to the agreement, since it is the product of years of legal experience.

BOILER ROOM place where high-pressure salespeople use banks of telephones to call lists of potential investors (known in the trade as sucker lists) in order to peddle speculative, even fraudulent, securities. They are called boiler rooms because of the high-pressure selling. Boiler room methods, if not illegal, clearly violate the National Association of Securities Dealers' RULES OF FAIR PRACTICE, particularly those requiring that recommendations be suitable to a customer's account. *See also* BUCKET SHOP.

BOLSA Spanish term for *stock exchange.* There are Bolsas in Spain, Mexico, Chile, Argentina, and many other Spanish-speaking countries. In French, the term is BOURSE; in Italian, Borsa.

BOLSA DE COMMERCIO DE SANTIAGO (SSE) is Chile's dominant stock exchange. SSE publishes three stock indices: the General Price Index (IGPA), a market capitalization weighted index of 161 companies that is rebalanced annually; the Selective Price Index (IPSA), a volume-weighted index 40 stocks most heavily traded in the prior year, that is rebalanced quarterly; and the Inter-10 Index, a volume weighted index of the 10 largest companies with ADRs, revised quarterly. Chile operates three stock exchanges: the Santiago Stock Exchange, the Bolsa Electronica, and the Valparaiso Stock Exchange. SSE, founded in 1893, is the largest, with close to 80% total trading. Bolsa Electronica, established in 1989, is a screen-based electronic stock exchange based in Santiago that accounts for more than 25% of total equity trading in the country. Bolsa de Valparaiso, established in

1892, is Chile's oldest exchange. Settlement usually occurs two days after a transaction, but can be accomplished earlier or by deferred payment on the last Wednesday of every month. Deferred transactions require a deposit and are allowed only in the shares of 124 companies. Open outcry at SSE is in three sessions: 10:30 A.M. to 11:20 A.M.; 12:30 P.M. to 1:20 P.M.; and 4 P.M. to 4:30 P.M. Low-volume shares trade on a computer system from 9:30 A.M. to 4:30 P.M. Shares are traded by auction once a day. There are no market makers, and most brokers trade for their own accounts.

BOLSA DE VALORES DE RIO DE JANIERO (BVRJ) is Brazil's second largest exchange. It calculates the IBV Index, covering the most actively-traded Rio stocks. Trading hours are 10:30 A.M. to 5:30 P.M. All stocks trade simultaneously on the floor and on the electronic system. There is a 30-minute pre-opening session. Physical settlement is on the second business day following the trade, and financial settlement is on the third business day at CLC, an independent clearing house that settles trades entered into the national trading system. The CLC is recognized by the Securities and Exchange Commission as a depository for U.S. institutional investors.

BOLSA DE VALORES DE SAO PAULO (BOVESPA) largest of Brazil's nine stock exchanges, it accounts for two-thirds of all stock transactions. The Bovespa Index is the most widely recognized. The Electric Power Index (IEE) is the first of a series of sector indices. Open outcry sessions are held in two sessions, from 10:30 A.M. to 1:30 P.M., and 2:30 P.M. to 5:30 P.M., Monday through Friday. Computer assisted trading system (CATS) sessions run simultaneously from 10:30 A.M. to 5:30 P.M. Stock and options of the 22 most actively traded companies are traded in the open outcry session; other stocks and options are traded only on CATS. Stock options and an option with a strike price quoted in points tied to the U.S. dollar are traded on the exchange as well. Physical settlement is on the second business day following the trade, and financial settlement is on the third business day at CALISPA, the exchange's wholly-owned subsidiary.

BOMBAY STOCK EXCHANGE (BSE) see NATIONAL STOCK EXCHANGE; THE STOCK EXCHANGE, MUMBAI (BSE).

BOND any interest-bearing or discounted government or corporate security that obligates the issuer to pay the bondholder a specified sum of money, usually at specific intervals, and to repay the principal amount of the loan at maturity. Bondholders have an IOU from the issuer, but no corporate ownership privileges, as stockholders do.

An owner of *bearer bonds* presents the bond coupons and is paid interest, whereas the owner of *registered bonds* appears on the records of the bond issuer.

A SECURED BOND is backed by collateral which may be sold by the bondholder to satisfy a claim if the bond's issuer fails to pay interest and principal when they are due. An *unsecured bond* or DEBENTURE is backed by the full faith and credit of the issuer, but not by any specific collateral.

A CONVERTIBLE bond gives its owner the privilege of exchange for other securities of the issuing company at some future date and under prescribed conditions.

Also, a bond, in finance, is the obligation of one person to repay a debt taken on by someone else, should that other person default. A bond can also be money or securities deposited as a pledge of good faith.

A surety or PERFORMANCE BOND is an agreement whereby an insurance company becomes liable for the performance of work or services provided by a contractor by an agreed-upon date. If the contractor does not do what was promised, the surety company is financially responsible. *See also* INDENTURE; ZERO COUPON SECURITY.

BOND ANTICIPATION NOTE (BAN) short-term debt instrument issued by a state or municipality that will be paid off with the proceeds of an upcoming bond issue. To the investor, BANs offer a safe, tax-free yield that may be higher than other tax-exempt debt instruments of the same maturity.

BOND BROKER broker who executes bond trades on the floor of an exchange. Also, one who trades corporate, U.S. government, or municipal debt issues over the counter, mostly for large institutional accounts.

BOND BUYER, THE daily publication containing most of the key statistics and indexes used in the fixed-income markets. *See also* BOND BUYER'S INDEX; THIRTY-DAY VISIBLE SUPPLY.

BOND BUYER'S MUNICIPAL BOND INDEX index published daily by the *BOND BUYER,* a newspaper covering the municipal bond market. The index tracks municipal bond prices and is composed of 40 actively traded general obligation and revenue issues rated A or better with a term portion of at least $50 million ($75 million for housing issues); at least 19 years remaining to maturity; a first call date between 7 and 16 years; and at least one call at par before redemption. Starting in July 1, 1995, noncallable bonds became eligible for inclusion in the index. The publication also tracks the Bond Buyer 20 Bond Index, which is an index of yields of 20 general obligation municipal bonds. Investors use the publication's Bond Buyer indices to plot interest rate patterns in the muni market. Traders use the daily Bond Buyer Index to trade municipal bond index futures and futures options at the CHICAGO BOARD OF TRADE.

BOND COUNSEL attorney or law firm that prepares the LEGAL OPINION for a municipal bond issue.

BOND CROWD exchange members who transact bond orders on the floor of the exchange. The work area in which they congregate is separate from the stock traders, hence the term bond crowd.

BOND DISCOUNT amount by which the MARKET PRICE of a bond is lower than its FACE VALUE. Outstanding bonds with fixed COUPONS go to discounts when market interest rates rise. Discounts are also caused when supply exceeds demand and when a bond's CREDIT RATING is reduced. When opposite conditions exist and market price is higher than face value, the difference is termed a *bond premium.* Premiums also occur when a bond issue with a CALL FEATURE is redeemed prior to maturity and the bondholder is compensated for lost interest. *See also* ORIGINAL ISSUE DISCOUNT.

BOND EQUIVALENT YIELD restatement of a DISCOUNT YIELD as its interest-bearing equivalent.

BONDHOLDER owner of a bond. Bondholders may be individuals or institutions such as corporations, banks, insurance companies, or mutual funds. Bondholders are entitled to regular interest payments as due and return of principal when the bond matures. Bondholders may own corporate, government, or municipal issues. For corporate bonds, bondholders' claims on the assets of the issuing corporation take precedence over claims of stockholders in the event of liquidation. Unlike stockholders, however, straight bondholders do not own an equity interest in the issuing company. Some bonds, such as convertible bonds, do have some claim on the equity of the issuing corporation.

BOND MARKET ASSOCIATION international trade association of banks and broker/dealers in U.S. government and federal agency securities, municipal securities, mortgage-backed securities and money-market securities.

BOND MUTUAL FUND mutual fund holding bonds. Such funds may specialize in a particular kind of bond, such as government, corporate, convertible, high-yield, mortgage-backed, municipal, foreign, or zero-coupon bonds. Other bond mutual funds will buy some or all of these kinds of bonds. Most bond mutual funds are designed to produce current income for shareholders. Bond funds also produce capital gains when interest rates fall and capital losses when interest rates rise. Unlike the bonds in these funds, the funds themselves never mature. There are two types of bond mutual funds: open- and closed-end. *Open-end funds* continually create new shares to accommodate new money as it flows into the funds and they always trade at NET ASSET VALUE. *Closed-end funds* issue a limited number of shares and trade on stock exchanges. Closed-end funds trade at either higher than their net asset value (a premium) or lower than their net asset value (a discount), depending on investor demand for the fund.

BOND PREMIUM *see* BOND DISCOUNT.

BOND POWER form used in the transfer of registered bonds from one owner to another. Sometimes called *assignment separate from certificate,* it accomplishes the same thing as the assignment form on the back of the bond certificate, but has a safety advantage in being separate.

Technically, the bond power appoints an attorney-in-fact with the power to make a transfer of ownership on the corporation's books.

BOND RATING method of evaluating the possibility of default by a bond issuer. Duff & Phelps/MCM, Standard & Poor's, Moody's Investors Service, and Fitch's Investors Service analyze the financial strength of each bond's issuer, whether a corporation or a government body. Their ratings range from AAA (highly unlikely to default) to D (in default). Bonds rated BB or below are not INVESTMENT GRADE—in other words, institutions that invest other people's money may not under most state laws buy them. *See also* RATING.

BOND RATIO *leverage* ratio measuring the percentage of a company's capitalization represented by bonds. It is calculated by dividing the total bonds due after one year by the same figure plus all equity. A bond ratio over 33% indicates high leverage—except in utilities, where higher bond ratios are normal. *See also* DEBT-TO-EQUITY RATIO.

BOND SWAP simultaneous sale of one bond issue and purchase of another. The motives for bond swaps vary: *maturity swaps* aim to stretch out maturities but can also produce a profit because of the lower prices on longer bonds; *yield swaps* seek to improve return and *quality swaps* seek to upgrade safety; *tax swaps* create tax-deductible losses through the sale, while the purchase of a substitute bond effectively preserves the investment. *See also* SWAP, SWAP ORDER.

BON VOYAGE BONUS *see* GREENMAIL.

BOOK
1. in an underwriting of securities, (1) preliminary indications of interest rate on the part of prospective buyers of the issue ("What is the book on XYZ Company?") or (2) record of activity in the syndicate account ("Who is managing the book on XYZ?").
2. record maintained by a specialist of buy and sell orders in a given security. The term derives from the notebook that specialists traditionally used for this purpose. Also, the aggregate of sell orders left with the specialist, as in BUY THE BOOK.
3. as a verb, to book is to give accounting recognition to something. ("They booked a profit on the transaction.")
4. collectively, books are the journals, ledgers, and other accounting records of a business.
   See also BOOK VALUE.

BOOK-ENTRY SECURITIES securities that are not represented by a certificate. Purchases and sales of some municipal bonds, for instance, are merely recorded on customers' accounts; no certificates change hands. This is increasingly popular because it cuts down on paperwork for brokers and leaves investors free from worry about their certificates. *See also* CERTIFICATELESS MUNICIPALS.

BOOK PROFIT OR LOSS *see* UNREALIZED PROFIT OR LOSS.

BOOK-TO-BILL RATIO The ratio of orders booked for future delivery to orders being shipped immediately, and therefore billed. The book-to-bill ratio is released on a monthly basis for the semiconductor industry because it provides a very sensitive indicator of whether orders for chips are rising or falling and at what pace. The release of the chip book-to-bill ratio can have a major impact on the stock prices of semiconductor stocks in particular and technology stocks in general.

BOOK VALUE

1. value at which an asset is carried on a balance sheet. For example, a piece of manufacturing equipment is put on the books at its cost when purchased. Its value is then reduced each year as depreciation is charged to income. Thus, its book value at any time is its cost minus accumulated depreciation. However, the primary purpose of accounting for depreciation is to enable a company to recover its cost, not replace the asset or reflect its declining usefulness. Book value may therefore vary significantly from other objectively determined values, most notably MARKET VALUE.

2. net asset value of a company's securities, calculated by using the following formula:

   Total assets *minus* intangible assets (goodwill, patents, etc.) *minus* current liabilities *minus* any long-term liabilities and equity issues that have a prior claim (subtracting them here has the effect of treating them as paid) *equals* total net assets available for payment of the issue under consideration.

   The total net asset figure, divided by the number of bonds, shares of preferred stock, or shares of common stock, gives the *net asset value*—or book value—per bond or per share of preferred or common stock.

   Book value can be a guide in selecting underpriced stocks and is an indication of the ultimate value of securities in liquidation. *See also* ASSET COVERAGE.

BOOT STRAP to help a company start from scratch. Entrepreneurs founding a company with little capital are said to be boot strapping it in order to become established.

BORROWED RESERVES funds borrowed by member banks from a FEDERAL RESERVE BANK for the purpose of maintaining the required reserve ratios. Actually, the proper term is *net borrowed reserves,* since it refers to the difference between borrowed reserves and excess or free reserves. Such borrowings, usually in the form of advances secured by government securities or eligible paper, are kept on deposit at the Federal Reserve bank in the borrower's region. Net borrowed reserves are an indicator of heavy loan demand and potentially TIGHT MONEY.

BORROWING POWER OF SECURITIES amount of money that customers can invest in securities on MARGIN, as listed every month on their brokerage account statements. This margin limit usually equals 50% of the value of their stocks, 30% of the value of their bonds, and the full value of their CASH EQUIVALENT assets, such as MONEY MARKET account funds. The term also refers to securities pledged (hypothecated) to a bank or other lender as loan COLLATERAL. The loan value in this case depends on lender policy and type of security.

BOSTON STOCK EXCHANGE (BSE) established in 1834, the BSE is the first American exchange to open its membership to foreign brokers. It is the only U.S. exchange with a foreign linkage—to the Montreal Exchange established in 1984—and the only U.S. exchange with an off-site backup trading floor, located in Woburn, Mass. The exchange trades only equities; its more than 2,000 listed securities represent the largest number of New York Stock Exchange listed companies in the U.S. Formerly known as a regional exchange, the BSE is in competition with other national stock exchanges, with 200 member firms and 160 of its own primary listed companies. In 1994, the exchange introduced the Competing Specialists Initiative (CSI) in an auction market environment. It also operates the BEACON automated trading system. The exchange moved to a state-of-the-art facility in downtown Boston in 1999. The BSE uses a three-day settlement. Trading hours are Monday through Friday, 9:30 A.M. to 4 P.M., with a limited crossing network at 5 P.M., matching the New York Stock Exchange's Session No. 1.

BOT
1. stockbroker shorthand for bought, the opposite of SL for sold.
2. in finance, abbreviation for balance of trade.
3. in the mutual savings bank industry, abbreviation for board of trustees.

BOTTOM
In general: support level for market prices of any type. When prices fall below that level and appear to be continuing downward without check, we say that the *bottom dropped out.* When prices begin to trend upward again, we say they have *bottomed out.*
Economics: lowest point in an economic cycle.
Securities: lowest market price of a security or commodity during a day, a season, a year, a cycle. Also, lowest level of prices for the market as a whole, as measured by any of the several indexes.

BOTTOM FISHER investor who is on the lookout for stocks that have fallen to their bottom prices before turning up. In extreme cases, bottom fishers buy stocks and bonds of bankrupt or near-bankrupt firms.

BOTTOM-UP APPROACH TO INVESTING search for outstanding performance of individual stocks before considering the impact of economic trends. The companies may be identified from research reports, stock screens, or personal knowledge of the products and services. This approach assumes that individual companies can do well, even in an industry that is not performing well. *See also* TOP-DOWN APPROACH TO INVESTING.

BOUGHT DEAL in securities underwriting, a FIRM COMMITMENT to purchase an entire issue outright from the issuing company. Differs from a STAND-BY COMMITMENT, wherein, with conditions, a SYNDICATE of investment bankers agrees to purchase part of an issue if it is not fully subscribed. Also differs from a BEST EFFORTS commitment, wherein the syndicate agrees to use its best efforts to sell the issue. Most issues in recent years have been bought deals. Typically, the syndicate puts up a portion of its own capital and borrows the rest from commercial banks. Then, perhaps through a selling group, the syndicate resells the issue to the public at slightly more than the purchase price.

BOUNCE return of a check by a bank because it is not payable, usually due to insufficient funds. In securities, the rejection and subsequent RECLAMATION of a security because of *bad delivery*. Term also refers to stock price's sudden decline and recovery.

BOURSE French term for *stock exchange. See* PARIS BOURSE.

BOUTIQUE small, specialized brokerage firm that deals with a limited clientele and offers a limited product line. A highly regarded securities analyst may form a research boutique, which clients use as a resource for buying and selling certain stocks. A boutique is the opposite of a FINANCIAL SUPERMARKET, which offers a wide variety of services to a wide variety of clients.

BOX physical location of securities or other documents held in safekeeping. The term derives from the large metal tin, or tray, in which brokerage firms and banks actually place such valuables. Depending on rules and regulations concerned with the safety and segregation of clients' securities, certificates held in safekeeping may qualify for stock loans or as bank loan collateral.

BRACKET CREEP edging into higher tax brackets as income rises to compensate for inflation.

BRADY BONDS public-issue, U.S. dollar-denominated bonds of developing countries, mainly in Latin America, that were exchanged in a restructuring for commercial bank loans in default. The securities, named for former Bush administration Treasury Secretary Nicholas Brady, are collateralized by U.S. Treasury zero-coupon bonds to ensure principal.

BRANCH OFFICE MANAGER person in charge of a branch of a securities brokerage firm or bank. Branch office managers who oversee the activities of three or more brokers must pass tests administered by various stock exchanges. A customer who is not able to resolve a conflict with a REGISTERED REPRESENTATIVE should bring it to the attention of the branch office manager, who is responsible for resolving such differences.

BREADTH OF THE MARKET percentage of stocks participating in a particular market move. Analysts say there was good breadth if two thirds of the stocks listed on an exchange rose during a trading session.

A market trend with good breadth is more significant and probably more long-lasting than one with limited breadth, since more investors are participating. Breadth-of-the-market indexes are alternatively called ADVANCE/DECLINE indexes.

BREAK

Finance: in a pricing structure providing purchasing discounts at different levels of volume, a point at which the price changes—for example, a 10% discount for ten cases.

Investments: (1) sudden, marked drop in the price of a security or in market prices generally; (2) discrepancy in the accounts of brokerage firms; (3) stroke of good luck.

BREAKEVEN POINT

Finance: the point at which sales equal costs. The point is located by breakeven analysis, which determines the volume of sales at which fixed and variable costs will be covered. All sales over the breakeven point produce profits; any drop in sales below that point will produce losses.

Because costs and sales are so complex, breakeven analysis has limitations as a planning tool and is being supplanted by computer based financial planning systems. *See also* LEVERAGE (operating).

Securities: dollar price at which a transaction produces neither a gain nor a loss.

In options strategy the term has the following definitions:
1. long calls and short uncovered calls: strike price plus premium.
2. long puts and short uncovered puts: strike price minus premium.
3. short covered call: purchase price minus premium.
4. short put covered by short stock: short sale price of underlying stock plus premium.

BREAKING THE SYNDICATE terminating the investment banking group formed to underwrite a securities issue. More specifically, terminating the AGREEMENT AMONG UNDERWRITERS, thus leaving the members free to sell remaining holdings without price restrictions. The agreement among underwriters usually terminates the syndicate 30 days after the selling group, but the syndicate can be broken earlier by agreement of the participants.

BREAKOUT rise in a security's price above a resistance level (commonly its previous high price) or drop below a level of support (commonly the former lowest price). A breakout is taken to signify a continuing move in the same direction. *See* chart on next page.

BREAKPOINT SALE in mutual funds, the dollar investment required to make the fundholder eligible for a lower sales charge. *See also* LETTER OF INTENT; RIGHT OF ACCUMULATION.

BREAKUP VALUE *see* PRIVATE MARKET VALUE.

BRETTON WOODS AGREEMENT OF 1944 *see* FIXED EXCHANGE RATE.

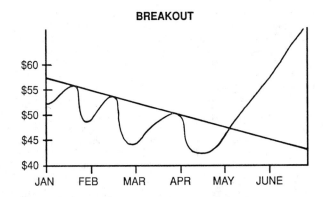

BRIDGE LOAN short-term loan, also called a *swing loan,* made in anticipation of intermediate-term or long-term financing.

BROAD TAPE enlargement of the Dow Jones news ticker tape, projected on a screen in the board room of a brokerage firm. It continually reports major news developments and financial information. The term can also refer to similar information provided by Associated Press, United Press International, Reuters, or Munifacts. The broad tape is not allowed on the exchange floor because it would give floor traders an unfair edge.

BROKER
Insurance: person who finds the best insurance deal for a client and then sells the policy to the client.
Real estate: person who represents the seller and gets a commission when the property is sold.
Securities: person who acts as an intermediary between a buyer and seller, usually charging a commission. A broker who specializes in stocks, bonds, commodities, or options acts as AGENT and must be registered with the exchange where the securities are traded. Hence the term *registered representative. See also* ACCOUNT EXECUTIVE; DEALER; DISCOUNT BROKER.

BROKER-DEALER *see* DEALER.

BROKERED CD CERTIFICATE OF DEPOSIT (CD) issued by a bank or thrift institution but bought in bulk by a brokerage firm and resold to brokerage customers. Brokered CDs pay as much as 1% more than those issued directly by major banks, carry federal deposit insurance up to $100,000, enjoy a liquid secondary market made by the broker, and do not require an investor to pay a commission.

BROKER LOAN RATE interest rate at which brokers borrow from banks to cover the securities positions of their clients. The broker loan rate usually hovers a percentage point or so above such short-term interest rates as the federal funds rate and the Treasury bill rate. Since brokers' loans and their customers' margin accounts are usually covered by the same collateral, the term REHYPOTHECATION is used synonymously with *broker loan borrowing.* Because broker loans are callable on 24-hour notice, the term *call loan rate* is also used, particularly in money rate tables published in newspapers.

BROUGHT OVER THE WALL when somebody in the research department of an investment bank is pressed into the service of the underwriting department in reference to a particular corporate client, the individual has been "brought over the ("Chinese") wall" that legally divides the two functions and, being thus privy to INSIDE INFORMATION, is precluded from providing opinions about the company involved. *See also* CHINESE WALL.

BRUSSELS STOCK EXCHANGE (BSE) was founded by Napoleonic decree in 1801. Tax relief legislation increased growth, and in 1990 BSE was established as a limited liability cooperative. It handles the majority of securities transactions in Belgium. A second exchange is in Antwerp, and it cooperates closely with the BSE. The Belgian market is fully open to foreign investors and can be accessed directly by foreign banks and brokerage firms that register as members. In April 1996, the exchange introduced a decentralized, order-driven trading system called NTS to replace open outcry in the cash market. All forward market stocks were transferred to NTS from the CATS automated trading system. Cash market settlement is on the third trading day following the transaction. For forward transactions, the settlement period is five business days. Cash market trading hours are 11:15 A.M. to 3:15 P.M.; forward market, 10 A.M. to 4:30 P.M. Both trade Monday through Friday.

BUCKET SHOP illegal brokerage firm, of a kind now almost extinct, which accepts customer orders but does not execute them right away as Securities and Exchange Commission regulations require. Bucket-shop brokers confirm the price the customer asked for, but in fact make the trade at a time advantageous to the broker, whose profit is the difference between the two prices. Sometimes bucket shops neglect to fill the customer's order and just pocket the money. *See also* BOILER ROOM.

BUDGET estimate of revenue and expenditure for a specified period. Of the many kinds of budgets, a CASH BUDGET shows cash flow, an expense budget shows projected expenditures, and a CAPITAL BUDGET shows anticipated capital outlays. The term refers to a preliminary financial plan. In a *balanced budget* revenues cover expenditures.

BUDGET DEFICIT excess of spending over income for a government, corporation, or individual over a particular period of time. A budget deficit accumulated by the federal government of the United States must be financed by the issuance of Treasury bonds. Corporate budget deficits must be reduced or eliminated by increasing sales and reducing expenditures, or the company will not survive in the long run. Similarly, individuals who consistently spend more than they earn will accumulate huge debts, which may ultimately force them to declare bankruptcy if the debt cannot be serviced.

BUDGET SURPLUS excess of income over spending for a government, corporation, or individual over a particular period of time. A government with a budget surplus may choose to start new programs or cut taxes. A corporation with a surplus may expand the business through investment or acquisition, or may choose to buy back its own stock. An individual with a budget surplus may choose to pay down debt or increase spending or investment.

BULGE quick, temporary price rise that applies to an entire commodities or stock market, or to an individual commodity or stock.

BULGE BRACKET the group of firms in an underwriting syndicate that share the largest participation. TOMBSTONE ads list the participants alphabetically within groupings organized by size of participation and presented in tiers. The first and lead grouping is the "bulge bracket." *See also* MEZZANINE BRACKET.

BULL person who thinks prices will rise. One can be bullish on the prospects for an individual stock, bond, or commodity, an industry segment, or the market as a whole. In a more general sense, bullish means optimistic, so a person can be bullish on the economy as a whole.

BULLION COINS coins composed of metal such as gold, silver, platinum, or palladium. Bullion coins provide the purest play on the "up or down" price moves of the underlying metal, and are the most actively traded. These coins trade at a slight premium over their metal content, unlike NUMISMATIC COINS, which trade on their rarity and artistic value. Some of the most popular bullion coins minted by major governments around the world include the American Eagle, the Canadian Maple Leaf, the South African Kruggerand, and the Australian Kangaroo. In addition to trading bullion in coin form, nearly pure precious metals also are available in bar form.

BULL MARKET prolonged rise in the prices of stocks, bonds, or commodities. Bull markets usually last at least a few months and are characterized by high trading volume.

BULL SPREAD option strategy, executed with puts or calls, that will be profitable if the underlying stock rises in value. The following are three varieties of bull spread:
Vertical spread: simultaneous purchase and sale of options of the same class at different strike prices, but with the same expiration date.
Calendar spread: simultaneous purchase and sale of options of the same class and the same price but at different expiration dates.

Diagonal spread: combination of vertical and calendar spreads wherein the investor buys and sells options of the same class at different strike prices and different expiration dates.

An investor who believes, for example, that XYZ stock will rise, perhaps only moderately, buys an XYZ 30 call for 1½ and sells an XYZ 35 call for ½; both options are OUT OF THE MONEY. The 30 and 35 are strike prices and the 1½ and ½ are premiums. The net cost of this spread, or the difference between the premiums, is $1. If the stock rises to 35 just prior to expiration, the 35 call becomes worthless and the 30 call is worth $5. Thus the spread provides a profit of $4 on an investment of $1. If on the other hand the price of the stock goes down, both options expire worthless and the investor loses the entire premium.

BUMP-UP CD certificate of deposit that gives its owner a one-time right to increase its yield for the remaining term of the CD if interest rates have risen from the date of issuance. The CD's yield will not be adjusted downward if rates fall, however. If rates remain stable or decline, the CD will pay its stated rate of interest until maturity.

BUNCHING
1. combining many round-lot orders for execution at the same time on the floor of an exchange. This technique can also be used with odd lot orders, when combining many small orders can save the odd-lot differential for each customer.
2. pattern on the ticker tape when a series of trades in the same security appear consecutively.
3. aggregating income items or deductions in a single year to minimize taxes in that year.

BURNOUT exhaustion of a tax shelter's benefits, when an investor starts to receive income from the investment. This income must be reported to the Internal Revenue Service, and taxes must be paid on it.

BURN RATE in venture capital financing, the rate at which a start-up company spends capital to finance overhead before generating a positive cash flow from operations.

BUSINESS COMBINATION *see* MERGER.

BUSINESS CYCLE recurrence of periods of expansion (RECOVERY) and contraction (RECESSION) in economic activity with effects on inflation, growth, and employment. One cycle extends from a GROSS DOMESTIC PRODUCT (GDP) base line through one rise and one decline and back to the base line, a period typically averaging about 2½ years. The 1990s, however, saw an extended period of expansion. A business cycle affects profitability and CASH FLOW, making it a key consideration in corporate dividend policy, and a factor in the rise and fall of the inflation rate, which in turn affects return on investments. *See also* SOFT LANDING.

BUSINESS DAY
    In general: hours when most businesses are in operation. Although individual working hours may differ, and particular firms may choose staggered schedules, the conventional business day is 9 A.M. to 5 P.M. **Finance and investments:** day when financial marketplaces are open for trading. In figuring the settlement date on a *regular way* securities transaction—which is the fifth business day after the trade date—Saturday, Sunday, and a legal holiday would not be counted, for example.

BUSINESS SEGMENT REPORTING reporting the results of the divisions, subsidiaries, or other segments of a business separately so that income, sales, and assets can be compared. When not a separate part of the business structure, a segment is generally defined as any grouping of products and services comprising a significant industry, which is one representing 10% or more of total revenues, assets, or income. Allocation of central corporate expenses is not required by the Financial Accounting Standards Board. Also called line of business reporting.

BUSTED CONVERTIBLES CONVERTIBLES that trade like fixed-income investments because the market price of the common stock they convert to has fallen so low as to render the conversion feature valueless.

BUST-UP TAKEOVER LEVERAGED BUYOUT in which TARGET COMPANY assets or activities are sold off to repay the debt that financed the TAKEOVER.

BUTTERFLY SPREAD complex option strategy that involves selling two calls and buying two calls on the same or different markets, with several maturity dates. One of the options has a higher exercise price and the other has a lower exercise price than the other two options. An investor in a butterfly spread will profit if the underlying security makes no dramatic movements because the premium income will be collected when the options are sold.

BUY acquire property in return for money. Buy can be used as a synonym for bargain.

BUY AND HOLD STRATEGY strategy that calls for accumulating shares in a company over the years. This allows the investor to pay favorable long-term capital gains tax on profits and requires far less attention than a more active trading strategy.

BUY AND WRITE STRATEGY conservative options strategy that entails buying stocks and then writing covered call options on them. Investors receive both the dividends from the stock and the premium income from the call options. However, the investor may have to sell the stock below the current market price if the call is exercised.

BUYBACK purchase of a long contract to cover a short position, usually arising out of the short sale of a commodity. Also, purchase of identical securities to cover a short sale. Synonym: *short covering. See also* STOCK BUYBACK.

Bond buyback: corporation's purchase of its own bonds at a discount in the open market. This is done in markets characterized by rapidly rising interest rates and commensurately declining bond prices.

BUY DOWN cash payment by a mortgage lender allowing the borrower to receive a lower rate of interest on a mortgage loan. For example, a home builder having trouble selling homes may offer a buy down with a local lender which will enable home buyers to qualify for mortgages that they would otherwise not qualify for. The buy down may lower the mortgage rate for the life of the loan, or sometimes just for the first few years of the loan.

BUYER'S MARKET market situation that is the opposite of a SELLER'S MARKET. Since there is more supply of a security or product than there is current demand, the prices tend to fall allowing buyers to set both the price and terms of the sale. It contrasts with a seller's market, characterized by excess demand, high prices, and terms suited to seller's desires.

BUY HEDGE *see* LONG HEDGE.

BUY IN

Options trading: procedure whereby the responsibility to deliver or accept stock can be terminated. In a transaction called *buying-in* or CLOSING PURCHASE, the writer buys an identical option (only the premium or price is different). The second of these options offsets the first, and the profit or loss is the difference in premiums.

Securities: transaction between brokers wherein securities are not delivered on time by the broker on the sell side, forcing the buy side broker to obtain shares from other sources.

BUYING CLIMAX rapid rise in the price of a stock or commodity, setting the stage for a quick fall. Such a surge attracts most of the potential buyers of the stock, leaving them with no one to sell their stock to at higher prices. This is what causes the ensuing fall. Technical chartists see a buying climax as a dramatic runup, accompanied by increased trading volume in the stock.

BUYING ON MARGIN buying securities with credit available through a relationship with a broker, called a MARGIN ACCOUNT. Arrangements of this kind are closely regulated by the Federal Reserve Board. *See also* MARGIN.

BUYING POWER amount of money available to buy securities, determined by tabulating the cash held in brokerage accounts, and adding the amount that could be spent if securities were margined to the limit. The market cannot rise beyond the available buying power. *See also* PURCHASING POWER.

BUY MINUS order to buy a stock at a price lower than the current market price. Traders try to execute a buy minus order on a temporary dip in the stock's price.

BUY ON THE BAD NEWS strategy based on the belief that, soon after a company announces bad news, the price of its stock will plummet. Those who buy at this stage assume that the price is about as low as it can go, leaving plenty of room for a rise when the news improves. If the adverse development is indeed temporary, this technique can be quite profitable. *See also* BOTTOM FISHER.

BUY ORDER in securities trading, an order to a broker to purchase a specified quality of a security at the MARKET PRICE or at another stipulated price.

BUYOUT purchase of at least a controlling percentage of a company's stock to take over its assets and operations. A buyout can be accomplished through negotiation or through a tender offer. A LEVERAGED BUYOUT occurs when a small group borrows the money to finance the purchase of the shares. The loan is ultimately repaid out of cash generated from the acquired company's operations or from the sale of its assets. *See also* GOLDEN PARACHUTE.

BUY STOP ORDER BUY ORDER marked to be held until the market price rises to the STOP PRICE, then to be entered as a MARKET ORDER to buy at the best available price. Sometimes called a *suspended market order,* because it remains suspended until a market transaction elects, activates, or triggers the stop. Such an order is not permitted in the over-the-counter market. *See also* STOP ORDER.

BUY THE BOOK order to a broker to buy all the shares available from the specialist in a security and from other brokers and dealers at the current offer price. The book is the notebook in which specialists kept track of buy and sell orders before computers. The most likely source of such an order is a professional trader or a large institutional buyer.

BYLAWS rules governing the internal management of an organization which, in the case of business corporations, are drawn up at the time of incorporation. The charter is concerned with such broad matters as the number of directors and the number of authorized shares; the bylaws, which can usually be amended by the directors themselves, cover such points as the election of directors, the appointment of executive and finance committees, the duties of officers, and how share transfers may be made. Bylaws, which are also prevalent in not-for-profit organizations, cannot countermand laws of the government.

BYPASS TRUST agreement allowing parents to pass assets on to their children to reduce estate taxes. The trust must be made irrevocable, meaning that the terms can never be changed. Assets put in such a trust usually exceed the amount that children and other heirs can receive tax-free at a parent's death. The estate tax exclusion amount was $625,000 in 1998, scheduled to increase gradually to $1 million in 2006 according to the TAXPAYER RELIEF ACT OF 1997. Parents can arrange to receive income from the assets during their lifetimes and may even be able to touch the principal in case of dire need. One variation of a bypass trust is the qualified terminable interest property trust, or Q-TIP TRUST.

C

CABINET CROWD members of the New York Stock Exchange who trade in infrequently traded bonds. Also called *inactive bond crowd* or *book crowd.* Buy and sell LIMIT ORDERS for these bonds are kept in steel racks, called cabinets, at the side of the bond trading floor; hence the name cabinet crowd. *See also* AUTOMATED BOND SYSTEM (ABS).

CABINET SECURITY stock or bond listed on a major exchange but not actively traded. There are a considerable number of such bonds and a limited number of such stocks, mainly those trading in ten-share units. Cabinets are the metal storage racks that LIMIT ORDERS for such securities are filed in pending execution or cancellation. *See also* AUTOMATED BOND SYSTEM (ABS); CABINET CROWD.

CAC 40 INDEX broad-based index of common stocks on the Paris Bourse, based on 40 of the 100 largest companies listed on the forward segment of the official list (reglement menseul); it has a base of 100. It is comparable to the Dow Jones Industrial Average. There are index futures and index options contracts based on the CAC 40 index.

CAFETERIA EMPLOYEE BENEFIT PLAN plan offering employees numerous options among their employee benefits. Each employee is able to pick the benefits that are most valuable in his or her particular situation. For example, a young employee with children may want to receive more life and health insurance than a mid-career employee who is more concerned with building up retirement plan assets.

CAGE section of a brokerage firm's back office where funds are received and disbursed.

Also, the installation where a bank teller works.

CALENDAR list of securities about to be offered for sale. Separate calendars are kept for municipal bonds, corporate bonds, government bonds, and new stock offerings.

CALENDAR SPREAD options strategy that entails buying two options on the same security with different maturities. If the EXERCISE PRICE is the same (a June 50 call and a September 50 call) it is a HORIZONTAL SPREAD. If the exercise prices are different (a June 50 call and a September 45 call), it is a DIAGONAL SPREAD. Investors gain or lose as the difference in price narrows or widens.

CALL

Banking: demand to repay a secured loan usually made when the borrower has failed to meet such contractual obligations as timely payment of interest. When a banker calls a loan, the entire principal amount is due immediately. *See also* BROKER LOAN RATE.

Bonds: right to redeem outstanding bonds before their scheduled maturity. The first dates when an issuer may call bonds are specified in the prospectus of every issue that has a call provision in its indenture. *See also* CALLABLE; CALL PRICE.

Options: right to buy a specific number of shares at a specified price by a fixed date. *See also* CALL OPTION.

CALLABLE redeemable by the issuer before the scheduled maturity. The issuer must pay the holders a premium price if such a security is retired early. Bonds are usually called when interest rates fall so significantly that the issuer can save money by floating new bonds at lower rates. *See also* CALL PRICE; DEMAND LOAN.

CALL DATE date on which a bond may be redeemed before maturity. If called, the bond may be redeemed at PAR or at a slight premium to par. For example, a bond may be scheduled to mature in 20 years but may have a provision that it can be called in 10 years if it is advantageous for the issuer to refinance the issue. The date 10 years from the issue date is the call date. When buying a bond, it is important to know the bond's call date, because you cannot be assured that you will receive interest from that bond beyond the call date.

CALLED AWAY term for a bond redeemed before maturity, or a call or put option exercised against the stockholder, or a delivery required on a short sale.

CALL FEATURE part of the agreement a bond issuer makes with a buyer, called the indenture, describing the schedule and price of redemptions before maturity. Most corporate and municipal bonds have 10-year call features (termed CALL PROTECTION by holders); government securities usually have none. *See also* CALL PRICE.

CALL LOAN any loan repayable on demand, but used in newspaper money rate tables as a synonym for *broker loan* or *broker overnight loan*. *See* BROKER LOAN RATE.

CALL LOAN RATE *see* BROKER LOAN RATE.

CALL OPTION right to buy 100 shares of a particular stock or stock index at a predetermined price before a preset deadline, in exchange for a premium. For buyers who think a stock will go up dramatically, call options permit a profit from a smaller investment than it would take to buy the stock. These options can also produce extra income for the seller, who gives up ownership of the stock if the option is exercised.

CALL PREMIUM amount that the buyer of a call option has to pay to the seller for the right to purchase a stock or stock index at a specified price by a specified date.

In bonds, preferreds, and convertibles, the amount over par that an issuer has to pay to an investor for redeeming the security early.

CALL PRICE price at which a bond or preferred stock with a *call provision* or CALL FEATURE can be redeemed by the issuer; also known as *redemption price.* To compensate the holder for loss of income and ownership, the call price is usually higher than the par value of the security, the difference being the CALL PREMIUM. *See also* CALL PROTECTION.

CALL PROTECTION length of time during which a security cannot be redeemed by the issuer. U.S. government securities are generally not callable, although there is an exception in certain 30-year Treasury bonds, which become callable after 25 years. Corporate and municipal issuers generally provide 10 years of call protection. Investors who plan to live off the income from a bond should be sure they have call protection, because without it the bond could be CALLED AWAY at any time specified in the indenture.

CALL PROVISION clause in a bond's INDENTURE that allows the issuer to redeem the bond before maturity. The call provision will spell out the first CALL DATE and whether the bond will be called at PAR or at a slight premium to par. Some preferred stock issues also have call provisions spelling out the conditions of a redemption.

CALL RISK risk to a bondholder that a bond may be redeemed before scheduled maturity. Bondholders should read the CALL PROVISIONS in a bond's INDENTURE to understand the earliest potential CALL DATE for their bond. The main risk of having a bond called before maturity is that the investor will be unable to replace the bond's yield with another similar-quality bond paying the same yield. The reason the bond issuer will call the bond is that interest rates will have fallen from the time of issuance, and the bond can be refinanced at lower rates.

CAMPS acronym for *Cumulative Auction Market Preferred Stocks,* Oppenheimer & Company's DUTCH AUCTION PREFERRED STOCK product.

CANADIAN DEALING NETWORK, INC. **(CDN)** the organized over-the-counter stock market of Canada. The CDN became a subsidiary of the TORONTO STOCK EXCHANGE in 1991. Previously, CDN was known as the Canadian Over-the-Counter Automated Trading System (COATS).

CANCEL
In general: void a negotiable instrument by annulling or paying it; also, prematurely terminate a bond or other contract.
Securities trading: void an order to buy or sell. *See also* GOOD TILL CANCELED ORDER.

CAP
Bonds: highest level interest rate that can be paid on a floating-rate debt instrument. For example, a variable-rate note might have a cap of 8%, meaning that the yield cannot exceed 8% even if the general level of interest rates goes much higher than 8%.
Mortgages: highest interest rate level that an adjustable-rate mortgage (ARM) can rise to over a particular period of time. For example, an

ARM contract may specify that the rate cannot jump more than two points in any year, or a total of six points during the life of the mortgage. **Stocks:** short for CAPITALIZATION, or the total current value of a company's outstanding shares in dollars. A stock's capitalization is determined by multiplying the total number of shares outstanding by the stock's price. Analysts also refer to small-, medium- and large-cap stocks as a way of distinguishing the capitalizations of companies they are interested in. Many mutual funds restrict themselves to the small-, medium- or large-cap universes. *See also* COLLAR.

CAPACITY

Debt: ability to repay loans, as measured by credit grantors. Creditors judge an applicant's ability to repay a loan based on assets and income, and assign a certain capacity to service debt. If someone has many credit cards and credit lines outstanding, even if there are no outstanding balances, that is using up that person's debt capacity.

Economics: the amount of productive capacity in the economy is known as *industrial capacity.* This figure is released on a monthly basis by the Federal Reserve to show how much of the nation's factories, mines, and utilities are in use. If more than 85% of industrial capacity is in use, economists worry that production bottlenecks may form and create inflationary pressure. On the other hand, if less than 80% of capacity is in use, industrial production may be slack and inflationary pressures low.

CAPACITY UTILIZATION RATE percentage of production capacity in use by a particular company, an industry, or the entire economy. While in theory a business can operate at 100% of its productive capacity, in practice the maximum output is less than that, because machines need to be repaired, employees take vacations, etc. The operating rate is expressed as a percentage of the potential 100% production output. For example, a company may be producing at an 85% operating rate, meaning its output is 85% of the maximum that could be produced with its existing resources. *See also* CAPACITY.

CAPITAL ASSET long-term asset that is not bought or sold in the normal course of business. Generally speaking, the term includes FIXED ASSETS—land, buildings, equipment, furniture and fixtures, and so on. The Internal Revenue Service definition of capital assets includes security investments.

CAPITAL ASSET PRICING MODEL (CAPM) sophisticated model of the relationship between *expected risk* and *expected return.* The model is grounded in the theory that investors demand higher returns for higher risks. It says that the return on an asset or a security is equal to the risk-free return—such as the return on a short-term Treasury security—plus a risk premium.

CAPITAL BUDGET program for financing long-term outlays such as plant expansion, research and development, and advertising. Among methods used in arriving at a capital budget are NET PRESENT VALUE (NPV), INTERNAL RATE OF RETURN (IRR), and PAYBACK PERIOD.

CAPITAL BUILDER ACCOUNT (CBA) brokerage account offered by Merrill Lynch that allows investors to buy and sell securities. It may be a cash or credit account that allows an investor to access the loan value of his or her eligible securities. Unlike a regular brokerage account, with a CBA one can choose from a money market fund or an insured money market deposit account to have one's idle cash invested or deposited on a regular basis, without losing access to the money.

CAPITAL CONSUMPTION ALLOWANCE amount of depreciation included in the GROSS DOMESTIC PRODUCT (GDP), normally around 11%. This amount is subtracted from GDP, on the theory that it is needed to maintain the productive capacity of the economy, to get net national product (NNP). When adjusted further for indirect taxes, NNP equals national income. Economists use GDP rather than NNP in the analyses we read every day largely because capital consumption allowance figures are not always available or reliable. *See also* DEPRECIATION.

CAPITAL EXPENDITURE outlay of money to acquire or improve CAPITAL ASSETS such as buildings and machinery.

CAPITAL FLIGHT movement of large sums of money from one country to another to escape political or economic turmoil or to seek higher rates of return. For example, periods of high inflation or political revolution have brought about an exodus of capital from many Latin American countries to the United States, which is seen as a safe haven.

CAPITAL FORMATION creation or expansion, through savings, of capital or of *producer's goods*—buildings, machinery, equipment— that produce other goods and services, the result being economic expansion.

CAPITAL GAIN difference between an asset's adjusted purchase price and selling price when the difference is positive. According to the TAX-PAYER RELIEF ACT OF 1997, a long-term capital gain is achieved once an asset such as a stock, bond, or mutual fund has been held for at least 12 months. Such long-term gains are taxed at a maximum rate of 20% for taxpayers in the 28% tax bracket or higher. Those in the 15% tax bracket pay a 10% tax on long-term capital gains. Selling assets for a profit after holding them for less than 12 months generates short-term capital gains, which are subject to regular income tax rates. Assets purchased starting January 1, 2000 and held for at least five years qualify for a maximum capital gains tax rate of 18% for those in the 28% tax bracket or higher, and 8% for those in the 15% tax bracket. Capital gains are reported on Schedule D of a tax return.

CAPITAL GAINS DISTRIBUTION mutual fund's distribution to shareholders of the profits derived from the sale of stocks or bonds.

Shareholders must pay long-term capital gains tax rates of as much as 20% if the fund held the securities for at least 12 months, no matter how long the shareholder owned shares in the mutual fund. Shareholders must pay short-term capital gains taxes at regular income tax rates on securities sold by the mutual fund that have been held for less than 12 months, no matter how long the shareholder owned shares in the mutual fund. Distributions which are reinvested by shareholders are taxed in the same way as distributions paid to shareholders in cash. If a capital gain distribution is declared in October, November, or December, but paid in January, the fund will still report the distribution as taxable in the year it was declared. Mutual funds report capital gains distributions to shareholders annually on FORM 1099-DIV.

CAPITAL GAINS TAX tax on profits from the sale of CAPITAL ASSETS. Traditionally, the tax law specified a minimum holding period after which a capital gain is taxed at a more favorable rate (recently a maximum of 20% for individuals) than ordinary income. A long-term capital gain is achieved once an asset such as a stock, bond, or mutual fund is held for at least 12 months. Such long-term gains are taxed at a maximum rate of 20% for taxpayers in the 28% tax bracket or higher. Those in the 15% tax bracket pay a 10% tax on long-term capital gains. Assets sold for a profit after having been held for less than 12 months generate short-term capital gains, which are subject to ordinary income tax rates. Assets purchased starting January 1, 2000 and held for at least five years qualify for a maximum capital gains tax rate of 18% for those in the 28% tax bracket or higher, and 8% for those in the 15% tax bracket.

CAPITAL GOODS goods used in the production of other goods—industrial buildings, machinery, equipment—as well as highways, office buildings, government installations. In the aggregate such goods form a country's productive capacity.

CAPITAL-INTENSIVE requiring large investments in CAPITAL ASSETS. Motor-vehicle and steel production are capital-intensive industries. To provide an acceptable return on investment, such industries must have a high margin of profit or a low cost of borrowing. Sometimes used to mean a high proportion of fixed assets to labor.

CAPITAL INTERNATIONAL INDEXES indexes maintained by Morgan Stanley's Capital International division which track most major stock markets throughout the world. The Capital International World Index tracks prices of major stocks in all the major markets worldwide. There are also many indexes for European, North American, and Asian markets. Most mutual funds and other institutional investors measure their performance against Capital International indexes.

CAPITAL INVESTMENT *see* CAPITAL EXPENDITURE.

CAPITALISM economic system in which (1) private ownership of property exists; (2) aggregates of property or capital provide income for the individuals or firms that accumulated it and own it; (3) individuals and firms are relatively free to compete with others for their own economic gain; (4) the profit motive is basic to economic life.

Among the synonyms for capitalism are LAISSEZ-FAIRE economy, private enterprise system, and free-price system. In this context *economy* is interchangeable with *system.*

CAPITALIZATION *see* CAPITALIZE; CAPITAL STRUCTURE; MARKET CAPITALIZATION.

CAPITALIZATION RATE rate of interest used to convert a series of future payments into a single PRESENT VALUE.

CAPITALIZATION RATIO analysis of a company's capital structure showing what percentage of the total is debt, preferred stock, common stock, and other equity. The ratio is useful in evaluating the relative RISK and leverage that holders of the respective levels of security have. *See also* BOND RATIO.

CAPITALIZE
1. convert a schedule of income into a principal amount, called *capitalized value,* by dividing by a rate of interest.
2. issue securities to finance *capital outlays* (rare).
3. record capital outlays as additions to asset accounts, not as expenses. *See also* CAPITAL EXPENDITURE.
4. convert a lease obligation to an asset/liability form of expression called a *capital lease,* that is, to record a leased asset as an owned asset and the lease obligation as borrowed funds.
5. turn something to one's advantage economically—for example, sell umbrellas on a rainy day.

CAPITAL LEASE lease that under Statement 13 of the Financial Accounting Standards Board must be reflected on a company's balance sheet as an asset and corresponding liability. Generally, this applies to leases where the lessee acquires essentially all of the economic benefits and risks of the leased property.

CAPITAL LOSS amount by which the proceeds from the sale of a CAPITAL ASSET are less than the adjusted cost of acquiring it. Capital losses are deducted first against capital gains, and then against up to $3,000 of other income for married couples filing jointly, and up to $1,500 for married couples filing separately. Any capital losses in excess of $3,000 may be carried over into future tax years. Short-term losses realized on assets sold less than 12 months after purchase are offset against short-term capital gains. Long-term capital losses on assets sold more than 12 months after purchase are offset against long-term capital gains. Capital losses are reported on Schedule D of a tax return. *See also* TAX LOSS CARRYBACK, CARRYFORWARD.

CAPITAL MARKETS markets where capital funds—debt and equity—are traded. Included are private placement sources of debt and equity as well as organized markets and exchanges. *See also* PRIMARY MARKET.

CAPITAL OUTFLOW exodus of capital from a country. A combination of political and economic factors may encourage domestic and foreign owners of assets to sell their holdings and move their money to other countries that offer more political stability and economic growth potential. If a capital outflow becomes large enough, some countries may try to restrict investors' ability to remove money from the country with currency controls or other measures.

CAPITAL OUTLAY *see* CAPITAL EXPENDITURE.

CAPITAL REQUIREMENTS
1. permanent financing needed for the normal operation of a business; that is, the long-term and working capital.
2. appraised investment in fixed assets and normal working capital. Whether patents, rights, and contracts should be included is moot.

CAPITAL SHARES one of the two classes of shares in a dual-purpose investment company. The capital shares entitle the owner to all appreciation (or depreciation) in value in the underlying portfolio in addition to all gains realized by trading in the portfolio. The other class of shares in a dual-purpose investment company are INCOME SHARES, which receive all income generated by the portfolio. If the fund guarantees a minimum level of income payable to the income shareholders, it may be necessary to sell some securities in the portfolio if the existing securities do not provide a high enough level of dividends and interest. In this case, the value of the capital shares will fall.

CAPITAL STOCK stock authorized by a company's charter and having PAR VALUE, STATED VALUE, or NO PAR VALUE. The number and value of issued shares are normally shown, together with the number of shares authorized, in the capital accounts section of the balance sheet.

Informally, a synonym for COMMON STOCK, though capital stock technically also encompasses PREFERRED STOCK.

CAPITAL STRUCTURE corporation's financial framework, including LONG-TERM DEBT, PREFERRED STOCK, and NET WORTH. It is distinguished from FINANCIAL STRUCTURE, which includes additional sources of capital such as short-term debt, accounts payable, and other liabilities. It is synonymous with *capitalization,* although there is some disagreement as to whether capitalization should include long-term loans and mortgages. Analysts look at capital structure in terms of its overall adequacy and its composition as well as in terms of the DEBT-TO-EQUITY RATIO, called *leverage. See also* CAPITALIZATION RATIO; PAR VALUE.

CAPITAL SURPLUS
1. EQUITY—or NET WORTH—not otherwise classifiable as CAPITAL STOCK or RETAINED EARNINGS. Here are five ways of creating surplus:
   a. from stock issued at a premium over par or stated value.
   b. from the proceeds of stock bought back and then sold again.
   c. from a reduction of par or stated value or a reclassification of capital stock.
   d. from donated stock.
   e. from the acquisition of companies that have capital surplus.
2. common umbrella term for more specific classifications such as ACQUIRED SURPLUS, ADDITIONAL PAID-IN CAPITAL, DONATED SURPLUS, and REEVALUATION SURPLUS (arising from appraisals). Most common synonyms: *paid-in surplus; surplus.*

CAPITAL TURNOVER annual sales divided by average stockholder equity (net worth). When compared over a period, it reveals the extent to which a company is able to grow without additional capital investment. Generally, companies with high profit margins have a low capital turnover and vice versa. Also called *equity turnover.*

CAPS acronym for *convertible adjustable preferred stock,* whose adjustable interest rate is pegged to Treasury security rates and which can be exchanged, during the period after the announcement of each dividend rate for the next period, for common stock (or, usually, cash) with a market value equal to the par value of the CAPS. CAPS solved a problem inherent with DUTCH AUCTION PREFERRED STOCK, which was that the investor could not be certain of the principal value of the preferred. *See also* MANDATORY CONVERTIBLES.

CAPTIVE AGENT insurance agent working exclusively for one company. Such an agent will tend to have more in-depth knowledge of that company's policies than an INDEPENDENT AGENT, who can sell policies from many companies. Captive agents are usually paid on a combination of salary and commissions earned from selling policies, in the first few years they sell policies. Later, they are usually paid exclusively on a commission basis.

CAPTIVE FINANCE COMPANY company, usually a wholly owned subsidiary, that exists primarily to finance consumer purchases from the parent company. Prominent examples are General Motors Acceptance Corporation and Ford Motor Credit Company. Although these subsidiaries stand on their own financially, parent companies frequently make SUBORDINATED LOANS to add to their equity positions. This supports the high leverage on which the subsidiaries operate and assures their active participation in the COMMERCIAL PAPER and bond markets.

CARDS acronym for *Certificates for Amortizing Revolving Debts,* a Salomon Brothers security collaterized by credit card accounts receivable. Also called *plastic bonds. See also* ASSET-BACKED SECURITIES

CARROT EQUITY British slang for an equity investment with a KICKER in the form of an opportunity to buy more equity if the company meets specified financial goals.

CARRYBACK, CARRYFORWARD *see* TAX LOSS CARRYBACK, CARRYFORWARD.

CARRYING CHARGE
Commodities: charge for carrying the actual commodity, including interest, storage, and insurance costs.
Margin accounts: fee that a broker charges for carrying securities on credit.
Real estate: carrying cost, primarily interest and taxes, of owning land prior to its development and resale.
Retailing: seller's charge for installment credit, which is either added to the purchase price or to unpaid installments.

CARRYOVER *see* TAX LOSS CARRYBACK, CARRYFORWARD.

CARS *see* CERTIFICATE FOR AUTOMOBILE RECEIVABLES.

CARTE BLANCHE full authority to take action. For example, an employee may be given carte blanche to enter into contracts with suppliers. The term also refers to the ability to fill in any amount on a blank check. For example, a father may sign a blank check and give it to his son to fill in when the son makes a major purchase. Carte Blanche is also the brand name of a widely used travel and entertainment card which requires that all balances be paid in full every month.

CARTEL group of businesses or nations that agree to influence prices by regulating production and marketing of a product. The most famous contemporary cartel is the Organization of Petroleum Exporting Countries (OPEC), which, notably in the 1970s, restricted oil production and sales and raised prices. A cartel has less control over an industry than a MONOPOLY. A number of nations, including the United States, have laws prohibiting cartels. TRUST is sometimes used as a synonym for cartel.

CASH asset account on a balance sheet representing paper currency and coins, negotiable money orders and checks, and bank balances. Also, transactions handled in cash. In the financial statements of annual reports, cash is usually grouped with CASH EQUIVALENTS, defined as all highly liquid securities with a known market value and a maturity, when acquirerest rate charged on the cash advance is usually different from the rate charged on purchases made with the same card. Frequently, the cash advance rate is higher. In many cases advance rates are variable, and are usually tied to a certain number of percentage points over the prime rate.

CASH ASSET RATIO balance sheet LIQUIDITY RATIO representing cash (and equivalents) and marketable securities divided by current liabilities. Stricter than the *quick ratio*.

CASH BASIS

Accounting: method that recognizes revenues when cash is received and recognizes expenses when cash is paid out. In contrast, the *accrual method* recognizes revenues when goods or services are sold and recognizes expenses when obligations are incurred. A third method, called *modified cash basis,* uses accrual accounting for long-term assets and is the basis usually referred to when the term cash basis is used.

Series EE Savings Bonds: paying the entire tax on these bonds when they mature. The alternative is to prorate the tax each year until the bonds mature.

CASHBOOK accounting book that combines cash receipts and disbursements. Its balance ties to the cash account in the general ledger on which the balance sheet is based.

CASH BUDGET estimated cash receipts and disbursements for a future period. A comprehensive cash budget schedules daily, weekly, or monthly expenditures together with the anticipated CASH FLOW from collections and other operating sources. Cash flow budgets are essential in establishing credit and purchasing policies, as well as in planning credit line usage and short-term investments in COMMERCIAL PAPER and other securities.

CASH COMMODITY commodity that is owned as the result of a completed contract and must be accepted upon delivery. Contrasts with futures contracts, which are not completed until a specified future date. The cash commodity contract specifications are set by the commodity exchanges.

CASH CONVERSION CYCLE elapsed time, usually expressed in days, from the outlay of cash for raw materials to the receipt of cash after the finished goods have been sold. Because a profit is built into the sales, the term *earnings cycle* is also used. The shorter the cycle, the more WORKING CAPITAL a business generates and the less it has to borrow. This cycle is directly affected by production efficiency, credit policy, and other controllable factors.

CASH COW business that generates a continuing flow of cash. Such a business usually has well-established brand names whose familiarity stimulates repeated buying of the products. For example, a magazine company that has a high rate of subscription renewals would be considered a cash cow. Stocks that are cash cows have dependable dividends.

CASH DISCOUNT TRADE CREDIT feature providing for a deduction if payment is made early. For example: trade terms of "2% 10 days net 30 days" allow a 2% cash discount for payment in 10 days. Term also refers to the lower price some merchants charge customers who pay in cash rather than with credit cards, in which case the merchant is passing on all or part of the merchant fee it would otherwise pay to the credit card company.

CASH DIVIDEND cash payment to a corporation's shareholders, distributed from current earnings or accumulated profits and taxable as income. Cash dividends are distinguished from STOCK DIVIDENDS, which are payments in the form of stock. *See also* YIELD.

INVESTMENT COMPANY cash dividends are usually made up of dividends, interest income, and capital gains received on its investment portfolio.

CASH EARNINGS cash revenues less cash expenses—specifically excluding noncash expenses such as DEPRECIATION.

CASH EQUIVALENTS instruments or investments of such high liquidity and safety that they are virtually as good as cash. Examples are a MONEY MARKET FUND and a TREASURY BILL. The FINANCIAL ACCOUNTING STANDARDS BOARD (FASB) defines cash equivalents for financial reporting purposes as any highly liquid security with a known market value and a maturity, when acquired, of less than three months.

CASH FLOW
1. in a larger financial sense, an analysis of all the changes that affect the cash account during an accounting period. The STATEMENT OF CASH FLOWS included in annual reports analyzes all changes affecting cash in the categories of operations, investments, and financing. For example: net operating income is an increase; the purchase of a new building is a decrease; and the issuance of stock or bonds is an increase. When more cash comes in than goes out, we speak of a *positive cash flow;* the opposite is a *negative cash flow.* Companies with assets well in excess of liabilities may nevertheless go bankrupt because they cannot generate enough cash to meet current obligations.
2. in investments, NET INCOME plus DEPRECIATION and other noncash charges. In this sense, it is synonymous with CASH EARNINGS. Investors focus on cash flow from operations because of their concern with a firm's ability to pay dividends. *See also* CASH BUDGET.

CASHIERING DEPARTMENT *see* CAGE.

CASHIER'S CHECK check that draws directly on a customer's account; the bank becomes the primary obligor. Consumers requiring a cashier's check must pay the amount of the check to the bank. The bank will then issue a check to a third party named by the consumer. Many businesses require that bills be paid by cashier's check instead of personal check, because they are assured that the funds are available with a cashier's check.

CASH INDEX PARTICIPATIONS (CIPS) *see* BASKET.

CASH MANAGEMENT
Corporate finance: efficient mobilization of cash into income-producing applications, using computers, telecommunications technology, innovative investment vehicles, and LOCK BOX arrangements.

Investing: broker's efficient movement of cash to keep it working. Merrill Lynch pioneered its proprietary Cash Management Account to combine securities trading, checking account services, money market investment services, and a debit (Visa) card.

CASH MARKET transactions in the cash or spot markets that are completed; that is, ownership of the commodity is transferred from seller to buyer and payment is given on delivery of the commodity. The cash market contrasts with the futures market, in which contracts are completed at a specified time in the future.

CASH-ON-CASH RETURN method of yield computation used for investments lacking an active secondary market, such as LIMITED PARTNERSHIPS. It simply divides the annual dollar income by the total dollars invested; a $10,000 investment that pays $1000 annually thus has a 10% cash-on-cash return. Investments having a market value and a predictable income stream to a designated maturity or call date, such as bonds, are better measured by CURRENT YIELD or YIELD-TO-MATURITY (or to call).

CASH ON DELIVERY (COD)
Commerce: transaction requiring that goods be paid for in full by cash or certified check or the equivalent at the point of delivery. The term *collect on delivery* has the same abbreviation and same meaning. If the customer refuses delivery, the seller has round-trip shipping costs to absorb or other, perhaps riskier, arrangements to make.
Securities: a requirement that delivery of securities to institutional investors be in exchange for assets of equal value—which, as a practical matter, means cash. Alternatively called *delivery against cost* (DAC) or *delivery versus payment* (DVP). On the other side of the trade, the term is *receive versus payment.*

CASH OR DEFERRED ARRANGEMENT (CODA) *see* 401(K) PLAN.

CASH RATIO ratio of cash and marketable securities to current liabilities; a refinement of the QUICK RATIO. The cash ratio tells the extent to which liabilities could be liquidated immediately. Sometimes called *liquidity ratio.*

CASH SETTLEMENT in the United States, settlement in cash on the TRADE DATE rather than the SETTLEMENT DATE of a securities transaction. In Great Britain, delivery and settlement on the first business day after the trade date.

CASH SURRENDER VALUE in insurance, the amount the insurer will return to a policyholder on cancellation of the policy. Sometimes abbreviated *CSVLI* (cash surrender value of life insurance), it shows up as an asset on the balance sheet of a company that has life insurance on its principals, called *key man insurance.* Insurance companies make loans against the cash value of policies, often at a better-than-market rate.

CASH VALUE INSURANCE life insurance that combines a death benefit with a potential tax-deferred buildup of money (called cash value) in the policy. The three main kinds of cash value insurance are WHOLE LIFE INSURANCE, VARIABLE LIFE INSURANCE, and UNIVERSAL LIFE INSURANCE. In whole life, cash value is accumulated based on the return on the company's investments in stocks, bonds, real estate, and other ventures. In variable life, the policyholder chooses how to allocate the money among stock, bond, and money market options. In universal life, a policyholder's cash value is invested in investments such as money market securities and medium-term Treasury bonds to build cash value. All cash values inside an insurance policy remain untaxed until they are withdrawn from the policy. Unlike cash value insurance, TERM LIFE INSURANCE offers only a death benefit, and no cash value buildup.

CASUALTY-INSURANCE insurance that protects a business or homeowner against property loss, damage, and related liability.

CASUALTY LOSS financial loss caused by damage, destruction, or loss of property as the result of an identifiable event that is sudden, unexpected, or unusual. Casualty and theft losses are considered together for tax purposes; are covered by most *casualty insurance* policies; and are tax deductible provided the loss is (1) not covered by insurance or (2) if covered, a claim has been made and denied.

CATASTROPHE CALL premature redemption of a municipal revenue bond because a catastrophe destroyed the source of the revenue backing the bond. For example, a bond backed by toll revenues from a bridge might be called, meaning bondholders will receive their principal back, if a storm destroyed the bridge. Usually, the proceeds for the payment will come from a commercial insurance policy covering the revenue-producing asset such as the bridge. A bond's INDENTURE will spell out the conditions under which a catastrophe call can be implemented.

CATS *see* CERTIFICATE OF ACCRUAL ON TREASURY SECURITIES.

CATS AND DOGS speculative stocks that have short histories of sales, earnings, and dividend payments. In bull markets, analysts say disparagingly that even the cats and dogs are going up.

CAVEAT EMPTOR, CAVEAT SUBSCRIPTOR *buyer beware, seller beware.* A variation on the latter is *caveat venditor.* Good advice when markets are not adequately protected, which was true of the stock market before the watchdog SECURITIES AND EXCHANGE COMMISSION was established in the 1930s.

CBO *see* COLLATERALIZED BOND OBLIGATION (CBO).

CEILING highest level allowable in a financial transaction. For example, someone buying a stock may place a ceiling on the stock's price, meaning they are not willing to pay more than that amount for the shares. The issuer of a bond may place a ceiling on the interest rate it is willing to pay. If market interest rates rise beyond that ceiling, the underwriter must cancel the issue. *See also* CAP.

CENTRAL BANK country's bank that (1) issues currency; (2) administers monetary policy, including OPEN MARKET OPERATIONS; (3) holds deposits representing the reserves of other banks; and (4) engages in transactions designed to facilitate the conduct of business and protect the public interest. In the United States, central banking is a function of the FEDERAL RESERVE SYSTEM.

CERTIFICATE formal declaration that can be used to document a fact, such as a birth certificate.

The following are certificates with particular relevance to finance and investments.

1. auditor's certificate, sometimes called certificate of accounts, or ACCOUNTANT'S OPINION.
2. bond certificate, certificate of indebtedness issued by a corporation containing the terms of the issuer's promise to repay principal and pay interest, and describing collateral, if any. Traditionally, bond certificates had coupons attached, which were exchanged for payment of interest. Now that most bonds are issued in registered form, coupons are less common. The amount of a certificate is the par value of the bond.
3. CERTIFICATE OF DEPOSIT.
4. certificate of INCORPORATION.
5. certificate of indebtedness, government debt obligation having a maturity shorter than a bond and longer than a treasury bill (such as a Treasury Note).
6. PARTNERSHIP certificate, showing the interest of all participants in a business partnership.
7. PROPRIETORSHIP certificate, showing who is legally responsible in an individually owned business.
8. STOCK CERTIFICATE, evidence of ownership of a corporation showing number of shares, name of issuer, amount of par or stated value represented or a declaration of no-par value, and rights of the shareholder. Preferred stock certificates also list the issuer's responsibilities with respect to dividends and voting rights, if any.

CERTIFICATE FOR AUTOMOBILE RECEIVABLES (CARS) PASS-THROUGH SECURITY backed by automobile loan paper of banks and other lenders. *See also* ASSET-BACKED SECURITIES.

CERTIFICATELESS MUNICIPALS MUNICIPAL BONDS that have no certificate of ownership for each bondholder. Instead, one certificate is valid for the entire issue. Certificateless municipals save paperwork for brokers and municipalities and allow investors to trade their bonds without having to transfer certificates. *See also* BOOK ENTRY SECURITIES.

CERTIFICATE OF ACCRUAL ON TREASURY SECURITIES (CATS) U.S. Treasury issues, sold at a deep discount from face value. A ZERO-COUPON security, they pay no interest during their lifetime, but return the full face value at maturity. They are appropriate for retirement or education planning. As TREASURY SECURITIES, CATS cannot be CALLED AWAY.

CERTIFICATE OF DEPOSIT (CD) debt instrument issued by a bank that usually pays interest. Institutional CDs are issued in denominations of $100,000 or more, and individual CDs start as low as $100. Maturities range from a few weeks to several years. Interest rates are set by competitive forces in the marketplace. *See also* BROKERED CD.

CERTIFIED CHECK check for which a bank guarantees payment. It legally becomes an obligation of the bank, and the funds to cover it are immediately withdrawn from the depositor's account.

CERTIFIED FINANCIAL PLANNER (CFP) person who has passed examinations accredited by the Denver-based Certified Financial Planner Board of Standards, testing the ability to coordinate a client's banking, estate, insurance, investment, and tax affairs. Financial planners usually specialize in one or more of these areas and consult outside experts as needed. Some planners charge only fees and make no money on the implementation of their plans. Others charge a commission on each product or service they sell. *See also* FINANCIAL PLANNER.

CERTIFIED FINANCIAL STATEMENTS financial statements accompanied by an ACCOUNTANT'S OPINION.

CERTIFIED PUBLIC ACCOUNTANT (CPA) accountant who has passed certain exams, achieved a certain amount of experience, reached a certain age, and met all other statutory and licensing requirements of the U.S. state where he or she works. In addition to accounting and auditing, CPAs prepare tax returns for corporations and individuals.

CHAIRMAN OF THE BOARD member of a corporation's board of directors who presides over its meetings and who is the highest ranking officer in the corporation. The chairman of the board may or may not have the most actual executive authority in a firm. The additional title of CHIEF EXECUTIVE OFFICER (CEO) is reserved for the principal executive, and depending on the particular firm, that title may be held by the chairman, the president, or even an executive vice president. In some corporations, the position of chairman is either a prestigious reward for a past president or an honorary position for a prominent person, a large stockholder, or a family member; it may carry little or no real power in terms of policy or operating decision making.

CHAPTER 7 *see* BANKRUPTCY.

CHAPTER 10 federal BANKRUPTCY law section providing for reorganization under a court-appointed independent manager (trustee in bankruptcy) rather than under existing management as in the case with Chapter 11.

CHAPTER 11 *see* BANKRUPTCY.

CHAPTER 13 *see* BANKRUPTCY.

CHARGE OFF *see* BAD DEBT.

CHARITABLE LEAD TRUST *see* CHARITABLE REMAINDER TRUST.

CHARITABLE REMAINDER TRUST IRREVOCABLE TRUST that pays income to one or more individuals until the GRANTOR'S death, at which time the balance, which is tax free, passes to a designated charity. It is a popular tax-saving alternative for individuals who have no children or who are wealthy enough to benefit both children and charity.

The charitable remainder trust is the reverse of a *charitable lead trust,* whereby a charity receives income during the grantor's life and the remainder passes to designated family members upon the grantor's death. The latter trust reduces estate taxes while enabling the family to retain control of the assets.

CHARTER *see* ARTICLES OF INCORPORATION.

CHARTERED FINANCIAL ANALYST (CFA) designation awarded by the Institute of Chartered Financial Analysts (ICFA) to experienced financial analysts who pass examinations in economics, financial accounting, portfolio management, security analysis, and standards of conduct.

CHARTERED FINANCIAL CONSULTANT (ChFC) designation awarded by American College, Bryn Mawr, PA, to a professional FINANCIAL PLANNER who completes a four-year program covering economics, insurance, taxation, real estate, and other areas related to finance and investing.

CHARTERED LIFE UNDERWRITER (CLU) designation granted by American College, Bryn Mawr, PA, the insurance and financial service industry's oldest and largest fully accredited institution of higher learning in the United States. Designation requires completion of ten college-level courses, three years of qualifying experience, and adherence to a strict code of ethics. All CLUs may join the American Society of CLU and ChFC, a professional association also headquartered in Bryn Mawr, for continuing education opportunities and other member services. The American Society has chapters in all 50 states.

CHARTIST technical analyst who charts the patterns of stocks, bonds, and commodities to make buy and sell recommendations to clients. Chartists believe recurring patterns of trading can help them forecast future price movements. *See also* TECHNICAL ANALYSIS.

CHASING THE MARKET purchasing a security at a higher price than intended because prices have risen sharply, or selling it at a lower level when prices fall. For example, an investor may want to buy shares of a stock at $20 and place a limit order to do so. But when the shares rise above $25, and then $28, the customer decides to enter a market order and buy the stock before it goes even higher. Investors can also chase the market when selling a stock. For example, if an investor wants to sell a stock at $20 and it declines to $15 and then $12, he may decide to sell it at the market price before it declines even further.

CHASTITY BONDS bonds that become redeemable at par value in the event of a TAKEOVER.

CHATTER *see* WHIPSAWED.

CHECK bill of exchange, or draft on a bank drawn against deposited funds to pay a specified sum of money to a specified person on demand. A check is considered as cash and is NEGOTIABLE when endorsed.

CHECKING THE MARKET canvassing securities market-makers by telephone or other means in search of the best bid or offer price.

CHICAGO BOARD OF TRADE (CBOT) formed in 1848 as a centralized marketplace for the grain trade, CBOT is a pioneer in the development of financial futures and options. Building on its agricultural and precious metals futures and options contracts on grains and silver and gold, CBOT launched GNMA futures in 1975 and grew to become the largest U.S. futures exchange based on volume with the introduction of U.S. Treasury bond and note futures, municipal bond index futures, and catastrophe insurance futures. In 1997, the exchange launched futures and futures options on the Dow Jones Industrial Average. The exchange has an international linkage with the LONDON INTERNATIONAL FINANCIAL FUTURES AND OPTIONS EXCHANGE, providing European markets with access to major U.S. government debt derivatives. Expanded trading sessions accommodate morning trading hours in Hong Kong, Sydney, Tokyo and Singapore. Project A, an electronic order-entry and matching system, enables members to trade futures and options outside of regular pit trading hours, supplementing open outcry. The CBOT Recyclables Exchange, a centralized market for paper, plastics, glass, rubber and other non-hazardous solid waste materials, operates on the Internet at http://cbot-recycle.com. The trading floor is open Monday through Friday, 7:20 A.M. to 2 P.M. Project A hours are Sunday through Thursday, 10:30 P.M. to 4:30 A.M. (agricultural products); and Sunday through Thursday, 10 P.M. to 6:45 A.M. and Monday through Thursday, 2:30 P.M. to 4:30 P.M. (financial products). *See also* SECURITIES AND COMMODITIES EXCHANGES.

CHICAGO BOARD OPTIONS EXCHANGE (CBOE) major U.S. marketplace exclusively for the trading of individual equity, index, and interest rate options. Among the most heavily-traded index options are contracts on the Dow Jones, Standard & Poor's, Russell and NASDAQ indices. CBOE also trades a family of country indices, including those for Japan, Mexico, and Israel. Sector indices cover real estate, technology, energy, metals, gaming and industrials. CBOE trades interest rate options and LEAPS, as well as structured products developed by Merrill Lynch, Bear Stearns, and other investment firms. There is active trading on CBOE Market Volatility Index, known as the VIX Index, which is a measure of the VOLATILITY of four S&P 100 contracts in the two nearby months. In 1998, CBOE consolidated operations with the PACIFIC EXCHANGE (PCX), combining the two exchange's product lines and operating under the CBOE name. Trading hours: Monday through Friday, from 7:20 A.M. to 3:15 P.M. *See also* SECURITIES AND COMMODITIES EXCHANGES.

CHICAGO MERCANTILE EXCHANGE (CME) U.S. derivatives exchange founded in 1874 trading futures and futures options on agriculture products, currencies, indices and interest rates. The CME's Globex automated trading system provides after-hours trading for the exchange's financial futures and options; MATIF and Reuters are the CME's partners in the system. OPEN OUTCRY is in use during regular trading sessions. The CME enjoys a mutual offset arrangement with the Singapore International Monetary Exchange, and with linkages the LONDON INTERNATIONAL FINANCIAL FUTURES AND OPTIONS EXCHANGE to trade short-term European interest rate contract, and with Matif to trade long-term European interest rate contracts. Trading hours: Monday through Friday, 7:20 A.M. to 3:15 P.M. *See also* SECURITIES AND COMMODITIES EXCHANGE.

CHICAGO STOCK EXCHANGE (CHX) founded in 1882, CHX is now a major exchange, particularly in extended trading hours. CHX merged with the stock exchanges in St. Louis, Minneapolis-St. Paul, and Cleveland in 1949 to form the Midwest Stock Exchange. Ten years later, the exchange in New Orleans also joined the Midwest Stock Exchange. The Midwest Stock Exchange changed its name to the Chicago Stock Exchange in 1993. CHX trades only stocks, more than 4,000 of which trade on the New York Stock Exchange, American Stock Exchange and NASDAQ Stock Market. Some issues are traded exclusively on CHX. There are 445 authorized memberships on CHX. The exchange provides retail services through its floor broker community. While trading is conducted on a trading floor, 90% of the trades are executed through the exchange's automated execution system, MAX. CHX is a leading market for executing block trades. Trading hours are 9:30 A.M. to 4:30 P.M.

CHIEF EXECUTIVE OFFICER (CEO) officer of a firm principally responsible for the activities of a company. CEO is usually an additional title held by the CHAIRMAN OF THE BOARD, the president, or another senior officer such as a vice chairman or an executive vice president.

CHIEF FINANCIAL OFFICER (CFO) executive officer who is responsible for handling funds, signing checks, keeping financial records, and financial planning for a corporation. He or she typically has the title of vice president-finance or financial vice president in large corporations, that of treasurer or controller (also spelled comptroller) in smaller companies. Since many state laws require that a corporation have a treasurer, that title is often combined with one or more of the other financial titles.

The controllership function requires an experienced accountant to direct internal accounting programs, including cost accounting, systems and procedures, data processing, acquisitions analysis, and financial planning. The controller may also have internal audit responsibilities.

The treasury function is concerned with the receipt, custody, investment, and disbursement of corporate funds and for borrowings and the maintenance of a market for the company's securities.

CHIEF OPERATING OFFICER (COO) officer of a firm, usually the president or an executive vice president, responsible for day-to-day management. The chief operating officer reports to the CHIEF EXECUTIVE OFFICER and may or may not be on the board of directors (presidents typically serve as board members). *See also* CHAIRMAN OF THE BOARD.

CHINESE WALL imaginary barrier between the investment banking, corporate finance, and research departments of a brokerage house and the sales and trading departments. Since the investment banking side has sensitive knowledge of impending deals such as takeovers, new stock and bond issues, divestitures, spinoffs and the like, it would be unfair to the general investing public if the sales and trading side of the firm had advance knowledge of such transactions. So several SEC and stock exchange rules mandate that a Chinese Wall be erected to prevent premature leakage of this market-moving information. It became law with the passage of SEC Rule 10b-5 of the Securities Exchange Act of 1934. The investment banking department uses code names and logs of the people who have access to key information in an attempt to keep the identities of the parties secret until the deal is publicly announced.

CHUNNEL tunnel crossing the English Channel between Great Britain and France. The Chunnel project took years to build and cost billions of dollars, but was finally opened for passenger and freight traffic in 1994. The Chunnel was built and is operated by Euro-Tunnel PLC.

CHURNING excessive trading of a client's account. Churning increases the broker's commissions, but usually leaves the client worse off or no better off than before. Churning is illegal under SEC and exchange rules, but is difficult to prove.

CINCINNATI STOCK EXCHANGE (CSE) stock exchange established in 1887, the exchange was the first—and still the only—fully automated stock exchange in the U.S., handling members' transactions using computers without a trading floor. CSE created the National Securities Trading System (NSTS), an electronic auction market. Participating brokerage firms enter orders into the NSTS computer system, along with specialists' bids and offers, which matches and clears orders back to brokers. The NSTS contains some of the features envisioned for a national exchange market system. Trading hours are 9:30 A.M. to 4 P.M.

CIRCLE underwriter's way of designating potential purchasers and amounts of a securities issue during the REGISTRATION period, before selling is permitted. Registered representatives canvass prospective buyers and report any interest to the underwriters, who then circle the names on their list.

CIRCUIT BREAKERS measures instituted by the major stock and commodities exchanges to halt trading temporarily in stocks and stock index futures when the market has fallen by an amount based on specified percentage declines in a specified period. For example, circuit breakers instituted at the NEW YORK STOCK EXCHANGE in spring 1998 halt stock trading when the Dow Jones Industrial Average falls 10%, 20%, and 30%, with the point settings revised quarterly on the first day of January, April, July, and October. Circuit breakers were originally instituted after BLACK MONDAY in 1987 and modified following another sharp market drop in October 1989. They are subject to change from time to time, but may include trading halts, curtailment of automated trading systems, and/or price movement limits on index futures. Their purpose is to prevent a market free-fall by permitting a rebalancing of buy and sell orders. *See also* PROGRAM TRADING.

CITIZEN BONDS form of CERTIFICATELESS MUNICIPALS. Citizen bonds may be registered on stock exchanges, in which case their prices are listed in daily newspapers, unlike other municipal bonds. *See also* BOOK-ENTRY SECURITIES.

CITY CODE ON TAKEOVERS AND MERGERS *see* DAWN RAID.

CIVILIAN LABOR FORCE all members of the population aged 16 or over in the United States who are not in the military or institutions such as prisons or mental hospitals and who are either employed or are unemployed and actively seeking and available for work. Every month, the U.S. Department of Labor releases the unemployment rate, which is the percentage of the civilian labor force who are unemployed. The Labor Department also releases the percentage of the civilian non-institutional population who are employed.

CLASS
1. securities having similar features. Stocks and bonds are the two main classes; they are subdivided into various classes—for example, mortgage bonds and debentures, issues with different rates of

interest, common and preferred stock, or Class A and Class B common. The different classes in a company's capitalization are itemized on its balance sheet.

2. options of the same type—put or call—with the same underlying security. A class of option having the same expiration date and EXERCISE PRICE is termed a SERIES.

CLASS A/CLASS B SHARES *see* CLASSIFIED STOCK.

CLASS ACTION legal complaint filed on behalf of a group of shareholders having an identical grievance. Shareholders in a class action are typically represented by one lawyer or group of attorneys, who like this kind of business because the awards tend to be proportionate to the number of parties in the class.

CLASSIFIED STOCK separation of equity into more than one CLASS of common, usually designated Class A and Class B. The distinguishing features, set forth in the corporation charter and bylaws, usually give an advantage to the Class A shares in terms of voting power, though dividend and liquidation privileges can also be involved. Classified stock is less prevalent today than in the 1920s, when it was used as a means of preserving minority control.

CLAYTON ANTI-TRUST ACT *see* ANTITRUST LAWS.

CLEAN
Finance: free of debt, as in a clean balance sheet. In banking, corporate borrowers have traditionally been required to *clean up* for at least 30 days each year to prove their borrowings were seasonal and not required as permanent working capital.
International trade: without documents, as in clean vs. documentary drafts.
Securities: block trade that matches buy or sell orders, sparing the block positioner any inventory risk. If the transaction appears on the exchange tape, it is said to be *clean on the tape.* Sometimes such a trade is called a *natural:* "We did a natural for 80,000 XYZ common."

CLEAR
Banking: COLLECTION of funds on which a check is drawn, and payment of those funds to the holder of the check. *See also* CLEARING HOUSE FUNDS.
Finance: asset not securing a loan and not otherwise encumbered. As a verb, to clear means to make a profit: "After all expenses, we *cleared* $1 million."
Securities: COMPARISON of the details of a transaction between brokers prior to settlement; final exchange of securities for cash on delivery.

CLEARING CORPORATIONS organizations, such as the NATIONAL SECURITIES CLEARING CORPORATION (NSCC), that are exchange-affiliated and facilitate the validation, delivery, and settlement of securities transactions.

CLEARING HOUSE FUNDS funds represented by checks or drafts that pass between banks through the FEDERAL RESERVE SYSTEM. Unlike FEDERAL FUNDS, which are drawn on reserve balances and are good the same day, clearing house funds require three days to clear. Also, funds used to settle transactions on which there is one day's FLOAT.

CLEAR TITLE title that is clear of all claims or disputed interests. It is necessary to have clear title to a piece of real estate before it can be sold by one party to another. In order to obtain a clear title, it is usually necessary to have a title search performed by a title company, which may find various clouds on the title such as an incomplete certificate of occupancy, outstanding building violations, claims by neighbors for pieces of the property, or an inaccurate survey. Once these objections have been resolved, the owner will have a clear and marketable title. *See also* BAD TITLE; CLOUD ON TITLE.

CLIFFORD TRUST trust set up for at least ten years and a day, which made it possible to turn over income-producing assets, then to reclaim the assets when the trust expired. Prior to the TAX REFORM ACT OF 1986, such trusts were popular ways of shifting income-producing assets from parents to children, whose income was taxed at lower rates. However, the 1986 Act made monies put into Clifford trusts after March 1, 1986, subject to taxation at the grantor's tax rate, thus defeating their purpose. For trusts established before that date, taxes are paid at the child's lower tax rate, but only if the child is under the age of 14. Since the Tax Act was implemented, few Clifford trusts are set up. *See also* INTER VIVOS TRUST.

CLONE FUND in a FAMILY OF FUNDS, new fund set up to emulate a successful existing fund.

CLOSE
1. the price of the final trade of a security at the end of a trading day.
2. the last half hour of a trading session on the exchanges.
3. in commodities trading, the period just before the end of the session when trades marked for execution AT THE CLOSE are completed.
4. to consummate a sale or agreement. In a REAL ESTATE closing, for example, rights of ownership are transferred in exchange for monetary and other considerations. At a *loan* closing, notes are signed and checks are exchanged. At the close of an *underwriting* deal, checks and securities are exchanged.
5. in accounting, the transfer of revenue and expense accounts at the end of the period—called *closing the books.*

CLOSE A POSITION to eliminate an investment from one's portfolio. The simplest example is the outright sale of a security and its delivery to the purchaser in exchange for payment. In commodities futures and options trading, traders commonly close out positions through offsetting transactions. Closing a position terminates involvement with the investment; HEDGING, though similar, requires further actions.

CLOSE MARKET market in which there is a narrow spread between BID and OFFER prices. Such a market is characterized by active trading and multiple competing market makers. In general, it is easier for investors to buy and sell securities and get good prices in a close market than in a wide market characterized by wide differences between bid and offer prices.

CLOSED CORPORATION corporation owned by a few people, usually management or family members. Shares have no public market. Also known as *private corporation* or *privately held corporation.*

CLOSED-END FUND type of fund that has a fixed number of shares usually listed on a major stock exchange. Unlike open-end mutual funds, closed end funds do not stand ready to issue and redeem shares on a continuous basis. They tend to have specialized portfolios of stocks, bonds, CONVERTIBLES, or combinations thereof, and may be oriented toward income, capital gains, or a combination of these objectives. Examples are the Korea Fund, which specializes in the stocks of Korean firms, and ASA Ltd., which specializes in South African gold mining stocks. Both are listed on the New York Stock Exchange. Because the managers of closed-end funds are perceived to be less responsive to profit opportunities than open-end fund managers, who must attract and retain shareholders, closed-end fund shares often sell at a discount from net asset value. *See also* DUAL-PURPOSE FUND.

CLOSED-END MANAGEMENT COMPANY INVESTMENT COMPANY that operates a mutual fund with a limited number of shares outstanding. Unlike an OPEN-END MANAGEMENT COMPANY, which creates new shares to meet investor demand, a closed-end fund has a set number of shares. These are often listed on an exchange. *See also* CLOSED-END FUND.

CLOSED-END MORTGAGE mortgage-bond issue with an indenture that prohibits repayment before maturity and the repledging of the same collateral without the permission of the bondholders; also called closed mortgage. It is distinguished from an OPEN-END MORTGAGE, which is reduced by amortization and can be increased to its original amount and secured by the original mortgage.

CLOSED FUND MUTUAL FUND that has become too large and is no longer issuing shares.

CLOSED OUT liquidated the position of a client unable to meet a margin call or cover a short sale. *See also* CLOSE A POSITION.

CLOSELY HELD corporation most of whose voting stock is held by a few shareholders; differs from a CLOSED CORPORATION because enough stock is publicly held to provide a basis for trading. Also, the shares held by the controlling group are not considered likely to be available for purchase.

CLOSING COSTS expenses involved in transferring real estate from a seller to a buyer, among them lawyer's fees, survey charges, title searches and insurance, and fees to file deeds and mortgages.

CLOSING PRICE price of the last transaction completed during a day's trading session on an organized securities exchange. *See also* CLOSING RANGE.

CLOSING PURCHASE option seller's purchase of another option having the same features as an earlier one. The two options cancel each other out and thus liquidate the seller's position.

CLOSING QUOTE last bid and offer prices recorded by a specialist or market maker at the close of a trading day.

CLOSING RANGE range of prices (in commodities trading) within which an order to buy or sell a commodity can be executed during one trading day.

CLOSING SALE sale of an option having the same features (i.e., of the same series) as an option previously purchased. The two have the effect of canceling each other out. Such a transaction demonstrates the intention to liquidate the holder's position in the underlying securities upon exercise of the buy.

CLOSING TICK gauge of stock market strength that nets the number of stocks whose New York Stock Exchange closing prices were higher than their previous trades, called an UPTICK or plus tick, against the number that closed on a DOWNTICK or minus tick. When the closing tick is positive, that is, when more stocks advanced than declined in the last trade, traders say the market closed on an uptick or was "buying at the close," a bullish sign. "Selling at the close," resulting in a minus closing tick or downtick, is bearish. *See also* TRIN.

CLOSING TRIN *see* TRIN.

CLOUD ON TITLE any document, claim, unreleased lien, or encumbrance that may superficially impair or injure the title to a property or make the title doubtful because of its apparent or possible validity. Clouds on title are usually uncovered in a TITLE SEARCH. These clouds range from a recorded mortgage paid in full, but with no satisfaction of mortgage recorded, to a property sold without a spouse's release of interest, to an heir of a prior owner with a questionable claim to the property. The property owner may initiate a quitclaim deed or a quiet title proceeding to remove the cloud on title from the record. Also called *bad title*.

CMO *see* COLLATERALIZED MORTGAGE OBLIGATION (CMO).

CMO REIT specialized type of REAL ESTATE INVESTMENT TRUST (REIT) that invests in the residual cash flows of COLLATERALIZED MORTGAGE

OBLIGATIONS (CMOs). CMO cash flows represent the spread (difference) between the rates paid by holders of the underlying mortgage loans and the lower, shorter term rates paid to investors in the CMOs. Spreads are subject to risks associated with interest rate levels and are considered risky investments. Also called *equity CMOs.*

COATTAIL INVESTING following on the coattails of other successful investors, usually institutions, by trading the same stocks when their actions are made public. This risky strategy assumes the research that guided the investor wearing the coat is still relevant by the time the coattail investor reads about it.

COBRA *See* CONSOLIDATED OMNIBUS BUDGET RECONCILIATION ACT (COBRA).

CODE OF PROCEDURE NATIONAL ASSOCIATION OF SECURITIES DEALERS (NASD) guide for its District Business Conduct Committees in hearing and adjudicating complaints filed between or against NASD members under its Rules of Fair Practice.

CODICIL legal document that amends a will.

C.O.D. TRANSACTION *see* DELIVERY VERSUS PAYMENT.

COFFEE, SUGAR AND COCOA EXCHANGE (CSCE) founded in 1882 as the Coffee Exchange of the City of New York. Sugar futures were added in 1914, and in 1979 the Coffee and Sugar Exchange merged with the New York Cocoa Exchange, which was founded in 1925. In 1998, CSCE merged with the NEW YORK COTTON EXCHANGE under an umbrella holding company, the Board of Trade of the City of New York, which provides joint clearing, back-office, and operational functions. The exchange continues to trade its derivative products under its name: futures and options in coffee, sugar, cocoa, basic formula price milk, nonfat dry milk, cheddar cheese and butter. CSCE also offers flexible options, comparable to over-the-counter options, for coffee, sugar, and cocoa. Trading is by open outcry. Contracts trade Monday through Friday, 9 A.M. to 2 P.M. *See also* SECURITIES AND COMMODITIES EXCHANGES.

COINCIDENT INDICATORS economic indicators that coincide with the current pace of economic activity. The Index of Coincident Indicators is published monthly by the Conference Board along with the Index of LEADING INDICATORS and the Index of LAGGING INDICATORS to give the public a reading on whether the economy is expanding or contracting and at what pace. The components of the Index of Coincident Indicators are: non-farm payroll workers, personal income less transfer payments, industrial production, manufacturing, and trade sales.

COINSURANCE sharing of an insurance risk, common when claims could be of such size that it would not be prudent for one company to underwrite the whole risk. Typically, the underwriter is liable up to a stated limit, and the coinsurer's liability is for amounts above that limit.

Policies on hazards such as fire or water damage often require coverage of at least a specified coinsurance percentage of the replacement cost. Such clauses induce the owners of property to carry full coverage or close to it.

COLA acronym for *cost-of-living adjustment,* which is an annual addition to wages or benefits to compensate employees or beneficiaries for the loss of purchasing power due to inflation. Many union contracts contain a COLA providing for salary increases at or above the change in the previous year's CONSUMER PRICE INDEX (CPI). Social Security recipients also have their monthly payments adjusted annually based on a COLA tied to the CPI.

COLD CALLING practice of making unsolicited calls to potential customers by brokers. Brokers hope to interest customers in stocks, bonds, mutual funds, financial planning, or other financial products and services in their cold calls. In some countries, such as Great Britain and parts of Canada, cold calling is severely restricted or even prohibited.

COLLAR
1. in new issue underwriting, the lowest rate acceptable to a buyer of bonds or the lowest price acceptable to the issuer. In an adjustable rate issue, refers to the maximum and minimum rates payable based on par value.
2. in ACQUISITION terminology, feature of an agreement that protects the acquirer from having to put up additional stock or cash in the event the market value of the acquirer falls between the agreement and closing.
3. in options trading, selling an OUT-OF-THE MONEY call and buying an IN-THE-MONEY put, thus limiting both upside and downside.
4. index level at which a CIRCUIT BREAKER is triggered.

COLLATERALIZE *see* ASSIGN; COLLATERAL; HYPOTHECATION.

COLLATERALIZED BOND OBLIGATION (CBO) INVESTMENT-GRADE bond backed by a pool of JUNK BONDS. CBOs are similar in concept to COLLATERALIZED MORTGAGE OBLIGATIONS (CMOs), but differ in that CBOs represent different degrees of credit quality rather than different maturities. Underwriters of CBOs package a large and diversified pool of high-risk, high-yield junk bonds, which is then separated into "tiers." Typically, a top tier represents the higher quality collateral and pays the lowest interest rate; a middle tier is backed by riskier bonds and pays a higher rate; the bottom tier represents the lowest credit quality and instead of receiving a fixed interest rate receives the residual interest payments—money that is left over after the higher tiers have been paid. CBOs, like CMOs, are substantially overcollateralized and this, plus the diversification of the pool backing them, earns them investment-grade bond ratings. Holders of third-tier CBOs stand to earn high yields or less money depending on the rate of defaults in the collateral pool. CBOs provide a way for big holders of junk bonds to reduce their portfolios and for securities firms to tap a new source of buyers in the disenchanted junk bond market of the early 1990s.

COLLATERALIZED MORTGAGE OBLIGATION (CMO) mortgage-backed bond that separates mortgage pools into different maturity classes, called *tranches*. This is accomplished by applying income (payments and prepayments of principal and interest) from mortgages in the pool in the order that the CMOs pay out. Tranches pay different rates of interest and can mature in a few months, or as long as 20 years. Issued by the Federal Home Loan Mortgage Corporation (Freddie Mac) and private issuers, CMOs are usually backed by government-guaranteed or other top-grade mortgages and have AAA ratings. In return for a lower yield, CMOs provide investors with increased security about the life of their investment compared to purchasing a whole mortgage-backed security. Even so, if mortgage rates drop sharply, causing a flood of refinancings, prepayment rates will soar and CMO tranches will be repaid before their expected maturity. CMOs are broken into different classes, called COMPANION BONDS or PLANNED AMORTIZATION CLASS (PAC) bonds.

COLLATERAL TRUST BOND corporate debt security backed by other securities, usually held by a bank or other trustee. Such bonds are backed by collateral trust certificates and are usually issued by parent corporations that are borrowing against the securities of wholly owned subsidiaries.

COLLECTIBLE rare object collected by investors. Examples: stamps, coins, oriental rugs, antiques, baseball cards, photographs. Collectibles typically rise sharply in value during inflationary periods, when people are trying to move their assets from paper currency as an inflation hedge, then drop in value during low inflation. Collectible trading for profit can be quite difficult, because of the limited number of buyers and sellers.

COLLECTION
1. presentation of a negotiable instrument such as a draft or check to the place at which it is payable. The term refers not only to check clearing and payment, but to such special banking services as foreign collections, coupon collection, and collection of returned items (bad checks).
2. referral of a past due account to specialists in collecting loans or accounts receivable, either an internal department or a private collection agency.
3. in a general financial sense, conversion of accounts receivable into cash.

COLLECTION PERIOD *see* COLLECTION RATIO.

COLLECTION RATIO ratio of a company's accounts receivable to its average daily sales. Average daily sales are obtained by dividing sales for an accounting period by the number of days in the accounting period—annual sales divided by 365, if the accounting period is a year. That result, divided into accounts receivable (an average of beginning and ending accounts receivable is more accurate), is the collection ratio—the average number of days it takes the company to convert receivables into cash. It is also called *average collection period. See* ACCOUNTS RECEIVABLE TURNOVER for a discussion of its significance.

COLLECTIVE BARGAINING process by which members of the labor force, operating through authorized union representatives, negotiate with their employers concerning wages, hours, working conditions, and benefits.

COLLEGE CONSTRUCTION LOAN INSURANCE ASSOCIATION federal agency established in 1987 to guarantee loans for college building programs. Informally called *Connie Lee.*

COLTS acronym for *Continuously Offered Longer-term Securities,* 3-year to 30-year fixed rate, variable rate, or zero-coupon bonds offered on an ongoing basis by the INTERNATIONAL BANK FOR RECONSTRUCTION AND DEVELOPMENT (World Bank). Bonds finance general operations of the bank and the terms are determined by bank management at the time of each new offering.

COMBINATION
1. arrangement of options involving two long or two short positions with different expiration dates or strike (exercise) prices. A trader could order a combination with a long call and a long put or a short call and a short put.
2. joining of competing companies in an industry to alter the competitive balance in their favor is called a combination in restraint of trade.
3. joining two or more separate businesses into a single accounting entity; also called *business combination. See also* MERGER.

COMBINATION ANNUITY *see* HYBRID ANNUITY.

COMBINATION BOND bond backed by the full faith and credit of the governmental unit issuing it as well as by revenue from the toll road, bridge, or other project financed by the bond.

COMBINATION ORDER *see* ALTERNATIVE ORDER.

COMBINED FINANCIAL STATEMENT financial statement that brings together the assets, liabilities, net worth, and operating figures of two or more affiliated companies. In its most comprehensive form, called a combining statement, it includes columns showing each affiliate on an "alone" basis; a column "eliminating" offsetting intercompany transactions; and the resultant combined financial statement. A combined statement is distinguished from a CONSOLIDATED FINANCIAL STATEMENT of a company and subsidiaries, which must reconcile investment and capital accounts. Combined financial statements do not necessarily represent combined credit responsibility or investment strength.

COMEX now a division of NEW YORK MERCANTILE EXCHANGE. Formerly known as the Commodity Exchange, it is the leading U.S. market for metals futures and futures options trading. Futures and futures options are traded on aluminum, copper, gold and silver, and the Eurotop 100 Index. Trading is conducted Monday through Friday, 8:10 A.M. to 2:35 P.M. *See also* NEW YORK MERCANTILE EXCHANGE; SECURITIES AND COMMODITIES EXCHANGES.

COMFORT LETTER

1. independent auditor's letter, required in securities underwriting agreements, to assure that information in the registration statement and prospectus is correctly prepared and that no material changes have occurred since its preparation. It is sometimes called *cold comfort letter*—cold because the accountants do not state positively that the information is correct, only that nothing has come to their attention to indicate it is not correct.

2. letter from one to another of the parties to a legal agreement stating that certain actions not clearly covered in the agreement will—or will not—be taken. Such declarations of intent usually deal with matters that are of importance only to the two parties and do not concern other signers of the agreement.

COMMERCIAL HEDGERS companies that take positions in commodities markets in order to lock in prices at which they buy raw materials or sell their products. For instance, Alcoa might hedge its holdings of aluminum with contracts in aluminum futures, or Eastman Kodak, which must buy great quantities of silver for making film, might hedge its holdings in the silver futures market.

COMMERCIAL LOAN short-term (typically 90-day) renewable loan to finance the seasonal WORKING CAPITAL needs of a business, such as purchase of inventory or production and distribution of goods. Commercial loans—shown on the balance sheet as notes payable—rank second only to TRADE CREDIT in importance as a source of short-term financing. Interest is based on the prime rate. *See also* CLEAN.

COMMERCIAL PAPER short-term obligations with maturities ranging from 2 to 270 days issued by banks, corporations, and other borrowers to investors with temporarily idle cash. Such instruments are unsecured and usually discounted, although some are interest-bearing. They can be issued directly—*direct issuers* do it that way—or through brokers equipped to handle the enormous clerical volume involved. Issuers like commercial paper because the maturities are flexible and because the rates are usually marginally lower than bank rates. Investors—actually lenders, since commercial paper is a form of debt—like the flexibility and safety of an instrument that is issued only by top-rated concerns and is nearly always backed by bank lines of credit. Both Moody's and Standard & Poor's assign ratings to commercial paper.

COMMERCIAL PROPERTY real estate that includes income-producing property, such as office buildings, restaurants, shopping centers, hotels, industrial parks, warehouses, and factories. Commercial property usually must be zoned for business purposes. It is possible to invest in commercial property directly, or through REAL ESTATE INVESTMENT TRUSTS or REAL ESTATE LIMITED PARTNERSHIPS. Investors receive income from rents and capital appreciation if the property is sold at a profit. Investing in commercial property also entails large risks, such as nonpayment of rent by tenants or a decline in property values because of overbuilding or low demand.

COMMERCIAL WELLS oil and gas drilling sites that are productive enough to be commercially viable. A limited partnership usually syndicates a share in a commercial well.

COMMINGLING
Securities: mixing customer-owned securities with those owned by a firm in its proprietary accounts. REHYPOTHECATION—the use of customers' collateral to secure brokers' loans—is permissible with customer consent, but certain securities and collateral must by law be kept separate.
Trust banking: pooling the investment funds of individual accounts, with each customer owning a share of the total fund. Similar to a MUTUAL FUND.

COMMISSION
Real estate: percentage of the selling price of the property, paid by the seller.
Securities: fee paid to a broker for executing a trade based on the number of shares traded or the dollar amount of the trade. Since 1975, when regulation ended, brokers have been free to charge whatever they like.

COMMISSION BROKER broker, usually a floor broker, who executes trades of stocks, bonds, or commodities for a commission.

COMMITMENT FEE lender's charge for contracting to hold credit available. Fee may be replaced by interest when money is borrowed or both fees and interest may be charged, as with a REVOLVING CREDIT.

COMMITTEE ON UNIFORM SECURITIES IDENTIFICATION PROCEDURES (CUSIP) committee that assigns identifying numbers and codes for all securities. These CUSIP numbers and symbols are used when recording all buy or sell orders. For International Business Machines the CUSIP symbol is IBM and the CUSIP number is 45920010.

COMMODITIES bulk goods such as grains, metals, and foods traded on a commodities exchange or on the SPOT MARKET. *See also* SECURITIES AND COMMODITIES EXCHANGES.

COMMODITIES EXCHANGE CENTER *see* SECURITIES AND COMMODITIES EXCHANGES.

COMMODITY-BACKED BOND bond tied to the price of an underlying commodity. An investor whose bond is tied to the price of silver or gold receives interest pegged to the metal's current price, rather than a fixed dollar amount. Such a bond is meant to be a hedge against inflation, which drives up the prices of most commodities.

COMMODITY FUTURES CONTRACT FUTURES CONTRACT tied to the movement of a particular commodity. This enables contract buyers to buy a specific amount of a commodity at a specified price on a particular date in the future. The price of the contract is determined using the OPEN OUTCRY system on the floor of a commodity exchange such as the Chicago Board of Trade or the Commodity Exchange in New York. There are commodity futures contracts based on meats such as cattle and pork bellies; grains such as corn, oats, soybeans and wheat; metals such as gold, silver, and platinum; and energy products such as heating oil, natural gas, and crude oil. For a complete listing of commodity futures contracts, *see* SECURITIES AND COMMODITIES EXCHANGES.

COMMODITY FUTURES TRADING COMMISSION (CFTC) independent agency created by Congress in 1974 responsible for regulating the U.S. commodity futures and options markets. The CFTC is responsible for insuring market integrity and protecting market participants against manipulation, abusive trade practices, and fraud.

COMMODITY INDICES indices that measure either the price or performance of physical commodities, or the price of commodities as represented by the price of futures contracts that are listed on commodity exchanges. The Journal of Commerce Index, Reuters Index and The Economist Index are three indices that measure industrial performance and raw commodities. Due to the complexities of holding physical commodities, however, investors tend to focus on futures indices that are liquid baskets of commodities. Institutional investors prohibited from investing directly in the futures market can include commodities in their portfolios through these indices. Among the commodity indices that measure futures price performance are:
Bankers Trust Commodity Index (BTCI) is a weighted, composite measure of the values of a basket of five commodities. Energy prices are based on NEW YORK MERCANTILE EXCHANGE contracts. Aluminum is based on the LONDON METAL EXCHANGE contract, while gold and silver are based on London spot fixings. The base prices used are the average prices of each component commodity over the first quarter of 1984. The components are: crude oil—45/\$30.191; gold—18/\$384.18; aluminum—

17/$1,543.67; heating oil—10/$0.8340; silver—10/$9.0043. The value of the index on any given day is calculated by multiplying the current price by the base weight and dividing this figure by the base price.

Chase Physical Commodity Index (CPCI) a value-weighted index of unleveraged physical commodity futures traded on U.S. exchanges. Unleveraged means the CPCI assumes investment in T-bills of a portion of the portfolio's total assets equal to 100% of the notional contract value, effectively collateralizing the long position. Only the risk and return of unleveraged changes in the constituent commodities' prices, augmented by the T-bills' yield, determine investment returns. The index is composed of five commodity categories: Energy (42.9%)—crude oil (19.4%), heating oil (8.02%), unleaded gasoline (5.24%), natural gas (10.24%); Livestock (20.55%)—lean hogs (7.92%), pork bellies (1.66%), live cattle (8.71%), feeder cattle (2.26%); Grain (16.78%)—wheat (6.16%), corn (4.94%), soybeans (3.61%), oats (2.07%); Food/Fiber (11.5%)—cotton (3.58%), coffee (2.59%), sugar (93.3%), cocoa (2.03%); Metals (8.27%)—copper (3%), gold (3.29%), silver (1.98%).

CRB/Bridge Index is made up of 17 commodities whose futures trade on U.S. exchanges. The index is viewed widely as a broad measure of overall commodity price trends. There are five component groups: industrials—crude oil, heating oil, natural gas, copper, cotton; grains—corn, wheat, soybeans; precious metals—gold, silver, platinum; livestock and meats—cattle, hogs; softs—coffee, cocoa, sugar, orange juice. Equal weighting is used for both arithmetic averaging of individual commodity months and for geometric averaging of the 21 commodity averages. As a result, no single month or commodity has undue impact on the index. Futures and options on the CRB/Bridge Index trade on the New York Futures Exchange (NYFE). Futures are settled at contract maturity by cash payment.

Energy and Metals Index (ENMET) is a geometrically weighted index based on the prices of futures contracts and developed by Merrill Lynch. ENMET is comprised of six commodities: crude oil (40%), natural gas (15%), gold (20%), silver (5%), copper (15%), aluminum (5%). The index is weighted to show optimal historic correlation with the CONSUMER PRICE INDEX and the PRODUCER PRICE INDEX. The index is computed daily.

Goldman Sachs Commodity Index (GSCI) consists of 22 commodities. All but the industrials, which trade on the LONDON METAL EXCHANGE, trade on U.S. futures markets. There are five component groups: Energy-crude oil (15.89%), natural gas (15.73%), heating oil (9.94%), unleaded gasoline (9.70%); Agriculture-wheat (8.87%), corn (6.34%), soybeans (2.99%), cotton (2.96%), sugar (2.84%), coffee (1.09%), cocoa (0.29%); Livestock-live cattle (9.35%), live hogs (4.24%); Industrials-aluminum (2.86%), copper (2.07%), zinc (0.77%), nickel (0.48%), lead (0.29%), tin (0.12%); Precious metals-gold (2.53%), platinum (0.40%), silver (0.26%). Each commodity is weighted by quantity of world production as a means of measuring the impact of commodity performance on the global economy. The index includes a rolling yield, achievable by continually rolling forward the futures positions, and it is investable. Price movement reflects spot price changes in the underlying commodities. Commodity yield reflects roll yield and Treasury bill yield. Because delivery of the underlying commodity never occurs, the investor can keep his money invested in Treasury bills. Additionally, there are six sub-indices, representing each of the commodity component groups, calculated daily on real-time prices. Futures and options on the index are traded on the CHICAGO MERCANTILE EXCHANGE. Other investment products based on the GSCI and the GSCI sub-indices include structured notes, swaps, customized over-the-counter options and principal-guaranteed annuity contracts.

Investable Commodity Index (ICI) is a broad-based index of 16 commodities based on exchange-traded commodity futures and developed by Intermarket Management, Inc. The index measures the reinvested total returns of an equally weighted, fully collateralized basket: Grains (19%)—wheat, corn, soybeans; Metals (19%)—gold, silver, copper; Energy (25%)—crude oil, heating oil, gasoline, natural gas; Livestock (12%)—live cattle, live hogs; Food and Fiber (25%)—cocoa, coffee, sugar, cotton. The ICI is a rolling index, and represents the compounded daily percentage change in the geometric mean of the 16 commodities' prices plus 100% of the daily compounded 13-week U.S. Treasury bill returns.

The J. P. Morgan Commodity Index (JPMCI) uses a dollar-weighted arithmetic average of total returns by investment in 11 metals and energy commodities. The index is composed of Base metals (22%)—aluminum (9%), copper (8%), nickel (2%), zinc (3%); Energy (55%)—West Texas Intermediate crude oil (33%), heating oil (10%), natural gas (7%), unleaded gasoline (5%); and Precious metals (23%)—gold (15%), silver (5%), platinum (3%). As a total return index, returns are derived from changes in commodity futures prices, from rolling long futures positions through time along a sloping forward curve, and by full collateralization of the value of the index with Treasury bills. The index has a positive correlation with growth and inflation, and a negative correlation with bond and equity returns. The index is rebalanced monthly to maintain constant dollar weight.

COMMODITY PAPER inventory loans or advances secured by commodities. If the commodities are in transit, a bill of lading is executed by a common carrier. If they are in storage, a trust receipt acknowledges that they are held and that proceeds from their sale will be transmitted to the lender; a warehouse receipt lists the goods.

COMMON MARKET *see* EUROPEAN ECONOMIC COMMUNITY.

COMMON STOCK units of ownership of a public corporation. Owners typically are entitled to vote on the selection of directors and other important matters as well as to receive dividends on their holdings. In the event that a corporation is liquidated, the claims of secured and unsecured creditors and owners of bonds and preferred stock take precedence over the claims of those who own common stock. For the most part, however, common stock has more potential for appreciation. *See also* CAPITAL STOCK.

COMMON STOCK EQUIVALENT preferred stock or bond convertible into common stock, or warrant to purchase common stock at a specified price or discount from market price. Common stock equivalents represent potential dilution of existing common shareholder's equity, and their conversion or exercise is assumed in calculating fully diluted earnings per share. *See also* FULLY DILUTED EARNINGS PER SHARE.

COMMON STOCK FUND MUTUAL FUND that invests only in common stocks.

COMMON STOCK RATIO percentage of total capitalization represented by common stock. From a creditor's standpoint a high ratio represents a margin of safety in the event of LIQUIDATION. From an investor's standpoint, however, a high ratio can mean a lack of *leverage.* What the ratio should be depends largely on the stability of earnings. Electric utilities can operate with low ratios because their earnings are stable. As a general rule, when an industrial company's stock ratio is below 30%, analysts check on earnings stability and fixed charge coverage in bad times as well as good.

COMMUNITY PROPERTY property and income accumulated by a married couple and belonging to them jointly. The two have equal rights to the income from stocks, bonds, and real estate, as well as to the appreciated value of those assets.

COMPANION BONDS one class of a COLLATERALIZED MORTGAGE OBLIGATION (CMO) which is paid off first when the underlying mortgages are prepaid as interest rates fall. When interest rates rise and there are fewer prepayments, the principal on companion bonds will be prepaid more slowly. Companion bonds therefore absorb most of the prepayment risk inherent in a CMO, and are therefore more volatile. In return, they pay higher yields than the other class within a CMO, called PLANNED AMORTIZATION CLASS (PAC) bonds.

COMPANY organization engaged in business as a proprietorship, partnership, corporation, or other form of enterprise. Originally, a firm made up of a group of people as distinguished from a sole proprietorship. However, since few proprietorships owe their existence exclusively to one person, the term now applies to proprietorships as well.

COMPANY DOCTOR executive, usually recruited from the outside, specialized in corporate turnarounds.

COMPARATIVE STATEMENTS financial statements covering different dates but prepared consistently and therefore lending themselves to comparative analysis, as accounting convention requires. Comparative figures reveal trends in a company's financial development and permit insight into the dynamics behind static balance sheet figures.

COMPARISON
1. short for *comparison ticket*, a memorandum exchanged prior to settlement by two brokers in order to confirm the details of a transaction to which they were parties. Also called comparison sheet.
2. verification of collateral held against a loan, by exchange of information between two brokers or between a broker and a bank.

COMPENSATING BALANCE *or* **COMPENSATORY BALANCE** average balance required by a bank for holding credit available. The more or less standard requirement for a bank line of credit, for example, is 10% of the line plus an additional 10% of the borrowings. Compensating balances increase the effective rate of interest on borrowings.

COMPETITIVE BID sealed bid, containing price and terms, submitted by a prospective underwriter to an issuer, who awards the contract to the bidder with the best price and terms. Many municipalities and virtually all railroads and public utilities use this bid system. Industrial corporations generally prefer NEGOTIATED UNDERWRITING on stock issues but do sometimes resort to competitive bidding in selecting underwriters for bond issues.

COMPETITIVE TRADER *see* REGISTERED COMPETITIVE TRADER.

COMPLETE AUDIT usually the same as an unqualified audit, because it is so thoroughly executed that the auditor's only reservations have to do with unobtainable facts. A complete audit examines the system of internal control and the details of the books of account, including subsidiary records and supporting documents. This is done with an eye to locality, mathematical accuracy, accountability, and the application of accepted accounting principles.

COMPLETED CONTRACT METHOD accounting method whereby revenues and expenses (and therefore taxes) on long-term contracts, such as government defense contracts, are recognized in the year the contract is concluded, except that losses are recognized in the year they are forecast. This method differs from the *percentage-of-completion method,* where sales and costs are recognized each year based on the value of the work performed. Under the TAX REFORM ACT OF 1986, manufacturers with long-term contracts must elect either the latter method or the *percentage-of-completion capitalized cost method,* requiring that 40% of the contract be included under the percentage-of-completion method and 60% under the taxpayer's normal accounting method.

COMPLETION PROGRAM oil and gas limited partnership that takes over drilling when oil is known to exist in commercial quantities. A completion program is a conservative way to profit from oil and gas drilling, but without the capital gains potential of exploratory wildcat drilling programs.

COMPLIANCE DEPARTMENT department set up in all organized stock exchanges to oversee market activity and make sure that trading complies with Securities and Exchange Commission and exchange regulations. A company that does not adhere to the rules can be delisted, and a trader or brokerage firm that violates the rules can be barred from trading.

COMPOSITE TAPE *see* TAPE.

COMPOUND ANNUAL RETURN investment return, discounted retroactively from a cumulative figure, at which money, compounded annually, would reach the cumulative total. Also called INTERNAL RATE OF RETURN.

COMPOUND GROWTH RATE rate of growth of a number, compounded over several years. Securities analysts check a company's compound growth rate of profits for five years to see the long-term trend.

COMPOUND INTEREST interest earned on principal plus interest that was earned earlier. If $100 is deposited in a bank account at 10%, the depositor will be credited with $110 at the end of the first year and $121 at the end of the second year. That extra $1, which was earned on the $10 interest from the first year, is the compound interest. This example involves interest compounded annually: interest can also be compounded on a daily, quarterly, half-yearly, or other basis. *See also* COMPOUND ANNUAL RETURN.

COMPTROLLER OF THE CURRENCY federal official, appointed by the President and confirmed by the Senate, who is responsible for chartering, examining, supervising, and liquidating all national banks. In response to the *comptroller's call,* national banks are required to submit *call reports* of their financial activities at least four times a year and to publish them in local newspapers. National banks can be declared insolvent only by the Comptroller of the Currency.

COMPUTERIZED MARKET TIMING SYSTEM system of picking buy and sell signals that puts together voluminous trading data in search of patterns and trends. Often, changes in the direction of moving average lines form the basis for buy and sell recommendations. These systems, commonly used by commodity funds and by services that switch between mutual funds, tend to work well when markets are moving steadily up or down, but not in trendless markets.

CONCERT PARTY person ACTING IN CONCERT.

CONCESSION
1. selling group's per-share or per-bond compensation in a corporate underwriting.
2. right, usually granted by a government entity, to use property for a specified purpose, such as a service station on a highway.

CONDEMNATION legal seizure of private property by a public authority for public use. Using the powers and legal procedures of EMINENT DOMAIN, a state, city, or town may condemn a property owner's home to make way for a highway, school, park, hospital, public housing project, parking facility, or other public project. The homeowners must give up the property even if they do not want to, and in return they must be compensated at fair market value by the public authority.

CONDITIONAL CALL OPTIONS form of CALL PROTECTION available to holders of some HIGH-YIELD BONDS. In the event the bond is called, the issuing corporation is obligated to substitute a non-callable bond having the same life and terms as the bond that is called.

CONDOMINIUM form of real estate ownership in which individual residents hold a deed and title to their houses or apartments and pay a maintenance fee to a management company for the upkeep of common property such as grounds, lobbies, and elevators as well as for other amenities. Condominium owners pay real estate taxes on their units and can sublet or sell as they wish. Some real estate limited partnerships specialize in converting rental property into condominiums. *See also* COOPERATIVE.

CONDUIT THEORY theory regulating investment companies such as REAL ESTATE INVESTMENT TRUSTS and MUTUAL FUNDS holding that since such companies are pure conduits for all capital gains, dividends, and interest to be passed through to shareholders, the investment company should not be taxed at the corporate level. As long as the investment company adheres to certain regulations, shareholders are therefore taxed only once—at the individual level—on income and capital gains. In contrast, shareholders of corporations are taxed twice: once at the corporate level in the form of corporate income taxes and once at the individual level in the form of individual income taxes on all dividends paid by the corporation.

CONFIRMATION
1. formal memorandum from a broker to a client giving details of a securities transaction. When a broker acts as a dealer, the confirmation must disclose that fact to the customer.
2. document sent by a company's auditor to its customers and suppliers requesting verification of the book amounts of receivables and payables. *Positive confirmations* request that every balance be confirmed, whereas *negative confirmations* request a reply only if an error exists.

CONFORMED COPY copy of an original document with the essential legal features, such as the signature and seal, being typed or indicated in writing.

CONFORMING LOANS mortgage loans that meet the qualifications of FREDDIE MAC or FANNIE MAE, which buy them from lenders and then issue PASS-THROUGH SECURITIES.

CONGLOMERATE corporation composed of companies in a variety of businesses. Conglomerates were popular in the 1960s, when they were thought to provide better management and sounder financial backing, and therefore to generate more profit, than small independent companies. However, some conglomerates became so complex that they were difficult to manage. In the 1980s and 1990s, many conglomerates sold off divisions and concentrated on a few core businesses. Analysts generally consider stocks of conglomerates difficult to evaluate because they are involved in so many unrelated businesses.

CONNIE LEE nickname for COLLEGE CONSTRUCTION LOAN INSURANCE ASSOCIATION.

CONSERVATOR individual appointed by a court to manage the property of a person who lacks the capacity to manage his own property. A conservator may be charged with liquidating the assets of a business in bankruptcy, or may have to take control of the personal finances of an incompetent individual who needs to be protected by the court.

CONSIDERATION something of value that one party gives to another in exchange for a promise or act. In law, a requirement of valid contracts. A consideration can be in the form of money, commodities, or personal services; in many industries the forms have become standardized.

CONSOLIDATED FINANCIAL STATEMENT financial statement that brings together all assets, liabilities, and operating accounts of a parent company and its subsidiaries. *See also* COMBINED FINANCIAL STATEMENT.

CONSOLIDATED MORTGAGE BOND bond issue that covers several units of property and may refinance separate mortgages on these properties. The consolidated mortgage with a single coupon rate is a traditional form of financing for railroads because it is economical to combine many properties in one agreement.

CONSOLIDATED OMNIBUS BUDGET RECONCILIATION ACT (COBRA) federal legislation under which group health plans sponsored by employers with 20 or more employees must offer continuation of coverage to employees who leave their jobs, voluntarily or otherwise, and their dependents. The employee must pay the entire premium up to 102% of the cost of coverage extended by COBRA. Depending on circumstances, COBRA permits employees to extend their coverage for up to 18 months and that of surviving dependents for up to 36 months. COBRA was designed to help former employees maintain health insurance coverage at group rates which may otherwise be unobtainable or unaffordable.

CONSOLIDATED TAPE combined tapes of the New York Stock Exchange and the American Stock Exchange. It became operative in June 1975. Network A covers NYSE-listed securities and identifies the originating market. Network B does the same for Amex-listed securities and also reports on securities listed on regional exchanges.

CONSOLIDATED TAX RETURN return combining the reports of the companies in what the tax law defines as an affiliated group. A firm is part of an affiliated group if it is at least 80% owned by a parent or other inclusive corporation. "Owned" refers to voting stock. (Before the TAX REFORM ACT OF 1986 it also included nonvoting stock.)

CONSOLIDATION LOAN loan that combines and refinances other loans or debt. It is normally an installment loan designed to reduce the dollar amount of an individual's monthly payments.

CONSORTIUM group of companies formed to promote a common objective or engage in a project of benefit to all the members. The relationship normally entails cooperation and a sharing of resources, sometimes even common ownership.

CONSTANT DOLLAR PLAN method of accumulating assets by investing a fixed amount of dollars in securities at set intervals. The investor buys more shares when the price is low and fewer shares when the price is high; the overall cost is lower than it would be if a constant number of shares were bought at set intervals. Also called *dollar cost averaging.*

CONSTANT DOLLARS dollars of a base year, used as a gauge in adjusting the dollars of other years in order to ascertain actual purchasing power. Denoted as C$ by the FINANCIAL ACCOUNTING STANDARDS BOARD (FASB), which defines constant dollars as hypothetical units of general purchasing power.

CONSTANT RATIO PLAN type of FORMULA INVESTING whereby a predetermined ratio is maintained between stock and FIXED INCOME INVESTMENTS through periodic adjustments. For example, an investor with $200,000 and a 50-50 formula might start out with $100,000 in stock and $100,000 in bonds. If the stock increased in value to $150,000 and the bonds remained unchanged over a given adjustment period, the investor would restore the ratio at $125,000-$125,000 by selling $25,000 of stock and buying $25,000 of bonds.

CONSTANT YIELD METHOD method of allocating annual interest on a ZERO-COUPON SECURITY for income tax purposes. IRS Publication 1212 explains how to figure taxable interest on such ORIGINAL ISSUE DISCOUNT securities.

CONSTRUCTION LOAN short-term real estate loan to finance building costs. The funds are disbursed as needed or in accordance with a prearranged plan, and the money is repaid on completion of the project, usually from the proceeds of a mortgage loan. The rate is normally higher than prime, and there is usually an origination fee. The effective yield on these loans tends to be high, and the lender has a security interest in the real property.

CONSTRUCTION LOAN NOTE (CLN) note issued by a municipality to finance the construction of multi-family housing projects. The notes, which typically mature in three years or less, are normally repaid out of the proceeds of a long-term bond issue.

CONSTRUCTIVE RECEIPT term used by Internal Revenue Service for the date when a taxpayer received dividends or other income. IRS rules say that constructive receipt of income is established if the taxpayer has the right to claim it, whether or not the choice is exercised. For instance, if a bond pays interest on December 29, the taxpayer must report the income in that tax year and not in the following year.

CONSUMER CREDIT debt assumed by consumers for purposes other than home mortgages. Interest on consumer loans had been 100% deductible until the TAX REFORM ACT OF 1986 mandated that the deduction be phased out by 1991. Consumers can borrow through credit cards, lines of credit, loans against insurance policies, and many other methods. The Federal Reserve Board releases the amount of outstanding consumer credit on a monthly basis.

CONSUMER CREDIT PROTECTION ACT OF 1968 landmark federal legislation establishing rules of disclosure that lenders must observe in dealings with borrowers. The act stipulates that consumers be told annual percentage rates, potential total cost, and any special loan terms. The act, enforced by the Federal Reserve Bank, is also known as the *Truth in Lending Act.*

CONSUMER DEBENTURE investment note issued by a financial institution and marketed directly to the public. Consumer debentures were a popular means of raising lendable funds for banks during tight money periods prior to deregulation, since these instruments, unlike certificates of deposit, could compete freely with other money-market investments in a high-rate market.

CONSUMER DURABLES products bought by consumers that are expected to last three years or more. These include automobiles, appliances, boats, and furniture. Economists look at the trend in consumer expenditure on durables as an important indicator of the strength of the economy, since consumers need confidence to make such large and expensive purchases. Stock market analysts also classify companies that produce appliances, furniture, cars, and similar items as consumer durables manufacturers, contrasting them with consumer non-durables manufacturers, which make consumable items such as food or drugs.

CONSUMER FINANCE COMPANY *see* FINANCE COMPANY.

CONSUMER GOODS goods bought for personal or household use, as distinguished from CAPITAL GOODS or *producer's goods,* which are used to produce other goods. The general economic meaning of consumer goods encompasses consumer services. Thus the *market basket* on which the CONSUMER PRICE INDEX is based includes clothing, food, and other goods as well as utilities, entertainment, and other services.

CONSUMER INTEREST interest paid on consumer loans. Consumer interest is paid on credit cards, bank lines of credit, retail purchases, car and boat loans, and educational loans. Since the end of 1991, such interest is no longer deductible for tax purposes, based on provisions of the TAX REFORM ACT OF 1986. That tax law distinguished nondeductible consumer interest from other forms of interest which can be deductible, including business interest, investment interest, and mortgage-related interest.

CONSUMER PRICE INDEX (CPI) measures prices of a fixed basket of goods bought by a typical consumer, including food, transportation, shelter, utilities, clothing, medical care, entertainment, and other items. The CPI, published by the Bureau of Labor Statistics in the Department of Labor, is based at 100 in 1982 and is released monthly. It is widely used as a cost-of-living benchmark to adjust Social Security payments and other payment schedules, union contracts, and tax brackets. Also known as the *cost-of-living index.*

CONSUMPTION TAX *see* VALUE-ADDED TAX (VAT).

CONTANGO
1. pricing situation in which futures prices get progressively higher as maturities get progressively longer, creating negative spreads as contracts go farther out. The increases reflect carrying costs, including storage, financing, and insurance. The reverse condition, an inverted market, is termed BACKWARDATION.
2. in finance, the costs that must be taken into account in analyses involving forecasts.

CONTINGENT BENEFICIARY person named in an insurance policy to receive the policy benefits if the primary beneficiary dies before the benefits become payable.

CONTINGENT DEFERRED SALES LOAD sales charge levied by a mutual fund if a customer sells fund shares within a specified number of years. Instead of charging a traditional FRONT END LOAD of 5%, for example, a brokerage firm may offer the same fund with a contingent deferred sales load. Customers who sell the fund within the first year pay a 5% load. In the second year, the charge would be 4%. Each year the charge declines by one percentage point until there is no fee for selling fund shares after the fifth year. Also called *back-end load.*

CONTINGENT LIABILITIES
Banking: potential obligation of a guarantor or accommodation endorser; or the position of a customer who opens a letter of credit and whose account will be charged if a draft is presented. The bank's own ultimate responsibility for letters of credit and other commitments, individually and collectively, is its contingent liability.
Corporate reports: pending lawsuits, judgments under appeal, disputed claims, and the like, representing potential financial liability.

CONTINGENT ORDER securities order whose execution depends on the execution of another order; for example, a sell order and a buy order with prices stipulated. Where the purpose is to effect a swap, a price difference might be stipulated as a condition of the order's execution. Generally, brokers discourage these orders, favoring firm instructions.

CONTINUOUS NET SETTLEMENT (CNS) method of securities clearing and settlement that eliminates multiple fails in the same securities. This is accomplished by using a clearing house, such as the National Securities Clearing Corporation, and a depository, such as DEPOSITORY TRUST COMPANY, to match transactions to securities available in the firm's position, resulting in one net receive or deliver position at the end of the day. By including the previous day's fail position in the next day's selling trades, the firm's position is always up-to-date and money settlement or withdrawals can be made at any time with the clearing house. The alternative to CNS is window settlement, where the seller delivers securities to the buyer's cashier and receives payment.

CONTRA BROKER broker on the opposite side—the buy side of a sell order or the sell side of a buy order.

CONTRACT in general, agreement by which rights or acts are exchanged for lawful consideration. To be valid, it must be entered into by competent parties, must cover a legal and moral transaction, must possess mutuality, and must represent a meeting of minds. Countless transactions in finance and investments are covered by contracts.

CONTRACTUAL PLAN plan by which fixed dollar amounts of mutual fund shares are accumulated through periodic investments for 10 or 15 years. The legal vehicle for such investments is the *plan company* or *participating unit investment trust,* a selling organization operating on behalf of the fund's underwriter. The plan company must be registered with the Securities and Exchange Commission, as the underlying fund must be, so the investor receives two prospectuses. Investors in these plans commonly receive other benefits in exchange for their fixed periodic payments, such as decreasing term life insurance. *See also* FRONT END LOAD.

CONTRARIAN investor who does the opposite of what most investors are doing at any particular time. According to contrarian opinion, if everyone is certain that something is about to happen, it won't. This is because most people who say the market is going up are fully invested and have no additional purchasing power, which means the market is at its peak. When people predict decline they have already sold out, so the market can only go up. Some mutual funds follow a contrarian investment strategy, and some investment advisers suggest only out-of-favor securities, whose price/earnings ratio is lower than the rest of the market or industry.

CONTRIBUTED CAPITAL payments made in cash or property to a corporation by its stockholders either to buy capital stock, to pay an assessment on the capital stock, or as a gift. **Also** called *paid-in capital.* The contributed or paid-in capital of a corporation is made up of capital stock and capital (or contributed) surplus, which is contributed (or paid-in) capital in excess of PAR value or STATED VALUE. Donated capital and DONATED SURPLUS are freely given forms of contributed (paid-in) capital, but DONATED STOCK refers to fully paid (previously issued) capital stock that is given as a gift to the issuing corporation.

CONTROLLED COMMODITIES commodities regulated by the Commodities Exchange Act of 1936, which set up trading rules for futures in commodities markets in order to prevent fraud and manipulation.

CONTROLLED WILDCAT DRILLING drilling for oil and gas in an area adjacent to but outside the limits of a proven field. Also known as a *field extension.* Limited partnerships drilling in this area take greater risks than those drilling in areas of proven energy reserves, but the rewards can be considerable if oil is found.

CONTROLLER *or* COMPTROLLER chief accountant of a company. In small companies the controller may also serve as treasurer. In a brokerage firm, the controller prepares financial reports, supervises internal audits, and is responsible for compliance with Securities and Exchange Commission regulations.

CONTROLLING INTEREST ownership of more than 50% of a corporation's voting shares. A much smaller interest, owned individually or by a group in combination, can be controlling if the other shares are widely dispersed and not actively voted.

CONTROL PERSON *see* AFFILIATED PERSON.

CONTROL STOCK shares owned by holders who have a CONTROLLING INTEREST.

CONVENTIONAL MORTGAGE residential mortgage loan, usually from a bank or savings and loan association, with a fixed rate and term. It is repayable in fixed monthly payments over a period usually 30 years or less, secured by real property, and not insured by the FEDERAL HOUSING ADMINISTRATION or guaranteed by the Veterans Administration.

CONVENTIONAL OPTION put or call contract arranged off the trading floor of a listed exchange and not traded regularly. It was commonplace when options were banned on certain exchanges, but is now rare.

CONVERGENCE movement of the price of a futures contract toward the price of the underlying CASH COMMODITY. At the start of the contract price is higher because of the time value. But as the contract nears expiration the futures price and the cash price converge.

CONVERSION
1. exchange of a convertible security such as a bond into a fixed number of shares of the issuing corporation's common stock.
2. transfer of mutual-fund shares without charge from one fund to another fund in a single family; also known as fund switching.
3. in insurance, switch from short-term to permanent life insurance.

CONVERSION FEATURE right to convert a particular holding to another form of holding, such as the SWITCHING within a mutual fund family, the right to convert certain preferred stock or bonds to common stock, or the right to switch from one type of insurance policy to another. *See also* CONVERTIBLES.

CONVERSION PARITY common-stock price at which a convertible security can become exchangeable for common shares of equal value.

CONVERSION PREMIUM amount by which the price of a convertible tops the market price of the underlying stock. If a stock is trading at $50 and the bond convertible at $45 is trading at $50, the premium is $5. If the premium is high the bond trades like any fixed income bond. If the premium is low the bond trades like a stock.

CONVERSION PRICE the dollar value at which convertible bonds, debentures, or preferred stock can be converted into common stock, as announced when the convertible is issued.

CONVERSION RATIO relationship that determines how many shares of common stock will be received in exchange for each convertible bond or preferred share when the conversion takes place. It is determined at the time of issue and is expressed either as a ratio or as a conversion price from which the ratio can be figured by dividing the par value of the convertible by the conversion price. The indentures of most convertible securities contain an antidilution clause whereby the conversion ratio may be raised (or the conversion price lowered) by the percentage amount of any stock dividend or split, to protect the convertible holder against dilution.

CONVERSION VALUE
In general: value created by changing from one form to another. For example, converting rental property to condominiums adds to the value of the property.

Convertibles: the price at which the exchange can be made for common stock.

CONVERTIBLE ADJUSTABLE PREFERRED STOCK *see* CAPS.

CONVERTIBLES corporate securities (usually preferred shares or bonds) that are exchangeable for a set number of another form (usually common shares) at a prestated price. Convertibles are appropriate for investors who want higher income than is available from common stock, together with greater appreciation potential than regular bonds offer. From the issuer's standpoint, the convertible feature is usually designed as a sweetener, to enhance the marketability of the stock or preferred.

CONVEXITY mathematical concept that measures sensitivity of the market price of an interest-bearing bond to changes in interest rate levels. *See also* DURATION.

COOK THE BOOKS to falsify the financial statements of a company intentionally. A firm in financial trouble may want to cook the books to prevent investors from pushing down the company's stock price. Companies may also falsify their records to lower their tax liabilities. Whatever the reason, the practice is illegal under SEC, IRS, and stock exchange rules as well as the ethical code of the accounting profession.

COOLING-OFF PERIOD
1. interval (usually 20 days) between the filing of a preliminary prospectus with the Securities and Exchange Commission and the offer of the securities to the public. *See also* REGISTRATION.
2. period during which a union is prohibited from striking, or an employer from locking out employees. The period, typically 30 to 90 days, may be required by law or provided for in a labor agreement.

COOPERATIVE organization owned by its members.

In real estate, a property whose residents own shares in a cooperative giving them exclusive use of their apartments. Decisions about common areas—hallways, elevators, grounds—are made by a vote of members' shares. Members also approve sales of apartments.

Agriculture cooperatives help farmers sell their products more efficiently. Food cooperatives buy food for their members at wholesale prices, but usually require members to help run the organization.

COPENHAGEN STOCK EXCHANGE only securities exchange in Denmark. Stocks, bonds futures and options are traded on ELECTRA, the electronic trading system to which all Danish stock brokerage houses are connected. ELECTRA combines trading, reporting, and information systems. Trading companies using the telephone market are legally obliged to report transactions in all listed securities within

90 seconds, ensuring all market participants the same transparent, real-time market. Transactions in Danish shares are settled three days after trading, and payment is due upon delivery of share certificates. FUTOP, the Danish derivatives market, trades futures and options on the KFX Stock Index, Danish government bonds and equities. FUTOP merged with the exchange in 1997.

CORE CAPITAL thrift institution's bedrock capital, which must be at least 2% of assets to meet proposed rules of the Federal Home Loan Bank. It comprises capital stock and surplus accounts, including perpetual preferred stock, plus minority interests in consolidated subsidiaries.

CORNERING THE MARKET purchasing a security or commodity in such volume that control over its price is achieved. A cornered market in a security would be unhappy news for a short seller, who would have to pay an inflated price to cover. Cornering has been illegal for some years.

CORPORATE BOND debt instrument issued by a private corporation, as distinct from one issued by a government agency or a municipality. Corporates typically have four distinguishing features: (1) they are taxable; (2) they have a par value of $1000; (3) they have a term maturity—which means they come due all at once—and are paid for out of a sinking fund accumulated for that purpose; (4) they are traded on major exchanges, with prices published in newspapers. *See also* BOND; MUNICIPAL BOND.

CORPORATE CHARTER *see* ARTICLES OF INCORPORATION.

CORPORATE EQUIVALENT YIELD comparison that dealers in government bonds include in their offering sheets to show the after-tax yield of government bonds selling at a discount and corporate bonds selling at par.

CORPORATE FINANCING COMMITTEE NATIONAL ASSOCIATION OF SECURITIES DEALERS standing committee that reviews documentation submitted by underwriters in compliance with Securities and Exchange Commission requirements to ensure that proposed markups are fair and in the public interest.

CORPORATE INCOME FUND (CIF) UNIT INVESTMENT TRUST with a fixed portfolio made up of high-grade securities and instruments, similar to a MONEY MARKET FUND. Most CIFs pay out investment income monthly.

CORPORATE INSIDER *see* INSIDER.

CORPORATION legal entity, chartered by a U.S. state or by the federal government, and separate and distinct from the persons who own it, giving rise to a jurist's remark that it has "neither a soul to damn nor

a body to kick." Nonetheless, it is regarded by the courts as an artificial person; it may own property, incur debts, sue, or be sued. It has three chief distinguishing features:
1. limited liability; owners can lose only what they invest.
2. easy transfer of ownership **through** the sale of shares of stock.
3. continuity of existence.

Other factors helping to explain the popularity of the corporate form of organization are its ability to obtain capital through expanded ownership, and the shareholders' ability to profit from the growth of the business.

CORPUS Latin for *body.*
1. in trust banking, the property in a trust—real estate, securities and other personal property, cash in bank accounts, and any other items included by **the** donor.
2. body of an investment or note, representing the principal or capital as distinct from the interest or income.

CORRECTION reverse movement, usually downward and exceeding 10%, in the price of an individual stock, bond, commodity, or index. If prices have been rising on the market as a whole, then fall dramatically, this is known as a *correction within an upward trend.* Technical analysts note that markets do not move straight up or down and that corrections are to be expected during any long-term move.

CORRECTION

CORRELATION COEFFICIENT statistical measure of the degree to which the movements of two variables are related.

CORRESPONDENT financial organization that regularly performs services for another in a market inaccessible to the other. In banking there is usually a depository relationship that compensates for expenses and facilitates transactions.

COST ACCOUNTING branch of accounting concerned with providing the information that enables the management of a firm to evaluate production costs.

COST BASIS original price of an asset, used in determining capital gains. It usually is the purchase price, but in the case of an inheritance it is the appraised value of the asset at the time of the donor's death.

COST-BENEFIT ANALYSIS method of measuring the benefits expected from a decision, calculating the cost of the decision, then determining whether the benefits outweigh the costs. Corporations use this method in deciding whether to buy a piece of equipment, and the government uses it in determining whether federal programs are achieving their goals.

COST OF CAPITAL rate of return that a business could earn if it chose another investment with equivalent risk—in other words, the OPPORTUNITY COST of the funds employed as the result of an investment decision. Cost of capital is also calculated using a weighted average of a firm's costs of debt and classes of equity. This is also called the *composite cost of capital.*

COST OF CARRY out-of-pocket costs incurred while an investor has an investment position, among them interest on long positions in margin accounts, dividends lost on short margin positions, and incidental expenses.

COST OF FUNDS interest cost paid by a financial institution for the use of money. Brokerage firms' cost of funds are comprised of the total interest éxpense to carry an inventory of stocks and bonds. In the banking and savings and loan industry, the cost of funds is the amount of interest the bank must pay on money market accounts, passbooks, CDs, and other liabilities. Many adjustable rate mortgage loans are tied to a cost-of-funds index, which rises and falls in line with the banks' interest expenses.

COST-OF-FUNDS INDEX (COFI) index used by mortgage lenders on adjustable rate mortgage loans. Borrower's mortgage payments rise or fall based on the widely published COFI, which is based on what financial institutions are paying on money market accounts, passbooks, CDs, and other liabilities. The COFI tends to move far more slowly, both up and down, than other indexes for adjustable rate mortgages, such as one-year Treasuries or the prime rate.

COST OF GOODS SOLD figure representing the cost of buying raw materials and producing finished goods. Depreciation is considered a part of this cost but is usually listed separately. Included in the direct costs are clear-cut factors such as direct factory labor as well as others that are less clear-cut, such as overhead. *Cost of sales* may be used as a synonym or may mean selling expenses. *See also* DIRECT OVERHEAD; FIRST IN, FIRST OUT; LAST IN, FIRST OUT.

COST-OF-LIVING ADJUSTMENT (COLA) adjustment of wages designed to offset changes in the cost of living, usually as measured by the CONSUMER PRICE INDEX. COLAs are key bargaining issues in labor contracts and are politically sensitive elements of Social Security payments and federal pensions because they affect millions of people.

COST-OF-LIVING INDEX *see* CONSUMER PRICE INDEX.

COST OF SALES *see* COST OF GOODS SOLD.

COST-PLUS CONTRACT contract basing the selling price of a product on the total cost incurred in making it plus a stated percentage or a fixed fee—called a *cost-plus-fixed-fee contract.* Cost-plus contracts are common when there is no historical basis for estimating costs and the producer would run a risk of loss—defense contracts involving sophisticated technology, for example. The alternative is a FIXED PRICE contract.

COST-PUSH INFLATION inflation caused by rising prices, which follow on the heels of rising costs. This is the sequence: When the demand for raw materials exceeds the supply, prices go up. As manufacturers pay more for these raw materials they raise the prices they charge merchants for the finished products, and the merchants in turn raise the prices they charge consumers. *See also* DEMAND-PULL INFLATION; INFLATION.

COST RECORDS
1. investor records of the prices at which securities were purchased, which provide the basis for computing capital gains.
2. in finance, anything that can substantiate the costs incurred in producing goods, providing services, or supporting an activity designed to be productive. Ledgers, schedules, vouchers, and invoices are cost records.

COUNCIL OF ECONOMIC ADVISERS group of economists appointed by the President of the United States to provide counsel on economic policy. The council helps to prepare the President's budget message to Congress, and its chairman frequently speaks for the administration's economic policy.

COUNTERCYCLICAL STOCKS stocks that tend to rise in value when the economy is turning down or is in recession. Traditionally, companies in industries with stable demand, such as drugs and food, are considered countercyclical. Some firms actually do better when the economy or stock market is in turmoil. For example, firms offering money market mutual funds may enjoy an inflow of cash when stock prices fall. Temporary-help firms may benefit if companies are cutting costs by laying off full-time employees and replacing them with temps. Companies that can perform various functions for other companies more efficiently and at lower cost (called *outsourcing firms*) will tend to benefit during economic downturns. *See also* CYCLICAL STOCKS.

COUPON interest rate on a debt security the issuer promises to pay to the holder until maturity, expressed as an annual percentage of face value. For example, a bond with a 10% coupon will pay $10 per $100 of the face amount per year, usually in installments paid every six months. The term derives from the small detachable segment of a bond certificate which, when presented to the bond's issuer, entitles the holder to the interest due on that date. As the REGISTERED BOND becomes more widespread, coupons are gradually disappearing.

COUPON BOND bond issued with detachable coupons that must be presented to a paying agent or the issuer for semiannual interest payment. These are bearer bonds, so whoever presents the coupon is entitled to the interest. Once universal, the coupon bond has been gradually giving way to the REGISTERED BOND, some of which pay interest through electronic transfers. *See also* BOOK-ENTRY SECURITIES; CERTIFICATELESS MUNICIPALS; COUPON.

COUPON COLLECTION *see* COLLECTION.

COUPON-EQUIVALENT RATE same as EQUIVALENT BOND YIELD.

COUPON PASS canvassing by the DESK of the Federal Reserve's Open-Market Committee of PRIMARY DEALERS to determine the inventory and maturities of their Treasury securities. Desk then decides whether to buy or sell specific issues (coupons) to add or withdraw reserves.

COUPON YIELD (OR RATE) *see* COUPON.

COVARIANCE statistical term for the correlation between two variables multiplied by the standard deviation for each of the variables.

COVENANT promise in a trust indenture or other formal debt agreement that certain acts will be performed and others refrained from. Designed to protect the lender's interest, covenants cover such matters as working capital, debt-equity ratios, and dividend payments. Also called *restrictive covenant* or *protective covenant.*

COVER
1. to buy back contracts previously sold; said of an investor who has sold stock or commodities short.
2. in corporate finance, to meet fixed annual charges on bonds, leases, and other obligations, out of earnings.
3. amount of net-asset value underlying a bond or equity security. Coverage is an important aspect of a bond's safety rating.

COVERAGE *see* FIXED-CHARGE COVERAGE.

COVERED OPTION option contract backed by the shares underlying the option. For instance, someone who owns 300 shares of XYZ and sells three XYZ call options is in a covered option position. If the XYZ stock price goes up and the option is exercised, the investor has the stock to deliver to the buyer. Selling a call brings a premium from the buyer. *See also* NAKED OPTION.

COVERED WRITER seller of covered options—in other words, an owner of stock who sells options against it to collect premium income. For example, when writing a CALL OPTION, if a stock price stays stable or drops, the seller will be able to hold onto the stock. If the price rises sharply enough, it will have to be given up to the option buyer.

COVERING SHORT *see* COVER.

CPI *see* CONSUMER PRICE INDEX (CPI).

CRAM-DOWN DEAL merger or leveraged buyout slang for situation in which stockholders are forced, for lack of attractive alternatives, to accept undesirable terms, such as JUNK BONDS instead of cash or equity.

CRASH precipitate drop in stock prices and economic activity, as in the crash of 1929 or BLACK MONDAY in 1987. Crashes are usually brought on by a loss in investor confidence following periods of highly inflated stock prices.

CREDIT
In general: loans, bonds, charge-account obligations, and open-account balances with commercial firms. Also, available but unused bank letters of credit and other standby commitments as well as a variety of consumer credit facilities.

On another level, discipline in which lending officers and industrial credit people are professionals. At its loftiest it is defined in Dun & Bradstreet's motto: "Credit—Man's Confidence in Man."
Accounting: entry—or the act of making an entry—that increases liabilities, owners' equity, revenue, and gains, and decreases assets and expenses. *See also* CREDIT BALANCE.
Customer's statement of account: adjustment in the customer's favor, or increase in equity.

CREDIT ANALYST person who (1) analyzes the record and financial affairs of an individual or a corporation to ascertain creditworthiness or (2) determines the credit ratings of corporate and municipal bonds by studying the financial condition and trends of the issuers.

CREDIT BALANCE
In general: account balance in the customer's favor. See *also* CREDIT.
Securities: in cash accounts with brokers, money deposited and remaining after purchases have been paid for, plus the uninvested pro-

ceeds from securities sold. In margin accounts, (1) proceeds from short sales, held in escrow for the securities borrowed for these sales; (2) free credit balances, or net balances, which can be withdrawn at will. SPECIAL MISCELLANEOUS ACCOUNT balances are not counted as free credit balances.

CREDIT BUREAU agency that gathers information about the credit history of consumers and relays it to credit grantors for a fee. Credit bureaus maintain files on millions of consumers detailing which lines of credit they have applied for and received, and whether they pay their bills in a timely fashion. Bureaus receive this information from credit grantors such as credit card issuers, retail stores, gasoline companies, and others. Credit grantors look at this information, which is constantly being updated, in making their decision as to whether or not to grant credit to a particular consumer, and if so, how much credit is appropriate. Consumers have rights under the FAIR CREDIT REPORTING ACT to see a copy of their credit report and to dispute any item they think is inaccurate. Credit data are maintained by 500 credit bureaus which operate off of three automated systems: Equifax, based in Georgia, Experian, based in California, and Trans Union, based in Illinois.

CREDIT CARD plastic card issued by a bank, savings and loan, retail store, oil company, or other credit grantor giving consumers the right to charge purchases and pay for them later. Most credit cards offer a grace period of about 25 days, during which interest charges do not accrue. After that, consumers pay nondeductible CONSUMER INTEREST on the remaining balance until it is paid off. Some credit cards start charging interest from the day the purchase is registered. Most credit cards also permit consumers to obtain cash on their card in the form of a CASH ADVANCE. *See also* CONSUMER CREDIT PROTECTION ACT OF 1968.

CREDIT ENHANCEMENT techniques used by debt issuers to raise the credit rating of their offering, and thereby lower their interest costs. A municipality may have their bond insured by one of the large insurance companies such as Municipal Bond Investor's Assurance (MBIA) or American Municipal Bond Assurance Corporation (AMBAC), thereby raising the bond's credit rating to AAA. A corporate bond issuer may arrange for a bank letter of credit to back its issue, raising its rating to AAA. While investors in such credit-enhanced issuers feel safer because an insurance company or bank stands ready to step in if there is a default by the underlying issuer, the yield received by the investor is lower than if the bond were uninsured.

CREDIT INSURANCE protection against *abnormal* losses from unpaid accounts receivable, often a requirement of banks lending against accounts receivable.

In consumer credit, life or accident coverage protecting the creditor against loss in the event of death or disability, usually stated as a percentage of the loan balance.

CREDIT LIMIT credit card term, meaning the maximum balance allowed for a particular customer.

CREDITOR party that extends credit, such as a trade supplier, a bank lender, or a bondholder.

CREDITOR'S COMMITTEE group representing firms that have claims on a company in financial difficulty or bankruptcy; sometimes used as an alternative to legal bankruptcy, especially by smaller firms.

CREDIT RATING formal evaluation of an individual's or company's credit history and capability of repaying obligations. Any number of firms investigate, analyze, and maintain records on the credit responsibility of individuals and businesses—Experian (individuals) and Dun & Bradstreet (commercial firms), for example. The bond ratings assigned by Standard & Poor's and Moody's are also a form of credit rating. Most large companies and lending institutions assign credit ratings to existing and potential customers.

CREDIT RISK financial and moral risk that an obligation will not be paid and a loss will result.

CREDIT SCORING objective methodology used by credit grantors to determine how much, if any, credit to grant to an applicant. Credit scoring is devised by three different methods: by a third-party firm, by the credit grantor, or by the credit bureau in cooperation with the credit grantor. Some of the most common factors in scoring are income, assets, length of employment, length of living in one place, and past record of using credit. Any negative events in the past, such as bankruptcies or tax delinquencies, will sharply reduce an applicant's credit score.

CREDIT SPREAD difference in the value of two options, when the value of the one sold exceeds the value of the one bought. The opposite of a DEBIT SPREAD.

CREDIT UNION not-for-profit financial institution typically formed by employees of a company, a labor union, or a religious group and operated as a cooperative. Credit unions may offer a full range of financial services and pay higher rates on deposits and charge lower rates on loans than commercial banks. Federally chartered credit unions are regulated and insured by the National Credit Union Administration.

CREDIT WATCH used by bond RATING agencies to indicate that a company's credit is under review and its rating subject to change. The implication is that if the rating is changed, it will be lowered, usually because of some event that affects the income statement or balance sheet adversely.

CREDITWORTHINESS general eligibility of a person or company to borrow money. *See* CREDIT RATING; CREDIT SCORING.

CREEPING TENDER OFFER strategy whereby individuals ACTING IN CONCERT circumvent WILLIAMS ACT provisions by gradually acquiring TARGET COMPANY shares from arbitrageurs and other sellers in the open market. *See also* TENDER OFFER.

CROSS securities transaction in which the same broker acts as agent in both sides of the trade. The practice—called crossing—is legal only if the broker first offers the securities publicly at a price higher than the bid.

CROSSED MARKET situation in which one broker's bid is higher than another broker's lowest offer, or vice versa. National Association of Securities Dealers (NASD) rules prohibit brokers from crossing the market deliberately.

CROSSED TRADE manipulative practice prohibited on major exchanges whereby buy and sell orders are offset without recording the trade on the exchange, thus perhaps depriving the investor of the chance to trade at a more favorable price. Also called *crossed sale*.

CROWD group of exchange members with a defined area of function tending to congregate around a trading post pending execution of orders. These are specialists, floor traders, odd-lot dealers, and other brokers as well as smaller groups with specialized functions—the INACTIVE BOND CROWD, for example.

CROWDING OUT heavy federal borrowing at a time when businesses and consumers also want to borrow money. Because the government can pay any interest rate it has to and individuals and businesses can't, the latter are crowded out of credit markets by high interest rates. Crowding out can thus cause economic activity to slow.

CROWN JEWELS the most desirable entities within a diversified corporation as measured by asset value, earning power and business prospects. The crown jewels usually figure prominently in takeover attempts; they typically are the main objective of the acquirer and may be sold by a takeover target to make the rest of the company less attractive.

CROWN LOAN demand loan by a high-income individual to a low-income relative, usually a child or elderly parent. This device was named for Chicago industrialist Harry Crown, who first used it. The money would be invested and the income would be taxable at the borrower's lower rates. For years, the crown loan provided a substantial tax benefit for all parties involved, since such loans could be made interest-free. In 1984 the U.S. Supreme Court ruled that such loans had to be made at the market rate of interest or be subject to gift taxes.

CUM DIVIDEND with dividend; said of a stock whose buyer is eligible to receive a declared dividend. Stocks are usually cum dividend for trades made on or before the fifth day preceding the RECORD DATE, when the register of eligible holders is closed for that dividend period. Trades after the fifth day go EX-DIVIDEND.

CUM RIGHTS with rights; said of stocks that entitle the purchaser to buy a specified amount of stock that is yet to be issued. The cut-off date when the stocks go from cum rights to EX-RIGHTS (without rights) is stipulated in the prospectus accompanying the rights distribution.

CUMULATIVE PREFERRED preferred stock whose dividends if omitted because of insufficient earnings or any other reason accumulate until paid out. They have precedence over common dividends, which cannot be paid as long as a cumulative preferred obligation exists. Most preferred stock issued today is cumulative.

CUMULATIVE VOTING voting method that improves minority shareholders' chances of naming representatives on the board of directors. In regular or statutory voting, stockholders must apportion their votes equally among candidates for director. Cumulative voting allows shareholders to cast all their votes for one candidate. Assuming one vote per share, 100 shares owned, and six directors to be elected, the regular method lets the shareholder cast 100 votes for each of six candidates for director, a total of 600 votes. The cumulative method lets the same 600 votes be cast for one candidate or split as the shareholder wishes. Cumulative voting is a popular cause among advocates of corporate democracy, but it remains the exception rather than the rule.

CURB *see* AMERICAN STOCK EXCHANGE.

CURRENCY FUTURES contracts in the futures markets that are for delivery in a major currency such as U.S. dollars, British pounds, French francs, German marks, Swiss francs, or Japanese yen. Corporations that sell products around the world can hedge their currency risk with these futures.

CURRENCY IN CIRCULATION paper money and coins circulating in the economy, counted as part of the total money in circulation, which includes DEMAND DEPOSITS in banks.

CURRENT ACCOUNT (1) an active TRADE CREDIT account; (2) an account with an extender of credit that is up to date; (3) *See* BALANCE OF PAYMENTS.

CURRENT ASSETS cash, accounts receivable, inventory, and other assets that are likely to be converted into cash, sold, exchanged, or expensed in the normal course of business, usually within a year.

CURRENT COUPON BOND corporate, federal, or municipal bond with a coupon within half a percentage point of current market rates. These bonds are less volatile than similarly rated bonds with lower coupons because the interest they pay is competitive with current market instruments.

CURRENT INCOME money that is received on an ongoing basis from investments in the form of dividends, interest, rents, or other income sources.

CURRENT LIABILITY debt or other obligation coming due within a year.

CURRENT MARKET VALUE present worth of a client's portfolio at today's market price, as listed in a brokerage statement every month—or more often if stocks are bought on margin or sold short. For listed stocks and bonds the current market value is determined by closing prices; for over-the-counter securities the bid price is used.

CURRENT MATURITY interval between the present time and the maturity date of a bond issue, as distinguished from original maturity, which is the **time** difference between the issue date and the maturity date. For example, in 2002 a bond issued in 2000 to mature in 2020 would have an original maturity of 20 years and a current maturity of 18 years.

CURRENT PRODUCTION RATE top interest rate allowed on current GOVERNMENT NATIONAL MORTGAGE ASSOCIATION mortgage-backed securities, usually half a percentage point below the current mortgage rate to defray administrative costs of the mortgage servicing company. For instance, when homeowners are paying 6½% on mortgages, an investor in a GNMA pool including those mortgages will get a current production rate of 6%.

CURRENT RATIO current assets divided by current liabilities. The ratio shows a company's ability to pay its current obligations from current assets. For the most part, a company that has a small inventory and readily collectible accounts receivable can operate safely with a lower current ratio than a company whose cash flow is less dependable. *See also* QUICK RATIO.

CURRENT YIELD annual interest on a bond divided by the market price. It is the actual income rate of return as opposed to the coupon rate (the two would be equal if the bond were bought at par) or the yield to maturity. For example, a 10% (coupon rate) bond with a face (or par) value of $1000 is bought at a market price of $800. The annual income from the bond is $100. But since only $800 was paid for the bond, the current yield is $100 divided by $800, or 12½%.

CUSHION
1. interval between the time a bond is issued and the time it can be called. Also termed CALL PROTECTION.
2. margin of safety for a corporation's financial ratios. For instance, if its DEBT-TO-EQUITY RATIO has a cushion of up to 40% debt, anything over that level might be cause for concern.
3. *see* LAST IN, FIRST OUT.

CUSHION BOND callable bond with a coupon above current market interest rates that is selling for a premium. Cushion bonds lose less of their value as rates rise and gain less in value as rates fall, making them suitable for conservative investors interested in high income.

CUSHION THEORY theory that a stock's price must rise if many investors are taking short positions in it, because those positions must be covered by purchases of the stock. Technical analysts consider it particularly bullish if the short positions in a stock are twice as high as the number of shares traded daily. This is because price rises force short sellers to cover their positions, making the stock rise even more.

CUSIP NUMBER number identifying all stocks and registered bonds, using the COMMITTEE ON UNIFORM SECURITIES IDENTIFICATION PROCEDURES (CUSIP). Brokers will use a security's CUSIP number to look it up on a computer terminal to get further information. The CUSIP number will also be listed on any trading confirmation tickets. The CUSIP system makes it easier to settle and clear trades. Foreign securities use a similar identification system called the CUSIP International Numbering System (CINS).

CUSTODIAL ACCOUNT account that is created for a minor, usually at a bank, brokerage firm, or mutual fund. Minors cannot make securities transactions without the approval of the custodian, who manages cash and other property gifted to minors under the UNIFORM GIFTS TO MINORS ACT or the Uniform Transfers to Minors Act. Any earnings or interest from the account up to $700 are tax-free if the child is under age 14. Earnings from $700 to $1400 are taxed at the child's tax rate. Any earnings over $1400 are taxed at the parents' rate. Once the child turns 14, the earnings are taxed at the child's tax rate. When the child reaches the age of majority, usually 18, they have full discretion over the account, unless the account is set up in a trust controlled by the parent. *See also* CLIFFORD TRUST; CROWN LOAN; UNIFORM GIFTS TO MINORS ACT.

CUSTODIAN bank or other financial institution that keeps custody of stock certificates and other assets of a mutual fund, individual, or corporate client. *See also* CUSTODIAL ACCOUNT.

CUSTODY legal responsibility for someone else's assets or for a child. Term implies management as well as safekeeping. The IRS does not require custodial parents or guardians to declare child support as income, nor is child support deductible by the noncustodial parent.

CUSTOMER'S LOAN CONSENT agreement signed by a margin customer permitting a broker to borrow margined securities to the limit of the customer's debit balance for the purpose of covering other customers' short positions and certain failures to complete delivery.

CUSTOMER'S MAN traditionally a synonym for *registered represen-tative, account executive,* or *account representative.* Now used rarely, as more women work in brokerages.

CUSTOMERS' NET DEBIT BALANCE total credit extended by New York Stock Exchange member firms to finance customer purchases of securities.

CUTOFF POINT in capital budgeting, the minimum rate of return acceptable on investments.

CYCLE *see* BUSINESS CYCLE.

CYCLICAL STOCK stock that tends to rise quickly when the economy turns up and to fall quickly when the economy turns down. Examples are housing, automobiles, and paper. Stocks of noncyclical indus-tries—such as foods, insurance, drugs—are not as directly affected by economic changes.

D

DAILY TRADING LIMIT maximum that many commodities and options markets are allowed to rise or fall in one day. When a market reaches its limit early and stays there all day, it is said to be having an up-limit or down-limit day. Exchanges usually impose a daily trading limit on each contract. For example, the Chicago Board of Trade limit is two points ($2000 per contract) up or down on its treasury bond futures options contract.

DAISY CHAIN trading between market manipulators to create the appearance of active volume as a lure for legitimate investors. When these traders drive the price up, the manipulators unload their holdings, leaving the unwary investors without buyers to trade with in turn.

DATA BASE store of information that is sorted, indexed, and summarized and accessible to people with computers. Data bases containing market and stock histories are available from a number of commercial sources.

DATED DATE date from which accrued interest is calculated on new bonds and other debt instruments. The buyer pays the issuer an amount equal to the interest accrued from the dated date to the issue's settlement date. With the first interest payment on the bond, the buyer is reimbursed.

DATE OF ISSUE
Bonds: date on which a bond is issued and effective. Interest accrues to bondholders from this date.
Insurance: date on which a policy is issued. Normally, the policy is also declared effective on that date, though not in every case.
Stocks: date on which a new stock is publicly issued and begins trading.

DATE OF RECORD date on which a shareholder must officially own shares in order to be entitled to a dividend. For example, the board of directors of a corporation might declare a dividend on November 1 payable on December 1 to stockholders of record on November 15. After the date of record the stock is said to be EX-DIVIDEND. Also called *record date.*

DATING in commercial transactions, extension of credit beyond the supplier's customary terms—for example, 90 days instead of 30 days. In industries marked by high seasonality and long lead time, dating, combined with ACCOUNTS RECEIVABLE FINANCING, makes it possible for manufacturers with lean capital to continue producing goods. Also called *seasonal dating, special dating.*

DAWN RAID British term for a practice whereby a RAIDER instructs brokers to buy all the available shares of another company at the opening of the market, thus giving the acquirer a significant holding before the

TARGET COMPANY gets wise to the undertaking. In London-based markets, the practice is restricted by the *City Code on Takeovers and Mergers. See also* SATURDAY NIGHT SPECIAL.

DAY LOAN loan from a bank to a broker for the purchase of securities pending delivery through the afternoon clearing. Once delivered the securities are pledged as collateral and the loan becomes a regular broker's call loan. Also called *morning loan.*

DAY OF DEPOSIT TO DAY OF WITHDRAWAL ACCOUNT bank account that pays interest based on the actual number of days that money is on deposit. Also called *actual balance method.*

DAY ORDER order to buy or sell securities that expires unless executed or canceled the day it is placed. All orders are day orders unless otherwise specified. The main exception is a GOOD-TILL-CANCELED ORDER, though even it can be executed the same day if conditions are right.

DAY TRADE purchase and sale of a position during the same day.

DEAD CAT BOUNCE sharp rise in stock prices after a severe decline. The saying refers to the fact that a dead cat dropped from a high place will bounce. Often, the bounce is the result of short-sellers covering their positions at a profit.

DEALER
1. individual or firm acting as a PRINCIPAL in a securities transaction. Principals trade for their own account and risk. When buying from a broker acting as a dealer, a customer receives securities from the firm's inventory; the confirmation must disclose this. When specialists trade for their own account, as they must as part of their responsibility for maintaining an orderly market, they act as dealers. Since most brokerage firms operate both as brokers and as principals, the term *broker-dealer* is commonly used.
2. one who purchases goods or services for resale to consumers. The element of inventory risk is what distinguishes a dealer from an agent or sales representative.

DEALER MARKET securities market in which transactions are between principals acting as DEALERS for their own accounts rather than between brokers acting as agents for buyers and sellers. Municipal and U.S. government securities are largely traded in dealer markets. *See also* AUCTION MARKET.

DEALER'S SPREAD *see* MARKDOWN; UNDERWRITING SPREAD.

DEAL FLOW rate of new deals being referred to the investment banking division of a brokerage firm. This might refer to proposals for new stock and bond issues, as well as mergers, acquisitions, and takeovers.

DEAL STOCK stock that may be rumored to be a TAKEOVER target or the party to some other major transaction such as a merger or leveraged buyout. The stock may be subject to a rumor of a prospective deal, or a deal may have been announced that attracts additional bidders and the company is said to be *in play.* Arbitrageurs and other speculators will attempt to buy deal stocks before the deal is finalized or profit when the stock price rises. Of course, if there is no deal, these speculators may lose money if the stock falls back to its pre-rumor price.

DEAR MONEY British equivalent of TIGHT MONEY.

DEATH-BACKED BONDS bonds backed by policyholder loans against life insurance policies. The loans will be repaid either by the policyholder while he or she is alive or from the proceeds of the insurance policy if the policyholder dies. Also called *policyholder loan bonds.*

DEATH BENEFIT amount of money to be paid to beneficiaries when a policyholder dies. The death benefit is the face value of the policy less any unpaid policy loans or other insurance company claims against the policy. Beneficiaries are not taxed on the death benefit when they receive it.

DEATH PLAY stock bought on the expectation that a key executive will die and the shares will gain value as a result. For example, there might be reason to believe that upon the imminent death of a CEO, a company will be broken up and that the shares will be worth more at their PRIVATE MARKET VALUE.

DEATH VALLEY CURVE venture capital term that describes a start-up company's rapid use of capital. When a company begins operations, it uses a great deal of its equity capital to set up its offices, hire personnel, and do research and development. It may be several months or even years before the company has products or services to sell, creating a stream of revenues. The Death Valley Curve is the time period before revenues begin, when it is difficult for the company to raise more equity or issue debt to help it through its cash-flow difficulties.

DEBENTURE general debt obligation backed only by the integrity of the borrower and documented by an agreement called an INDENTURE. An *unsecured bond* is a debenture.

DEBENTURE STOCK stock issued under a contract providing for fixed payments at scheduled intervals and more like preferred stock than a DEBENTURE, since their status in liquidation is equity and not debt.

Also, a type of bond issued by Canadian and British corporations, which refer to debt issues as stock.

DEBIT BALANCE
  1. account balance representing money owed to the lender or seller.
  2. money a margin customer owes a broker for loans to purchase securities.

DEBIT CARD card issued by a bank to allow customers access to their funds electronically. Debit cards could replace checks as a method of payment for goods and services, and are more convenient because they are more widely accepted than checks. Debit cards can also be used to withdraw cash from automatic teller machines. Unlike credit cards, however, consumers do not have the advantage of the FLOAT on their money since funds are withdrawn immediately.

DEBIT SPREAD difference in the value of two options, when the value of the one bought exceeds the value of the one sold. The opposite of a CREDIT SPREAD.

DEBT
1. money, goods, or services that one party is obligated to pay to another in accordance with an expressed or implied agreement. Debt may or may not be secured.
2. general name for bonds, notes, mortgages, and other forms of paper evidencing amounts owed and payable on specified dates or on demand.

DEBT BOMB situation in which a major financial institution defaults on its obligations, causing major disruption to the financial system of the institution's home country. If a major multinational bank were to run into such trouble, it could have a major negative impact on the global financial system.

DEBT CEILING *see* DEBT LIMIT.

DEBT INSTRUMENT written promise to repay a debt; for instance, a BILL, NOTE, BOND, banker's ACCEPTANCE, CERTIFICATE OF DEPOSIT, or COMMERCIAL PAPER.

DEBTOR any individual or company that owes money. If debt is in the form of a loan from a financial institution, you might use *borrower*. If indebtedness is in the form of securities, such as bonds, you would refer to the *issuer*. *See also* OBLIGOR.

DEBT LIMIT maximum amount of debt that a municipality can incur. If a municipality wants to issue bonds for an amount greater than its debt limit, it usually requires approval from the voters.

DEBT RETIREMENT repayment of debt. The most common method of retiring corporate debt is to set aside money each year in a SINKING FUND.
    Most municipal bonds and some corporates are issued in serial form, meaning different portions of an issue—called series—are retired at different times, usually on an annual or semiannual schedule.
    Sinking fund bonds and serial bonds are not classes of bonds, just methods of retiring them that are adaptable to debentures, convertibles, and so on. *See also* REFUNDING.

DEBT SECURITY security representing money borrowed that must be repaid and having a fixed amount, a specific maturity or maturities, and usually a specific rate of interest or an original purchase discount. For instance, a BILL, BOND, COMMERCIAL PAPER, or a NOTE.

DEBT SERVICE cash required in a given period, usually one year, for payments of interest and current maturities of principal on outstanding debt. In corporate bond issues, the annual interest plus annual sinking fund payments; in government bonds, the annual payments into the debt service fund. *See also* ABILITY TO PAY.

DEBT SERVICE COVERAGE

Corporate finance: amount, usually expressed as a ratio, of CASH FLOW available to meet annual interest and principal payments on debt, including SINKING FUND payments.

Government finance: export earnings required to cover annual principal and interest payments on a country's external debts.

Personal finance: ratio of monthly installment debt payments, excluding mortgage loans and rent, to monthly take-home pay.

See also FIXED-CHARGE COVERAGE.

DEBT SWAP exchange, between banks, of a loan, usually to a third-world country in local currency. *See also* SWAP.

DEBT-TO-EQUITY RATIO

1. total liabilities divided by total shareholders' equity. This shows to what extent owner's equity can cushion creditors' claims in the event of liquidation.
2. total long-term debt divided by total shareholders' equity. This is a measure of LEVERAGE—the use of borrowed money to enhance the return on owners' equity.
3. long-term debt and preferred stock divided by common stock equity. This relates securities with fixed charges to those without fixed charges.

DECIMAL TRADING quotation of stock prices in decimals. Several stock markets around the world trade stocks in decimals, and it is anticipated that American markets including the New York and American Exchanges and the NASDAQ Stock Market will convert from quoting stocks in fractions of a dollar to the decimal system sometime early in the 21st century. Proponents of decimal trading maintain that it saves investors money by narrowing the spread between BID AND ASKED prices, and by making stock prices easier to understand. An interim step towards decimal trading was the reduction in the minimum increment in stock prices from one-eighth to one-sixteenth by all the stock exchanges in the late 1990s.

DECLARATION DATE date on which a company announces the amount and date of its next dividend payment. There is normally an interim period of a few days between the declaration date and the EX-STOCK DIVIDEND date which allows people to buy shares and still qualify to receive the upcoming dividend.

DECLARE authorize the payment of a dividend on a specified date, an act of the board of directors of a corporation. Once declared, a dividend becomes an obligation of the issuing corporation.

DECREASING TERM LIFE INSURANCE form of life insurance coverage in which premiums remain constant for the life of the policy while the death benefit declines. Term insurance premiums usually increase every year as the policyholder ages, and the policy is renewed. If there is less need for coverage because, for example, children have become self-sufficient, it may be prudent to decrease the amount of outstanding coverage.

DEDUCTIBLE
Insurance: amount of money that the policyholders must pay out of their pockets before reimbursements from the insurance company begin. The deductible is usually set as a fixed dollar amount, though in some cases it can also be a percentage of the premium paid or some other formula. Some group health insurance plans set the deductible at a set percentage of the employee's salary, for example. In general, the higher a deductible a policyholder will accept, the lower insurance premiums will be. The insurance company is willing to lower its premiums because the company is no longer liable for small claims.
Taxes: *see* TAX DEDUCTIBLE.

DEDUCTION
1. expense allowed by the Internal Revenue Service as a subtraction from adjusted gross income in arriving at a person's taxable income. Such deductions include some interest paid, state and local taxes, charitable contributions.
2. adjustment to an invoice allowed by a seller for a discrepancy, shortage, and so on.

DEED written instrument containing some transfer, bargain, or contract relating to property—most commonly, conveying the legal title to real estate from one party to another.

DEEP DISCOUNT BOND bond selling for a discount of more than about 20% from its face value. Unlike a CURRENT COUPON BOND, which has a higher interest rate, a deep discount bond will appreciate faster as interest rates fall and drop faster as rates rise. Unlike ORIGINAL ISSUE DISCOUNT bonds, deep discounts were issued at a par value of $1000.

DEEP IN/OUT OF THE MONEY CALL OPTION whose exercise price is well below the market price of the underlying stock (deep *in* the money) or well above the market price (deep *out of* the money). The situation would be exactly the opposite for a PUT OPTION. The premium for buying a deep-in-the-money option is high, since the holder has the right to purchase the stock at a striking price considerably below the current price of the stock. The premium for buying a deep-out-of-the-money option is very small, on the other hand, since the option may never be profitable.

DEFAULT failure of a debtor to make timely payments of interest and principal as they come due or to meet some other provision of a bond indenture. In the event of default, bondholders may make claims against the assets of the issuer in order to recoup their principal.

DEFAULT RISK risk that a debtholder will not receive interest and principal when due. One way to gauge default risk is the RATINGS issued by credit rating agencies such as Fitch Investors Service, Moody's, and Standard & Poor's. The higher the rating (AAA or Aaa is highest), the less risk of default. Some issues, such as Treasury bonds backed by the full faith and credit of the U.S. government, are considered free of default risk. Other bonds, such as JUNK BONDS, carry a much higher default risk. One investor defense against default for municipal bonds is MUNICIPAL BOND INSURANCE.

DEFEASANCE

In general: provision found in some debt agreements whereby the contract is nullified if specified acts are performed.

Corporate finance: short for in-substance defeasance, a technique whereby a corporation discharges old, low-rate debt without repaying it prior to maturity. The corporation uses newly purchased securities with a lower face value but paying higher interest or having a higher market value. The objective is a cleaner (more debt free) balance sheet and increased earnings in the amount by which the face amount of the old debt exceeds the cost of the new securities. The use of defeasance in modern corporate finance began in 1982 when Exxon bought and put in an irrevocable trust $312 million of U.S. government securities yielding 14% to provide for the repayment of principal and interest on $515 million of old debt paying 5.8% to 6.7% and maturing in 2009. Exxon removed the defeased debt from its balance sheet and added $132 million—the after-tax difference between $515 million and $312 million—to its earnings that quarter.

In another type of defeasance, a company instructs a broker to buy, for a fee, the outstanding portion of an old bond issue of the company. The broker then exchanges the bond issue for a new issue of the company's stock with an equal market value. The broker subsequently sells the stock at a profit.

DEFENSIVE SECURITIES stocks and bonds that are more stable than average and provide a safe return on an investor's money. When the stock market is weak, defensive securities tend to decline less than the overall market.

DEFERRAL OF TAXES postponement of tax payments from this year to a later year. For instance, an INDIVIDUAL RETIREMENT ACCOUNT (IRA) defers taxes until the money is withdrawn.

DEFERRED ACCOUNT account that postpones taxes until a later date. Some examples: ANNUITY, INDIVIDUAL RETIREMENT ACCOUNT, KEOGH PLAN accounts, PROFIT-SHARING PLAN, SALARY REDUCTION PLAN, SIMPLI-FIED EMPLOYEE PENSION (SEP) PLAN.

DEFERRED ANNUITY *see* DEFERRED PAYMENT ANNUITY.

DEFERRED CHARGE expenditure carried forward as an asset until it becomes relevant, such as an advance rent payment or insurance premium. The opposite is *deferred income,* such as advance rent received.

DEFERRED COMPENSATION currently earned compensation that, under the terms of a profit-sharing, pension, or stock option plan, is not actually paid until a later date and is therefore not taxable until that date.

DEFERRED INTEREST BOND bond that pays interest at a later date. A ZERO COUPON BOND, which pays interest and repays principal in one lump sum at maturity, is in this category. In effect, such bonds automatically reinvest the interest at a fixed rate. Prices are more volatile for a deferred interest bond than for a CURRENT COUPON BOND.

DEFERRED PAYMENT ANNUITY ANNUITY whose contract provides that payments to the annuitant be postponed until a number of periods have elapsed—for example, when the annuitant attains a certain age. Also called a *deferred annuity.*

DEFERRED SALES CHARGE *see* BACK-END LOAD.

DEFICIENCY LETTER written notice from the Securities and Exchange Commission to a prospective issuer of securities that the preliminary prospectus needs revision or expansion. Deficiency letters require prompt action; otherwise, the registration period may be prolonged.

DEFICIT
1. excess of liabilities and debts over income and assets. Deficits usually are corrected by borrowing or by selling assets.
2. in finance, an excess of expenditures over budget.

DEFICIT FINANCING borrowing by a government agency to make up for a revenue shortfall. Deficit financing stimulates the economy for a time but eventually can become a drag on the economy by pushing up interest rates. *See also* CROWDING OUT; KEYNESIAN ECONOMICS.

DEFICIT NET WORTH excess of liabilities over assets and capital stock, perhaps as a result of operating losses. Also called *negative net worth.*

DEFICIT SPENDING excess of government expenditures over government revenue, creating a shortfall that must be financed through borrowing. *See also* DEFICIT FINANCING.

DEFINED ASSET FUND a UNIT INVESTMENT TRUST with a fixed portfolio of securities offered by Merrill Lynch, Salomon Smith Barney,

Prudential Securities, Morgan Stanley Dean Witter, and Paine Webber. Defined Asset Funds own particular kinds of stocks, such as BLUE CHIPS, REAL ESTATE INVESTMENT TRUSTS, UTILITIES, or the highest yielding stocks in a major index such as the Dow Jones Industrials or the United Kingdom's Footsie Index. There is usually a sales charge to buy shares in one of these trusts. Defined Asset Funds also have a set time period—one to two years, typically—after which they expire. Proceeds can either be taken in cash or rolled over into another Defined Asset Fund. Defined Asset Funds are also called Equity Investor Funds, and net asset values are available in *Barron's. See also* DOGS OF THE DOW.

DEFINED BENEFIT PENSION PLAN plan that promises to pay a specified amount to each person who retires after a set number of years of service. Such plans pay no taxes on their investments. Employees contribute to them in some cases; in others, all contributions are made by the employer.

DEFINED CONTRIBUTION PENSION PLAN pension plan in which the level of contributions is fixed at a certain level, while benefits vary depending on the return from the investments. In some cases, such as 401(k), 403(b), and 457 plans, employees make voluntary contributions into a tax-deferred account, which may or may not be matched by employers. The level of contribution may be selected by the employee within a range set by the employer, such as between 2% and 10% of annual salary. In other cases, contributions are made by an employer into a profit-sharing account based on each employee's salary level, years of service, age, and other factors. Defined contribution pension plans, unlike DEFINED BENEFIT PENSION PLANS, give the employee options of where to invest the account, usually among stock, bond and money market accounts. Defined contribution plans have become increasingly popular in recent years because they limit a company's pension outlay and shift the liability for investment performance from the company's pension plan to employees.

DEFLATION decline in the prices of goods and services. Deflation is the reverse of INFLATION; it should not be confused with DISINFLATION, which is a slowing down in the rate of price increases. Generally, the economic effects of deflation are the opposite of those produced by inflation, with two notable exceptions: (1) prices that increase with inflation do not necessarily decrease with deflation—union wage rates, for example; (2) while inflation may or may not stimulate output and employment, marked deflation has always affected both negatively.

DEFLATOR statistical factor used to convert current dollar activity into inflation-adjusted activity—in effect, a measure of prices. The change in the gross domestic product (GDP) deflator, for example, is a measure of economy-wide inflation.

DEFLECTION OF TAX LIABILITY legal shift of one person's tax burden to someone else through such methods as the CLIFFORD TRUST, CUSTODIAL ACCOUNTS, and SPOUSAL REMAINDER TRUSTS. Such devices were curtailed but not eliminated by the TAX REFORM ACT OF 1986.

DELAYED DELIVERY delivery of securities later than the scheduled date, which is ordinarily five business days after the trade date. A contract calling for delayed delivery, known as a SELLER'S OPTION, is usually agreed to by both parties to a trade. *See also* DELIVERY DATE.

DELAYED OPENING postponement of the start of trading in a stock until a gross imbalance in buy and sell orders is overcome. Such an imbalance is likely to follow on the heels of a significant event such as a takeover offer.

DELINQUENCY failure to make a payment on an obligation when due. In finance company parlance, the amount of past due balances, determined either on a contractual or recency-of-payment basis.

DELISTING removal of a company's security from an exchange because the firm did not abide by some regulation or the stock does not meet certain financial ratios or sales levels.

DELIVERABLE BILLS financial futures and options trading term meaning Treasury bills that meet all the criteria of the exchange on which they are traded. One such criterion is that the deliverable T-bill is the current bill for the week in which settlement takes place.

DELIVERY *see* DELIVERY DATE; GOOD DELIVERY.

DELIVERY DATE
1. first day of the month in which delivery is to be made under a futures contract. Since sales are on a SELLER'S OPTION basis, delivery can be on any day of the month, as long as proper notice is given.
2. third business day following a REGULAR WAY transaction of stocks or bonds. Seller's option delivery can be anywhere from 3 to 60 days, though there may be a purchase-price adjustment to compensate for DELAYED DELIVERY. The SETTLEMENT DATE was changed from 5 days to 3 days effective June 1, 1995, after approval by the SEC. New deadline is known as *T* (for trade)-*plus-three*.

DELIVERY NOTICE
1. notification from the seller to the buyer of a futures contract indicating the date when the actual commodity is to be delivered.
2. in general business transactions, a formal notice documenting that goods have been delivered or will be delivered on a certain date.

DELIVERY VERSUS PAYMENT securities industry procedure, common with institutional accounts, whereby delivery of securities sold is made to the buying customer's bank in exchange for payment, usually in the form of cash. (Institutions are required by law to require "assets of equal value" in exchange for delivery.) Also called CASH ON DELIV-ERY, delivery against payment, delivery against cash, or, from the sell side, RECEIVE VERSUS PAYMENT.

DELTA

1. measure of the relationship between an option price and the under-lying futures contract or stock price. For a call option, a delta of 0.50 means a half-point rise in premium for every dollar that the stock goes up. For a put option contract, the premium rises as stock prices fall. As options near expiration, IN-THE-MONEY contracts approach a delta of 1.
2. on the London Stock Exchange, *delta stocks* were the smallest cap-italization issues before the system was replaced with today's NOR-MAL MARKET SIZE.

DELTA HEDGING HEDGING method used in OPTION trading and based on the change in premium (option price) caused by a change in the price of the underlying instrument. The change in the premium for each one-point change in the underlying security is called DELTA and the relation-ship between the two price movements is called the *hedge ratio*. For example, if a call option has a hedge ratio of 40, the call should rise 40% of the change in the security move if the stock goes down. The delta of a put option, conversely, has a negative value. The value of the delta is usually good the first one-point move in the underlying security over a short time period. When an option has a high hedge ratio, it is usually more profitable to buy the option than to be a WRITER because the greater percentage movement vis-à-vis the underlying security's price and the relatively little time value erosion allow the purchaser greater leverage. The opposite is true for options with a low hedge ratio.

DEMAND DEPOSIT account balance which, without prior notice to the bank, can be drawn on by check, cash withdrawal from an automatic teller machine, or by transfer to other accounts using the telephone or home computers. Demand deposits are the largest component of the U.S. MONEY SUPPLY, and the principal medium through which the Federal Reserve implements monetary policy. *See also* COMPENSATING BALANCE.

DEMAND LOAN loan with no set maturity date that can be called for repayment when the lender chooses. Banks usually bill interest on these loans at fixed intervals.

DEMAND-PULL INFLATION price increases occurring when supply is not adequate to meet demand. *See also* COST-PUSH INFLATION.

DEMONETIZATION withdrawal from circulation of a specified form of currency. For example, the Jamaica Agreement between major INTER-NATIONAL MONETARY FUND countries officially demonetized gold starting in 1978, ending its role as the major medium of international settlement.

DENKS acronym for *dual-employed, no kids,* referring to a family unit in which both husband and wife work, and there are no children.

Without the expense and responsibility for children, DENKS have a larger disposable income than couples with children, making them a prime target for marketers of luxury goods and services, particularly various types of investments.

DENOMINATION face value of currency units, coins, and securities. *See also* PAR VALUE.

DEPLETION accounting treatment available to companies that extract oil and gas, coal, or other minerals, usually in the form of an allowance that reduces taxable income. Oil and gas limited partnerships pass the allowance on to their limited partners, who can use it to reduce other tax liabilities.

DEPOSIT
1. cash, checks, or drafts placed with a financial institution for credit to a customer's account. Banks broadly differentiate between demand deposits (checking accounts on which the customer may draw at any time) and time deposits, which usually pay interest and have a specified maturity or require 30 days' notice before withdrawal.
2. securities placed with a bank or other institution or with a person for a particular purpose.
3. sums lodged with utilities, landlords, and service companies as security.
4. money put down as evidence of an intention to complete a contract and to protect the other party in the event that the contract is not completed.

DEPOSITARY RECEIPT *see* AMERICAN DEPOSITARY RECEIPT.

DEPOSIT INSURANCE *see* CREDIT UNION; FEDERAL DEPOSIT INSURANCE CORPORATION.

DEPOSITORY INSTITUTIONS DEREGULATION AND MONETARY CONTROL ACT federal legislation of 1980 providing for deregulation of the banking system. The act established the Depository Institutions Deregulation Committee, composed of five voting members, the Secretary of the Treasury and the chair of the Federal Reserve Board, the Federal Home Loan Bank Board, the Federal Deposit Insurance Corporation, and the National Credit Union Administration, and one nonvoting member, the Comptroller of the Currency. The committee was charged with phasing out regulation of interest rates of banks and savings institutions over a six-year period (passbook accounts were de-regulated effective April, 1986, under a different federal law). The act authorized interest-bearing NEGOTIABLE ORDER OF WITHDRAWAL (NOW) accounts to be offered anywhere in the country. The act also overruled state usury laws on home mortgages over $25,000 and otherwise modernized mortgages by eliminating dollar limits, permitting second mortgages, and ending territorial restrictions in mortgage lending. Another part of the law permitted stock brokerages to offer checking accounts. *See also* DEREGULATION.

DEPOSITORY TRUST COMPANY central securities repository where stock and bond certificates are exchanged. Most of these exchanges now take place electronically, and few paper certificates actually change hands. The DTC is a member of the Federal Reserve System and is owned by most of the brokerage houses on Wall Street and the New York Stock Exchange.

DEPRECIATED COST original cost of a fixed asset less accumulated DEPRECIATION; this is the *net book value* of the asset.

DEPRECIATION
Economics: consumption of capital during production—in other words, wearing out of plant and capital goods, such as machines and equipment.
Finance: amortization of fixed assets, such as plant and equipment, so as to allocate the cost over their depreciable life. Depreciation reduces taxable income but does not reduce cash.

   Among the most commonly used methods are STRAIGHT-LINE DEPRECIATION; ACCELERATED DEPRECIATION; the ACCELERATED COST RECOVERY SYSTEM, and the MODIFIED ACCELERATED COST RECOVERY SYSTEM. Others include the annuity, appraisal, compound interest, production, replacement, retirement, and sinking fund methods.
Foreign exchange: decline in the price of one currency relative to another.

DEPRESSED MARKET market characterized by more supply than demand and therefore weak (depressed) prices. *See also* SYSTEMATIC RISK.

DEPRESSED PRICE price of a product, service, or security that is weak because of a DEPRESSED MARKET. Also refers to the market price of a stock that is low relative to comparable stocks or to its own ASSET VALUE because of perceived or actual risk. Such stocks are identified by high dividend yield, abnormally low PRICE/EARNINGS RATIOS and other such yardsticks. *See also* FUNDAMENTAL ANALYSIS.

DEPRESSION economic condition characterized by falling prices, reduced purchasing power, an excess of supply over demand, rising unemployment, accumulating inventories, deflation, plant contraction, public fear and caution, and a general decrease in business activity. The Great Depression of the 1930s, centered in the United States and Europe, had worldwide repercussions.

DEREGULATION greatly reducing government regulation in order to allow freer markets to create a more efficient marketplace. After the stock-brokerage industry was deregulated in the mid-1970s, commissions were no longer fixed. After the banking industry was deregulated in the early 1980s, banks were given greater freedom in setting interest rates on deposits and loans. Industries such as communications and transportation have also been deregulated, with similar results: increased competition, heightened innovation, and mergers among weaker competitors. Some government oversight usually remains after deregulation.

DERIVATIVE short for *derivative instrument,* a contract whose value is based on the performance of an underlying financial asset, index, or other investment. For example, an ordinary *option* is a derivative because its value changes in relation to the performance of an underlying stock. A more complex example would be an option on a FUTURES CONTRACT, where the option value varies with the value of the futures contract which, in turn, varies with the value of an underlying commodity or security. Derivatives are available based on the performance of assets, interest rates, currency exchange rates, and various domestic and foreign indexes. Derivatives afford leverage and, when used properly by knowledgeable investors, can enhance returns and be useful in HEDGING portfolios. They gained notoriety in the late '80s, however, because of problems involved in PROGRAM TRADING, and in the '90s, when a number of mutual funds, municipalities, corporations, and leading banks suffered large losses because unexpected movements in interest rates adversely affected the value of derivatives. *See also* BEARS, CERTIFICATES OF ACCRUAL ON TREASURY SECURITIES (CATS), COLLATERALIZED BOND OBLIGATION (CBO); COLLATERALIZED MORTGAGE OBLIGATION (CMO); CUBS; DIAMONDS; INDEX OPTIONS; OEX; SPDR; STRIP; SUBSCRIPTION RIGHT; SUBSCRIPTION WARRANT; SWAP; TIGER.

DERIVATIVE INSTRUMENT *see* DERIVATIVE.

DESCENDING TOPS chart pattern wherein each new high price for a security is lower than the preceding high. The trend is considered bearish.

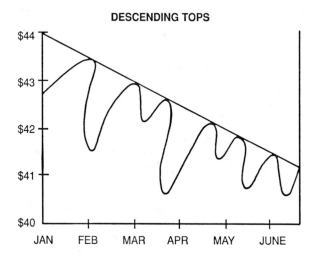

DESCENDING TOPS

DESIGNATED ORDER TURNAROUND (DOT) electronic system used by the New York Stock Exchange to expedite execution of small MARKET ORDERS by routing them directly from the member firm to the SPECIALIST, thus bypassing the FLOOR BROKER. A related system called *Super DOT* routes LIMIT ORDERS.

DESK trading desk, or Securities Department, at the New York FEDERAL RESERVE BANK, which is the operating arm of the FEDERAL OPEN MARKET COMMITTEE. The Desk executes all transactions undertaken by the FEDERAL RESERVE SYSTEM in the money market or the government securities market, serves as the Treasury Department's eyes and ears in these and related markets, and encompasses a foreign desk which conducts transactions in the FOREIGN EXCHANGE market.

DEUTSCHE BORSE AG operating company for the German securities and derivatives markets. In 1998, it changed its name to Eurex Frankfurt GmbH. It operates the FRANKFURT STOCK EXCHANGE, the country's leading stock exchange, and seven others in Dusseldorf, Munich, Hamburg, Berlin, Stuttgart, Hanover and Bremen. Deutsche Borse also operates DEUTSCHE TERMINBORSE, Germany's only futures exchange, and is responsible for settlement of all securities and futures exchange transactions in Germany. The eight exchanges have different official trading hours. General trading hours are 10:30 A.M. to 1:30 P.M., Monday through Friday. The IBIS system runs from 8:30 A.M. to 5 P.M.

DEUTSCHE TERMINBORSE (DTB) Germany's first fully computerized exchange, and the first German exchange for trading financial futures, opened in January 1990. In January 1994, DTB merged with DEUTSCHE BORSE AG. DTB changed its name to Eurex Deutschland in 1998, when it joined with the SWISS OPTIONS AND FINANCIAL FUTURES EXCHANGE (SOFFEX) to form Eurex. Eurex trades futures and options contracts formerly traded on the two exchanges: futures and options on the DAX Index (the German stock index) and the Swiss Market Index (SMI); futures and future options on the DAX future, BOBL national government bonds (3.3 to 5 years), BUND national government bonds (8.5 to 10 years), Swiss government bonds (Conf), Dow Jones STOXX 50 and Dow Jones Euro STOXX 50; futures on the one-month Euromark, three-month Euromark, Mid-Cap DAX and Jumbo Pfandbrief; stock options on German and Swiss blue chip equities; and U.S. dollar/Deutschemark options.

DEVALUATION lowering of the value of a country's currency relative to gold and/or the currencies of other nations. Devaluation can also result from a rise in value of other currencies relative to the currency of a particular country.

DEVELOPMENTAL DRILLING PROGRAM drilling for oil and gas in an area with proven reserves to a depth known to have been productive in the past. Limited partners in such a program, which is considerably less risky than an EXPLORATORY DRILLING PROGRAM or WILD-CAT DRILLING, have a good chance of steady income, but little chance of enormous profits.

DEWKS acronym for *dual-employed, with kids,* referring to a family unit in which both husband and wife work and there are children. Marketers selling products for children, including various investments, target DEWKS.

DIAGONAL SPREAD strategy based on a long and short position in the same class of option (two puts or two calls in the same stock) at different striking prices and different expiration dates. Example: a six-month call sold with a striking price of 40 and a three-month call sold with a striking price of 35. *See also* CALENDAR SPREAD; VERTICAL SPREAD.

DIALING AND SMILING expression for COLD CALLING by securities brokers and other salespeople. Brokers must not only make unsolicited telephone calls to potential customers, but also gain the customer's confidence with their upbeat tone of voice and sense of concern for the customer's financial well-being.

DIALING FOR DOLLARS expression for COLD CALLING in which brokers make unsolicited telephone calls to potential customers, hoping to find people with investable funds. The term has a derogatory implication, and is typically applied to salespeople working in BOILER ROOMS, selling speculative or fraudulent investments such as PENNY STOCKS.

DIAMOND INVESTMENT TRUST unit trust that invests in high-quality diamonds. Begun in the early 1980s by Thomson McKinnon, these trusts let shareholders invest in diamonds without buying and holding a particular stone. Shares in these trusts do not trade actively and are therefore difficult to sell if diamond prices fall, as they did soon after the first trust was set up.

DIAMONDS represent units of beneficial interest in the DIAMONDS Trust, a UNIT INVESTMENT TRUST that holds the 30 component stocks of the Dow Jones Industrial Average. First introduced in January, 1998, DIAMONDS trade under the ticker symbol "DIA" like any other stock on the American Stock Exchange. They are designed to offer investors a low-cost means of tracking the DJIA, the most widely recognized indicator of the American stock market. DIAMONDS pay monthly DIVIDENDS (which can be reinvested into more shares of the trust) that correspond to the dividend yields of the DJIA component stocks and pay capital gains distributions once a year. DIAMONDS are designed to trade at about 1/100 the level of the Dow Jones Industrial Average. So if the DJIA is at 9000, DIAMONDS will trade at about $90 per unit.

For those speculating that stock market prices will fall, it is possible to SELL SHORT using DIAMONDS. Short sellers have an additional advantage: DIAMONDS are not subject to the UPTICK RULE that applies to stocks, meaning they can be sold regardless of which direction the price is moving.

Unlike open-end mutual funds, DIAMONDS trade like stocks, allowing investors to buy or sell at any time during the trading day, whereas index mutual funds are only priced once at the end of each trading day. Like open-end index funds, DIAMONDS charge low management fees because there is little research or trading conducted by the trust's management. There are also no LOADS to buy DIAMONDS, though normal brokerage commissions do apply to trades. Whereas closed-end funds often trade at discounts to their NET ASSET VALUES, investors can create an unlimited number of DIAMONDS trading units, which helps insure they will correlate closely with the performance of the DJIA stocks in the portfolio. *See also* INDEX FUND; SPDR.

DIFF short for *Euro-rate differential,* a futures contract traded on the Chicago Mercantile Exchange that is based on the interest rate spread between the U.S. dollar and the British pound, the German mark, or the Japanese yen.

DIFFERENTIAL small extra charge sometimes called the *odd-lot-differential*—usually ⅛ of a point—that dealers add to purchases and subtract from sales in quantities less than the standard trading unit or ROUND LOT. Also, the extent to which a dealer widens his round lot quote to compensate for lack of volume.

DIGITS DELETED designation on securities exchange tape meaning that because the tape has been delayed, some digits have been dropped. For example, 26½… 26⅝… 26⅛ becomes 6½… 6⅝… 6⅛.

DILUTION effect on earnings per share and book value per share if all convertible securities were converted or all warrants or stock options were exercised. *See* FULLY DILUTED EARNINGS PER (COMMON) SHARE.

DINKS acronym for *dual-income, no kids,* referring to a family unit in which there are two incomes and no children. The two incomes may result from both husband and wife working, or one spouse holding down two jobs. Since the couple do not have children, they typically have more disposable income than those with children, and therefore are the prime targets of marketers selling luxury products and services, including various investments. *See also* DENKS; DEWKS.

DIP slight drop in securities prices after a sustained uptrend. Analysts often advise investors to buy on dips, meaning buy when a price is momentarily weak. *See* chart on next page.

DIRECT INVESTMENT (1) purchase of a controlling interest in a foreign (international) business or subsidiary. (2) in domestic finance, the purchase of a controlling interest or a minority interest of such size and influence that active control is a feasible objective.

DIRECTOR *see* BOARD OF DIRECTORS.

DIP

DIRECT OVERHEAD portion of overhead costs—rent, lights, insurance—allocated to manufacturing, by the application of a standard factor termed a *burden rate*. This amount is absorbed as an INVENTORY cost and ultimately reflected as a COST OF GOODS SOLD.

DIRECT PARTICIPATION PROGRAM program letting investors participate directly in the cash flow and tax benefits of the underlying investments. Such programs are usually organized as LIMITED PARTNERSHIPS, although their uses as tax shelters have been severely curtailed by tax legislation affecting PASSIVE investments.

DIRECT PLACEMENT direct sale of securities to one or more professional investors. Such securities may or may not be registered with the SECURITIES AND EXCHANGE COMMISSION. They may be bonds, private issues of stock, limited partnership interests, mortgage-backed securities, venture capital investments, or other sophisticated instruments. These investments typically require large minimum purchases, often in the millions of dollars. Direct placements offer higher potential returns than many publicly offered securities, but also present more risk. Buyers of direct placements are large, sophisticated financial institutions including insurance companies, banks, mutual funds, foundations, and pension funds that are able to evaluate such offerings. Also called *private placement.*

DIRECT PURCHASE purchasing shares in a no-load or low-load OPEN-END MUTUAL FUND directly from the fund company. Investors making direct purchases deal directly with the fund company over the phone, in person at investor centers, or by mail. This contrasts with the method of purchasing shares in a LOAD FUND through a financial intermediary such as a broker or financial planner, who collects a commission for offering advice on which fund is appropriate for the client. Many companies also now allow shareholders to purchase "no-load" stock directly from the company, thereby avoiding brokers and sales commissions. *See also* TREASURY DIRECT.

DIRTY STOCK stock that fails to meet the requirements for GOOD DELIVERY.

DISABILITY INCOME INSURANCE insurance policy that pays benefits to a policyholder when that person becomes incapable of performing one or more occupational duties, either temporarily or on a long-term basis, or totally. The policy is designed to replace a portion of the income lost because of the insured's disability. Payments begin after a specified period, called the *elimination period,* of several weeks or months.

Some policies remain in force until the person is able to return to work, or to return to a similar occupation, or is eligible to receive benefits from another program such as Social Security disability. Disability insurance payments are normally tax-free to beneficiaries as long as they paid the policy premiums. Many employers offer disability income insurance to their employees, though people are able to buy coverage on an individual basis as well.

DISBURSEMENT paying out of money in the discharge of a debt or an expense, as distinguished from a distribution.

DISCHARGE OF BANKRUPTCY order terminating bankruptcy proceedings, ordinarily freeing the debtor of all legal responsibility for specified obligations.

DISCHARGE OF LIEN order removing a lien on property after the originating legal claim has been paid or otherwise satisfied.

DISCLAIMER OF OPINION auditor's statement, sometimes called an *adverse opinion,* that an ACCOUNTANT'S OPINION cannot be provided because of limitations on the examination or because some condition or situation exists, such as pending litigation, that could impair the financial strength or profitability of the client.

DISCLOSURE release by companies of all information, positive or negative, that might bear on an investment decision, as required by the Securities and Exchange Commission and the stock exchanges. *See also* FINANCIAL PUBLIC RELATIONS; INSIDE INFORMATION; INSIDER.

DISCONTINUED OPERATIONS operations of a business that have been sold, abandoned, or otherwise disposed of. Accounting regulations require that continuing operations be reported separately in the income statement from discontinued operations, and that any gain or loss from the disposal of a segment (an entity whose activities represent a separate major line of business or class of customer) be reported along with the operating results of the discontinued segment.

DISCOUNT
1. difference between a bond's current market price and its face or redemption value.
2. manner of selling securities such as treasury bills, which are issued at less than face value and are redeemed at face value.
3. relationship between two currencies. The French franc may sell at a discount to the English pound, for example.

4. to apply all available news about a company in evaluating its current stock price. For instance, taking into account the introduction of an exciting new product.

5. method whereby interest on a bank loan or note is deducted in advance.

6. reduction in the selling price of merchandise or a percentage off the invoice price in exchange for quick payment.

DISCOUNT BOND bond selling below its redemption value. *See also* DEEP DISCOUNT BOND.

DISCOUNT BROKER brokerage house that executes orders to buy and sell securities at commission rates sharply lower than those charged by a FULL SERVICE BROKER.

DISCOUNT DIVIDEND REINVESTMENT PLAN *see* DIVIDEND REINVESTMENT PLAN.

DISCOUNTED CASH FLOW value of future expected cash receipts and expenditures at a common date, which is calculated using NET PRESENT VALUE or INTERNAL RATE OF RETURN and is a factor in analyses of both capital investments and securities investments. The net present value (NPV) method applies a rate of discount (interest rate) based on the marginal cost of capital to future cash flows to bring them back to the present. The internal rate of return (IRR) method finds the average return on investment earned through the life of the investment. It determines the discount rate that equates the present value of future cash flows to the cost of the investment.

DISCOUNTING THE NEWS bidding a firm's stock price up or down in anticipation of good or bad news about the company's prospects.

DISCOUNT POINTS *see* POINT.

DISCOUNT RATE

1. interest rate that the Federal Reserve charges member banks for loans, using government securities or ELIGIBLE PAPER as collateral. This provides a floor on interest rates, since banks set their loan rates a notch above the discount rate.

2. interest rate used in determining the PRESENT VALUE of future CASH FLOWS. *See also* CAPITALIZATION RATE.

DISCOUNT WINDOW place in the Federal Reserve where banks go to borrow money at the DISCOUNT RATE. Borrowing from the Fed is a privilege, not a right, and banks are discouraged from using the privilege except when they are short of reserves.

DISCOUNT YIELD yield on a security sold at a discount—U.S. treasury bills sold at $9750 and maturing at $10,000 in 90 days, for instance. Also called *bank discount basis.* To figure the annual yield, divide the discount ($250) by the face amount ($10,000) and multiply that number by the approximate number of days in the year (360) divided by the number of days to maturity (90). The calculation looks like this:

$$\frac{\$250}{\$10,000} \times \frac{360}{90} = .025 \times 4 = .10 = 10\%.$$

DISCRETIONARY ACCOUNT account empowering a broker or adviser to buy and sell without the client's prior knowledge or consent. Some clients set broad guidelines, such as limiting investments to blue chip stocks.

DISCRETIONARY INCOME amount of a consumer's income spent after essentials like food, housing, and utilities and prior commitments have been covered. The total amount of discretionary income can be a key economic indicator because spending this money can spur the economy.

DISCRETIONARY ORDER order to buy a particular stock, bond, or commodity that lets the broker decide when to execute the trade and at what price.

DISCRETIONARY TRUST
1. mutual fund or unit trust whose investments are not limited to a certain kind of security. The management decides on the best way to use the assets.
2. personal trust that lets the trustee decide how much income or principal to provide to the beneficiary. This can be used to prevent the beneficiary from dissipating funds.

DISHONOR to refuse to pay, as in the case of a check that is returned by a bank because of insufficient funds.

DISINFLATION slowing down of the rate at which prices increase—usually during a recession, when sales drop and retailers are not always able to pass on higher prices to consumers. Not to be confused with DEFLATION, when prices actually drop.

DISINTERMEDIATION movement of funds from low-yielding accounts at traditional banking institutions to higher-yielding investments in the general market—for example, withdrawal of funds from a passbook savings account paying 5½% to buy a Treasury bill paying 10%. As a counter move, banks may pay higher rates to depositors, then charge higher rates to borrowers, which leads to tight money and reduced economic activity. Since banking DEREGULATION, disintermediation is not the economic problem it once was.

DISINVESTMENT reduction in capital investment either by disposing of capital goods (such as plant and equipment) or by failing to maintain or replace capital assets that are being used up·

DISPOSABLE INCOME personal income remaining after personal taxes and noncommercial government fees have been paid. This money can be spent on essentials or nonessentials or it can be saved. *See also* DISCRETIONARY INCOME.

DISTRESS SALE sale of property under distress conditions. For example, stock, bond, mutual fund or futures positions may have to be sold in a portfolio if there is a MARGIN CALL. Real estate may have to be sold because a bank is in the process of FORECLOSURE on the property. A brokerage firm may be forced to sell securities from its inventory if it has fallen below various capital requirements imposed by stock exchanges and regulators. Because distress sellers are being forced to sell, they usually do not receive as favorable a price as if they were able to wait for ideal selling conditions.

DISTRIBUTING SYNDICATE group of brokerage firms or investment bankers that join forces in order to facilitate the DISTRIBUTION of a large block of securities. A distribution is usually handled over a period of time to avoid upsetting the market price. The term distributing syndicate can refer to a primary distribution or a secondary distribution, but the former is more commonly called simply a syndicate or an underwriting syndicate.

DISTRIBUTION

Corporate finance: allocation of income and expenses to the appropriate subsidiary accounts.

Economics: (1) movement of goods from manufacturers; (2) way in which wealth is shared in any particular economic system.

Estate law: parceling out of assets to the beneficiaries named in a will, as carried out by the executor under the guidance of a court.

Mutual funds and closed-end investment companies: payout of realized capital gains on securities in the portfolio of the fund or closed-end investment company.

Securities: sale of a large block of stock in such manner that the price is not adversely affected. Technical analysts look on a pattern of distribution as a tipoff that the stock will soon fall in price. The opposite of distribution, known as ACCUMULATION, may signal a rise in price.

DISTRIBUTION AREA price range in which a stock trades for a long time. Sellers who want to avoid pushing the price down will be careful not to sell below this range. ACCUMULATION of shares in the same range helps to account for the stock's price stability. Technical analysts consider distribution areas in predicting when stocks may break up or down from that price range. *See also* ACCUMULATION AREA.

DISTRIBUTION PERIOD period of time, usually a few days, between the date a company's board of directors declares a stock dividend, known as the DECLARATION DATE, and the DATE OF RECORD, by which the shareholder must officially own shares to be entitled to the dividend.

DISTRIBUTION PLAN plan adopted by a mutual fund to charge certain distribution costs, such as advertising, promotion and sales incentives, to shareholders. The plan will specify a certain percentage, usually .75% or less, which will be deducted from fund assets annually. *See also* 12b-1 MUTUAL FUND.

DISTRIBUTION STOCK stock part of a block sold over a period of time in order to avoid upsetting the market price. May be part of a primary (underwriting) distribution or a secondary distribution following SHELF REGISTRATION.

DISTRIBUTOR wholesaler of goods to dealers that sell to consumers.

DIVERSIFICATION
1. spreading of risk by putting assets in several categories of investments—stocks, bonds, money market instruments, and precious metals, for instance, or several industries, or a mutual fund, with its broad range of stocks in one portfolio.
2. at the corporate level, entering into different business areas, as a CONGLOMERATE does.

DIVERSIFIED INVESTMENT COMPANY mutual fund or unit trust that invests in a wide range of securities. Under the Investment Company Act of 1940, such a company may not have more than 5 percent of its assets in any one stock, bond, or commodity and may not own more than 10 percent of the voting shares of any one company.

DIVESTITURE disposition of an asset or investment by outright sale, employee purchase, liquidation, and so on.
Also, one corporation's orderly distribution of large blocks of another corporation's stock, which were held as an investment. Du Pont was ordered by the courts to divest itself of General Motors stock, for example.

DIVIDEND distribution of earnings to shareholders, prorated by class of security and paid in the form of money, stock, scrip, or, rarely, company products or property. The amount is decided by the board of directors and is usually paid quarterly. Dividends must be declared as income in the year they are received.
Mutual fund dividends are paid out of income, usually on a quarterly basis from the fund's investments. The tax on such dividends depends on whether the distributions resulted from capital gains, interest income, or dividends received by the fund. *See also* EQUALIZING DIVIDEND; EXTRA DIVIDEND.

DIVIDEND CAPTURE *See* DIVIDEND ROLLOVER PLAN.

DIVIDEND COVER British equivalent of the dividend PAYOUT RATIO.

DIVIDEND DISCOUNT MODEL mathematical model used to determine the price at which a stock should be selling based on the discounted value of projected future dividend payments. It is used to identify undervalued stocks representing capital gains potential.

DIVIDEND EXCLUSION pre-TAX REFORM ACT OF 1986 provision allowing for subtraction from dividends qualifying as taxable income under Internal Revenue Service rules—$100 for individuals and $200 for married couples filing jointly. The 1986 Tax Act eliminated this exclusion effective for the 1987 tax year.

   Domestic corporations may exclude from taxable income 70% of dividends received from other domestic corporations. The exclusion was 85% prior to the 1986 Act, which reduced it to 80%.

DIVIDEND IN ARREARS ACCUMULATED DIVIDEND on CUMULATIVE PREFERRED stock, which is payable to the current holder. Preferred stock in a TURNAROUND situation can be an attractive buy when it is selling at a discount and has dividends in arrears.

DIVIDEND PAYOUT RATIO percentage of earnings paid to shareholders in cash. In general, the higher the payout ratio, the more mature the company. Electric and telephone utilities tend to have the highest payout ratios, whereas fast-growing companies usually reinvest all earnings and pay no dividends.

DIVIDEND RECORD publication of Standard & Poor's Corporation that provides information on corporate policies and payment histories.

DIVIDEND REINVESTMENT PLAN automatic reinvestment of shareholder dividends in more shares of the company's stock. Some companies absorb most or all of the applicable brokerage fees, and some also discount the stock price. Dividend reinvestment plans allow shareholders to accumulate capital over the long term using DOLLAR COST AVERAGING. For corporations, dividend reinvestment plans are a means of raising capital funds without the FLOTATION COSTS of a NEW ISSUE.

DIVIDEND REQUIREMENT amount of annual earnings necessary to pay contracted dividends on preferred stock.

DIVIDEND ROLLOVER PLAN method of buying and selling stocks around their EX-DIVIDEND dates so as to collect the dividend and make a small profit on the trade. This entails buying shares about two weeks before a stock goes ex-dividend. After the ex-dividend date the price will drop by the amount of the dividend, then work its way back up to the earlier price. By selling slightly above the purchase price, the investor can cover brokerage costs, collect the dividend, and realize a small capital gain in three or four weeks. Also called *dividend capture*. *See also* TRADING DIVIDENDS.

DIVIDENDS PAYABLE dollar amount of dividends that are to be paid, as reported in financial statements. These dividends become an obligation once declared by the board of directors and are listed as liabilities in annual and quarterly reports.

DIVIDENDS-RECEIVED DEDUCTION tax deduction allowed to a corporation owning shares in another corporation for the dividends it receives. In most cases, the deduction is 70%, but in some cases it may be as high as 100% depending on the level of ownership the dividend-receiving company has in the dividend-paying entity.

DIVIDEND YIELD annual percentage of return earned by an investor on a common or preferred stock. The yield is determined by dividing the amount of the annual dividends per share by the current market price per share of the stock. For example, a stock paying a $1 dividend per year that sells for $10 a share has a 10% dividend yield. The dividend yields of stocks are listed in the stock tables of most daily newspapers.

DOCUMENTARY DRAFT *see* DRAFT.

DOGS OF THE DOW strategy of buying the 10 high-yielding stocks in the DOW JONES INDUSTRIAL AVERAGE. Over one-year periods, these 10 stocks tend to outperform all 30 Dow stocks because investors are buying them at depressed prices and earning the highest yields, and the stocks tend to bounce back. Investors can execute this strategy by buying all 10 stocks once a year, or by buying DEFINED ASSET FUNDS or other UNIT INVESTMENT TRUSTS specializing in this technique. The strategy of buying the 10 high-yielding stocks in an index has spread far from just the Dow Jones Industrials, as investors now practice it with shares in the United Kingdom, Hong Kong and many other indices. The Dogs of the Dow strategy was popularized by Michael B. O'Higgins and John Downes in their book and newsletter *Beating the Dow*. (Downes is the co-author of this *Dictionary*.)

DOLLAR BEARS traders who think the dollar will fall in value against other foreign currencies. Dollar bears may implement a number of investment strategies to capitalize on a falling dollar, such as buying Japanese yen, Deutsche marks, British pounds or other foreign currencies directly, or buying futures or options contracts on those currencies.

DOLLAR BOND
1. municipal revenue bond quoted and traded on a dollar price basis instead of yield to maturity.
2. bond denominated in U.S. dollars but issued outside the United States, principally in Europe.
3. bond denominated in U.S. dollars and issued in the United States by foreign companies.
   See also EUROBOND; EURODOLLAR BOND.

DOLLAR COST AVERAGING *see* CONSTANT DOLLAR PLAN.

DOLLAR DRAIN amount by which a foreign country's imports from the United States exceed its exports to the United States. As the country spends more dollars to finance the imports than it receives in payment for the exports, its dollar reserves drain away.

DOLLAR PRICE bond price expressed as a percentage of face value (normally $1000) rather than as a yield. Thus a bond quoted at 97½ has a dollar price of $975, which is 97½% of $1000.

DOLLAR SHORTAGE situation in which a country that imports from the United States can no longer pay for its purchases without U.S. gifts or loans to provide the necessary dollars. After World War II a worldwide dollar shortage was alleviated by massive infusions of American money through the European Recovery Program (Marshall Plan) and other grant and loan programs.

DOLLAR-WEIGHTED RETURN portfolio accounting method that measures changes in total dollar value, treating additions and withdrawals of capital as a part of the RETURN along with income and capital gains and losses. For example, a portfolio (or group of portfolios) worth $100 million at the beginning of a reporting period and $120 million at the end would show a return of 20%; this would be true even if the investments lost money, provided enough new money was infused. While dollar weighting enables investors to compare absolute dollars with financial goals, manager-to-manager comparisons are not possible unless performance is isolated from external cash flows; this is accomplished with the TIME-WEIGHTED RETURN method.

DOMESTIC ACCEPTANCE *see* ACCEPTANCE.

DOMESTIC CORPORATION corporation doing business in the U.S. state in which it was incorporated. In all other U.S. states its legal status is that of a FOREIGN CORPORATION.

DOMICILE place where a person has established permanent residence. It is important to establish a domicile for the purpose of filing state and local income taxes, and for filing estate taxes upon death. The domicile is created based on obtaining a driver's license, registering to vote, and having a permanent home to which one returns. Usually, one must be a resident in a state for at least six months of the year to establish a domicile.

DONATED STOCK fully paid capital stock of a corporation contributed without CONSIDERATION to the same issuing corporation. The gift is credited to the DONATED SURPLUS account at PAR VALUE.

DONATED SURPLUS shareholder's equity account that is credited when contributions of cash, property, or the firm's own stock are freely given to the company. Also termed *donated capital*. Not to be confused with contributed surplus or contributed capital, which is the balances in CAPITAL STOCK accounts plus capital contributed in excess of par or STATED VALUE accounts.

DO NOT INCREASE abbreviated *DNI.* Instruction on good-till-cancelled buy limit and sell stop orders that prevent the quantity from changing in the event of a stock SPLIT or stock dividend.

DO NOT REDUCE (DNR) instruction on a LIMIT ORDER to buy, or on a STOP ORDER to sell, or on a STOP-LIMIT ORDER to sell, not to reduce the order when the stock goes EX-DIVIDEND and its price is reduced by the amount of the dividend as usually happens. DNRs do not apply to rights or stock dividends.

DONOR individual who donates property to another through a TRUST. Also called a *grantor.* Donors also make tax-deductible charitable contributions of securities or physical property to nonprofit institutions such as schools, philanthropic groups, and religious organizations.

DON'T FIGHT THE TAPE don't trade against the market trend. If stocks are falling, as reported on the BROAD TAPE, some analysts say it would be foolish to buy aggressively. Similarly, it would be fighting the tape to sell short during a market rally.

DON'T KNOW Wall Street slang for a *questioned trade.* Brokers exchange comparison sheets to verify the details of transactions between them. Any discrepancy that turns up is called a don't know or a *QT.*

DOT (and SUPER-DOT) SYSTEM acronym for *Designated Order Turnaround,* New York Stock Exchange AUTOMATED ORDER ENTRY SYSTEMS for expediting small and moderate-sized orders. DOT handles market orders and Super DOT limited price orders. The systems bypass floor brokers and rout orders directly to the SPECIALIST, who executes through a CONTRA BROKER or against the SPECIALIST'S BOOK.

DOUBLE AUCTION SYSTEM *see* AUCTION MARKET.

DOUBLE-BARRELED municipal revenue bond whose principal and interest are guaranteed by a larger municipal entity. For example, a bridge authority might issue revenue bonds payable out of revenue from bridge tolls. If the city or state were to guarantee the bonds, they would be double-barreled, and the investor would be protected against default in the event that bridge usage is disappointing and revenue proves inadequate.

DOUBLE BOTTOM technical chart pattern showing a drop in price, then a rebound, then another drop to the same level. The pattern is usually interpreted to mean the security has much support at that price and should not drop further. However, if the price does fall through that level, it is considered likely to reach a new low. *See also* DOUBLE TOP.

DOUBLE BOTTOM

DOUBLE-DECLINING-BALANCE DEPRECIATION METHOD (DDB) method of accelerated depreciation, approved by the Internal Revenue Service, permitting twice the rate of annual depreciation as the straight-line method. It is also called the 200 percent declining-balance method. The two methods are compared below, assuming an asset with a total cost of $1000, a useful life of four years, and no SALVAGE VALUE.

With STRAIGHT-LINE DEPRECIATION the useful life of the asset is divided into the total cost to arrive at the uniform annual charge of $250, or 25% a year. DDB permits twice the straight-line annual percentage rate—50% in this case—to be applied each year to the undepreciated value of the asset. Hence: 50% × $1000 = $500 the first year, 50% × $500 = $250 the second year, and so on.

YEAR	STRAIGHT LINE		DOUBLE DECLINING BALANCE	
	Expense	Cumulative	Expense	Cumulative
1	$250	$250	$500	$500
2	250	500	250	750
3	250	750	125	875
4	250	1000	63	938
	$1000		$938	

A variation of DDB, called *150 percent declining balance method,* uses 150% of the straight-line annual percentage rate.

A switch to straight-line from declining balance depreciation is permitted once in the asset's life—logically, at the third year in our example. When the switch is made, however, salvage value must be considered. *See also* MODIFIED ACCELERATED COST RECOVERY SYSTEM; DEPRECIATION.

DOUBLE TAXATION taxation of earnings at the corporate level, then again as stockholder dividends.

DOUBLE TOP technical chart pattern showing a rise to a high price, then a drop, then another rise to the same high price. This means the security is encountering resistance to a move higher. However, if the price does move through that level, the security is expected to go on to a new high. *See also* DOUBLE BOTTOM.

DOUBLE TOP

DOUBLE UP sophisticated stock buying (or selling short) strategy that reaffirms the original rationale by doubling the risk when the price goes (temporarily it is hoped) the wrong way. For example, an investor with confidence in XYZ buys 10,000 shares at $40. When the price drops to $35, the investor buys 10,000 additional shares, thus doubling up on a stock he feels will ultimately rise.

DOUBLE WITCHING DAY day when two related classes of options and futures expire. For example, index options and index futures on the same underlying index may expire on the same day, leading to various strategies by ARBITRAGEURS to close out positions. *See also* TRIPLE WITCHING HOUR.

DOW DIVIDEND THEORY *see* DOGS OF THE DOW.

DOW JONES AVERAGES *see* STOCK INDICES AND AVERAGES.

DOW JONES INDUSTRIAL AVERAGE *see* STOCK INDEXES AND AVERAGES.

DOWNSIDE RISK estimate that a security will decline in value and the extent of the decline, taking into account the total range of factors affecting market price.

DOWNSIZING term for a corporate strategy popular in the 1990s whereby a company reduces its size and complexity, thereby presumably increasing its efficiency and profitability. Downsizing is typically accomplished through RESTRUCTURING, which means reducing the number of employees and, often, the SPIN-OFF of activities unrelated to the company's core business.

DOWNSTREAM flow of corporate activity from parent to subsidiary. Financially, it usually refers to loans, since dividends and interest generally flow upstream.

DOWNTICK sale of a security at a price below that of the preceding sale. If a stock has been trading at $15 a share, for instance, the next trade is a downtick if it is at 14⅞. Also known as MINUS TICK.

DOWNTURN shift of an economic or stock market cycle from rising to falling.

DOW THEORY theory that a major trend in the stock market must be confirmed by a similar movement in the Dow Jones Industrial Average and the Dow Jones Transportation Average. According to Dow Theory, a significant trend is not confirmed until both Dow Jones indexes reach the new highs or lows; if they don't, the market will fall back to its former trading range. Dow Theory proponents often disagree on when a true breakout has occurred and, in any case, miss a major portion of the up or down move while waiting for their signals.

DRAFT signed, written order by which one party (drawer) instructs another party (drawee) to pay a specified sum to a third party (payee). Payee and drawer are usually the same person. In foreign transactions, a draft is usually called a *bill of exchange.* When prepared without supporting papers, it is a *clean draft.* With papers or documents attached, it is a *documentary draft.* A *sight draft* is payable on demand. *A time draft* is payable either on a definite date or at a fixed time after sight or demand.

DRAINING RESERVES actions by the Federal Reserve System to decrease the money supply by curtailing the funds banks have available to lend. The Fed does this in three ways: (1) by raising reserve requirements, forcing banks to keep more funds on deposit with Federal Reserve banks; (2) by increasing the rate at which banks borrow to maintain reserves, thereby making it unattractive to deplete reserves by making loans; and (3) by selling bonds in the open market at such attractive rates that dealers reduce their bank balances to buy them. *See also* MULTIPLIER.

DRAWBACK rebate of taxes or duties paid on imported goods that have been reexported. It is in effect a government subsidy designed to encourage domestic manufacturers to compete overseas.

DRAWER *see* DRAFT.

DRESSING UP A PORTFOLIO practice of money managers to make their portfolio look good at the end of a reporting period. For example, a mutual fund or pension fund manager may sell certain stocks that performed badly during the quarter shortly before the end of that quarter to avoid having to report that holding to shareholders. Or they may buy stocks that have risen during the quarter to show shareholders that they owned winning stocks. Because these portfolio changes are largely cosmetic, they have little effect on portfolio performance except they increase transaction costs. In the final few days of a quarter, market analysts frequently comment that certain stocks rose or fell because of end-of-quarter WINDOW DRESSING.

DRILLING PROGRAM *see* BALANCED DRILLING PROGRAM; COMPLETION PROGRAM; DEVELOPMENTAL DRILLING PROGRAM; EXPLORATORY DRILLING PROGRAM; OIL AND GAS LIMITED PARTNERSHIP.

DRIP *see* DIVIDEND REINVESTMENT PLAN.

DRIP FEED supplying capital to a new company as its growth requires it, rather than in a lump sum at the beginning. *See also* EVERGREEN FUNDING.

DROP-DEAD DAY day on which a deadline, such as the expiration of the national debt limit, becomes absolutely final.

DROP-DEAD FEE British term meaning a fee paid to a lender only if a deal requiring financing from that lender falls through.

DROPLOCK SECURITY FLOATING RATE NOTE or bond that becomes a FIXED INCOME INVESTMENT when the rate to which it is pegged drops to a specified level.

DUAL BANKING U.S. system whereby banks are chartered by the state or federal government. This makes for differences in banking regulations, in lending limits, and in services available to customers.

DUAL LISTING listing of a security on more than one exchange, thus increasing the competition for bid and offer prices as well as the liquidity of the securities. Furthermore, being listed on an exchange in the East and another in the West would extend the number of hours when the stock can be traded. Securities may not be listed on both the New York and American stock exchanges.

DUAL PURPOSE FUND exchange-listed CLOSED-END FUND that has two classes of shares. Preferred shareholders receive all the income (dividends and interest) from the portfolio, while common shareholders receive all the capital gains. Such funds are set up with a specific expiration date when preferred shares are redeemed at a predetermined price and common shareholders claim the remaining assets, voting either to liquidate or to continue the fund on an open-end basis. Dual purpose funds are not closely followed on Wall Street, and there is little trading in them.

DUAL TRADING commodities traders' practice of dealing for their own and their clients' accounts at the same time. Reformers favor restricting dual trading to prevent FRONT RUNNING; advocates claim the practice is harmless in itself and economically vital to the industry.

DUE BILL *see* BILL.

DUE DATE date on which a debt-related obligation is required to be paid.

DUE DILIGENCE MEETING meeting conducted by the underwriter of a new offering at which brokers can ask representatives of the issuer questions about the issuer's background and financial reliability and the intended use of the proceeds. Brokers who recommend investment in new offerings without very careful due diligence work may face lawsuits if the investment should go sour later. Although, in itself, the legally required due diligence meeting typically is a perfunctory affair, most companies, recognizing the importance of due diligence, hold informational meetings, often in different regions of the country, at which top management representatives are available to answer questions of securities analysts and institutional investors.

DUE-ON-SALE CLAUSE clause in a mortgage contract requiring the borrower to pay off the full remaining principal outstanding on a mortgage when the mortgaged property is sold, transferred, or in any way encumbered. Due-on-sale clauses prevent the buyer of the property from assuming the mortgage loan.

DUMPING
    International finance: selling goods abroad below cost in order to eliminate a surplus or to gain an edge on foreign competition. The U.S. Antidumping Act of 1974 was designed to prevent the sale of imported goods below cost in the United States.
    Securities: offering large amounts of stock with little or no concern for price or market effect.

DUN & BRADSTREET (D & B) company that combines credit information obtained directly from commercial firms with data solicited from their creditors, then makes this available to subscribers in reports and a ratings directory. D & B also offers an accounts receivable collection service and publishes financial composite ratios and other financial information. A subsidiary, MOODY'S INVESTOR'S SERVICE, rates bonds and commercial paper.

DUN'S NUMBER short for Dun's Market Identifier. It is published as part of a list of firms giving information such as an identification number, address code, number of employees, corporate affiliations, and trade styles. Full name: Data Universal Numbering System.

DURABLE POWER OF ATTORNEY legal document by which a person with assets (the principal) appoints another person (the agent) to act on the principal's behalf, even if the principal becomes incompetent. If the power of attorney is not "durable," the agent's authority to act ends if the principal becomes incompetent. The agent's power to act for the principal may be broadly stated, allowing the agent to buy and sell securities, or narrowly stated to limit activity to selling a car.

DURATION concept first developed by Frederick Macaulay in 1938 that measures bond price VOLATILITY by measuring the "length" of a bond. It is a weighted-average term-to-maturity of the bond's cash flows, the weights being the present value of each cash flow as a percentage of the bond's full price. A Salomon Smith Barney study compared it to a series of tin cans equally spaced on a seesaw. The size of each can represents the cash flow due, the contents of each can represent the present values of those cash flows, and the intervals between them represent the payment periods. Duration is the distance to the fulcrum that would balance the seesaw. The duration of a zero-coupon security would thus equal its maturity because all the cash flows—all the weights—are at the other end of the seesaw. The greater the duration of a bond, the greater its percentage volatility. In general, duration rises with maturity, falls with the frequency of coupon payments, and falls as the yield rises (the higher yield reduces the present values of the cash flows.) Duration (the term *modified duration* is used in the strict sense because of modifications to Macaulay's formulation) as a measure of percentage of volatility is valid only for small changes in yield. For working purposes, duration can be defined as the approximate percentage change in price for a 100-basis-point change in yield. A duration of 5, for example, means the price of the bond will change by approximately 5% for a 100-basis point change in yield.

For larger yield changes, volatility is measured by a concept called *convexity*. That term derives from the price-yield curve for a normal bond, which is convex. In other words, the price is always falling at a slower rate as the yield increases. The more convexity a bond has, the merrier, because it means the bond's price will fall more slowly and rise more quickly on a given movement in general interest rate levels. As with duration, convexity on straight bonds increases with lower coupon, lower yield, and longer maturity. Convexity measures the rate of change of duration, and for an option-free bond it is always positive because changes in yield do not affect cash flows. When a bond has a call option, however, cash flows are affected. In that case, duration gets smaller as yield decreases, resulting in *negative convexity.*

When the durations of the assets and the liabilities of a portfolio, say that of a pension fund, are the same, the portfolio is inherently protected against interest-rate changes and you have what is called *immunization*. The high volatility and interest rates in the early 1980s caused institutional investors to use duration and convexity as tools in immunizing their portfolios.

DUTCH AUCTION auction system in which the price of an item is gradually lowered until it meets a responsive bid and is sold. U.S. Treasury bills are sold under this system. Contrasting is the two-sided or DOUBLE AUCTION SYSTEM exemplified by the major stock exchanges. *See also* BILL.

DUTCH AUCTION PREFERRED STOCK type of adjustable-rate PREFERRED STOCK whose dividend is determined every seven weeks in a DUTCH AUCTION process by corporate bidders. Shares are bought and sold at FACE VALUES ranging from $100,000 to $500,000 per share. Also known as *auction rate preferred stock, Money Market Preferred Stock* (Lehman Brothers Inc.), and by such proprietary acronyms as DARTS (Salomon Smith Barney Inc.). *See also* AMPS; APS.

DUTY tax imposed on the importation, exportation, or consumption of goods. *See also* TARIFF.

DWARFS pools of mortgage-backed securities, with original maturity of 15 years, issued by the Federal National Mortgage Association (FAN-NIE MAE).

E

EACH WAY commission made by a broker involved on both the purchase and the sale side of a trade. *See also* CROSSED TRADE.

EAFE acronym for the *Europe and Australasia, Far East Equity* index, calculated by the Morgan Stanley Capital International (MSCI) group. EAFE is composed of stocks screened for liquidity, cross-ownership, and industry representation. Stocks are selected by MSCI's analysts in Geneva. The index acts as a benchmark for managers of international stock portfolios. There are financial futures and options contracts based on EAFE.

EARLY WITHDRAWAL PENALTY charge assessed against holders of fixed-term investments if they withdraw their money before maturity. Such a penalty would be assessed, for instance, if someone who has a six-month certificate of deposit withdrew the money after four months.

EARNED INCOME income (especially wages and salaries) generated by providing goods or services. Also, pension or annuity income.

EARNED INCOME CREDIT TAX CREDIT for qualifying taxpayers with at least one child in residence for more than half the year and incomes below a specified dollar level.

EARNED SURPLUS *see* RETAINED EARNINGS.

EARNEST MONEY good faith deposit given by a buyer to a seller prior to consummation of a transaction. Earnest money is usually forfeited in the event the buyer is unwilling or unable to complete the sale. In real estate, earnest money is the down payment, which is usually put in an escrow account until the closing.

EARNING ASSET income-producing asset. For example, a company's building would not be an earning asset normally, but a financial investment in other property would be if it provided rental income.

EARNINGS BEFORE TAXES corporate profits after interest has been paid to bondholders, but before taxes have been paid.

EARNINGS MOMENTUM pattern of increasing rate of growth in EARNINGS PER SHARE from one period to another, which usually causes a stock price to go up. For example, a company whose earnings per share are up 15% one year and 35% the next has earnings momentum and should see a gain in its stock price.

EARNINGS PER SHARE portion of a company's profit allocated to each outstanding share of common stock. For instance, a corporation that earned $10 million last year and has 10 million shares outstanding would report earnings of $1 per share. The figure is calculated after paying taxes and after paying preferred shareholders and bond-holders. Under new accounting rules adopted in 1998, companies must report earnings per share on two bases: BASIC EARNINGS PER SHARE which doesn't count stock options, warrants, and convertible securities, and (fully) *diluted earnings per share,* which includes those securities. *See also* FULLY DILUTED EARNINGS PER (COMMON) SHARE.

EARNINGS-PRICE RATIO relationship of earnings per share to current stock price. Also known as *earnings yield,* it is used in comparing the relative attractiveness of stocks, bonds, and money market instruments. Inverse of PRICE-EARNINGS RATIO.

EARNINGS REPORT statement issued by a company to its shareholders and the public at large reporting its earnings for the latest period, which is either on a quarterly or annual basis. The report will show revenues, expenses, and net profit for the period. Earnings reports are released to the press and reported in newspapers and electronic media, and are also mailed to shareholders of record. Also called *profit and loss statement* (P&L) or *income statement.*

EARNINGS SURPRISE EARNINGS REPORT that reports a higher or lower profit than analysts have projected. If earnings are higher than expected, a company's stock price will usually rise sharply. If profits are below expectations, the company's stock will often plunge. Many analysts on Wall Street study earnings surprises very carefully on the theory that when a company reports a positive or negative surprise, it is typically followed by another surprise in the same direction. Three firms that follow general trends in earnings surprises are FIRST CALL; I/B/E/S INTERNATIONAL INC; and ZACKS ESTIMATE SYSTEM.

EARNINGS YIELD *see* EARNINGS-PRICE RATIO.

EARN-OUT in mergers and acquisitions, supplementary payments, not part of the original ACQUISITION COST, based on future earnings of the acquired company above a predetermined level.

EASY MONEY *see* TIGHT MONEY.

EATING SOMEONE'S LUNCH expression that an aggressive competitor is beating their rivals. For example, an analyst might say that one retailer is "eating the lunch" of a competitive retailer in the same town if it is gaining market share through an aggressive pricing strategy. The implication of the expression is that the winning competitor is taking food away from the losing company or individual.

EATING STOCK a block positioner or underwriter who can't find buyers may find himself eating stock, that is, buying it for his own account.

ECM *see* EMERGING COMPANY MARKETPLACE (ECM).

ECONOMETRICS use of computer analysis and modeling techniques to describe in mathematical terms the relationship between key economic forces such as labor, capital, interest rates, and government policies, then test the effects of changes in economic scenarios. For instance, an econometric model might show the relationship of housing starts and interest rates.

ECONOMIC GROWTH RATE rate of change in the GROSS NATIONAL PRODUCT, as expressed in an annual percentage. If adjusted for inflation, it is called the *real economic growth rate.* Two consecutive quarterly drops in the growth rate mean recession, and two consecutive advances in the growth rate reflect an expanding economy.

ECONOMIC INDICATORS key statistics showing the direction of the economy. Among them are the unemployment rate, inflation rate, factory utilization rate, and balance of trade. *See also* LEADING INDICATORS.

ECONOMIC RECOVERY TAX ACT OF 1981 (ERTA) tax-cutting legislation. Among the key provisions:
1. across-the-board tax cut, which took effect in three stages ending in 1983.
2. indexing of tax brackets to the inflation rate.
3. lowering of top tax rates on long-term capital gains from 28% to 20%. The top rate on dividends, interest, rents, and royalties income dropped from 70% to 50%.
4. lowering of MARRIAGE PENALTY tax, as families with two working spouses could deduct 10% from the salary of the lower-paid spouse, up to $3000.
5. expansion of INDIVIDUAL RETIREMENT ACCOUNTS to all working people, who can contribute up to $2000 a year, and $250 annually for nonworking spouses. Also, expansion of the amount self-employed people can contribute to KEOGH PLAN account contributions.
6. creation of the *all-savers certificate,* which allowed investors to exempt up to $1000 a year in earned interest. The authority to issue these certificates expired at the end of 1982.
7. deductions for reinvesting public utility dividends.
8. reductions in estate and gift taxes, phased in so that the first $600,000 of property can be given free of estate tax starting in 1987. Annual gifts that can be given free of gift tax were raised from $3000 to $10,000. Unlimited deduction for transfer of property to a spouse at death.
9. lowering of rates on the exercise of stock options.
10. change in rules on DEPRECIATION and INVESTMENT CREDIT.
    See also TAX REFORM ACT OF 1986.

ECONOMICS study of the economy. Classic economics concentrates on how the forces of supply and demand allocate scarce product and service resources. MACROECONOMICS studies a nation or the world's economy as a whole, using data about inflation, unemployment and industrial production to understand the past and predict the future. MICROECONOMICS studies the behavior of specific sectors of the economy, such as companies, industries, or households. Over the years, various schools of economic thought have gained prominence, including KEYNESIAN ECONOMICS, MONETARISM and SUPPLY-SIDE ECONOMICS.

ECONOMIES OF SCALE economic principle that as the volume of production increases, the cost of producing each unit decreases. Therefore, building a large factory will be more efficient than a small factory because the large factory will be able to produce more units at a lower cost per unit than the smaller factory. The introduction of mass production techniques in the early twentieth century, such as the assembly line production of Ford Motor Company's Model T, put the theory of economies of scale into action.

ECU *see* EUROPEAN CURRENCY UNIT (ECU).

EDGE ACT banking legislation, passed in 1919, which allows national banks to conduct foreign lending operations through federal or state chartered subsidiaries, called Edge Act corporations. Such corporations can be chartered by other states and are allowed, unlike domestic banks, to own banks in foreign countries and to invest in foreign commercial and industrial firms. The act also permitted the FEDERAL RESERVE SYSTEM to set reserve requirements on foreign banks that do business in America. Edge Act corporations benefited further from the 1978 International Banking Act, which instructs the Fed to strike any regulations putting American banks at a disadvantage compared with U.S. operations of foreign banks.

EDUCATION IRA form of INDIVIDUAL RETIREMENT ACCOUNT created in the TAXPAYER RELIEF ACT OF 1997 allowing parents to contribute up to $500 per year for each child up to the age of 18. This $500 limit is reduced for married couples filing jointly with ADJUSTED GROSS INCOMES between $150,000 and $160,000, or singles reporting incomes between $95,000 and $110,000. Couples with incomes over $160,000 and singles with incomes over $110,000 may not contribute to Education IRAs. Contributions to Education IRAs do not generate tax deductions. However, assets inside the Education IRA grow tax-free and principal and earnings can be withdrawn tax-free as long as the proceeds are used to pay for education expenses at a postsecondary school, including tuition, fees, books, supplies and room and board. In a family with two or more children, Education IRA money not used by the first child can be used by the second or subsequent children if the first child does not attend college. The assets in the Education IRA must be spent on education before the child reaches age 30. If the assets are not used for college expenses, the account must be liquidated and taxes paid on the proceeds at regular income tax rates.

Money inside Education IRAs can be invested in stocks, bonds, mutual funds and other investments suitable for regular IRAs.

EEC *see* EUROPEAN ECONOMIC COMMUNITY.

EFFECTIVE DATE

In general: date on which an agreement takes effect.

Securities: date when an offering registered with the Securities and Exchange Commission may commence, usually 20 days after filing the registration statement. *See also* SHELF REGISTRATION.

Banking and insurance: time when an insurance policy goes into effect. From that day forward, the insured party is covered by the contract.

EFFECTIVE DEBT total debt owed by a firm, including the capitalized value of lease payments.

EFFECTIVE NET WORTH net worth plus subordinated debt, as viewed by senior creditors. In small business banking, loans payable to principals are commonly subordinated to bank loans. The loans for principals thus can be regarded as effective net worth as long as a bank loan is outstanding and the subordination agreement is in effect.

EFFECTIVE RATE yield on a debt instrument as calculated from the purchase price. The effective rate on a bond is determined by the price, the coupon rate, the time between interest payments, and the time until maturity. Every bond's effective rate thus depends on when it was bought. The effective rate is a more meaningful yield figure than the coupon rate. *See also* RATE OF RETURN.

EFFECTIVE SALE price of a ROUND LOT that determines the price at which the next ODD LOT will be sold. If the last round-lot price was 15, for instance, the odd-lot price might be 15⅛. The added fraction is the *odd-lot differential.*

EFFECTIVE TAX RATE tax rate paid by a taxpayer. It is determined by dividing the tax paid by the taxable income in a particular year. For example, if a taxpayer with a taxable income of $100,000 owes $30,000 in a year, he has an effective tax rate of 30%. The effective tax rate is useful in tax planning, because it gives a taxpayer a realistic understanding of the amount of taxes he is paying after allowing for all deductions, credits, and other factors affecting tax liability.

EFFICIENT MARKET theory that market prices reflect the knowledge and expectations of all investors. Those who adhere to this theory consider it futile to seek undervalued stocks or to forecast market movements. Any new development is reflected in a firm's stock price, they say, making it impossible to beat the market. This vociferously disputed hypothesis also holds that an investor who throws darts at a newspaper's stock listings has as good a chance to outperform the market as any professional investor.

EFFICIENT PORTFOLIO portfolio that has a maximum expected return for any level of risk or a minimum level of risk for any expected return. It is arrived at mathematically, taking into account the expected return and standard deviation of returns for each security, as well as the covariance of returns between different securities in the portfolio.

EITHER-OR ORDER *see* ALTERNATIVE ORDER.

ELASTICITY OF DEMAND AND SUPPLY
Elasticity of demand: responsiveness of buyers to changes in price. Demand for luxury items may slow dramatically if prices are raised, because these purchases are not essential, and can be postponed. On the other hand, demand for necessities such as food, telephone service, and emergency surgery is said to be inelastic. It remains about the same despite price changes because buyers cannot postpone their purchases without severe adverse consequences.
Elasticity of supply: responsiveness of output to changes in price. As prices move up, the supply normally increases. If it does not, it is said to be inelastic. Supply is said to be elastic if the rise in price means a rise in production.

ELECT
In general: choose a course of action. Someone who decides to incorporate a certain provision in a will elects to do so.
Securities trading: make a conditional order into a market order. If a customer has received a guaranteed buy or sell price from a specialist on the floor of an exchange, the transaction is considered elected when that price is reached. If the guarantee is that a stock will be sold when it reaches 20, and a stop order is put at that price, the sale will be elected at 20.

ELEPHANTS expression describing large institutional investors. The term implies that such investors, including mutual funds, pension funds, banks, and insurance companies, tend to move their billions of dollars in assets in a herd-like manner, driving stock and bond prices up and down in concert. CONTRARIAN investors specialize in doing the opposite of the elephants—buying when institutions are selling and selling when the elephants are buying. The opposite of elephants are SMALL INVESTORS, who buy and sell far smaller quantities of stocks and bonds.

ELEVEN BOND INDEX average yield on a particular day of 11 selected general obligation municipal bonds with an average AA rating, maturing in 20 years. It is comprised of 11 of the 20 bonds in the Twenty Bond Index, also referred to as the BOND BUYER'S MUNICIPAL BOND INDEX, published by the *BOND BUYER* and used as a benchmark in tracking municipal bond yields.

ELIGIBLE PAPER commercial and agricultural paper, drafts, bills of exchange, banker's acceptances, and other negotiable instruments that were acquired by a bank at a discount and that the Federal Reserve Bank will accept for rediscount.

ELIGIBILITY REQUIREMENTS

Insurance: requirements by an insurance company to qualify for coverage. For example, a life insurance company may require that because of a person's health condition, a potential policyholder would need to pay a higher premium to obtain coverage. In this circumstance, the policyholder's ability to pay becomes a primary issue.

For employer group health insurance coverage, an employer may require a person be a full-time employee for coverage of the employee and the employee's dependents.

Pensions: conditions an employee must satisfy to become a participant in a pension plan, such as completing one year of service and reaching the age of 21. Federal pension laws allow plan participants to become VESTED after five years of service. Alternatively, some companies implement a graduated vesting schedule. Public pension plans sponsored by federal, state, and local governments have their own eligibility requirements.

ELVES ten technical analysts who predict the direction of stock prices over the next six months on the "Wall Street Week" television show on the Public Broadcasting System. If five or more analysts are bullish or bearish at one time, the Wall Street Week Elves Index is giving a signal to buy or sell.

EMANCIPATION freedom to assume certain legal responsibilities normally associated only with adults, said of a minor who is granted this freedom by a court. If both parents die in an accident, for instance, the 16-year-old eldest son may be emancipated by a judge to act as guardian for his younger brothers and sisters.

EMBARGO government prohibition against the shipment of certain goods to another country. An embargo is most common during wartime, but is sometimes applied for economic reasons as well. For instance, the Organization of Petroleum Exporting Countries placed an embargo on the shipment of oil to the West in the early 1970s to protest Israeli policies and to raise the price of petroleum.

EMERGENCY FUND cash reserve that is available to meet financial emergencies, such as large medical bills or unexpected auto or home repairs. Most financial planners advocate maintaining an emergency reserve of two to three months' salary in a liquid interest-bearing account such as a money market mutual fund or bank money market deposit account.

EMERGENCY HOME FINANCE ACT OF 1970 act creating the quasigovernmental Federal Home Loan Mortgage Corporation, also known as Freddie Mac, to stimulate the development of a secondary mortgage market. The act authorized Freddie Mac to package and sell

Federal Housing Administration- and Veterans Administration-guaranteed mortgage loans. More than half the home mortgages were subsequently packaged and sold to investors in the secondary market in the form of pass-through securities.

EMERGING COMPANY MARKETPLACE (ECM) discontinued service of the AMERICAN STOCK EXCHANGE that focused on the needs of small growth companies meeting special listing requirements. ECM provided matching of public orders, short sale protection, specialist oversight and support, and offered other services and programs designed to promote corporate visibility (through separate listings in newspaper stock tables, for example).

EMERGING MARKETS FREE (EMF) INDEX index developed by Morgan Stanley Capital International to follow stock markets in Mexico, Malaysia, Chile, Jordan, Thailand, the Philippines, and Argentina, countries selected because of their accessibility to foreign investors.

EMINENT DOMAIN right of a government entity to seize private property for the purpose of constructing a public facility. Federal, state, and local governments can seize people's homes under eminent domain laws as long as the homeowner is compensated at fair market value. Some public projects that may necessitate such CONDEMNATION include highways, hospitals, schools, parks, or government office buildings.

EMPLOYEE RETIREMENT INCOME SECURITY ACT (ERISA) 1974 law governing the operation of most private pension and benefit plans. The law eased pension eligibility rules, set up the PENSION BENEFIT GUARANTY CORPORATION, and established guidelines for the management of pension funds.

EMPLOYEE STOCK OWNERSHIP PLAN (ESOP) program encouraging employees to purchase stock in their company. Employees may participate in the management of the company and even take control to rescue the company or a particular plant that would otherwise go out of business. Employees may offer wage and work rule concessions in return for ownership privileges in an attempt to keep a marginal facility operating.

EMPTY HEAD AND PURE HEART TEST SEC Rule 14e-3, subparagraph (b), which, with strict exceptions, prohibits any party other than the bidder in a TENDER OFFER to trade in the stock while having INSIDE INFORMATION.

ENCUMBERED owned by one party but subject to another party's valid claim. A homeowner owns his mortgaged property, for example, but the bank has a security interest in it as long as the mortgage loan is outstanding.

ENDORSE transfer ownership of an asset by signing the back of a negotiable instrument. One can endorse a check to receive payment or endorse a stock or bond certificate to transfer ownership.

See also QUALIFIED ENDORSEMENT.

ENDOWMENT permanent gift of money or property to a specified institution for a specified purpose. Endowments may finance physical assets or be invested to provide ongoing income to finance operations.

ENERGY MUTUAL FUND mutual fund that invests solely in energy stocks such as oil, oil service, gas, solar energy, and coal companies and makers of energy-saving devices.

ENTERPRISE a business firm. The term often is applied to a newly formed venture.

ENTREPRENEUR person who takes on the risks of starting a new business. Many entrepreneurs have technical knowledge with which to produce a saleable product or to design a needed new service. Often, VENTURE CAPITAL is used to finance the startup in return for a piece of the equity. Once an entrepreneur's business is established, shares may be sold to the public as an INITIAL PUBLIC OFFERING, assuming favorable market conditions.

ENVIRONMENTAL FUND MUTUAL FUND specializing in stocks of companies having a role in the bettering of the environment. Not to be confused with a SOCIALLY CONSCIOUS MUTUAL FUND, which aims in part to satisfy social values, an environmental fund is designed to capitalize on financial opportunities related to the environmental movement.

EOM DATING arrangement—common in the wholesale drug industry, for example—whereby all purchases made through the 25th of one month are payable within 30 days of the end of the following month; EOM means *end of month.* Assuming no prompt payment discount, purchases through the 25th of April, for example, will be payable by the end of June. If a discount exists for payment in ten days, payment would have to be made by June 10th to take advantage of it. End of month dating with a 2% discount for prompt payment (10 days) would be expressed in the trade either as: *2%-10 days, EOM, 30,* or *2/10 prox. net 30,* where prox., or proximo, means "the next."

EPS *see* EARNINGS PER SHARE.

EQUAL CREDIT OPPORTUNITY ACT federal legislation passed in the mid-1970s prohibiting discrimination in granting credit, based on race, religion, sex, ethnic background, or whether a person is receiving public assistance or alimony. The Federal Trade Commission enforces the act.

EQUALIZING DIVIDEND special dividend paid to compensate investors for income lost because a change was made in the quarterly dividend payment schedule.

EQUILIBRIUM PRICE
1. price when the supply of goods in a particular market matches demand.
2. for a manufacturer, the price that maximizes a product's profitability.

EQUILIBRIUM PRICE

EQUIPMENT LEASING PARTNERSHIP limited partnership that buys equipment such as computers, railroad cars, and airplanes, then leases it to businesses. Limited partners receive income from the lease payments as well as tax benefits such as depreciation. Whether a partnership of this kind works out well depends on the GENERAL PARTNER'S expertise. Failure to lease the equipment can be disastrous, as happened with railroad hopper cars in the mid-1970s.

EQUIPMENT TRUST CERTIFICATE bond, usually issued by a transportation company such as a railroad or shipping line, used to pay for new equipment. The certificate gives the bondholder the first right to the equipment in the event that interest and principal are not paid when due. Title to the equipment is held in the name of the trustee, usually a bank, until the bond is paid off.

EQUITABLE OWNER beneficiary of property held in trust.

EQUITY
In general: fairness. Law courts, for example, try to be equitable in their judgments when splitting up estates or settling divorce cases.
Banking: difference between the amount a property could be sold for and the claims held against it.
Brokerage account: excess of securities over debit balance in a margin account. For instance, equity would be $28,000 in a margin

account with stocks and bonds worth $50,000 and a debit balance of
$22,000.

Investments: ownership interest possessed by shareholders in a corporation—stock as opposed to bonds.

EQUITY CMO *see* CMO REIT.

EQUITY COMMITMENT NOTES *see* MANDATORY CONVERTIBLES.

EQUITY CONTRACT NOTES *see* MANDATORY CONVERTIBLES.

EQUITY FINANCING raising money by issuing shares of common or
preferred stock. Usually done when prices are high and the most capital can be raised for the smallest number of shares.

EQUITY FUNDING type of investment combining a life insurance policy and a mutual fund. The fund shares are used as collateral for a loan
to pay the insurance premiums, giving the investor the advantages of
insurance protection and investment appreciation potential.

EQUITY KICKER offer of an ownership position in a deal that
involves loans. For instance, a mortgage real estate limited partnership
that lends to real estate developers might receive as an equity kicker a
small ownership position in a building that can appreciate over time.
When the building is sold, limited partners receive the appreciation
payout. In return for that equity kicker, the lender is likely to charge a
lower interest rate on the loan. Convertible features and warrants are
offered as equity kickers to make securities attractive to investors.

EQUITY REIT REAL ESTATE INVESTMENT TRUST that takes an ownership
position in the real estate it invests in. Stockholders in equity REITs
earn dividends on rental income from the buildings and earn appreciation if properties are sold for a profit. The opposite is a MORTGAGE
REIT.

EQUIVALENT BOND YIELD comparison of discount yields and
yields on bonds with coupons. Also called *coupon-equivalent rate.* For
instance, if a 10%, 90-day Treasury bill with a face value of $10,000
cost $9750, the equivalent bond yield would be:

$$\frac{\$250}{\$9750} \quad \times \quad \frac{365}{90} \quad = \quad 10.40\%$$

EQUIVALENT TAXABLE YIELD comparison of the taxable yield on
a corporate or government bond and the tax-free yield on a municipal
bond. Depending on the tax bracket, an investor's aftertax return may
be greater with a municipal bond than with a corporate or government
bond offering a highest interest rate. For someone in a 31% federal tax
bracket, for instance, a 7% municipal bond would have an equivalent
taxable yield of 10.4%. An investor living in a state that levies state
income tax should add in the state tax bracket to get a true measure of

the equivalent taxable yield. *See* YIELD EQUIVALENCE for method of calculation.

ERISA *see* EMPLOYEE RETIREMENT INCOME SECURITY ACT.

ERM acronym for *exchange rate mechanism,* by which participating member countries agree to maintain the value of their own currencies through intervention.

ERTA *see* ECONOMIC RECOVERY TAX ACT OF 1981.

ESCALATOR CLAUSE provision in a contract allowing cost increases to be passed on. In an employment contract, an escalator clause might call for wage increases to keep employee earnings in line with inflation. In a lease, an escalator clause could obligate the tenant to pay for increases in fuel or other costs.

ESCHEAT return of property (for example, land, bank balances, insurance policies) to the state if abandoned or left by a person who died without making a will. If rightful owners or heirs later appear, they can claim the property.

ESCROW money, securities, or other property or instruments held by a third party until the conditions of a contract are met.

ESCROWED TO MATURITY (ETM) holding proceeds from a new bond issue in a separate escrow account to pay off an existing bond issue when it matures. Bond issuers will implement an ADVANCE REFUNDING when interest rates have fallen significantly, making it advantageous to pay off the existing issue before scheduled maturity at the first CALL DATE. The funds raised by the refunding are invested in government securities in the escrow account until the principal is used to prepay the original bond issue at the first call date. The escrowed funds may also pay some of the interest on the original issue up until the bonds are redeemed.

ESCROW RECEIPT in options trading, a document provided by a bank to guarantee that the UNDERLYING SECURITY is on deposit and available for potential delivery.

ESSENTIAL PURPOSE (or FUNCTION) BOND *see* PUBLIC PURPOSE BOND.

ESTATE all the assets a person possesses at the time of death—such as securities, real estate, interests in business, physical possessions, and cash. The estate is distributed to heirs according to the dictates of the person's will or, if there is no will, a court ruling.

ESTATE PLANNING planning for the orderly handling, disposition, and administration of an estate when the owner dies. Estate planning includes drawing up a will, setting up trusts, and minimizing estate taxes, perhaps by passing property to heirs before death or by setting up a BYPASS TRUST or a TESTAMENTARY TRUST.

ESTATE TAX tax imposed by a state or the federal government on assets left to heirs. Under the ECONOMIC RECOVERY TAX ACT OF 1981, there is no estate tax on transfers of property between spouses, an action known as the MARITAL DEDUCTION. According to the TAXPAYER RELIEF ACT OF 1997, the amount of assets that each person can exclude from federal estate taxes is $625,000 in 1998, rising to $1 million in 2006 and later years. This limit rises to $650,000 in 1999, $675,000 in 2000 and 2001, $700,000 in 2002 and 2003, $850,000 in 2004, $950,000 in 2005 and $1 million in 2006. The law created a special $1.3 million limit for qualifying farmers and small business owners starting January 1, 1998. Any assets passed to beneficiaries over these limits that are not protected by TRUSTS are assessed estate taxes at rates as high as 55%. Many states impose their own estate taxes on top of the federal levies. Careful ESTATE PLANNING, involving the writing of a will and the establishment of trusts, is essential for those wishing to minimize estate taxes.

ESTIMATED TAX amount of estimated tax for the coming year, minus tax credits, based on the higher of regular or ALTERNATIVE MINIMUM TAX (AMT). Corporations, estates and trusts, self-employed persons, and persons for whom less than a fixed percentage of income is withheld by employers must compute estimated tax and make quarterly tax payments to the IRS and state tax authorities, if required. Generally, a taxpayer must pay at least 90% of his or her total tax liability for the year in withholding and/or quarterly estimated tax payments. Alternatively, taxpayers may base their current year's estimated tax on the prior year's income tax. For taxpayers with adjusted gross income (AGI) in the prior tax year of $150,000 or less, estimated taxes must equal 100% of the prior year's tax. For those reporting AGI of more than $150,000, the current year's estimated taxes must be based on 110% of the prior year's tax liability. Thus, for someone reporting an AGI of more than $150,000 who paid $50,000 in taxes in the prior year, estimated taxes of at least $55,000 will be due in the current tax year. Severe penalties are imposed by the IRS and state tax authorities for underpayment of estimated taxes.

ETHICAL FUND *see* SOCIAL CONSCIOUSNESS MUTUAL FUND.

EUREX German-Swiss electronic derivatives exchange. *See* DEUTSCHE TERMINBORSE (DTB); SWISS OPTIONS AND FINANCIAL FUTURES EXCHANGE (SOFFEX).

EURO common currency adopted by 11 European nations starting January 1, 1999. The 11 countries are: Austria, Belgium, Finland, France, Germany, Ireland, Italy, Luxembourg, the Netherlands, Portugal and Spain. On that date, the conversion rates of the participating currencies are irrevocably fixed, both among themselves and against the Euro. At first, the Euro will be used in financial markets by companies and governments issuing bonds. Credit cards will also be denominated in Euros. Starting January 1, 2002, the Euro will begin to replace all national currencies as Euro notes and coins are put into circulation. By July 1, 2002, all national notes and coins will be withdrawn from circulation. Euro notes will be issued in denominations of 5, 10, 20, 50, 100, 200 and 500 Euro. There will be eight different coins ranging from one cent (one hundredth of a Euro) to 2 Euro. The Euro replaced the ECU (European Currency Unit) on January 1, 1999.

The EUROPEAN CENTRAL BANK, based in Brussels, started conducting monetary policy for participating European countries starting on January 1, 1999. The bank's role is to protect the value of the Euro and foster economic growth with low inflation. The bank will conduct monetary and foreign-exchange operations in Euros, issue Euro notes and coins, and withdraw national currency from circulation.

The common currency was adopted by the Treaty on European Union, signed in Maastricht, the Netherlands in February, 1992 and ratified on behalf of the people by the parliaments of the member states. In some countries, there were direct popular referendums endorsing the single currency. The economic rationale behind the move was that a single, stable currency should make it easier to create a single market for trade among the European states, and between Europe and the rest of the world. The introduction of the Euro is designed to help companies cut their costs because they will not have the expense of conducting business in several currencies. Only Denmark and the United Kingdom opted not to use the Euro as their currencies.

In order for a country to use the Euro, it must meet a series of economic conditions, known as the convergence criteria:

• Its government deficit must equal 3% of its GDP or less, with government debt below the reference value of 60% of GDP.
• Inflation cannot exceed by more than 1.5 percentage points the rate of the 3 best performing countries.
• The country's currency must have remained within the normal fluctuation margins of the European Monetary System (EMS) for at least two years.
• The country's long-term interest rates should not exceed by more than 2 percentage points the average of the three countries with the lowest inflation rates in the European Union.

The 11 countries that will use the Euro met these conditions, as certified by the European Commission in March 1998. These 11 countries will become known as "Euroland."

EUROBOND bond denominated in U.S. dollars or other currencies and sold to investors outside the country whose currency is used. The bonds are usually issued by large underwriting groups composed of banks and issuing houses from many countries. An example of a Eurobond transaction might be a dollar-denominated debenture issued by a Belgian corporation through an underwriting group comprised of the overseas affiliate of a New York investment banking house, a bank in Holland, and a consortium of British merchant banks; a portion of the issue is sold to French investors through Swiss investment accounts. The Eurobond market is an important source of capital for multinational companies and foreign governments, including Third World governments.

EUROCURRENCY money deposited by corporations and national governments in banks away from their home countries, called *Eurobanks*. The terms Eurocurrency and Eurobanks do not necessarily mean the currencies or the banks are European, though more often than not, that is the case. For instance, dollars deposited in a British bank or Italian lire deposited in a Japanese bank are considered to be Eurocurrency. The Eurodollar is only one of the Eurocurrencies, though it is the most prevalent. Also known as *Euromoney*.

EURODOLLAR U.S. currency held in banks outside the United States, mainly in Europe, and commonly used for settling international transactions. Some securities are issued in Eurodollars—that is, with a promise to pay interest in dollars deposited in foreign bank accounts.

EURODOLLAR BOND bond that pays interest and principal in Eurodollars, U.S. dollars held in banks outside the United States, primarily in Europe. Such a bond is not registered with the Securities and Exchange Commission, and because there are fewer regulatory delays and costs in the Euromarket, Eurodollar bonds generally can be sold at lower than U.S. interest rates. *See also* EUROBOND.

EURODOLLAR CERTIFICATE OF DEPOSIT CDs issued by banks outside the United States, primarily in Europe, with interest and principal paid in dollars. Such CDs usually have minimum denominations of $100,000 and short-term maturities of less than two years. The interest rate on these CDs is usually pegged to the LONDON INTERBANK OFFERED RATE (LIBOR).

EURO.NM a pan-European network of regulated markets dedicated to growth companies. Formed March 1, 1996, members of this umbrella market include the PARIS BOURSE (LE NOUVEAU MARCHE), DEUTSCHE BORSE AG (Neuer Markt), AMSTERDAM EXCHANGES (NMAX) and the BRUSSELS STOCK EXCHANGE (EURO.NM Belgium). The network has hundreds of listings, many of them dually listed on other exchanges such as NASDAQ, the TORONTO STOCK EXCHANGE, and the SWISS ELECTRONIC BOURSE (EBS). The official EURO.NM All-Share Index represents the markets. NASDAQ is the model for EURO.NM, whose objective is to develop a fully integrated, pan-European network of high-growth stock markets providing single points of access for market information and trading across. Convergent regulatory and operational standards have been adopted. EURO.NM provides cross-membership between its markets, and members are linking their existing systems to form a common electronic system for trading and market information.

EUROPEAN CENTRAL BANK (ECB) bank founded to oversee monetary policy for the 11 countries that convert their local currencies into the EURO on January 1, 1999. The 11 countries are: Austria, Belgium, Finland, France, Germany, Ireland, Italy, Luxembourg, the Netherlands, Portugal, and Spain. Based in Brussels, Belgium, the bank's primary mission is to maintain price stability and issue Euro currency. It replaces the Frankfurt-based European Monetary Institute (EMI), which was established in 1994 to prepare the way for a single currency. The economic and monetary policy of Europe is set by the EU Council of Economics and Finance Ministers (known as the Ecofin Council). The European Central Bank's mission is to implement that policy. The bank is run by a Governing Council, which is composed of members of the Executive Board and the Governors of National Central Banks. The Executive Board consists of a president, vice president, and four other members appointed for a non-renewable term of up to 8 years.

The Governing Council formulates monetary policy, decisions relating to monetary objectives, key interest rates, and the supply of reserves in the European System of Central Banks (ESCB). The Executive Board implements the policy by instructing the National Central Banks. The National Central Banks will not disappear, but will form, along with the European Central Bank, the ESCB. The ESCB will implement the common European monetary policy, conduct foreign exchange operations, and manage foreign reserves of the member states.

EUROPEAN COMMUNITY (EC) with ratification of the Maastricht Treaty on European Union in November 1993, the former name of European Economic Community was dropped. The EC is part of the EUROPEAN UNION. The EC is an economic and, increasingly, political alliance formed in 1957 by Germany, France, Belgium, Luxembourg, the Netherlands and Italy to foster trade and cooperation among its members and "an ever closer union among the peoples of Europe." Membership was subsequently extended to the UK, Ireland and Denmark (1973); Greece (1981); and Spain and Portugal (1986). Austria, Finland, and Sweden became members in 1995. Norway rejected membership in November 1994. Tariff barriers between the member states have been abolished, and import duties vis-a-vis non-EC countries have been standardized. Many former European dependencies in African, Caribbean, and Pacific countries have preferential trade terms with the EC through the Rome Convention. EC headquarters is in Brussels, administered by the European Commission, the executive arm of the European Union. By December 1992, most remaining non-tariff trade barriers between the member states had been eliminated, and common standards in many industries had been adopted. Also known as the *European Union,* of which it is a part and, anachronistically, the *Common Market.*

EUROPEAN CURRENCY UNIT (ECU) one of two international currency substitutes ("artificial currencies"), the other being the SPECIAL DRAWING RIGHTS (SDRs) of the INTERNATIONAL MONETARY FUND (IMF). Like the SDR, the ECU is a currency basket comprised of a predetermined amount of a number of different currencies. Whereas SDRs represent five currencies, ECUs include all the EUROPEAN ECONOMIC COMMUNITY (EEC) currencies except the Spanish peseta and the

Portuguese escudo. Currency substitutes are less volatile than the currencies making them up and are expected to be used increasingly for commercial purposes as the European Community develops.

EUROPEAN OPTIONS EXCHANGE (EOE) the Dutch derivatives exchange merged in 1996 with the Amsterdam Stock Exchange to form the Amsterdam Exchanges. *See also* AMSTERDAM EXCHANGES (AEX).

EUROPEAN-STYLE EXERCISE system of exercising options contracts in which the option buyer can exercise the contract only on the last business day prior to expiration (normally Friday). This system is widely used with index options traded on various U.S. exchanges.

EUROPEAN UNION (EU) umbrella term referring to a "three-pillar" construction comprising the EUROPEAN COMMUNITY (EC) and two new pillars: Common Foreign and Security Policy (including defense) and Justice and Home Affairs (notably cooperation between police and other authorities on crime, terrorism, and immigration issues). The EU is governed by a five-part institutional system, including the European Commission, the EU Council of Ministers, the European Parliament and the European Court of Justice, and the Court of Auditors, which monitors EU budget spending. Under the Maastricht Treaty on European Union of Nov. 1, 1993, the directly elected Parliament gained co-decision powers with the Council and Commission.

EUROYEN BOND EUROCURRENCY deposits in Japanese yen.

EVALUATOR independent expert who appraises the value of property for which there is limited trading—antiques in an estate, perhaps, or rarely traded stocks or bonds. The fee for this service is sometimes a flat amount, sometimes a percentage of the appraised value.

EVENT RISK risk that a bond will suddenly decline in credit quality and warrant a lower RATING because of a TAKEOVER-related development, such as additional debt or a RECAPITALIZATION. Corporations whose INDENTURES include protective COVENANTS, such as POISON PUT provisions, are assigned *Event Risk Covenant Rankings* by Standard & Poor's Corporation. Ratings range from E-1, the highest, to E-5 and supplement basic bond ratings.

EVERGREEN FUNDING similar to DRIP FEED, British term for the gradual infusion of capital into a new or recapitalized enterprise. In the United States, banks use the term *evergreen* to describe short-term loans that are continuously renewed rather than repaid.

EXACT INTEREST interest paid by a bank or other financial institution and calculated on a 365-days-per-year basis, as opposed to a 360-day basis, called ordinary interest. The difference—the ratio is 1.0139—can be material when calculating daily interest on large sums of money.

EX-ALL sale of a security without dividends, rights, warrants, or any other privileges associated with that security.

EXCESS MARGIN equity in a brokerage firm's customer account, expressed in dollars, above the legal minimum for a margin account or the maintenance requirement. For instance, with a margin requirement of $25,000, as set by REGULATION T and a maintenance requirement of $12,500 set by the stock exchange, the client whose equity is $100,000 would have excess margin of $75,000 and $87,500 in terms of the initial and maintenance requirements, respectively.

EXCESS PROFITS TAX extra federal taxes placed on the earnings of a business. Such taxes may be levied during a time of national emergency, such as in wartime, and are designed to increase national revenue. The excess profits tax differs from the WINDFALL PROFITS TAX, designed to prevent excessive corporate profits in special circumstances.

EXCESS RESERVES money a bank holds over and above the RESERVE REQUIREMENT. The money may be on deposit with the Federal Reserve System or with an approved depository bank, or it may be in the bank's possession. For instance, a bank with a reserve requirement of $5 million might have $4 million on deposit with the Fed and $1.5 million in its vaults and as till cash. The $500,000 in excess reserves is available for loans to other banks or customers or for other corporate uses.

EXCHANGE
Barter: to trade goods and services with another individual or company for other goods and services of equal value.
Corporate finance: offer by a corporation to exchange one security for another. For example, a company may want holders of its convertible bonds to exchange their holdings for common stock. Or a company in financial distress may want its bondholders to exchange their bonds for stock in order to reduce or eliminate its debt load. *See also* SWAP.
Currency: trading of one currency for another. Also known as *foreign exchange.*
Mutual funds: process of switching from one mutual fund to another, either within one fund family or between fund families, if executed through a brokerage firm offering funds from several companies. In many cases, fund companies will not charge an additional LOAD if the assets are kept within the same family. If one fund is sold to buy another, a taxable event has occurred, meaning that capital gains or losses have been realized, unless the trade was executed within a tax-deferred account, such as an IRA or Keogh account.
Trading: central location where securities or futures trading takes place. The New York and American Stock Exchanges are the largest centralized place to trade stocks in the United States, for example. Futures exchanges in Chicago, Kansas City, New York, and elsewhere

facilitate the trading of futures contracts. *See also* SECURITIES AND COMMODITIES EXCHANGES.

EXCHANGEABLE DEBENTURE like CONVERTIBLES, with the exception that this type of debenture can be converted to the common stock of a SUBSIDIARY or AFFILIATE of the issuer.

EXCHANGE CONTROLS government regulation of foreign exchange (currency trading).

EXCHANGE DISTRIBUTION block trade carried out on the floor of an exchange between customers of a member firm. Someone who wants to sell a large block of stock in a single transaction can get a broker to solicit and bunch a large number of orders. The seller transmits the securities to the buyers all at once, and the trade is announced on the BROAD TAPE as an exchange distribution. The seller, not the buyers, pays a special commission to the broker who executes the trade.

EXCHANGE MEMBERS *see* MEMBER FIRM; SEAT.

EXCHANGE PRIVILEGE right of a shareholder to switch from one mutual fund to another within one fund family—often, at no additional charge. This enables investors to put their money in an aggressive growth-stock fund when they expect the market to turn up strongly, then switch to a money-market fund when they anticipate a downturn. Some discount brokers allow shareholders to switch between fund families in pursuit of the best performance.

EXCHANGE RATE price at which one country's currency can be converted into another's. The exchange rate between the U.S. dollar and the British pound is different from the rate between the dollar and the German mark, for example. A wide range of factors influences exchange rates, which generally change slightly each trading day. Some rates are fixed by agreement; *see* FIXED EXCHANGE RATE.

EXCHANGE STOCK PORTFOLIO (ESP) *see* BASKET.

EXCISE TAX federal or state tax on the sale or manufacture of a commodity, usually a luxury item. Examples: federal and state taxes on alcohol and tobacco.

EXCLUSION
Contracts: item not covered by a contract. For example, an insurance policy may list certain hazards, such as acts of war, that are excluded from coverage.
Taxes: on a tax return, items that must be reported, but not taxed. For example, corporations are allowed to exclude 70% of dividends received from other domestic corporations. Gift tax rules allow DONORS to exclude up to $10,000 worth of gifts to donees annually.

EXCLUSIVE LISTING written listing agreement giving an agent the right to sell a specific property for a period of time with a definite termination date, frequently three months. There are two types of exclusive listings. With the exclusive agency, the owner reserves the right to sell the property himself without owing a commission; the exclusive agent is entitled to a commission if he or she personally sells the property, or if it is sold by anyone other than the seller. Under the exclusive right to sell, a broker is appointed as exclusive agent, entitled to a commission if the property is sold by the owner, the broker, or anyone else. "Right to sell" means the right to find a buyer. Sellers opt for exclusive listings because they think an agent will give their property more attention. An agent with an exclusive listing will not have to share the commission with any other agent as they would under a multiple-listing arrangement. If the property is not sold within the specified time, the seller may expand the selling group through an open, multiple listing.

EX-DIVIDEND interval between the announcement and the payment of the next dividend. An investor who buys shares during that interval is not entitled to the dividend. Typically, a stock's price moves up by the dollar amount of the dividend as the ex-dividend date approaches, then falls by the amount of the dividend after that date. A stock that has gone ex-dividend is marked with an x in newspaper listings.

EX-DIVIDEND DATE date on which a stock goes EX-DIVIDEND, typically about three weeks before the dividend is paid to shareholders of record. Shares listed on the New York Stock Exchange go ex-dividend four business days before the RECORD DATE. This NYSE rule is generally followed by the other exchanges.

EXECUTION
Law: the signing, sealing, and delivering of a contract or agreement making it valid.
Securities: carrying out a trade. A broker who buys or sells shares is said to have executed an order.

EXECUTOR/EXECUTRIX administrator of the estate who gathers the estate assets; files the estate tax returns and final personal income tax returns, and administers the estate; pays the debts of and charges against the estate; and distributes the balance in accordance with the terms of the will. The executor's responsibility is relatively short term, one to three years, ending when estate administration is completed. An executor (executrix if a female) may be a bank trust officer, a lawyer, or a family member or trusted friend.

EXEMPTION IRS-allowed direct reductions from gross income. Personal and dependency exemptions are allowed for: individual taxpayers; elderly and disabled taxpayers; dependent children and other dependents more than half of whose support is provided; total or partial blindness; and a taxpayer's spouse.

EXEMPT SECURITIES stocks and bonds exempt from certain Securities and Exchange Commission and Federal Reserve Board rules. For instance, government and municipal bonds are exempt from SEC registration requirements and from Federal Reserve Board margin rules.

EXERCISE make use of a right available in a contract. In options trading a buyer of a call contract may exercise the right to buy underlying shares at a particular price by informing the option seller. A put buyer's right is exercised when the underlying shares are sold at the agreed-upon price.

EXERCISE LIMIT limit on the number of option contracts of any one class that can be exercised in a span of five business days. For options on stocks, the exercise limit is usually 2000 contracts.

EXERCISE NOTICE notification by a broker that a client wants to exercise a right to buy the underlying stock in an option contract. Such notice is transmitted to the option seller through the Options Clearing Corporation, which ensures that stock is delivered as agreed upon.

EXERCISE PRICE price at which the stock or commodity underlying a call or put option can be purchased (call) or sold (put) over the specified period. For instance, a call contract may allow the buyer to purchase 100 shares of XYZ at any time in the next three months at an exercise or STRIKE PRICE of $63.

EXHAUST PRICE price at which broker must liquidate a client's holding in a stock that was bought on margin and has declined, but has not had additional funds put up to meet the MARGIN CALL.

EXIMBANK *see* EXPORT-IMPORT BANK.

EXIT FEE *see* BACK-END LOAD.

EX-LEGAL municipal bond that does not have the legal opinion of a bond law firm printed on it, as most municipal bonds do. When such bonds are traded, buyers must be warned that legal opinion is lacking.

EXPECTED RETURN *see* MEAN RETURN.

EXPENSE RATIO amount, expressed as a percentage of total investment, that shareholders pay annually for mutual fund operating expenses and management fees. These expenses include shareholder service, salaries for money managers and administrative staff, and investor centers, among many others. The expense ratio, which may be as low as 0.2% or as high as 2% of shareholder assets, is taken out of the fund's current income and is disclosed in the prospectus to shareholders.

EXPERIENCE RATING insurance company technique to determine the correct price of a policy premium. The company analyzes past loss experience for others in the insured group to project future claims. The premium is then set at a rate high enough to cover those potential claims and still earn a profit for the insurance company. For example, life insurance companies charge higher premiums to smokers than to non-smokers because smokers' experience rating is higher, meaning their chance of dying is much higher.

EXPIRATION
Banking: date on which a contract or agreement ceases to be effective.
Options trading: last day on which an option can be exercised. If it is not, traders say that the option *expired worthless.*

EXPIRATION CYCLE cycle of expiration dates used in short-term options trading. For example, contracts may be written for one of three cycles: January, April, July, October; February, May, August, November; March, June, September, December. Since options are traded in three-, six-, and nine-month contracts, only three of the four months in the set are traded at once. In our example, when the January contract expires, trading begins on the October contract. Commodities futures expiration cycles follow other schedules.

EX-PIT TRANSACTION purchase of commodities off the floor of the exchange where they are regularly traded and at specified terms.

EXPLORATORY DRILLING PROGRAM search for an undiscovered reservoir of oil or gas—a very risky undertaking. Exploratory wells are called *wildcat* (in an unproven area); *controlled wildcat* (in an area outside the proven limits of an existing field); or *deep test* (within a proven field but to unproven depths). Exploratory drilling programs are usually syndicated, and units are sold to limited partners.

EXPORT-IMPORT BANK (EXIMBANK) bank set up by Congress in 1934 to encourage U.S. trade with foreign countries. Eximbank is an independent entity that borrows from the U.S. Treasury to (1) finance exports and imports; (2) grant direct credit to non-U.S. borrowers; (3) provide export guarantees, insurance against commercial and political risk, and discount loans.

EX-RIGHTS without the RIGHT to buy a company's stock at a discount from the prevailing market price, which was distributed until a particular date. Typically, after that date the rights trade separately from the stock itself. *See also* EX-WARRANTS.

EX-STOCK DIVIDENDS interval between the announcement and payment of a stock dividend. An investor who buys shares during that interval is not entitled to the announced stock dividend; instead, it goes to the seller of the shares, who was the owner on the last recorded date before the books were closed and the stock went EX-DIVIDEND. Stocks cease to be ex-dividend after the payment date.

EXTENDED COVERAGE insurance protection that is extended beyond the original term of the contract. For example, consumers can buy extended warranties when they purchase cars or appliances, which will cover repairs beyond the original warranty period.

EXTENSION OF TIME FOR FILING TAXES time period beyond the original tax filing date. For example, taxpayers who file Form 4868 may get an automatic extension of four months to file their tax returns with the IRS. Though the return will then be due on August 15, the estimated tax is still due on the original filing date of April 15.

EXTERNAL FUNDS funds brought in from outside the corporation, perhaps in the form of a bank loan, or the proceeds from a bond offering, or an infusion of cash from venture capitalists. External funds supplement internally generated CASH FLOW and are used for expansion, as well as for seasonal WORKING CAPITAL needs.

EXTRA DIVIDEND dividend paid to shareholders in addition to the regular dividend. Such a payment is made after a particularly profitable year in order to reward shareholders and engender loyalty.

EXTRAORDINARY CALL early redemption of a revenue bond by the issuer due to elimination of the source of revenue to pay the stipulated interest. For example, a mortgage revenue municipal bond may be subject to an extraordinary call if the issuer is unable to originate mortgages to homeowners because mortgage rates have dropped sharply, making the issuer's normally below-market mortgage interest rate suddenly higher than market rates. In this case, the bond issuer is required to return the money raised from the bond issue to bondholders because the issuer will not be able to realize the expected interest payments from mortgages. Extraordinary calls may also be necessary if another revenue-producing project such as a road or bridge is not able to be built for some reason. Calls are usually made at PAR. Also called a *special call.*

EXTRAORDINARY ITEM nonrecurring occurrence that must be explained to shareholders in an annual or quarterly report. Some examples: writeoff of a division, acquisition of another company, sale of a large amount of real estate, or uncovering of employee fraud that negatively affects the company's financial condition. Earnings are usually reported before and after taking into account the effects of extraordinary items.

EX-WARRANTS stock sold with the buyer no longer entitled to the WARRANT attached to the stock. Warrants allow the holder to buy stock at some future date at a specified price. Someone buying a stock on June 3 that had gone ex-warrants on June 1 would not receive those warrants. They would be the property of the stockholder of record on June 1.

F

FACE-AMOUNT CERTIFICATE debt security issued by face-amount certificate companies, one of three categories of mutual funds defined by the INVESTMENT COMPANY ACT OF 1940. The holder makes periodic payments to the issuer, and the issuer promises to pay the purchaser the face value at maturity or a surrender value if the certificate is presented prior to maturity.

FACE VALUE value of a bond, note, mortgage, or other security as given on the certificate or instrument. Corporate bonds are usually issued with $1000 face values, municipal bonds with $5000 face values, and federal government bonds with $10,000 face values. Although the bonds fluctuate in price from the time they are issued until redemption, they are redeemed at maturity at their face value, unless the issuer defaults. If the bonds are retired before maturity, bondholders normally receive a slight premium over face value. The face value is the amount on which interest payments are calculated. Thus, a 10% bond with a face value of $1000 pays bondholders $100 per year. Face value is also referred to as PAR VALUE or *nominal value.*

FACTORING type of financial service whereby a firm sells or transfers title to its accounts receivable to a factoring company, which then acts as principal, not as agent. The receivables are sold without recourse, meaning that the factor cannot turn to the seller in the event accounts prove uncollectible. Factoring can be done either on a *notification basis,* where the seller's customers remit directly to the factor, or on a *non-notification basis,* where the seller handles the collections and remits to the factor. There are two basic types of factoring:
1. **Discount factoring** arrangement whereby seller receives funds from the factor prior to the average maturity date, based on the invoice amount of the receivable, less cash discounts, less an allowance for estimated claims, returns, etc. Here the factor is compensated by an interest rate based on daily balances and typically 2% to 3% above the bank prime rate.
2. **Maturity factoring** arrangement whereby the factor, who performs the entire credit and collection function, remits to the seller for the receivables sold each month on the average due date of the factored receivables. The factor's commission on this kind of arrangement ranges from 0.75% to 2%, depending on the bad debt risk and the handling costs.

    Factors also accommodate clients with "overadvances," loans in anticipation of sales, which permit inventory building prior to peak selling periods. Factoring has traditionally been most closely associated with the garment industry, but is used by companies in other industries as well.

FAIL POSITION securities undelivered due to the failure of selling clients to deliver the securities to their brokers so the latter can deliver them to the buying brokers. Since brokers are constantly buying and selling, receiving and delivering, the term usually refers to a net delivery position—that is, a given broker owes more securities to other brokers on sell transactions than other brokers owe to it on buy transactions. *See also* FAIL TO DELIVER; FAIL TO RECEIVE.

FAIL TO DELIVER situation where the broker-dealer on the sell side of a contract has not delivered securities to the broker-dealer on the buy side. A fail to deliver is usually the result of a broker not receiving delivery from its selling customer. As long as a fail to deliver exists. the seller will not receive payment. *See also* FAIL TO RECEIVE.

FAIL TO RECEIVE situation where the broker-dealer on the buy side of a contract has not received delivery of securities from the broker-dealer on the sell side. As long as a fail to receive exists, the buyer will not make payment for the securities. *See also* FAIL TO DELIVER.

FAIR CREDIT BILLING ACT federal law designed to facilitate the handling of credit complaints and eliminate abusive credit billing practices. For example, the law requires that bills be sent within a prescribed length of time and that consumers' complaints about credit bills be answered promptly.

FAIR CREDIT REPORTING ACT (FCRA) federal law enacted in 1971 giving persons the right to see their credit records at credit reporting bureaus. Designed to improve the confidentiality and accuracy of credit reports, the law is enforced by the FEDERAL TRADE COMMISSION (FTC) and state consumer protection agencies. Individuals may challenge and correct negative aspects of their record if they can prove there is a mistake. Consumers may also submit statements explaining why they received certain negative credit marks. Congress passed amendments to the FCRA that went into effect on October 1, 1997 which augmented consumers' privacy rights and further protected the accuracy of credit report information. For example, the amendments made it a civil law violation for someone to obtain a consumer report without a permissible purpose. Consumers must now give written permission before their credit reports are obtained for employment purposes. Consumers also have the right not to be included in direct mail or telemarketing solicitations based on prescreened lists obtained from credit bureaus. The amendments also state that when a consumer disputes information, the consumer reporting agency and the original furnisher of the information must investigate the claim. Agencies must finish their investigations within 30 days and report their results back to consumers. Consumers can to obtain a copy of their consumer report for a fee not to exceed $8. The law also stipulates that there be a "date certain" for the calculation of the length of time that information can remain in consumer report files in situations involving collections or charge-offs. *See also* CREDIT RATING.

FAIR MARKET VALUE price at which an asset or service passes from a willing seller to a willing buyer. It is assumed that both buyer and seller are rational and have a reasonable knowledge of relevant facts. *See also* MARKET.

FAIRNESS OPINION professional judgment offered for a fee by an investment banker on the fairness of the price being offered in a merger, takeover, or leveraged buyout. For example, if management is trying to take over a company in a leveraged buyout, it will need a fairness opinion from an independent source to verify that the price being offered is adequate and in the best interests of shareholders. If shareholders sue on the grounds that the offer is not adequate, management will rely on the fairness opinion in court to prove its case. Fairness opinions are also obtained when a majority shareholder is trying to buy out the minority shareholders of a company.

FAIR RATE OF RETURN level of profit that a utility is allowed to earn as determined by federal and/or state regulators. Public utility commissions set the fair rate of return based on the utility's needs to maintain service to its customers, pay adequate dividends to shareholders and interest to bondholders, and maintain and expand plant and equipment.

FAIR TRADE ACTS state laws protecting manufacturers from price-cutting by permitting them to establish minimum retail prices for their goods. Fair trade pricing was effectively eliminated in 1975 when Congress repealed the federal laws upholding resale price maintenance.

FALLEN ANGELS bonds that were INVESTMENT GRADE at the time they were issued but have since declined in quality to below investment grade (BB or lower). Fallen angels are a type of JUNK BOND, but the latter term is usually reserved for bonds that are originally issued with ratings of BB or lower.

FALL OUT OF BED sharp drop in a stock's price, usually in response to negative corporate developments. For example, a stock may fall out of bed if a takeover deal falls apart or if profits in the latest period fall far short of expectations.

FAMILY OF FUNDS *see* FUND FAMILY.

FANNIE MAE (FEDERAL NATIONAL MORTGAGE ASSOCIATION) publicly owned, government-sponsored corporation established in 1938 to purchase both government-backed and conventional mortgages from lenders and securitize them. Its objective is to increase the affordability of home mortgage funds for low-, moderate- and middle-income home buyers. Fannie Mae is a congressionally chartered, shareholder-owned company, and the largest source of home mortgage funds in the United States. Fannie Mae is a large issuer of debt securities which are used to finance its activities. Equity shares of Fannie Mae are traded on the New York Stock Exchange.

FARMER MAC *see* FEDERAL AGRICULTURAL MORTGAGE CORPORATION.

FARMER'S HOME ADMINISTRATION (FHA) federal agency under the Department of Agriculture that makes loans in low-income, rural areas of the United States for farms, homes, and community facilities.

FAR MONTH trading month that is farthest in the future in an options or futures contract. This may be a few months or up to a year or more. Under normal conditions, there is far less trading activity in the far month contracts than in the NEAREST MONTH or SPOT DELIVERY MONTH contracts. Also called *furthest month.*

FARTHER OUT; FARTHER IN relative length of option-contract maturities with reference to the present. For example, an options investor in January would call an option expiring in October farther out than an option expiring in July. The July option is farther in than the October option. *See also* DIAGONAL SPREAD.

FASB *see* FINANCIAL ACCOUNTING STANDARDS BOARD.

FAT CAT wealthy person who has become lazy living off the dividends and interest from investments. Fat cats also tend to be offered special treatment by brokers and other financial professionals because they have so much money and their accounts can therefore generate large fees and commissions.

FAVORABLE TRADE BALANCE situation that exists when the value of a nation's exports is in excess of the value of its imports. *See* BALANCE OF PAYMENTS; BALANCE OF TRADE.

FAVORITE FIFTY *See* NIFTY FIFTY.

FEDERAL AGENCY SECURITY debt instrument issued by an agency of the federal government such as the Federal National Mortgage Association, Federal Farm Credit Bank, and the Tennessee Valley Authority (TVA). Though not general obligations of the U.S. Treasury, such securities are sponsored by the government and therefore have high safety ratings.

FEDERAL AGRICULTURAL MORTGAGE CORPORATION federal agency established in 1988 to provide a secondary market for farm mortgage loans. Informally called *Farmer Mac.*

FEDERAL DEFICIT (SURPLUS) federal shortfall that results when the government spends more in a fiscal year than it receives in revenue. To cover the shortfall, the government usually borrows from the public by floating long- and short-term debt. Federal deficits, which started to rise in the 1970s, exploded to enormous proportions of hundreds of billions of dollars per year in the 80s and 90s. By the late 90s, revenues from an extended period of strong economic growth and soaring stock prices were applied to eliminate the deficit in accordance with budget balancing legislation which resulted in a *federal surplus.* Though this scenario did not come to pass in the '80s and '90s, some economists think that massive federal deficits can lead to high interest rates and inflation, since they compete with private borrowing by consumers and businesses. Deficits also add to the demand for money from the FEDERAL RESERVE BANK. *See also* CROWDING OUT; NATIONAL DEBT.

FEDERAL DEPOSIT INSURANCE CORPORATION (FDIC) federal agency established in 1933 that guarantees (within limits) funds on deposit in member banks and thrift institutions and performs other functions such as making loans to or buying assets from member institutions to facilitate mergers or prevent failures. In 1989, Congress passed savings and loan association bailout legislation that reorganized FDIC into two insurance units: the BANK INSURANCE FUND (BIF) continues the traditional FDIC functions with respect to banking institutions; the SAVINGS ASSOCIATION INSURANCE FUND (SAIF) insures thrift institution deposits, replacing the FEDERAL SAVINGS AND LOAN INSURANCE CORPORATION (FSLIC), which ceased to exist. *See also* OFFICE OF THRIFT SUPERVISION (OTS).

FEDERAL FARM CREDIT BANK government-sponsored institution that consolidates the financing activities of the Federal Land Banks, the Federal Intermediate Credit Banks, and the Banks for Cooperatives. *See* FEDERAL FARM CREDIT SYSTEM.

FEDERAL FARM CREDIT SYSTEM system established by the Farm Credit Act of 1971 to provide credit services to farmers and farm-related enterprises through a network of 12 Farm Credit districts. Each district has a Federal Land Bank, a Federal Intermediate Credit Bank, and a Bank for Cooperatives to carry out policies of the system. The system sells short-term (5- to 270-day) notes in increments of $50,000 on a discounted basis through a national syndicate of securities dealers. Rates are set by the FEDERAL FARM CREDIT BANK, a unit established to consolidate the financing activities of the various banks. An active secondary market is maintained by several dealers. The system also issues Federal Farm Credit System Consolidated Systemwide Bonds on a monthly basis with 6- and 9-month maturities. The bonds are sold in increments of $5000 with rates set by the system. The bonds enjoy a secondary market even more active than that for the discounted notes. *See also* SECONDARY MARKET.

FEDERAL FINANCING BANK (FFB) U.S. government-owned bank that consolidates financing activities of government AGENCIES in order to reduce borrowing costs.

FEDERAL FUNDS
   1. funds deposited by commercial banks at Federal Reserve Banks, including funds in excess of bank reserve requirements. Banks may lend federal funds to each other on an overnight basis at the federal funds rate. Member banks may also transfer funds among themselves or on behalf of customers on a same-day basis by debiting and crediting balances in the various reserve banks. *See* FED WIRE.

   2. money used by the Federal Reserve to pay for its purchases of government securities.

   3. funds used to settle transactions where there is no FLOAT.

FEDERAL FUNDS RATE interest rate charged by banks with excess reserves at a Federal Reserve district bank to banks needing overnight loans to meet reserve requirements. The federal funds rate is the most sensitive indicator of the direction of interest rates, since it is set daily by the market, unlike the PRIME RATE and the DISCOUNT RATE, which are periodically changed by banks and by the Federal Reserve Board, respectively.

FEDERAL GIFT TAX federal tax imposed on the transfer of securities, property, or other assets. The donor must pay the tax based on the fair market value of the transferred assets. However, federal law allows donors to give up to $10,000 per year to any individual without incurring gift tax liability. So, a husband and wife may gift $20,000 to their child in one year without tax if each parent gives $10,000. This practice is known as GIFT SPLITTING. According to the TAXPAYER RELIEF ACT OF 1997, this gift tax limit is indexed to inflation in $1,000 increments, starting on January 1, 1999. For those making gifts over the limit, a gift tax return using IRS Form 709 must be filed by April 15th of the year following the year of the gift.

FEDERAL HOME LOAN BANK SYSTEM system supplying credit reserves for SAVINGS AND LOANS, cooperative banks, and other mortgage lenders in a manner similar to the Federal Reserve's role with commercial banks. The Federal Home Loan Bank System is made up of 12 regional Federal Home Loan Banks. It raises money by issuing notes and bonds and lends money to savings and loans and other mortgage lenders based on the amount of collateral the institution can provide. The system was established in 1932 after a massive wave of bank failures. In 1989, Congress passed savings and loan bailout legislation revamping the regulatory structure of the industry. The Federal Home Loan Bank Board was dismantled and replaced with the FEDERAL HOUSING FINANCE BOARD, which now oversees the home loan bank system. *See also* OFFICE OF THRIFT SUPERVISION (OTS).

FEDERAL HOME LOAN MORTGAGE CORPORATION (FHLMC) publicly chartered agency that buys qualifying residential mortgages from lenders, packages them into new securities backed by those pooled mortgages, provides certain guarantees, and then resells the securities on the open market. The corporation's stock is owned by savings institutions across the U.S. and is held in trust by the Federal Home Loan Bank System. The corporation, nicknamed Freddie Mac, has created an enormous secondary market, which provides more funds for mortgage lending and allows investors to buy high-yielding securities backed by federal guarantees. Freddie Mac formerly packaged only mortgages backed by the Veteran's Administration or the

Federal Housing Administration, but now it also resells nongovernmentally backed mortgages. The corporation was established in 1970. *See also* MORTGAGE BACKED CERTIFICATES.

FEDERAL HOUSING ADMINISTRATION (FHA) federally sponsored agency that insures lenders against loss on residential mortgages. It was founded in 1934 in response to the Great Depression to execute the provisions of the National Housing Act. The FHA was the forerunner of a group of government agencies responsible for the growing secondary market for mortgages, such as the Government National Mortgage Association (Ginnie Mae) and the Federal National Mortgage Association (Fannie Mae).

FEDERAL HOUSING FINANCE BOARD (FHFB) U.S. government agency created by Congress in 1989 to assume oversight of the FEDERAL HOME LOAN BANK SYSTEM from the dismantled Federal Home Loan Bank Board. *See also* OFFICE OF THRIFT SUPERVISION (OTS).

FEDERAL INCOME TAXES *see* INCOME TAXES.

FEDERAL INSURANCE CONTRIBUTIONS ACT (FICA) commonly known as Social Security, the federal law requiring employers to withhold wages and make payments to a government trust fund providing retirement and other benefits. *See also* SOCIAL SECURITY.

FEDERAL INTERMEDIATE CREDIT BANK one of 12 banks that make funds available to production credit associations, commercial banks, agricultural credit corporations, livestock loan companies, and other institutions extending credit to crop farmers and cattle raisers. Their stock is owned by farmers and ranchers, and the banks raise funds largely from the public sale of short-term debentures. *See also* FEDERAL FARM CREDIT BANK; FEDERAL FARM CREDIT SYSTEM.

FEDERAL LAND BANK one of 12 banks under the U.S. Farm Credit Administration that extends long-term mortgage credit to crop farmers and cattle raisers for buying land, refinancing debts, or other agricultural purposes. To obtain a loan, a farmer or rancher must purchase stock equal to 5% of the loan in any one of approximately 500 local land bank associations; these, in turn, purchase an equal amount of stock in the Federal Land Bank. The stock is retired when the loan is repaid. The banks raise funds by issuing Consolidated Systemwide Bonds to the public. *See also* FEDERAL FARM CREDIT BANK; FEDERAL FARM CREDIT SYSTEM.

FEDERAL NATIONAL MORTGAGE ASSOCIATION (FNMA) publicly owned, government-sponsored corporation chartered in 1938 to purchase mortgages from lenders and resell them to investors. The agency, known by the nickname Fannie Mae, mostly packages mortgages backed by the Federal Housing Administration, but also sells some nongovernmentally backed mortgages. Shares of FNMA itself, known as Fannie Maes, are traded on the New York Stock Exchange.

The price usually soars when interest rates fall and plummets when interest rates rise, since the mortgage business is so dependent on the direction of interest rates.

FEDERAL OPEN-MARKET COMMITTEE (FOMC) committee that sets interest rate and credit policies for the Federal Reserve System, the United States' central bank. The FOMC has 12 members. Seven are the members of the Federal Reserve Board, appointed by the president of the United States. The other five are presidents of the 12 regional Federal Reserve banks. Of the five, four are picked on a rotating basis; the other is the president of the Federal Reserve Bank of New York, who is a permanent member. The Committee decides whether to increase or decrease interest rates through open-market operations of buying or selling government securities. The Committee's decisions are closely watched and interpreted by economists and stock and bond market analysts, who try to predict whether the Fed is seeking to tighten credit to reduce inflation or to loosen credit to stimulate the economy.

FEDERAL RESERVE BANK one of the 12 banks that, with their branches, make up the FEDERAL RESERVE SYSTEM. These banks are located in Boston, New York, Philadelphia, Cleveland, Richmond, Atlanta, Chicago, St. Louis, Minneapolis, Kansas City, Dallas, and San Francisco. The role of each Federal Reserve Bank is to monitor the commercial and savings banks in its region to ensure that they follow Federal Reserve Board regulations and to provide those banks with access to emergency funds from the DISCOUNT WINDOW. The reserve banks act as depositories for member banks in their regions, providing money transfer and other services. Each of the banks is owned by the member banks in its district.

FEDERAL RESERVE BOARD (FRB) governing board of the FEDERAL RESERVE SYSTEM. Its seven members are appointed by the president of the United States, subject to Senate confirmation, and serve 14-year terms. The Board establishes Federal Reserve System policies on such key matters as reserve requirements and other bank regulations, sets the discount rate, tightens or loosens the availability of credit in the economy, and regulates the purchase of securities on margin.

FEDERAL RESERVE OPEN MARKET COMMITTEE *see* FEDERAL OPEN MARKET COMMITTEE.

FEDERAL RESERVE SYSTEM system established by the Federal Reserve Act of 1913 to regulate the U.S. monetary and banking system. The Federal Reserve System (the Fed) is comprised of 12 regional Federal Reserve Banks, their 24 branches, and all national and state banks that are part of the system. National banks are stockholders of the FEDERAL RESERVE BANK in their region.

The Federal Reserve System's main functions are to regulate the national money supply, set reserve requirements for member banks, supervise the printing of currency at the mint, act as clearinghouse for the transfer of funds throughout the banking system, and examine member banks to make sure they meet various Federal Reserve regulations. Although the members of the system's governing board are appointed by the President of the United States and confirmed by the Senate, the Federal Reserve System is considered an independent entity, which is supposed to make its decisions free of political influence. Governors are appointed for terms of 14 years, which further assures their independence. *See also* FEDERAL OPEN MARKET COMMITTEE; FEDERAL RESERVE BOARD; OPEN MARKET OPERATIONS.

FEDERAL SAVINGS AND LOAN ASSOCIATION federally chartered institution with a primary responsibility to collect people's savings deposits and to provide mortgage loans for residential housing. Federal Savings and Loans may be owned either by stockholders, who can trade their shares on stock exchanges, or by depositors, in which case the associations are considered mutual organizations. Federal Savings and Loans are members of the Federal Home Loan Bank System. After deregulation, S&Ls expanded into nonhousing-related financial services such as discount stock brokerage, financial planning, credit cards, and consumer loans. *See also* FINANCIAL SUPERMARKET; MUTUAL ASSOCIATION; OFFICE OF THRIFT SUPERVISION (OTS); SAVINGS AND LOAN ASSOCIATION.

FEDERAL SAVINGS AND LOAN INSURANCE CORPORATION (FSLIC) federal agency established in 1934 to insure deposits in member savings institutions. In 1989, Congress passed savings and loan bailout legislation revamping the regulatory structure of the industry. FSLIC was disbanded and its insurance activities were assumed by a new agency, SAVINGS ASSOCIATION INSURANCE FUND (SAIF), a unit of the FEDERAL DEPOSIT INSURANCE CORPORATION (FDIC). Responsibility for insolvent institutions previously under FSLIC's jurisdiction was assumed by another newly created agency, RESOLUTION FUNDING CORPORATION (REFCORP). *See also* OFFICE OF THRIFT SUPERVISION (OTS).

FEDERAL SURPLUS *see* FEDERAL DEFICIT (SURPLUS).

FEDERAL TRADE COMMISSION (FTC) federal agency established in 1914 to foster free and fair business competition and prevent monopolies and activities in restraint of trade. It administers both antitrust and consumer protection legislation.

FEDERAL UNEMPLOYMENT TAX ACT (FUTA) legislation under which federal and state governments require employers (and in some states, such as New Jersey, employees) to contribute to a fund that pays unemployment insurance benefits.

FED PASS move by the Federal Reserve to add reserves to the banking system, thereby making credit more available. The Fed will initiate an open-market operation when it wants to add or subtract reserves in the banking system. It transacts these operations through a group of dealers called PRIMARY DEALERS, banks or security houses with which the Fed has agreed to do business. For example, the buying of securities by the Federal Reserve can be done in such a way that will make reserves more available, thus encouraging banks to lend and making credit easier to obtain by consumer and business borrowers.

FED WIRE high-speed, computerized communications network that connects all 12 Federal Reserve Banks, their 24 branches, the Federal Reserve Board office in Washington, D.C., U.S. Treasury offices in Washington, D.C., and Chicago, and the Washington, D.C. office of the Commodity Credit Corporation; also spelled FedWire and Fedwire. The Fed wire has been called the central nervous system of money transfer in the United States. It enables banks to transfer reserve balances from one to another for immediate available credit and to transfer balances for business customers. Using the Fed wire, Federal Reserve Banks can settle interdistrict transfers resulting from check collections, and the Treasury can shift balances from its accounts in different reserve banks quickly and without cost. It is also possible to transfer bearer short-term government securities within an hour at no cost. This is done through a procedure called CPD (Commissioner of Public Debt of the Treasury) transfers, whereby one Federal Reserve Bank "retires" a seller's security, while another reserve bank makes delivery of a like amount of the same security from its unissued stock to the buyer.

FICA *see* FEDERAL INSURANCE CONTRIBUTIONS ACT.

FICO *see* FINANCING CORPORATION.

FICTITIOUS CREDIT the credit balance in a securities MARGIN ACCOUNT representing the proceeds from a short sale and the margin requirement under Federal Reserve Board REGULATION T (which regulates margin credit). Because the proceeds, which are held as security for the loan of securities made by the broker to effect the short sale, and the margin requirement are both there to protect the broker's position, the money is not available for withdrawal by the customer; hence the term "fictitious" credit. It is in contrast to a free credit balance, which can be withdrawn anytime.

FIDELITY BOND *see* BLANKET FIDELITY BOND.

FIDUCIARY person, company, or association holding assets in trust for a beneficiary. The fiduciary is charged with the responsibility of investing the money wisely for the beneficiary's benefit. Some examples of fiduciaries are executors of wills and estates, receivers in bankruptcy, trustees, and those who administer the assets of underage or incompetent beneficiaries. Most U.S. states have laws about what a fiduciary may or may not do with a beneficiary's assets. For instance, it is illegal for fiduciaries to invest or misappropriate the money for their personal gain. *See also* LEGAL LIST; PRUDENT MAN RULE.

FIFO *see* FIRST IN, FIRST OUT.

FILING STATUS category a taxpayer chooses in filing a tax return. It determines the filing requirements, standard deduction, eligibility to claim certain deductions and credits, and tax rates. Filing status is determined on the last day of the tax year. The four filing status categories are single, married filing jointly, married filing separately, and head of household. Depending upon the taxpayer's family situation and income, it is more advantageous to file using one category over others. Many accountants figure out a taxpayer's liability using two filing statuses—filing jointly or filing separately—to calculate which one results in the lower tax.

FILL execute a customer's order to buy or sell a stock, bond, or commodity. An order is filled when the amount of the security requested is supplied. When less than the full amount of the order is supplied, it is known as a *partial fill.*

FILL OR KILL (FOK) order to buy or sell a particular security which, if not executed immediately, is canceled. Often, fill or kill orders are placed when a client wants to buy a large quantity of shares of a particular stock at a particular price. If the order is not executed because it will significantly upset the market price for that stock, the order is withdrawn.

FINANCE CHARGE cost of credit, including interest, paid by a customer for a consumer loan. Under the Truth in Lending Act, the finance charge must be disclosed to the customer in advance. *See also* CONSUMER CREDIT PROTECTION ACT OF 1968; REGULATION Z.

FINANCE COMPANY company engaged in making loans to individuals or businesses. Unlike a bank, it does not receive deposits but rather obtains its financing from banks, institutions, and other money market sources. Generally, finance companies fall into three categories: (1) consumer finance companies, also known as *small loan* or *direct loan companies,* lend money to individuals under the small loan laws of the individual U.S. states; (2) sales finance companies, also called *acceptance companies,* purchase retail and wholesale paper from automobile and other consumer and capital goods dealers; (3) commercial finance companies, also called *commercial credit companies,* make loans to manufacturers and wholesalers; these loans are secured by accounts receivable, inventories, and equipment. Finance companies typically enjoy high credit ratings and are thus able to borrow at the lowest market rates, enabling them to make loans at rates not much higher than banks. Even though their customers usually do not qualify for bank credit, these companies have experienced a low rate of default. Finance companies in general tend to be interest rate-sensitive—increases and decreases in market interest rates affect their profits directly. For this reason, publicly held finance companies are sometimes referred to as money stocks. *See also* CAPTIVE FINANCE COMPANY.

FINANCIAL ACCOUNTING STANDARDS BOARD (FASB) independent board responsible for establishing and interpreting generally accepted accounting principles. It was formed in 1973 to succeed and continue the activities of the Accounting Principles Board (APB). *See* GENERALLY ACCEPTED ACCOUNTING PRINCIPLES.

FINANCIAL ADVISER professional adviser offering financial counsel. Some financial advisers charge a fee and earn commissions on the products they recommend to implement their advice. Other advisers only charge fees, and do not sell any products or accept commissions. Some financial advisers are generalists, while others specialize in specific areas such as investing, insurance, estate planning, taxes, or other areas.

FINANCIAL ANALYSIS analysis of the FINANCIAL STATEMENT of a company. *See also* FUNDAMENTAL ANALYSIS.

FINANCIAL ASSETS assets in the form of stocks, bonds, rights, certificates, bank balances, etc., as distinguished from tangible, physical assets. For example, real property is a physical asset, but shares in a REAL ESTATE INVESTMENT TRUST (REIT) or the stock or bonds of a company that held property as an investment would be financial assets.

FINANCIAL FUTURE FUTURES CONTRACT based on a financial instrument. Such contracts usually move under the influence of interest rates. As rates rise, contracts fall in value; as rates fall, contracts gain in value. Examples of instruments underlying financial futures contracts: Treasury bills, Treasury notes, Government National Mortgage Association (Ginnie Mae) pass-throughs, foreign currencies, and certificates of deposit. Trading in these contracts is governed by the federal Commodities Futures Trading Commission. Traders use these futures to speculate on the direction of interest rates. Financial institutions (banks, insurance companies, brokerage firms) use them to hedge financial portfolios against adverse fluctuations in interest rates.

FINANCIAL GUARANTEE INSURANCE covers losses from specific financial transactions. The coverage guarantees investors in debt instruments that they will receive timely payment of principal and interest if there is a default on underlying debts. For example, this insurance backs loan portfolios composed of credit card and auto loans.

FINANCIAL INSTITUTION institution that collects funds from the public to place in financial assets such as stocks, bonds, money market instruments, bank deposits, or loans. Depository institutions (banks, savings and loans, savings banks, credit unions) pay interest on deposits and invest the deposit money mostly in loans. Nondepository institutions (insurance companies, pension plans) collect money by selling insurance policies or receiving employer contributions and pay it out for legitimate claims or for retirement benefits. Increasingly, many institutions are performing both depository and nondepository functions. For instance, brokerage firms now place customers' money in certificates of deposit and money market funds and sell insurance. *See* FINANCIAL SUPERMARKET.

FINANCIAL INSTITUTIONS REFORM, RECOVERY AND ENFORCEMENT ACT OF 1989 (FIRREA) legislation enacted into law on August 9, 1989, to resolve the crisis affecting U.S. savings and loan associations. Known as the *bailout bill,* it revamped the regulatory, insurance, and financing structures and established the OFFICE OF THRIFT SUPERVISION. The act created (1) the RESOLUTION TRUST CORPORATION (RTC), which, operating under the management of the FEDERAL DEPOSIT INSURANCE CORPORATION (FDIC), was charged with closing or merging institutions that had become insolvent beginning in 1989; (2) the RESOLUTION FUNDING CORPORATION (REFCORP), charged with borrowing from private capital markets to fund RTC activities and to manage the remaining assets and liabilities taken over by the FEDERAL SAVINGS AND LOAN INSURANCE CORPORATION (FSLIC) prior to 1989; (3) the SAVINGS ASSOCIATION INSURANCE FUND (SAIF) (pronounced "safe"), to replace FSLIC as insurer of thrift deposits and to be administered by the FDIC separately from its bank deposit insurance program, which became the BANK INSURANCE FUND (BIF); and (4) the FEDERAL HOUSING FINANCE BOARD (FHFB), charged with overseeing the FEDERAL HOME LOAN BANKS.

The RTC was authorized to accept additional insolvent institutions through June 1995; after that date, responsibilities for newly failed institutions shifted to the SAIF.

See also BAILOUT BOND.

FINANCIAL INTERMEDIARY commercial bank, savings and loan, mutual savings bank, credit union, or other "middleman" that smooths the flow of funds between "savings surplus units" and "savings deficit units." In an economy viewed as three sectors—households, businesses, and government—a *savings surplus unit* is one where income exceeds consumption; a *savings deficit unit* is one where current expenditures exceed current income and external sources must be called upon to make up the difference. As a whole, households are savings surplus units, whereas businesses and governments are savings deficit units. Financial intermediaries redistribute savings into productive uses and, in the process, serve two other important functions: By making savers infinitesimally small "shareholders" in huge pools of capital, which in turn are loaned out to a wide number and variety of borrowers, the intermediaries provide both diversification of risk and liquidity to the individual saver. *See also* DISINTERMEDIATION; FINDER'S FEE.

FINANCIAL LEASE lease in which the service provided by the lessor to the lessee is limited to financing equipment. All other responsibilities related to the possession of equipment, such as maintenance, insurance, and taxes, are borne by the lessee. A financial lease is usually noncancellable and is fully paid out *(amortized)* over its term.

FINANCIAL LEVERAGE *see* LEVERAGE.

FINANCIAL MARKET market for the exchange of capital and credit in the economy. Money markets concentrate on short-term debt instruments; capital markets trade in long-term debt and equity instruments. Examples of financial markets: stock market, bond market, commodities market, and foreign exchange market.

FINANCIAL NEEDS APPROACH technique to assess the proper amount of life insurance for an individual. The person, either on his or her own or with the help of an insurance adviser, must estimate the financial needs of survivors in case the person dies unexpectedly. Projections for expenses, income, taxes, funeral costs, and other financial factors lead to an understanding of the amount of insurance proceeds that would be needed to allow the survivors to continue in their present lifestyle. Once the optimal amount of insurance protection is determined, various kinds of TERM and CASH VALUE INSURANCE programs can be designed to meet these needs.

FINANCIAL PLANNER professional who analyzes personal financial circumstances and prepares a program to meet financial needs and objectives. Financial planners, who may be accountants, bankers, lawyers, insurance agents, real estate or securities brokers, or independent practitioners, should have knowledge in the areas of wills and estate planning, retirement planning, taxes, insurance, family budgeting, debt management, and investments.

Fee-only planners charge on the basis of service and time and have nothing to sell. *Commission-only planners* offer their services for free but sell commission-producing products such as MUTUAL FUNDS, LIMITED PARTNERSHIPS, insurance products, stocks, and bonds. *Fee-plus-commission planners* charge an upfront fee for consultation and their written plan, then charge commissions on the financial products they sell. *Fee-offset planners* charge fees against which they apply credits when they sell commission-producing products.

The Certified Financial Planner Board of Standards, Inc., in Denver, Colorado, issues the CERTIFIED FINANCIAL PLANNER (CFP) license, and the Institute of Certified Financial Planners, also in Denver, maintains a referral list. The International Association for Financial Planning (IAFP) in Atlanta, Georgia, provides a list of financial planners with CFA, CFP, ChFC, or CPA designation; a law or financial planning degree; or those who have completed its Practical Knowledge Examination. The American Institute of Certified Public Accountants in New York City, provides a list of CPAs who offer financial planning services; The National Association of Personal Financial Advisors (NAPFA) in Buffalo Grove, Illinois, lists fee-only planners. The National Endowment for Financial Education, in Denver, offers a financial planning starter kit to consumers, on request.

FINANCIAL POSITION status of a firm's assets, liabilities, and equity accounts as of a certain time, as shown on its FINANCIAL STATEMENT. Also called *financial condition*.

FINANCIAL PUBLIC RELATIONS branch of public relations specializing in corporate disclosure responsibilities, stockholder relations, and relations with the professional investor community. Financial public relations is concerned not only with matters of corporate image and the cultivation of a favorable financial and investment environment but also with legal interpretation and adherence to Securities and Exchange Commission and other government regulations, as well as with the DISCLOSURE requirements of the securities exchanges. Its practitioners, therefore, include lawyers with expertise in such areas as tender offers and takeovers, public offerings, proxy solicitation, and insider trading. *See also* INVESTOR RELATIONS DEPARTMENT.

FINANCIAL PYRAMID

1. risk structure many investors aim for in spreading their investments between low-, medium-, and high-risk vehicles. In a financial pyramid, the largest part of the investor's assets is in safe, liquid investments that provide a decent return. Next, some money is invested in stocks and bonds that provide good income and the possibility for long-term growth of capital. Third, a smaller portion of one's capital is committed to speculative investments which may offer higher returns if they work out well. At the top of the financial pyramid, where only a small amount of money is committed, are high-risk ventures that have a slight chance of success, but which will provide substantial rewards if they succeed.

2. acquisition of holding company assets through financial leverage. *See* PYRAMIDING.

   Financial pyramid is not to be confused with fraudulent selling schemes, also sometimes called *pyramiding*.

FINANCIAL PYRAMID

High Risk

Speculation

Income and Long-Term Growth

Liquidity and Safety

FINANCIAL STATEMENT written record of the financial status of an individual, association, or business organization. The financial statement includes a BALANCE SHEET and an INCOME STATEMENT (or operating statement or profit and loss statement) and may also include a STATEMENT OF CASH FLOWS, a statement of changes in retained earnings, and other analyses.

FINANCIAL STRUCTURE makeup of the right-hand side of a company's BALANCE SHEET, which includes all the ways its assets are financed, such as trade accounts payable and short-term borrowings as well as long-term debt and ownership equity. Financial structure is distinguished from CAPITAL STRUCTURE, which includes only long-term debt and equity. A company's financial structure is influenced by a number of factors, including the growth rate and stability of its sales, its competitive situation (i.e., the stability of its profits), its asset structure, and the attitudes of its management and its lenders. It is the basic frame of reference for analyses concerned with financial leveraging decisions.

FINANCIAL SUPERMARKET company that offers a wide range of financial services under one roof. For example, some large retail organizations offer stock, insurance, and real estate brokerage, as well as banking services. For customers, having all their assets with one institution can make financial transactions and planning more convenient and efficient, since money does not constantly have to be shifted from one institution to another. For institutions, such all-inclusive relationships are more profitable than dealing with just one aspect of a customer's financial needs. Institutions often become financial supermarkets in order to capture all the business of their customers.

FINANCIAL TABLES tables found in newspapers listing prices, dividends, yields, price/earnings ratios, trading volume, and other important data on stocks, bonds, mutual funds, and futures contracts. While local newspapers may carry limited tables, more extensive listings are available in *Barron's, Investor's Business Daily,* the *Wall Street Journal,* and other publications.

FINANCING CORPORATION (FICO) agency set up by Congress in 1987 to issue bonds and bail out the FEDERAL SAVINGS AND LOAN INSURANCE CORPORATION (FSLIC). *See also* BAILOUT BOND.

FINDER'S FEE fee charged by a person or company acting as a finder (intermediary) in a transaction.

FINEX financial derivatives division of the NEW YORK COTTON EXCHANGE with a trading floor in Dublin, FINEX Europe, creating a 24-hour market in most FINEX contracts. FINEX/FINEX Europe trades futures and futures options on the U.S. Dollar Index, currencies, and cross-rate currencies. Futures and options on Treasury auction five-year U.S. Treasury note futures and Treasury auction two-year U.S. Treasury note futures are traded only in New York. *See also* SECURITIES AND COMMODITIES EXCHANGES.

FINITE LIFE REAL ESTATE INVESTMENT TRUST (FREIT) REAL ESTATE INVESTMENT TRUST (REIT) that promises to try to sell its holdings within a specified period to realize CAPITAL GAINS.

FIREWALL the legal separation of banking and broker/dealer operations within a financial institution. Under the GLASS-STEAGALL ACT OF

1933, banks are not allowed to own or control broker/dealers, though in recent years banks have offered many of the services traditionally provided by brokers. A firewall would prevent a bank from lending money to a securities affiliate, for example. To some extent, the separation is maintained to protect the FDIC insurance fund and insured bank deposits from the risks associated with the brokerage business.

FIRM

1. general term for a business, corporation, partnership, or proprietorship. Legally, a firm is not considered a corporation since it may not be incorporated and since the firm's principals are not recognized as separate from the identity of the firm itself. This might be true of a law or accounting firm, for instance.
2. solidity with which an agreement is made. For example, a firm order with a manufacturer or a firm bid for a stock at a particular price means that the order or bid is assured.

FIRM COMMITMENT

Lending: term used by lenders to refer to an agreement to make a loan to a specific borrower within a specific period of time and, if applicable, on a specific property. *See also* COMMITMENT FEE.

Securities underwriting: arrangement whereby investment bankers make outright purchases from the issuer of securities to be offered to the public; also called *firm commitment underwriting*. The underwriters, as the investment bankers are called in such an arrangement, make their profit on the difference between the purchase price—determined through either competitive bidding or negotiation—and the public offering price. Firm commitment underwriting is to be distinguished from conditional arrangements for distributing new securities, such as standby commitments and best efforts commitments. The word *underwriting* is frequently misused with respect to such conditional arrangements. It is used correctly only with respect to firm commitment underwritings or, as they are sometimes called, BOUGHT DEALS. *See also* BEST EFFORT; STANDBY COMMITMENT.

FIRM ORDER

Commercial transaction: written or verbal order that has been confirmed and is not subject to cancellation.

Securities: (1) order to buy or sell for the proprietary account of the broker-dealer firm; (2) buy or sell order not conditional upon the customer's confirmation.

FIRM QUOTE securities industry term referring to any round lot bid or offer price of a security stated by a market maker and not identified as a nominal (or subject) quote. Under National Association of Securities Dealers' (NASD) rules and practice, quotes requiring further negotiation or review must be identified as nominal quotes. *See also* NOMINAL QUOTATION.

FIRREA *see* FINANCIAL INSTITUTIONS REFORM AND RECOVERY ACT.

FIRST BOARD delivery dates for futures as established by the Chicago Board of Trade and other exchanges trading in futures.

FIRST CALL Boston-based global investment research service providing research opinion and data on over 7000 companies from more than 400 brokers. First Call delivers fully-integrated global equity and fixed income research notes and reports, consensus earnings estimates and related information, corporate news and broker buy/sell/hold/ recommendations. First Call Corporate Services provides investor relations services to companies. *See also* I/B/E/S/ INTERNATIONAL INC.; ZACKS ESTIMATE SYSTEM.

FIRST CALL DATE first date specified in the indenture of a corporate or municipal bond contract on which part or all of the bond may be redeemed at a set price. An XYZ bond due in 2030, for instance, may have a first call date of May 1, 2013. This means that, if XYZ wishes, bondholders may be paid off starting on that date in 2013. Bond brokers typically quote yields on such bonds with both yield to maturity (in this case, 2030) and yield to call (in this case, 2013). *See also* DURATION; YIELD TO CALL; YIELD TO MATURITY.

FIRST IN, FIRST OUT (FIFO) method of accounting for inventory whereby, quite literally, the inventory is assumed to be sold in the chronological order in which it was purchased. For example, the following formula is used in computing the cost of goods sold:

Under the FIFO method, inventory costs flow from the oldest purchases forward, with beginning inventory as the starting point and ending inventory representing the most recent purchases. The FIFO method contrasts with the LIFO or LAST IN, FIRST OUT method, which is FIFO in reverse. The significance of the difference becomes apparent when inflation or deflation affects inventory prices. In an inflationary period, the FIFO method produces a higher ending inventory, a lower cost of goods sold figure, and a higher gross profit. LIFO, on the other hand, produces a lower ending inventory, a higher cost of goods sold figure, and a lower reported profit.

In accounting for the purchase and sale of securities for tax purposes, FIFO is assumed by the IRS unless it is advised of the use of an alternative method.

FIRST MORTGAGE real estate loan that gives the mortgagee (lender) a primary lien against a specified piece of property. A primary lien has precedence over all other mortgages in case of default. *See also* JUNIOR MORTGAGE; SECOND MORTGAGE.

FIRST PREFERRED STOCK preferred stock that has preferential claim on dividends and assets over other preferred issues and common stock.

FISCAL AGENT
1. usually a bank or a trust company acting for a corporation under a corporate trust agreement. The fiscal agent handles such matters as disbursing funds for dividend payments, redeeming bonds and coupons, handling taxes related to the issue of bonds, and paying rents.
2. agent of the national government or its agencies or of a state or municipal government that performs functions relating to the issue and payment of bonds. For example, the Federal Reserve is the U.S. government's fiscal agent.

FISCAL POLICY federal taxation and spending policies designed to level out the business cycle and achieve full employment, price stability, and sustained growth in the economy. Fiscal policy basically follows the economic theory of the 20th-century English economist John Maynard Keynes that insufficient demand causes unemployment and excessive demand leads to inflation. It aims to stimulate demand and output in periods of business decline by increasing government purchases and cutting taxes, thereby releasing more disposable income into the spending stream, and to correct overexpansion by reversing the process. Working to balance these deliberate fiscal measures are the so-called built-in stabilizers, such as the progressive income tax and unemployment benefits, which automatically respond countercyclically. Fiscal policy is administered independently of MONETARY POLICY, by which the Federal Reserve Board attempts to regulate economic activity by controlling the money supply. The goals of fiscal and monetary policy are the same, but Keynesians and Monetarists disagree as to which of the two approaches works best. At the basis of their differences are questions dealing with the velocity (turnover) of money and the effect of changes in the money supply on the equilibrium rate of interest (the rate at which money demand equals money supply). *See also* KEYNESIAN ECONOMICS.

FISCAL YEAR (FY) accounting period covering 12 consecutive months, 52 consecutive weeks, 13 four-week periods, or 365 consecutive days, at the end of which the books are closed and profit or loss is determined. A company's fiscal year is often, but not necessarily, the same as the calendar year. A seasonal business will frequently select a fiscal rather than a calendar year, so that its year-end figures will show it in its most liquid condition, which also means having less inventory to verify physically. The FY of the U.S. government ends September 30.

FIT a situation where the features of a particular investment perfectly match the portfolio requirements of an investor.

FITCH INVESTORS SERVICE, INC. New York- and Denver-based RATING firm, which rates corporate and municipal bonds, preferred stock, commercial paper, and obligations of health-care and not-for-profit institutions.

FITCH SHEETS sheets indicating the successive trade prices of securities listed on the major exchanges. They are published by Francis Emory Fitch, Inc. in New York City.

FIVE HUNDRED DOLLAR RULE REGULATION T provision of the Federal Reserve that exempts deficiencies in margin requirements amounting to $500 or less from mandatory remedial action. Brokers are thus not forced to resort to the liquidation of an account to correct a trivial deficiency in a situation where, for example, a customer is temporarily out of town and cannot be reached. *See also* MARGIN CALL.

FIVE PERCENT RULE one of the Rules of Fair Practice of the National Association of Securities Dealers (NASD). It proposes an ethical guideline for spreads in dealer transactions and commissions in brokerage transactions, including PROCEEDS SALES and RISKLESS TRANSACTIONS.

FIXATION setting of a present or future price of a commodity, such as the twice-daily London GOLD FIXING. In other commodities, prices are fixed further into the future for the benefit of both buyers and sellers of that commodity.

FIXED ANNUITY investment contract sold by an insurance company that guarantees fixed payments, either for life or for a specified period, to an annuitant. In fixed annuities, the insurer takes both the investment and the mortality risks. A fixed annuity contrasts with a VARIABLE ANNUITY, where payments depend on an uncertain outcome, such as prices in the securities markets. See *also* ANNUITY.

FIXED ASSET tangible property used in the operations of a business, but not expected to be consumed or converted into cash in the ordinary course of events. Plant, machinery and equipment, furniture and fixtures, and leasehold improvements comprise the fixed assets of most companies. They are normally represented on the balance sheet at their net depreciated value.

FIXED BENEFITS payments to a BENEFICIARY that are fixed rather than variable.

FIXED-CHARGE COVERAGE ratio of profits before payment of interest and income taxes to interest on bonds and other contractual long-term debt. It indicates how many times interest charges have been earned by the corporation on a pretax basis. Since failure to meet interest payments would be a default under the terms of indenture agreements, the coverage ratio measures a margin of safety. The amount of safety desirable depends on the stability of a company's earnings. (Too much safety can be an indication of an undesirable lack of leverage.) In cyclical companies, the fixed-charge coverage in periods of recession is a telling ratio. Analysts also find it useful to calculate the number of times that a company's *cash flow*—i.e., *after*-tax earnings plus noncash expenses (for example, depreciation)—covers fixed charges. Also known as *times fixed charges.*

FIXED COST cost that remains constant regardless of sales volume. Fixed costs include salaries of executives, interest expense, rent, depreciation, and insurance expenses. They contrast with *variable costs* (direct labor, materials costs), which are distinguished from *semivariable costs.* Semivariable costs vary, but not necessarily in direct relation to sales. They may also remain fixed up to a level of sales, then increase when sales enter a higher range. For example, expenses associated with a delivery truck would be fixed up to the level of sales where a second truck was required. Obviously, no costs are purely fixed; the assumption, however, serves the purposes of cost accounting for limited planning periods. Cost accounting is also concerned with the allocation of portions of fixed costs to inventory costs, also called indirect costs, overhead, factory overhead, and supplemental overhead. *See also* DIRECT OVERHEAD; VARIABLE COST.

FIXED EXCHANGE RATE set rate of exchange between the currencies of countries. At the Bretton Woods international monetary conference in 1944, a system of fixed exchange rates was set up, which existed until the early 1970s, when a FLOATING EXCHANGE RATE system was adopted.

FIXED EXPENSES *see* FIXED COSTS.

FIXED-INCOME INVESTMENT security that pays a fixed rate of return. This usually refers to government, corporate, or municipal bonds, which pay a fixed rate of interest until the bonds mature, and to preferred stock, paying a fixed dividend. Such investments are advantageous in a time of low inflation, but do not protect holders against erosion of buying power in a time of rising inflation, since the bondholder or preferred shareholder gets the same amount of interest or dividends, even though consumer goods cost more.

FIXED PREMIUM equal installments payable to an insurance company for INSURANCE or an ANNUITY. *See also* SINGLE-PREMIUM DEFERRED ANNUITY (SPDA) and SINGLE-PREMIUM LIFE INSURANCE.

FIXED PRICE
Contracts: type of contract where the price is preset and invariable, regardless of the actual costs of production. *See also* COST-PLUS CONTRACT.
Investment: in a public offering of new securities, price at which investment bankers in the underwriting SYNDICATE agree to sell the issue to the public. The price remains fixed as long as the syndicate remains in effect. The proper term for this kind of system is *fixed price offering system.* In contrast, Eurobonds, which are also sold through

underwriting syndicates, are offered on a basis that permits discrimination among customers; i.e., the underwriting spread may be adjusted to suit the particular buyer. *See also* EUROBOND.

FIXED RATE (LOAN) type of loan in which the interest rate does not fluctuate with general market conditions. There are fixed rate mortgage (also known as conventional mortgage) and consumer installment loans, as well as fixed rate business loans. Fixed rate loans tend to have higher original interest rates than flexible rate loans such as an ADJUSTABLE RATE MORTGAGE (ARM), because lenders are not protected against a rise in the cost of money when they make a fixed rate loan.

The term fixed rate may also refer to fixed currency exchange rates. *See* FIXED EXCHANGE RATE.

FIXED TERM REVERSE MORTGAGE mortgage granted by a bank or other lending institution providing payments to a homeowner for a fixed number of years. A retired couple who have paid off their traditional mortgage might be interested in such a plan if they do not want to move out of their house, but want to be able to tap the equity in their house for current cash income.

FIXED TRUST UNIT INVESTMENT TRUST that has a fixed portfolio of previously agreed upon securities; also called *fixed investment trust.* The securities are usually of one type, such as corporate, government, or municipal bonds, in order to afford a regular income to holders of units. A fixed trust is distinguished from a PARTICIPATING TRUST.

FIXTURE attachment to real property that is not intended to be moved and would create damage to the property if it were moved—for example, a plumbing fixture. Fixtures are classified as part of real estate when they share the same useful life. Otherwise, they are considered equipment.

FLAG technical chart pattern resembling a flag shaped like a parallelogram with masts on either side, showing a consolidation within a trend. It results from price fluctuations within a narrow range, both preceded and followed by sharp rises or declines. If the flag—the consolidation period—is preceded by a rise, it will usually be followed by a rise; a fall will follow a fall. *See* chart on next page.

FLASH tape display designation used when volume on an exchange is so heavy that the tape runs more than five minutes behind. The flash interrupts the display to report the current price—called the *flash price*—of a heavily traded security. Current prices of two groups of 50 stocks are flashed at five-minute intervals as long as the tape is seriously behind.

FLAT
  1. in bond trading, without accrued interest. This means that accrued interest will be received by the buyer if and when paid but that no

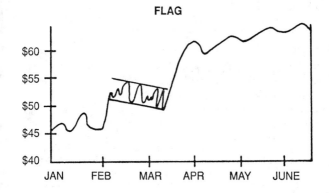

FLAG

accrued interest is payable to the seller. Issues in default and INCOME BONDS are normally quoted and traded flat. The opposite of a flat bond is an AND INTEREST bond. *See also* LOANED FLAT.

2. inventory of a market maker with a net zero position—i.e., neither long nor short.

3. position of an underwriter whose account is completely sold.

FLAT MARKET market characterized by HORIZONTAL PRICE MOVEMENT. It is usually the result of low activity. However, STABILIZATION, consolidation, and DISTRIBUTION are situations marked by both horizontal price movement and active trading.

FLAT SCALE

Industry: labor term denoting a uniform rate of pay that makes no allowance for volume, frequency, or other factors.

Municipal bonds: bond trader's term describing a situation where shorter and longer term yields show little difference over the maturity range of a new serial bond issue.

FLAT TAX tax applied at the same rate to all levels of income. It is often discussed as an alternative to the PROGRESSIVE TAX. Proponents of a flat tax argue that people able to retain larger portions of higher income would have an added incentive to earn, thus stimulating the economy. Advocates also note its simplicity. Opponents argue it is a REGRESSIVE TAX in effect, comparing it to the sales tax, a uniform tax that puts a greater burden on households with lower incomes. The TAX REFORM ACT OF 1986 instituted a modified flat tax system—a progressive tax with fewer tax brackets and lower rates. However, the trend towards a flat tax was reversed with the REVENUE RECONCILIATION ACT OF 1993, which added another tax bracket and a tax surcharge to the income tax system.

FLEXIBLE BUDGET statement of projected revenue and expenditure based on various levels of production. It shows how costs vary with different rates of output or at different levels of sales volume.

FLEXIBLE EXCHANGE RATE *see* FLOATING EXCHANGE RATE.

FLEXIBLE EXPENSES in personal finance, expenses that can be adjusted or eliminated, such as those for luxuries, as opposed to fixed expenses, such as rent or car payments.

FLEXIBLE MUTUAL FUND fund that can invest in stocks, bonds, and cash in whatever proportion the fund manager thinks will maximize returns to shareholders at the lowest level of risk. Flexible funds, also called ASSET ALLOCATION funds, can provide high returns if they are fully invested in stocks when stock prices soar, and they can also protect shareholders' assets by going largely to cash during a stock bear market. Flexible mutual funds are popular because the fund manager, not the shareholder, must make the difficult decisions on asset allocation and market timing. Some flexible funds allow managers to buy securities anywhere in the world in their quest to maximize shareholder returns.

FLIGHT OF CAPITAL *see* CAPITAL FLIGHT.

FLIGHT TO QUALITY moving capital to the safest possible investment to protect oneself from loss during an unsettling period in the market. For example, when a major bank fails, cautious money market investors may buy only government-backed money market securities instead of those issued by major banks. A flight to quality can be measured by the differing yields resulting from such a movement of capital. In the example just given, the yields on bank-issued money market paper will rise since there will be less demand for it, and the rates on government securities will fall, because there will be more demand for them.

FLIP-IN POISON PILL *see* POISON PILL.

FLIP-OVER POISON PILL *see* POISON PILL.

FLIPPING buying shares in an INITIAL PUBLIC OFFERING and selling them immediately for a profit. Brokerage firms underwriting new stock issues tend to discourage flipping, and will often try to allocate shares to investors who say they plan to hold on to the shares for some time. Still, the temptation to flip a new issue once it has risen in price sharply is too irresistible for many investors lucky enough to be allocated shares in a HOT ISSUE. An investor who flips stocks is called a *flipper.*

FLOAT
Banking: time between the deposit of a check in a bank and payment. Long floats are to the advantage of checkwriters, whose money may earn interest until a check clears. They are to the disadvantage of

depositors, who must wait for a check to clear before they have access to the funds. As a rule, the further away the paying bank is from the deposit bank, the longer it will take for a check to clear. Some U.S. states limit the amount of float a bank can impose on the checks of its depositors. *See also* UNCOLLECTED FUNDS.

Investments: number of shares of a corporation that are outstanding and available for trading by the public. A small float means the stock will be more volatile, since a large order to buy or sell shares can influence the stock's price dramatically. A larger float means the stock will be less volatile.

FLOATER

Bonds: debt instrument with a variable interest rate tied to another interest rate, e.g., the rate paid by Treasury bills. A FLOATING RATE NOTE, for instance, provides a holder with additional interest if the applicable interest rate rises and less interest if the rate falls. It is generally best to buy floaters if it appears that interest rates will rise. If the outlook is for falling rates, investors typically favor fixed rate instruments. Floaters spread risk between issuers and debtholders.

Insurance: endorsement to a homeowner's or renter's insurance policy, a form of property insurance for items that are moved from location to location. Typically, a floater is bought to cover jewelry, furs, and other items whose full value is not covered in standard homeowner's or renter's policies. A standard homeowner's policy typically covers $1000 to $2000 for jewelry, furs, and watches. Also called a *rider.*

FLOATING AN ISSUE *see* NEW ISSUE; UNDERWRITE.

FLOATING DEBT continuously renewed or refinanced short-term debt of companies or governments used to finance ongoing operating needs.

FLOATING EXCHANGE RATE movement of a foreign currency exchange rate in response to changes in the market forces of supply and demand; also known as *flexible exchange rate.* Currencies strengthen or weaken based on a nation's reserves of hard currency and gold, its international trade balance, its rate of inflation and interest rates, and the general strength of its economy. Nations generally do not want their currency to be too strong, because this makes the country's goods too expensive for foreigners to buy. A weak currency, on the other hand, may signify economic instability if it has been caused by high inflation or a weak economy. The opposite of the floating exchange rate is the FIXED EXCHANGE RATE system. *See also* PAR VALUE OF CURRENCY.

FLOATING RATE NOTE debt instrument with a variable interest rate. Interest adjustments are made periodically, often every six months, and are tied to a money-market index such as Treasury bill rates. Floating rate notes usually have a maturity of about five years. They provide holders with protection against rises in interest rates, but pay lower yields than fixed rate notes of the same maturity. Also known as a FLOATER.

FLOATING SECURITIES
1. securities bought for the purpose of making a quick profit on resale and held in a broker's name.
2. outstanding stock of a corporation that is traded on an exchange.
3. unsold units of a newly issued security.

FLOATING SUPPLY
Bonds: total dollar amount of municipal bonds in the hands of speculators and dealers that is for sale at any particular time as offered in the BLUE LIST. Someone might say, for instance, "There is $10 billion in floating supply available now in the municipal bond market."
Stocks: number of shares of a stock available for purchase. A dealer might say, "The floating supply in this stock is about 200,000 shares." Sometimes called simply the *float.*

FLOOR in general, the lower limit of something. In securities, the part of a stock exchange where active trading takes place or the price at which a STOP LOSS order is activated. *See also* FLOOR BROKER.

FLOOR BROKER member of an exchange who is an employee of a member firm and executes orders, as agent, on the floor of the exchange for clients. The floor broker receives an order via teletype machine from his firm's trading department, then proceeds to the appropriate trading post on the exchange floor. There he joins other brokers and the specialist in the security being bought or sold, and executes the trade at the best competitive price available. On completion of the transaction, the customer is notified through his registered representative back at the firm, and the trade is printed on the consolidated ticker tape, which is displayed electronically around the country. A floor broker should not be confused with a FLOOR TRADER, who trades as a principal for his or her own account, rather than as a broker.

FLOOR OFFICIAL securities exchange employee, who is present on the floor of the exchange to settle disputes in the auction procedure, such as questions about priority or precedence in the settling of an auction. The floor official makes rulings on the spot and his or her judgment is usually accepted.

FLOOR TICKET summary of the information entered on the ORDER TICKET by the registered representative on receipt of a buy or sell order from a client. The floor ticket gives the floor broker the information needed to execute a securities transaction. The information required on floor tickets is specified by securities industry rules.

FLOOR TRADER member of a stock or commodities exchange who trades on the floor of that exchange for his or her own account. The floor trader must abide by trading rules similar to those of the exchange specialists who trade on behalf of others. The term should not be confused with FLOOR BROKER. *See also* REGISTERED COMPETITIVE TRADER.

FLOTATION (FLOATATION) COST cost of issuing new stocks or bonds. It varies with the amount of underwriting risk and the job of physical distribution. It comprises two elements: (1) the compensation earned by the investment bankers (the underwriters) in the form of the spread between the price paid to the issuer (the corporation or government agency) and the offering price to the public, and (2) the expenses of the issuer (legal, accounting, printing, and other out-of-pocket expenses). Securities and Exchange Commission studies reveal that flotation costs are higher for stocks than for bonds, reflecting the generally wider distribution and greater volatility of common stock as opposed to bonds, which are usually sold in large blocks to relatively few investors. The SEC also found that flotation costs as a percentage of gross proceeds are greater for smaller issues than for larger ones. This occurs because the issuer's legal and other expenses tend to be relatively large and fixed; also, smaller issues tend to originate with less established issuers, requiring more information development and marketing expense. An issue involving a RIGHTS OFFERING can involve negligible underwriting risk and selling effort and therefore minimal flotation cost, especially if the underpricing is substantial.

The UNDERWRITING SPREAD is the key variable in flotation cost, historically ranging from 23.7% of the size of a small issue of common stock to as low as 1.25% of the par value of high-grade bonds. Spreads are determined by both negotiation and competitive bidding.

FLOWER BOND type of U.S. government bond that, regardless of its cost price, is acceptable at par value in payment of estate taxes if the decedent was the legal holder at the time of death; also called *estate tax anticipation bond.* Flower bonds were issued as recently as 1971, and the last of them, with a 3½% coupon, will mature in 1998.

FLOW OF FUNDS
Economics: in referring to the national economy, the way funds are transferred from savings surplus units to savings deficit units through financial intermediaries. *See also* FINANCIAL INTERMEDIARY.

Municipal bonds: statement found in the bond resolutions of municipal revenue issues showing the priorities by which municipal revenue will be applied. Typically, the flow of funds in decreasing order of priority is operation and maintenance, bond debt service, expansion of the facility, and sinking fund for retirement of debt prior to maturity. The flow of funds statement varies in detail from issue to issue.

Mutual funds: movement of money into or out of mutual funds or between various fund sectors. Heavy inflows and outflows are viewed respectively as bullish or bearish indicators for the stock market in general or for stock prices of the underlying companies in different sectors.

FLUCTUATION
1. change in prices or interest rates, either up or down. Fluctuation may refer to either slight or dramatic changes in the prices of stocks, bonds, or commodities. *See also* FLUCTUATION LIMIT.
2. the ups and downs in the economy.

FLUCTUATION LIMIT limits placed on the daily ups and downs of futures prices by the commodity exchanges. The limit protects traders from losing too much on a particular contract in one day. If a commodity reaches its limit, it may not trade any further that day. *See also* LIMIT UP, LIMIT DOWN.

FLURRY sudden increase in trading activity in a particular security. For example, there will be a flurry of trading in the stock of a company that was just the target of a surprise takeover bid. There are often trading flurries right after a company releases its quarterly earnings.

FNMA *see* FEDERAL NATIONAL MORTGAGE ASSOCIATION.

FOB *see* FREE ON BOARD.

FOCUS REPORT FOCUS is an acronym for the Financial and Operational Combined Uniform Single report, which broker-dealers are required to file monthly and quarterly with self-regulatory organizations (SROs). The SROs include exchanges, securities associations, and clearing organizations registered with the Securities and Exchange Commission and required by federal securities laws to be self-policing. The FOCUS report contains figures on capital, earnings, trade flow, and other required details.

FOOTSIE popular name for the *Financial Times'* FT-SE 100 Index (Financial Times-Stock Exchange 100 stock index), a market-value (capitalization)-weighted index of 100 blue chip stocks traded on the London Stock Exchange.

FORBES 500 annual listing by *Forbes* magazine of the largest U.S. publicly-owned corporations ranked four ways: by sales, assets, profits, and market value. *See also* FORTUNE 500.

FORCED CONVERSION when a CONVERTIBLE security is called in by its issuer. Convertible owners may find it to their financial advantage either to sell or to convert their holdings into common shares of the underlying company or to accept the call price. Such a conversion usually takes place when the convertible is selling above its CALL PRICE because the market value of the shares of the underlying stock has risen sharply. *See also* CONVERTIBLE.

FORECASTING projecting current trends using existing data.
    Stock market forecasters predict the direction of the stock market by relying on technical data of trading activity and fundamental statistics on the direction of the economy.
    Economic forecasters foretell the strength of the economy, often by utilizing complex econometric models as a tool to make specific

predictions of future levels of inflation, interest rates, and employment. *See also* ECONOMETRICS.

Forecasting can also refer to various PROJECTIONS used in business and financial planning.

FORECLOSURE process by which a homeowner who has not made timely payments of principal and interest on a mortgage loses title to the home. The holder of the mortgage, whether it be a bank, a savings and loan, or an individual, must go to court to seize the property, which may then be sold to satisfy the claims of the mortgage.

FOREIGN CORPORATION
1. corporation chartered under the laws of a state other than the one in which it conducts business. Because of inevitable confusion with the term ALIEN CORPORATION, *out-of-state corporation* is preferred.
2. corporation organized under the laws of a foreign country; the term ALIEN CORPORATION is usually preferred.

FOREIGN CORRUPT PRACTICES SECURITIES EXCHANGE ACT OF 1934 amendment passed in 1977 providing internal controls and penalties aimed at curtailing bribery by publicly held companies of foreign government officials and personnel.

FOREIGN CROWD New York Stock Exchange members who trade on the floor in foreign bonds.

FOREIGN CURRENCY FUTURES AND OPTIONS futures and options contracts based on foreign currencies, such as the Japanese yen, Deutsche mark, British pound, and French franc. The buyer of a foreign currency futures contract acquires the right to buy a particular amount of that currency by a specific date at a fixed rate of exchange, and the seller agrees to sell that currency at the same fixed price. *Call options* give call buyers the right, but not the obligation, to buy the underlying currency at a particular price by a particular date. Call options on foreign currency futures give call buyers the right to a long underlying futures contracts. Those buying *put options* have the right to sell the underlying currencies at a specific price by a specific date. Most buyers and sellers of foreign currency futures and options do not exercise their rights to buy or sell, but trade out of their contracts at a profit or loss before they expire. SPECULATORS hope to profit by buying or selling a foreign currency futures or options contract before a currency rises or falls in value. HEDGERS buy or sell such contracts to protect their cash market position from fluctuations in currency values. These contracts are traded on SECURITIES AND COMMODITIES EXCHANGES throughout the world, including the CHICAGO MERCANTILE EXCHANGE (CME), FINEX, the Mid-America Commodity Exchange, and the PHILADELPHIA STOCK EXCHANGE (PHLX).

FOREIGN DIRECT INVESTMENT
1. investment in U.S. businesses by foreign citizens; usually involves majority stock ownership of the enterprise.
2. joint ventures between foreign and U.S. companies.

FOREIGN EXCHANGE instruments employed in making payments between countries—paper currency, notes, checks, bills of exchange, and electronic notifications of international debits and credits.

FOREIGN EXCHANGE RATE *see* EXCHANGE RATE. *See also* FOREIGN EXCHANGE.

FORFEITURE loss of rights or assets due to failure to fulfill a legal obligation or condition and as compensation for resulting losses or damages.

FORM 8-K Securities and Exchange Commission required form that a publicly held company must file, reporting on any material event that might affect its financial situation or the value of its shares, ranging from merger activity to amendment of the corporate charter or bylaws. The SEC considers as material all matters about which an average, prudent investor ought reasonably to be informed before deciding whether to buy, sell, or hold a registered security. Form 8-K must be filed within a month of the occurrence of the material event. Timely disclosure rules may require a corporation to issue a press release immediately concerning an event subsequently reported on Form 8-K.

FORM 4 document, filed with the Securities and Exchange Commission and the pertinent stock exchange, which is used to report changes in the holdings of (1) those who own at least 10% of a corporation's outstanding stock and (2) directors and officers, even if they own no stock. When there has been a major change in ownership, Form 4 must be filed within ten days of the end of the month in which the change took place. Form 4 filings must be constantly updated during a takeover attempt of a company when the acquirer buys more than 10% of the outstanding shares.

FORM T National Association of Securities Dealers (NASD) form for reporting equity transaction executed after the market's normal hours.

FORM 10-K annual report required by the Securities and Exchange Commission of every issuer of a registered security, every exchange-listed company, and any company with 500 or more shareholders or $1 million or more in gross assets. The form provides for disclosure of total sales, revenue, and pretax operating income, as well as sales by separate classes of products for each of a company's separate lines of business for each of the past five years. A source and application of funds statement presented on a comparative basis for the last two fiscal years is also required. Form 10-K becomes public information when filed with the SEC.

FORM 10-Q quarterly report required by the Securities and Exchange Commission of companies with listed securities. Form 10-Q is less comprehensive than the FORM 10-K annual report and does not require that figures be audited. It may cover the specific quarter or it may be cumulative. It should include comparative figures for the same period of the previous year.

FORM 13D form used to comply with SCHEDULE 13D.

FORM 13G short form of SCHEDULE 13D for positions acquired in the ordinary course of business and not to assume control or influence.

FORM 3 form filed with the Securities and Exchange Commission and the pertinent stock exchange by all holders of 10% or more of the stock of a company registered with the SEC and by all directors and officers, even if no shares are owned. Form 3 details the number of shares owned as well as the number of warrants, rights, convertible bonds, and options to purchase common stock. Individuals required to file Form 3 are considered insiders, and they are required to update their information whenever changes occur. Such changes are reported on FORM 4.

FORMULA INVESTING investment technique based on a predetermined timing or asset allocation model that eliminates emotional decisions. One type of formula investing, called dollar cost averaging, involves putting the same amount of money into a stock or mutual fund at regular intervals, so that more shares will be bought when the price is low and less when the price is high. Another formula investing method calls for shifting funds from stocks to bonds or vice versa as the stock market reaches particular price levels. If stocks rise to a particular point, a certain amount of the stock portfolio is sold and put in bonds. On the other hand, if stocks fall to a particular low price, money is brought out of bonds into stocks. *See also* CONSTANT DOLLAR PLAN; CONSTANT RATIO PLAN.

FORTUNE 500 listings of the top 500 U.S. corporations compiled by *Fortune* magazine. The companies are ranked by 12 indices, among them revenues; profits; assets; stockholders' equity; market value; profits as a percentage of revenues, assets, and stockholders' equity; earnings per share growth over a 10-year span; total return to investors in the year; and the 10-year annual rate of total return to investors. In separate listings, companies also are ranked by performance and within states. Headquarters city, phone number, and the name of the chief executive officer are included. In another listing 1,000 companies are ranked within 61 different industry groups.

FORWARD CONTRACT purchase or sale of a specific quantity of a commodity, government security, foreign currency, or other financial instrument at the current or SPOT PRICE, with delivery and settlement at a specified future date. Because it is a completed contract—as opposed to an options contract, where the owner has the choice of completing or not completing—a forward contract can be a COVER for the sale of a FUTURES CONTRACT. *See* HEDGE.

FORWARD EXCHANGE TRANSACTION purchase or sale of foreign currency at an exchange rate established now but with payment and delivery at a specified future time. Most forward exchange contracts have one-, three-, or six-month maturities, though contracts in major currencies can normally be arranged for delivery at any specified date up to a year, and sometimes up to three years.

FORWARD PRICING Securities and Exchange Commission requirement that open-end investment companies, whose share price is always determined by the NET ASSET VALUE of the outstanding shares, base all incoming buy and sell orders on the next net asset valuation of fund shares. *See also* INVESTMENT COMPANY.

FOR YOUR INFORMATION (FYI) prefix to a security price quote by a market maker that indicates the quote is "for your information" and is not a firm offer to trade at that price. FYI quotes are given as a courtesy for purposes of valuation. FVO (for valuation only) is sometimes used instead.

401(k) PLAN plan whereby employees may elect, as an alternative to receiving taxable cash in the form of compensation or a bonus, to contribute pretax dollars to a qualified tax-deferred retirement plan. Elective deferrals are limited to $10,000 a year (the amount is revised each year by the IRS based on inflation). Many companies, to encourage employee participation in the plan, match employee contributions anywhere from 10% to 100% annually. All employee contributions and employer matching funds can be invested in several options, usually including several stock mutual funds, bond mutual funds, a GUARANTEED INVESTMENT CONTRACT, a money market fund, and company stock. Employees control how the assets are allocated among the various choices, and can usually move the money at least once a year, and sometimes even daily. Withdrawals from 401(k) plans prior to age 59½ are subject to a 10% penalty tax except for death, disability, termination of employment, or qualifying hardship. Withdrawals after the age of 59½ are subject to taxation in the year the money is withdrawn. "Highly compensated" employees are subject to special limitations. 401(k) plans have become increasingly popular in recent years, in many cases supplanting traditional DEFINED BENEFIT PENSION PLANS. Employees favor them because they cut their tax bills in the year of contribution and their savings grow tax deferred until retirement. Companies favor these plans because they are less costly than traditional pension plans and also shift the responsibility for asset allocation to employees. Also called *cash or deferred arrangement* (CODA) or *salary reduction plan.*

403(b) PLAN type of INDIVIDUAL RETIREMENT ACCOUNT (IRA) covered in Section 403(b) of the Internal Revenue Code that permits employees of qualifying nonprofit organizations to set aside tax-deferred funds.

FOURTH MARKET direct trading of large blocks of securities between institutional investors to save brokerage commissions. The fourth market is aided by computers, notably by a computerized subscriber service called *INSTINET,* an acronym for Institutional Networks Corporation. INSTINET is registered with the Securities and Exchange Commission as a stock exchange and numbers among its subscribers a large number of mutual funds and other institutional investors linked to each other by computer terminals. The system permits subscribers to display tentative volume interest and bid-ask quotes to others in the system.

FRACTIONAL DISCRETION ORDER buy or sell order for securities that allows the broker discretion within a specified fraction of a point. For example, "Buy 1000 XYZ at 28, discretion ½ point" means that the broker may execute the trade at a maximum price of 28½.

FRACTIONAL SHARE unit of stock less than one full share. For instance, if a shareholder is in a dividend reinvestment program, and the dividends being reinvested are not adequate to buy a full share at the stock's current price, the shareholder will be credited with a fractional share until enough dividends accumulate to purchase a full share.

FRANCHISE
In general: (1) privilege given a dealer by a manufacturer or franchise service organization to sell the franchisor's products or services in a given area, with or without exclusivity. Such arrangements are sometimes formalized in *a franchise agreement,* which is a contract between the franchisor and franchisee wherein the former may offer consultation, promotional assistance, financing, and other benefits in exchange for a percentage of sales or profits. (2) The business owned by the franchisee, who usually must meet an initial cash investment requirement.
Government: legal right given to a company or individual by a government authority to perform some economic function. For example, an electrical utility might have the right, under the terms of a franchise, to use city property to provide electrical service to city residents.

FRANCHISED MONOPOLY monopoly granted by the government to a company. The firm will be protected from competition by government exclusive license, permit, patent, or other device. For example, an electric utility will be granted the exclusive right to generate and sell electricity in a particular locality in return for agreeing to be subject to governmental rate regulation.

FRANCHISE TAX state tax, usually regressive (that is, the rate decreases as the tax base increases), imposed on a state-chartered corporation for the right to do business under its corporate name. Franchise taxes are usually levied on a number of value bases, such as capital stock, capital stock plus surplus, capital, profits, or property in the state.

FRANKFURT STOCK EXCHANGE the largest of eight German securities exchanges, operated by DEUTSCHE BORSE AG. There are three membership classes: banks and other credit institutions that trade securities for their own accounts or on behalf of third parties; Kursmaklers, official brokers who act as intermediaries for securities trades in the Official Market and at the same time determine their prices; and Free Maklers, free brokers who act as intermediaries in any securities. Branches of foreign brokerage firms, which under national laws are not banks, are treated as banks. Stocks, fixed-income securities and warrants are traded on the floor and in two electronic trading systems— Xetra for stocks and IBIS-R for fixed income securities. Settlement has been computerized since 1970, and takes place on the second business day after the trade. Trading hours are 10:30 A.M. to 1:30 P.M., Monday through Friday. The IBIS system runs from 8:30 A.M. to 5 P.M.

FRAUD intentional misrepresentation, concealment, or omission of the truth for the purpose of deception or manipulation to the detriment of a person or an organization. Fraud is a legal concept and the application of the term in a specific instance should be determined by a legal expert.

FREDDIE MAC
1. nickname for FEDERAL HOME LOAN MORTGAGE CORPORATION (FHLMC).
2. mortgage-backed securities, issued in minimum denominations of $25,000, that are packaged, guaranteed, and sold by the FHLMC. Mortgage-backed securities are issues in which residential mortgages are packaged and sold to investors.

FREE AND OPEN MARKET market in which price is determined by the free, unregulated interchange of supply and demand. The opposite is a *controlled market,* where supply, demand, and price are artificially set, resulting in an *inefficient market.*

FREE BOX securities industry jargon for a secure storage place ("box") for fully paid ("free") customers' securities, such as a bank vault or the DEPOSITORY TRUST COMPANY.

FREED UP securities industry jargon meaning that the members of an underwriting syndicate are no longer bound by the price agreed upon and fixed in the AGREEMENT AMONG UNDERWRITERS. They are thus free to trade in the security on a market basis.

FREE ON BOARD (FOB) transportation term meaning that the invoice price includes delivery at the seller's expense to a specified point and no further. For example, "FOB our Newark warehouse" means that the buyer must pay all shipping and other charges associated with transporting the merchandise from the seller's warehouse in Newark to the buyer's receiving point. Title normally passes from seller to buyer at the FOB point by way of a bill of lading.

FREERIDING
1. practice, prohibited by the Securities and Exchange Commission and the National Association of Securities Dealers, whereby an underwriting SYNDICATE member withholds a portion of a new

securities issue and later resells it at a price higher than the initial offering price.

2. practice whereby a brokerage client buys and sells a security in rapid order without putting up money for the purchase. The practice violates REGULATION T of the Federal Reserve Board concerning broker-dealer credit to customers. The penalty requires that the customer's account be frozen for 90 days. *See also* FROZEN ACCOUNT.

FREE RIGHT OF EXCHANGE ability to transfer securities from one name to another without paying the charge associated with a sales transaction. The free right applies, for example, where stock in STREET NAME (that is, registered in the name of a broker-dealer) is transferred to the customer's name in order to be eligible for a dividend reinvestment plan. *See also* REGISTERED SECURITY.

FREE STOCK (1) stock that is fully paid for and is not assigned as collateral. (2) stock held by an issuer following a PRIVATE PLACEMENT but that can be traded free of the restrictions bearing on a LETTER SECURITY.

FREEZE OUT put pressure on minority shareholders after a takeover to sell their shares to the acquirer.

FREIT *see* FINITE LIFE REAL ESTATE INVESTMENT TRUST.

FRICTIONAL COST in an INDEX FUND, the amount by which the fund's return is less than that of the index it replicates. The difference, assuming it is not otherwise adjusted, represents the fund's management fees and transaction costs.

FRIENDLY TAKEOVER merger supported by the management and board of directors of the target company. The board will recommend to shareholders that they approve the takeover offer, because it represents fair value for the company's shares. In many cases, the acquiring company will retain many of the existing managers of the acquired company to continue to run the business. A friendly takeover is in contrast to a HOSTILE TAKEOVER, in which management actively resists the acquisition attempt by another company or RAIDER.

FRINGE BENEFITS compensation to employees in addition to salary. Some examples of fringe benefits are paid holidays, retirement plans, life and health insurance plans, subsidized cafeterias, company cars, stock options, and expense accounts. In many cases, fringe benefits can add significantly to an employee's total compensation, and are a key ingredient in attracting and retaining employees. For the most part, fringe benefits are not taxable to the employee, though they are generally tax-deductible for the employer.

FRONT-END LOAD sales charge applied to an investment at the time of initial purchase. There may be a front-end load on a mutual fund, for instance, which is sold by a broker. Annuities, life insurance policies, and limited partnerships can also have front-end loads. From the investor's point of view, the earnings from the investment should make up for this up-front fee within a relatively short period of time. *See also* INVESTMENT COMPANY.

FRONT OFFICE sales personnel in a brokerage, insurance, or other financial services operation. Front office workers produce revenue, in contrast to BACK OFFICE workers, who perform administrative and other support functions for the front office.

FRONT RUNNING practice whereby a securities or commodities trader takes a POSITION to capitalize on advance knowledge of a large upcoming transaction expected to influence the market price. In the stock market, this might be done by buying an OPTION on stock expected to benefit from a large BLOCK transaction. In commodities, DUAL TRADING is common practice and provides opportunities to profit from front running.

FROZEN ACCOUNT
Banking: bank account from which funds may not be withdrawn until a lien is satisfied and a court order is received freeing the balance.
   A bank account may also be frozen by court order in a dispute over the ownership of property.
Investments: brokerage account under disciplinary action by the Federal Reserve Board for violation of REGULATION T. During the period an account is frozen (90 days), the customer may not sell securities until their purchase price has been fully paid and the certificates have been delivered. The penalty is invoked commonly in cases of FREERIDING.

FULL COUPON BOND bond with a coupon rate that is near or above current market interest rates. If interest rates are generally about 8%, for instance, a 7½% or 9% bond is considered a full coupon bond.

FULL DISCLOSURE
In general: requirement to disclose all material facts relevant to a transaction.
Securities industry: public information requirements established by the Securities Act of 1933, the Securities Exchange Act of 1934, and the major stock exchanges.
   See also DISCLOSURE.

FULL FAITH AND CREDIT phrase meaning that the full taxing and borrowing power, *plus* revenue other than taxes, is pledged in payment of interest and repayment of principal of a bond issued by a government entity. U.S. government securities and general obligation bonds of states and local governments are backed by this pledge.

FULL REPLACEMENT COVERAGE *see* GUARANTEED REPLACEMENT COST COVERAGE INSURANCE.

FULL-SERVICE BROKER broker who provides a wide range of services to clients. Unlike a DISCOUNT BROKER, who just executes trades, a full-service broker offers advice on which stocks, bonds, commodities, and mutual funds to buy or sell. A full-service broker may also offer an ASSET MANAGEMENT ACCOUNT; advice on financial planning, tax shelters, and INCOME LIMITED PARTNERSHIPS; and new issues of stock. A full-service broker's commissions will be higher than those of a discount broker. The term *brokerage* is gradually being replaced by variations of the term *financial services* as the range of services offered by brokers expands.

FULL TRADING AUTHORIZATION freedom, even from broad guidelines, allowed a broker or adviser under a DISCRETIONARY ACCOUNT.

FULLY DEPRECIATED said of a fixed asset to which all the DEPRECIATION the tax law allows has been charged. Asset is carried on the books at its RESIDUAL VALUE, although its LIQUIDATING VALUE may be higher or lower.

FULLY DILUTED EARNINGS PER (COMMON) SHARE figure showing earnings per common share after assuming the exercise of warrants and stock options, and the conversion of convertible bonds and preferred stock (all potentially *dilutive* securities). Actually, it is more analytically correct to define the term as the smallest earnings per common share that can be obtained by computing EARNINGS PER SHARE (EPS) for all possible combinations of assumed exercise or conversion (because antidilutive securities—securities whose conversion would add to EPS—may not be assumed to be exercised or converted). Under accounting rules adopted in 1998, companies must report EPS on two bases: Basic EPS, which does not count stock options, warrants, and convertible securities, and (fully) Diluted EPS, which includes those securities. *See also* DILUTION; EARNINGS PER SHARE; PRIMARY EARNINGS PER (COMMON) SHARE.

FULLY DISTRIBUTED term describing a new securities issue that has been completely resold to the investing public (that is, to institutions and individuals and other investors rather than to dealers).

FULLY INVESTED said of an investor or a portfolio when funds in cash or CASH EQUIVALENTS are minimal and assets are totally committed to other investments, usually stock. To be fully invested is to have an optimistic view of the market.

FULLY VALUED said of a stock that has reached a price at which analysts think the underlying company's fundamental earnings power has been recognized by the market. If the stock goes up from that price, it is called OVERVALUED. If the stock goes down, it is termed UNDERVALUED.

FUND *see* FUND FAMILY; FUNDING; MUTUAL FUND.

FUNDAMENTAL ANALYSIS

Economics: research of such factors as interest rates, gross national product, inflation, unemployment, and inventories as tools to predict the direction of the economy.

Investment: analysis of the balance sheet and income statements of companies in order to forecast their future stock price movements. Fundamental analysts consider past records of assets, earnings, sales, products, management, and markets in predicting future trends in these indicators of a company's success or failure. By appraising a firm's prospects, these analysts assess whether a particular stock or group of stocks is UNDERVALUED or OVERVALUED at the current market price. The other major school of stock market analysis is TECHNICAL ANALYSIS, which relies on price and volume movements of stocks and does not concern itself with financial statistics.

FUNDED DEBT

1. debt that is due after one year and is formalized by the issuing of bonds or long-term notes.
2. bond issue whose retirement is provided for by a SINKING FUND. *See also* FLOATING DEBT.

FUNDED PENSION PLAN pension plan in which all liabilities are fully funded. A pension plan's administrator knows the potential payments necessary to make to pensioners over the coming years. In order to be funded, the plan must have enough capital contributions from the plan sponsor, plus returns from investments, to pay those claims. Employees are notified annually of the financial strength of their pension plans, and whether or not the plans are fully funded. If the plans are not funded, the PENSION BENEFIT GUARANTY CORPORATION (PBGC), which guarantees pension plans, will act to try to get the plan sponsor to contribute more money to the plan. If a company fails with an underfunded pension plan, the PBGC will step in to make the promised payments to pensioners.

FUND FAMILY mutual fund company offering funds with many investment objectives. A fund family may offer several types of stock, bond, and money market funds and allow free switching among their funds. Large no-load fund families include American Century, Fidelity, Dreyfus, T. Rowe Price, Scudder, Strong, and Vanguard. Most major brokerage houses such as Merrill Lynch, Smith Barney, and PaineWebber also sponsor fund families of their own. Many independent firms such as American Funds, Loomis-Sayles, Putnam, and Pioneer distribute their funds with a sales charge through brokerage firms and financial planners. Many investors find it convenient to place most of their assets with one or two fund families because of the convenience offered by such switching privileges. In recent years, several discount brokerage firms have offered the ability to shift assets from one fund family to another, making it less important than it had been to consolidate assets in one fund family. *See also* INVESTMENT COMPANY.

FUNDING
1. refinancing a debt on or before its maturity; also called REFUNDING and, in certain instances, PREREFUNDING.
2. putting money into investments or another type of reserve fund, to provide for future pension or welfare plans.
3. in corporate finance, the word *funding* is preferred to *financing* when referring to bonds in contrast to stock. A company is said to be funding its operations if it floats bonds.
4. to provide funds to finance a project, such as a research study
    See also SINKING FUND.

FUND MANAGER manager of a pool of money such as a mutual fund, pension fund, insurance fund, or bank-pooled fund. Their job is to maximize the fund's returns at the least risk possible. Each fund manager tries his or her best to realize the fund's objectives, whether it be growth, income, or some combination of the two. Different fund managers use different styles to accomplish their objectives. For example, some stock fund managers use the value style of investing, while others concentrate on growth stocks. In picking a fund, it is important to know the fund manager's style, and how long he or she has been managing the fund. This information is generally available for publicly offered mutual funds from fund company literature or fund representatives.

FUND OF FUNDS mutual fund that invests in other mutual funds. The concept behind such funds is that they are able to move money between the best funds in the industry, and thereby increase shareholders' returns with more diversification than is offered by a single fund. The fund of funds has been criticized as adding another layer of management expenses on shareholders, however, because fees are paid to the fund's management company as well as to all the underlying fund management companies. The SEC limits the total amount of fees that shareholders can pay in such a fund. Funds of funds are usually organized in a fund family of their own, offering funds that will specialize in international stocks, aggressive growth, income, and other objectives. Funds of funds were extremely popular in the 1960s, but then faded in popularity in the 1970s because of a scandal involving Equity Funding, which was a fund of funds. They have enjoyed a modest comeback in recent years, however.

FUND SWITCHING moving money from one mutual fund to another, within the same FUND FAMILY. Purchases and sales of funds may be done to time the ups and downs of the stock and bond markets, or because investors' financial needs have changed. Several newsletters and fund managers specialize in advising clients on which funds to switch into and out of, based on market conditions. Switching among funds within a fund family is usually allowed without sales charges. Discount brokerages allow convenient switching of funds among fund families. Unless practiced inside a tax-deferred account such as an IRA or Keogh account, a fund switch creates a taxable event, since CAPITAL GAINS OR LOSSES are realized.

FUNGIBLES bearer instruments, securities, or goods that are equivalent, substitutable, and interchangeable. Commodities such as soybeans or wheat, common shares of the same company, and dollar bills are all familiar examples of fungibles.

Fungibility (interchangeability) of listed options, by virtue of their common expiration dates and strike prices, makes it possible for buyers and sellers to close out their positions by putting offsetting transactions through the OPTIONS CLEARING CORPORATION. *See also* OFFSET; STRIKE PRICE.

FUN MONEY money that is not necessary for everyday living expenses, and can therefore be risked in volatile, but potentially highly profitable, investments. If the investment pans out, the investor has had some fun speculating. If the investment turns sour, the investor's lifestyle has not been put at risk because he or she could afford to lose the money.

FURTHEST MONTH in commodities or options trading, the month that is furthest away from settlement of the contract. For example, Treasury bill futures may have outstanding contracts for three, six, or nine months. The six- and nine-month contracts would be the furthest months, and the three-month contract would be the NEAREST MONTH.

FUTA *see* FEDERAL UNEMPLOYMENT TAX ACT (FUTA).

FUTOP the screen-traded, Danish derivatives market which merged with the COPENHAGEN STOCK EXCHANGE in 1997. FUTOP offers futures and options on the KFX Stock Index, Danish government bonds, and Danish equities.

FUTURES CONTRACT agreement to buy or sell a specific amount of a commodity or financial instrument at a particular price on a stipulated future date. The price is established between buyer and seller on the floor of a commodity exchange, using the OPEN OUTCRY system. A futures contract obligates the buyer to purchase the underlying commodity and the seller to sell it, unless the contract is sold to another before settlement date, which may happen if a trader waits to take a profit or cut a loss. This contrasts with options trading, in which the option buyer may choose whether or not to exercise the option by the exercise date. *See also* FORWARD CONTRACT; FUTURES MARKET.

FUTURES MARKET exchange where futures contracts and options on futures contracts are traded. Different exchanges specialize in particular kinds of contracts. The major exchanges in the U.S. are the COFFEE, SUGAR AND COCOA EXCHANGE; COMEX; FINEX; NEW YORK COTTON EXCHANGE; NEW YORK MERCANTILE EXCHANGE; and the NEW YORK FUTURES EXCHANGE, all in New York; the CHICAGO BOARD OF TRADE; INTERNATIONAL MONETARY MARKET; CHICAGO MERCANTILE EXCHANGE; and the CHICAGO RICE AND COTTON EXCHANGE, all in Chicago; and the KANSAS CITY BOARD OF TRADE, in Kansas City, MO.

Futures markets from around the world are also described elsewhere in this *Dictionary* including: DEUTSCHE TERMINBORSE; EUREX; INTERNATIONAL PETROLEUM EXCHANGE; LONDON INTERNATIONAL FINANCIAL FUTURES AND OPTIONS EXCHANGE (LIFFE); MARCHE A TERME INTERNATIONAL DE FRANCE (MATIF); MONTREAL EXCHANGE; SWISS OPTIONS AND FINANCIAL FUTURES EXCHANGE (SOFFEX); SYDNEY FUTURES EXCHANGE (SFE); TORONTO FUTURES EXCHANGE AND WINIPEG COMMODITY EXCHANGE. *See also* SECURITIES AND COMMODITIES EXCHANGES; SPOT MARKET.

FUTURES OPTION OPTION on a FUTURES CONTRACT.

FUTURE VALUE reverse of PRESENT VALUE.

FVO (FOR VALUATION ONLY) *see* FOR YOUR INFORMATION.

G

GAAP *see* GENERALLY ACCEPTED ACCOUNTING PRINCIPLES (GAAP).

GAIJIN non-Japanese investor in Japan. The Japanese refer to foreign competitors, on both the individual and institutional levels, as gaijin. In particular, the large, prestigious American and European brokerage firms that compete with the major Japanese brokerage firms, such as Nomura and Nikko, are called gaijin.

GAIN profit on a securities transaction. A gain is realized when a stock, bond, mutual fund, futures contract, or other financial instrument is sold for more than its purchase price. If the instrument was held for more than a year, the gain is taxable at more favorable capital gains tax rates. If held for under a year, the gain is taxed at regular income tax rates.

GAMMA STOCKS obsolete classification of stocks traded on the London Stock Exchange. Ranking third behind ALPHA and BETA stocks in capitalization and activity, gamma stocks are less regulated, requiring just two market makers quoting indicative share prices. *See also* NORMAL MARKET SIZE (NMS).

GAP
Finance: amount of a financing need for which provision has yet to be made. For example, ABC company might need $1.5 million to purchase and equip a new plant facility. It arranges a mortgage loan of $700,000, secures equipment financing of $400,000, and obtains new equity of $150,000. That leaves a gap of $250,000 for which it seeks gap financing. Such financing may be available from state and local governments concerned with promoting economic development.
Securities: securities industry term used to describe the price movement of a stock or commodity when one day's trading range for the stock or commodity does not overlap the next day's, causing a range, or gap, in which no trade has occurred. This usually takes place because of some extraordinary positive or negative news about the company or commodity. *See* chart on next page. *See also* PRICE GAP.

GAP OPENING opening price for a stock that is significantly higher or lower than the previous day's closing price. For example, if XYZ Company was the subject of a $50 takeover bid after the market closed with its shares trading at $30, its share price might open the next morning at $45 a share. There would therefore be a gap between the closing price of $30 and the opening price of $45. The same phenomenon can occur on the downside if a company reports disappointing earnings or a takeover bid falls through, for example. Stocks trading on the New York or American Stock Exchange may experience a delayed opening when such an event occurs as the specialist deals with the rush of buy or sell orders to find the stock's appropriate price level.

GARAGE annex floor on the north side of the main trading floor of the New York Stock Exchange.

GARBATRAGE stock traders' term, combining garbage and ARBITRAGE, for activity in stocks swept upward by the psychology surrounding a major takeover. For example, when two leading entertainment stocks, Time, Inc., and Warner Communications, Inc., were IN PLAY in 1989, stocks with insignificant involvement in the entertainment sector became active. Garbatrage would not apply to activity in bona fide entertainment stocks moving on speculation that other mergers would follow in the wake of Time-Warner. *See also* RUMORTRAGE.

GARNISHMENT court order to an employer to withhold all or part of an employee's wages and send the money to the court or to a person who has won a lawsuit against the employee. An employee's wages will be *garnished* until the court-ordered debt is paid. Garnishing may be used in a divorce settlement or for repayment of creditors.

GATHER IN THE STOPS stock-trading tactic that involves selling a sufficient amount of stock to drive down the price to a point where stop orders (orders to buy or sell at a given price) are known to exist. The stop orders are then activated to become market orders (orders to buy or sell at the best available price), in turn creating movement which touches off other stop orders in a process called SNOWBALLING. Because this can cause sharp trading swings, floor officials on the exchanges have the authority to suspend stop orders in individual securities if that seems advisable. *See also* STOP ORDER.

GDP IMPLICIT PRICE DEFLATOR ratio of current-dollar GROSS DOMESTIC PRODUCT (GDP) to constant-dollar GDP. Changes in the implicit price deflator reflect both changes in prices of all goods and services that make up GDP and changes in the composite of GDP. Over time, the implicit price deflator understates inflation because people tend to shift consumption from goods that have high prices or rapidly increasing prices to goods that have less rapidly increasing prices. Therefore, theoretically, prices of all goods and service could increase and the implicit price deflator could decrease. *See also* PERSONAL INFLATION RATE.

G-8 FINANCE MINISTERS the finance ministers of the eight largest industrial countries: Canada, France, Germany, Great Britain, Italy, Japan, Russia and the United States. Meetings of the G-8 take place at least once a year and are important in coordinating economic policy among the major industrial countries. The political leaders of the G-8 countries also meet once a year, usually in July, at the Economic Summit, which is held in one of the eight countries. Before the admission of Russia in 1998, the group was called G-7 Finance Ministers and that designation was still being used in the late 1990s.

GENERAL ACCOUNT Federal Reserve Board term for brokerage customer margin accounts subject to REGULATION T, which covers extensions of credit by brokers for the purchase and short sale of securities. The Fed requires that all transactions in which the broker advances credit to the customer be made in this account. *See also* MARGIN ACCOUNT.

GENERAL AGREEMENT ON TARIFFS AND TRADE (GATT) United Nations-associated international treaty organization headquartered in Geneva that works to eliminate barriers to trade between nations. In December 1994 Congress approved a pact that reduced tariffs, enhanced international copyright protections, and generally liberalized trade. *See also* WORLD TRADE ORGANIZATION (WTO).

GENERAL LEDGER formal ledger containing all the financial statement accounts of a business. It contains offsetting debit and credit accounts, the totals of which are proved by a trial balance. Certain accounts in the general ledger, termed *control accounts,* summarize the detail booked on separate subsidiary ledgers.

GENERAL LIEN LIEN against an individual that excludes real property. The lien carries the right to seize personal property to satisfy a debt. The property seized need not be the property that gave rise to the debt.

GENERAL LOAN AND COLLATERAL AGREEMENT continuous agreement under which a securities broker-dealer borrows from a bank against listed securities to buy or carry inventory, finance the underwriting of new issues, or carry the margin accounts of clients. Synonymous with *broker's loan. See also* BROKER LOAN RATE; MARGIN ACCOUNT; UNDERWRITE.

GENERALLY ACCEPTED ACCOUNTING PRINCIPLES (GAAP) conventions, rules, and procedures that define accepted accounting practice, including broad guidelines as well as detailed procedures.

The basic doctrine was set forth by the Accounting Principles Board of the American Institute of Certified Public Accountants, which was superseded in 1973 by the FINANCIAL ACCOUNTING STANDARDS BOARD (FASB), an independent self-regulatory organization.

GENERAL MORTGAGE mortgage covering all the mortgageable properties of a borrower and not restricted to any particular piece of property. Such a blanket mortgage can be lower in priority of claim in liquidation than one or more other mortgages on specific parcels.

GENERAL OBLIGATION BOND municipal bond backed by the FULL FAITH AND CREDIT (which includes the taxing and further borrowing power) of a municipality. A *GO bond,* as it is known, is repaid with general revenue and borrowings, in contrast to the revenue from a specific facility built with the borrowed funds, such as a tunnel or a sewer system. *See also* REVENUE BOND.

GENERAL PARTNER
1. one of two or more partners who are jointly and severally responsible for the debts of a partnership.
2. managing partner of a LIMITED PARTNERSHIP, who is responsible for the operations of the partnership and, ultimately, any debts taken on by the partnership. The general partner's liability is unlimited. In a real estate partnership, the general partner will pick the properties to be bought and will manage them. In an oil and gas partnership, the general partner will select drilling sites and oversee drilling activity. In return for these services, the general partner collects certain fees and often retains a percentage of ownership in the partnership.

GENERAL REVENUE when used in reference to state and local governments taken separately, the term refers to total revenue less revenue from utilities, sales of alcoholic beverages, and insurance trusts. When speaking of combined state and local total revenue, the term refers only to taxes, charges, and miscellaneous revenue, which avoids the distortion of overlapping intergovernmental revenue.

GENERAL REVENUE SHARING unrestricted funds (which can be used for any purpose) provided by the federal government until 1987 to the 50 states and to more than 38,000 cities, towns, counties, townships, Indian tribes, and Alaskan native villages under the State and Local Fiscal Assistance Act of 1972.

GENERATION-SKIPPING TRANSFER OR TRUST arrangement whereby your principal goes into a TRUST when you die, and transfers to your grandchildren when your children die, but which provides income to your children while they live. Once a major tax loophole for the wealthy because taxes were payable only at your death and your grandchildren's death, now only $1 million can be transferred tax-free to the grandchildren. Otherwise, a special generation-skipping tax—with rates equal to the maximum ESTATE TAX rate—applies to transfers to grandchildren, whether the gifts are direct or from a trust.

GHOSTING illegal manipulation of a company's stock price by two or more market makers. One firm will push a stock's price higher or lower, and the other firms will follow their lead in collusion to drive the stock's price up or down. The practice is called ghosting because the investing public is unaware of this coordinated activity among market makers who are supposed to be competing with each other.

GIC *see* GUARANTEED INVESTMENT CONTRACT.

GIFT INTER VIVOS gift of property from one living person to another, without consideration.

GIFT SPLITTING dividing a gift into $10,000 pieces to avoid GIFT TAX. For example, a husband and wife wanting to give $20,000 to their child will give $10,000 each instead of $20,000 from one parent, so that no gift tax is due.

GIFT TAX graduated tax, levied on the donor of a gift by the federal government and most state governments when assets are transferred from one person to another. The more money given as a gift, the higher the tax rate. The ECONOMIC RECOVERY TAX ACT OF 1981 allowed a $10,000 federal gift tax exemption per recipient. This means that individuals can gift $10,000 a year free of gift tax to another person ($20,000 from a married couple). The gift tax is computed on the fair market value of the asset being transferred above the $10,000 exemption level. According to the TAXPAYER RELIEF ACT OF 1997, this gift tax limit is indexed to inflation in $1,000 increments, starting on January 1, 1999. For those making gifts over the limit, a federal gift tax return using IRS Form 709 must be filed by April 15th of the year following the year of the gift. Gifts between spouses are not subject to gift tax. Many states match the $10,000 gift tax exemption, but some allow a smaller amount to be gifted free of tax. *See also* FEDERAL GIFT TAX; GIFT SPLITTING.

GILT-EDGED SECURITY stock or bond of a company that has demonstrated over a number of years that it is capable of earning sufficient profits to cover dividends on stocks and interest on bonds with great dependability. The term is used with corporate bonds more often than with stocks, where the term BLUE CHIP is more common.

GILTS bonds issued by the British government. Gilts are the equivalent of Treasury securities in the United States in that they are perceived to have no risk of default. Income earned from investing in gilts is therefore guaranteed. Gilt yields act as the benchmark against which all other British bond yields are measured. Gilt futures are traded on the LONDON INTERNATIONAL FINANCIAL FUTURES AND OPTIONS EXCHANGE (LIFFE). The name gilt is derived from the original British government certificates, which had gilded edges.

GINNIE MAE nickname for the GOVERNMENT NATIONAL MORTGAGE ASSOCIATION and the securities guaranteed by that agency. *See also* GINNIE MAE PASS-THROUGH.

GINNIE MAE PASS-THROUGH security, backed by a pool of mortgages and guaranteed by the GOVERNMENT NATIONAL MORTGAGE ASSOCIATION (Ginnie Mae), which passes through to investors the interest and principal payments of homeowners. Homeowners make their mortgage payments to the bank or savings and loan that originated their mortgage. After deducting a service charge (usually ½%), the bank forwards the mortgage payments to the pass-through buyers, who may be institutional investors or individuals. Ginnie Mae guarantees that investors will receive timely principal and interest payments even if homeowners do not make mortgage payments on time.

The introduction of Ginnie Mae pass-throughs has benefited the home mortgage market, since more capital has become available for lending. Investors, who are able to receive high, government-guaranteed interest payments, have also benefited. For investors, however, the rate of principal repayment on a Ginnie Mae pass-through is uncertain. If interest rates fall, principal will be repaid faster, since homeowners will refinance their mortgages. If rates rise, principal will be repaid more slowly, since homeowners will hold onto the underlying mortgages. *See also* HALF-LIFE.

GIVE UP
1. term used in a securities transaction involving three brokers, as illustrated by the following scenario: Broker A, a FLOOR BROKER, executes a buy order for Broker B, another member firm broker who has too much business at the time to execute the order. The broker with whom Broker A completes the transaction (the sell side broker) is Broker C. Broker A "gives up" the name of Broker B, so that the record shows a transaction between Broker B and Broker C even though the trade was actually executed between Broker A and Broker C.
2. another application of the term: A customer of brokerage firm ABC Co. travels out of town and, finding no branch office of ABC, places an order with DEF Co., saying he is an account of ABC. After confirming the account relationship, DEF completes a trade with GHI Co., advising GHI that DEF is acting for ABC ("giving up" ABC's name). ABC will then handle the clearing details of the transaction with GHI. Alternatively, DEF may simply send the customer's order directly to ABC for execution. Whichever method is used, the customer pays only one commission.

GLAMOR STOCK stock with a wide public and institutional following. Glamor stocks achieve this following by producing steadily rising sales and earnings over a long period of time. In bull (rising) markets, glamor stocks tend to rise faster than market averages. Although a glamor stock is often in the category of a BLUE CHIP stock, the glamor is characterized by a higher earnings growth rate.

GLASS-STEAGALL ACT OF 1933 legislation passed by Congress authorizing deposit insurance and prohibiting commercial banks from owning full-service brokerage firms. Under Glass-Steagall, these banks were prohibited from investment banking activities, such as underwriting corporate securities or municipal revenue bonds. The law was designed to insulate bank depositors from the risk involved when a bank deals in securities and to prevent a bank collapse like the one that occurred during the Great Depression. The original separation of commercial and investment banking has been significantly eroded in recent years, however, since banks now own discount brokerage operations, sell mutual funds and can perform some corporate and municipal underwriting operations, and can provide other investment services.

GLOBAL DEPOSITARY RECEIPT receipt for shares in a foreign-based corporation traded in capital markets around the world. While AMERICAN DEPOSITARY RECEIPTS permit foreign corporations to offer shares to American citizens, Global Depositary Receipts (GDRs) allow companies in Europe, Asia, the United States and Latin America to offer shares in many markets around the world. The advantage to the issuing company is that they can raise capital in many markets, as opposed to just their home market. The advantage of GDRs to local investors is that they do not have to buy shares through the issuing company's home exchange, which may be difficult and expensive. In addition, the share price and all dividends are converted into the shareholder's home currency. Many GDRs are issued by companies in emerging markets such as China, India, Brazil, and South Korea and are traded on major stock exchanges, particularly the London SEAQ International Trading system. Because the companies issuing GDRs are not as well established and do not use the same accounting systems as traditional Western corporations, their stocks tend to be more volatile and less liquid.

GLOBAL MUTUAL FUND mutual fund that can invest in stocks and bonds throughout the world. Such funds typically have a portion of their assets in American markets as well as Europe, Asia, and developing countries. Global funds differ from INTERNATIONAL MUTUAL FUNDS, which invest only in non-U.S. securities. The advantage of global funds is that the fund managers can buy stocks or bonds anywhere they think has the best opportunities for high returns. Thus if one market is underperforming, they can shift assets to markets with better potential. Though some global funds invest in both stocks and bonds, most funds specialize in either stocks or bonds.

GNOMES OF ZÜRICH term coined by Labour ministers of Great Britain, during the sterling crisis of 1964, to describe the financiers and bankers in Zürich, Switzerland, who were engaged in foreign exchange speculation.

GNP *see* GROSS NATIONAL PRODUCT.

GOAL financial objective set by an individual or institution. For example, an individual investor might set a goal to accumulate enough capital to finance a child's college education. A pension fund's goal is to build up enough money to pay pensioners their promised benefits. Investors may also set specific price objectives when buying a security. For example, an investor buying a stock at $30 may set a price goal of $50, at which point he or she will sell shares, or at least reevaluate whether or not to continue holding the stock. Also called *target price.*

GO AROUND term used to describe the process whereby the trading desk at the New York Federal Reserve Bank ("the DESK"), acting on behalf of the FEDERAL OPEN MARKET COMMITTEE, contacts primary dealers for bid and offer prices. Primary dealers are those banks and investment houses approved for direct purchase and sale transactions with the Federal Reserve System in its OPEN MARKET OPERATIONS.

GODFATHER OFFER takeover offer that is so generous that management of the target company is unable to refuse it out of fear of shareholder lawsuits.

GO-GO FUND MUTUAL FUND that invests in highly risky but potentially rewarding stocks. During the 1960s many go-go funds shot up in value, only to fall dramatically later and, in some cases, to go out of business as their speculative investments fizzled.

GOING AHEAD unethical securities brokerage act whereby the broker trades first for his own account before filling his customers' orders. Brokers who go ahead violate the RULES OF FAIR PRACTICE of the National Association of Securities Dealers.

GOING AWAY bonds purchased by dealers for immediate resale to investors, as opposed to bonds purchased *for stock*—that is, to be held in inventory for resale at some future time. The significance of the difference is that bonds bought going away will not overhang the market and cause adverse pressure on prices.

　　The term is also used in new offerings of serial bonds to describe large purchases, usually by institutional investors, of the bonds in a particular maturity grouping (or series).

GOING-CONCERN VALUE value of a company as an operating business to another company or individual. The excess of going-concern value over asset value, or LIQUIDATING VALUE, is the value of the operating organization as distinct from the value of its assets. In acquisition accounting, going-concern value in excess of asset value is treated as an intangible asset, termed *goodwill.* Goodwill is generally understood to represent the value of a well-respected business name, good customer relations, high employee morale, and other such factors expected to translate into greater than normal earning power. However, because this intangible asset has no independent market or liquidation value, accepted accounting principles require that goodwill be written off over a period of time. The Revenue Reconciliation Act of 1993 provides that goodwill and related intangible assets can be deducted ratably over a 15-year (180-month) period on a straight-line method.

GOING LONG purchasing a stock, bond, or commodity for investment or speculation. Such a security purchase is known as a LONG POSITION. The opposite of going long is GOING SHORT, when an investor sells a security he does not own and thereby creates a SHORT POSITION.

GOING PRIVATE movement from public ownership to private ownership of a company's shares either by the company's repurchase of shares or through purchases by an outside private investor. A company usually goes private when the market price of its shares is substantially below their BOOK VALUE and the opportunity thus exists to buy the assets cheaply. Another motive for going private is to ensure the tenure of existing management by removing the company as a takeover prospect.

GOING PUBLIC securities industry phrase used when a private company first offers its shares to the public. The firm's ownership thus shifts from the hands of a few private stockowners to a base that includes public shareholders. At the moment of going public, the stock is called an INITIAL PUBLIC OFFERING. From that point on, or until the company goes private again, its shares have a MARKET VALUE. *See also* NEW ISSUE; GOING PRIVATE.

GOING SHORT selling a stock or commodity that the seller does not have. An investor who goes short borrows stock from his or her broker, hoping to purchase other shares of it at a lower price. The investor will then replace the borrowed stock with the lower priced stock and keep the difference as profit. *See also* SELLING SHORT; GOING LONG.

GOLD BARS bars made out of 99.5% to 99.99% pure gold which can be traded for investment purposes or held by central banks. Gold bars range in size from 400 troy ounces to as little as 1 ounce of gold; an individual can either hold on to these bars or store them in a safe deposit box. Central banks store gold bars weighing 400 troy ounces in vaults. In the United States, gold is stored at a few Federal Reserve banks and Fort Knox, for example. In the past, this gold directly backed the American currency, but now it serves more as a symbolic backing for dollars issued by the Federal Reserve.

GOLD BOND bond backed by gold. Such debt obligations are issued by gold-mining companies, who peg interest payments to the level of gold prices. Investors who buy these bonds therefore anticipate a rising gold price. Silver mining firms similarly issue silver-backed bonds.

GOLDBUG analyst enamored of gold as an investment. Goldbugs usually are worried about possible disasters in the world economy, such as a depression or hyperinflation, and recommend gold as a HEDGE.

GOLD BULLION gold in its purest form. The metal may be smelted into GOLD COINS or GOLD BARS of different sizes. The price of gold bullion is set by market forces of supply and demand. Twice a day, the latest gold price is fixed at the London GOLD FIXING. Gold bullion is traded in physical form, and also through futures and options contracts. Certain gold-oriented mutual funds also hold small amounts of gold bullion.

GOLD CERTIFICATE paper certificate providing evidence of ownership of gold bullion. An investor not wanting to hold the actual gold in his or her home because of lack of security, for example, may prefer to hold gold in certificate form; the physical gold backing the certificate is held in a secure bank vault. Certificate owners pay a small custodial charge each year to the custodian bank.

GOLD COIN coin minted in gold. Bullion coins are minted by governments and are traded mostly on the value of their gold content. Major gold bullion coins include the American Eagle, the Canadian Maple Leaf, the Mexican Peso, the Australian Kangaroo, and the South African Kruggerand. Other gold coins, called NUMISMATIC COINS, are minted in limited quantity and trade more on the basis of their aesthetic value and rarity, rather than on their gold content. Numismatic coins are sold at a hefty markup to their gold content, and are therefore not as pure a play on gold prices as bullion coins.

GOLDEN BOOT inducement, using maximum incentives and financial benefits, for an older worker to take "voluntary" early retirement, thus circumventing age discrimination laws.

GOLDEN HANDCUFFS contract that ties a broker to a brokerage firm. If the broker stays at the firm, he or she will earn lucrative commissions, bonuses, and other compensation. But if the broker leaves and tries to lure clients to another firm, the broker must promise to give back to the firm much of the compensation received while working there. Golden handcuffs are a response by the brokerage industry to the frequent movement of brokers from one firm to another.

GOLDEN HANDSHAKE generous payment by a company to a director, senior executive, or consultant who is let go before his or her contract expires because of a takeover or other development. *See also* GOLDEN PARACHUTE.

GOLDEN HELLO bonus paid by a securities firm, usually in England, to get a key employee away from a competing firm.

GOLDEN PARACHUTE lucrative contract given to a top executive to provide lavish benefits in case the company is taken over by another firm, resulting in the loss of the job. A golden parachute might include generous severance pay, stock options, or a bonus. The TAX REFORM ACT OF 1984 eliminated the deductibility of "excess compensation" and imposed an excise tax. The TAX REFORM ACT OF 1986 covered matters of clarification.

GOLD FIXING daily determination of the price of gold by selected gold specialists and bank officials in London, Paris, and Zürich. The price is fixed at 10:30 A.M. and 3:30 P.M. London time every business day, according to the prevailing market forces of supply and demand.

GOLDILOCKS ECONOMY term coined in the mid-90s to describe an economy that was "not too hot, not too cold, just right," as was the porridge in the children's story of "Goldilocks and the Three Bears." Adroit MONETARY POLICY was credited for an economy that enjoyed steady growth with a nominal rate of inflation. *See also* SOFT LANDING.

GOLD MUTUAL FUND mutual fund investing in gold mining shares. Some funds limit themselves to shares in North American mining companies, while others can buy shares anywhere in the world, including predominantly South Africa and Australia. Such mutual funds offer investors diversification among many gold mining companies, somewhat reducing risks. Still, such funds tend to be volatile, since the prices of gold mining shares tend to move up or down far more than the price of gold itself. Gold funds also tend to pay dividends, since many gold mining companies pay dividends based on gold sales.

GOLD STANDARD monetary system under which units of currency are convertible into fixed amounts of gold. Such a system is said to be anti-inflationary. The United States has been on the gold standard in the past but was taken off in 1971. *See also* HARD MONEY.

GOODBYE KISS *see* GREENMAIL.

GOOD DELIVERY securities industry designation meaning that a certificate has the necessary endorsements and meets all other requirements (signature guarantee, proper denomination, and other qualifications), so that title can be transferred by delivery to the buying broker, who is then obligated to accept it. Exceptions constitute *bad delivery. See also* DELIVERY DATE.

GOOD FAITH DEPOSIT
In general: token amount of money advanced to indicate intent to pursue a contract to completion.
Commodities: initial margin deposit required when buying or selling a futures contract. Such deposits generally range from 2% to 10% of the contract value.
Securities:
1. deposit, usually 25% of a transaction, required by securities firms of individuals who are not known to them but wish to enter orders with them.
2. deposit left with a municipal bond issuer by a firm competing for the underwriting business. The deposit typically equals 1% to 5% of the principal amount of the issue and is refundable to the unsuccessful bidders.

GOOD MONEY
Banking: federal funds, which are good the same day, in contrast to CLEARING HOUSE FUNDS. Clearing house funds are understood in two

ways: (1) funds requiring three days to clear and (2) funds used to settle transactions on which there is a one-day FLOAT.

Gresham's Law: theory that money of superior intrinsic value, "good money," will eventually be driven out of circulation by money of lesser intrinsic value. *See also* GRESHAM'S LAW.

GOOD-THIS-MONTH ORDER (GTM) order to buy or sell securities (usually at a LIMIT PRICE or STOP PRICE set by the customer) that remains in effect until the end of the month. In the case of a limit price, the customer instructs the broker either to buy at the stipulated limit price or anything lower, or to sell at the limit price or anything higher. In the case of a stop price, the customer instructs the broker to enter a market order once a transaction in the security occurs at the stop price specified.

A variation on the GTM order is the *good-this-week-order* (GTW), which expires at the end of the week if it is not executed.

See also DAY ORDER; GOOD-TILL-CANCELED ORDER; LIMIT ORDER; OPEN ORDER; STOP ORDER.

GOOD THROUGH order to buy or sell securities or commodities at a stated price for a stated period of time, unless canceled, executed, or changed. It is a type of LIMIT ORDER and may be specified GTW (good this week), GTM (GOOD-THIS-MONTH ORDER), or for shorter or longer periods.

GOOD-TILL-CANCELED ORDER (GTC) brokerage customer's order to buy or sell a security, usually at a particular price, that remains in effect until executed or canceled. If the GTC order remains unfilled after a long period of time, a broker will usually periodically confirm that the customer still wants the transaction to occur if the stock reaches the target price. *See also* DAY ORDER; GOOD-THIS-MONTH ORDER; OPEN ORDER; TARGET PRICE.

GOODWILL *see* GOING-CONCERN VALUE.

GOVERNMENT NATIONAL MORTGAGE ASSOCIATION (GNMA) government-owned corporation, nicknamed Ginnie Mae, which is an agency of the U.S. Department of Housing and Urban Development. GNMA guarantees, with the full faith and credit of the U.S. Government, full and timely payment of all monthly principal and interest payments on the mortgage-backed PASS-THROUGH SECURITIES of registered holders. The securities, which are issued by private firms, such as MORTGAGE BANKERS and savings institutions, and typically marketed through security broker-dealers, represent pools of residential mortgages insured or guaranteed by the Federal Housing Administration (FHA), the Farmer's Home Administration (FmHA), or the Veterans Administration (VA). *See also* FEDERAL HOME LOAN MORTGAGE CORPORATION; FEDERAL NATIONAL MORTGAGE ASSOCIATION; GINNIE MAE PASS-THROUGH.

GOVERNMENT OBLIGATIONS U.S. government debt instruments (Treasury bonds, bills, notes, savings bonds) the government has pledged to repay. *See* GOVERNMENTS.

GOVERNMENTS
1. securities issued by the U.S. government, such as Treasury bills, bonds, notes, and savings bonds. Governments are the most credit-worthy of all debt instruments since they are backed by the FULL FAITH AND CREDIT of the U.S. government, which if necessary can print money to make payments. Also called TREASURIES.
2. debt issues of federal agencies, which are not directly backed by the U.S. government. *See also* GOVERNMENT SECURITIES.

GOVERNMENT SECURITIES securities issued by U.S. government agencies, such as the RESOLUTION FUNDING CORPORATION (REFCORP) or the Federal Land Bank; also called *agency securities.* Although these securities have high credit ratings, they are not considered to be GOVERNMENT OBLIGATIONS and therefore are not directly backed by the FULL FAITH AND CREDIT of the government as TREASURIES are. *See also* AGENCY SECURITIES.

GRACE PERIOD period of time provided in most loan contracts and insurance policies during which default or cancellation will not occur even though payment is due.
Credit cards: number of days between when a credit card bill is sent and when the payment is due without incurring interest charges. Most banks offer credit card holders a 25-day grace period, though some offer more and others fewer days.
Insurance: number of days, typically 30, during which insurance cov-erage is in force and premiums have not been paid.
Loans: provision in some long-term loans, particularly EUROCUR-RENCY syndication loans to foreign governments and multinational firms by groups of banks, whereby repayment of principal does not begin until some point well into the lifetime of the loan. The grace period, which can be as long as five years for international transac-tions for corporations, is an important point of negotiation between a borrower and a lender; borrowers sometimes will accept a higher interest rate to obtain a longer grace period.

GRADUATED CALL WRITING strategy of writing (selling) covered CALL OPTIONS at gradually higher EXERCISE PRICES so that as the price of the underlying stock rises and the options are exercised, the seller winds up with a higher average price than the original exercise price. The premiums naturally rise as the underlying stock rises, representing income to the seller that helps offset the loss if the stock should decline.

GRADUATED LEASE longer-term lease in which payments, instead of being fixed, are adjusted periodically based on appraisals or a bench-mark rate, such as increases in the CONSUMER PRICE INDEX.

GRADUATED-PAYMENT MORTGAGE (GPM) mortgage featuring lower monthly payments at first, which steadily rise until they level off after a few years. GPMs, also known as "jeeps," are designed for young couples whose income is expected to grow as their careers advance. A graduated-payment mortgage allows such a family to buy a house that would be unaffordable if mortgage payments started out at a high level. Persons planning to take on such a mortgage must be confident that their income will be able to keep pace with the rising payments. *See also* ADJUSTABLE-RATE MORTGAGE; CONVENTIONAL MORTGAGE; REVERSE-ANNUITY MORTGAGE; VARIABLE-RATE MORTGAGE.

GRADUATED SECURITY security whose listing has been upgraded by moving from one exchange to another—for example, from the American Stock Exchange to the more prestigious New York Stock Exchange, or from a regional exchange to a national exchange. An advantage of such a transfer is to widen trading in the security.

GRAHAM AND DODD METHOD OF INVESTING investment approach outlined in Benjamin Graham and David Dodd's landmark book *Security Analysis,* published in the 1930s. Graham and Dodd founded the modern discipline of security analysis with their work. They believed that investors should buy stocks with undervalued assets and that eventually those assets would appreciate to their true value in the marketplace. Graham and Dodd advocated buying stocks in companies where current assets exceed current liabilities and all long-term debt, and where the stock is selling at a low PRICE/EARNINGS RATIO. They suggested that the stocks be sold after a profit objective of between 50% and 100% was reached, which they assumed would be three years or less from the time of purchase. Analysts today who call themselves Graham and Dodd investors hunt for stocks selling below their LIQUIDATING VALUE and do not necessarily concern themselves with the potential for earnings growth.

GRANDFATHER CLAUSE provision included in a new rule that exempts from the rule a person or business already engaged in the activity coming under regulation. For example, the Financial Accounting Standards Board might adopt a rule effective in 1998 relating, say, to depreciation that, under a grandfather clause, would exempt assets put in service before 1998.

GRANTOR
Investments: options trader who sells a CALL OPTION or a PUT OPTION and collects PREMIUM INCOME for doing so. The grantor sells the right to buy a security at a certain price in the case of a call, and the right to sell at a certain price in the case of a put.
Law: one who executes a deed conveying title to property or who creates a trust. Also called a *settlor.*

GRANTOR RETAINED INCOME TRUST (GRIT) type of TRUST designed to save estate taxes in the event the GRANTOR outlives the trust termination date. Under such a trust, which must be irrevocable and have a life of at least 15 years, the grantor transfers property immediately to the beneficiary but receives income until termination, at which time the beneficiary begins receiving it. At that point the grantor pays a GIFT TAX based on the original value of the gift. When the grantor dies, the gift is added back to the grantor's estate at the value as of the day of the gift, not its (presumably) higher current value.

GRAVEYARD MARKET bear market wherein investors who sell are faced with substantial losses, while potential investors prefer to stay liquid, that is, to keep their money in cash or cash equivalents until market conditions improve. Like a graveyard, those who are in can't get out and those who are out have no desire to get in.

GRAY KNIGHT acquiring company that, acting to advance its own interests, outbids a WHITE KNIGHT but that, not being unfriendly, is preferable to a hostile bidder.

GRAY MARKET
Consumer goods: sale of products by unauthorized dealers, frequently at discounted prices. Consumers who buy gray market goods may find that the manufacturer refuses to honor the product warranty. In some cases, gray market goods may be sold in a country they were not intended for, so, for example, instructions may be in another language than the home market language.
Securities: sale of securities that have not officially been issued yet by a firm that is not a member of the underwriting syndicate. Such trading in the when-issued, or gray, market can provide a good indication of the amount of demand for an upcoming new stock or bond issue.

GREATER FOOL THEORY theory that even though a stock or the market as a whole is FULLY VALUED, speculation is justified because there are enough fools to push prices further upward.

GREENMAIL payment of a premium to a raider trying to take over a company through a proxy contest or other means. Also known as BON VOYAGE BONUS, it is designed to thwart the takeover. By accepting the payment, the raider agrees not to buy any more shares or pursue the takeover any further for a specified number of years. *See also* GOODBYE KISS.

GREEN SHOE clause in an underwriting agreement saying that, in the event of exceptional public demand, the issuer will authorize additional shares for distribution by the syndicate.

GRESHAM'S LAW theory in economics that bad money drives out good money. Specifically, people faced with a choice of two currencies of the same nominal value, one of which is preferable to the other because of metal content or because it resists mutilation, will hoard the good money and spend the bad money, thereby driving the good money out of circulation. The observation is named for Sir Thomas Gresham, master of the mint in the reign of Queen Elizabeth I.

GRIT *see* GRANTOR RETAINED INCOME TRUST (GRIT).

GROSS DOMESTIC PRODUCT (GDP) market value of the goods and services produced by labor and property in the United States. GDP is made up of consumer and government purchases, private domestic investments, and net exports of goods and services. Figures for GDP are released by the Commerce Department on a quarterly basis. Growth of the U.S. economy is measured by the change in inflation-adjusted GDP, or real GDP. Formerly called *Gross National Product.*

GROSS EARNINGS personal taxable income before adjustments made to arrive at ADJUSTED GROSS INCOME.

GROSS ESTATE total value of a person's assets before liabilities such as debts and taxes are deducted. After someone dies, the executor of the will makes an assessment of the stocks, bonds, real estate, and personal possessions that comprise the gross estate. Debts and taxes are paid, as are funeral expenses and estate administration costs. Beneficiaries of the will then receive their portion of the remainder, which is called the *net estate.*

GROSS INCOME total personal income before exclusions and deductions.

GROSS LEASE property lease under which the lessor (landlord) agrees to pay all the expenses normally associated with ownership (insurance, taxes, utilities, repairs). An exception might be that the lessee (tenant) would be required to pay real estate taxes above a stipulated amount or to pay for certain special operating expenses (snow removal, grounds care in the case of a shopping center, or institutional advertising, for example). Gross leases are the most common type of lease contract and are typical arrangements for short-term tenancy. They normally contain no provision for periodic rent adjustments, nor are there preestablished renewal arrangements. *See also* NET LEASE.

GROSS NATIONAL PRODUCT (GNP) *see* GROSS DOMESTIC PRODUCT.

GROSS PER BROKER gross amount of commission revenues attributable to a particular REGISTERED REPRESENTATIVE during a given period. Brokers, who typically keep one third of the commissions they generate, are often expected by their firms to meet productivity quotas based on their gross.

GROSS PROFIT net sales less the COST OF GOODS SOLD. Also called *gross margin. See also* NET PROFIT.

GROSS SALES total sales at invoice values, not reduced by customer discounts, returns or allowances, or other adjustments. *See also* NET SALES.

GROSS SPREAD difference (spread) between the public offering price of a security and the price paid by an underwriter to the issuer. The spread breaks down into the manager's fee, the dealer's (or underwriter's) discount, and the selling concession (i.e., the discount offered to a selling group). *See also* CONCESSION; FLOTATION (FLOATATION) COST.

GROUND LEASE lease on the land. Typically, the land will be under a building, which will have its own leases with tenants.

GROUP INSURANCE insurance coverage bought for and provided to a group instead of an individual. For example, an employer may buy disability, health, and term life insurance for its employees at a far better rate than the employees could obtain on their own. Credit unions, trade associations, and other groups may also offer their members preferential group insurance rates. Group insurance is not only advantageous to employees or group members because it is cheaper than they could obtain on their own, but some people may be able to get coverage under the group umbrella when they would be denied coverage individually because of preexisting conditions or other factors.

GROUP OF TEN ten major industrialized countries that try to coordinate monetary and fiscal policies to create a more stable world economic system. The ten are Belgium, Canada, France, Germany, Italy, Japan, the Netherlands, Sweden, the United Kingdom, and the United States. Also known as the *Paris Club.*

GROUP ROTATION tendency of stocks in one industry to outperform and then underperform other industries. This may be due to the economic cycle or what industry is popular or unpopular with investors at any particular time. For example, CYCLICAL stocks in the auto, paper, or steel industry may be group leaders when the economy is showing robust growth, while stocks of stable-demand firms such as drug or food companies may be market leaders in a recession. Alternatively, investor demand for stocks in certain industries, such as biotechnology, computer software, or real estate investment trusts may rise and fall because of enthusiasm or disappointment with the group, creating rotation into or out of such stocks. Market analysts watch which industry group is coming into and going out of vogue in recommending stocks that might lead or lag in coming months.

GROUP SALES term used in securities underwriting that refers to block sales made to institutional investors. The securities come out of a syndicate "pot" with credit for the sale prorated among the syndicate members in proportion to their original allotments.

GROUP UNIVERSAL LIFE POLICY (GULP) UNIVERSAL LIFE INSURANCE offered on a group basis, and therefore more cheaply than one could obtain it personally, to employees and, sometimes, their family members.

GROWING EQUITY MORTGAGE (GEM) mortgage with a fixed interest rate and growing payments. This technique allows the homeowner to build equity in the underlying home faster than if they made the same mortgage payment for the life of the loan. Borrowers who take on GEM loans should be confident in their ability to make higher payments over time based on their prospects for rising income.

GROWTH AND INCOME FUND MUTUAL FUND that seeks earnings growth as well as income. These funds invest mainly in the common stock of companies with a history of capital gains but that also have a record of consistent dividend payments.

GROWTH FUND mutual fund that invests in growth stocks. The goal is to provide capital appreciation for the fund's shareholders over the long term. Growth funds are more volatile than more conservative income or money market funds. They tend to rise faster than conservative funds in bull (advancing) markets and to drop more sharply in bear (falling) markets. *See also* GROWTH STOCK.

GROWTH RATE percentage rate at which the economy, stocks, or earnings are growing. The economic growth rate is normally determined by the growth of the GROSS DOMESTIC PRODUCT. Individual companies try to establish a rate at which their earnings grow over time. Firms with long-term earnings growth rates of more than 15% are considered fast-growing companies. Analysts also apply the term *growth rate* to specific financial aspects of a company's operations, such as dividends, sales, assets, and market share. Analysts use growth rates to compare one company to another within the same industry.

GROWTH STOCK stock of a corporation that has exhibited faster-than-average gains in earnings over the last few years and is expected to continue to show high levels of profit growth. Over the long run, growth stocks tend to outperform slower-growing or stagnant stocks. Growth stocks are riskier investments than average stocks, however, since they usually sport higher price/earnings ratios and make little or no dividend payments to shareholders. *See also* PRICE/EARNINGS RATIO.

GUARANTEE to take responsibility for payment of a debt or performance of some obligation if the person primarily liable fails to perform. A guarantee is a CONTINGENT LIABILITY of the guarantor—that is, it is a potential liability not recognized in accounts until the outcome becomes probable in the opinion of the company's accountant.

GUARANTEED BOND bond on which the principal and interest are guaranteed by a firm other than the issuer. Such bonds are nearly always railroad bonds, arising out of situations where one road has leased the road of another and the security holders of the leased road require assurance of income in exchange for giving up control of the property. Guaranteed securities involved in such situations may also include preferred or common stocks when dividends are guaranteed. Both guaranteed stock and guaranteed bonds become, in effect, DEBENTURE (unsecured) bonds of the guarantor, although the status of the stock may be questionable in the event of LIQUIDATION. In any event, if the guarantor enjoys stronger credit than the railroad whose securities are being guaranteed, the securities have greater value.

Guaranteed bonds may also arise out of parent-subsidiary relationships where bonds are issued by the subsidiary with the parent's guarantee.

GUARANTEED INSURABILITY feature offered as an option in life and health insurance policies that enables the insured to add coverage at specified future times and at standard rates without evidence of insurability.

GUARANTEED INVESTMENT CONTRACT contract between an insurance company and a corporate profit-sharing or pension plan that guarantees a specific rate of return on the invested capital over the life of the contract. Many defined contribution plans, such as 401(k) and 403(b) plans, offer guaranteed investment contracts as investment options to employees. Although the insurance company takes all market, credit, and interest rate risks on the investment portfolio, it can profit if its return exceeds the guaranteed amount. Only the insurance company backs the guarantee, not any governmental agency, so if the insurer fails, it is possible that there could be a default on the contract. For pension and profit-sharing plans, guaranteed investment contracts, also known as GICs, are a conservative way of assuring beneficiaries that their money will achieve a certain rate of return. *See also* BANK INVESTMENT CONTRACT.

GUARANTEED RENEWABLE POLICY INSURANCE policy that requires the insurer to renew the policy for a period specified in the contract provided premiums are paid in a timely fashion. The insurer cannot make any changes in the provisions of the policy other than a change in the premium rate for all insureds in the same class.

GUARANTEED REPLACEMENT COST COVERAGE INSURANCE policy that pays for the full cost of replacing damaged property without a deduction for depreciation and without a dollar limit. This policy is different from an actual cash value policy, which takes into account depreciation for lost and damaged items, if the damage resulted from an insured peril.

GUARANTEED STOCK *see* GUARANTEED BOND.

GUARANTEE LETTER letter by a commercial bank that guarantees payment of the EXERCISE PRICE of a client's PUT OPTION (the right to sell a given security at a particular price within a specified period) if or when a notice indicating its exercise, called an assignment notice, is presented to the option seller (writer).

GUARANTEE OF SIGNATURE certificate issued by a bank or brokerage firm vouching for the authenticity of a person's signature. Such a document may be necessary when stocks, bonds, or other registered securities are transferred from a seller to a buyer. Banks also require guarantees of signature before they will process certain transactions.

GUARDIAN individual who has the legal right to care for another person as a parent or to act as an administrator of the assets of a person declared incompetent for mental or physical reasons. Guardians can be *testamentary*, meaning appointed in a parent's will; *general,* meaning having the general responsibility to care for another person and that person's estate; or *special,* meaning the guardian has limited authority, such as half the responsibility of a general guardian but not the other.

GULP *see* GROUP UNIVERSAL LIFE POLICY (GULP).

GUN JUMPING
1. trading securities on information before it becomes publicly disclosed.
2. illegally soliciting buy orders in an underwriting, before a Securities and Exchange Commission REGISTRATION is complete.

GUNSLINGER aggressive portfolio manager who buys speculative stocks, often on margin. In the great bull market of the 1960s, several hot fund managers gained reputations and had huge followings as gunslingers by producing enormous returns while taking great risks. However, the bear market of the early 1970s caused many of these gunslingers to lose huge amounts of money, and in most cases, their followings. The term is still used when referring to popular managers who take big risks in search of high returns.

H

HAIRCUT securities industry term referring to the formulas used in the valuation of securities for the purpose of calculating a broker-dealer's net capital. The haircut varies according to the class of a security, its market risk, and the time to maturity. For example, cash equivalent GOVERNMENTS could have a 0% haircut, equities could have an average 30% haircut, and fail positions (securities with past due delivery) with little prospect of settlement could have a 100% haircut. *See also* CASH EQUIVALENTS; FAIL POSITION.

HALF-LIFE point in time in which half the principal has been repaid in a mortgage-backed security guaranteed or issued by the GOVERNMENT NATIONAL MORTGAGE ASSOCIATION, the FEDERAL NATIONAL MORTGAGE ASSOCIATION, or the FEDERAL HOME LOAN MORTGAGE CORPORATION. Normally, it is assumed that such a security has a half-life of 12 years. But specific mortgage pools can have vastly longer or shorter half-lives, depending on interest rate trends. If interest rates fall, more homeowners will refinance their mortgages, meaning that principal will be paid off more quickly, and half-lives will drop. If interest rates rise, homeowners will hold onto their mortgages longer than anticipated, and half-lives will rise.

HALF-STOCK common or preferred stock with a $50 PAR value instead of the more conventional $100 par value.

HAMMERING THE MARKET intense selling of stocks by those who think prices are inflated. Speculators who think the market is about to drop, and therefore sell short, are said to be hammering the market. *See also* SELLING SHORT.

HANDS-OFF INVESTOR investor willing to take a passive role in the management of a corporation. An individual or corporation with a large stake in another company may decide to adopt a "hands-off" policy if it is satisfied with the current performance of management. However, if management falters, it may become more actively involved in corporate strategy.

HANDS-ON INVESTOR investor who takes an active role in the management of the company whose stock he or she has bought.

HANG SENG INDEX the major indicator of stock market performance in Hong Kong. The index is comprised of 33 companies, divided into four sub-indices: financial (4), property (9), utilities (6), commerce and industry (14). It is computed on an arithmetic basis, weighted by market capitalization, and strongly influenced by large capitalization stocks such as Hongkong Bank, Hang Seng Bank, Hongkong Land and Cheung Kong.

HARD DOLLARS actual payments made by a customer for services, including research, provided by a brokerage firm. For instance, if a broker puts together a financial plan for a client, the fee might be $1000 in hard dollars. This contrasts with SOFT DOLLARS, which refers to compensation by way of the commissions a broker would receive if he were to carry out any trades called for in that financial plan. Brokerage house research is sold for either hard or soft dollars.

HARD MONEY (HARD CURRENCY)

1. currency in which there is widespread confidence. It is the currency of an economically and politically stable country, such as the U.S. or Switzerland. Countries that have taken out loans in hard money generally must repay them in hard money.
2. gold or coins, as contrasted with paper currency, which is considered *soft money*. Some hard-money enthusiasts advocate a return to the GOLD STANDARD as a method of reducing inflation and promoting economic growth.

HEAD AND SHOULDERS patterns resembling the head and shoulders outline of a person, which is used to chart stock price trends. The pattern signals the reversal of a trend. As prices move down to the right shoulder, a head and shoulders top is formed, meaning that prices should be falling. A reverse head and shoulders pattern has the head at the bottom of the chart, meaning that prices should be rising.

HEAD AND SHOULDERS

HEAD OF HOUSEHOLD tax filing status available in the tax code to individuals who provide more than half of the financial support to their household during the tax year. Heads of household can be married or single, as long as they support dependent children or grandchildren, parents, or other close relatives living at home. Those qualifying for head-of-household status pay the same tax rates as singles and married couples filing jointly, but the rates apply at different income levels. For example, a head of household pays a 28% tax rate on taxable income between $33,051 and $85,350, while a single pays the same tax rate on income between $24,651 and $59,750, and a married couple filing jointly pays 28% on $41,201 to $99,600.

HEALTH INSURANCE in popular usage, any insurance plan that covers medical expenses or health care services, including HMOs, insured plans, preferred provider organizations, etc. In insurance, protection against loss by sickness or bodily injury, in which sense it is synonymous with accident and health, accident and sickness, accident, or disability income insurance.

HEAVY MARKET stock, bond, or commodity market with falling prices resulting from a larger supply of offers to sell than bids to buy.

HEDGE/HEDGING strategy used to offset investment risk. A perfect hedge is one eliminating the possibility of future gain or loss.

A stockholder worried about declining stock prices, for instance, can hedge his or her holdings by buying a PUT OPTION on the stock or selling a CALL OPTION. Someone owning 100 shares of XYZ stock, selling at $70 per share, can hedge his position by buying a put option giving him the right to sell 100 shares at $70 at any time over the next few months. This investor must pay a certain amount of money, called a PREMIUM, for these rights. If XYZ stock falls during that time, the investor can exercise his option—that is, sell the stock at $70—thereby preserving the $70 value of the XYZ holdings. The same XYZ stockholder can also hedge his position by selling a call option. In such a transaction, he sells the right to buy XYZ stock at $70 per share for the next few months. In return, he receives a premium. If XYZ stock falls in price, that premium income will offset to some extent the drop in value of the stock.

SELLING SHORT is another widely used hedging technique.

Investors often try to hedge against inflation by purchasing assets that will rise in value faster than inflation, such as gold, real estate, or other tangible assets.

Large commercial firms that want to be assured of the price they will receive or pay for a commodity will hedge their position by buying and selling simultaneously in the FUTURES MARKET. For example, Hershey's, the chocolate company, will hedge its supplies of cocoa in the futures market to limit the risk of a rise in cocoa prices.

Managers of large pools of money such as pension and mutual funds frequently hedge their exposure to currency or interest rate risk by buying or selling futures or options contracts. For example, a GLOBAL MUTUAL FUND manager with a large position in Japanese stocks who thinks the Japanese yen is about to fall in value against the U.S. dollar may buy futures or options on the Japanese yen to offset the projected loss on the currency.

HEDGE CLAUSE disclaimer seen in market letters, security research reports, or other printed matter having to do with evaluating investments, which purports to absolve the writer from responsibility for the accuracy of information obtained from usually reliable sources. Despite such clauses, which may mitigate liability, writers may still be charged with negligence in their use of information. Typical language of a hedge clause: "The information furnished herein has been obtained from sources believed to be reliable, but its accuracy is not guaranteed."

HEDGED TENDER SELLING SHORT a portion of the shares being tendered to protect against a price drop in the event all shares tendered are not accepted. For example, ABC Company or another company wishing to acquire ABC Company announces a TENDER OFFER at $52 a share when ABC shares are selling at a market price of $40. The market price of ABC will now rise to near the tender price of $52. An investor wishing to sell all his or her 2000 shares at $52 will tender 2000 shares, but cannot be assured all shares will be accepted. To lock in the $52 price on the tendered shares the investor thinks might not be accepted—say half of them or 1000 shares—he or she will sell short that many shares. Assuming the investor has guessed correctly and only 1000 shares are accepted, when the tender offer expires and the market price of ABC begins to drop, the investor will still have sold all 2000 shares for $52 or close to it—half to the tenderer and the other half when the short sale is consummated.

HEDGE FUND private investment partnership (for U.S. investors) or an off-shore investment corporation (for non-U.S. or tax-exempt investors) in which the general partner has made a substantial personal investment, and whose offering memorandum allows for the fund to take both long and short positions, use leverage and derivatives, and invest in many markets. Hedge funds often take large risks on speculative strategies, including PROGRAM TRADING, SELLING SHORT, SWAPS, and ARBITRAGE. A fund need not employ all of these tools all of the time; it must merely have them at its disposal. Since hedge funds are not limited to buying securities, they can potentially profit in any market environment, including one with sharply declining prices. Because they move billions of dollars in and out of markets quickly, hedge funds can have a significant impact on the day-to-day trading developments in the stock, bond, and futures markets.

Hedge funds entitle the general partner to an additional incentive management fee based upon positive returns—the higher the returns, the higher their fee. Hedge funds require that 65% of all investors be of the *accredited* type, defined as an individual or couple who have a net worth of at least $1 million, or an individual who had income in the previous year of at least $200,000, or a couple with at least $300,000 of income in the previous year. In reality, though, an investor needs much more than that.

The funds also require substantial minimum investments that can make it hard even for accredited investors to ante up. Minimums typically range from about $250,000 to $10 million. An investor gives up liquidity in hedge funds. They typically have a one-year lock-up for first-time investors.

HEDGE WRAPPER options strategy where the holder of a long position in an underlying stock buys an OUT OF THE MONEY put and sells an out of the money call. It defines a range where the stock will be sold at expiration of the option, whatever way the stock moves. The maximum profit is made if the call is exercised at expiration, since the holder gets the strike price plus any dividends. The maximum loss occurs if the put option is exercised, and represents the cost of the hedge wrapper less the strike price plus dividends received. The cost of the hedge wrapper less dividends received is the breakeven point. The strategy produces a loss whenever the breakeven price is higher than the strike price of the call.

HEIR one who inherits some or all of the estate of a deceased person by virtue of being in the direct line (*heir of the body*), or being designated in a will or by a legal authority (*heir at law*).

HEMLINE THEORY whimsical idea that stock prices move in the same general direction as the hemlines of women's dresses. Short skirts in the 1920s and 1960s were considered bullish signs that stock prices would rise, whereas longer dresses in the 1930s and 1940s were considered bearish (falling) indicators. Despite its sometimes uncanny way of being prophetic, the hemline theory has remained more in the area of wishful thinking than serious market analysis.

HEX LTD., HELSINKI STOCK AND DERIVATIVES EXCHANGE, clearing house formed in 1997 through the merger of the Helsinki Stock Exchange and SOM Ltd., Finnish Securities and Derivatives Exchange, Clearing House. HEX Ltd. is the parent company of two subsidiaries: EL-EX Electricity Exchange Ltd. and Somtel Ltd. Under an existing cooperation agreement between SOM and OM Stockholm AB, the Swedish exchange, SOM products can be traded in Stockholm and at the market operated by OM's London-based exchange, OMLX. OM's products, in turn, are traded in Finland. The agreement also covers some cooperation on the equity market. The HEX Index includes all shares quoted on the exchange; share price indices are computed for industry groups. Futures and options are traded on the Finnish Options Index (FOX), currencies, and stocks. Futures are offered on the FIM government bond. Trading is fully automated through the HETI trading system, which is available in English. Clearing and settlement is through the Finnish Central Securities Depository's KATI clearing system. Trading hours: Monday through Friday, 9:30 A.M. to 5 P.M., with a pre-market session from 9 A.M. to 9:25 A.M., and an after-market session from 5:05 P.M. to 5:30 P.M.

HIBOR acronym for *Hong Kong Interbank Offer Rate,* the annualized offer rate paid by banks for Hong Kong dollar-denominated three-month deposits. It acts as a benchmark for many interest rates throughout the Far East.

HIDDEN LOAD sales charge which may not be immediately apparent to an investor. For example, a 12b-1 MUTUAL FUND assesses an annual asset base charge of up to 0.75% to cover marketing, distribution, and promotion expenses incurred by the fund. Even though it has been disclosed in the prospectus, many investors do not realize that they are paying this load. The sales charges levied on insurance policies are also hidden, because they are not explicitly disclosed to customers, and are instead subtracted from premiums paid by policyholders.

HIDDEN VALUES assets owned by a company but not yet reflected in its stock price. For example, a manufacturing firm may own valuable real estate that could be sold at a much higher price than it appears on the company's books, which is usually the price at which the real estate was purchased. Other undervalued assets that could have significant value include patents, trademarks, or exclusive contracts. Value-oriented money managers search for stocks with hidden values on their balance sheet in the hope that some day, those values will be realized through a higher stock price either by actions of the current management or by a takeover.

HIGH CREDIT
Banking: maximum amount of loans outstanding recorded for a particular customer.
Finance: the highest amount of TRADE CREDIT a particular company has received from a supplier at one time.

HIGH CURRENT INCOME MUTUAL FUND mutual fund with the objective of paying high income to shareholders. Such funds usually take higher risks than more conservative, but lower-yielding funds in order to provide an above-market rate of current yield. For example, JUNK BOND funds buy corporate bonds with below investment grade credit ratings in order to pay higher levels of income to shareholders than would be available from Treasury or high-quality corporate bonds. Another example of a high current income mutual fund is an international bond fund.

HIGH FLYER high-priced and highly speculative stock that moves up sharply over a short period. The stock of unproven high-technology companies might be high flyers, for instance.

HIGH-GRADE BOND bond rated triple-A or double-A by Standard & Poor's, Moody's, and other RATING services.

HIGHJACKING Japanese term for a TAKEOVER.

HIGHLY CONFIDENT LETTER letter from an investment banking firm that it is "highly confident" that it will be able to arrange financing for a securities deal. This letter might be used to finance a leveraged buyout or multibillion-dollar takeover offer, for example. The board of directors of the target firm might request a highly confident letter in evaluating whether a proposed takeover can be financed. After the letter has been issued and the deal approved, the investment bankers will attempt to line up financing from banks, private investors, stock and bond offerings, and other sources. Though the investment banker professes to be highly confident he can arrange financing, the letter is not an ironclad guarantee of his ability to do so.

HIGHLY LEVERAGED TRANSACTION (HLT) loan, usually by a bank, to an already highly LEVERAGED COMPANY.

HIGH-PREMIUM CONVERTIBLE DEBENTURE bond with a long-term, high-premium, common stock conversion feature and also offering a fairly competitive interest rate. Premium refers in this case to the difference between the market value of the CONVERTIBLE security and the value at which it is convertible into common stock. Such bonds are designed for bond-oriented portfolios, with the "KICKER," the added feature of convertibility to stock, intended as an inflation hedge.

HIGHS stocks that have hit new high prices in daily trading for the current 52-week period. (They are listed as "highs" in daily newspapers.) Technical analysts consider the ratio between new highs and new LOWS in the stock market to be significant for pointing out stock market trends.

HIGH-TECH STOCK stock of companies involved in high-technology fields (computers, semiconductors, biotechnology, robotics, electronics). Successful high-tech stocks have above-average earnings growth and therefore typically very volatile stock prices.

HIGH-TICKET ITEMS items with a significant amount of value, such as jewelry and furs. Most standard homeowner's/renter's policies have limits on specific types of high-ticket items. Most policies have a limit of $1000–$2000 for all jewelry and furs. To provide appropriate coverage for these items, they should be scheduled separately in the form of a FLOATER or endorsement. Also called *valuables*.

HIGH-YIELD BOND bond that has RATING of BB or lower and that pays a higher yield to compensate for its greater risk. *See also* JUNK BOND.

HISTORICAL COST accounting principle requiring that all financial statement items be based on original cost or acquisition cost. The dollar is assumed to be stable for the period involved.

HISTORICAL TRADING RANGE price range within which a stock, bond, or commodity has traded since going public. A VOLATILE stock will have a wider trading range than a more conservative stock. Technical analysts see the top of a historical range as the RESISTANCE LEVEL and the bottom as the SUPPORT LEVEL. They consider it highly significant if a security breaks above the resistance level or below the support level. Usually such a move is interpreted to mean that the security will go onto new highs or new lows, thus expanding its historical trading range.

HISTORICAL YIELD yield provided by a mutual fund, typically a money market fund, over a particular period of time. For instance, a money market fund may advertise that its historical yield averaged 5% over the last year.

HISTORIC REHABILITATION LIMITED PARTNERSHIP partnership designed to take advantage of the historic rehabilitation tax credit available in the Internal Revenue Code. These partnerships rehabilitate structures to their original condition, and limited partners receive credits that reduce partners' taxes dollar for dollar. For example, $5000 in tax credits reduces the amount of taxes due by $5000. Tax credits of 20% are available if the partnership rehabilitates a historic structure built before 1936. Tax credits of 10% are available for the restoration of buildings built before 1936 that are not certified as historic by the Department of the Interior. Historic rehabilitation limited partnerships can be assembled by local builders and investors, or by professional general partners specializing in such projects.

HIT informally, a significant securities loss or a development having a major impact on corporate profits, such as a large WRITE-OFF. Term is also used in the opposite sense to describe an investing success, similar to a "hit" in show business.

HIT THE BID to accept the highest price offered for a stock. For instance, if a stock's ask price is $50¼ and the current bid price is $50, a seller will hit the bid if he or she accepts $50 a share.

HOLD
Banking: retaining an asset in an account until the item has been collected. For example, a hold can be put on a certain amount of funds in a checking account if a certified check has been issued for that amount.
Securities: maintaining ownership of a stock, bond, mutual fund, or other security for a long period of time. Proponents of the BUY AND HOLD STRATEGY try to buy high-quality securities which they hope will grow in value over many years. By holding for a long time, the investor can delay capital gains taxes until the position is sold many years in the future.
        Securities analysts also issue a HOLD recommendation if they are not enthusiastic enough about a security to recommend purchasing it, yet are not pessimistic enough to recommend selling it. However, many analysts who downgrade a stock from a buy to a hold rating are in fact saying that investors should sell the stock, since there are better opportunities to invest elsewhere.

HOLDER OF RECORD owner of a company's securities as recorded on the books of the issuing company or its TRANSFER AGENT as of a particular date. Dividend declarations, for example, always specify payability to holders of record as of a specific date.

HOLDING COMPANY corporation that owns enough voting stock in another corporation to influence its board of directors and therefore to control its policies and management. A holding company need not own a majority of the shares of its subsidiaries or be engaged in similar activities. However, to gain the benefits of tax consolidation, which include tax-free dividends to the parent and the ability to share operating losses, the holding company must own 80% or more of the subsidiary's voting stock.

Among the advantages of a holding company over a MERGER as an approach to expansion are the ability to control sizeable operations with fractional ownership and commensurately small investment; the somewhat theoretical ability to take risks through subsidiaries with liability limited to the subsidiary corporation; and the ability to expand through unobtrusive purchases of stock, in contrast to having to obtain the approval of another company's shareholders.

Among the disadvantages of a holding company are partial multiple taxation when less than 80% of a subsidiary is owned, plus other special state and local taxes; the risk of forced DIVESTITURE (it is easier to force dissolution of a holding company than to separate merged operations); and the risks of negative leverage effects in excessive PYRAMIDING.

The following types of holding companies are defined in special ways and subject to particular legislation: public utility holding company (*see* PUBLIC UTILITY HOLDING COMPANY ACT), BANK HOLDING COMPANY, railroad holding company, and air transport holding company.

HOLDING PERIOD length of time an asset is held by its owner. Capital assets held for 12 months or more qualify for preferential capital gains tax treatment. Assets sold after being held for more than 12 months are subject to a maximum capital gains tax rate of 20%, while assets sold after being held for less than 12 months are taxed at regular income tax rates as high as 39.6%. *See also* ANTICIPATED HOLDING PERIOD; CAPITAL GAIN; INVESTMENT LETTER.

HOLDING THE MARKET entering the market with sufficient buy orders to create price support for a security or commodity, for the purpose of stabilizing a downward trend. The Securities and Exchange Commission views "holding" as a form of illegal manipulation except in the case of stabilization of a new issue cleared with the SEC beforehand.

HOME BANKING service offered by banks allowing consumers and small businesses to perform many banking functions at home through computers, telephones, and cable television links to the bank, thereby providing them with a number of convenience services. Bank customers are able to shift money between accounts, apply for loans and make loan payments, pay bills, check balances, and buy and sell securities, among other services. As home banking becomes easier and more convenient to use, more and more consumers sign up for it. It offers the advantages of privacy, speed, accuracy and the ability to perform transactions at any time. Most banks charge an extra fee for access to home banking services. Home banking does not currently offer the ability to obtain cash, for which customers must still visit a bank teller or automatic teller machine.

HOMEOWNER'S EQUITY ACCOUNT credit line offered by banks, savings and loans, brokerage firms, credit unions and other mortgage lenders allowing a homeowner to tap the built-up equity in his or her home. Such an account is, in effect, a REVOLVING CREDIT second mortgage, which owners can access with the convenience of a check. Most lenders will provide a line of credit up to 70% or 80% of the appraised value of a home, minus any outstanding first mortgage debt. Some home equity lenders will lend as much as 125% of the home's value, although this is risky for both the lender and the borrower; if the borrower defaults, he must come up with 25% more equity than his home is worth to satisfy the loan. When a homeowner receives the loan, a LIEN is automatically placed against the house and removed when the loan is repaid. A homeowner's equity account often carries a lower interest rate than a second mortgage; typically, the rate is tied to the PRIME RATE. Often, a lender will offer a below-market rate at or below the prime rate for some introductory period of six months to a year to entice the borrower. After that, many banks charge between the prime rate and two percentage points over prime for the long term. Most programs require an initial sign-up fee, an annual maintenance fee and payment of additional fees called POINTS when the credit line is tapped. Interest on such loans is tax deductible up to $100,000, no matter how loan proceeds are used. Interest on loans exceeding $100,000 may be deductible if the proceeds are used to purchase investments or for business purposes. Consult a tax specialist for the latest information on what qualifies as a deduction. *See also* SECOND MORTGAGE LENDING.

HOMEOWNER'S INSURANCE POLICY policy protecting a homeowner against property and casualty perils. A basic HO-3 policy (HO stands for homeowner's) is a standard policy and the most comprehensive. It will cover damage to the home from natural causes such as fire, lightning, windstorms, hail, rain, or volcanic eruption. In addition, man-made disasters such as riots, vandalism, damage from cars or airplanes, explosions, and theft will also be reimbursed. Damage caused by falling objects, the weight of ice, snow or sleet, freezing of plumbing, heating or air conditioning systems, electrical discharges, or the rupture of water heating or protective sprinkler systems also fall under the HO-3 policy. Flood, earthquake, war, and nuclear accident are not covered; flood and earthquake insurance can be purchased separately. Other types of homeowner's policies include HO-4 for renters (which also could include co-ops), HO-6 for condominium owners, and HO-8 for older homes. In general, homeowners should try to purchase coverage that will pay for the replacement of damaged or stolen items at current market prices, not at the prices for which those items may have been acquired years ago. There are dollar limits for high-ticket items such as jewelry. A FLOATER or an endorsement, purchased separately, can provide the additional coverage needed.

The average homeowner's or renter's policy provides approximately $100,000 of liability protection. A special policy is required for homeowner's business risk coverage. Home business owners need both property and liability insurance, since the homeowner's policy provides only limited coverage for business equipment, in most cases up to $2,500 for business equipment in the home and $250 away from the home.

Most mortgage lenders require homeowners to obtain adequate insurance coverage before they agree to provide a mortgage.

HOME RUN large gain by an investor in a short period of time. Someone who aims to hit an investment home run may be looking for a potential TAKEOVER target, for example, since takeover bids result in sudden price spurts. Such investing is inherently more risky than the strategy of holding for the long term.

HORIZON ANALYSIS method of measuring the discounted cash flow (timeadjusted return) from an investment, using time periods or series *(horizons)* that differ from the investment's contractual maturity. The horizon date might be the end of a BUSINESS CYCLE or some other date determined in the perspective of the investor's overall portfolio requirements. Horizon analysis calculations, which include reinvestment assumptions, permit comparison with alternative investments that is more realistic in terms of individual portfolio requirements than traditional YIELD-TO-MATURITY calculations.

HORIZONTAL MERGER *see* MERGER.

HORIZONTAL PRICE MOVEMENT movement within a narrow price range over an extended period of time. A stock would have a horizontal price movement if it traded between $47 and $51 for over six months, for instance. Also known as *sideways price movement. See* chart on next page. *See also* FLAT MARKET.

HORIZONTAL SPREAD options strategy that involves buying and selling the same number of options contracts with the same exercise price, but with different maturity dates; also called a CALENDAR SPREAD. For instance, an investor might buy ten XYZ call options with a striking price of $70 and a maturity date of October. At the same time, he would sell ten XYZ call options with the same striking price of $70 but a maturity date of July. The investor hopes to profit by moves in XYZ stock by this means.

HOSPITAL REVENUE BOND bond issued by a municipal or state agency to finance construction of a hospital or nursing home. The latter is then operated under lease by a not-for-profit organization or a for-profit corporation such as Columbia/ HCA. A hospital revenue bond, which is a variation on the INDUSTRIAL DEVELOPMENT BOND, is tax exempt, but there may be limits to the exemption. *See also* REVENUE BOND.

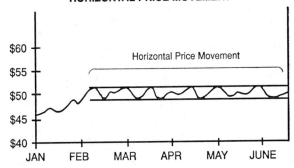

HORIZONTAL PRICE MOVEMENT

HOSTILE TAKEOVER takeover of a company against the wishes of current management and the board of directors. This takeover may be attempted by another company or by a well-financed RAIDER. If the price offered is high enough, shareholders may vote to accept the offer even if management resists and claims that the company is actually worth even more. If the acquirer raises the price high enough, management may change its attitude, converting the hostile takeover into a friendly one. Management has many weapons at its disposal to fend off a hostile takeover, such as GREENMAIL, POISON PILLS, the SCORCHED EARTH POLICY, and SUICIDE PILLS, among others. Also called *unfriendly takeover. See also* TAKEOVER.

HOT ISSUE newly issued stock that is in great public demand. Hot issue stocks usually shoot up in price at their initial offering, since there is more demand than there are shares available. Special National Association of Securities Dealers rules apply to the distribution of hot issues by the selling investment banking syndicate. *See also* UNDER-WRITE.

HOT MONEY investment funds capriciously seeking high, short-term yields. Borrowers attracting hot money, such as banks issuing high-yielding CERTIFICATES OF DEPOSIT, should be prepared to lose it as soon as another borrower offers a higher rate.

HOT STOCK
1. stock that has been stolen.
2. newly issued stock that rises quickly in price. *See* HOT ISSUE.

HOUSE
1. firm or individual engaged in business as a broker-dealer in securities and/or investment banking and related services.
2. nickname for the London Stock Exchange.

HOUSE ACCOUNT account handled at the main office of a brokerage firm or managed by an executive of the firm; in other words, an account distinguished from one that is normally handled by a salesperson in the territory. Ordinarily, a salesperson does not receive a commission on a house account, even though the account may actually be in his or her territory.

HOUSE CALL brokerage house notification that the customer's EQUITY in a MARGIN ACCOUNT is below the maintenance level. If the equity declines below that point, a broker must call the client, asking for more cash or securities. If the client fails to deliver the required margin, his or her position will be liquidated. House call limits are usually higher than limits mandated by the National Association of Securities Dealers (NASD), a self-regulatory group, and the major exchanges with jurisdiction over these rules. Such a margin MAINTENANCE REQUIREMENT is in addition to the initial margin requirements set by REGULATION T of the Federal Reserve Board. *See also* HOUSE MAINTENANCE REQUIREMENT; MARGIN CALL.

HOUSE MAINTENANCE REQUIREMENT internally set and enforced rules of individual broker-dealers in securities with respect to a customer's MARGIN ACCOUNT. House maintenance requirements set levels of EQUITY that must be maintained to avoid putting up additional equity or having collateral sold out. These levels are normally higher than maintenance levels required by the NATIONAL ASSOCIATION OF SECURITIES DEALERS (NASD) and the stock exchange. *See also* HOUSE CALL; MINIMUM MAINTENANCE.

HOUSE OF ISSUE investment banking firm that underwrites a stock or bond issue and offers the securities to the public. *See also* UNDERWRITE.

HOUSE POOR short of cash because the bulk of your money is tied up in your house. Implication is that without the real estate investment and associated mortgage, you would be financially comfortable.

HOUSE RULES securities industry term for internal rules and policies of individual broker-dealer firms concerning the opening and handling of customers' accounts and the activities of the customers in such accounts. House rules are designed to assure that firms are in comfortable compliance with the requirements of outside regulatory authorities and in most cases are more stringent than the outside regulations. *See also* HOUSE CALL; HOUSE MAINTENANCE REQUIREMENT.

HOUSING AFFORDABILITY INDEX *see* AFFORDABILITY INDEX.

HOUSING AND URBAN DEVELOPMENT, DEPARTMENT OF (HUD) cabinet-level federal agency, founded in 1965, which is responsible for stimulating housing development in the United States. HUD has several programs to subsidize low- and moderate-income housing and urban renewal projects, often through loan guarantees. The GOV-

ERNMENT NATIONAL MORTGAGE ASSOCIATION (Ginnie Mae), which fosters the growth of the secondary mortgage market, is within HUD.

HOUSING BOND short- or long-term bond issued by a local housing authority to finance short-term construction of (typically) low- or middle-income housing or long-term commitments for housing, plants, pollution control facilities, or similar projects. Such bonds are free from federal income taxes and from state and local taxes where applicable.

Shorter-term bonds sell in $5000 denominations and have maturities from 18 months to 4 years. They cannot be called (redeemed prior to maturity) and are paid at maturity with the proceeds from Federal Housing Administration-insured loans. Longer-term bonds are typically issued by local authorities under federal agency contracts, thus providing complete safety. Yields are competitive.

HOUSING STARTS category of residential construction monitored by the Department of Commerce. Housing starts represent the start of construction of a house or apartment building, which means the digging of the foundation. Other categories are housing permits, housing completions, and new home sales. In the aggregate, residential construction accounts for roughly 3% of GROSS DOMESTIC PRODUCT.

HULBERT RATING rating by *Hulbert Financial Digest* of Alexandria, Virginia, of how well the recommendations of various investment advisory newsletters have performed. The ratings cover performance as far back as 1980, if data are available. The *Digest* ranks over 150 investment advisory newsletters covering stocks, bonds, mutual funds, futures, and options by tabulating the profits and losses subscribers would have received had they followed the newsletter's advice exactly.

HUMAN CAPITAL skills acquired by a worker through formal education and experience that improve the worker's productivity and increase his or her income.

HUNG UP term used to describe the position of an investor whose stocks or bonds have dropped in value below their purchase price, presenting the problem of a substantial loss if the securities were sold.

HUNKERING DOWN trader's term for working to sell off a big position in a stock.

HURDLE RATE term used in the budgeting of capital expenditures, meaning the REQUIRED RATE OF RETURN in a DISCOUNTED CASH FLOW analysis. If the EXPECTED RATE OF RETURN on an investment is below the hurdle rate, the project is not undertaken. The hurdle rate should be equal to the INCREMENTAL COST OF CAPITAL.

HYBRID ANNUITY contract offered by an insurance company that allows an investor to mix the benefits of both fixed and variable annuities. Also called *combination annuity.* For instance, an annuity buyer may put a portion of his assets in a FIXED ANNUITY, which promises a certain rate of return, and the remainder in a stock or bond fund VARIABLE ANNUITY, which offers a chance for higher return but takes more risk.

HYBRID INVESTMENT OR SECURITY investment vehicle that combines two different kinds of underlying investments. For example, a structured note, which is a form of a bond, may have the interest rate it pays tied to the rise and fall of a commodity's price. Hybrid investments are also called *derivatives.*

HYPERINFLATION *see* INFLATION.

HYPOTHECATION
Banking: pledging property to secure a loan. Hypothecation does not transfer title, but it does transfer the right to sell the hypothecated property in the event of default.
Securities: pledging of securities to brokers as collateral for loans made to purchase securities or to cover short sales, called margin loans. When the same collateral is pledged by the broker to a bank to collateralize a broker's loan, the process is called *rehypothecation.*

I

IBC'S MONEY FUND REPORT AVERAGE average for all major taxable and tax-free money market mutual fund yields published weekly for 7- and 30-day simple and compound (assumes reinvested dividends) yields. IBC also tracks the average maturity of securities in money fund portfolios. A short maturity of about 30 days or less reflects the conviction of fund managers that interest rates will rise, and a long maturity of 60 days or more reflects a sentiment that rates will fall. Investors can compare the yield and average maturity against the industry average to ascertain if their money fund's return is competitive, and how their fund manager's views on the direction of interest rates compares to industry peers. IBC's Money Fund Report Average is published in major newspapers, including *The Wall Street Journal, The New York Times,* and *Barron's. Barron's* also publishes a list of the 7- and 30-day yields of most money market mutual funds, along with each fund's net assets and average maturity as compiled by the IBC Organization of Ashland, Massachusetts.

I/B/E/S INTERNATIONAL INC. provides the I/B/E/S data base, which comprises analysts' estimates of future earnings for thousands of publicly traded companies. These estimates are tabulated, and companies whose estimates have increased or decreased significantly are pinpointed. Reports also detail how many estimates are available on each company and the high, low, and average estimates for each. *See also* EARNINGS SURPRISE; FIRST CALL; ZACKS ESTIMATE SYSTEM.

I-BONDS inflation-indexed SAVINGS BONDS issued by the United States Treasury in eight denominations ranging from $50 to $10,000 with a 30-year maturity. Unlike other inflation-adjusted bonds, but like other savings bonds, the securities, which were introduced in 1998, offer special tax benefits. As long as investors hold their bonds, they may defer paying taxes on their earnings, which are automatically reinvested and added to the principal. Like other Treasury bonds, I-Bonds are exempt from state and local income taxes. If the bond is redeemed to pay for college tuition or other college fees, investors may exclude part or all of the income in calculating their taxes. The payout on the bonds is determined by two rates. A fixed rate, ranging from 3% to 3.5% when the bonds were first introduced, is set by the Treasury Department. The second rate, a rate of inflation, is determined every six months by the Bureau of Labor Statistics to reflect changes in a version of the Consumer Price Index. Some protection against deflation exists in that any decline in the CONSUMER PRICE INDEX (CPI) could eat into the fixed rate, but not affect the underlying principal. *See also* INFLATION INDEXED SECURITIES.

IDENTIFIED SHARES shares of stock or a mutual fund identified as having been bought at a particular price on a particular date. If a shareholder wishes to minimize his tax liability when selling shares, he must identify which shares were bought at what price in order to determine his cost basis. If he has acquired shares over a long period of time, through a CONSTANT DOLLAR PLAN or a DIVIDEND REINVESTMENT PLAN, for example, he will have many shares at many different prices. By identifying the shares with the highest cost basis, he will generally pay lower capital gains taxes than if he identified shares bought at a lower cost. If shares are sold at a loss, the shareholder can pick how large or small a loss he wants to take based on which shares he identifies. In addition, if the identified shares were held for 12 months or more, the investor qualifies for long-term capital gains tax rates. If the identified shares were held for less than 12 months, he will have to pay regular income tax rates on the gain.

ILLEGAL DIVIDEND dividend declared by a corporation's board of directors in violation of its charter or of state laws. Most states, for example, stipulate that dividends be paid out of current income or RETAINED EARNINGS; they prohibit dividend payments that come out of CAPITAL SURPLUS or that would make the corporation insolvent. Directors who authorize illegal dividends may be sued by stockholders and creditors and may also face civil and criminal penalties. Stockholders who receive such dividends may be required to return them in order to meet the claims of creditors.

ILLIQUID
Finance: firm that lacks sufficient CASH FLOW to meet current and maturing obligations.
Investments: not readily convertible into cash, such as a stock, bond, or commodity that is not traded actively and would be difficult to sell at once without taking a large loss. Other assets for which there is not a ready market, and which therefore may take some time to sell, include real estate and collectibles such as rare stamps, coins, or antique furniture.

IMBALANCE OF ORDERS too many orders of one kind—to buy or to sell—without matching orders of the opposite kind. An imbalance usually follows a dramatic event such as a takeover, the death of a key executive, or a government ruling that will significantly affect the company's business. If it occurs before the stock exchange opens, trading in the stock is delayed. If it occurs during the trading day, the specialist suspends trading until enough matching orders can be found to make for an orderly market.

IMF *see* INTERNATIONAL MONETARY FUND.

IMMEDIATE FAMILY parents, brothers, sisters, children, relatives supported financially, father-in-law, mother-in-law, sister-in-law, and brother-in-law. This definition is incorporated in the NATIONAL ASSOCIATION OF SECURITIES DEALERS RULES OF FAIR PRACTICE on abuses of *hot issues* through such practices as FREERIDING and WITHHOLDING. The ruling prohibits the sale of such securities to members of a broker-dealer's own family or to persons buying and selling for institutional accounts and their families.

IMMEDIATE OR CANCEL ORDER order requiring that all or part of the order be executed as soon as the broker enters a bid or offer; the portion not executed is automatically canceled. Such stipulations usually accompany large orders.

IMMEDIATE PAYMENT ANNUITY annuity contract bought with a single payment and with a specified payout plan that starts right away. Payments may be for a specified period or for the life of the annuitant and are usually on a monthly basis. *See also* ANNUITIZE.

IMMUNIZATION *see* DURATION.

IMPAIRED CAPITAL total capital that is less than the stated or par value of the company's CAPITAL STOCK. *See also* DEFICIT NET WORTH.

IMPAIRED CREDIT deterioration in the credit rating of a borrower, which may result in a reduction in the amount of credit made available by lenders. For example, a company may launch a product line that is a failure, and the resulting losses will seriously weaken the company's finances. Concerned lenders may reduce the firm's credit lines as a result. The same process can apply to an individual who has been late paying bills, or in an extreme case, has filed for bankruptcy protection. Also called *adverse credit.*

IMPORT DUTY *see* TARIFF.

IMPUTED INTEREST interest considered to have been paid in effect even though no interest was actually paid. For example, the Internal Revenue Service requires that annual interest be recognized on a ZERO-COUPON SECURITY.

IMPUTED VALUE logical or implicit value that is not recorded in any accounts. Examples: in projecting annual figures, values are imputed for months about which actual figures are not yet available; cash invested unproductively has an imputed value consisting of what it would have earned in a productive investment (OPPORTUNITY COST); in calculating national income, the U.S. Department of Commerce imputes a dollar value for wages and salaries paid in kind, such as food and lodging provided on ships at sea.

INACTIVE ASSET asset not continually used in a productive way, such as an auxiliary generator.

INACTIVE BOND CROWD *see* CABINET CROWD.

INACTIVE POST trading post on the New York Stock Exchange at which inactive stocks are traded in 10-share units rather than the regular 100-share lots. Known to traders as *Post 30. See also* ROUND LOT.

INACTIVE STOCK/BOND security traded relatively infrequently, either on an exchange or over the counter. The low volume makes the security ILLIQUID, and small investors tend to shy away from it.

IN-AND-OUT TRADER one who buys and sells the same security in one day, aiming to profit from sharp price moves. *See also* DAY TRADE.

INCENTIVE FEE compensation for producing above-average results. Incentive fees are common for commodities trading advisers who achieve or top a preset return, as well as for a GENERAL PARTNER in a real estate or oil and gas LIMITED PARTNERSHIP.

INCENTIVE STOCK OPTION plan created by the ECONOMIC RECOVERY TAX ACT OF 1981 (ERTA) under which qualifying options are free of tax at the date of grant and the date of exercise. Profits on shares sold after being held at least two years from the date of grant or one year from the date of transfer to the employee are subject to favorable CAPITAL GAINS TAX rates. *See also* QUALIFYING STOCK OPTION.

INCESTUOUS SHARE DEALING buying and selling of shares in each other's companies to create a tax or other financial advantage.

INCOME AVAILABLE FOR FIXED CHARGES *see* FIXED-CHARGE COVERAGE.

INCOME AVERAGING method of computing personal income tax whereby tax is figured on the average of the total of current year's income and that of the three preceding years. According to 1984 U.S. tax legislation, income averaging was used when a person's income for the current year exceeded 140% of the average taxable income in the preceding three years. The TAX REFORM ACT OF 1986 repealed income averaging.

INCOME BOND obligation on which the payment of interest is contingent on sufficient earnings from year to year. Such bonds are traded FLAT—that is, with no accrued interest—and are often an alternative to bankruptcy. *See also* ADJUSTMENT BOND.

INCOME DIVIDEND payout to shareholders of interest, dividends, or other income received by a mutual fund. By law, all such income must be distributed to shareholders, who may choose to take the money in cash or reinvest it in more shares of the fund. All income dividends are taxable to shareholders in the year they are received, unless the fund is held in a tax-deferred account such as an IRA or Keogh plan.

INCOME EXCLUSION RULE INCOME TAX rule excluding certain items from taxable income. Personal exclusions include interest on tax-exempt securities, returns of capital, life insurance death benefits, dividends on veterans' life insurance, child support, welfare payments, disability benefits paid by the Veterans Administration, and amounts received from an insurer because of the loss of use of a home. *See also* EXCLUSION.

INCOME INVESTMENT COMPANY management company that operates an income-oriented MUTUAL FUND for investors who value income over growth. These funds may invest in bonds or high-dividend stocks or may write covered call options on stocks. *See also* INVESTMENT COMPANY.

INCOME LIMITED PARTNERSHIP real estate, oil and gas, or equipment leasing LIMITED PARTNERSHIP whose aim is high income, much of which may be taxable. Such a partnership may be designed for tax-sheltered accounts like Individual Retirement Accounts, Keogh plan accounts, or pension plans.

INCOME MUTUAL FUND mutual fund designed to produce current income for shareholders. Some examples of income funds are government, mortgage-backed security, municipal, international, and junk bond funds. Several kinds of equity-oriented funds also can have income as their primary investment objective, such as utilities income funds and equity income funds. All distributions from income funds are taxable in the year received by the shareholder unless the fund is held in a tax-deferred account such as an IRA or Keogh or the distributions come from tax-exempt bonds, such as with a municipal bond fund.

INCOME PROPERTY real estate bought for the income it produces. The property may be placed in an INCOME LIMITED PARTNERSHIP, or it may be owned by individuals or corporations. Buyers also hope to achieve capital gains when they sell the property.

INCOME SHARES one of two kinds or classes of capital stock issued by a DUAL-PURPOSE FUND or split investment company, the other kind being *capital shares*. Holders of income shares receive dividends from both classes of shares, generated from income (dividends and interest) produced by the portfolio, whereas holders of capital shares receive capital gains payouts on both classes. Income shares normally have a minimum income guarantee, which is cumulative.

INCOME STATEMENT *see* PROFIT AND LOSS STATEMENT.

INCOME STOCK stock paying high and regular dividends to shareholders. Some industries known for income stocks include gas, electric, and telephone utilities; real estate investment trusts; banks; and insurance companies. High-quality income stocks have established a long history of paying dividends, and in many cases have a track record of regularly increasing dividends. All dividends paid to shareholders of income stocks are taxable in the year received unless the stock is held in a tax-deferred account such as an IRA or Keogh plan.

INCOME TAX annual tax on income levied by the federal government and by certain state and local governments. There are two basic types: the personal income tax, levied on incomes of households and unincorporated businesses, and the corporate (or corporation) income tax, levied on net earnings of corporations.

The U.S. income tax was instituted in 1913 by the Sixteenth Amendment to the Constitution. Typically, it accounts for more than half the federal government's total annual revenue. Most states tax individual and corporate incomes, as do some cities, though sales and property taxes are the main sources of state and local revenue. The personal income tax, and to a lesser extent the corporate income tax, were designed to be progressive—that is, to take a larger percentage of higher incomes than lower incomes. The ranges of incomes to which progressively higher rates apply are called TAX BRACKETS, which also determine the value of DEDUCTIONS, such as business costs and expenses, state and local income taxes, or charitable contributions.

Under present tax law, there are effectively five tax brackets for individual taxpayers: 15%, 28%, 31%, 36% and 39.6%. The levels of TAXABLE INCOME for each bracket differs according to filing status (such as married filing jointly, singles, or heads of household) and is revised slightly every year. Long-term CAPITAL GAINS receive preferential tax treatment both for individuals and corporations. Assets held for more than 12 months are taxed at a top rate of 20%, versus a top rate of 39.6% for short-term gains on assets held for less than 12 months. Because capital gains rates rewarded taxpayers in a position to take risks, and since LOOPHOLES and TAX SHELTERS enabled the wealthiest corporations and individuals to escape the higher tax brackets, the progressiveness of the tax system has often been more theoretical than real. There have been many sweeping changes in the tax code, creating an enormous amount of complexity. In 1998, the INTERNAL REVENUE SERVICE RESTRUCTURING AND REFORM ACT OF 1998 instituted numerous changes in the way the Internal Revenue Service conducts business, including shifting the burden of proof from taxpayers to the IRS in court disputes over the amount of taxes owed by a taxpayer. The progression of changes in the tax code is described in great detail in other *Dictionary* entries, including: ECONOMIC RECOVERY TAX ACT OF 1981 (ERTA); INTERNAL REVENUE SERVICE RESTRUCTURING AND REFORM ACT OF 1998; REVENUE RECONCILIATION ACT OF 1993; TAX EQUITY AND FISCAL RESPONSIBILITY ACT OF 1982 (TEFRA); TAX REFORM ACT OF 1976; TAX REFORM ACT OF 1984; TAX REFORM ACT OF 1986; and the TAXPAYER RELIEF ACT OF 1997.

INCONTESTABILITY CLAUSE provision in a life insurance contract stating that the insurer cannot revoke the policy after it has been in force for one or two years if the policyholder concealed important facts from the company during the application process. For example, a policyholder who stated that he had never had a heart attack, but in fact had experienced one, would still be covered by the policy if the insurance company had not discovered this discrepancy within one or two years. However, if a policyholder lies about his age on the application, the policy's death benefit can be adjusted higher retroactively to account for the insured's true age.

INCORPORATION process by which a company receives a state charter allowing it to operate as a corporation. The fact of incorporation must be acknowledged in the company's legal name, using the word *incorporated*, the abbreviation *inc.*, or other acceptable variations. *See also* ARTICLES OF INCORPORATION.

INCREMENTAL CASH FLOW net of cash outflows and inflows attributable to a corporate investment project.

INCREMENTAL COST OF CAPITAL weighted cost of the additional capital raised in a given period. Weighted cost of capital, also called *composite cost of capital*, is the weighted average of costs applicable to the issues of debt and classes of equity that compose the firm's capital structure. Also called *marginal cost of capital*.

INDEMNIFY agree to compensate for damage or loss. The word is used in insurance policies promising that, in the event of a loss, the insured will be restored to the financial position that existed prior to the loss.

INDENTURE formal agreement, also called a deed of trust, between an issuer of bonds and the bondholder covering such considerations as: (1) form of the bond; (2) amount of the issue; (3) property pledged (if not a debenture issue); (4) protective COVENANTS including any provision for a sinking fund; (5) WORKING CAPITAL and CURRENT RATIO; and (6) redemption rights or call privileges. The indenture also provides for the appointment of a trustee to act on behalf of the bondholders, in accordance with the TRUST INDENTURE ACT OF 1939.

INDEPENDENT AGENT agent representing several insurance companies. The agent is independent from all the companies he or she sells for, and can therefore in theory evaluate different insurance policies objectively. Independent agents pay all their own expenses and keep their own records and earn their income from commissions on the policies they sell. The opposite of an independent agent is a CAPTIVE AGENT, who works exclusively for one company.

INDEPENDENT AUDITOR certified public accountant (CPA) who provides the ACCOUNTANT'S OPINION.

INDEPENDENT BROKER New York Stock Exchange member who executes orders for other floor brokers who have more volume than they can handle, or for firms whose exchange members are not on the floor. Formerly called $2 brokers because of their commission for a round lot trade, independent brokers are compensated by commission brokers with fees that once were fixed but are now negotiable. *See also* GIVE UP.

INDEX statistical composite that measures changes in the economy or in financial markets, often expressed in percentage changes from a base period or from the previous month. For instance, the CONSUMER PRICE INDEX uses 1982–84 as the base period. That index, made up of the prices for key consumer goods and services, moves up and down as the rate of inflation changes. By the late '90s the index climbed from 100 in 1982–84 to 160 and higher, meaning that the basket of goods the index was based on rose in price by more than 60%.

Indices also measure the ups and downs of stock, bond, and commodities markets, reflecting market prices and the number of shares outstanding for the companies in the index. Some well-known indices are the Dow Jones Averages, the New York Stock Exchange Composite Index, the American Stock Exchange Composite Index, the Standard & Poor's 500 Index, the NASDAQ Composite Index, the Russell 2000 Index and the Value Line Composite Index. Subindices for industry groups such as drugs, railroads, or computers are also tracked. Stock market indices form the basis for trading in INDEX OPTIONS. *See also* STOCK INDICES AND AVERAGES.

INDEX ARBITRAGE *see* ARBITRAGE.

INDEXATION *see* INDEXING, at meaning (2).

INDEX BOND bond whose cash flow is linked to the purchasing power of the dollar or a foreign currency. For example, a bond indexed to the CONSUMER PRICE INDEX (CPI) would ensure that the bondholder receives real value by making an upward adjustment in the interest rate to reflect higher prices.

INDEX FUND mutual fund that has a portfolio matching that of a broad-based portfolio. This may include the Dow Jones Industrial Average, Standard & Poor's 500 Index, indices of mid- and small-capitalization stocks, foreign stock indices, and bond indices, to name a few. Many institutional and individual investors, especially believers in the EFFICIENT MARKET theory, put money in index funds on the assumption that trying to beat the market averages over the long run is futile, and their investments in these funds will at least keep pace with the index being tracked. In addition, since the cost of managing an index fund is far cheaper than the cost of running an actively managed portfolio, index funds have a built-in cost advantage.

INDEXING
1. weighting one's portfolio to match a broad-based index such as Standard & Poor's so as to match its performance—or buying shares in an INDEX FUND.
2. tying wages, taxes, or other rates to an index. For example, a labor contract may call for indexing wages to the consumer price index to protect against loss of purchasing power in a time of rising inflation.

INDEX OF LEADING INDICATORS *see* LEADING INDICATORS.

INDEX OPTIONS calls and puts on indexes of stocks. These options are traded on the New York, American, and Chicago Board Options Exchanges, among others. Broad-based indexes cover a wide range of companies and industries, whereas narrow-based indexes consist of stocks in one industry or sector of the economy. Index options allow investors to trade in a particular market or industry group without having to buy all the stocks individually. For instance, someone who thought oil stocks were about to fall could buy a put on the oil index instead of selling short shares in half a dozen oil companies.

INDEX PARTICIPATION *see* BASKET.

INDICATED YIELD coupon or dividend rate as a percentage of the current market price. For fixed rate bonds it is the same as CURRENT YIELD. For common stocks, it is the market price divided into the annual dividend. For preferred stocks, it is the market price divided into the contractual dividend.

INDICATION approximation of what a security's TRADING RANGE (bid and offer prices) will be when trading resumes after a delayed opening or after being halted because of an IMBALANCE OF ORDERS or another reason. Also called *indicated market.*

INDICATION OF INTEREST securities underwriting term meaning a dealer's or investor's interest in purchasing securities that are still *in registration* (awaiting clearance by) the Securities and Exchange Commission. A broker who receives an indication of interest should send the client a preliminary prospectus on the securities. An indication of interest is not a commitment to buy, an important point because selling a security while it is in registration is illegal. *See also* CIRCLE.

INDICATOR technical measurement securities market analysts use to forecast the market's direction, such as investment advisory sentiment, volume of stock trading, direction of interest rates, and buying or selling by corporate insiders.

INDIRECT COST AND EXPENSE *see* DIRECT OVERHEAD; FIXED COST.

INDIRECT LABOR COSTS wages and related costs of factory employees, such as inspectors and maintenance crews, whose time is not charged to specific finished products.

INDIVIDUAL RETIREMENT ACCOUNT (IRA) personal, tax-deferred, retirement account that an employed person can set up with a deposit limited to $2,000 per year ($4,000 for a married couple filing jointly, whether or not both spouses work.) IRA contributions are deductible regardless of income if neither the taxpayer nor the taxpayer's spouse is covered by a QUALIFIED PLAN OR TRUST. If the taxpayer is covered by a qualified plan, they may deduct IRA contributions if ADJUSTED GROSS INCOME (AGI) is below $50,000 on a joint return, or $30,000 on a single return. Couples with incomes of $50,000 to $60,000 and single taxpayers with incomes of $30,000 to $40,000 are allowed partial deductions in amounts reduced proportionately over the $10,000 range with a minimum deduction of $200. Taxpayers with incomes over $60,000 (joint) and $40,000 (single) are not allowed deductions, but may make the same contributions (treated as a nontaxable RETURN OF CAPITAL upon withdrawal) and thus gain the benefit of tax-deferral. Under the TAXPAYER RELIEF ACT OF 1997, income limits gradually climb through the year 2007 to $80,000 for a couple and $50,000 for a single. Over those limits, the deduction phases out for the next $10,000 in income. For singles, the deduction is phased out completely once income tops $60,000 in 2005. For married couples filing jointly, the deduction is phased out once income exceeds $100,000 in 2007. Taxpayers who cannot make deductible contributions because of participation in qualified retirement plans may make nondeductible contributions.

Withdrawals from IRAs prior to age 59½ are generally subject to a 10% (of principal) penalty tax. Withdrawals after age 59½ are fully taxable if the original contributions generated deductions. If the original contributions were nondeductible, taxes need not be paid on the amount of those contributions. No IRA withdrawals are required until age 70½, when mandatory distributions must be made according to an IRS schedule based on life expectancy.

The 1997 tax law also created the ROTH IRA, named after Delaware Republican Senator William V. Roth, Jr. who championed the idea. Starting on January 1, 1998, individuals can invest up to $2,000 a year in earnings into a Roth IRA, even after reaching the age of 70½. As long as the assets have remained inside the account for five years, all earnings and principal can be withdrawn totally tax-free after age 59½. Unlike regular IRAs, participants do not have to take distributions from a Roth IRA starting at age 70½. In fact, they don't have to take distributions at all in their lifetimes, allowing them to pass the assets in the Roth to beneficiaries income-tax free. Contributors to Roth IRAs do not receive a tax deduction for making the contribution, but the value of tax-free withdrawals often exceeds the tax break from upfront deductions. Roth IRA rules also permit participants to withdraw assets without the usual 10% early withdrawal penalty if they use the money for the purchase of a first home (withdrawals are limited to up to $10,000), for college expenses, or if they become disabled. Only married couples with AGIs of $150,000 or less and singles with AGIs of $95,000 or less can contribute the full amount to Roth IRAs. The amount they can contribute is phased out for income between $150,000 and $160,000 for married couples, and between $95,000 and $110,000 for singles. No contributions are allowed over these income limits. For those with AGIs of $100,000 or less, the tax law allows ROLLOVERS of existing deductible and nondeductible IRA balances into a Roth IRA. Taxpayers who rollover, however, must pay income tax on all previously untaxed contributions and earnings. If they execute such a rollover before January 1, 1999, they can spread the resulting tax bill over 4 years. Starting in 1999, the rollover is fully taxable in the year it is completed.

The 1997 tax act also created another form of IRA called the EDUCATION IRA. It allows parents to contribute up to $500 per year for each child up to the age of 18. This $500 limit is reduced for married couples filing jointly with AGIs between $150,000 and $160,000, or singles reporting between $95,000 and $110,000 in income. Couples with incomes over $160,000 and singles with incomes over $110,000 may not contribute to Education IRAs. Contributions to Education IRAs do not generate tax deductions, however, assets inside the Education IRA grow tax-free and principal and earnings can be withdrawn tax-free as long as the proceeds are used to pay for education expenses at a postsecondary school, including tuition, fees, books, supplies and room and board. In a family with two or more children, Education IRA money not used by the first child can be used by the second or subsequent children if the first child does not attend college. The assets in the Education IRA must be spent on education before the child reaches age 30. If the assets are not used for college expenses, the account must be liquidated and taxes paid on the proceeds at regular income tax rates.

IRAs can be invested in almost every kind of instrument including stocks, bonds, mutual funds, certificates of deposit, annuities and precious metals. Physical real estate cannot be among an IRA's assets.

See also EDUCATION IRA; ROTH IRA; SIMPLIFIED EMPLOYEE PENSION (SEP) PLAN; SELF-DIRECTED IRA; SIMPLE IRA.

INDIVIDUAL RETIREMENT ACCOUNT (IRA) ROLLOVER provision of the IRA law that enables persons receiving LUMP-SUM payments from their company's pension, profit-sharing, or SALARY REDUCTION PLAN—due to retirement or other termination of employment—to roll over the amount into an IRA investment plan within 60 days. Also, current IRAs may be transferred to other investment options or financial institutions within a 60-day period. Through an IRA rollover, the capital continues to accumulate tax-deferred until time of withdrawal. In order to avoid a 20% withholding by the IRA trustee, assets should be rolled over from one place to another as a *direct transfer*, made by instructing the IRA trustee to transfer the assets directly to another IRA trustee. Tax-free rollovers may only occur once in a one-year period starting on the date of the first distribution. Otherwise, the distribution amount would be subject to regular income tax and a 10% premature distribution penalty. IRA account holders can also take advantage of the rollover rules to borrow funds from their IRAs for a 60-day loan. As long as the money is redeposited within 60 days, there is no tax on the withdrawal, which is considered a tax-free rollover. *See also* ROLLOVER.

INDIVIDUAL TAX RETURN tax return filed by an individual instead of a corporation. The 1040 tax form used by individuals comes in three basic varieties: the 1040EZ basic form, the 1040A short form, and the 1040 long form. Attached to the 1040 are several schedules, including Schedule A for itemized deductions, Schedule B for interest and dividend income, Schedule C for profits and losses from a business, Schedule D for reporting capital gains and losses, Schedule E for supplemental income and losses, Schedule F for profit or loss from farming, Schedule H for household employment taxes, Schedule K-1 for a limited partner's share of gains, losses, and credits, Schedule R for the credit for the elderly or the disabled and Schedule SE for self-employment tax. The 1040PC allows taxpayers to file their tax returns electronically through what is known as an *IRS e-file*. Form 1040X allows taxpayers to amend their return if they discover mistakes in their original filing. Form 1040 ES is designed for taxpayers making quarterly estimated tax payments.

INDUSTRIAL in stock market vernacular, general, catch-all category including firms producing or distributing goods and services that are not classified as utility, transportation, or financial companies. *See also* STOCK INDICES AND AVERAGES; FORBES 500; FORTUNE 500.

INDUSTRIAL DEVELOPMENT BOND (IDB) type of MUNICIPAL REVENUE BOND issued to finance FIXED ASSETS that are then leased to private firms, whose payments AMORTIZE the debt. IDBs were traditionally tax-exempt to buyers, but under the TAX REFORM ACT OF 1986, large IDB issues ($1 million plus) became taxable effective August 15, 1986, while tax-exempt small issues for commercial and manufacturing purposes were prohibited after 1986 and 1989 respectively. Also, effective August 7, 1986, banks lost their 80% interest deductibility on borrowings to buy IDBs.

INDUSTRIAL PRODUCTION monthly statistic released by the FEDERAL RESERVE BOARD on the total output of all U.S. factories and mines. These numbers are a key ECONOMIC INDICATOR.

INDUSTRIAL REVENUE BOND *see* INDUSTRIAL DEVELOPMENT BOND.

INEFFICIENCY IN THE MARKET failure of investors to recognize that a particular stock or bond has good prospects or may be headed for trouble. According to the EFFICIENT MARKET theory, current prices reflect all knowledge about securities. But some say that those who find out about securities first can profit by exploiting that information; stocks of small, little-known firms with a large growth potential most clearly reflect the market's inefficiency, they say.

INELASTIC DEMAND OR SUPPLY *see* ELASTICITY OF DEMAND OR SUPPLY.

IN ESCROW *see* ESCROW.

INFANT INDUSTRY ARGUMENT case made by developing sectors of the economy that their industries need protection against international competition while they establish themselves. In response to such pleas, the government may enact a TARIFF or import duty to stifle foreign competition. The infant industry argument is frequently made in developing nations that are trying to lessen their dependence on the industrialized world. In Brazil, for example, such infant industries as automobile production argue that they need protection until their technological capability and marketing prowess are sufficient to enable competition with well-established foreigners.

INFLATION rise in the prices of goods and services, as happens when spending increases relative to the supply of goods on the market—in other words, too much money chasing too few goods. Moderate inflation is a common result of economic growth. Hyperinflation, with prices rising at 100% a year or more, causes people to lose confidence in the currency and put their assets in hard assets like real estate or gold, which usually retain their value in inflationary times. *See also* COST-PUSH INFLATION; DEMAND-PULL INFLATION.

INFLATION ACCOUNTING showing the effects of inflation in financial statements. The Financial Accounting Standards Board (FASB) requires major companies to supplement their traditional financial reporting with information showing the effects of inflation. The ruling applies to public companies having inventories and fixed assets of more than $125 million or total assets of more than $1 billion.

INFLATION HEDGE investment designed to protect against the loss of purchasing power from inflation. Traditionally, gold and real estate have a reputation as good inflation hedges, though growth in stocks also can offset inflation in the long run. Money market funds, which pay higher yields as interest rates rise during inflationary times, can also be a good inflation hedge. In the case of hyperinflation, hard assets such as precious metals and real estate are normally viewed as inflation hedges, while the value of paper-based assets such as stocks, bonds, and currency erodes rapidly.

INFLATION-INDEXED SECURITIES bonds or notes that guarantee a return that beats INFLATION if held to maturity. Also applied to shares in mutual funds that hold such securities. Inflation-indexed Treasury securities were introduced in 1997 in 10-year maturities and were subsequently issued as 5-year notes. Similar offerings followed by issuers such as the Tennessee Valley Authority and the Federal Home Loan Bank. In April, 1998, the first 30-year inflation-indexed Treasury bonds were issued. Inflation-indexed Treasuries offer a fixed rate of return, as well as a fluctuating rate of return that matches inflation. The fixed portion is paid out as INTEREST, while the indexed portion is represented by an annual adjustment of PRINCIPAL. For example, a $1,000 inflation-indexed Treasury is issued at auction with a 3.5% INTEREST RATE and inflation that year turns out to be 3%. The 3.5% interest on $1,000 would be paid out and, at the end of the year, the inflation rate would adjust the principal, bringing it to $1,030. The following year, the fixed 3.5% interest rate would be applied to the new principal of $1,030 and the principal would again be adjusted according to that year's inflation rate. With low inflation prevailing in the late '90s, anti-inflation securities met a lackluster reception, although longer-term bonds were in somewhat greater demand. Chief drawbacks are the prospect of DEFLATION, a lack of LIQUIDITY, and the fact that the inflation adjustment is taxable annually but not paid out until maturity.

INFLATION RATE rate of change in prices. Two primary U.S. indicators of the inflation rate are the CONSUMER PRICE INDEX and the PRODUCER PRICE INDEX, which track changes in prices paid by consumers and by producers. The rate can be calculated on an annual, monthly, or other basis.

INFLATION RISK *see* RISK.

INFLEXIBLE EXPENSES *see* FLEXIBLE EXPENSES.

INFRASTRUCTURE a nation's basic system of transportation, communication, and other aspects of its physical plant. Building and maintaining road, bridge, sewage, and electrical systems provides millions of jobs nationwide. For developing countries, building an infrastructure is a first step in economic development.

INGOT bar of metal. The Federal Reserve System's gold reserves are stored in ingot form. Individual investors may take delivery of an ingot of a precious metal such as gold or silver or may buy a certificate entitling them to a share in an ingot.

INHERITANCE part of an estate acquired by an HEIR.

INHERITANCE TAX RETURN state counterpart to the federal ESTATE TAX return, required of the executor or administrator to determine the amount of state tax due on the inheritance.

INITIAL MARGIN amount of cash or eligible securities required to be deposited with a broker before engaging in margin transactions. A margin transaction is one in which the broker extends credit to the customer in a margin account. Under REGULATION T of the Federal Reserve Board, the initial margin is currently 50% of the purchase price when buying eligible stock or convertible bonds or 50% of the proceeds of a short sale. *See also* MAINTENANCE REQUIREMENT; MARGIN CALL; MARGIN REQUIREMENT; MARGIN SECURITY.

INITIAL PUBLIC OFFERING (IPO) corporation's first offering of stock to the public. IPO's are almost invariably an opportunity for the existing investors and participating venture capitalists to make big profits, since for the first time their shares will be given a market value reflecting expectations for the company's future growth. *See also* HOT ISSUE.

INJUNCTION court order instructing a defendant to refrain from doing something that would be injurious to the plaintiff, or face a penalty. The usual procedure is to issue a temporary restraining order, then hold hearings to determine whether a permanent injunction is warranted.

IN PLAY stock affected by TAKEOVER rumors or activities.

INSIDE INFORMATION corporate affairs that have not yet been made public. The officers of a firm would know in advance, for instance, if the company was about to be taken over, or if the latest earnings report was going to differ significantly from information released earlier. Under Securities and Exchange Commission rules, an INSIDER is not allowed to trade on the basis of such information.

INSIDE MARKET bid or asked quotes between dealers trading for their own inventories. Distinguished from the retail market, where quotes reflect the prices that customers pay to dealers. Also known as *interdealer market; wholesale market.*

INSIDER person with access to key information before it is announced to the public. Usually the term refers to directors, officers, and key employees, but the definition has been extended legally to include relatives and others in a position to capitalize on INSIDE INFORMATION. Insiders are prohibited from trading on their knowledge.

INSIDER TRADING practice of buying and selling shares in a company's stock by that company's management or board of directors, or by a holder of more than 10% of the company's shares. Managers may trade their company's stock as long as they disclose their activity within ten days of the close of the month within the time the transactions took place. However, it is illegal for insiders to trade based on their knowledge of material corporate developments that have not been announced publicly. Developments that would be considered *material* include news of an impending takeover, introduction of a new product line, a divestiture, a key executive appointment, or other news that could affect the company's stock positively or negatively. Insider trading laws have been extended to other people who have knowledge of these developments but who are not members of management, including investment bankers, lawyers, printers of financial disclosure documents, or relatives of managers and executives who learn of these material developments.

INSIDER TRADING SANCTIONS ACT OF 1984 amendment to the SECURITIES EXCHANGE ACT OF 1934 that outlined civil and criminal penalties for insider trading violations. Fines up to triple the amount of illegal gains can be levied. The amendment applies not only to people who buy or sell using material nonpublic information, but to anyone who gives them such information or aids and abets them.

INSOLVENCY inability to pay debts when due. *See also* BANKRUPTCY; CASH FLOW; SOLVENCY.

INSTALLMENT SALE
   In general: sale made with the agreement that the purchased goods or services will be paid for in fractional amounts over a specified period of time.

Securities: transaction with a set contract price, paid in installments over a period of time. Gains or losses are generally taxable on a prorated basis.

INSTINET *see* FOURTH MARKET.

INSTITUTIONAL BROKER broker who buys and sells securities for banks, mutual funds, insurance companies, pension funds, or other institutional clients. Institutional brokers deal in large volumes of securities and generally charge their customers lower per-unit commission rates than individuals pay.

INSTITUTIONAL INVESTOR organization that trades large volumes of securities. Some examples are mutual funds, banks, insurance companies, pension funds, labor union funds, corporate profit-sharing plans, and college endowment funds. Typically, upwards of 70% of the daily trading on the New York Stock Exchange is on behalf of institutional investors.

INSTRUMENT legal document in which some contractual relationship is given formal expression or by which some right is granted—for example, notes, contracts, agreements. *See also* NEGOTIABLE INSTRUMENT.

INSTRUMENTALITY federal agency whose obligations, while not direct obligations of the U.S. Government, are sponsored or guaranteed by the government and backed by the FULL FAITH AND CREDIT of the government. Well over 100 series of notes, certificates, and bonds have been issued by such instrumentalities as Federal Home Loan Bank, and Student Loan Marketing Association.

INSURABILITY conditions under which an insurance company is willing to insure a risk. Each insurance company applies its own standards based on its own underwriting criteria. For example, some life insurance companies do not insure people with high-risk occupations such as stuntmen or firefighters, while other companies consider these people insurable, though the premiums they must pay are higher than for those in low-risk professions.

INSURABLE INTEREST relationship between an insured person or property and the potential beneficiary of the policy. For example, a wife has an insurable interest in her husband's life, because she would be financially harmed if he were to die. Therefore, she could receive the proceeds of the insurance policy if he were to die while the policy was in force. If there is no insurable interest, an insurance company will not issue a policy.

INSURANCE system whereby individuals and companies that are concerned about potential hazards pay premiums to an insurance company, which reimburses them in the event of loss. The insurer profits by investing the premiums it receives. Some common forms of insurance cover business risks, automobiles, homes, boats, workers' compensation, and health. Life insurance guarantees payment to the beneficiaries when the insured person dies. In a broad economic sense, insurance transfers risk from individuals to a larger group, which is better able to pay for losses.

INSURANCE AGENT representative of an insurance company who sells the firm's policies. CAPTIVE AGENTS sell the policies of only one company, while INDEPENDENT AGENTS sell the policies of many companies. Agents must be licensed to sell insurance in the states where they solicit customers.

INSURANCE BROKER independent broker who searches for the best insurance coverage at the lowest cost for the client. Insurance brokers do not work for insurance companies, but for the buyers of insurance products. They constantly are comparing the merits of competing insurance companies to find the best deal for their customers.

INSURANCE CLAIM request for payment from the insurance company by the insured. For example, a homeowner files a claim if he or she suffered damage because of a fire, theft, or other loss. In life insurance, survivors submit a claim when the insured dies. The insurance company investigates the claim and pays the appropriate amount if the claim is found to be legitimate, or denies the claim if it determines the loss was fraudulent or not covered by the policy.

INSURANCE DIVIDEND money paid to cash value life insurance policyholders with participating policies, usually once a year. Dividend rates are based on the insurance company's mortality experience, administrative expenses, and investment returns. Lower mortality experience (the number of policyholders dying) and expenses, combined with high investment returns, will increase dividends. Technically, dividends are considered a return of the policyholder's premiums, and are thus not considered taxable income by the IRS. Policyholders may choose to take these dividends in cash or may purchase additional life insurance.

INSURANCE POLICY insurance contract specifying what risks are insured and what premiums must be paid to keep the policy in force. Policies also spell out DEDUCTIBLES and other terms. Policies for life insurance specify whose life is insured and which beneficiaries will receive the insurance proceeds. HOMEOWNER'S INSURANCE POLICIES specify which property and casualty perils are covered. *Health insurance policies* detail which medical procedures, drugs, and devices are reimbursed. *Auto insurance policies* describe the conditions under which car owners will be covered in case of accidents, theft, or other damage to their cars. *Disability policies* specify the qualifying conditions of disability and how long payments will continue. *Business insurance policies* describe which liabilities are reimbursable. The policy is the written document that both insured and insurance company refer to when determining whether or not a claim is covered.

INSURANCE PREMIUM payment made by the insured in return for insurance protection. Premiums are set based on the probability of risk of loss and competitive pressures with other insurers. An insurance company's actuary will figure out the expected loss ratio on a particular class of customers, and then individual applicants will be evaluated based on whether they present higher or lower risks than the class as a whole. If a policyholder does not pay the premium, the insurance or policy may lapse. If the policy is a cash value policy, the policyowner can choose to take a paid-up insurance policy with a lower face value amount or an extended term policy.

INSURANCE SETTLEMENT payment of proceeds from an insurance policy to the insured under the terms of an insurance contract. Insurance settlements may be either in the form of one lump-sum payment or a series of payments.

INSURED individual, group, or property that is covered by an INSURANCE POLICY. The policy specifies exactly which perils the insured is indemnified against. The insured may be a particular individual, such as someone covered by a life insurance policy. It may be a group of people, such as those covered by a group life insurance policy purchased by a company on behalf of its employees. The insured may also refer to property, such as a house and its possessions which are covered by a HOMEOWNER'S INSURANCE POLICY.

INSURED ACCOUNT account at a bank, savings and loan association, credit union, or brokerage firm that belongs to a federal or private insurance organization. Bank accounts are insured by the BANK INSURANCE FUND (BIF), and savings and loan deposits are insured by the SAVINGS ASSOCIATION INSURANCE FUND (SAIF); both programs are administered by the FEDERAL DEPOSIT INSURANCE CORPORATION (FDIC). Credit union accounts are insured by the *National Credit Union Administration.* Brokerage accounts are insured by the SECURITIES INVESTOR PROTECTION CORPORATION. Such insurance protects depositors against loss in the event that the institution becomes insolvent. Federal insurance systems were set up in the 1930s, after bank failures threatened the banking system with collapse. Some money market funds are covered by private insurance companies.

INSURED BONDS municipal bonds that are insured against default by a MUNICIPAL BOND INSURANCE company. The company pledges to make all interest and principal payments when due if the issuer of the bonds defaults on its obligations. In return, the bond's issuer pays a premium to the insurance company. Insured bonds usually trade based on the credit rating of the insurer rather than the rating of the underlying issuer, since the insurance company is ultimately at risk for the repayment of principal and interest. Insured bonds will pay slightly lower yields, because of the cost of the insurance protection, than comparable noninsured bonds. Some of the major municipal bond insurance firms include MBIA and AMBAC Indemnity Corporation.

INTANGIBLE ASSET right or nonphysical resource that is presumed to represent an advantage to the firm's position in the marketplace. Such assets include copyrights, patents, TRADEMARKS, goodwill, computer programs, capitalized advertising costs, organization costs, licenses, LEASES, FRANCHISES, exploration permits, and import and export permits.

INTANGIBLE COST tax-deductible cost. Such costs are incurred in drilling, testing, completing, and reworking oil and gas wells—labor, core analysis, fracturing, drill stem testing, engineering, fuel, geologists' expenses; also abandonment losses, management fees, delay rentals, and similar expenses.

INTERBANK RATE *see* LONDON INTERBANK OFFERED RATE (LIBOR).

INTERCOMMODITY SPREAD spread consisting of a long position and a short position in different but related commodities—for example, a long position in gold futures and a short position in silver futures. The investor hopes to profit from the changing price relationship between the commodities.

INTERDELIVERY SPREAD futures or options trading technique that entails buying one month of a contract and selling another month in the same contract—for instance, buying a June wheat contract and simultaneously selling a September wheat contract. The investor hopes to profit as the price difference between the two contracts widens or narrows.

INTEREST
1. cost of using money, expressed as a rate per period of time, usually one year, in which case it is called an annual rate of interest.
2. share, right, or title in property.

INTEREST COVERAGE *see* FIXED-CHARGE COVERAGE.

INTEREST DEDUCTION DEDUCTION allowable for certain types of interest expense, such as for interest on a home mortgage or interest on a MARGIN ACCOUNT.

INTEREST EQUALIZATION TAX (IET) tax of 15% on interest received by foreign borrowers in U.S. capital markets, imposed in 1963 and removed in 1974.

INTEREST-ONLY LOAN form of loan where the only current obligation is interest and where repayment of principal is deferred.

INTEREST OPTION insurance policyholder's choice to reinvest dividends with the insurer to earn a guaranteed rate of interest. A beneficiary may also reinvest proceeds to earn interest.

INTEREST RATE rate of interest charged for the use of money, usually expressed at an annual rate. The rate is derived by dividing the amount of interest by the amount of principal borrowed. For example, if a bank charged $10 per year in interest to borrow $100, they would be charging a 10% interest rate. Interest rates are quoted on bills, notes, bonds, credit cards, and many kinds of consumer and business loans.

INTEREST-RATE FUTURES CONTRACT futures contract based on a debt security or inter-bank deposit. In theory, the buyer of a bond futures contract agrees to take delivery of the underlying bonds when the contract expires, and the contract seller agrees to deliver the debt instrument. However, most contracts are not settled by delivery, but instead are traded out before expiration. The value of the contract rises and falls inversely to changes in interest rates. For example, if Treasury bond yields rise, futures contracts on Treasury bonds will fall in price. Conversely, when yields fall, Treasury bond futures prices rise. There are many kinds of interest rate futures contracts, including those on Treasury bills, notes, and bonds; Government National Mortgage Association (GNMA) mortgage-backed securities; municipal bonds; and inter-bank deposits such as Eurodollars. Speculators believing that interest rates are about to rise or fall trade these futures. Also, companies with exposure to fluctuations in interest rates, such as brokerage firms, banks, and insurance companies, may use these contracts to HEDGE their holdings of Treasury bonds and other debt instruments or their costs of future borrowings. For a list of interest rate futures contracts, *see* SECURITIES AND COMMODITIES EXCHANGES.

INTEREST-RATE OPTIONS CONTRACT options contract based on an underlying debt security. Options, unlike futures, give their buyers the right, but not the obligation, to buy the underlying bond at a fixed price before a specific date in the future. Option sellers promise to sell the bonds at a set price anytime until the contract expires. In return for granting this right, the option buyer pays a premium to the option seller. Yield-based calls become more valuable as yields rise, and puts become more valuable as yields decline. There are interest rate options on Treasury bills, notes, and bonds; GNMA mortgage-backed securities; certificates of deposit; municipal bonds; and other interest-sensitive instruments. For a complete list of these contracts, *see* SECURITIES AND COMMODITIES EXCHANGES.

INTEREST-RATE RISK RISK that changes in interest rates will adversely affect the value of an investor's securities portfolio. For example, an investor with large holdings in long-term bonds and utilities has assumed a significant interest-rate risk, because the value of those bonds and utility stocks will fall if interest rates rise. Investors can take various precautionary measures to HEDGE their interest-rate risk, such as buying INTEREST-RATE FUTURES or INTEREST-RATE OPTIONS CONTRACTS.

INTEREST-SENSITIVE INSURANCE POLICY cash value life insurance with dividend rates tied to the fluctuations in interest rates. For example, holders of UNIVERSAL LIFE INSURANCE policies will be credited with a greater increase in cash values when interest rates rise and a slower rate of increase in cash values when interest rates fall.

INTEREST-SENSITIVE STOCK stock of a firm whose earnings change when interest rates change, such as a bank or utility, and which therefore tends to go up or down on news of rate movements.

INTERIM DIVIDEND DIVIDEND declared and paid before annual earnings have been determined, generally quarterly. Most companies strive for consistency and plan quarterly dividends they are sure they can afford, reserving changes until fiscal year results are known.

INTERIM FINANCING temporary, short-term loan made conditional on a TAKEOUT by intermediate or long-term financing. Also called *bridge loan* financing.

INTERIM LOAN *see* CONSTRUCTION LOAN.

INTERIM STATEMENT financial report covering only a portion of a fiscal year. Public corporations supplement the annual report with quarterly statements informing shareholders of changes in the balance sheet and income statement, as well as other newsworthy developments.

INTERLOCKING DIRECTORATE membership on more than one company's board of directors. This is legal so long as the companies are not competitors. Consumer activists often point to interlocking directorates as an element in corporate conspiracies. The most flagrant abuses were outlawed by the Clayton Anti-Trust Act of 1914.

INTERMARKET SPREAD *see* INTERDELIVERY SPREAD.

INTERMARKET SURVEILLANCE INFORMATION SYSTEM (ISIS) DATABASE sharing information provided by the major stock exchanges in the United States. It permits the identification of CONTRA BROKERS and aids in preventing violations.

INTERMARKET TRADING SYSTEM (ITS) video-computer display system that links the posts of specialists at the New York, American, Boston, Chicago, Philadelphia Stock Exchanges, and the Pacific Exchange, as well as the NASD market makers who are trading the same securities. The quotes are displayed and are firm (good) for at least 100 shares. A broker at one exchange may direct an order to another exchange where the quote is better by sending the order through the electronic workstation. A transaction that is accepted by the broker at the other exchange is analogous to an electronic handshake and constitutes a contract.

INTERMEDIARY person or institution empowered to make investment decisions for others. Some examples are banks, savings and loan institutions, insurance companies, brokerage firms, mutual funds, and credit unions. These specialists are knowledgeable about investment alternatives and can achieve a higher return than the average investor can. Furthermore, they deal in large dollar volumes, have lower transaction costs, and can diversify their assets easily. Also called *financial intermediary*.

INTERMEDIATE TERM period between the short and long term, the length of time depending on the context. Stock analysts, for instance, mean 6 to 12 months, whereas bond analysts most often mean 3 to 10 years.

INTERMEDIATION placement of money with a financial INTERMEDIARY like a broker or bank, which invests it in bonds, stocks, mortgages, or other loans, money-market securities, or government obligations so as to achieve a targeted return. More formally called *financial intermediation.* The opposite is DISINTERMEDIATION, the withdrawal of money from an intermediary.

INTERNAL AUDITOR employee of a company who examines records and procedures to ensure against fraud and to make certain board directives and management policies are being properly executed.

INTERNAL CONTROL method, procedure, or system designed to promote efficiency, assure the implementation of policy, and safeguard assets.

INTERNAL EXPANSION asset growth financed out of internally generated cash—usually termed INTERNAL FINANCING—or through ACCRETION or APPRECIATION. *See also* CASH EARNINGS.

INTERNAL FINANCING funds produced by the normal operations of a firm, as distinguished from external financing, which includes borrowings and new equity. *See also* INTERNAL EXPANSION.

INTERNAL RATE OF RETURN (IRR) discount rate at which the present value of the future cash flows of an investment equal the cost of the investment. It is found by a process of trial and error; when the net present values of cash outflows (the cost of the investment) and cash inflows (returns on the investment) equal zero, the rate of discount being used is the IRR. When IRR is greater than the required return—called the hurdle rate in capital budgeting—the investment is acceptable

INTERNAL REVENUE CODE blanket term for complexity of statutes comprising the federal TAX law.

INTERNAL REVENUE SERVICE (IRS) U.S. agency charged with collecting nearly all federal taxes, including personal and corporate income taxes, social security taxes, and excise and gift taxes. Major exceptions include taxes having to do with alcohol, tobacco, firearms, and explosives, and customs duties and tariffs. The IRS administers the rules and regulations that are the responsibility of the U.S. Department of the Treasury and investigates and prosecutes (through the U.S. Tax Court) tax illegalities.

INTERNAL REVENUE SERVICE RESTRUCTURING AND REFORM ACT OF 1998 legislation designed to reform the Internal Revenue Service, lower the holding period for CAPITAL GAINS, and make various technical corrections in the TAXPAYER RELIEF ACT OF 1997. Some of the major provisions of law, which was enacted in the summer of 1998, include:

1. **Reduction in the capital gains holding period:** Under the Taxpayer Relief Act of 1997, the holding period to qualify for preferential long-term 20% (10% for those in the 15% tax bracket) capital gains tax rates had been raised from 12 to 18 months. This law lowered the holding period back to 12 months, effective retroactively to January 1, 1998.

2. **Restructuring the Internal Revenue Service:** The IRS Commissioner was instructed to modify the organization and governance of the agency by replacing the National-Regional-District structure with operating units to serve particular groups of taxpayers such as individuals, small businesses, big businesses, and tax-exempt organizations. In addition, the Act created an independent Oversight Board to supervise strategic IRS plans and modernization. The National Taxpayer Advocate was made independent of IRS control, now reporting directly to the Treasury Secretary. Local Taxpayer Advocates will help taxpayers resolve disputes separate from IRS examination, collection, and appeals functions.

3. **Taxpayer protections and rights:** Several sections of the law were designed to help taxpayers in disputes with the IRS during the audit and collection process:

   Shift in burden of proof: The burden of proof shifts from the taxpayer to the IRS in any court proceeding on income, gift, estate, or generation-skipping tax liability on factual issues. This applies only if the taxpayer introduces credible evidence on factual issues, maintains records and substantiates claims, and cooperates with reasonable IRS requests for meetings, interviews, witnesses, information, and documents. These rules apply to all court proceedings arising from audits after the Act was signed into law in July 1998. It does not apply to court proceedings started before that date. The burden of proof remains on corporations, trusts, and partnerships with a net worth over $7 million.

   Confidentiality privilege: The Act extends the existing attorney-client privilege of confidentiality to non-lawyers who are authorized to practice before the IRS, such as accountants or enrolled agents. This privilege may be asserted in any noncriminal tax proceeding before the IRS or federal courts.

   Innocent spouse relief: Spouses who become divorced, legally separated, or live apart for at least 12 months are entitled to relief from tax liabilities if their former mates made tax mistakes without their knowledge. Spouses may elect to make a separate-liability claim if the taxes paid were understated as late as two years after the IRS has initiated collection activities. The IRS also must inform taxpayers of their joint and several liability and innocent spouse rights.

   Liberalizes installment agreements and offers-in-compromise: The Act makes offers-in-compromise and installment agreements more flexible and accessible to taxpayers. The IRS is directed to try to negotiate deals with taxpayers instead of battling them in drawn-out court proceedings. If the taxpayer owes $10,000 or less, the IRS is required to allow the tax liability to be paid in installments.

Increases safeguards against IRS collection abuses: The Act imposes a list of "due-process" procedures the IRS must follow as it attempts to collect taxes. For example, taxpayers can request a hearing before Tax Court before property is seized and they can appeal IRS liens more easily. Higher dollar amounts were instituted for property that is exempt from liens and levies. The IRS must follow fair debt collection practices imposed on private-sector collection agencies, such as the prohibition against late-night calls to taxpayers.

Interest and penalty relief: The Act suspends interest and time-related penalties if the IRS does not provide appropriate notice of tax liability to a taxpayer within 18 months after a timely return is filed. In addition, taxpayers are entitled to a 0% interest rate when outstanding overpayments and underpayments of income and self-employment taxes are equal. The interest rate paid on refunds was raised to the same rate as the underpayment interest rate.

4. **Electronic filing incentives:** The Act encourages more filing of returns electronically, with the goal of limiting paper returns to 20% of all returns by the year 2007. By 2002, taxpayers who prepare their returns electronically but send a printout to the IRS will be required to file electronically. Those who file information returns electronically after 1999 get an extra month to file, from February 28 under the old law to March 31 under the new rules.

5. **Limit the tax benefits of "paired-share" REITs:** A small number of Real Estate Investment Trusts, called "paired-share" REITs, had been taking advantage of a tax loophole allowing them to put the revenues from operating businesses through their tax-sheltered REIT structures. This practice was curtailed.

6. **Changes to Roth IRA rules:** Several changes were made to clarify regulations related to the Roth IRA, which was created in the TAXPAYER RELIEF ACT OF 1997. For example, those who convert to Roth IRAs from regular IRAs may elect to recognize all income in the year of conversion rather than over four years. In addition, taxpayers have until the due date of their return to change their minds about any Roth IRA conversion that took place at any time in the past tax year. This rule was designed to help taxpayers who incorrectly projected the size of their adjusted gross income as less than $100,000 when converting assets from a regular IRA to a Roth IRA.

7. **Pre-rata gains from sales of principal residences:** The Act settled the question of how to apply the capital gain exclusion to the sale of a residence that had been owned and occupied for less than two years. Such homeowners can now exclude the amount of the capital gain ($500,000 for couples and $250,000 for singles) that is equal to the fraction of the two years that the property was owned and occupied.

INTERNATIONAL BANK FOR RECONSTRUCTION AND DEVELOPMENT (IBRD) organization set up by the Bretton Woods Agreement of 1944 to help finance the reconstruction of Europe and Asia after World War II. That task accomplished, the *World Bank,* as IBRD is known, turned to financing commercial and infrastructure projects, mostly in developing nations. It does not compete with commercial banks, but it may participate in a loan set up by a commercial bank. World Bank loans must be backed by the government in the borrowing country.

INTERNATIONAL MARKET INDEX market-value weighted proprietary index of the American Stock Exchange which tracks the performance of 50 American Depositary Receipts traded on the American Stock Exchange, New York Stock Exchange and NASDAQ Market. Options are no longer traded on the index.

INTERNATIONAL MONETARY FUND (IMF) organization set up by the Bretton Woods Agreement in 1944. Unlike the World Bank, whose focus is on foreign exchange reserves and the balance of trade, the IMF focus is on lowering trade barriers and stabilizing currencies. While helping developing nations pay their debts, the IMF usually imposes tough guidelines aimed at lowering inflation, cutting imports, and raising exports. IMF funds come mostly from the treasuries of industrialized nations. *See also* INTERNATIONAL BANK FOR RECONSTRUCTION AND DEVELOPMENT.

INTERNATIONAL MONETARY MARKET (IMM) division of the Chicago Mercantile Exchange that trades futures in U.S. Treasury bills, foreign currency, certificates of deposit, and Eurodollar deposits.

INTERNATIONAL MUTUAL FUND mutual fund that invests in securities markets throughout the world so that if one market is in a slump, profits can still be earned in others. Fund managers must be alert to trends in foreign currencies as well as in world stock and bond markets. Otherwise, seemingly profitable investments in a rising market could lose money if the national currency is falling against the dollar. While international mutual funds tend to concentrate only on non-American securities, GLOBAL MUTUAL FUNDS buy both foreign and domestic stocks and bonds.

INTERNATIONAL PETROLEUM EXCHANGE (IPE) London-based energy futures and options exchange, trading Brent crude oil futures and options, gas oil futures and options, and natural gas futures. Brent crude futures are also traded through a mutual offset link on the SIMEX. There are three classes of IPE membership: floor members who are voting members, hold SEATS on the exchange and own a share of the exchange; trade associates, which are companies with direct interests in producing, refining, or trading oil and oil products; and local floor members, individuals who can trade on the exchange floor. Locals also have voting rights and a share of the exchange, while trade associates do not. Brent crude oil and gas oil are traded on the IPE floor through floor members; natural gas is traded electronically on the IPE's Energy Trading System (ETS). The IPE coordinates trading with the NEW YORK MERCANTILE EXCHANGE through the ETS 2/NYMEX ACCESS 2000 trading system. The IPE also trades electricity, carbon dioxide emissions, European natural gas and fuel oil. Anyone can trade through floor members. Locals can trade for their own accounts or for floor members and other locals, but not directly for clients. Trading hours are 9:27 A.M. to 8:12 P.M.

INTERNATIONAL STOCK EXCHANGE OF THE U.K. AND THE REPUBLIC OF IRELAND (ISE) organization formed after BIG BANG to replace the London Stock Exchange following its merger with the International Securities Regulatory Organization (ISRO). ISRO is a professional trade association of brokers and dealers in the United Kingdom that functions as a self-regulatory organization. The term *London Stock Exchange* persists in investment parlance despite the name change.

INTERPOLATION estimation of an unknown number intermediate between known numbers. Interpolation is a way of approximating price or yield using bond tables that do not give the net yield on every amount invested at every rate of interest and for every maturity. Interpolation is based on the assumption that a certain percentage change in yield will result in the same percentage change in price. The assumption is not altogether correct, but the variance is small enough to ignore.

INTERPOSITIONING placement of a second broker in a securities transaction between two principals or between a customer and a marketmaker. The practice is regulated by the Securities and Exchange Commission, and abuses such as interpositioning to create additional commission income are illegal.

INTERSTATE COMMERCE COMMISSION (ICC) federal agency created by the Interstate Commerce Act of 1887 to insure that the public receives fair and reasonable rates and services from carriers and transportation service firms involved in interstate commerce. Legislation enacted in the 1970s and 80s substantially curtailed the regulatory activities of the ICC, particularly in the rail, truck, and bus industries.

INTER VIVOS TRUST trust established between living persons—for instance, between father and child. In contrast, a TESTAMENTARY TRUST goes into effect when the person who establishes the trust dies. Also called *living trust.*

INTESTACY; INTESTATE a person who dies without a valid will is said to die *intestate* or *in intestacy.* State law determines who is entitled to inherit and who is entitled to manage the decedent's estate.

INTESTATE DISTRIBUTION distribution of assets to beneficiaries from the estate of a person who dies without a written will of instructions. This distribution is overseen by a PROBATE court and the appointed EXECUTOR of the estate. Each state has specific laws outlining how intestate distributions are to be made.

IN THE MONEY option contract on a stock whose current market price is above the striking price of a call option or below the striking price of a put option. A call option on XYZ at a striking price of 100 would be in the money if XYZ were selling for 102, for instance, and a put option with the same striking price would be in the money if XYZ were selling for 98. *See also* AT THE MONEY; OUT OF THE MONEY.

IN THE TANK slang expression meaning market prices are dropping rapidly. Stock market observers may say, "The market is in the tank" after a day in which stock prices fell.

INTRACOMMODITY SPREAD futures position in which a trader buys and sells contracts in the same commodity on the same exchange, but for different months. For instance, a trader would place an intracommodity spread if he bought a pork bellies contract expiring in December and at the same time sold a pork bellies contract expiring in April. His profit or loss would be determined by the price difference between the December and April contracts.

INTRADAY within the day; often used in connection with high and low prices of a stock, bond, or commodity. For instance, "The stock hit a new intraday high today" means that the stock reached an all-time high price during the day but fell back to a lower price by the end of the day. The listing of the high and low prices at which a stock is traded during a day is called the *intraday price range.*

INTRASTATE OFFERING securities offering limited to one state in the United States. *See also* BLUE-SKY LAW.

INTRINSIC VALUE
Financial analysis: valuation determined by applying data inputs to a valuation theory or model. The resulting value is comparable to the prevailing market price.
Options trading: difference between the EXERCISE PRICE or strike price of an option and the market value of the underlying security. For example, if the strike price is $53 on a call option to purchase a stock with a market price of $55, the option has an intrinsic value of $2. Or, in the case of a put option, if the strike price was $55 and the market price of the underlying stock was $53, the intrinsic value of the option would also be $2. Options AT THE MONEY or OUT OF THE MONEY have no intrinsic value.

INVENTORY
Corporate finance: value of a firm's raw materials, work in process, supplies used in operations, and finished goods. Since inventory value changes with price fluctuations, it is important to know the method of valuation. There are a number of inventory valuation methods; the most widely used are FIRST IN, FIRST OUT (FIFO) and LAST IN, FIRST OUT

(LIFO). Financial statements normally indicate the basis of inventory valuation, generally the lower figure of either cost price or current market price, which precludes potentially overstated earnings and assets as the result of sharp increases in the price of raw materials.

Personal finance: list of all assets owned by an individual and the value of each, based on cost, market value, or both. Such inventories are usually required for property insurance purposes and are sometimes required with applications for credit.

Securities: net long or short position of a dealer or specialist. Also, securities bought and held by a dealer for later resale.

INVENTORY FINANCING

Factoring: sometimes used as a synonym for overadvances in FAC-TORING, where loans in excess of accounts receivable are made against inventory in anticipation of future sales.

Finance companies: financing by a bank or sales finance company of the inventory of a dealer in consumer or capital goods. Such loans, also called wholesale financing or *floorplanning*, are secured by the inventory and are usually made as part of a relationship in which retail installment paper generated by sales to the public is also financed by the lender. *See also* FINANCE COMPANY.

INVENTORY TURNOVER ratio of annual sales to inventory, which shows how many times the inventory of a firm is sold and replaced during an accounting period; sometimes called *inventory utilization ratio*. Compared with industry averages, a low turnover might indicate a company is carrying excess stocks of inventory, an unhealthy sign because excess inventory represents an investment with a low or zero rate of return and because it makes the company more vulnerable to falling prices. A steady drop in inventory turnover, in comparison with prior periods, can reveal lack of a sufficiently aggressive sales policy or ineffective buying.

Two points about the way inventory turnover may be calculated: (1) Because sales are recorded at market value and inventories are normally carried at cost, it is more realistic to obtain the turnover ratio by dividing inventory into cost of goods sold rather than into sales. However, it is conventional to use sales as the numerator because that is the practice of Dun & Bradstreet and other compilers of published financial ratios, and comparability is of overriding importance. (2) To minimize the seasonal factor affecting inventory levels, it is better to use an average inventory figure, obtained by adding yearly beginning and ending inventory figures and dividing by 2.

INVERSE FLOATER derivative instrument whose coupon rate is inversely related to some multiple of a specified market rate of interest. Typically a cap and floor are placed on the coupon. As interest rates go down, the amount of interest the inverse floater pays goes up. For example, if the inverse floater rate is 32% and the multiple is four times the London Interbank Offered Rate (LIBOR) of 7%, the coupon is valued at 4%. If the LIBOR goes to 6%, the new coupon is 8%. Many inverse floaters are based on pieces of mortgage-backed securities such as COL-LATERALIZED MORTGAGE OBLIGATIONS which react inversely to movements in interest rates.

INVERTED SCALE serial bond offering where earlier maturities have higher yields than later maturities. *See also* SERIAL BOND.

INVERTED YIELD CURVE unusual situation where short-term interest rates are higher than long-term rates. Normally, lenders receive a higher yield when committing their money for a longer period of time; this situation is called a POSITIVE YIELD CURVE. An inverted YIELD CURVE occurs when a surge in demand for short-term credit drives up short-term rates on instruments like Treasury bills and money-market funds, while long-term rates move up more slowly, since borrowers are not willing to commit themselves to paying high interest rates for many years. This situation happened in the early 1980s, when short-term interest rates were around 20%, while long-term rates went up to only 16% or 17%. The existence of an inverted yield curve can be a sign of an unhealthy economy, marked by high inflation and low levels of confidence. Also called *negative yield curve.*

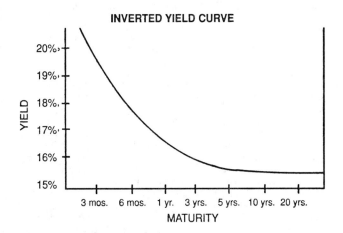

INVESTMENT use of capital to create more money, either through income-producing vehicles or through more risk-oriented ventures designed to result in capital gains. *Investment* can refer to a financial investment (where an investor puts money into a vehicle) or to an investment of effort and time on the part of an individual who wants to reap profits from the success of his labor. Investment connotes the idea that safety of principal is important. SPECULATION, on the other hand, is far riskier.

INVESTMENT ADVISERS ACT legislation passed by Congress in 1940 that requires all investment advisers to register with the Securities and Exchange Commission. The Act is designed to protect the public from fraud or misrepresentation by investment advisers. One requirement, for example, is that advisers must disclose all potential *conflicts of interest* with any recommendations they make to those they advise. A potential conflict of interest might exist where the adviser had a position in a security he was recommending. *See also* INVESTMENT ADVISORY SERVICE.

INVESTMENT ADVISORY SERVICE service providing investment advice for a fee. Investment advisers must register with the Securities and Exchange Commission and abide by the rules of the INVESTMENT ADVISERS ACT. Investment advisory services usually specialize in a particular kind of investment—for example, emerging growth stocks, international stocks, mutual funds, or commodities. Some services only offer advice through a newsletter; others will manage a client's money. The performance of many investment advisory services is ranked by the *Hulbert Financial Digest. See* HULBERT RATING.

INVESTMENT BANKER firm, acting as underwriter or agent, that serves as intermediary between an issuer of securities and the investing public. In what is termed FIRM COMMITMENT underwriting, the investment banker, either as manager or participating member of an investment banking syndicate, makes outright purchases of new securities from the issuer and distributes them to dealers and investors, profiting on the spread between the purchase price and the selling (public offering) price. Under a conditional arrangement called BEST EFFORT, the investment banker markets a new issue without underwriting it, acting as agent rather than principal and taking a commission for whatever amount of securities the banker succeeds in marketing. Under another conditional arrangement, called STANDBY COMMITMENT, the investment banker serves clients issuing new securities by agreeing to purchase for resale any securities not taken by existing holders of RIGHTS.

Where a client relationship exists, the investment banker's role begins with pre-underwriting counseling and continues after the distribution of securities is completed, in the form of ongoing expert advice and guidance, often including a seat on the board of directors. The direct underwriting responsibilities include preparing the Securities and Exchange Commission registration statement; consulting on pricing of the securities; forming and managing the syndicate; establishing a selling group if desired; and PEGGING (stabilizing) the price of the issue during the offering and distribution period.

In addition to new securities offerings, investment bankers handle the distribution of blocks of previously issued securities, either through secondary offerings or through negotiations; maintain markets for securities already distributed; and act as finders in the private placement of securities.

Along with their investment banking functions, the majority of investment bankers also maintain broker-dealer operations, serving both wholesale and retail clients in brokerage and advisory capacities and offering a growing number of related financial services. *See also* FLOTATION COST; SECONDARY DISTRIBUTION; UNDERWRITE.

INVESTMENT CERTIFICATE certificate evidencing investment in a savings and loan association and showing the amount of money invested. Investment certificates do not have voting rights and do not involve stockholder responsibility. Also called *mutual capital certificate. See also* MUTUAL ASSOCIATION.

INVESTMENT CLIMATE economic, monetary, and other conditions affecting the performance of investments.

INVESTMENT CLUB group of people who pool their assets in order to make joint investment decisions. Each member of the club contributes a certain amount of capital, with additional money to be invested every month or quarter. Decisions on which stocks or bonds to buy are made by a vote of members. Besides helping each member become more knowledgeable about investing, these clubs allow people with small amounts of money to participate in larger investments, own part of a more diversified portfolio, and pay lower commission rates than would be possible for individual members on their own. The trade group for investment clubs is the National Association of Investors Corporation (NAIC) in Madison Heights, Michigan. The NAIC helps clubs get started and offers several programs, such as the Low-Cost Investment Plan allowing clubs to purchase an initial share of individual stocks at low commissions and reinvest dividends automatically at no charge.

INVESTMENT COMPANY firm that, for a management fee, invests the pooled funds of small investors in securities appropriate for its stated investment objectives. It offers participants more diversification, liquidity, and professional management service than would normally be available to them as individuals.

There are two basic types of investment companies: (1) *open-end,* better known as a MUTUAL FUND, which has a floating number of outstanding shares (hence the name *open-end*) and stands prepared to sell or redeem shares at their current NET ASSET VALUE; and (2) *closed-end*, also known as an *investment trust,* which, like a corporation, has a fixed number of outstanding shares that are traded like a stock, often on the New York and American Stock Exchanges.

Open-end management companies are basically divided into two categories, based on the way they distribute their funds to customers. The first category is *load funds,* which are sold in the over-the-counter market by broker-dealers, who do not receive a sales commission; instead a "loading charge" is added to the net asset value at time of purchase. For many years the charge was 8½%, but more recently it has been reduced to 4.5%–5%. Many load funds do not charge an upfront load, but instead impose a BACK-END LOAD which customers must pay if they sell fund shares within a certain number of years, usually five. The second category is *no-load funds,* which are bought directly from sponsoring fund companies. Such companies do not charge a loading fee, although some funds levy a redemption fee if shares are sold within a specified number of years.

Some funds, both load and no-load, are called 12b-1 MUTUAL FUNDS because they levy an annual 12b-1 charge of up to 0.75% of assets to pay for promotional and marketing expenses.

Dealers in closed-end investment companies obtain their revenue from regular brokerage commissions, just as they do in selling any individual stock.

Both open-end and closed-end investment companies charge annual management fees, typically ranging from 0.25% to 2% of the value of the assets in the fund.

Under the INVESTMENT COMPANY ACT OF 1940, the registration statement and prospectus of every investment company must state its specific investment objectives. Investment companies fall into many categories, including: diversified common stock funds (with growth of capital as the principal objective); balanced funds (mixing common and preferred stocks, bonds, and cash); bond and preferred stock funds (emphasizing current income); specialized funds (by industry, groups of industries, geography, or size of company); income funds buying high-yield stocks and bonds; dual-purpose funds (a form of closed-end investment company offering a choice of income shares or capital gains shares); and money market funds which invest in money market instruments.

INVESTMENT COMPANY ACT OF 1940 legislation passed by Congress requiring registration and regulation of investment companies by the Securities and Exchange Commission. The Act sets the standards by which mutual funds and other investment vehicles of investment companies operate, in such areas as promotion, reporting requirements, pricing of securities for sale to the public, and allocation of investments within a fund portfolio. *See also* INVESTMENT COMPANY.

INVESTMENT COUNSEL person with the responsibility for providing investment advice to clients and executing investment decisions. *See also* PORTFOLIO MANAGER.

INVESTMENT CREDIT reduction in income tax liability granted by the federal government over the years to firms making new investments in certain asset categories, primarily equipment; also called *investment tax credit.* The investment credit, designed to stimulate the economy by encouraging capital expenditure, has been a feature of tax legislation on and off, and in varying percentage amounts, since 1962; in 1985 it was 6% or 10% of the purchase price, depending on the life of the asset. As a credit, it has been deducted from the tax bill, not from pretax income, and it has been independent of DEPRECIATION. The TAX REFORM ACT OF 1986 generally repealed the investment credit retroactively for any property placed in service after January 1, 1986. The 1986 Act also provided for a 35% reduction of the value of credits carried over from previous years, which was later changed to 50%.

INVESTMENT GRADE bond with a RATING of AAA to BBB. *See also* JUNK BOND.

INVESTMENT HISTORY body of prior experience establishing "normal investment practice" with respect to the account relationship between a member firm and its customer. For example, the Rules of Fair Practice of the National Association of Securities Dealers (NASD) prohibit the sale of a new issue to members of a distributing dealer's immediate family, but if there was sufficient precedent in the investment history of this particular dealer-customer relationship, the sale would not be a violation.

INVESTMENT INCOME income from securities and other nonbusiness investments; such as DIVIDENDS, INTEREST, OPTION PREMIUMS, and income from a ROYALTY or ANNUITY. Under the TAX REFORM ACT OF 1986, interest on MARGIN ACCOUNTS may be used to offset investment income without limitation. Investment income earned by passive activities must be treated separately from other PASSIVE income. The REVENUE RECONCILIATION ACT OF 1993 eliminated net gains from selling investment property from the definition of *investment income.* Expenses incurred to generate investment income can reduce investment income to the extent they exceed 2% of adjusted gross income. By excluding capital gains from the calculation, the 1993 Act, in effect, prevents a taxpayer from claiming an ordinary deduction for margin interest incurred to carry an investment that is taxable at the favorable capital gains rate. Also called UNEARNED INCOME and *portfolio income.*

INVESTMENT LETTER in the private placement of new securities, a letter of intent between the issuer of securities and the buyer establishing that the securities are being bought as an investment and are not for resale. This is necessary to avoid having to register the securities with the Securities and Exchange Commission. (Under provisions of SEC Rule 144, a purchaser of such securities may eventually resell them to the public if certain specific conditions are met, including a minimum holding period of at least two years.) Use of the investment letter gave rise to the terms *letter stock* and *letter bond* in referring to unregistered issues. *See also* LETTER SECURITY.

INVESTMENT MANAGEMENT in general, the activities of a portfolio manager. More specifically, it distinguishes between managed and unmanaged portfolios, examples of the latter being UNIT INVESTMENT TRUSTS and INDEX FUNDS, which are fixed portfolios not requiring ongoing decisions.

INVESTMENT OBJECTIVE financial objective that an investor uses to determine which kind of investment is appropriate. For example, if the investor's objective is growth of capital, he may opt for growth-oriented mutual funds or individual stocks. If he is more interested in income, he might purchase income-oriented mutual funds or individual bonds instead. Consideration of investment objectives, combined with the risk tolerance of investors, helps an investor narrow his search to an investment vehicle designed for his needs at a particular time.

INVESTMENT PHILOSOPHY style of investment practiced by an individual investor or money manager. For example, some investors follow the growth philosophy, concentrating on stocks with steadily rising earnings. Others are value investors, searching for stocks that have fallen out of favor, and are therefore cheap relative to the true value of their assets. Some managers favor small-capitalization stocks, while others stick with large blue-chip companies. Some managers have a philosophy of remaining fully invested at all times, while others believe in market timing, so that their portfolios can accumulate cash if the managers think stock or bond prices are about to fall.

INVESTMENT SOFTWARE software designed to aid investors' decision-making. Some software packages allow investors to perform TECHNICAL ANALYSIS, charting stock prices, volume, and other indicators. Other programs allow FUNDAMENTAL ANALYSIS, permitting investors to SCREEN STOCKS based on financial criteria such as earnings, price/earnings ratios, book value, and dividend yields. Some software offers recordkeeping, so that an investor can keep track of the value of his portfolio and the prices at which he bought or sold securities. Many software packages allow investors to tap into databases to update securities prices, scan news items, and execute trades. Specialty programs allow investors to value options, calculate yield analysis on bonds, and screen mutual funds.

INVESTMENT STRATEGY plan to allocate assets among such choices as stocks, bonds, CASH EQUIVALENTS, commodities, and real estate. An investment strategy should be formulated based on an investor's outlook on interest rates, inflation, and economic growth, among other factors, and also taking into account the investor's age, tolerance for risk, amount of capital available to invest, and future needs for capital, such as for financing children's college educations or buying a house. An investment adviser will help to devise such a strategy. *See also* INVESTMENT ADVISORY SERVICE.

INVESTMENT STRATEGY COMMITTEE committee in the research department of a brokerage firm that sets the overall investment strategy the firm recommends to clients. The director of research, the chief economist, and several top analysts typically sit on this committee. The group advises clients on the amount of money that should be placed into stocks, bonds, or CASH EQUIVALENTS, as well as the industry groups or individual stocks or bonds that look particularly attractive.

INVESTMENT TAX CREDIT *see* INVESTMENT CREDIT.

INVESTMENT TRUST *see* INVESTMENT COMPANY.

INVESTMENT VALUE OF A CONVERTIBLE SECURITY estimated price at which a CONVERTIBLE security (CV) would be valued by the marketplace if it had no stock conversion feature. The investment value for CVs of major companies is determined by investment advisory services and, theoretically, should never fall lower than the price of the related stock. It is arrived at by estimating the price at which a nonconvertible ("straight") bond or preferred share of the same issuing company would sell. The investment value reflects the interest rate; therefore, the market price of the security will go up when rates are down and vice versa. *See also* PREMIUM OVER BOND VALUE.

INVESTOR party who puts money at risk; may be an individual or an institutional investor.

INVESTOR RELATIONS DEPARTMENT in major listed companies, a staff position responsible for investor relations, reporting either to the chief financial officer or to the director of public relations. The actual duties will vary, depending on whether the company retains an outside financial public relations firm, but the general responsibilities are as follows:
- to see that the company is understood, in terms of its activities and objectives, and is favorably regarded in the financial and capital markets and the investment community; this means having input into the annual report and other published materials, coordinating senior management speeches and public statements with the FINANCIAL PUBLIC RELATIONS effort, and generally fostering a consistent and positive corporate image.
- to ensure full and timely public DISCLOSURE of material information, and to work with the legal staff in complying with the rules of the SEC, the securities exchanges, and other regulatory authorities.
- to respond to requests for reports and information from shareholders, professional investors, brokers, and the financial media.
- to maintain productive relations with the firm's investment bankers, the specialists in its stock, major broker-dealers, and institutional investors who follow the company or hold sizeable positions in its securities.
- to take direct measures, where necessary, to see that the company's shares are properly valued. This involves identifying the firm's particular investment audience and the professionals controlling its stock float, arranging analysts' meetings and other presentations, and generating appropriate publicity.

The most successful investor relations professionals have been those who follow a policy of full and open dissemination of relevant information, favorable and unfavorable, on a consistent basis. The least successful, over the long run, have been the "touts"—those who emphasize promotion at the expense of credibility.

INVESTORS SERVICE BUREAU New York Stock Exchange public service that responds to written inquiries of all types concerning securities investments.

INVOICE bill prepared by a seller of goods or services and submitted to the purchaser. The invoice lists all the items bought, together with amounts.

INVOLUNTARY BANKRUPTCY *see* BANKRUPTCY.

IRA *see* INDIVIDUAL RETIREMENT ACCOUNT.

IRA ROLLOVER *see* INDIVIDUAL RETIREMENT ACCOUNT ROLLOVER.

IRREDEEMABLE BOND
1. bond without a CALL FEATURE (issuer's right to redeem the bond before maturity) or a REDEMPTION privilege (holder's right to sell the bond back to the issuer before maturity).
2. PERPETUAL BOND.

IRREVOCABLE something done that cannot legally be undone, such as an IRREVOCABLE TRUST.

IRREVOCABLE LIVING TRUST trust usually created to achieve some tax benefit, or to provide a vehicle for managing assets of a person the creator believes cannot or should not be managing his or her own property. This trust cannot be changed or reversed by the creator of the trust.

IRREVOCABLE TRUST trust that cannot be changed or terminated by the one who created it without the agreement of the BENEFICIARY.

IRS *see* INTERNAL REVENUE SERVICE.

IRS PRIVATE LETTER RULING *see* PRIVATE LETTER RULING.

ISIS *see* INTERMARKET SURVEILLANCE INFORMATION SYSTEM (ISIS).

INTERNATIONAL SECURITIES REGULATORY ORGANIZATION (ISRO) *see* INTERNATIONAL STOCK EXCHANGE OF THE UNITED KINGDOM AND THE REPUBLIC OF IRELAND (ISE).

ISSUE
1. stock or bonds sold by a corporation or a government entity at a particular time.
2. selling new securities by a corporation or government entity, either through an underwriter or by a private placement.

3. descendants, such as children and grandchildren. For instance, "This man's estate will be passed, at his death, to his issue."

ISSUED AND OUTSTANDING shares of a corporation, authorized in the corporate charter, which have been issued and are outstanding. These shares represent capital invested by the firm's shareholders and owners, and may be all or only a portion of the number of shares authorized. Shares that have been issued and subsequently repurchased by the company are called *treasury stock,* because they are held in the corporate treasury pending reissue or retirement. Treasury shares are legally issued but are not considered outstanding for purposes of voting, dividends, or earnings per share calculations. Shares authorized but not yet issued are called *unissued shares.* Most companies show the amount of authorized, issued and outstanding, and treasury shares in the capital section of their annual reports. *See also* TREASURY STOCK.

ISSUER legal entity that has the power to issue and distribute a security. Issuers include corporations, municipalities, foreign and domestic governments and their agencies, and investment trusts. Issuers of stock are responsible for reporting on corporate developments to shareholders and paying dividends once declared. Issuers of bonds are committed to making timely payments of interest and principal to bondholders.

ITALIAN DERIVATIVES MARKET (IDEM) operated by the Italian Stock Exchange Council, the IDEM trades on a national computerized system based on the Swedish OM system. The exchange began operations in November 1994. It trades futures and options on the MIB 30 Index and individual stock options.

ITALIAN STOCK EXCHANGE (ISE) based in Milan, ISE is the national computerized, order-driven trading system, resulting from a major reform program that united Italy's 10 national exchanges in 1991. Three institutions are responsible for market regulation and management: the Consiglio di Borsa (Consob), the market watchdog; the Bank of Italy; and the Italian Stock Exchange Council, which instituted computerized trading. Since 1994, all listed securities have been traded electronically. The electronic trading system is managed by the ISE Council and operated by CED Borsa, a private company. A network connects all authorized securities firms throughout Italy, enabling real-time trading in all securities. The main indices are the MIB and the MIBTEL, based on the prices of all listed shares, and the MIB 30, based on a sample of the 30 most liquid and highly capitalized shares. The Comit Index is calculated daily by the Banca Commerciale Italiana, and includes all ISE listed shares. Trading is conducted Monday through Friday. The main market offers an opening auction from 8 A.M. to 9:30 A.M., with continuous trading from 10 A.M. to 5 P.M. An electronic auction in the second market runs from

3 P.M. to 5 P.M. Trading on Italy's second market, Mercato Ristretto, is regulated and conducted by stockbrokers.

ITEMIZED DEDUCTION item that allows a taxpayer to reduce adjusted gross income on his or her tax return. For example, mortgage interest, charitable contributions, state and local income and property taxes, unreimbursed business expenses, IRA contributions, and other miscellaneous items are considered deductible under certain conditions, and are listed as itemized deductions on Schedule A of an individual's tax return. However, at certain income levels, deductions are phased out. For example, in the 1998 tax year, itemized deductions for married couples filing jointly were phased out by 3% of the excess of adjusted gross income over $121,200 (if married and filing separately, then $60,600) adjusted annually for inflation. Some deductions are not subject to the 3% reduction, including medical and dental expenses, investment interest, casualty and theft losses and gambling losses.

J

JANUARY BAROMETER market forecasting tool popularized by *The Stock Traders Almanac,* whose statistics show that with 88% consistency since 1950, the market has risen in years when the STANDARD & POOR'S INDEX of 500 stocks was up in January and dropped when the index for that month was down.

JANUARY EFFECT phenomenon that stocks (especially small stocks) have historically tended to rise markedly during the period starting on the last day of December and ending on the fourth trading day of January. The January Effect is owed to year-end selling to create tax losses, recognize capital gains, effect portfolio WINDOW DRESSING, or raise holiday cash; since such selling depresses the stocks but has nothing to do with their fundamental worth, bargain hunters quickly buy in, causing the January rally.

JEEP *see* GRADUATED PAYMENT MORTGAGE.

JOBBER
1. wholesaler, especially one who buys in small lots from manufacturers, importers, and/or other wholesalers and sells to retailers.
2. London Stock Exchange term for MARKET MAKER.

JOHANNESBURG STOCK EXCHANGE (JSE) largest stock exchange in Africa, established in 1886 to raise financing for the mining industry. In 1995, the JSE opened its doors to foreign and corporate members. The following year, the Johannesburg electronic trading system, JET, was introduced, moving stocks off the floor and into the system. A specialist manages an electronic order book for ODD LOTS, and market makers voluntarily quote prices. The mining sector dominates market capitalization of quoted companies, but financial services is a growing area. The JSE All Share Index tracks the overall ordinary share market. Shares are grouped in five sectors, each with a separate index: overall, mining producers, mining finance, financial and industrial. Two subsidiary markets are traded: the development capital market (DCM) aimed at smaller, developing companies that need to raise capital; and the venture capital market (VCM), to facilitate the listing of venture capital companies. Orders are matched electronically in the JET system and transferred electronically to the Equity Clearing House, a department in the exchange. The exchange has moved to a rolling settlement, ultimately 3 days after a trade. Trading hours: 8:30 A.M. to 6 P.M., Monday through Friday.

JOINT ACCOUNT bank or brokerage account owned jointly by two or more people. Joint accounts may be set up in two ways: (1) either all parties to the account must sign checks and approve all withdrawals or brokerage transactions or (2) any one party can take such actions on his or her own. *See also* JOINT TENANTS WITH RIGHT OF SURVIVORSHIP.

JOINT ACCOUNT AGREEMENT form needed to open a JOINT ACCOUNT at a bank or brokerage. It must be signed by all parties to the account regardless of the provisions it may contain concerning signatures required to authorize transactions.

JOINT AND SURVIVOR ANNUITY annuity that makes payments for the lifetime of two or more beneficiaries, often a husband and wife. When one of the annuitants dies, payments continue to the survivor annuitant in the same amount or in a reduced amount as specified in the contract.

JOINT BOND bond that has more than one obligator or that is guaranteed by a party other than the issuer; also called *joint and several bond.* Joint bonds are common where a parent corporation wishes to guarantee the bonds of a subsidiary. *See* GUARANTEED BOND.

JOINT LIABILITY mutual legal responsibility by two or more parties for claims on the assets of a company or individual. *See also* LIABILITY.

JOINTLY AND SEVERALLY
In general: legal phrase used in definitions of liability meaning that an obligation may be enforced against all obligators jointly or against any one of them separately.
Securities: term used to refer to municipal bond underwritings where the account is undivided and syndicate members are responsible for unsold bonds in proportion to their participations. In other words, a participant with 5% of the account would still be responsible for 5% of the unsold bonds, even though that member might already have sold 10%. *See also* SEVERALLY BUT NOT JOINTLY.

JOINT OWNERSHIP equal ownership by two or more people, who have right of survivorship.

JOINT STOCK COMPANY form of business organization that combines features of a corporation and a partnership. Under U.S. law, joint stock companies are recognized as corporations with unlimited liability for their stockholders. As in a conventional corporation, investors in joint stock companies receive shares of stock they are free to sell at will without ending the corporation; they also elect directors. Unlike in a limited liability corporation, however, each shareholder in a joint stock company is legally liable for all debts of the company.

There are some advantages to this form of organization compared with limited-liability corporations: fewer taxes, greater ease of formation under the common law, more security for creditors, mobility, and freedom from regulation, for example. However, the disadvantages—such as the fact that the joint stock company usually cannot hold title to real estate and, particularly, the company's unlimited liability—tend to outweigh the advantages, with the result that it is not a popular form of organization.

JOINT TAX RETURN tax return filed by two people, usually a married couple. Both parties must sign the return and they are equally responsible for paying the taxes due. Thus if one party does not pay the taxes, the IRS can come after the other party to make the required payment. Because of the way the tax tables are designed, it is frequently more advantageous for a married couple to file a joint return than for them to file separate returns. *See also* FILING STATUS; HEAD OF HOUSEHOLD.

JOINT TENANCY *see* TENANCY IN COMMON. *See also* JOINT TENANTS WITH RIGHT OF SURVIVORSHIP.

JOINT TENANTS WITH RIGHT OF SURVIVORSHIP when two or more people maintain a JOINT ACCOUNT with a brokerage firm or a bank, it is normally agreed that, upon the death of one account holder, ownership of the account assets passes to the remaining account holders. This transfer of assets escapes probate, but estate taxes may be due, depending on the amount of assets transferred.

JOINT VENTURE agreement by two or more parties to work on a project together. Frequently, a joint venture will be formed when companies with complementary technology wish to create a product or service that takes advantage of the strengths of the participants. A joint venture, which is usually limited to one project, differs from a partnership, which forms the basis for cooperation on many projects.

JOINT WILL single document setting forth the testamentary instructions of a husband and wife. The use of joint wills is not common in the United States, and it may create tax and other problems.

JONESTOWN DEFENSE tactics taken by management to ward off a hostile TAKEOVER that are so extreme that they appear suicidal for the company. For example, the company may try to sell its CROWN JEWELS or take on a huge amount of debt to make the company undesirable to the potential acquirer. The term refers to the mass suicide led by Jim Jones in Jonestown, Guyana, in the early 1980s. *See also* SCORCHED EARTH POLICY.

JUDGMENT decision by a court of law ordering someone to pay a certain amount of money. For instance, a court may order someone who illegally profited by trading on INSIDE INFORMATION to pay a judgment amounting to all the profits from the trade, plus damages. The term also refers to condemnation awards by government entities in payment for private property taken for public use.

JUMBO CERTIFICATE OF DEPOSIT certificate with a minimum denomination of $100,000. Jumbo CDs are usually bought and sold by large institutions such as banks, pension funds, money market funds, and insurance companies.

JUMBO LOANS loans in amounts exceeding the national guidelines of FREDDIE MAC and FANNIE MAE.

JUNIOR ISSUE issue of debt or equity that is subordinate in claim to another issue in terms of dividends, interest, principal, or security in the event of liquidation. *See also* JUNIOR SECURITY; PREFERRED STOCK; PRIORITY; PRIOR LIEN BOND: PRIOR PREFERRED STOCK.

JUNIOR MORTGAGE mortgage that is subordinate to other mortgages—for example, a second or a third mortgage. If a debtor defaults, the first mortgage will have to be satisfied before the junior mortgage.

JUNIOR REFUNDING refinancing government debt that matures in one to five years by issuing new securities that mature in five years or more.

JUNIOR SECURITY security with lower priority claim on assets and income than a SENIOR SECURITY. For example, a PREFERRED STOCK is junior to a DEBENTURE, but a debenture, being an unsecured bond, is junior to a MORTGAGE BOND. COMMON STOCK is junior to all corporate securities. Some companies—finance companies, for example—have senior SUBORDINATED and junior subordinated issues, the former having priority over the latter, but both ranking lower than senior (unsubordinated) debt.

JUNK BOND bond with a credit rating of BB or lower by RATING agencies. Although commonly used, the term has a pejorative connotation, and issuers and holders prefer the securities be called *high-yield bonds*. Junk bonds are issued by companies without long track records of sales and earnings, or by those with questionable credit strength. In the 1980s, they were a popular means of financing TAKEOVERS. Since they are more volatile and pay higher yields than INVESTMENT GRADE bonds, many risk-oriented investors specialize in trading them. Institutions with FIDUCIARY responsibilities are regulated (*see* PRUDENT-MAN RULE). *See also* FALLEN ANGELS.

JURISDICTION defined by the American Bankers Association as "the legal right, power or authority to hear and determine a cause; as in the jurisdiction of a court." The term frequently comes up in finance and investment discussions in connection with the jurisdictions of the various regulatory authorities bearing on the field. For example, the Federal Reserve Board, not the Securities and Exchange Commission (as might be supposed), has jurisdiction in a case involving a brokerage MARGIN ACCOUNT (*see also* REGULATION T).

   The term also is important with respect to EUROCURRENCY loan agreements, where it is possible for a loan to be funded in one country but made in another by a group of international banks each from different countries, to a borrower in still another country. The determination of jurisdiction, not to mention the willingness of courts in different countries to accept that jurisdiction, is a matter of obvious urgency in such cases.

JURY OF EXECUTIVE OPINION forecasting method whereby a panel of experts—perhaps senior corporate financial executives—

prepare individual forecasts based on information made available to all of them. Each expert then reviews the others' work and modifies his or her own forecasts accordingly. The resulting composite forecast is supposed to be more realistic than any individual effort could be. Also known as *Delphi forecast.*

JUSTIFIED PRICE fair market price an informed buyer will pay for an asset, whether it be a stock, a bond, a commodity, or real estate. *See also* FAIR MARKET VALUE.

JUST TITLE title to property that is supportable against all legal claims. Also called *clear title, good title, proper title.*

K

KAFFIRS informal term for South African gold mining shares traded on the LONDON STOCK EXCHANGE. These shares are traded over the counter in the U.S. in the form of American Depositary Receipts, which are claims to share certificates deposited in a foreign bank. Under South African law, Kaffirs must pay out almost all their earnings to shareholders as dividends. These shares thus not only provide stockholders with a gold investment to hedge against inflation, but also afford substantial income in the form of high dividend payments. However, investors in Kaffirs must also consider the political risks of investing in South Africa, as well as the risk of fluctuations in the price of gold. *See also* AMERICAN DEPOSITARY RECEIPT.

KANGAROOS nickname for Australian stocks. The term normally refers to stocks in the ALL ORDINARIES INDEX, and refers to the animal most closely associated with Australia.

KANSAS CITY BOARD OF TRADE (KCBT) formed in 1856 as a chamber of commerce, it reorganized after the Civil War as an exchange. The KCBT trades red winter wheat futures and options; Western natural gas futures and options; Value Line Index futures; and Mini Value Line futures and options. Trading hours: 8:30 A.M. to 3:15 P.M., Monday to Friday. *See also* SECURITIES AND COMMODITIES EXCHANGES.

KEOGH PLAN tax-deferred pension account designated for employees of unincorporated businesses or for persons who are self-employed (either full-time or part-time). Eligible people can contribute up to 25% of earned income, up to a maximum of $30,000. Like the INDIVIDUAL RETIREMENT ACCOUNT (IRA), the Keogh plan allows all investment earnings to grow tax deferred until capital is withdrawn, as early as age 59½ and starting no later than age 70½. Almost any investment except precious metals or collectibles can be used for a Keogh account. Typically, people place Keogh assets in stocks, bonds, money-market funds, certificates of deposit, mutual funds, or limited partnerships. The Keogh plan, named after U.S. Representative Eugene James Keogh, was established by Congress in 1962 and was expanded in the ECONOMIC RECOVERY TAX ACT OF 1981 (ERTA).

KEY INDUSTRY industry of primary importance to a nation's economy. For instance, the defense industry is called a key industry since it is crucial to maintaining a country's safety. The automobile industry is also considered key since so many jobs are directly or indirectly dependent on it.

KEY MAN (OR WOMAN) INSURANCE life insurance policy bought by a company, usually a small business, on the life of a key executive, with the company as beneficiary.

KEYNESIAN ECONOMICS body of economic thought originated by the British economist and government adviser, John Maynard Keynes (1883–1946), whose landmark work, *The General Theory of Employment, Interest and Money,* was published in 1935. Writing during the Great Depression, Keynes took issue with the classical economists, like Adam Smith, who believed that the economy worked best when left alone. Keynes believed that active government intervention in the marketplace was the only method of ensuring economic growth and stability. He held essentially that insufficient demand causes unemployment and that excessive demand results in inflation; government should therefore manipulate the level of aggregate demand by adjusting levels of government expenditure and taxation. For example, to avoid depression Keynes advocated increased government spending and EASY MONEY, resulting in more investment, higher employment, and increased consumer spending.

Keynesian economics has had great influence on the public economic policies of industrial nations, including the United States. In the 1980s, however, after repeated recessions, slow growth, and high rates of inflation in the U.S., a contrasting outlook, uniting monetarists and "supply siders," blamed excessive government intervention for troubles in the economy.

See also AGGREGATE SUPPLY; LAISSEZ-FAIRE; MACROECONOMICS; MONETARIST; SUPPLY-SIDE ECONOMICS.

KICKBACK
Finance: practice whereby sales finance companies reward dealers who discount installment purchase paper through them with cash payments.
Government and private contracts: payment made secretly by a seller to someone instrumental in awarding a contract or making a sale—an illegal payoff.
Labor relations: illegal practice whereby employers require the return of a portion of wages established by law or union contract, in exchange for employment.

KICKER added feature of a debt obligation, usually designed to enhance marketability by offering the prospect of equity participation. For instance, a bond may be convertible to stock if the shares reach a certain price. This makes the bond more attractive to investors, since the bondholder potentially gets the benefit of an equity security in addition to interest payments. Other examples of equity kickers are RIGHTS and WARRANTS. Some mortgage loans also include kickers in the form of ownership participation or in the form of a percentage of gross rental receipts. Kickers are also called *sweeteners.*

KIDDIE TAX tax filed by parents on Form 8615 for the investment income of children under age 14 exceeding $1,400. Tax is at parent's top tax rate. In some cases, however, parents may elect to report such children's income on their own returns.

KILLER BEES those who aid a company in fending off a takeover bid. "Killer bees" are usually investment bankers who devise strategies to make the target less attractive or more difficult to acquire.

KITING

Commercial banking: (1) depositing and drawing checks between accounts at two or more banks and thereby taking advantage of the FLOAT—that is, the time it takes the bank of deposit to collect from the paying bank. (2) fraudently altering the figures on a check to increase its face value.

Securities: driving stock prices to high levels through manipulative trading methods, such as the creation of artificial trading activity by the buyer and the seller working together and using the same funds.

KNOCK-OUT OPTION form of derivative that gives the buyer the right, but not the obligation, to buy an underlying commodity, currency, or other position at a preset price. Unlike regular options, however, knock-out options expire worthless, or are "knocked out" if the underlying commodity or currency goes through a particular price level. For example, a knock-out option based on the value of the U.S. dollar against the German mark gets knocked out if the dollar falls below a specified exchange rate against the mark. Regular options can have unlimited moves up or down. Knock-out options are much cheaper to buy than regular options, allowing buyers to take larger positions with less money than regular options. Knock-out options are frequently used by hedge funds and other speculators.

KNOW YOUR CUSTOMER ethical concept in the securities industry either stated or implied by the rules of the exchanges and the other authorities regulating broker-dealer practices. Its meaning is expressed in the following paragraph from Article 3 of the NASD Rules of Fair Practice: "In recommending to a customer the purchase, sale or exchange of any security, a member shall have reasonable grounds for believing that the recommendation is suitable for such customer upon the basis of the facts, if any, disclosed by such customer as to his other security holdings and as to his financial situation and needs." Customers opening accounts at brokerage firms must supply financial information that satisfies the know your customer requirement for routine purposes.

KONDRATIEFF WAVE theory of the Soviet economist Nikolai Kondratieff in the 1920s that the economies of the Western capitalist world were prone to major up-and-down "supercycles" lasting 50 to 60 years. He claimed to have predicted the economic crash of 1929–30 based on the crash of 1870, 60 years earlier. The Kondratieff wave theory has adherents, but is controversial among economists. Also called *Kondratieff cycle.*

KRUGGERAND gold bullion coin minted by the Republic of South Africa which comes in one-ounce, half-ounce, quarter-ounce and one-tenth-ounce sizes. Kruggerands usually sell for slightly more than the current value of their gold content. Kruggerands, which had been the dominant gold coin in the world, were banned from being imported into the United States in 1985 because of the South African government's policy of apartheid. The ban was lifted on July 10, 1991. Other GOLD COINS traded in addition to the Kruggerand include the United States Eagle, Canadian Maple Leaf, Mexican Peso, Austrian Philharmonic, and Australian Kangaroo.

KUALA LUMPUR COMMODITY EXCHANGE exchange trading futures in crude palm oil by open outcry. Trading hours: 11 A.M. to 7 P.M., Monday to Friday.

KUALA LUMPUR OPTIONS & FINANCIAL FUTURES EXCHANGE BARHAD (KLOFFE) launched in December 1995, it trades the KLSE Composite Index, the benchmark of the KUALA LUMPUR STOCK EXCHANGE. Trading is electronic. Trading hours: 11 A.M. to 7 P.M., Monday to Friday.

KUALA LUMPUR STOCK EXCHANGE largest securities exchange in Malaysia, formerly affiliated with Singapore as the Stock Exchange of Malaysia. The KLSE Composite Index is the benchmark index, with 11 other sector indices traded. *SCORE,* the System on Computerized Order Routing and Execution, the exchange's semi-automated trading system, was introduced in 1989 and open outcry was discontinued. Settlement is through the Central Depository System (CDS), by book entry, with CDS accounts of buyers credited on the fifth day but held in lien until payment by the seventh market day; sellers are debited on the fifth market day. Trading hours: 9:30 A.M. to 12:30 P.M., and 2:30 P.M. to 5 P.M., Monday through Friday.

L

LABOR-INTENSIVE requiring large pools of workers. Said of an industry in which labor costs are more important than capital costs. Deep-shaft coal mining, for instance, is labor-intensive.

LADY MACBETH STRATEGY TAKEOVER tactic whereby a third party poses as a white knight then turns coat and joins an unfriendly bidder.

LAFFER CURVE curve named for U.S. economics professor Arthur Laffer, postulating that economic output will grow if marginal tax rates are cut. The curve is used in explaining SUPPLY-SIDE ECONOMICS, a theory that noninflationary growth is spurred when tax policies encourage productivity and investment.

LAGGING INDICATORS economic indicators that lag behind the overall pace of economic activity. The Conference Board publishes the Index of Lagging Indicators monthly along with the index of LEADING INDICATORS and the index of COINCIDENT INDICATORS. The six components of the lagging indicators are the unemployment rate, business spending, unit labor costs, bank loans outstanding, bank interest rates, and the book value of manufacturing and trade inventories.

LAISSEZ-FAIRE doctrine that interference of government in business and economic affairs should be minimal. Adam Smith's *The Wealth Of Nations* (1776) described laissez-faire economics in terms of an "invisible hand" that would provide for the maximum good for all, if businessmen were free to pursue profitable opportunities as they saw them. The growth of industry in England in the early 19th century and American industrial growth in the late 19th century both occurred in a laissez-faire capitalist environment. The laissez-faire period ended by the beginning of the 20th century, when large monopolies were broken up and government regulation of business became the norm. The Great Depression of the 1930s saw the birth of KEYNESIAN ECONOMICS, an influential approach advocating government intervention in economic affairs. The movement toward deregulation of business in the United States that began in the 1970s and 80s is to some extent a return to the laissez-faire philosophy. Laissez-faire is French for "allow to do."

LAND CONTRACT creative real estate financing method whereby a seller with a mortgage finances a buyer by taking a down payment and being paid installments but not yielding title until the mortgage is repaid. Also called *contract for deed* and *installment sales contract.*

LANDLORD owner of property who rents it to a TENANT.

LAPSE expiration of a right or privilege because one party did not live up to its obligations during the time allowed. For example, a life insurance policy will lapse if the policyholder does not make the required premium payments on time. This means that the policyholder is no longer protected by the policy.

LAPSED OPTION OPTION that reached its expiration date without being exercised and is thus without value.

LARGE CAP stock with a large capitalization (numbers of shares outstanding times the price of the shares). Large Cap stocks typically have at least $5 billion in outstanding MARKET VALUE. Numerous mutual funds specialize in Large Cap stocks, and many have the words Large Cap in their names.

LAST IN FIRST OUT (LIFO) method of accounting for INVENTORY that ties the cost of goods sold to the cost of the most recent purchases. The formula for cost of goods sold is:

beginning inventory + purchases − ending inventory = cost of goods sold

In contrast to the FIRST IN, FIRST OUT (FIFO) method, in a period of rising prices LIFO produces a higher cost of goods sold and a lower gross profit and taxable income. The artificially low balance sheet inventories resulting from the use of LIFO in periods of inflation give rise to the term *LIFO cushion.*

LAST SALE most recent trade in a particular security. Not to be confused with the final transaction in a trading session, called the CLOSING SALE. The last sale is the point of reference for two Securities and Exchange Commission rules: (1) On a national exchange, no SHORT SALE may be made below the price of the last regular sale. (2) No short sale may be made at the same price as the last sale unless the last sale was at a price higher than the preceding different price. PLUS TICK, MINUS TICK, ZERO MINUS TICK, and ZERO PLUS TICK, used in this connection, refer to the last sale.

LAST TRADING DAY final day during which a futures contract may be settled. If the contract is not OFFSET, either an agreement between the buying and selling parties must be arranged or the physical commodity must be delivered from the seller to the buyer.

LATE CHARGE fee charged by a grantor of credit when the borrower fails to make timely payment.

LATE TAPE delay in displaying price changes because trading on a stock exchange is particularly heavy. If the tape is more than five minutes late, the first digit of a price is deleted. For instance, a trade at 62¾ is reported as 2¾. *See also* DIGITS DELETED.

LAUNDER to make illegally acquired cash look as if it were acquired legally. The usual practice is to transfer the money through foreign banks, thereby concealing its purpose. SEC Rule 17a-8 prohibits using broker-dealers for this purpose.

LAW OF LARGE NUMBERS statistical concept holding that the greater the number of units in a projection, the less important each unit becomes. Group insurance, which gets cheaper as the group gets larger, is an example of the principle in application; actuarial abnormalities have less influence on total claims.

LAY OFF
Investment banking: reduce the risk in a standby commitment, under which the bankers agree to purchase and resell to the public any portion of a stock issue not subscribed to by shareowners who hold rights. The risk is that the market value will fall during the two to four weeks when shareholders are deciding whether to exercise or sell their rights. To minimize the risk, investment bankers (1) buy up the rights as they are offered and, at the same time, sell the shares represented by these rights; and (2) sell short an amount of shares proportionate to the rights that can be expected to go unexercised—to ½% of the issue, typically. Also called *laying off.*
Labor: temporarily or permanently remove an employee from a payroll because of an economic slowdown or a production cutback, not because of poor performance or an infraction of company rules.

LEADER
1. stock or group of stocks at the forefront of an upsurge or a downturn in a market. Typically, leaders are heavily bought and sold by institutions that want to demonstrate their own market leadership.
2. product that has a large market share.

LEADING INDICATORS components of indicators released monthly by the Conference Board, along with the Index of LAGGING INDICATORS and the Index of COINCIDENT INDICATORS. The 11 components are: the average workweek of production workers; average weekly claims for state unemployment insurance; manufacturers' new orders for consumer goods and materials; vendor performance (companies receiving slower deliveries from suppliers); contracts and orders for plant and equipment; building permits; change in manufacturers' unfilled orders for durable goods; changes in sensitive materials prices; stock prices; MONEY SUPPLY (M-2); and index of consumer expectations. The index of leading indicators, the components of which are adjusted for inflation, accurately forecasts the ups and downs of the business cycle.

LEAD REGULATOR leading self-regulatory organization (SRO) taking responsibility for investigation of a particular section of the law and all the cases that pertain to it. In the securities business, for example, the New York Stock Exchange may take the lead in investigating certain kinds of fraud or suspicious market activity, while the American Stock Exchange or NASDAQ may be the lead regulator in other areas. The lead regulator will report its findings to the other self-regulatory organizations, and ultimately to a government oversight agency, such as the Securities and Exchange Commission.

LEAPS acronym for Long-Term Equity AnticiPation Securities, LEAPS are long-term equity options traded on U.S. exchanges and over the counter. Instead of expiring in two near-term and two farther out months as most equity OPTIONS do, LEAPS expire in two to five years, giving the buyer a longer time for his strategy to come to fruition. LEAPS are traded on many individual stocks listed on the New York Stock Exchange, the American Stock Exchange, and NASDAQ.

LEARNING CURVE predictable improvements following the early part of the life of a production contract, when costly mistakes are made.

LEASE contract granting use of real estate, equipment, or other fixed assets for a specified time in exchange for payment, usually in the form of rent. The owner of the leased property is called the lessor, the user the lessee. *See also* CAPITAL LEASE; FINANCIAL LEASE; OPERATING LEASE; SALE AND LEASEBACK.

LEASE ACQUISITION COST price paid by a real estate LIMITED PARTNERSHIP, when acquiring a lease, including legal fees and related expenses. The charges are prorated to the limited partners.

LEASEBACK transaction in which one party sells property to another and agrees to lease the property back from the buyer for a fixed period of time. For example, a building owner wanting to get cash out of the building may decide to sell the building to a real estate or leasing company and sign a long-term lease to occupy the space. The original owner is thereby able to receive cash for the value of his property, which he can reinvest in his business, as well as remain in the property. The new owner is assured of the stability of a long-term tenant and a steady income. Leaseback deals (also called sale and leaseback deals) also are executed for business equipment such as computers, cars, trucks, and airplanes. Partial ownership interests in leasing deals are sold to investors in LIMITED PARTNERSHIP form, and are designed to produce a fixed level of income to limited partners for the lease term.

LEASEHOLD asset representing the right to use property under a LEASE.

LEASEHOLD IMPROVEMENT modification of leased property. The cost is added to fixed assets and then amortized.

LEASE-PURCHASE AGREEMENT agreement providing that portions of LEASE payments may be applied toward the purchase of the property under lease.

LEG
1. sustained trend in stock market prices. A prolonged bull or bear market may have first, second, and third legs.
2. one side of a spread transaction. For instance, a trader might buy a CALL OPTION that has a particular STRIKE PRICE and expiration date,

then combine it with a PUT OPTION that has the same striking price and a different expiration date. The two options are called legs of the spread. Selling one of the options is termed LIFTING A LEG.

LEGACY gift under a WILL of cash or some other specific item of personal property, such as a stock certificate, a car, or a piece of jewelry. The legacy usually is conditioned, meaning the legatee is required to be employed by the TESTATOR—the person who makes the will—or related to the testator by marriage. In other cases, a legacy to a legatee who has not attained a particular age at the testator's death will be held in trust for the legatee, instead of being distributed outright.

LEGAL computerized data base maintained by the New York Stock Exchange to track enforcement actions against member firms, audits of member firms, and customer complaints. LEGAL is not an acronym, but is written in all capitals.

LEGAL AGE age at which a person can enter into binding contracts or agree to other legal acts without the consent of another adult. In most states, the legal age, also called the *age of majority,* is 18 years old.

LEGAL ENTITY person or organization that has the legal standing to enter into a contract and may be sued for failure to perform as agreed in the contract. A child under legal age is not a legal entity; a corporation is a legal entity since it is a person in the eyes of the law.

LEGAL INVESTMENT investment permissible for investors with FIDUCIARY responsibilities. INVESTMENT GRADE bonds, as rated by Standard & Poor's or Moody's, usually qualify as legal investments. Guidelines designed to protect investors are set by the state in which the fiduciary operates. *See also* LEGAL LIST.

LEGAL LIABILITY (1) monies owed, shown on a balance sheet. (2) individual's or company's obligation to act responsibly or face compensatory penalties. *See also* LIABILITY.

LEGAL LIST securities selected by a state agency, usually a banking department, as permissible holdings of mutual savings banks, pension funds, insurance companies, and other FIDUCIARY institutions. To protect the money that individuals place in such institutions, only high quality debt and equity securities are generally included. As an alternative to the legal list, some states apply the PRUDENT MAN RULE.

LEGAL MONOPOLY exclusive right to offer a particular service within a particular territory. In exchange, the company agrees to have its policies and rates regulated. Electric and water utilities are legal monopolies.

LEGAL OPINION
  1. statement as to legality, written by an authorized official such as a city attorney or an attorney general.

2. statement as to the legality of a MUNICIPAL BOND issue, usually written by a law firm specializing in public borrowings. It is part of the *official statement,* the municipal equivalent of a PROSPECTUS. Unless the legality of an issue is established, an investor's contract is invalid at the time of issue and he cannot sue under it. The legal opinion is therefore required by a SYNDICATE MANAGER and customarily accompanies the transfer of municipal securities as long as they are outstanding.

LEGAL TRANSFER transaction that requires documentation other than the standard stock or bond power to validate the transfer of a stock certificate from a seller to a buyer—for example, securities registered to a corporation or to a deceased person. It is the selling broker's responsibility to supply proper documentation to the buying broker in a legal transfer.

LEGISLATIVE RISK risk that a change in legislation could have a major positive or negative effect on an investment. For instance, a company that is a large exporter may be a beneficiary of a trade agreement that lowers tariff barriers, and therefore may see its stock price rise. On the other hand, a company that is a major polluter may be harmed by laws that stiffen fines for polluting the air or water, thereby making its share price fall.

LEMON product or investment producing poor performance. A car that continually needs repairs is a lemon, and consumers are guaranteed a full refund in several states under so-called lemon laws. A promising stock that fails to live up to expectations is also called a lemon.

LENDER individual or firm that extends money to a borrower with the expectation of being repaid, usually with interest. Lenders create debt in the form of loans, and in the event of LIQUIDATION they are paid off before stockholders receive distributions. But the investor deals in both debt (bonds) and equity (stocks). It is useful to remember that investors in commercial paper, bonds, and other debt instruments are in fact lenders with the same rights and powers enjoyed by banks.

LENDER OF LAST RESORT
1. characterization of a central bank's role in bolstering a bank that faces large withdrawals of funds. The U.S. lender of last resort is the FEDERAL RESERVE BANK. Member banks may borrow from the DISCOUNT WINDOW to maintain reserve requirements or to meet large withdrawals. The Fed thereby maintains the stability of the banking system, which would be threatened if major banks were to fail.
2. government small business financing programs and municipal economic development organizations whose precondition to making loans to private enterprises is an inability to obtain financing elsewhere.

LENDING AGREEMENT contract between a lender and a borrower. *See also* INDENTURE; REVOLVING CREDIT; TERM LOAN.

LENDING AT A PREMIUM term used when one broker lends securities to another broker to cover customer's short position and imposes a charge for the loan. Such charges, which are passed on to the customer, are the exception rather than the rule, since securities are normally LOANED FLAT between brokers, that is, without interest. Lending at a premium might occur when the securities needed are in very heavy demand and are therefore difficult to borrow. The premium is in addition to any payments the customer might have to make to the lending broker to MARK TO THE MARKET or to cover dividends or interest payable on the borrowed securities.

LENDING AT A RATE paying interest to a customer on the credit balance created from the proceeds of a SHORT SALE. Such proceeds are held in ESCROW to secure the loan of securities, usually made by another broker, to cover the customer's short position. Lending at a rate is the exception rather than the rule.

LENDING SECURITIES securities borrowed from a broker's inventory, other MARGIN ACCOUNTS, or from other brokers, when a customer makes a SHORT SALE and the securities must be delivered to the buying customer's broker. As collateral, the borrowing broker deposits with the lending broker an amount of money equal to the market value of the securities. No interest or premium is ordinarily involved in the transaction. The Securities and Exchange Commission requires that brokerage customers give permission to have their securities used in loan transactions, and the point is routinely covered in the standard agreement signed by customers when they open general accounts.

LESS DEVELOPED COUNTRIES (LDC) countries that are not fully industrialized or do not have sophisticated financial or legal systems. These countries, also called members of the *Third World,* typically have low levels of per-capita income, high inflation and debt, and large trade deficits. The World Bank may be helping them by providing loan assistance. Loans to such countries are commonly called *LDC debt.*

LESSEE *see* LEASE.

LESSOR *see* LEASE.

LETTER BOND *see* LETTER SECURITY.

LETTER OF CREDIT (L/C) instrument or document issued by a bank guaranteeing the payment of a customer's drafts up to a stated amount for a specified period. It substitutes the bank's credit for the buyer's and eliminates the seller's risk. It is used extensively in international trade. A *commercial letter of credit* is normally drawn in favor of a third party, called the beneficiary. A *confirmed letter of credit* is provided by a correspondent bank and guaranteed by the issuing bank. A *revolving letter of credit* is issued for a specified amount and automatically renewed for the same amount for a specified period, permitting any number of drafts to be drawn so long as they do not exceed its overall limit. A *traveler's letter of credit* is issued for the convenience of a traveling customer and typically lists correspondent banks at which drafts will be honored. A *performance letter of credit* is issued to guarantee performance under a contract.

LETTER OF INTENT

1. any letter expressing an intention to take (or not take) an action, sometimes subject to other action being taken. For example, a bank might issue a letter of intent stating it will make a loan to a customer, subject to another lender's agreement to participate. The letter of intent, in this case, makes it possible for the customer to negotiate the participation loan.

2. preliminary agreement between two companies that intend to merge. Such a letter is issued after negotiations have been satisfactorily completed.

3. promise by a MUTUAL FUND shareholder to invest a specified sum of money monthly for about a year. In return, the shareholder is entitled to lower sales charges.

4. INVESTMENT LETTER for a LETTER SECURITY.

LETTER OF LAST INSTRUCTIONS letter placed with a WILL containing instructions on carrying out the provisions of the will. These letters generally are not binding on the executors, but many executors feel morally bound to follow the wishes of the TESTATORS who appointed them. Florida is one of several states where the law allows these letters to be incorporated by reference if the language of the will shows this intent and identifies the letter's purpose clearly.

LETTER SECURITY stock or bond that is not registered with the Securities and Exchange Commission and therefore cannot be sold in the public market. When an issue is sold directly by the issuer to the investor, registration with the SEC can be avoided if a LETTER OF INTENT, called an INVESTMENT LETTER, is signed by the purchaser establishing that the securities are being bought for investment and not for resale. The letter's integral association with the security gives rise to the terms *letter security, letter stock,* and *letter bond.*

LETTER STOCK *see* LETTER SECURITY.

LEVEL DEBT SERVICE provision in a municipal charter stipulating that payments on municipal debt be approximately equal every year. This makes it easier to project the amount of tax revenue needed to meet obligations.

LEVERAGE

Operating leverage: extent to which a company's costs of operating are fixed (rent, insurance, executive salaries) as opposed to variable

(materials, direct labor). In a totally automated company, whose costs are virtually all fixed, every dollar of increase in sales is a dollar of increase in operating income once the BREAKEVEN POINT has been reached, because costs remain the same at every level of production. In contrast, a company whose costs are largely variable would show relatively little increase in operating income when production and sales increased because costs and production would rise together. The leverage comes in because a small change in sales has a magnified percentage effect on operating income and losses. The *degree of operating leverage*—the ratio of the percentage change in operating income to the percentage change in sales or units sold—measures the sensitivity of a firm's profits to changes in sales volume. A firm using a high degree of operating leverage has a breakeven point at a relatively high sales level.
Financial leverage: debt in relation to equity in a firm's capital structure—its LONG-TERM DEBT (usually bonds), PREFERRED STOCK, and SHAREHOLDERS' EQUITY—measured by the DEBT-TO-EQUITY RATIO. The more long-term debt there is, the greater the financial leverage. Shareholders benefit from financial leverage to the extent that return on the borrowed money exceeds the interest costs and the market value of their shares rises. For this reason, financial leverage is popularly called *trading on the equity*. Because leverage also means required interest and principal payments and thus ultimately the risk of default, how much leverage is desirable is largely a question of stability of earnings. As a rule of thumb, an industrial company with a debt to equity ratio of more than 30% is highly leveraged, exceptions being firms with dependable earnings and cash flow, such as electric utilities.

Since long-term debt interest is a fixed cost, financial leverage tends to take over where operating leverage leaves off, further magnifying the effects on earnings per share of changes in sales levels. In general, high operating leverage should accompany low financial leverage, and vice versa.
Investments: means of enhancing return or value without increasing investment. Buying securities on margin is an example of leverage with borrowed money, and extra leverage may be possible if the leveraged security is convertible into common stock. RIGHTS, WARRANTS, and OPTION contracts provide leverage, not involving borrowings but offering the prospect of high return for little or no investment.

LEVERAGED BUYOUT takeover of a company, using borrowed funds. Most often, the target company's assets serve as security for the loans taken out by the acquiring firm, which repays the loan out of cash flow of the acquired company. Management may use this technique to retain control by converting a company from public to private. A group of investors may also borrow funds from banks, using their own assets as collateral, to take over another firm. In almost all leveraged buyouts, public shareholders receive a premium over the current market value for their shares. When a company that has gone private in a leveraged buyout offers shares to the public again, it is called a REVERSE LEVERAGED BUYOUT.

LEVEL LOAD sales charge that does not change over time. In mutual funds, level load shares are called *C class shares,* compared to *A class* for upfront loads and *B class* for back-end loads. A level load will typically be 1% to 2% of assets each year, which is lower than an upfront load of 4% to 5% or the back-end load, which starts at 5% and declines each year until it disappears if the fund shares are held for five years. Though the level load may be lower than an upfront or back-end load, an investor ends up paying a higher commission if he holds the fund for many years.

LEVEL PLAYING FIELD condition in which competitors operate under the same rules. For example, all banks must follow the same regulations set down by the Federal Reserve. In some situations, competitors complain to regulators or Congress that they are not playing on a level playing field. For example, banks contend that brokerage firms can offer certain banking services without the same rules imposed on banks. Companies wanting to export to a particular country may complain that domestic companies are protected by various trade barriers, creating an uneven playing field. Various sections of the tax code may favor some companies more than others, prompting cries from the disadvantaged firms to "level the playing field."

LEVEL TERM INSURANCE life insurance policy with a fixed face value and rising insurance premiums.

LEVERAGED COMPANY company with debt in addition to equity in its capital structure. In its popular connotation, the term is applied to companies that are highly leveraged. Although the judgment is relative, industrial companies with more than one third of their capitalization in the form of debt are considered highly leveraged. *See also* LEVERAGE.

LEVERAGED EMPLOYEE STOCK OWNERSHIP PLAN (LESOP) EMPLOYEE STOCK OWNERSHIP PLAN (ESOP) in which employee pension plans and profit-sharing plans borrow money to purchase stock in the company or issue CONVERTIBLES exchangeable for common stock. In addition to the usual advantages of employee ownership, the LESOP is a way to ensure that majority ownership remains in friendly hands.

LEVERAGED INVESTMENT COMPANY
1. open-end INVESTMENT COMPANY, or MUTUAL FUND, that is permitted by its charter to borrow capital from a bank or other lender.
2. dual-purpose INVESTMENT COMPANY, which issues both income and capital shares. Holders of income shares receive dividends and interest on investments, whereas holders of capital shares receive all capital gains on investments. In effect each class of shareholder leverages the other.

LEVERAGED LEASE LEASE that involves a lender in addition to the lessor and lessee. The lender, usually a bank or insurance company, puts up a percentage of the cash required to purchase the asset, usually more than half. The balance is put up by the lessor, who is both the equity participant and the borrower. With the cash the lessor acquires the asset, giving the lender (1) a mortgage on the asset and (2) an assignment of the lease and lease payments. The lessee then makes periodic payments to the lessor, who in turn pays the lender. As owner of the asset, the lessor is entitled to tax deductions for DEPRECIATION on the asset and INTEREST on the loan.

LEVERAGED RECAPITALIZATION corporate strategy to fend off potential acquirers by taking on a large amount of debt and making a large cash distribution to shareholders. For example, XYZ Company, selling at $50 a share, may borrow $3 billion to make a one-time distribution of $20 a share to stockholders. After the distribution, the stock price will drop to $30. By replacing equity with $3 billion in debt, XYZ is a far less attractive takeover target for a raider or other company than it was before. Also called *leveraged recap* for short.

LEVERAGED STOCK stock financed with credit, as in a MARGIN ACCOUNT. Although not, strictly speaking, leveraged stock, securities that are convertible into common stock provide an extra degree of leverage when bought on margin. Assuming the purchase price is reasonably close to the INVESTMENT VALUE and CONVERSION VALUE, the downside risk is no greater than it would be with the same company's common stock, whereas the appreciation value is much greater.

LIABILITY claim on the assets of a company or individual—excluding ownership EQUITY. Characteristics: (1) It represents a transfer of assets or services at a specified or determinable date. (2) The firm or individual has little or no discretion to avoid the transfer. (3) The event causing the obligation has already occurred. *See also* BALANCE SHEET.

LIABILITY INSURANCE insurance for money the policyholder is legally obligated to pay because of bodily injury or property damage caused to another person and covered in the policy. Liabilities may result from property damage, bodily injury, libel, or any other damages caused by the insured. The insurance company agrees to pay for such damages if they are awarded by a court, up to the limitations specified in the insurance contract. The insurer may also cover legal expenses incurred in defending the suit.

LIBOR *see* LONDON INTERBANK OFFERED RATE.

LICENSE legal document issued by a regulatory agency permitting an individual to conduct a certain activity, usually because the person has passed a training course qualifying him. For example, a securities license is required for a broker to sell stocks, bonds, and mutual funds. An insurance license is required before someone can sell insurance products. Before a driver's license is granted, a driver must pass an examination proving that he knows how to drive safely. If the licensed individual violates the regulations, the license can be revoked.

LIEN creditor's claim against property. For example, a mortgage is a lien against a house; if the mortgage is not paid on time, the house can be seized to satisfy the lien. Similarly, a bond is a lien against a company's assets; if interest and principal are not paid when due, the assets may be seized to pay the bondholders. As soon as a debt is paid, the lien is removed. Liens may be granted by courts to satisfy judgments. *See also* MECHANIC'S LIEN.

LIFE ANNUITY ANNUITY that makes a guaranteed fixed payment for the rest of the life of the annuitant. After the annuitant dies, beneficiaries receive no further payments.

LIFE CYCLE most common usage refers to an individual's progression from cradle to grave and the assumption that the choice of appropriate investments changes. Term also applies to the life of a product or of a business, consisting of inception, development, growth, expansion, maturity, and decline (or change). Recently, the term has entered into the vocabulary of the family-owned business, referring to generations of management. The post-World War II baby boom produced entrepreneurs who built businesses that now approach a juncture where a second generation either takes over management or sells out.

LIFE CYCLE PLANNING planning contemplated by the concept of LIFE CYCLE.

LIFE EXPECTANCY age to which an average person can be expected to live, as calculated by an ACTUARY. Insurance companies base their projections of benefit payouts on actuarial studies of such factors as sex, heredity, and health habits and base their rates on actuarial analysis. Life expectancy can be calculated at birth or at some other age and generally varies according to age. Thus, all persons at birth might have an average life expectancy of 70 years and all persons aged 40 years might have an average life expectancy of 75 years.

Life expectancy projections determine such matters as the ages when an INDIVIDUAL RETIREMENT ACCOUNT may start and finish withdrawing funds. Annuities payable for lifetimes are usually based on separate male or female tables, except that a QUALIFIED PLAN OR TRUST must use unisex tables.

LIFE INSURANCE insurance policy that pays a death benefit to beneficiaries if the insured dies. In return for this protection, the insured pays a premium, usually on an annual basis. *Term insurance* pays off upon the insured's death but provides no buildup of cash value in the policy. Term premiums are cheaper than premiums for *cash value policies* such as whole life, variable life, and universal life, which pay death benefits and also provide for the buildup of cash values in the policy. The cash builds up tax-deferred in the policy and is invested in stocks, bonds, real estate, and other investments. Policyholders can take out loans against their policies, which reduce the death benefit if they are not repaid. Some life insurance provides benefits to policyholders while they are still living, including income payments. *See also* SINGLE PREMIUM LIFE INSURANCE.

LIFE INSURANCE IN FORCE amount of life insurance that a company has issued, including the face amount of all outstanding policies together with all dividends that have been paid to policyholders. Thus a life insurance policy for $500,000 on which dividends of $10,000 have been paid would count as life insurance in force of $510,000.

LIFE INSURANCE POLICY contract between an insurance company and the insured setting out the provisions of the life insurance coverage. These provisions include premiums, loan procedures, face amounts, and the designation of beneficiaries, among many other clauses. Policies may be for term or permanent cash value types of coverage.

LIFETIME REVERSE MORTGAGE type of reverse mortgage agreement whereby a homeowner borrows against the value of the home, retains title, and makes no payments while living in the home. When the home ceases to be the primary residence of the borrower, as when the borrower dies, the lender sells the property, repays the loan, and remits any surplus to the borrower's estate. Such arrangements may be appropriate for older people who need cash and are HOUSE POOR. *See also* REVERSE ANNUITY MORTGAGE (RAM).

LIFFE *see* LONDON INTERNATIONAL FINANCIAL FUTURES AND OPTIONS EXCHANGE.

LIFO *see* LAST IN, FIRST OUT.

LIFT rise in securities prices as measured by the Dow Jones Industrial Average or other market averages, usually caused by good business or economic news.

LIFTING A LEG closing one side of a HEDGE, leaving the other side as a long or short position. A leg, in Wall Street parlance, is one side of a hedged transaction. A trader might have a STRADDLE—that is, a call and a put on the same stock, at the same price, with the same expiration date. Making a closing sale of the put, thereby lifting a leg—or *taking off a leg,* as it is sometimes called—would leave the trader with the call, or the LONG LEG.

LIGHTEN UP to sell a portion of a stock or bond position in a portfolio. A money manager with a large profit in a stock may decide to realize some of the gains because he is unsure that the stock will continue to rise, or because he is concerned too much of the fund's assets are tied up in the stock. As a result, he will say that he is "lightening up" his position in the stock. However, some of the stock remains in the portfolio.

LIMIT *see* LIMIT ORDER; LIMIT UP, LIMIT DOWN.

LIMITED COMPANY form of business most common in Britain, where registration under the Companies Act is comparable to incorporation under state law in the United States. It is abbreviated Ltd. or PLC.

LIMITED DISCRETION agreement between broker and client allowing the broker to make certain trades without consulting the client—for instance, sell an option position that is near expiration or sell a stock on which there has just been adverse news.

LIMITED LIABILITY underlying principle of the CORPORATION and the LIMITED PARTNERSHIP in the United States and the LIMITED COMPANY in the United Kingdom that LIABILITY is limited to an investor's original investment. In contrast, a general partner or the owner of a PROPRIETORSHIP has unlimited liability.

LIMITED PARTNERSHIP organization made up of a GENERAL PARTNER, who manages a project, and limited partners, who invest money but have limited liability, are not involved in day-to-day management, and usually cannot lose more than their capital contribution. Usually limited partners receive income, capital gains, and tax benefits; the general partner collects fees and a percentage of capital gains and income. Typical limited partnerships are in real estate, oil and gas, and equipment leasing, but they also finance movies, research and development, and other projects. Typically, public limited partnerships are sold through brokerage firms, for minimum investments of $5000, whereas private limited partnerships are put together with fewer than 35 limited partners who invest more than $20,000 each. *See also* INCOME LIMITED PARTNERSHIP; MASTER LIMITED PARTNERSHIP; OIL AND GAS LIMITED PARTNERSHIP; PASSIVE; RESEARCH AND DEVELOPMENT LIMITED PARTNERSHIP; UNLEVERAGED PROGRAM.

LIMITED PAYMENT POLICY LIFE INSURANCE contract that provides protection for one's whole life but requires premiums for a lesser number of years.

LIMITED RISK risk in buying an options contract. For example, someone who pays a PREMIUM to buy a CALL OPTION on a stock will lose nothing more than the premium if the underlying stock does not rise during the life of the option. In contrast, a FUTURES CONTRACT entails *unlimited risk,* since the buyer may have to put up more money in the event of an adverse move. Thus options trading offers limited risk unavailable in futures trading.

Also, stock analysts may say of a stock that has recently fallen in price, that it now has limited risk, reasoning that the stock is unlikely to fall much further.

LIMITED TAX BOND MUNICIPAL BOND backed by the full faith of the issuing government but not by its full taxing power; rather it is secured by the pledge of a special tax or group of taxes, or a limited portion of the real estate tax.

LIMITED TRADING AUTHORIZATION *see* LIMITED DISCRETION.

LIMITED WARRANTY warranty that imposes certain limitations, and is therefore not a full warranty. For example, an automaker may issue a warranty that covers parts, but not labor, for a particular period of time.

LIMIT ON CLOSE ORDER order to buy or sell a stated amount of a stock at the closing price, to be executed only if the closing price is a specified price or better, e.g., an order to sell XYZ at the close, if the closing price is $30 or higher.

LIMIT ORDER order to buy or sell a security or commodity at a specific price or better. The broker will execute the trade only within the price restriction. For example, a customer puts in a limit order to buy XYZ Corp. at 30 when the stock is selling for 32. Even if the stock reached 30⅛ the broker will not execute the trade. Similarly, if the client put in a limit order to sell XYZ Corp. at 33 when the price is 31, the trade will not be executed until the stock price hits 33.

LIMIT ORDER INFORMATION SYSTEM electronic system that informs subscribers about securities traded on participating exchanges, showing the specialist, the exchange, the order quantities, and the bid and offer prices. This allows subscribers to shop for the most favorable prices.

LIMIT PRICE price set in a LIMIT ORDER. For example, a customer might put in a limit order to sell shares at 45 or to buy at 40. The broker executes the order at the limit price or better.

LIMIT UP, LIMIT DOWN maximum price movement allowed for a commodity FUTURES CONTRACT during one trading day. In the face of a particularly dramatic development, a future's price may move limit up or limit down for several consecutive days.

LINE category of insurance, such as the *liability line,* or the amount of insurance on a given property, such as a $500,000 line on the buildings of the XYZ Company. Term is also used generally, to refer to a product line. *See also* BANK LINE.

LINE OF CREDIT *see* BANK LINE.

LIPPER MUTUAL FUND INDUSTRY AVERAGE average performance level of all mutual funds, as reported by Lipper Analytical Services of New York. The performance of all mutual funds is ranked quarterly and annually, by type of fund—such as aggressive growth fund or income fund. Mutual fund managers try to beat the industry average as well as the other funds in their category. *See also* MUTUAL FUND.

LIQUID ASSET cash or easily convertible into cash. Some examples: money-market fund shares, U.S. Treasury bills, bank deposits. An investor in an ILLIQUID investment such as a real estate or oil and gas LIMITED PARTNERSHIP is required to have substantial liquid assets, which would serve as a cushion if the illiquid deal did not work out favorably.

   In a corporation's financial statements, liquid assets are cash, marketable securities, and accounts receivable.

LIQUIDATING DIVIDEND distribution of assets in the form of a DIVIDEND from a corporation that is going out of business. Such a payment may come when a firm goes bankrupt or when management decides to sell off a company's assets and pass the proceeds on to shareholders.

LIQUIDATING VALUE projected price for an asset of a company that is going out of business—for instance, a real estate holding or office equipment. Liquidating value, also called *auction value,* assumes that assets are sold separately from the rest of the organization; it is distinguished from GOING CONCERN VALUE, which may be higher because of what accountants term *organization value* or *goodwill.*

LIQUIDATION
1. dismantling of a business, paying off debts in order of priority, and distributing the remaining assets in cash to the owners. Involuntary liquidation is covered under Chapter 7 of the federal BANKRUPTCY law. *See also* JUNIOR SECURITY; PREFERRED STOCK.
2. forced sale of a brokerage client's securities or commodities after failure to meet a MARGIN CALL. *See also* SELL OUT.

LIQUIDITY ability to buy or sell an asset quickly and in large volume without substantially affecting the asset's price. Shares in large blue-chip stocks like General Motors or General Electric are liquid, because they are actively traded and therefore the stock price will not be dramatically moved by a few buy or sell orders. However, shares in small companies with few shares outstanding, or commodity markets with limited activity, generally are not considered liquid, because one or two big orders can move the price up or down sharply. A high level of liquidity is a key characteristic of a good market for a security or a commodity.

   Liquidity also refers to the ability to convert to cash quickly. For example, a money market mutual fund provides instant liquidity since shareholders can write checks on the fund. Other examples of liquid accounts include checking accounts, bank money market deposit accounts, passbook accounts, and Treasury bills.

LIQUIDITY DIVERSIFICATION purchase of bonds whose maturities range from short to medium to long term, thus helping to protect against sharp fluctuations in interest rates.

LIQUIDITY FUND Emeryville, California, company that buys REAL ESTATE LIMITED PARTNERSHIP interests 25% to 35% below the current appraised value of the real estate assets. The company also buys REAL ESTATE INVESTMENT TRUSTS.

LIQUIDITY RATIO measure of a firm's ability to meet maturing short-term obligations. *See also* CASH ASSET RATIO; CURRENT RATIO; NET QUICK ASSETS; QUICK RATIO.

LISBON STOCK EXCHANGE (LSE) founded in January 1769, the exchange trades stocks, bonds, and unit trusts. The BVL General Index is the exchange's official index, and includes all listed shares on the LSE official market. Shares in the official market are traded through TRADIS, a computer-linked system. Physical settlement is three days after the trade; cash settlement is four days. Trading hours: Monday through Friday, 9 A.M to 10 A.M. pre-opening, 10 A.M. to 4 P.M. for continuous trading, and 10 A.M. to 4 P.M. for daily calls.

LISTED FIRM company whose stock trades on the New York Stock Exchange or American Stock Exchange. The company has to meet certain LISTING REQUIREMENTS or it will be delisted. Listed firms are distinguished from unlisted companies, whose stock trades over-the-counter on the NASDAQ market.

LISTED OPTION put or call OPTION that an exchange has authorized for trading, properly called an *exchange-traded option.*

LISTED SECURITY stock or bond that has been accepted for trading by one of the organized and registered securities exchanges in the United States, which list more than 6000 issues of securities of some 3500 corporations. Generally, the advantages of being listed are that the exchanges provide (1) an orderly marketplace; (2) liquidity; (3) fair price determination; (4) accurate and continuous reporting on sales and quotations; (5) information on listed companies; and (6) strict regulations for the protection of security holders. Each exchange has its own listing requirements, those of the New York Stock Exchange being most stringent. Listed securities include stocks, bonds, convertible bonds, preferred stocks, warrants, rights, and options, although not all forms of securities are accepted on all exchanges. Unlisted securities are traded in the OVER-THE-COUNTER market. *See also* LISTING REQUIREMENTS; STOCK EXCHANGE.

LISTING written employment agreement between a property owner and a real estate broker authorizing the broker to find a buyer or tenant for certain property. Oral listings, while not specifically illegal, are unenforceable under many state fraud statutes, and generally are not recommended. The most common form of listing is the exclusive-right-to-sell listing. Others include open listings, net listings and exclusive-agency listings. Listings are personal service contracts and cannot be assigned to another broker, but brokers can delegate the work to other members of the sales office. The listing usually states the amount of commission the seller will pay the broker and the time limit. In a buyer's listing, the buyer hires the broker to locate a property.

LISTING BROKER licensed real estate broker (agent) who secures a listing of a property for sale. A *listing* involves a contract authorizing the broker to perform services for the selling property owner. The listing broker may sell the property, but it may also be sold by the *selling broker,* a different agent, with the two sharing commissions, usually equally.

LISTING REQUIREMENTS rules that must be met before a stock is listed for trading on an exchange. Among the requirements of the New York Stock Exchange: a corporation must have a minimum of one million publicly held shares with a minimum aggregate market value of $16 million as well as an annual net income topping $2.5 million before federal income tax.

LIST PRICE suggested retail price for a product according to the manufacturer. The list price is designed to guide retailers, though they remain free to sell products above or below list price.

LITTLE DRAGONS nickname for developing Asian nations such as Singapore, Hong Kong, South Korea, and Taiwan that pose a threat to Japan (the Big Dragon) because of their lower labor costs, high productivity, and pro-business attitudes. Also known as the *tigers.* Called an "economic miracle" for most of the 1990s, the so-called Pacific Rim region lost its economic underpinnings in 1997, causing currencies and securities markets to plunge.

LIVING BENEFITS life insurance benefits upon which the insured can draw cash while still alive. Some policies allow benefits to be paid to the insured in cases of terminal illness or illness involving certain long-term care costs. Beneficiaries receive any balance upon the insured's death. Also known as *accelerated benefits.*

LIVING DEAD *see* ZOMBIES.

LIVING TRUST *see* INTER VIVOS TRUST.

LLOYD'S OF LONDON a gathering place in London, England for insurance UNDERWRITERS. Lloyd's is a marketplace made up of hundreds of underwriting syndicates, each of them in effect a mini-insurer. Lloyd's sets standards for its members, but does not issue policies itself. Each syndicate is managed by an underwriter who decides which risks to accept. Typically, a risk underwritten at Lloyd's will be shared by many syndicates. The number of individual investors, known as "names," in a particular syndicate may vary from a few to hundreds. The Lloyd's market is also a major international reinsurer, allowing other insurance companies to limit their risks.

LOAD sales charge paid by an investor who buys shares in a load MUTUAL FUND or ANNUITY. Loads are usually charged when shares or units are purchased; a charge for withdrawing is called a BACK-END LOAD (or *rear-end load*). A fund that does not charge this fee is called a NO-LOAD FUND. *See also* INVESTMENT COMPANY.

LOAD FUND MUTUAL FUND that is sold for a sales charge by a brokerage firm or other sales representative. Such funds may be stock, bond, or commodity funds, with conservative or aggressive objectives. The stated advantage of a load fund is that the salesperson will explain the fund to the customer, and advise him or her when it is appropriate to sell the fund, as well as when to buy more shares. A NO-LOAD FUND, which is sold without a sales charge directly to investors by a fund company, does not give advice on when to buy or sell. Increasingly, traditional no-load funds are becoming *low-load funds,* imposing up-front charges of 3% or less with no change in services. *See also* INVESTMENT COMPANY.

LOAD SPREAD OPTION method of allocating the annual sales charge on some contractual mutual funds. In a CONTRACTUAL PLAN, the investor accumulates shares in the fund through periodic fixed payments. During the first four years of the contract, up to 20% of any single year's contributions to the fund may be credited against the sales charge, provided that the total charges for these four years do not exceed 64% of one year's contributions. The sales charge is limited to 9% of the entire contract.

LOAN transaction wherein an owner of property, called the LENDER, allows another party, the *borrower,* to use the property. The borrower customarily promises to return the property after a specified period with payment for its use, called INTEREST. The documentation of the promise is called a PROMISSORY NOTE when the property is cash.

LOAN AMORTIZATION reduction of debt by scheduled, regular payments of principal and interest sufficient to repay the loan at maturity.

LOAN COMMITMENT lender's agreement to make money available to a borrower in a specified amount, at a specified rate, and within a specified time. *See also* COMMITMENT FEE.

LOAN CROWD stock exchange members who lend or borrow securities required to cover the positions of brokerage customers who sell short—called a crowd because they congregate at a designated place on the floor of the exchange. *See also* LENDING SECURITIES.

LOANED FLAT loaned without interest, said of the arrangement whereby brokers lend securities to one another to cover customer SHORT SALE positions. *See also* LENDING AT A PREMIUM; LENDING AT A RATE; LENDING SECURITIES.

LOAN ORIGINATION FEE *see* POINT.

LOAN STOCK *see* LENDING SECURITIES.

LOAN-TO-VALUE RATIO (LTV) ratio of money borrowed to fair market value, usually in reference to real property. Residential mortgage loans conventionally have a maximum LTV of 80% (an $80,000 loan on a $100,0000 house).

LOAN VALUE

1. amount a lender is willing to lend against collateral. For example, at 50% of appraised value, a piece of property worth $800,000 has a loan value of $400,000.
2. with respect to REGULATION T of the FEDERAL RESERVE BOARD, the maximum percentage of the current market value of eligible securities that a broker can lend a margin account customer. Regulation T applies only to securities formally registered or having an unlisted trading privilege on a national securities exchange. For securities exempt from Regulation T, which comprise U.S. government securities, municipal bonds, and bonds of the International Bank for Reconstruction and Development, loan value is a matter of the individual firm's policy.

LOCAL member of a futures exchange who trades for his or her own account. The traders in a futures pit are composed of locals and employees of various brokerage firms. Locals initiate their own transactions on the floor of the exchange. Some, termed *dual traders,* also execute orders on behalf of customers.

LOCAL TAXES taxes paid by an individual to his or her locality. This includes city income, property, sewer, water, school, and other taxes. These taxes are usually deductible on the taxpayer's federal income tax return.

LOCK BOX

1. cash management system whereby a company's customers mail payments to a post office box near the company's bank. The bank collects checks from the lock box—sometimes several times a day—deposits them to the account of the firm, and informs the company's cash manager by telephone of the deposit. This reduces processing FLOAT and puts cash to work more quickly. The bank's fee for its services must be weighed against the savings from reduced float to determine whether this arrangement is cost-effective.
2. bank service that entails holding a customer's securities and, as agent, receiving and depositing income such as dividends on stock and interest on bonds.
3. box rented in a post office where mail is stored until collected.

LOCKED IN

1. unable to take advantage of preferential tax treatment on the sale of an asset because the required HOLDING PERIOD has not elapsed. *See also* CAPITAL GAIN.
2. commodities position in which the market has an up or down limit day, and investors cannot get in or out of the market.

3. said of a rate of return that has been assured for a length of time through an investment such as a certificate of deposit or a fixed rate bond; also said of profits or yields on securities or commodities that have been protected through HEDGING techniques.

LOCKED MARKET highly competitive market environment with identical bid and ask prices for a stock. The appearance of more buyers and sellers unlocks the market.

LOCK-UP OPTION privilege offered a WHITE KNIGHT (friendly acquirer) by a TARGET COMPANY of buying CROWN JEWELS or additional equity. The aim is to discourage a hostile TAKEOVER.

LONDON COMMODITY EXCHANGE (LCE) merged with the LONDON INTERNATIONAL FINANCIAL FUTURES & OPTIONS EXCHANGE (LIFFE) in September 1996.

LONDON INTERNATIONAL FINANCIAL FUTURES AND OPTIONS EXCHANGE (LIFFE) merged with the London Commodity Exchange in September 1996, adding futures and options on robust coffee, No. 7 cocoa, No. 5 white sugar, Baltic freight (Biffex), EU wheat, EU barley, and potatoes. The LCE conducts trade on its FAST electronic trading system from 9:30 A.M. to 5:30 P.M., Monday through Friday. LIFFE trades futures and options contracts on long-term and short-term interest rates, denominated in world currencies: three-month sterling (short sterling), three-month Eurodollar, three-month Euromark, three-month EuroSwiss franc (Euroswiss) and three-month Eurolira; three-month ECU and one-month Euromark futures; and long gilt futures and options. Bond trading includes German government bond (bund) futures and options, Italian government bond (BTP) futures and options, and Japanese government bond (JGB) futures. LIFFE trades futures and options on the FT-SE 100 Index and the FT-SE 250 Index, as well as equity options. Hours: 7:30 A.M. to 4:15 P.M., Monday through Friday. Short sterling, Euromarks, Euroswiss, Long Gilt, bund, BTP, and Bobl futures contracts are traded after hours on the exchange's Automated Pit Trading (APT) system, between 4:20 P.M. and 8 P.M.; the JGB trades from 7 A.M. to 4 P.M. The exchange has links with the TOKYO INTERNATIONAL FINANCIAL FUTURES EXCHANGE, the TOKYO STOCK EXCHANGE, the CHICAGO BOARD OF TRADE and the CHICAGO MERCANTILE EXCHANGE.

LONDON INTERBANK OFFERED RATE (LIBOR) rate that the most creditworthy international banks dealing in EURODOLLARS charge each other for large loans. The LIBOR rate is usually the base for other large Eurodollar loans to less creditworthy corporate and government borrowers. For instance, a Third World country may have to pay one point over LIBOR when it borrows money.

LONDON METAL EXCHANGE (LME) principal-to-principal market for base metals trading established in 1877. LME trades cash and 3-

month contracts on aluminum, copper, nickel, lead, zinc, tin and aluminum alloy. Traded options contracts are available against the underlying futures contracts. LME operates as a 24-hour market, with the majority of its business conducted outside of the twice-daily official floor trading sessions, or "rings." During the first ring, beginning at 11:45 A.M. Greenwich Mean Time (GMT), each contract trades in turn for five minutes; after a 10-minute break, the process is repeated. The second part of this session results in settlement and official prices, at or near 1:15 P.M. GMT. After official prices are announced, a period of trading called "the kerb" begins, usually lasting around 15 minutes, with all contracts trading simultaneously. The second ring, or the afternoon session, begins at 3:20 P.M. GMT, following the structure of the first ring and ending with a 25-minute kerb period from 4:35 P.M. to 5 P.M. GMT. LME prices are used as reference prices in many world markets by metals producers and fabricators of metal products. LME contracts assume an eventual delivery of physical metal on the prompt date, but this generally does not occur, since the majority of LME business is for trade hedging. Both floor and interoffice trading are covered by a matching system run by the London Clearing House Ltd., which acts as a central counterpart to trades executed between clearing members of the exchange.

LONDON STOCK EXCHANGE (LSE) originated as New Jonathan's Coffee House in 1773. In 1973, it joined the United Kingdom's six regional exchanges to form the Stock Exchange of Great Britain and Ireland. Regional trading floors ceased in the late '80s, and in 1995 after the Dublin Stock Exchange left the alliance, the exchange became known as the London Stock Exchange. Six regional offices operate in the UK. The FT-SE 100 Index (known as the *Footsie*), based on the 100 largest listed companies by market capitalization, is the dominant index; it is calculated on a minute-by-minute basis. The Eurotrack 100 Index tracks the top Continental European and Irish shares using real-time prices through the exchange's Stock Exchange Automatic Quotation (SEAQ) and SEAQ International systems; this index is calculated once a minute in Deutschemarks. Traders can act as both market makers and agents as long as they are member firms of the LSE. The exchange introduced two major electronic systems in August 1996: Sequence, the electronic equity trading system, and Crest, the electronic share settlement system. Settlement is done on a five-day rolling basis. Trading hours: Monday to Friday, 8:30 A.M. to 4:30 P.M.

LONG BOND in general, bond that matures in more than 10 years. Since these bonds commit investors' money for a long time, they normally pay investors a higher yield. In Wall Street parlance, the "long bond" is the 30-year Treasury.

LONG COUPON

   1. bond issue's first interest payment covering a longer period than the remaining payments, or the bond issue itself. Conventional schedules call for interest payments at six-month intervals. A long COUPON results when a bond is issued more than six months before the date of the first scheduled payment. *See also* SHORT COUPON.

2. interest-bearing bond maturing in more than 10 years.

LONG HEDGE

1. FUTURES CONTRACT bought to protect against a rise in the cost of honoring a future commitment. Also called a *buy hedge.* The hedger benefits from a narrowing of the BASIS (difference between cash price and future price) if the future is bought below the cash price, and from a widening of the basis if the future is bought above the cash price.

2. FUTURES CONTRACT or CALL OPTION bought in anticipation of a drop in interest rates, so as to lock in the present yield on a fixed-income security.

LONG LEG
part of an OPTION SPREAD representing a commitment to buy the underlying security. For instance, if a spread consists of a long CALL OPTION and a short PUT OPTION, the long call is the long LEG.

LONG POSITION

1. ownership of a security, giving the investor the right to transfer ownership to someone else by sale or by gift; the right to receive any income paid by the security; and the right to any profits or losses as the security's value changes.

2. investor's ownership of securities held by a brokerage firm.

LONG TERM

1. holding period of 12 months or longer and applicable in calculating the CAPITAL GAINS TAX.

2. investment approach to the stock market in which an investor seeks appreciation by holding a stock for 12 months or more.

3. bond with a maturity of 10 years or longer.

See also CAPITAL GAIN; LONG BOND; LONG-TERM DEBT; LONG-TERM FINANCING; LONG-TERM GAIN; LONG-TERM INVESTOR; LONG-TERM LOSS; SHORT TERM.

LONG-TERM DEBT
liability due in a year or more. Normally, interest is paid periodically over the term of the loan, and the principal amount is payable as notes or bonds mature. Also, a LONG BOND with a maturity of 10 years or more.

LONG-TERM DEBT RATIO
see DEBT-TO-EQUITY RATIO (2). *See also* RATIO ANALYSIS.

LONG-TERM FINANCING
liabilities not repayable in one year and all equity. *See also* LONG-TERM DEBT.

LONG-TERM GAIN
gain on the sale of a CAPITAL ASSET where the HOLDING PERIOD was 12 months or more and the profit was subject to the long-term CAPITAL GAINS TAX.

LONG-TERM GOALS financial goals that an individual sets for five years or longer. Some examples of long-term goals include assembling a retirement fund, saving for a down payment on a house or for college tuition, buying a second home, or starting a business.

LONG-TERM INVESTOR someone who invests in stocks, bonds, mutual funds or other investment vehicles for a long time, typically at least five years, in order to fund long-term goals. A long-term investor looks for solid investments with a good long-term track record, such as a BLUE CHIP stock or a mutual fund with exemplary performance. As long as the investor holds his investments for 12 months, he will pay preferential CAPITAL GAINS TAXES at a top 20% tax rate instead of paying higher regular income tax rates, which are due when assets are sold after having been held for less than 12 months.

LONG-TERM LIABILITIES any monies owed that are not payable on demand or within one year. The *current portion of long-term debt* is a current liability, as distinguished from a long-term liability.

LONG-TERM LOSS negative counterpart to LONG-TERM GAIN as defined by the same legislation. A long-term loss is realized when an asset held for more than 12 months is sold at a lower price than its adjusted purchase price. A CAPITAL LOSS can be used to offset a CAPITAL GAIN plus $3000 of ORDINARY INCOME except that short-term losses exceeding short-term gains must first be applied to long-term gains, if any.

LONG-TERM PLANNING financial planning to accomplish LONG-TERM GOALS. A long-term plan will project how much money will be needed to fund retirement, pay college tuition, or buy a house in five years or more by designing an investment strategy to meet that goal.

LOOPHOLE technicality making it possible to circumvent a law's intent without violating its letter. For instance, a TAX SHELTER may exploit a loophole in the tax law, or a bank may take advantage of a loophole in the GLASS STEAGALL ACT to acquire a DISCOUNT BROKER.

LOOSE CREDIT policy by the Federal Reserve Board to make loans less expensive and thus widely available in the economy. The Fed implements a loose credit policy by reducing interest rates through OPEN MARKET OPERATIONS by buying Treasury securities, which gives banks more funds they need to satisfy loan demand. The Fed initiates a loose credit policy when the economy is weak and inflation is low, in order to stimulate a faster pace of economic activity. Also called *easy money.* The opposite policy is called TIGHT MONEY, in which the Fed sells securities and makes it more difficult and expensive to borrow, and thereby hopes to slow down economic activity. Tight money policy is used to dampen inflation in an overheated economy.

LOSS opposite of PROFIT.

LOSS-CONTROL ACTIVITIES actions initiated by a company or individual at the urging of its insurance company to prevent accidents, losses or other insurance claims. For example, a home insurer may require smoke alarms. A commercial insurer may require certain safety procedures in a manufacturing plant.

LOSS LEADER concept, primarily in retailing, where an item is priced at a loss and widely advertised in order to draw trade into the store. The loss is considered a cost of promotion and is offset by the profits on other items sold. Concept is sometimes used by DISCOUNT BROKERS, who will advertise a particular transaction at a loss price to attract customers, who will enter into other transactions at a profit to the broker.

LOSS-OF-INCOME INSURANCE insurance coverage replacing income lost by a policyholder. For example, *business interruption insurance* will pay employee wages if a business is temporarily out of operation because of a fire, flood, or other disaster. *Disability insurance* will replace a portion of an insured disabled person's income while he or she is disabled due to injury or illness. *Worker's compensation insurance* will reimburse a worker who was injured on the job for lost wages during the disability period.

LOSS PREVENTION programs instituted by individuals or companies to prevent losses. Businesses implement safety programs to prevent workplace injuries. Individuals install fire detectors, burglar alarms, and other protective devices to prevent losses caused by fire and theft. Car owners install special locks to prevent auto theft. Insurance companies usually offer discounts to businesses or individuals taking loss prevention measures.

LOSS RATIO ratio of losses paid or accrued by an insurer to premiums earned, usually for a one-year period. *See also* BAD DEBT.

LOSS RESERVE *see* BAD DEBT.

LOT in a general business sense, a lot is any group of goods or services making up a transaction. *See also* ODD LOT; ROUND LOT.

LOW bottom price paid for a security over the past year or since trading in the security began; in the latter sense also called *historic low.*

LOW BALANCE METHOD interest computation method on savings accounts where interest is based on the lowest balance during the period.

LOW GRADE bond RATING of B or lower.

LOW-INCOME HOUSING LIMITED PARTNERSHIP limited partnership investment in housing complexes occupied by low- and moderate-income tenants paying rent that cannot exceed statutory limits. Such partnerships offer investors annual tax credits over a 10-year period that total approximately 130% to 150% of the amount invested.

Due to the restricted rents as required under the tax law, anticipated cash flow during the holding period is minimal. Properties can be sold after a 15-year holding period, which may return some or all of the original investment. The primary investment motivation for limited partners is a predictable stream of annual tax benefits. Limited partners use IRS Form 8586 to claim the credit.

LOW-LOAD FUND *see* LOAD FUND.

LUMP SUM large payment of money received at one time instead of in periodic payments. People retiring from or leaving a company may receive a lump-sum distribution of the value of their pension, salary reduction or profit-sharing plan. (Special tax rules apply to such lump-sum distributions unless the money is rolled into an IRA rollover account.) Some annuities, called *single premium deferred annuities* (SPDAs) require one upfront lump sum which is invested. Beneficiaries of life insurance policies may receive a death benefit in a lump sum. A consumer making a large purchase such as a car or boat may decide to pay in one lump sum instead of financing the purchase over time.

LUXURY TAX tax on goods considered nonessential. For example, in the early '90s a 10% luxury tax was imposed on purchases of cars selling for $30,000 or more, airplanes, boats, furs and expensive jewelry. The result of the tax, however, was that purchases of these items dropped sharply, harming the producers and retailers of these goods severely. That luxury tax was repealed in the REVENUE RECONCILIATION ACT OF 1993.

M

MA BELL nickname for AT&T Corporation. Before the Bell System was broken up in 1984, AT&T controlled both local and long distance telephone service in the United States. After the breakup, local phone service was performed by the seven regional phone companies and AT&T concentrated on long distance, telecommunications research, equipment and computer manufacturing. Even though it no longer enjoys the monopoly it once had, people still refer to AT&T as Ma Bell. The stock is also a component of the Dow Jones Industrial Average, and is one of the most widely held and actively traded stocks on the New York Stock Exchange.

MACARONI DEFENSE defensive tactic used by a corporation trying to defeat a TAKEOVER attempt by a RAIDER or unfriendly bidder. The target corporation will issue a massive amount of bonds that must be redeemed at a mandatory higher redemption value if the company is taken over. The redemption value of these bonds therefore expands when the company is threatened—like macaroni when it is cooked—making the takeover prohibitively expensive to complete.

MACD *see* MOVING AVERAGE CONVERGENCE/DIVERGENCE.

MACROECONOMICS analysis of a nation's economy as a whole, using such aggregate data as price levels, unemployment, inflation, and industrial production. *See also* MICROECONOMICS.

MADRID STOCK EXCHANGE (BOLSA DE MADRID) largest and most international of Spain's four stock exchanges. More than 90% of trading is through the Spanish Stock Market Interconnection System (SIBE), linking the other exchanges in Barcelona, Bilbao, and Valencia. All fixed-income securities are traded through the on-line, fixed income electronic system. Using SIBE, data can be displayed simultaneously on 72 different shares; trading can occur in any of the shares without interrupting the information flow. The Madrid Stock Exchange General Index is made up of 110 stocks and represents more than 90% of total market capitalization, excluding foreign stocks. Banks, utilities, and communications firms account for 70% of the index's capitalization. Settlement is three business days after the trade date. Trading on the continuous market owned by the four exchanges is Monday to Friday, from 10 A.M. to 5 P.M., with pre-opening trading from 9:30 A.M. to 10 A.M.

MACRS *see* MODIFIED ACCELERATED COST RECOVERY SYSTEM (MACRS).

MAINTENANCE BOND a bond that guarantees against defects in workmanship or materials for a specified period following completion of a contract.

MAINTENANCE CALL call for additional money or securities when a brokerage customer's margin account equity falls below the requirements of the National Association of Securities Dealers (NASD), of the exchanges, or of the brokerage firm. Unless the account is brought up to the levels complying with equity maintenance rules, some of the client's securities may be sold to remedy the deficiency. *See also* MAINTENANCE REQUIREMENT; MINIMUM MAINTENANCE; SELL OUT.

MAINTENANCE FEE annual charge to maintain certain types of brokerage accounts. Such a fee may be attached to an ASSET MANAGEMENT ACCOUNT, which combines securities and money market accounts. Banks and brokers may also charge a maintenance fee for an INDIVIDUAL RETIREMENT ACCOUNT (IRA).

MAINTENANCE REQUIREMENT *see* MINIMUM MAINTENANCE.

MAJORITY SHAREHOLDER one of the shareholders who together control more than half the outstanding shares of a corporation. If the ownership is widely scattered and there are no majority shareholders, effective control may be gained with far less than 51% of the outstanding shares. *See also* WORKING CONTROL.

MAKE A MARKET maintain firm bid and offer prices in a given security by standing ready to buy or sell ROUND LOTS at publicly quoted prices. The dealer is called a *market maker* in the over-the-counter market and a SPECIALIST on the exchanges. A dealer who makes a market over a long period is said to *maintain* a market. See *also* REGISTERED COMPETITIVE MARKET MAKER.

MAKE A PRICE *see* MAKE A MARKET.

MALAYSIA COMMODITY EXCHANGE trades interest rate futures on the 3-month KIBOR (Kuala Lumpur Interbank Offered Rate). The exchange is a subsidiary of the KUALA LUMPUR COMMODITY EXCHANGE.

MALONEY ACT legislation, also called the Maloney Amendment, enacted in 1938 to amend the SECURITIES EXCHANGE ACT OF 1934 by adding Section 15A, which provides for the regulation of the OVER-THE-COUNTER market (OTC) through national securities associations registered with the Securities and Exchange Commission. *See also* NATIONAL ASSOCIATION OF SECURITIES DEALERS (NASD).

MANAGED ACCOUNT investment account consisting of money that one or more clients entrust to a manager, who decides when and where to invest it. Such an account may be handled by a bank trust department or by an investment advisory firm. Clients are charged a MANAGEMENT FEE And share in proportion to their participation in any losses and gains.

MANAGEMENT combined fields of policy and administration and the people who provide the decisions and supervision necessary to implement the owners' business objectives and achieve stability and growth.

The formulation of policy requires analysis of all factors having an effect on short- and long-term profits. The administration of policies is carried out by the CHIEF EXECUTIVE OFFICER, his or her immediate staff, and everybody else who possesses authority delegated by people with supervisory responsibility. Thus the size of management can range from one person in a small organization to multilayered management hierarchies in large, complex organizations. The top members of management, called senior management, report to the owners of a firm; in large corporations, the CHAIRMAN OF THE BOARD, the PRESIDENT, and sometimes other key senior officers report to the BOARD OF DIRECTORS, comprising elected representatives of the owning stockholders. The application of scientific principles to decision-making is called management science. *See also* ORGANIZATION CHART.

MANAGEMENT BUYIN purchase of a large, and often controlling, interest in a company by an outside investor group that chooses to retain existing management. In many cases, the outside investors are venture capitalists who believe the company's products, services, and management have bright prospects. The investor group will usually place its representatives on the company's board of directors to monitor the progress of the company.

MANAGEMENT BUYOUT purchase of all of a company's publicly held shares by the existing management, which takes the company private. Usually, management will have to pay a premium over the current market price to entice public shareholders to go along with the deal. If management has to borrow heavily to finance the transaction, it is called a LEVERAGED BUYOUT (LBO). Managers may want to buy their company for several reasons: They want to avoid being taken over by a raider who would bring in new management; they no longer want the scrutiny that comes with running a public company; or they believe they can make more money for themselves in the long run by owning a larger share of the company, and eventually reap substantial profits by going public again with a REVERSE LEVERAGED BUYOUT.

MANAGEMENT COMPANY same as INVESTMENT COMPANY.

MANAGEMENT FEE charge against investor assets for managing the portfolio of an open- or closed-end MUTUAL FUND as well as for such services as shareholder relations or administration. The fee, as disclosed in the PROSPECTUS, is a fixed percentage of the fund's net asset value, typically between 0.5% and 2% per year. The fee also applies to a MANAGED ACCOUNT. The management fee is deducted automatically from a shareholder's assets once a year.

MANAGING UNDERWRITER leading—and originating—investment banking firm of an UNDERWRITING GROUP organized for the purchase and distribution of a new issue of securities. The AGREEMENT AMONG UNDERWRITERS authorizes the managing underwriter, or syndicate manager, to act as agent for the group in purchasing, carrying, and distributing the issue as well as complying with all federal and state requirements; to form the selling group; to determine the allocation of securities to each member; to make sales to the selling group at a specified discount—or CONCESSION—from the public offering price; to engage in open market transactions during the underwriting period to stabilize the market price of the security; and to borrow for the syndicate account to cover costs. *See also* FLOTATION COST; INVESTMENT BANKER; UNDERWRITE.

MANDATORY CONVERTIBLES debt-equity hybrids that became popular in the 1980s to meet the strong demand by banks for the raising of capital. One type, *equity contract notes,* is exchangeable at maturity for common stock having a market value equal to the principal amount of the notes. If the holder of the notes does not choose to receive equities at maturity, the issuer will sell the equity on behalf of the holder. Another type, *equity commitment notes,* does not require the holder to purchase equity with the notes but rather commits the issuer to redeem the notes with the proceeds of an equity issue at some future date. The Federal Reserve requires issuers to fund a third of the equity in the first four years, another third in the second four years, and the balance by maturity in the third four years. CAPS are still another form of mandatory convertible.

MANIPULATION buying or selling a security to create a false appearance of active trading and thus influence other investors to buy or sell shares. This may be done by one person or by a group acting in concert. Those found guilty of manipulation are subject to criminal and civil penalties. *See also* MINI-MANIPULATION.

MAPLE LEAF bullion coin minted by the government of Canada in gold (99.99% pure), silver (99.99% pure) and platinum (99.95% pure). The gold and platinum coins are available in one ounce, one-half ounce, one-quarter ounce, one-tenth ounce, one-fifteenth ounce and one-twentieth ounce sizes. The silver coin is available only in the one-ounce size. The Maple Leaf is actively traded throughout the world along with the American Eagle, South African Kruggerand, and other coins. The Maple Leaf usually sells at a slight premium to the bullion value of the coin. *See also* GOLD COIN.

MARGIN
In general: amount a customer deposits with a broker when borrowing from the broker to buy securities. Under Federal Reserve Board regulation, the initial margin required since 1945 has ranged from 50 to 100 percent of the security's purchase price. In the mid-1990s the minimum was 50% of the purchase or short sale price, in cash or eligible securities, with a minimum of $2000. Thereafter, MINIMUM MAINTENANCE requirements are imposed by the National Association of Securities Dealers (NASD) and the New York Stock Exchange, and by the individual brokerage firm, whose requirement is typically higher.

Banking: difference between the current market value of collateral backing a loan and the face value of the loan. For instance, if a $100,000 loan is backed by $50,000 in collateral, the margin is $50,000.

Corporate finance: difference between the price received by a company for its products and services and the cost of producing them. Also known as *gross profit margin.*

Futures trading: good-faith deposit an investor must put up when buying or selling a contract. If the futures price moves adversely, the investor must put up more money to meet margin requirements.

MARGINABLE SECURITIES see MARGIN SECURITY.

MARGIN ACCOUNT brokerage account allowing customers to buy securities with money borrowed from the broker. Margin accounts are governed by REGULATION T, by the National Association of Securities Dealers (NASD), by the New York Stock Exchange, and by individual brokerage house rules. Margin requirements can be met with cash or with eligible securities. In the case of securities sold short, an equal amount of the same securities is normally borrowed without interest from another broker to cover the sale, while the proceeds are kept in escrow as collateral for the lending broker. *See also* MINIMUM MAINTENANCE.

MARGIN AGREEMENT document that spells out the rules governing a MARGIN ACCOUNT, including the HYPOTHECATION of securities, how much equity the customer must keep in the account, and the interest rate on margin loans. Also known as *hypothecation agreement.*

MARGINAL COST increase or decrease in the total costs of a business firm as the result of one more or one less unit of output. Also called *incremental cost* or *differential cost.* Determining marginal cost is important in deciding whether or not to vary a rate of production. In most manufacturing firms, marginal costs decrease as the volume of output increases due to economies of scale, which include factors such as bulk discounts on raw materials, specialization of labor, and more efficient use of machinery. At some point, however, diseconomies of scale enter in and marginal costs begin to rise; diseconomies include factors like more intense managerial supervision to control a larger work force, higher raw materials costs because local supplies have been exhausted, and generally less efficient input. The marginal cost curve is typically U-shaped on a graph.

A firm is operating at optimum output when marginal cost coincides with average total unit cost. Thus, at less than optimum output, an increase in the rate of production will result in a marginal unit cost lower than average total unit cost; production in excess of the optimum point will result in marginal cost higher than average total unit cost. In other words, a sale at a price higher than marginal unit cost will increase the net profit of the manufacturer even though the sales price does not cover average total unit cost; marginal cost is thus the lowest amount at which a sale can be made without adding to the producer's loss or subtracting from his profits.

MARGINAL COST

MARGINAL EFFICIENCY OF CAPITAL annual percentage yield earned by the last additional unit of capital. It is also known as *marginal productivity of capital, natural interest rate, net capital productivity,* and *rate of return over cost.* The significance of the concept to a business firm is that it represents the market rate of interest at which it begins to pay to undertake a capital investment. If the market rate is 10%, for example, it would not pay to undertake a project that has a return of 9½%, but any return over 10% would be acceptable. In a larger economic sense, marginal efficiency of capital influences long-term interest rates. This occurs because of the law of diminishing returns as it applies to the yield on capital. As the highest yielding projects are exhausted, available capital moves into lower yielding projects and interest rates decline. As market rates fall, investors are able to justify projects that were previously uneconomical. This process is called *diminishing marginal productivity* or *declining marginal efficiency of capital.*

MARGINAL REVENUE change in total revenue caused by one additional unit of output. It is calculated by determining the difference between the total revenues produced before and after a one-unit increase in the rate of production. As long as the price of a product is constant, price and marginal revenue are the same; for example, if baseball bats are being sold at a constant price of $10 apiece, a one-unit increase in sales (one baseball bat) translates into an increase in total revenue of $10. But it is often the case that additional output can be sold only if the price is reduced, and that leads to a consideration of

MARGINAL COST—the added cost of producing one more unit. Further production is not advisable when marginal cost exceeds marginal revenue since to do so would result in a loss. Conversely, whenever marginal revenue exceeds marginal cost, it is advisable to produce an additional unit. Profits are maximized at the rate of output where marginal revenue equals marginal cost.

MARGINAL TAX RATE amount of tax imposed on an additional dollar of income. In the U.S. progressive income tax system, the marginal tax rate increases as income rises. Economists believing in SUPPLY-SIDE ECONOMICS hold that this reduces the incentive to be productive and discourages business investment. In urging that marginal tax rates be cut for individuals and businesses, they argue that the resulting increased work effort and business investment would reduce STAGFLATION. *See also* FLAT TAX.

MARGINAL UTILITY in economics, the addition to total satisfaction from goods or services (called *utility*) that is derived from consuming one more unit of that good or service.

MARGIN CALL demand that a customer deposit enough money or securities to bring a margin account up to the INITIAL MARGIN or MINIMUM MAINTENANCE requirements. If a customer fails to respond, securities in the account may be liquidated. *See also* FIVE HUNDRED DOLLAR RULE; SELL OUT.

MARGIN DEPARTMENT section within a brokerage firm that monitors customer compliance with margin regulations, keeping track of debits and credits, short sales, and purchases of stock on margin, and all other extensions of credit by the broker. Also known as the *credit department. See also* MARK TO THE MARKET.

MARGIN OF PROFIT relationship of gross profits to net sales. Returns and allowances are subtracted from gross sales to arrive at net sales. Cost of goods sold (sometimes including depreciation) is subtracted from net sales to arrive at gross profit. Gross profit is divided by net sales to get the profit margin, which is sometimes called the *gross margin.* The result is a ratio, and the term is also written as *margin of profit ratio.*

The term profit margin is less frequently used to mean the *net margin,* obtained by deducting operating expenses in addition to cost of goods sold and dividing the result by net sales. Operating expenses are usually shown on profit and loss statements as "selling, general and administrative (SG&A) expenses."

Both gross and net profit margins, when compared with prior periods and with industry statistics, can be revealing in terms of a firm's operating efficiency and pricing policies and its ability to compete successfully with other companies in its field.

MARGIN REQUIREMENT minimum amount that a client must deposit in the form of cash or eligible securities in a margin account as spelled out in REGULATION T of the Federal Reserve Board. Reg T requires a minimum of $2000 or 50% of the purchase price of eligible securities bought on margin or 50% of the proceeds of short sales. Also called INITIAL MARGIN. *See also* MARGIN; MARGIN SECURITY; MINIMUM MAINTENANCE; SELLING SHORT.

MARGIN SECURITY security that may be bought or sold in a margin account. REGULATION T defines margin securities as (1) any *registered security* (a LISTED SECURITY or a security having UNLISTED TRADING privileges); (2) any *OTC margin stock* or *OTC margin bond,* which are defined as any UNLISTED SECURITY that the Federal Reserve Board (FRB) periodically identifies as having the investor interest, marketability, disclosure, and solid financial position of a listed security; (3) any OTC security designated as qualified for trading in the NATIONAL MARKET SYSTEM under a plan approved by the Securities and Exchange Commission; (4) any mutual fund or unit investment trust registered under the Investment Company Act of 1940. Other securities that are not EXEMPT SECURITIES must be transacted in cash.

MARITAL DEDUCTION provision in the federal estate and gift tax law allowing spouses to transfer unlimited amounts of property to each other free of tax. Such transfers may be made during the life or at the death of the transferor, and are intended to treat a couple as an economic unit for transfer tax purposes. Although the deduction is unlimited, passing all assets to a spouse may create transfer tax problems in the surviving spouse's estate; planners should try to fully use each spouse's UNIFIED CREDIT, which offsets up to $625,000 in transfers in 1998, and equalize the rate of transfer taxes for both spouses to reduce taxes for the couple. According to the TAXPAYER RELIEF ACT OF 1997, the amount of assets that each person can exclude from federal estate taxes is $625,000 in 1998, rising to $1 million in 2006 and later years. This limit rises to $650,000 in 1999; $675,000 in 2000 and 2001; $700,000 in 2002 and 2003; $850,000 in 2004; $950,000 in 2005; and $1 million in 2006.

MARKDOWN
1. amount subtracted from the selling price, when a customer sells securities to a dealer in the OVER THE COUNTER market. Had the securities been purchased from the dealer, the customer would have paid a *markup,* or an amount added to the purchase price. The National Association of Securities Dealers (NASD) RULES OF FAIR PRACTICE established 5% as a reasonable guideline in markups and markdowns, though many factors enter into the question of fairness, and exceptions are common.
2. reduction in the price at which the underwriters offer municipal bonds after the market has shown a lack of interest at the original price.
3. downward adjustment of the value of securities by banks and investment firms, based on a decline in market quotations.

4. reduction in the original retail selling price, which was determined by adding a percentage factor, called a markon, to the cost of the merchandise. Anything added to the markon is called a markup, and the term markdown does not apply unless the price is dropped below the original selling price.

MARKET

1. public place where products or services are bought and sold, directly or through intermediaries. Also called *marketplace.*
2. aggregate of people with the present or potential ability and desire to purchase a product or service; equivalent to demand.
3. securities markets in the aggregate, or the New York Stock Exchange in particular.
4. short for *market value,* the value of an asset based on the price it would command on the open market, usually as determined by the MARKET PRICE at which similar assets have recently been bought and sold.
5. as a verb, to sell. *See also* MARKETING.

MARKETABILITY speed and ease with which a particular security may be bought and sold. A stock that has a large amount of shares outstanding and is actively traded is highly marketable and also liquid. In common use, marketability is interchangeable with LIQUIDITY, but liquidity implies the preservation of value when a security is bought or sold.

MARKETABLE SECURITIES securities that are easily sold. On a corporation's balance sheet, they are assets that can be readily converted into cash—for example, government securities, banker's acceptances, and commercial paper. In keeping with conservative accounting practice, these are carried at cost or market value, whichever is lower.

MARKETABLE TITLE title to a piece of real estate that is reasonably free from risk of litigation over possible defects, and while it may not be perfect, it is free from plausible or reasonable objections, and is one that a court of law would order the buyer to accept. A seller under a contract of sale is required to deliver marketable title at final closing; this requirement is implicit in law and does not need to be stated in the contract. Usually the property buyer will engage a title insurance company to ensure that the seller has CLEAR TITLE to the real estate before entering into a purchase contract. This search generally is not ordered until financing has been secured. Once the title company has researched the history of ownership of the property and feels sure that the seller owns it, it will issue a title insurance policy. The seller is thus assured that he has a marketable title, which allows him to transfer ownership to the buyer. *See also* BAD TITLE; CLOUD ON TITLE.

MARKET ANALYSIS

1. research aimed at predicting or anticipating the direction of stock, bond, or commodity markets, based on technical data about the

movement of market prices or on fundamental data such as corporate earnings prospects or supply and demand.

2. study designed to define a company's markets, forecast their directions, and decide how to expand the company's share and exploit any new trends.

MARKET BASKET *see* BASKET.

MARKET BREAK any sudden drop (BREAK) in the stock market as measured by STOCK INDEXES AND AVERAGES. In SEC parlance, BLACK MONDAY, when the Dow Jones Industrial Average dropped 508 points.

MARKET BREADTH *see* BREADTH OF THE MARKET.

MARKET CAPITALIZATION value of a corporation as determined by the market price of its issued and outstanding common stock. It is calculated by multiplying the number of outstanding shares by the current market price of a share. Institutional investors often use market capitalization as one investment criterion, requiring, for example, that a company have a market capitalization of $100 million or more to qualify as an investment. Analysts look at market capitalization in relation to book, or accounting, value for an indication of how investors value a company's future prospects.

MARKET EYE financial information service that emanates from the British Broadcasting Company under the sponsorship of the INTERNATIONAL STOCK EXCHANGE OF THE UK AND THE REPUBLIC OF IRELAND (ISE). Market Eye supplies current market information plus statistical information on particular equity and debt issues and is a supplement to the Stock Exchange Automated Quotations System (SEAQ), which records trades.

MARKET IF TOUCHED ORDER (MIT) order to buy or sell a security or commodity as soon as a preset market price is reached, at which point it becomes a MARKET ORDER. When corn is selling for $4.75 a bushel, someone might enter a market if touched order to buy at $4.50. As soon as the price is dropped to $4.50, the contract would be bought on the customer's behalf at whatever market price prevails when the order is executed.

MARKET INDEX numbers representing weighted values of the components that make up the index. A stock market index, for example, is weighted according to the prices and number of outstanding shares of the various stocks. The Standard & Poor's 500 Stock Index is one of the most widely followed, but myriad other indexes track stocks in various industry groups.

MARKETING moving goods and services from the provider to consumer. This involves product origination and design, development, distribution, advertising, promotion, and publicity as well as market analysis to define the appropriate market.

MARKET OPENING the start of formal trading on an exchange, usually referring to the New York Stock Exchange (NYSE) and marked by an opening bell. All stocks do not necessarily open trading at the bell, since there may be order imbalances causing a DELAYED OPENING. *See also* OPD; OPENING.

MARKET JITTERS state of widespread fear among investors, which may cause them to sell stocks and bonds, pushing prices downward. Investors may fear lower corporate earnings, negative economic news, tightening of credit by the Federal Reserve, foreign currency fluctations, or many other factors. In some cases, news may be good, but is interpreted as bad because investors are so fearful. For example, investors may think that positive economic or corporate earnings news is putting more pressure on the Federal Reserve to raise interest rates, which would hurt stock and bond prices.

MARKET LETTER newsletter provided to brokerage firm customers or written by an independent market analyst, registered as an investment adviser with the Securities and Exchange Commission, who sells the letter to subscribers. These letters assess the trends in interest rates, the economy, and the market in general. Brokerage letters typically reiterate the recommendations of their own research departments. Independent letters take on the personality of their writers—concentrating on growth stocks, for example, or basing their recommendations on technical analysis. A HULBERT RATING is an evaluation of such a letter's performance.

MARKET MAKER *see* MAKE A MARKET.

MARKET-ON-CLOSE (MOC) ORDER order to buy or sell stocks or futures and options contracts as near as possible to when the market closes for the day. Such an order may be a LIMIT ORDER which had not yet been executed during the trading day.

MARKET ORDER order to buy or sell a security at the best available price. Most orders executed on the exchanges are market orders.

MARKET OUT CLAUSE escape clause sometimes written into FIRM COMMITMENT underwriting agreements which essentially allows the underwriters to be released from their purchase commitment if material adverse developments affect the securities markets generally. It is not common practice for the larger investment banking houses to write "outs" into their agreements, since the value of their commitment is a matter of paramount concern. *See also* UNDERWRITE.

MARKET PERFORMANCE COMMITTEE (MPC) New York Stock Exchange (NYSE) SPECIALIST oversight group consisting of members and ALLIED MEMBERS. MOC monitors specialists' effectiveness in maintaining fair prices and orderly markets and is authorized to assign or reassign new or existing issues to specialist units based on their capability.

MARKETPLACE *see* MARKET.

MARKET PRICE last reported price at which a security was sold on an exchange. For stocks or bonds sold OVER THE COUNTER, the combined bid and offer prices available at any particular time from those making a market in the stock. For an inactively traded security, evaluators or other analysts may determine a market price if needed—to settle an estate, for example.

In the general business world, market price refers to the price agreed upon by buyers and sellers of a product or service, as determined by supply and demand.

MARKET RESEARCH exploration of the size, characteristics, and potential of a market to find out, before developing any new product or service, what people want and need. Market research is an early step in marketing—which stretches from the original conception of a product to its ultimate delivery to the consumer.

In the stock market, market research refers to TECHNICAL ANALYSIS of factors such as volume, price advances and declines, and market breadth, which analysts use to predict the direction of prices.

MARKET RISK *see* SYSTEMATIC RISK.

MARKET SHARE percentage of industry sales of a particular company or product.

MARKET SWEEP second offer to institutional investors, made following a public TENDER OFFER, aimed at increasing the buyer's position from a significant interest to a controlling interest. The second offering is usually at a slightly higher price than the original tender offer.

MARKET TIMING decisions on when to buy or sell securities, in light of economic factors such as the strength of the economy and the direction of interest rates, or technical indications such as the direction of stock prices and the volume of trading. Investors in mutual funds may implement their market timing decisions by switching from a stock fund to a bond fund to a money market fund and back again, as the market outlook changes.

MARKET TONE general health and vigor of a securities market. The market tone is good when dealers and market makers are trading actively on narrow bid and offer spreads; it is bad when trading is inactive and bid and offer spreads are wide.

MARKET VALUE
In general: market price—the price at which buyers and sellers trade similar items in an open marketplace. In the absence of a market price, it is the estimated highest price a buyer would be warranted in paying and a seller justified in accepting, provided both parties were fully informed and acted intelligently and voluntarily.

Investments: current market price of a security—as indicated by the latest trade recorded.

Accounting: technical definition used in valuing inventory or marketable securities in accordance with the conservative accounting principle of "lower of cost or market." While cost is simply acquisition cost, market value is estimated net selling price less estimated costs of carrying, selling, and delivery, and, in the case of an unfinished product, the costs to complete production. The market value arrived at this way cannot, however, be lower than the cost at which a normal profit can be made.

MARKET VALUE-WEIGHTED INDEX index whose components are weighted according to the total market value of their outstanding shares. Also called *capitalization-weighted index.* The impact of a component's price change is proportional to the issue's overall market value, which is the share price times the number of shares outstanding. For example, the AMEX Market Value Index (AMVI) has more than 800 component stocks. The weighting of each stock constantly shifts with changes in the stock's price and the number of shares outstanding. The index fluctuates in line with the price moves of the stocks.

MARKING UP OR DOWN increasing or decreasing the price of a security based on supply and demand forces. A securities dealer may mark up the price of a stock or bond if prices are rising, and may be forced to mark it down if demand is declining. The markup is the difference, or spread, between the price the dealer paid for the security and the price at which he sells it to the retail customer. *See also* MARKDOWN.

MARK TO THE MARKET
1. adjust the valuation of a security or portfolio to reflect current market values. For example, MARGIN ACCOUNTS are marked to the market to ensure compliance with maintenance requirements. OPTION and FUTURES CONTACTS are marked to the market at year end with PAPER PROFIT OR LOSS recognized for tax purposes.
2. in a MUTUAL FUND, the daily net asset value reported to shareholders is the result of marking the fund's current portfolio to current market prices.

MARKUP *see* MARKDOWN.

MARRIAGE PENALTY effect of a tax code that makes a married couple pay more than the same two people would pay if unmarried and filing singly. For example, the REVENUE RECONCILIATION ACT OF 1993 may penalize low-end taxpayers whose combined income disqualifies them for the EARNED INCOME CREDIT they would have received as single taxpayers. High-end married taxpayers, on the other hand, may find that, combined, their incomes become subject to the SURTAX on incomes over $250,000.

MARRIED PUT option to sell a certain number of securities at a particular price by a specified time, bought simultaneously with securities of the underlying company so as to hedge the price paid for the securities. *See also* OPTION; PUT OPTION.

MASTER LIMITED PARTNERSHIP (MLP) public LIMITED PARTNER-SHIP composed of corporate assets spun off *(roll out)* or private limited partnerships *(roll up)* with income, capital gains, and/or TAX SHELTER orientations. Interests are represented by depositary receipts traded in the SECONDARY MARKET. Investors thus enjoy LIQUIDITY. Flow-through tax benefits, previously possible within PASSIVE income restrictions, were limited by tax legislation passed in 1987 that would treat most MLPs as corporations after a GRANDFATHER CLAUSE expired in 1998.

MATCHED AND LOST report of the results of flipping a coin by two securities brokers locked in competition to execute equal trades.

MATCHED BOOK term used for the accounts of securities dealers when their borrowing costs are equal to the interest earned on loans to customers and other brokers.

MATCHED MATURITIES coordination of the maturities of a financial institution's assets (such as loans) and liabilities (such as certificates of deposit and money-market accounts). For instance, a savings and loan might issue 10-year mortgages at 10%, funded with money received for 10-year CDs at 7% yields. The bank is thus positioned to make a three-percentage-point profit for 10 years. If a bank granted 20-year mortgages at a fixed 10%, on the other hand, using short-term funds from money-market accounts paying 7%, the bank would be vulnerable to a rapid rise in interest rates. If yields on the money-market accounts surged to 14%, the bank could lose a large amount of money, since it was earning only 10% from its assets. Such a situation, called a *maturity mismatch,* can cause tremendous problems for financial institutions if it persists, as it did in the early 1980s.

MATCHED ORDERS
1. illegal manipulative technique of offsetting buy and sell orders to create the impression of activity in a security, thereby causing upward price movement that benefits the participants in the scheme.
2. action by a SPECIALIST to create an opening price reasonably close to the previous close. When an accumulation of one kind of order—either buy or sell—causes a delay in the opening of trading on an exchange, the specialist tries to find counterbalancing orders or trades long or short from his own inventory in order to narrow the spread.

MATCHED SALE PURCHASE TRANSACTION FEDERAL OPEN MAR-KET COMMITTEE procedure whereby the Federal Reserve Bank of New York sells government securities to a nonbank dealer against payment in FEDERAL FUNDS. The agreement requires the dealer to sell the securities back by a specified date, which ranges from one to 15 days. The Fed pays the dealer a rate of interest equal to the discount rate. These transactions, also called reverse repurchase agreements, decrease the money supply for temporary periods by reducing dealer's bank balances and thus excess reserves. The Fed is thus able to adjust an abnormal monetary expansion due to seasonal or other factors. *See also* REPURCHASE AGREEMENT.

MATERIALITY characteristic of an event or information that is sufficiently important (or *material*) to have a large impact on a company's stock price. For example, if a company was about to report its earnings, or make a takeover bid for another company, that would be considered material information. Material information is information the reasonable investor needs to make an informed decision about an investment.

MATIF SA France's futures exchange, formally known as Marche a Terme International de France. MATIF uses a combination of open outcry (9 A.M. to 4:30 P.M.) and after-hours trading. MATIF participates in the French NCS electronic trading system developed by SB-Paris Bourse. MATIF also is linked with the CHICAGO MERCANTILE EXCHANGE so that its long-term interest rate products can be traded in Chicago. MATIF trades futures and options in the notional bond, ECU bond, three-month PIBOR (Paris Interbank Offered Rate) and white sugar; CAC 40 INDEX futures; potato, rapeseed and milling wheat futures; and currency options.

MATRIX TRADING bond swapping whereby traders seek to take advantage of temporary aberrations in YIELD SPREAD differentials between bonds of the same class but with different ratings or between bonds of different classes.

MATURE ECONOMY economy of a nation whose population has stabilized or is declining, and whose economic growth is no longer robust. Such an economy is characterized by a decrease in spending on roads or factories and a relative increase in consumer spending. Many of Western Europe's economies are considerably more mature than that of the United States and in marked contrast to the faster-growing economies of the Far East.

MATURITY
1. reaching the date at which a debt instrument is due and payable. A bond due to mature on January 1, 2010, will return the bondholder's principal and final interest payment when it reaches maturity on that date. Bond yields are frequently calculated on a YIELD-TO-MATURITY basis.
2. when referring to a company or economy, *maturity* means that it is well-established, and has little room for dynamic growth. For example, economists will say that an aging industrial economy has reached maturity. Or stock analysts will refer to a company's market as mature, meaning that demand for the company's products is stagnant.

MATURITY DATE
1. date on which the principal amount of a note, draft, acceptance bond, or other debt instrument becomes due and payable. Also

termination or due date on which an installment loan must be paid in full.

2. in FACTORING, average due date of factored receivables, when the factor remits to the seller for receivables sold each month.

MATURITY MATCHING *see* DURATION *(immunization).*

MAXIMUM CAPITAL GAINS MUTUAL FUND fund whose objective is to produce large capital gains for its shareholders. During a bull market it is likely to rise much faster than the general market or conservative mutual funds. But in a falling market, it is likely to drop much farther than the market averages. This increased volatility results from a policy of investing in small, fast-growing companies whose stocks characteristically are more volatile than those of large, well-established companies.

MAY DAY May 1, 1975, when fixed minimum brokerage commissions ended in the United States. Instead of a mandated rate to execute exchange trades, brokers were allowed to charge whatever they chose. The May Day changes ushered in the era of discount brokerage firms that execute buy and sell orders for low commissions, but give no investment advice. The end of fixed commissions also marked the beginning of diversification by the brokerage industry into a wide range of financial services utilizing computer technology and advanced communications systems.

McCARRAN-FERGUSON ACT OF 1945 federal law in which Congress declared that the states will continue to regulate the insurance business. As a result, insurers are granted a limited exemption to federal antitrust legislation.

MEALS AND ENTERTAINMENT EXPENSE expense for meals and entertainment that qualifies for a tax deduction. Under current tax law, employers may deduct 50% of meals and entertainment expenses that have a bona fide business purpose. For example, a business meal must include a discussion producing a direct business benefit.

MEAN RETURN in security analysis, expected value, or mean, of all the likely returns of investments comprising a portfolio; in capital budgeting, mean value of the probability distribution of possible returns. The portfolio approach to the analysis of investments aims at quantifying the relationship between risk and return. It assumes that while investors have different risk-value preferences, rational investors will always seek the maximum rate of return for every level of acceptable risk. It is the mean, or expected, return that an investor attempts to maximize at each level of risk. Also called *expected return. See also* CAPITAL ASSET PRICING MODEL, EFFICIENT PORTFOLIO, PORTFOLIO THEORY.

MECHANIC'S LIEN LIEN against buildings or other structures, allowed by some states to contractors, laborers, and suppliers of materials used in their construction or repair. The lien remains in effect until these people have been paid in full and may, in the event of a liquidation before they have been paid, give them priority over other creditors.

MEDIAN midway value between two points. There are an equal number of points above and below the median. For example, the number 5 is the median between the numbers 1 and 9, since there are 4 numbers above and below 5 in this sequence. Several important economic numbers use medians, including median household income and median home price.

MEDIUM-TERM BOND bond with a maturity of 2 to 10 years. *See also* INTERMEDIATE TERM; LONG TERM; SHORT TERM.

MEFF RENTA FIJA Spain's screen-based derivatives exchange in Barcelona, listing futures and options on fixed-interest securities and on interest rates, including the 90-day MIBOR (Madrid Interbank Offered Rate) and 1-year MIBOR; and 3-year and 10-year government bond futures and options contracts. Trading hours: 9 A.M. to 5:15 P.M., Monday through Friday.

MEFF RENTA VARIABLE Spain's screen-based stock index and equity derivatives market, located in Madrid, trading futures and options on the Iberian Exchange (IBEX)-35 Index and on individual stocks: Fecsa, Iberdrola, Endesa, Telefonica, Repsol, Union Fenosa, Autopistas C.E.S.A., Argentaria, Banco Santander, Sevillana and BBV. The IBEX-35 is the official index of the continuous market of the Spanish Sociedad de Bolsas, owned by the four exchanges. It is composed of the 35 most liquid stocks on the SIBE electronic trading system. Trading hours: 10 A.M. to 5:15 P.M., Monday through Friday.

MELLO ROOS FINANCING financing of real estate developments in California authorized by legislation in 1982 sponsored by Henry Mello and Mike Roos of the California legislature. The bill allowed municipalities to float bonds to be repaid from the proceeds of tax revenues generated by real estate sales. The bonds financed construction of a community's infrastructure, such as sewers, roads, and electricity, which developers then finished with homes and businesses.

MEMBER BANK bank that is a member of the FEDERAL RESERVE SYSTEM, including all nationally chartered banks and any state-chartered banks that apply for membership and are accepted. Member banks are required to purchase stock in the FEDERAL RESERVE BANK in their districts. Half of that investment is carried as an asset of the member bank. The other half is callable by the Fed at any time. Member banks are also required to maintain a percentage of their deposits as reserves in the form of currency in their vaults and balances on deposit at their Fed district banks. These reserve balances make possible a range of money transfer and other services using the FED WIRE system to connect banks in different parts of the country.

MEMBER FIRM brokerage firm that has at least one membership on a major stock exchange, even though, by exchange rules, the membership is in the name of an employee and not of the firm itself. Such a firm enjoys the rights and privileges of membership, such as voting on exchange policy, together with the obligations of membership, such as the commitment to settle disputes with customers through exchange arbitration procedures.

MEMBER SHORT SALE RATIO ratio of the total shares sold short for the accounts of New York Stock Exchange members in one week divided by the total short sales for the same week. Because the specialists, floor traders, and off-the-floor traders who trade for members' accounts are generally considered the best minds in the business, the ratio is a valuable indicator of market trends. A ratio of 82% or higher is considered bearish; a ratio of 68% or lower is positive and bullish. The member short sale ratio appears with other NYSE round lot statistics in the Monday edition of *The Wall Street Journal* and in *Barron's,* a weekly financial newspaper.

MERC nickname for the Chicago Mercantile Exchange. The exchange trades many types of futures, futures options, and foreign currency futures contracts. *See also* SECURITIES AND COMMODITIES EXCHANGES.

MERCANTILE AGENCY organization that supplies businesses with credit ratings and reports on other firms that are or might become customers. Such agencies may also collect past due accounts or trade collection statistics, and they tend to industry and geographical specialization. The largest of the agencies, DUN & BRADSTREET, was founded in 1841 under the name Mercantile Agency. It provides credit information on companies of all descriptions along with a wide range of other credit and financial reporting services.

MERCATO ITALIANO FUTURES (MIF) the Italian futures market, based in Rome. The MIF is a screen-based market, trading 10-year and 5-year Italian Treasury bond (BTP) futures. The market uses the same computer network that handles the underlying secondary market in Italian government securities.

MERCHANT BANK
1. European financial institution that engages in investment banking, counseling, and negotiating in mergers and acquisitions, and a variety of other services including securities portfolio management for customers, insurance, the acceptance of foreign bills of exchange, dealing in bullion, and participating in commercial ventures. Deposits in merchant banks are negligible, and the prominence of such names as Rothschild, Baring, Lazard, and Hambro attests to their role as counselors and negotiators in large-scale acquisitions, mergers, and the like.
2. part of an American bank that engages in investment banking functions, such as advising clients in mergers and acquisitions, underwriting securities, and taking debt or equity positions. The Federal Reserve permits commercial banks to underwrite corporate debt and common stock deals.

3. American bank that has entered into an agreement with a merchant to accept deposits generated by bank credit/charge card transactions.

MERGER combination of two or more companies, either through a POOLING OF INTERESTS, where the accounts are combined; a purchase, where the amount paid over and above the acquired company's book value is carried on the books of the purchaser as goodwill; or a consolidation, where a new company is formed to acquire the net assets of the combining companies. Strictly speaking, only combinations in which one of the companies survives as a legal entity are called mergers or, more formally, statutory mergers; thus consolidations, or statutory consolidations, are technically not mergers, though the term merger is commonly applied to them. Mergers meeting the legal criteria for pooling of interests, where common stock is exchanged for common stock, are nontaxable and are called tax-free mergers. Where an acquisition takes place by the purchase of assets or stock using cash or a debt instrument for payment, the merger is a taxable capital gain to the selling company or its stockholders. There is a potential benefit to such taxable purchase acquisitions, however, in that the acquiring company can write up the acquired company's assets by the amount by which the market value exceeds the book value; that difference can then be charged off to depreciation with resultant tax savings.

Mergers can also be classified in terms of their economic function. Thus a *horizontal merger* is one combining direct competitors in the same product lines and markets; a *vertical merger* combines customer and company or supplier and company; a *market extension merger* combines companies selling the same products in different markets; a *product extension merger* combines companies selling different but related products in the same market; a *conglomerate merger* combines companies with none of the above relationships or similarities. *See also* ACQUISITION.

MEXICAN STOCK EXCHANGE the only stock exchange in Mexico, formally known as the Bolsa Mexicana de Valores, and owned by the 33 casas de bolsa, or stock brokerage companies, five of which are foreign. The Indice de Precios y Cotizaciones, or IPC Index, consists of the 35 most representative stocks chosen every two months. The INMEX Index is an underlying index for derivative products, based on 20 companies and reviewed every six months so a single issuer cannot account for more than 10% of the index. Trading is conducted through a combination of open outcry and an automated system, BMV-SENTRA. The electronic system is used for trading debt instruments, warrants and about 50% of the stocks on the exchange. Trades are settled two days after the trade date. Trading hours: 8:30 A.M. to 3 P.M., Monday to Friday.

MEZZANINE BRACKET members of a securities underwriting group whose participations are of such a size as to place them in the tier second to the largest participants. In the newspaper TOMBSTONE advertisements that announce new securities offerings, the underwriters are listed in alphabetical groups, first the lead underwriters, then the mezzanine bracket, then the remaining participants.

MEZZANINE LEVEL stage of a company's development just prior to its going public, in VENTURE CAPITAL language. Venture capitalists entering at that point have a lower risk of loss than at previous stages and can look forward to early capital appreciation as a result of the MARKET VALUE gained by an INITIAL PUBLIC OFFERING.

MICROECONOMICS study of the behavior of basic economic units such as companies, industries, or households. Research on the companies in the airline industry would be a microeconomic concern, for instance. *See also* MACROECONOMICS.

MID CAP stock with a middle-level capitalization (numbers of shares outstanding times the price of the shares). Mid Cap stocks typically have between $1 billion and $5 billion in outstanding market value. Many mutual funds specializing in mid cap stocks will use the words mid cap in their names.

MIG-1 *see* MOODY'S INVESTMENT GRADE.

MILAN STOCK EXCHANGE largest of regional stock exchanges in Italy, accounting for more than 90% of trading volume. The MIB indices, based on the prices of all listed shares, and the COMIT Index, calculated by the Banca Commerciale Italiana, are the most widely used. Extensive reforms and reorganization in Italy created the Consiglio di Borsa, the Italian Stock Exchange Council, which instituted computerized trading and a block market. The regional exchanges are located in Rome, Turin, Genoa, Bologna, Florence, Naples, Palermo, Trieste, and Venice. Electronic trading is conducted Monday through Friday from 8:45 A.M. to 10 A.M. (order entry, automatic fixing of opening price), and from 10 A.M. to 4 P.M. (continuous trading with automatic matching of buy and sell orders). An open outcry system is used in the second market, from 9 A.M. to 10 A.M. Milan's second market, Mercato Ristretto, is the largest in the country. Trades are settled on a monthly basis, between 15 and 45 days after the trade date.

MILL one-tenth of a cent, the unit most often used in expressing property tax rates. For example, if a town's tax rate is 5 mills per dollar of assessed valuation, and the assessed valuation of a piece of property is $100,000, the tax is $500, or 0.005 times $100,000.

MINI-MANIPULATION trading in a security underlying an option contract so as to manipulate the stock's price, thus causing an increase in the value of the options. In this way the manipulator's profit can be multiplied many times, since a large position in options can be purchased with a relatively small amount of money.

MINIMUM FLUCTUATION smallest possible price movement of a security or options or futures contract. For example, most stocks on the New York Stock Exchange trade with a minimum fluctuation of one-eighth of a point. Some low-priced options contracts trade with a minimum fluctuation of one-sixteenth of a point. Minimum fluctuations are set by the securities, futures, or options exchanges regulating each security or contract. Also called MINIMUM TICK.

MINIMUM MAINTENANCE equity level that must be maintained in brokerage customers' margin accounts, as required by the New York Stock Exchange (NYSE), the National Association of Securities Dealers (NASD), and individual brokerage firms. Under REGULATION T, $2000 in cash or securities must be deposited with a broker before *any* credit can be extended; then an INITIAL MARGIN requirement must be met, currently 50% of the market value of eligible securities long or short in customers' accounts. The NYSE and NASD, going a step further, both require that a margin be *maintained* equal to 25% of the market value of securities in margin accounts. Brokerage firm requirements are typically a more conservative 30%. When the market value of margined securities falls below these minimums a MARGIN CALL goes out requesting additional equity. If the customer fails to comply, the broker may sell the margined stock and close the customer out. *See also* MARGIN REQUIREMENT; MARGIN SECURITY; MARK TO THE MARKET; SELL OUT.

MINIMUM PAYMENT minimum amount that a consumer is required to pay on a revolving charge account in order to keep the account in good standing. If the minimum payment is not made, late payment penalties are due. If the minimum is still not paid within a few months, credit privileges may be revoked. If a consumer pays just the minimum due, interest charges continue to accrue on all outstanding balances. In some cases, a credit card issuer will waive the minimum payment for a month or two, as long as the cardholder has demonstrated a good payment history. If the cardholder does not make any minimum payment in such a case, interest charges accrue on the entire outstanding balance.

MINIMUM TICK *see* MINIMUM FLUCTUATION.

MINI-WAREHOUSE LIMITED PARTNERSHIP partnership that invests in small warehouses where people can rent space to store belongings. Such partnerships offer tax benefits such as depreciation allowances, but mostly they provide income derived from rents. When the partnership is liquidated, the general partner may sell the warehouse for a profit, providing capital gains to limited partners.

MINORITY INTEREST interest of shareholders who, in the aggregate, own less than half the shares in a corporation. On the consolidated balance sheets of companies whose subsidiaries are not wholly owned, the minority interest is shown as a separate equity account or as a liability of indefinite term. On the income statement, the minority's share of income is subtracted to arrive at consolidated net income.

MINOR'S ACCOUNT bank savings account in the name of a minor, in which the minor has the power to deposit and withdraw. The minor must be able to sign for the account, but minimum deposit requirements and charges are waived until the child reaches majority (age 18 in most states).

MINUS symbol (–) preceding a fraction or number in the change column at the far right of newspaper stock tables designating a closing sale lower than that of the previous day.

MINUS TICK *see* DOWNTICK.

MISERY INDEX index that combines the unemployment and inflation rates. The index was devised in the 1970s when both inflation and unemployment rose sharply. The misery index is often credited with political significance, since it may be difficult for a president to be re-elected if there is a high misery index. The misery index is also linked to consumer confidence—the lower the index, in general, the more confident consumers tend to be.

MISSING THE MARKET failing to execute a transaction on terms favorable to a customer and thus being negligent as a broker. If the order is subsequently executed at a price demonstrably less favorable, the broker, as the customer's agent, may have to make up the loss.

MIXED ACCOUNT brokerage account in which some securities are owned (in long positions) and some borrowed (in short positions).

MLP *see* MASTER LIMITED PARTNERSHIP (MLP).

MOB SPREAD difference in yield between a tax-free MUNICIPAL BOND and a Treasury bond with the same maturity. Term is an acronym for *municipals-over-bonds* SPREAD, which will always exist because municipals involve different degrees of risk while Treasuries are risk-free as to principal. The spread between a "muni" of a given rating and a Treasury with the same maturity has significance in tax decisions and in transactions involving financial futures contracts.

MOBILE HOME CERTIFICATE mortgage-backed security guaranteed by the GOVERNMENT NATIONAL MORTGAGE ASSOCIATION consisting of mortgages on mobile homes. Although the maturity tends to be shorter on these securities than on single-family homes, they have all the other characteristics of regular Ginnie Maes, and the timely payment of interest and the repayment of principal are backed by the FULL FAITH AND CREDIT of the U.S. government.

MOCK TRADING simulated trading of stocks, bonds, commodities and mutual funds. Real money is not used. Students learning about investing in schools or brokerage training classes may go through exercises in mock trading, in which securities prices are tracked on a daily basis and fictional trades are made. With commodity futures and options, this may take the form of going through a simulated trading session on the trading floor or using computer programs to illustrate the futures and options strategies.

MODELING designing and manipulating a mathematical representation of an economic system or corporate financial application so that the effect of changes can be studied and forecast. For example, in ECONOMETRICS, a complex economic model can be drawn up, entered into a computer, and used to predict the effect of a rise in inflation or a cut in taxes on economic output.

MODERN PORTFOLIO THEORY *see* PORTFOLIO THEORY.

MODIFIED ACCELERATED COST RECOVERY SYSTEM (MACRS) provision, originally called the Accelerated Cost Recovery System (ACRS), instituted by the Economic Recovery Tax Act of 1981 (ERTA) and modified by the Tax Reform Act of 1986, which establishes rules for the DEPRECIATION (the recovery of cost through tax deductions) of qualifying assets. With certain exceptions, the 1986 Act modifications, which generally provide for greater acceleration over longer periods of time than ERTA rules, are effective for property placed in service after 1986.

   Under the modified rules, depreciable assets other than buildings fall within a 3-, 5-, 7-, 10-, 15-, or 20-year class life. The 3-, 5-, 7-, and 10-year classes use the DOUBLE DECLINING BALANCE DEPRECIATION METHOD, with a switch to STRAIGHT LINE DEPRECIATION. Instead of the 200% rate, you may elect a 150% rate. For 15- and 20-year property, the 150% declining balance method is used with a switch to straight line. The conversion to straight line occurs when larger annual deductions may be claimed over the remaining life. Real estate uses the straight line basis. Residential rental property placed in service after December 31, 1986, is depreciated over 27.5 years, while nonresidential property placed in service between December 1, 1986, and May 13, 1993, is depreciated over 31.5 years. A 39-year period applies to nonresidential property placed in service after May 12, 1993, although certain transition rules apply.

MOMENTUM rate of acceleration of an economic, price, or volume movement. An economy with strong growth that is likely to continue is said to have a lot of momentum. In the stock market, technical analysts study stock momentum by charting price and volume trends. *See also* EARNINGS MOMENTUM.

MOMENTUM INDICATORS indicators, called oscillators, used in technical analysis to measure the velocity of price movements (momentum), both up and down. In his book, *Introduction to Technical Analysis,* Martin Pring says, "All momentum series have the characteristics of an oscillator as they move from one extreme to the other. These extremes are known as OVERBOUGHT and OVERSOLD levels. An unruly dog taking a walk strains at the leash, moving from one side of the walk to the other. One moment the dog roams to the curb on his extreme left and the next he scampers back toward the lawns on his right, as far as the leash will allow him. Momentum works in a similar manner, so that when an oscillator is at an overextended reading on the upside, it is said to be overbought. When it reaches the opposite end of the spectrum on the downside, the condition is known as oversold. The horizontal line in between these extremes is called the equilibrium line."

Some of the most widely used momentum indicators are the RELATIVE STRENGTH INDICATOR (RSI), the MOVING AVERAGE CONVERGENCE/DIVERGENCE (MACD) and the STOCHASTICS INDEX. The basic characteristics of any momentum oscillator are illustrated below.

TYPICAL MOMENTUM OSCILLATOR

M-1, M-2 and M-3 three measures of the money supply as defined by the Federal Reserve Board:

M1 is the narrowest measure of money supply. It includes currency in circulation, checking account balances, NOW accounts and share draft accounts at credit unions, and travelers' checks. M1 represents all money that can be spent or readily converted to cash for immediate spending.

M2 includes everything in M1 plus savings accounts and time deposits such as CDs, money market deposit accounts, and repurchase agreements.

M3 includes everything in M2 plus large CDs and money market fund balances held by institutions. M3 is the broadest measure of money supply tracked by the Fed.

Federal Reserve policymakers carefully watch the growth rate of all three money supply measures, but especially M2, as key indicators of economic growth and the potential for inflation. Most economists maintain that most economic growth and inflation is determined by the rate of growth in the money supply.

MONEP (Marche des Options Negociables de Paris) subsidiary of the PARIS BOURSE, continuously trading stock and index options through open outcry and the STAMP electronic screen system. Two index classes and 50 stock classes are traded. The exchange trades CAC 40 INDEX short-term (American style) and long-term (European style) options, and equity options. The CAC 40 INDEX is the underlying index for derivative products traded on the MONEP and MATIF SA. Trading hours are 10 A.M. to 5 P.M., Monday through Friday.

MONETARIST economist who believes that the MONEY SUPPLY is the key to the ups and downs in the economy. Monetarists such as Milton Friedman think that the money supply has far more impact on the economy's future course than, say, the level of federal spending—a factor on which KEYNESIAN ECONOMICS puts great stress. Monetarists advocate slow but steady growth in the money supply.

MONETARY INDICATORS economic gauges of the effects of MONETARY POLICY, such as various measures of credit market conditions, U.S. Treasury BILL rates, and the Dow Jones Industrial Average (of common stocks).

MONETARY POLICY FEDERAL RESERVE BOARD decisions on the MONEY SUPPLY. To make the economy grow faster, the Fed can supply more credit to the banking system through its OPEN MARKET OPERATIONS, or it can lower the member bank reserve requirement or lower the DISCOUNT RATE—which is what banks pay to borrow additional reserves from the Fed. If, on the other hand, the economy is growing too fast and inflation is an increasing problem, the Fed might withdraw money from the banking system, raise the reserve requirement, or raise the discount rate, thereby putting a brake on economic growth. Other instruments of monetary policy range from selective credit controls to simple but often highly effective MORAL SUASION. Monetary policy differs from FISCAL POLICY, which is carried out through government spending and taxation. Both seek to control the level of economic activity as measured by such factors as industrial production, employment, and prices.

MONETIZE THE DEBT to finance the national debt by printing new money, causing inflation.

MONEY legal tender as defined by a government and consisting of currency and coin. In a more general sense, money is synonymous with CASH, which includes negotiable instruments, such as checks, based on bank balances.

MONEY CENTER BANK bank in one of the major financial centers of the world, among them New York, Chicago, San Francisco, Los Angeles, London, Paris, and Tokyo. These banks play a major national and international economic role because they are large lenders, depositories, and buyers of money market instruments and securities as well as large lenders to international governments and corporations. In the stock market, bank analysts usually categorize the money center banks as separate from regional banks—those that focus on one area of the country. Also known as *money market bank.*

MONEY MANAGEMENT financial planner's responsibility for the general management of monetary matters, including banking, credit management, budgeting, taxation, and borrowing. Term is also a synonym for PORTFOLIO MANAGEMENT.

MONEY MANAGER *see* PORTFOLIO MANAGER.

MONEY MARKET market for SHORT-TERM DEBT INSTRUMENTS—negotiable certificates of deposit, Eurodollar certificates of deposit, commercial paper, banker's acceptances, Treasury bills, and discount notes of the Federal Home Loan Bank, Federal National Mortgage Association, and Federal Farm Credit System, among others. Federal funds borrowings between banks, bank borrowings from the Federal Reserve Bank WINDOW, and various forms of repurchase agreements are also elements of the money market. What these instruments have in common are safety and LIQUIDITY. The money market operates through dealers, MONEY CENTER BANKS, and the Open Market Trading DESK at the New York Federal Reserve Bank. New York City is the leading money market, followed by London and Tokyo. The dealers in the important money markets are in constant communication with each other and with major borrowers and investors to take advantage of ARBITRAGE opportunities, a practice which helps keep prices uniform worldwide. *See also* MONEY MARKET FUND.

MONEY MARKET DEPOSIT ACCOUNT market-sensitive bank account that has been offered since December 1982. Under Depository Institutions Deregulatory Committee rules, such accounts had a minimum of $1000 (eliminated in 1986) and only three checks may be drawn per month, although unlimited transfers may be carried out at an automated teller machine. The funds are therefore liquid—that is, they are available to depositors at any time without penalty. The interest rate is generally comparable to rates on money market mutual funds, though any individual bank's rate may be higher or lower. These accounts are insured by the FEDERAL DEPOSIT INSURANCE CORPORATION.

MONEY MARKET FUND open-ended MUTUAL FUND that invests in commercial paper, banker's acceptances, repurchase agreements, government securities, certificates of deposit, and other highly liquid and safe securities, and pays money market rates of interest. Launched in the middle 1970s, these funds were especially popular in the early 1980s when interest rates and inflation soared. Management's fee is less than 1% of an investor's assets; interest over and above that amount is credited to shareholders monthly. The fund's net asset value remains a constant $1 a share—only the interest rate goes up or down. Such funds usually offer the convenience of checkwriting privileges.

Most funds are not federally insured, but some are covered by private insurance. Some funds invest only in government-backed securities, which give shareholders an extra degree of safety.

Many money market funds are part of fund families. This means that investors can switch their money from one fund to another and back again without charge. Money in an ASSET MANAGEMENT ACCOUNT usually is automatically swept into a money market fund until the accountholder decides where to invest it next. *See also* IBC'S MONEY FUND REPORT AVERAGE; FAMILY OF FUNDS; MONEY MARKET DEPOSIT ACCOUNT; TAX-EXEMPT MONEY MARKET FUND.

MONEY ORDER financial instrument that can be easily converted into cash by the payee named on the money order. The money order lists both the payee and the person who bought the instrument, known as the payor. Money orders are issued by banks, telephone companies, post offices, and traveler's check issuers to people presenting cash or other forms of acceptable payment. A personal money order from a bank can be considered a one-stop checking account, because the purchaser has the ability to stop payment on it; this does not hold true for money orders from other sources. Money orders often are used by people who do not have checking accounts. They can be used to pay bills or any outstanding debts.

MONEY PURCHASE PLAN program for buying a pension annuity that provides for specified, regular payments, usually based on salary.

MONEY SPREAD *see* VERTICAL SPREAD.

MONEY SUPPLY total stock of money in the economy, consisting primarily of (1) currency in circulation and (2) deposits in savings and checking accounts. Too much money in relation to the output of goods tends to push interest rates down and push prices and inflation up; too little money tends to push interest rates up, lower prices and output, and cause unemployment and idle plant capacity. The bulk of money is in demand deposits with commercial banks, which are regulated by the Federal Reserve Board. It manages the money supply by raising or lowering the reserves that banks are required to maintain and the DISCOUNT RATE at which they can borrow from the Fed, as well as by its OPEN MARKET OPERATIONS—trading government securities to take money out of the system or put it in.

Changes in the financial system, particularly since banking deregulation in the 1980s, have caused controversy among economists as to what really constitutes the money supply at a given time. In response to this, a more comprehensive analysis and breakdown of money was developed. Essentially, the various forms of money are now grouped into two broad divisions: M-1, M-2, and M-3, representing money and NEAR MONEY; and L, representing longer-term liquid funds. The table on the next page shows a detailed breakdown of all four categories. *See also* MONETARY POLICY.

MONEY SUPPLY

Classification	Components
M-1	currency in circulation
	commercial bank demand deposits
	NOW and ATS (automatic transfer from savings) accounts
	credit union share drafts
	mutual savings bank demand deposits
	nonbank travelers checks
M-2	M-1
	overnight repurchase agreements issued by commercial banks
	overnight Eurodollars
	savings accounts
	time deposits under $100,000
	money market mutual fund shares
M-3	M-2
	time deposits over $100,000
	term repurchase agreements
L	M-3 and other liquid assets such as:
	Treasury bills
	savings bonds
	commercial paper
	bankers' acceptances
	Eurodollar holdings of United States residents (nonbank)

MONOPOLY control of the production and distribution of a product or service by one firm or a group of firms acting in concert. In its pure form, monopoly, which is characterized by an absence of competition, leads to high prices and a general lack of responsiveness to the needs and desires of consumers. Although the most flagrant monopolistic practices in the United States were outlawed by ANTITRUST LAWS enacted in the late 19th century and early 20th century, monopolies persist in some degree as the result of such factors as patents, scarce essential materials, and high startup and production costs that discourage competition in certain industries. *Public monopolies*—those operated by the government, such as the post office, or closely regulated by the government, such as utilities—ensure the delivery of essential products and services at acceptable prices and generally avoid the disadvantages produced by private monopolies. MONOPSONY, the dominance of a market by one buyer or group of buyers acting together, is less prevalent than monopoly. *See also* CARTEL; OLIGOPOLY; PERFECT COMPETITION.

MONOPSONY situation in which one buyer dominates, forcing sellers to agree to the buyer's terms. For example, a tobacco grower may have no choice but to sell his tobacco to one cigarette company that is the only buyer for his product. The cigarette company therefore virtually controls the price at which it buys tobacco. The opposite of a monopsony is a MONOPOLY.

MONTHLY COMPOUNDING OF INTEREST *see* COMPOUND INTEREST.

MONTHLY INVESTMENT PLAN plan whereby an investor puts a fixed dollar amount into a particular investment every month, thus building a position at advantageous prices by means of *dollar cost averaging (see* CONSTANT DOLLAR PLAN).

MONTREAL EXCHANGE/BOURSE DE MONTREAL Canada's oldest stock exchange and second-largest in dollar value of trading. In 1996, the ME and its sister Canadian exchanges became the first in North America to introduce a decimal pricing system of trading and abandon the old "pieces of eight" system. Stocks, bonds, futures and options are traded through a specialist system combined with automated systems, including the Electronic Order Book for registering market and limit orders; MORRE, an electronic order execution system; and Montreal Direct Access, which provides access to the Electronic Order Board through existing terminals for the trading desks of member firms. Futures trading is conducted by traditional open outcry. A system-to-system link between the Montreal Exchange (ME) and the BOSTON STOCK EXCHANGE (BSE) enables ME member firms to electronically route retail orders for U.S. securities directly to BSE for automatic execution and confirmation at the best prevailing price in the Intermarket Trading System. The Canadian Market Portfolio Index (XXM) tracks the market performance of the 25 highest capitalized stocks traded on at least two Canadian exchanges, and is the ME's main index. Trading hours are 9:30 A.M. to 4 P.M. EST, Monday through Friday; extended sessions of 8:15 A.M. to 9:15 A.M., and 4:15 P.M. to 5:15 P.M., are offered. In addition, six sector indices track banking, forest products, industrial products, mining and minerals, oil and gas and utilities. In the derivatives market, the exchange trades 10-year Government of Canada bond futures (CGB) and options (OGB) and 3-month Canadian bankers' acceptance (BAX) futures and options (OBX); 1-month Canadian bankers' acceptance futures (BAR) and 5-year Government of Canada bond futures (CGF); equity options and long-term equity options; Canadian bond options; and LEAPS. Futures are traded from 8 A.M. to 3 P.M.; options, from 8:20 A.M. to 4 P.M. Settlement for securities is the third business day following the trade date; for futures and options, it is the day after a transaction by direct payment to the Canadian Derivatives Clearing Corporation.

MOODY'S INVESTMENT GRADE rating assigned by MOODY'S INVESTORS SERVICE to certain municipal short-term debt securities, classified as MIG-1, 2, 3, and 4 to signify best, high, favorable, and adequate quality, respectively. All four are investment grade or bank quality.

MOODY'S INVESTORS SERVICE headquartered with its parent company, Dun & Bradstreet, in downtown Manhattan, Moody's is one of the two best known bond rating agencies in the country, the other being Standard & Poor's. Moody's also rates commercial paper, preferred and common stocks, and municipal short-term issues. The six bound manuals it publishes annually, supplemented weekly or semiweekly, provide great detail on issuers and securities. The company also publishes the quarterly *Moody's Handbook of Common Stocks,* which charts more than 500 companies, showing industry group trends and company stock price performance. Also included are essential statistics for the past decade, an analysis of the company's financial background, recent financial developments, and the outlook. Moody's rates most of the publicly held corporate and municipal bonds and many Treasury and government agency issues, but does not usually rate privately placed bonds.

MORAL OBLIGATION BOND tax-exempt bond issued by a municipality or a state financial intermediary and backed by the moral obligation pledge of a state government. (State financial intermediaries are organized by states to pool local debt issues into single bond issues, which can be used to tap larger investment markets.) Under a moral obligation pledge, a state government indicates its intent to appropriate funds in the future if the primary OBLIGOR, the municipality or intermediary, defaults. The state's obligation to honor the pledge is moral rather than legal because future legislatures cannot be legally obligated to appropriate the funds required.

MORAL SUASION persuasion through influence rather than coercion, said of the efforts of the FEDERAL RESERVE BOARD to achieve member bank compliance with its general policy. From time to time, the Fed uses moral suasion to restrain credit or to expand it.

MORGAN STANLEY CAPITAL INTERNATIONAL INDICES indices maintained and calculated by Morgan Stanley's Capital International group (MSCI) which track more than 45 equity markets throughout the world. The MSCI indices are market capitalization weighted and cover both developed and emerging markets. In addition to the country indices, MSCI also calculates aggregate indices for the world, Europe, North America, Asia, and Latin America. Most international mutual funds and other international institutional investors measure their performance against MSCI indices.

MORNINGSTAR RATING SYSTEM system for rating open- and closed-end mutual funds and annuities by Morningstar Inc. of Chicago. The system rates funds from one to five stars, using a risk-adjusted performance rating in which performance equals total return of the fund.

The system rates funds assessing down-side risk, which is linked to the three-month U.S. Treasury bill. If a fund underperforms the Treasury bill, it will lower the fund's rating. The score is plotted on a bell curve, and is applied to four distinct categories: all equities, fixed income, hybrids, municipals. The top 10% receive five stars; the top 22.5%, four stars; the top 35%, three stars; the bottom 22.5%, two stars; and the bottom 10%, one star. Morningstar is a subscription-based company, offering its ratings in binders, software, and CD-ROM form. It sells its data to America Online and Realities Telescan Analyzer and other databases, as well as metropolitan newspapers. Morningstar also sells information on U.S. equities and American Depositary Receipts (ADRs), but star ratings are not calculated for them.

MORTGAGE debt instrument by which the borrower (mortgagor) gives the lender (mortgagee) a lien on property as security for the repayment of a loan. The borrower has use of the property, and the lien is removed when the obligation is fully paid. A mortgage normally involves real estate. For personal property, such as machines, equipment, or tools, the lien is called a *chattel mortgage. See also* ADLUSTABLE RATE MORTGAGE; CLOSED-END MORTGAGE; CONSOLIDATED MORTGAGE BOND; MORTGAGE BOND; OPEN-END MORTGAGE; VARIABLE RATE MORTGAGE.

MORTGAGE-BACKED CERTIFICATE security backed by mortgages. Such certificates are issued by the FEDERAL HOME LOAN MORTGAGE CORPORATION, and the FEDERAL NATIONAL MORTGAGE ASSOCIATION. Others are guaranteed by the GOVERNMENT NATIONAL MORTGAGE ASSOCIATION. Investors receive payments out of the interest and principal on the underlying mortgages. Sometimes banks issue certificates backed by CONVENTIONAL MORTGAGES, selling them to large institutional investors. The growth of mortgage-backed certificates and the secondary mortgage market in which they are traded has helped keep mortgage money available for home financing. *See also* PASS-THROUGH SECURITY.

MORTGAGE-BACKED SECURITY *see* MORTGAGE-BACKED CERTIFICATE.

MORTGAGE BANKER company, or individual, that originates mortgage loans, sells them to other investors, services the monthly payments, keeps related records, and acts as escrow agent to disperse funds for taxes and insurance. A mortgage banker's income derives from origination and servicing fees, profits on the resale of loans, and the spread between mortgage yields and the interest paid on borrowings while a particular mortgage is held before resale. To protect against negative spreads or mortgages that can't be resold, such companies seek commitments from institutional lenders or buy them from the FEDERAL NATIONAL MORTGAGE ASSOCIATION or the GOVERNMENT NATIONAL MORTGAGE ASSOCIATION. Mortgage bankers thus play an important role in the flow of mortgage funds even though they are not significant mortgage holders.

MORTGAGE BOND bond issue secured by a mortgage on the issuer's property, the lien on which is conveyed to the bondholders by a deed of trust. A mortgage bond may be designated senior, underlying, first, prior, overlying, junior, second, third, and so forth, depending on the priority of the lien. Most of those issued by corporations are first mortgage bonds secured by specific real property and also representing unsecured claims on the general assets of the firm. As such, these bonds enjoy a preferred position relative to unsecured bonds of the issuing corporation. *See also* CONSOLIDATED MORTGAGE BOND; MORTGAGE.

MORTGAGE BROKER one who places mortgage loans with lenders for a fee, but does not originate or service loans.

MORTGAGE INTEREST DEDUCTION federal tax deduction for mortgage interest paid in a taxable year. Interest on a mortgage to acquire, construct, or substantially improve a residence is deductible for indebtedness of up to $1 million. In addition, interest on a home equity loan of up to $100,000 is deductible. These amounts are halved for married taxpayers filing separately.

MORTGAGE LIFE INSURANCE policy that pays off the balance of a mortgage on the death of the insured.

MORTGAGE POOL group of mortgages sharing similar characteristics in terms of class of property, interest rate, and maturity. Investors buy participations and receive income derived from payments on the underlying mortgages. The principal attractions to the investor are DIVERSIFICATION and LIQUIDITY, along with a relatively attractive yield. Those backed by government-sponsored agencies such as the FEDERAL HOME LOAN MORTGAGE CORPORATION, FEDERAL NATIONAL MORTGAGE ASSOCIATION, and GOVERNMENT NATIONAL MORTGAGE ASSOCIATION have become popular not only with individual investors but with life insurance companies, pension funds, and even foreign investors.

MORTGAGE REIT invests in loans secured by real estate. These mortgages either may be originated and underwritten by the REAL ESTATE INVESTMENT TRUST or the REIT may purchase preexisting secondary mortgages. The funds the REIT invests may come from either shareholder equity capital or debt borrowed from other lenders. Mortgage REITs earn income from the interest they are paid and fees generated. This net income is generated from the excess of their interest and fee income and their interest expense and administrative fees. The other kind of real estate investment trust—called an EQUITY REIT—takes an ownership position in real estate, as opposed to acting as a lender. Some REITs, called *hybrid REITs,* take equity positions and make mortgage loans.

MORTGAGE SERVICING administration of a mortgage loan, including collecting monthly payments and penalties on late payments, keeping track of the amount of principal and interest that has been paid at any particular time, acting as escrow agent for funds to cover taxes and insurance, and, if necessary, curing defaults and foreclosing when a homeowner is seriously delinquent. For mortgage loans that are sold in the secondary market and packaged into a MORTGAGE-BACKED CERTIFICATE the local bank or savings and loan that originated the mortgage typically continues servicing the mortgages for a fee.

MOSCOW INTERBANK CURRENCY EXCHANGE (MICEX) the most liquid and best organized financial exchange in Russia. MICEX was established in 1992 to handle currency transactions from the former Gosbank of the USSR. It is a closed joint-stock company with ownership spread among major Russian commercial banks and the Central Bank of Russia. The Central Bank owns 6%, while less than 0.5% is held by the Association of Russian Banks, the Government of Moscow, and the Ministry of Finance of the Russian Federation. The rest of the shares are evenly split among 30 Russian and CIS banks. MICEX offers four market divisions which operate separately: electronic markets in foreign currencies, government securities, company shares and derivatives. Seven regional exchanges are linked to the MICEX trading and depository system; some 1,000 remote terminals are connected to the MICEX government securities trading system either directly or through regional trading floors. The MICEX Settlement House provides settlement services for the four divisions. The exchange trades 10 foreign currencies, including the larger CIS currencies. The MICEX Derivatives Division, launched in 1996, trades cash-settled futures on the U.S. dollar, Russian T-bill (GKO), MICEX Composite Stock Index and deliverable futures on individual Russian stocks. Some 20 members trade derivatives in the trading hall. The exchange's trading system, developed by Computershare Systems of Australia, enables traders to trade GKOs and stocks alongside GKO futures, deliverable stock futures, and MICEX Composite Index futures. Trading hours are 11 A.M. to 3 P.M.

MOST ACTIVE LIST stocks with the most shares traded on a given day. Unusual VOLUME can be caused by TAKEOVER activity, earnings releases, institutional trading in a widely held issue, and other factors.

MOVING AVERAGE average of security or commodity prices constructed on a period as short as a few days or as long as several years and showing trends for the latest interval. For example, a thirty-day moving average includes yesterday's figures; tomorrow the same average will include today's figures and will no longer show those for the earliest date included in yesterday's average. Thus every day it picks up figures for the latest day and drops those for the earliest day *See* chart on the next page.

MOVING AVERAGE CONVERGENCE/DIVERGENCE (MACD) TECHNICAL ANALYSIS oscillator developed by Gerald Appel that measures OVERBOUGHT and OVERSOLD conditions. MACD, informally called "MacD," uses three exponential MOVING AVERAGES: a short one, a long one, and a third that plots the moving average of the difference

MOVING AVERAGE

between the other two and forms a signal line on an MACD graph. (MACD is usually shown as a histogram, which plots the difference between the signal line and the MACD line). Trend reversals are signaled by the convergence and divergence of these moving averages. A positive BREAKOUT occurs when the histogram crosses the zero line upward (a buy signal) and a negative breakout occurs when the histogram crosses the zero (equilibrium) line downward (a sell signal). One of the most popular MACDs is the 8/17/9 MACD. On a daily MACD, the short moving average would be 8 days, the long one 17 days, and the signal line 9 days. On a weekly MACD, the same numbers would refer to weeks instead of days. The weekly MACD overrides chatter (*see* WHIPSAWED) and is a better indicator of how strongly the market feels about a stock and how likely it is the current trend will continue. *See also* MOMENTUM INDICATORS.

MTN initials standing for *medium-term notes* that are issued by corporations and distributed by investment banks acting as agents, similar to shorter-term COMMERCIAL PAPER.

MUD acronym for *municipal utility district,* a political subdivision that provides utility-related services and may issue SPECIAL ASSESSMENT BONDS.

MULTINATIONAL CORPORATION corporation that has production facilities or other fixed assets in at least one foreign country and makes its major management decisions in a global context. In marketing, production, research and development, and labor relations, its decisions must be made in terms of host-country customs and traditions. In finance, many of its problems have no domestic counterpart—the payment of dividends in another currency, for example, or the need to shelter working capital from the risk of devaluation, or the choices between owning and licensing. Economic and legal questions must be dealt with in drastically different ways. In addition to foreign exchange risks and the special business risks of operating in unfamiliar environments, there is the specter of political risk—the risk that sovereign governments may interfere with operations or terminate them altogether.

MULTIPLE *see* PRICE-EARNINGS RATIO.

MULTIPLE LISTING listing agreement used by a broker who is a member of a multiple-listing organization that is an exclusive right to sell with an additional authority and obligation on the part of the listing broker to distribute the listing to other brokers in the organization. These listings then are distributed in a multiple-listing service publication. Generally, the listing broker and the selling broker will split the commission, but terms for division can vary. A multiple-listing agreement benefits the seller by exposing his property to a wider group of potential buyers than would be available from one exclusive broker, which should allow the sale to be completed more quickly, and for a higher price. The multiple-listing service, however, has come under close scrutiny by consumer groups and justice departments for alleged antitrust practices.

MULTIPLE PERIL INSURANCE policy that incorporates several different types of property insurance coverage, such as flood, fire, wind, etc. In its broadest application, the term is synonymous with *all-risks insurance,* which covers loss or damage to property from fortuitous circumstances not specifically excluded from coverage. Do not confuse multiple peril insurance with *multiple protection insurance,* which is a form of life insurance policy combining features of term and whole life insurance.

MULTIPLIER the multiplier has two major applications in finance and investments.
   1. *investment multiplier* or *Keynesian multiplier:* multiplies the effects of investment spending in terms of total income. An investment in a small plant facility, for example, increases the incomes of the workers who built it, the merchants who provide supplies, the distributors who supply the merchants, the manufacturers who supply the distributors, and so on. Each recipient spends a portion of the income and saves the rest. By making an assumption as to the percentage each recipient saves, it is possible to calculate the total income produced by the investment.
   2. *deposit multiplier* or *credit multiplier:* magnifies small changes in bank deposits into changes in the amount of outstanding credit and the money supply. For example, a bank receives a deposit of $100,000, and the RESERVE REQUIREMENT is 20%. The bank is thus required to keep $20,000 in the form of reserves. The remaining $80,000 becomes a loan, which is deposited in the borrower's bank. When the borrower's bank sets aside the $16,000 required reserve out of the $80,000, $64,000 is available for another loan and another deposit, and so on. Carried out to its theoretical limit, the original deposit of $100,000 could expand into a total of $500,000 in deposits and $400,000 in credit.

MUNICIPAL BOND debt obligation of a state or local government entity. The funds may support general governmental needs or special projects. Prior to the TAX REFORM ACT OF 1986, the terms *municipal* and *tax-exempt* were synonymous, since virtually all municipal obligations were exempt from federal income taxes and most from state and local income taxes, at least in the state of issue. The 1986 Act, however, divided municipals into two broad groups: (1) PUBLIC PURPOSE BONDS, which remain tax-exempt and can be issued without limitation, and (2) PRIVATE PURPOSE BONDS, which are taxable unless specifically exempted. The tax distinction between public and private purpose is based on the percentage extent to which the bonds benefit private parties; if a tax-exempt public purpose bond involves more than a 10% benefit to private parties, it is taxable. Permitted private purpose bonds (those specified as tax-exempt) are generally TAX PREFERENCE ITEMS in computing the ALTERNATIVE MINIMUM TAX, and effective August 15, 1986, are subject to volume caps. *See also* ADVANCE REFUNDING; GENERAL OBLIGATION BOND; HOSPITAL REVENUE BOND; INDUSTRIAL DEVELOPMENT BOND; LIMITED TAX BOND; MUNICIPAL INVESTMENT TRUST; MUNICIPAL REVENUE BOND; SINGLE STATE MUNICIPAL BOND FUND; SPECIAL ASSESSMENT BOND; TAXABLE MUNICIPAL BOND; TAX-EXEMPT SECURITY; UNDERLYING DEBT; YIELD BURNING.

MUNICIPAL BOND INSURANCE policies underwritten by private insurers guaranteeing municipal bonds in the event of default. The insurance can be purchased either by the issuing government entity or the investor; it provides that bonds will be purchased from investors at par should default occur. Such insurance is available from a number of large insurance companies, but a major portion is written by the following "monoline" companies, so-called because their primary business is insuring municipal bonds: AMBAC Idemnity Corporation (AMBAC); Capital Guaranty Insurance Company (CGIC); Connie Lee Insurance Company; Financial Guaranty Insurance Company (FGIC); Financial Security Assurance, Inc. (FSA); and Municipal Bond Investors Assurance Corporation (MBIA). Insured municipal bonds generally enjoy the highest rating resulting in greater marketability and lower cost to their issuers. From the investor's standpoint, however, their yield is typically lower than similarly rated uninsured bonds because the cost of the insurance is passed on by the issuer to the investor. Some unit investment trusts and mutual funds feature insured municipal bonds for investors willing to trade marginally lower yield for the extra degree of safety.

MUNICIPAL IMPROVEMENT CERTIFICATE certificate issued by a local government in lieu of bonds to finance improvements or services, such as widening a sidewalk, or installing a sewer, or repairing a street. Such an obligation is payable from a special tax assessment against those who benefit from the improvement, and the payments may be collected by the contractor performing the work. Interest on the certificate is usually free of federal, state, and local taxes. *See also* GENERAL OBLIGATION BOND.

MUNICIPAL INVESTMENT TRUST (MIT) UNIT INVESTMENT TRUST that buys municipal bonds and passes the tax-free income on to shareholders. Bonds in the trust's portfolio are normally held until maturity, unlike the constant trading of bonds in an open-ended municipal bond fund's portfolio. MITs are sold through brokers, typically for a sales charge of about 3% of the principal paid, with a minimum investment of $1000. The trust offers diversification, professional management of the portfolio, and monthly interest, compared with the semiannual payments made by individual municipal bonds.

Many MITs invest in the securities of just one state. For California residents who buy a California-only MIT, for example, all the interest is free of federal, state, and local taxes. In contrast, a Californian who buys a national MIT might have to pay state and local taxes on interest derived from out-of-state bonds in the trust's portfolio.

MUNICIPAL NOTE in common usage, a municipal debt obligation with an original maturity of two years or less.

MUNICIPAL REVENUE BOND bond issued to finance public works such as bridges or tunnels or sewer systems and supported directly by the revenues of the project. For instance, if a municipal revenue bond is issued to build a bridge, the tolls collected from motorists using the bridge are committed for paying off the bond. Unless otherwise specified in the indenture, holders of these bonds have no claims on the issuer's other resources.

MUNICIPAL SECURITIES RULEMAKING BOARD *see* SELF-REGULATORY ORGANIZATION.

MUTILATED SECURITY certificate that cannot be read for the name of the issue or the issuer, or for the detail necessary for identification and transfer, or for the exercise of the holder's rights. It is then the seller's obligation to take corrective action, which usually means having the transfer agent guarantee the rights of ownership to the buyer.

MUTUAL ASSOCIATION SAVINGS AND LOAN ASSOCIATION organized as a cooperative owned by its members. Members' deposits represent shares; shareholders vote on association affairs and receive income in the form of dividends. Unlike state-chartered corporate S&Ls, which account for a minority of the industry, mutual associations are not permitted to issue stock, and they are usually chartered by the OFFICE OF THRIFT SUPERVISION (OTS) and belong to the SAVINGS ASSOCIATION INSURANCE FUND (SAIF). Deposits are technically subject to a waiting period before withdrawal, although in practice withdrawals are usually allowed on demand.

MUTUAL COMPANY corporation whose ownership and profits are distributed among members in proportion to the amount of business they do with the company. The most familiar examples are (1) mutual insurance companies, whose members are policy holders entitled to name the directors or trustees and to receive dividends or rebates on future premiums; (2) state-chartered MUTUAL SAVINGS BANKS, whose members are depositors sharing in net earnings but having nothing to do with management; and (3) federal savings and loan associations, MUTUAL ASSOCIATIONS whose members are depositors entitled to vote and receive dividends.

MUTUAL EXCLUSION DOCTRINE doctrine which established that interest from municipal bonds is exempt from federal taxation. In return for this federal tax exemption, states and localities are not allowed to tax interest generated by federal government securities, such as Treasury bills, notes, and bonds.

MUTUAL FUND fund operated by an INVESTMENT COMPANY that raises money from shareholders and invests it in stocks, bonds, options, futures, currencies, or money market securities. These funds offer investors the advantages of diversification and professional management. A management fee is charged for these services, typically between 0.5% and 2% of assets per year. Funds also levy other fees such as 12B-1 FEES, EXCHANGE FEES and other administrative charges. Funds that are sold through brokers are called LOAD FUNDS, and those sold to investors directly from the fund companies are called NO-LOAD FUNDS. Mutual fund shares are redeemable on demand at NET ASSET VALUE by shareholders. All shareholders share equally in the gains and losses generated by the fund.

Mutual funds come in many varieties. Some invest aggressively for capital appreciation, while others are conservative and are designed to generate income for shareholders. Investors need to assess their tolerance for risk before they decide which fund would be appropriate for them. In addition, the timing of buying or selling depends on the outlook for the economy, the state of the stock and bond markets, interest rates, and other factors.

MUTUAL FUND CASH-TO-ASSETS RATIO amount of mutual fund assets held in cash instruments. A fund manager may choose to keep a large cash position if he is bearish on the stock or bond market, or if he cannot find securities he thinks are attractive to buy. A large cash position (10% or more of the fund's assets in liquid instruments) may also accumulate if many investors buy fund shares and the fund manager cannot put all the money to work at once. On the other hand, a low cash-to-assets ratio is an indication that the fund manager is bullish, because he is fully invested and expects stock or bond prices to rise. Some analysts consider this ratio to be an important indicator of bullish or bearish sentiment among sophisticated investment managers. If many fund managers are increasing their cash positions, the fund managers are becoming more bearish—though some analysts consider it bullish for the market because the managers will have more cash to buy securities. The ratio for the entire mutual fund industry is released on a monthly basis by the Investment Company Institute, the largest mutual fund trade group.

MUTUAL FUND CUSTODIAN commercial bank or trust company that provides safekeeping for the securities owned by a mutual fund and may also act as TRANSFER AGENT, making payments to and collecting investments from shareholders. Mutual fund custodians must comply with the rules set forth in the INVESTMENT COMPANY ACT OF 1940.

MUTUAL IMPROVEMENT CERTIFICATE certificate issued by a local government in lieu of bonds to finance improvements or services, such as widening a sidewalk, or installing a sewer, or repairing a street. Such an obligation is payable from a special tax assessment against those who benefit from the improvement, and the payments may be collected by the contractor performing the work. Interest on the certificate is free of federal, state, and local taxes. *See also* GENERAL OBLIGATION BOND.

MUTUAL SAVINGS BANK SAVINGS BANK organized under state charter for the ownership and benefit of its depositors. A local board of trustees makes major decisions as fiduciaries, independently of the legal owners. Traditionally, income is distributed to depositors after expenses are deducted and reserve funds are set aside as required. In recent times, many mutual savings banks have begun to issue stock and offer consumer services such as credit cards and checking accounts, as well as commercial services such as corporate checking accounts and commercial real estate loans.

N

NAKED OPTION OPTION for which the buyer or seller has no underlying security position. A writer of a naked CALL OPTION, therefore, does not own a LONG POSITION in the stock on which the call has been written. Similarly, the writer of a naked PUT OPTION does not have a SHORT POSITION in the stock on which the put has been written. Naked options are very risky—although potentially very rewarding. If the underlying stock or stock index moves in the direction sought by the investor, profits can be enormous, because the investor would only have had to put down a small amount of money to reap a large return. On the other hand, if the stock moved in the opposite direction, the writer of the naked option could be subject to huge losses.

For instance, if someone wrote a naked call option at $60 a share on XYZ stock without owning the shares, and if the stock rose to $70 a share, the writer of the option would have to deliver XYZ shares to the call buyer at $60 a share. In order to acquire those shares, he or she would have to go into the market and buy them for $70 a share, sustaining a $10-a-share loss on his or her position. If, on the other hand, the option writer already owned XYZ shares when writing the option, he or she could just turn those shares over to the option buyer. This latter strategy is known as writing a COVERED CALL.

NAKED POSITION securities position that is not hedged from market risk—for example, the position of someone who writes a CALL or PUT option without having the corresponding LONG POSITION or SHORT POSITION on the underlying security. The potential risk or reward of naked positions is greater than that of covered positions. *See* COVERED CALL; HEDGE; NAKED OPTION.

NAMED PERILS INSURANCE property insurance that covers risks specified in the policy. Contrasts with *all-risks insurance,* which specifies exclusions.

NARROWING THE SPREAD closing the SPREAD between the bid and asked prices of a security as a result of bidding and offering by market makers and specialists in a security. For example, a stock's bid price—the most anyone is willing to pay—may be $10 a share, and the asked price—the lowest price at which anyone will sell—may be $10¼. If a broker or market maker offers to buy shares at $10¼, while the asked price remains at $10¼, the spread has effectively been narrowed.

NARROW MARKET securities or commodities market characterized by light trading and greater fluctuations in prices relative to volume than would be the case if trading were active. The market in a particular stock is said to be narrow if the price falls more than a point between ROUND LOT trades without any apparent explanation, suggesting lack of interest and too few orders. The terms THIN MARKET and *inactive market* are used as synonyms for narrow market.

NASDAQ National Association of Securities Dealers Automated Quotations system, which is owned and operated by the NATIONAL ASSOCIATION OF SECURITIES DEALERS. NASDAQ is a computerized system that provides brokers and dealers with price quotations for securities traded OVER THE COUNTER as well as for many New York Stock Exchange listed securities. NASDAQ quotes are published in the financial pages of most newspapers. *See also* NATIONAL MARKET SYSTEM.

NASDAQ SMALL CAPITALIZATION COMPANIES separately listed group of some 2000 companies that have smaller capitalizations and are less actively traded than NASDAQ NATIONAL MARKET SYSTEM stocks, but that meet NASDAQ price and market value listing criteria and have at least two MARKET MAKERS.

NASDAQ STOCK MARKET the first electronic stock market listing nearly 5,500 companies, operated by the NASDAQ Stock Market, Inc., a wholly owned subsidiary of the NATIONAL ASSOCIATION OF SECURITIES DEALERS (NASD). Some 530 market makers provide more than 60,000 competing bids to buy, offer, and sell NASDAQ stocks through an international computer network that displays the best quotations in 52 countries. The computer network is capable of trading more than 1 billion shares per day. Market makers use their own capital to buy and sell NASDAQ securities. The NASDAQ Stock Market is composed of two separate markets. The NASDAQ National Market, the market for NASDAQ'S largest and most actively traded securities, lists more than 4,400 securities. This market comprises some of the best known companies in the world, among them Microsoft and Intel. The NASDAQ SmallCap Market lists nearly 1,800 emerging growth companies. As these companies become established, they move up to the NASDAQ National Market. NASDAQ also operates NASDAQ International Ltd., a United Kingdom corporation based in London that helps non-U.S. companies list on the NASDAQ Stock Market directly through American Depositary Receipts. NASDAQ is developing a new communications infrastructure, called Enterprise Wide Network II (EWN II) that will handle 4-8 billion shares daily.

In 1998, the AMERICAN STOCK EXCHANGE and the PHILADELPHIA STOCK EXCHANGE (PHLX) merged with NASD, making the Amex and PHLX subsidiaries of NASD. Under the terms of the mergers, the Amex equity and options markets continue to operate separately from the NASDAQ Stock Market and NASDAQ International, both operated by the NASD. The Philadelphia Stock Exchange trading floor continues to operate separately for up to five years from the date of the merger.

NASD FORM FR-1 form required of foreign dealers in securities subscribing to new securities issues in the process of distribution, whereby they agree to abide by NATIONAL ASSOCIATION OF SECURITIES DEALERS rules concerning a HOT ISSUE. Under NASD Rules of Fair Practice, firms participating in the distribution must make a bona fide public offering at the public offering price. Any sale designed to capitalize on a hot issue—one that on the first day of trading sells at a substantial premium over the public offering price—would be in violation of NASD rules. Violations include a sale to a member of the dealer's family or to an employee, assuming such sales could not be defended as "normal investment practice." Also called *blanket certification form.*

NATIONAL ASSOCIATION OF INVESTORS CORPORATION not-for-profit educational association that helps investment clubs become established. Investment clubs are formed by people who pool their money and make common decisions about how to invest those assets. The NAIC is located in Madison Heights, Michigan. *See also* INVESTMENT CLUB.

NATIONAL ASSOCIATION OF SECURITIES DEALERS (NASD) nonprofit organization formed under the joint sponsorship of the Investment Bankers' Conference and the Securities and Exchange Commission to comply with the MALONEY ACT. NASD members include virtually all investment banking houses and firms dealing in the OVER THE COUNTER market. Operating under the supervision of the SEC, the NASD's basic purposes are to (1) standardize practices in the field, (2) establish high moral and ethical standards in securities trading, (3) provide a representative body to consult with the government and investors on matters of common interest, (4) establish and enforce fair and equitable rules of securities trading, and (5) establish a disciplinary body capable of enforcing the above provisions. The NASD also requires members to maintain quick assets in excess of current liabilities at all times. Periodic examinations and audits are conducted to ensure a high level of solvency and financial integrity among members. A special Investment Companies Department is concerned with the problems of investment companies and has the responsibility of reviewing companies' sales literature in that segment of the securities industry. *See also* NASDAQ; NASDAQ SMALL CAPITALIZATION COMPANIES; NASDAQ STOCK MARKET.

NATIONAL BANK commercial bank whose charter is approved by the U.S. Comptroller of the Currency rather than by a state banking department. National banks are required to be members of the FEDERAL RESERVE SYSTEM and to purchase stock in the FEDERAL RESERVE BANK in their district *(see* MEMBER BANK). They must also belong to the FEDERAL DEPOSIT INSURANCE CORPORATION.

NATIONAL CREDIT UNION ADMINISTRATION independent federal agency based in Washington, D.C., established by Congress to oversee the federal credit union system. The NCUA is funded by credit unions and does not receive any tax dollars. The agency supervises nearly 7600 federal credit unions and federally insures member accounts in approximately 4600 state-chartered credit unions. The National Credit Union Share Insurance Fund is the agency's arm that insures member accounts up to $100,000. It is backed by the full faith and credit of the U.S. government and is managed by the NCUA Board, which is comprised of three members appointed by the President.

NATIONAL DEBT debt owed by the federal government. The national debt is made up of such debt obligations as Treasury bills, Treasury notes, and Treasury bonds. Congress imposes a ceiling on the national debt, which has been increased on occasion when accumulated deficits near the ceiling. By the late 1990s, the national debt stood at more than $5.5 trillion. The interest due on the national debt is one of the major expenses of the federal government. The national debt, which is the total debt accumulated by the government over many decades, should not be confused with the federal budget deficit, which is the excess of spending over income by the federal government in one fiscal year.

NATIONAL FOUNDATION FOR CONSUMER CREDIT a nonprofit national organization based in Silver Spring, Maryland, created in 1951 to help the increasing number of consumers who have taken on too much debt. The NFCC has more than 200 members operating 1100 locations providing consumers with money management, budget, and wise-credit-use education workshops and counseling sessions. While counselors work with creditors to work out a payment plan, the NFCC does not provide credit or financial assistance. Most members do not charge for counseling; however some members charge a low fee for services such as debt repayment or counseling. No one is turned away due to the inability to pay.

NATIONALIZATION takeover of a private company's assets or operations by a government. The company may or may not be compensated for the loss of assets. In developing nations, an operation is typically nationalized if the government feels the company is exploiting the host country and exporting too high a proportion of the profits. By nationalizing the firm, the government hopes to keep profits at home. In developed countries, industries are often nationalized when they need government subsidies to survive. For instance, the French government nationalized steel and chemical companies in the mid-1980s in order to preserve jobs that would have disappeared if free market forces had prevailed. In some developed countries, however, nationalization is carried out as a form of national policy, often by Socialist governments, and is not designed to rescue ailing industries.

NATIONAL MARKET ADVISORY BOARD board appointed by the Securities and Exchange Commission under provisions of the 1975 Securities Act to study and advise the commission on a national exchange market system (NEMS). NEMS is envisioned as a highly automated, national exchange with continuous auction markets and competing specialist or market makers, but one that would preserve the existing regional exchanges.

NATIONAL MARKET EXCHANGES formed by the BOSTON STOCK EXCHANGE, CHICAGO STOCK EXCHANGE, PACIFIC EXCHANGE and PHILADELPHIA STOCK EXCHANGE to help stock investors better understand the role of the NATIONAL MARKET SYSTEM and the Intermarket Trading System in the U.S. *See also* NATIONAL MARKET SYSTEM.

NATIONAL MARKET SYSTEM (NMS) developed in 1975 by the Securities and Exchange Commission following a mandate by the U.S. Congress to foster greater competition among the stock exchanges in the U.S. NMS consists of every major market center in the U.S.—the NEW YORK STOCK EXCHANGE, AMERICAN STOCK EXCHANGE, BOSTON STOCK EXCHANGE, CHICAGO STOCK EXCHANGE, CINCINNATI STOCK EXCHANGE, PACIFIC EXCHANGE, PHILADELPHIA STOCK EXCHANGE and the NATIONAL ASSOCIATION OF SECURITIES DEALERS. Its Intermarket Trading System (ITS) is an electronic linkage among all of the NMS exchanges that displays current bid and offer prices for all eligible stocks at a given exchange. It also displays the current bid and offer prices at all markets in the system and the best prices available nationwide. *See also* NATIONAL MARKET ADVISORY BOARD.

NATIONAL QUOTATION BUREAU daily service to subscribers that collects bid and offer quotes from MARKET MAKERS in stocks and bonds traded OVER THE COUNTER. Quotes are distributed on PINK SHEETS (for stocks) and YELLOW SHEETS (for corporate bonds). The Bureau is located in Cedar Grove, New Jersey. *See also* OTC BULLETIN BOARD.

NATIONAL SECURITIES CLEARING CORPORATION (NSCC) securities clearing organization formed in 1977 by merging subsidiaries of the New York and American Stock Exchanges with the National Clearing Corporation. It functions essentially as a medium through which brokerage firms, exchanges, and other clearing corporations reconcile accounts with each other. *See also* CONTINUOUS NET SETTLEMENT.

NATIONAL STOCK EXCHANGE (NSE) established in India in 1994 to provide a more transparent alternative to the Bombay Stock Exchange. Creation of a wholesale debt market was concurrent with its establishment. NSE serves as a national exchange, integrating the country's stock markets through nationwide automated on-line screen operations and electronic clearing and settlement. NSE is India's second-largest stock exchange. Settlement, on an account period basis, takes one week. Trading hours: 10 A.M. to 2:30 P.M., Monday through Friday, with a carry-forward session on Saturday from 11 A.M. to 3:30 P.M.

NEARBYS months of futures or options contracts that are nearest to delivery (for futures) or expiration (for options). For example, in January, futures and options contracts settling in February and March would be considered nearbys. In general, nearby contracts are far more actively traded than contracts for more distant months. *See also* FURTHEST MONTH, NEAREST MONTH.

NEAREST MONTH in commodity futures or OPTION trading, the expiration dates, expressed as months, closest to the present. For a commodity or an option that had delivery or expiration dates available in September, December, March, and June, for instance, the nearest month would be September if a trade were being made in August. Nearest month contracts are always more heavily traded than FURTHEST MONTH contracts.

NEAR MONEY CASH EQUIVALENTS and other assets that are easily convertible into cash. Some examples are government securities, bank TIME DEPOSITS, and MONEY MARKET FUND shares. Bonds close to REDEMPTION date are also called near money.

NEGATIVE AMORTIZATION financing arrangement in which monthly payments are less than the true amortized amounts and the loan balance increases over the term of the loan rather than decreases; the interest shortage is added to the unpaid principal. In some cases, the interest shortage is added back to the loan and payable at maturity. For example, amortized payments for the first six months of a 30-year mortgage loan would be based on a 13% rate, but interest would be charged against equity at 18%; this rate charge would fluctuate every six-month period. In some loans, the negative amounts may be made up by applying such deficits against the borrower's down payment equity. Federal law requires mortgage lenders to make sure that borrowers understand the potential impact of negative amortization in several interest rate scenarios through a series of extensive disclosure documents.

NEGATIVE CARRY situation in which the cost of money borrowed to finance securities or financial futures positions is higher than the return on those positions. For example, if an investor borrowed at 10% to finance, or "carry," a bond yielding 8%, the bond position would have a negative carry. Negative carry does not necessarily mean a loss to the investor, however, and a positive yield can result on an aftertax basis. In this case, the yield from the 8% bond may be tax-exempt, whereas interest on the 10% loan is tax-deductible. In commodities, this would occur in any month in a BACKWARDATION where the price is higher than the spot month. With the negative carry, if the investor holds the physical position in copper, for example, it will continue to lose value.

NEGATIVE CASH FLOW situation in which a business spends more cash than it receives through earnings or other transactions in an accounting period. *See also* CASH FLOW.

NEGATIVE INCOME TAX proposed system of providing financial aid to poverty-level individuals and families, using the mechanisms already in place to collect income taxes. After filing a tax return showing income below subsistence levels, instead of paying an income tax, low-income people would receive a direct subsidy, called a negative income tax, sufficient to bring them up to the subsistence level.

NEGATIVE PLEDGE CLAUSE negative covenant or promise in an INDENTURE agreement that states the corporation will not pledge any of its assets if doing so would result in less security to the debtholders covered under the indenture agreement. Also called *covenant of equal coverage.*

NEGATIVE WORKING CAPITAL situation in which the current liabilities of a firm exceed its current assets. For example, if the total of cash, MARKETABLE SECURITIES, ACCOUNTS RECEIVABLE and notes receivable, inventory, and other current assets is less than the total of ACCOUNTS PAYABLE, short-term notes payable, long-term debt due in one year, and other current liabilities, the firm has a negative working capital. Unless the condition is corrected, the firm will not be able to pay debts when due, threatening its ability to keep operating and possibly resulting in bankruptcy.

To remedy a negative working capital position, a firm has these alternatives: (1) it can convert a long-term asset into a current asset—for example, by selling a piece of equipment or a building, by liquidating a long-term investment, or by renegotiating a long-term loan receivable; (2) it can convert short-term liabilities into long-term liabilities—for example, by negotiating the substitution of a current account payable with a long-term note payable; (3) it can borrow long term; (4) it can obtain additional equity through a stock issue or other sources of paid-in capital; (5) it can retain or "plow back" profits. *See also* WORKING CAPITAL.

NEGATIVE YIELD CURVE situation in which yields on short-term securities are higher than those on long-term securities of the same quality. Normally, short-term rates are lower than long-term rates because those who commit their money for longer periods are taking more risk. But if interest rates climb high enough, borrowers become unwilling to lock themselves into high rates for long periods and borrow short-term instead. Therefore, yields rise on short-term funds and fall or remain stable on long-term funds. Also called an INVERTED YIELD CURVE. *See also* YIELD CURVE.

NEGOTIABLE
In general:
1. something that can be sold or transferred to another party in exchange for money or as settlement of an obligation.
2. matter of mutual concern to one or more parties that involves conditions to be worked out to the satisfaction of the parties. As examples: In a lender-borrower arrangement, the interest rate may be negotiable; in securities sales, brokerage commissions are now negotiable, having historically been fixed; and in divorce cases involving children, the terms of visiting rights are usually negotiable.

Finance: instrument meeting the qualifications of the Uniform Commercial Code dealing with negotiable instruments. *See* NEGOTIABLE INSTRUMENT.

Investments: type of security the title to which is transferable by delivery. A stock certificate with the stock power properly signed is negotiable, for example.

NEGOTIABLE CERTIFICATE OF DEPOSIT large-dollar-amount, short-term certificate of deposit. Such certificates are issued by large banks and bought mainly by corporations and institutional investors. They are payable either to the bearer or to the order of the depositor, and, being NEGOTIABLE, they enjoy an active SECONDARY MARKET, where they trade in round lots of $5 million. Although they can be issued in any denomination from $100,000 up, the typical amount is $1 million. They have a minimum original maturity of 14 days; most original maturities are under six months. Also called a JUMBO CERTIFICATE OF DEPOSIT.

NEGOTIABLE INSTRUMENT unconditional order or promise to pay an amount of money, easily transferable from one person to another. Examples: check, promissory note, draft (bill of exchange). The Uniform Commercial Code requires that for an instrument to be negotiable it must be signed by the maker or drawer, must contain an unconditional promise or order to pay a specific amount of money, must be payable on demand or at a specified future time, and must be payable to order or to the bearer.

NEGOTIABLE ORDER OF WITHDRAWAL a bank or savings and loan withdrawal ticket that is a NEGOTIABLE INSTRUMENT. The accounts from which such withdrawals can be made, called NOW accounts, are thus, in effect, interest-bearing checking accounts. They were first introduced in the late 1970s and became available nationally in January 1980. In the early and mid-1980s the interest rate on NOW accounts was capped at 5½%; the cap was phased out in the late 1980s. *See also* SUPER NEGOTIABLE ORDER OF WITHDRAWAL (NOW) ACCOUNT.

NEGOTIATED COMMISSION brokerage COMMISSION that is determined through negotiation. Prior to 1975, commissions were fixed. Since then, brokerage firms have been free to charge what they want and, although they have minimums and commission schedules, will negotiate commissions on large transactions.

NEGOTIATED UNDERWRITING underwriting of new securities issue in which the SPREAD between the purchase price paid to the issuer and the public offering price is determined through negotiation rather than multiple competitive bidding. The spread, which represents the compensation to the investment bankers participating in the underwriting (collectively called the *syndicate),* is negotiated between the issuing company and the MANAGING UNDERWRITER, with the consent of the group. Most corporate stock and bond issues and municipal revenue bond issues are priced through negotiation, whereas municipal general obligation bonds and new issues of public utilities are generally priced through competitive bidding. Competitive bidding is mandatory for new issues of public utilities holding companies. *See also* COMPETITIVE BID.

NEO abbreviation for *nonequity options.* This refers to options contracts on foreign currencies, bonds and other debt issues, commodities, metals, and stock indexes. In contrast, equity options have individual stocks as underlying values.

NEST EGG assets put aside for a person's retirement. Such assets are usually invested conservatively to provide the retiree with a secure standard of living for the rest of his or her life. Investment in an INDIVIDUAL RETIREMENT ACCOUNT would be considered part of a nest egg.

NET

In general: figure remaining after all relevant deductions have been made from the gross amount. For example: net sales are equal to gross sales minus discounts, returns, and allowances; net profit is gross profit less operating (sales, general, and administrative) expenses; net worth is assets (worth) less liabilities.

Investments: dollar difference between the proceeds from the sale of a security and the seller's adjusted cost of acquisition—that is, the gain or loss.

As a verb:

1. to arrive at the difference between additions and subtractions or plus amounts and minus amounts. For example, in filing tax returns, capital losses are netted against capital gains.
2. to realize a net profit, as in "last year we netted a million dollars after taxes."

NET AFTERTAX GAIN capital gain after income taxes.

NET ASSETS difference between a company's total assets and liabilities; another way of saying *owner's equity* or NET WORTH. *See* ASSET COVERAGE for a discussion of net asset value per unit of bonds, preferred stock, or common stock.

NET ASSET VALUE (NAV)

1. in mutual funds, the market value of a fund share, synonymous with *bid price*. In the case of no-load funds, the NAV, market price, and offering price are all the same figure, which the public pays to **buy** shares; load fund market or offer prices are quoted after adding the sales charge to the net asset value. NAV is calculated by most funds after the close of the exchanges each day by taking the closing market value of all securities owned plus all other assets such as cash, subtracting all liabilities, then dividing the result (total net assets) by the total number of shares outstanding. The number of shares outstanding can vary each day depending on the number of purchases and redemptions.
2. book value of a company's different classes of securities, usually stated as net asset value per bond, net asset value per share of preferred stock, and net book value per common share of common stock. The formula for computing net asset value is total assets less any INTANGIBLE ASSET less all liabilities and securities having a prior claim, divided by the number of units outstanding (i.e., bonds, preferred shares, or common shares). *See* BOOK VALUE for a discussion

of how these values are calculated and what they mean. *See also* DEFINED ASSET FUNDS.

NET CAPITAL REQUIREMENT Securities and Exchange Commission requirement that member firms as well as nonmember broker-dealers in securities maintain a maximum ratio of indebtedness to liquid capital of 15 to 1; also called *net capital rule* and *net capital ratio.* Indebtedness covers all money owed to a firm, including MARGIN loans and commitments to purchase securities, one reason new public issues are spread among members of underwriting syndicates. Liquid capital includes cash and assets easily converted into cash.

NET CHANGE difference between the last trading price on a stock, bond, commodity, or mutual fund from one day to the next. The net change in individual stock prices is listed in newspaper financial pages. The designation +2½, for example, means that a stock's final price on that day was $2.50 higher than the final price on the previous trading day. The net changes in prices of NASDAQ STOCK MARKET stocks is usually the difference between bid prices from one day to the next.

NET CURRENT ASSETS difference between current assets and current liabilities; another name for WORKING CAPITAL. Some security analysts divide this figure (after subtracting preferred stock, if any) by the number of common shares outstanding to arrive at working capital per share. Believing working capital per share to be a conservative measure of LIQUIDATING VALUE (on the theory that fixed and other noncurrent assets would more than compensate for any shrinkage in current assets if assets were to be sold), they compare it with the MARKET VALUE of the company's shares. If the net current assets per share figure, or "minimum liquidating value," is higher than the market price, these analysts view the common shares as a bargain (assuming, of course, that the company is not losing money and that its assets are conservatively valued). Other analysts believe this theory ignores the efficiency of capital markets generally and, specifically, obligations such as pension plans, which are not reported as balance sheet liabilities under present accounting rules.

NET EARNINGS *see* NET INCOME.

NET ESTATE *see* GROSS ESTATE.

NET INCOME
In general: sum remaining after all expenses have been met or deducted; synonymous with *net earnings* and with *net profit* or *net loss* (depending on whether the figure is positive or negative).
For a business: difference between total sales and total costs and expenses. Total costs comprise cost of goods sold including depreciation; total expenses comprise selling, general, and administrative expenses, plus INCOME DEDUCTIONS. Net income is usually specified as to whether it is before income taxes or after income taxes. Net income after taxes is the *bottom line* referred to in popular vernacular. It is out of this figure that dividends are normally paid. See *also* OPERATING PROFIT (OR LOSS).

For an individual: gross income less expenses incurred to produce gross income. Those expenses are mostly deductible for tax purposes.

NET INCOME PER SHARE OF COMMON STOCK amount of profit or earnings allocated to each share of common stock after all costs, taxes, allowances for depreciation, and possible losses have been deducted. Net income per share is stated in dollars and cents and is usually compared with the corresponding period a year earlier. For example, XYZ might report that second-quarter net income per share was $1.20, up from 90 cents in the previous year's second quarter. Also known as *earnings per common share* (EPS).

NET INCOME TO NET WORTH RATIO *see* RETURN ON EQUITY.

NET INTEREST COST (NIC) total amount of interest that a corporate or municipal bond entity will end up paying when issuing a debt obligation. The net interest cost factors in the coupon rate, any premiums or discounts, and reduces this to an average annual rate for the number of years until the bond matures or is callable. Underwriters compete to offer issuers the lowest NIC when they bid for the deal. The underwriting syndicate with the lowest NIC is normally awarded the contract.

NET INVESTMENT INCOME PER SHARE income received by an investment company from dividends and interest on securities investments during an accounting period, less management fees and administrative expenses and divided by the number of outstanding shares. Short-term trading profits (net profits from securities held for less than six months) are considered dividend income. The dividend and interest income is received by the investment company, which in turn pays shareholders the net investment income in the form of dividends prorated according to each holder's share in the total PORTFOLIO.

NET LEASE financial lease stipulating that the user (rather than the owner) of the leased property shall pay all maintenance costs, taxes, insurance, and other expenses. Many real estate and oil and gas limited partnerships are structured as net leases with ESCALATOR CLAUSES, to provide limited partners with both depreciation tax benefits and appreciation of investment, minus cash expenses. *See also* GROSS LEASE.

NET OPERATING LOSS (NOL) tax term for the excess of business expenses over income in a tax year. Under TAX LOSS CARRYBACK, CARRYFORWARD provisions, NOLs can (if desired) be carried back three years and forward 15 years.

NET PRESENT VALUE (NPV) method used in evaluating investments whereby the net present value of all cash outflows (such as the cost of the investment) and cash inflows (returns) is calculated using a given discount rate, usually a REQUIRED RATE OF RETURN. An investment is acceptable if the NPV is positive. In capital budgeting, the discount rate used is called the HURDLE RATE and is usually equal to the INCREMENTAL COST OF CAPITAL.

NET PROCEEDS amount (usually cash) received from the sale or disposition of property, from a loan, or from the sale or issuance of securities after deduction of all costs incurred in the transaction. In computing the gain or loss on a securities transaction for tax purposes, the amount of the sale is the amount of the net proceeds.

NET PROFIT *see* NET INCOME.

NET PROFIT MARGIN NET INCOME as a percentage of NET SALES. A measure of operating efficiency and pricing strategy, the ratio is usually computed using net profit before extraordinary items and taxes— that is, net sales less COST OF GOODS SOLD and SELLING, GENERAL, AND ADMINISTRATIVE (SG&A) EXPENSES.

NET QUICK ASSETS cash, MARKETABLE SECURITIES, and ACCOUNTS RECEIVABLE, minus current liabilities. *See also* QUICK RATIO.

NET REALIZED CAPITAL GAINS PER SHARE amount of CAPITAL GAINS that an investment company realized on the sale of securities, net of CAPITAL LOSSES, and divided by the number of outstanding shares. Such net gains are distributed annually to shareholders in proportion to their shares in the total portfolio. The distributions are eligible for favorable CAPITAL GAINS TAX rates if the positions were held for at least 12 months. If held for less than 12 months, the gains would be subject to regular income taxes at the shareholder's tax bracket. *See also* REGULATED INVESTMENT COMPANY.

NET SALES gross sales less returns and allowances, freight out, and cash discounts allowed. Cash discounts allowed is seen less frequently than in past years, since it has become conventional to report as net sales the amount finally received from the customer. Returns are merchandise returned for credit; allowances are deductions allowed by the seller for merchandise not received or received in damaged condition; freight out is shipping expense passed on to the customer.

NET TANGIBLE ASSETS PER SHARE total assets of a company, less any INTANGIBLE ASSET such as goodwill, patents, and trademarks, less all liabilities and the par value of preferred stock, divided by the number of common shares outstanding. *See* BOOK VALUE for a discussion of what this calculation means and how it can be varied to apply to bonds or preferred stock shares. *See also* NET ASSET VALUE.

NET TRANSACTION securities transaction in which the buyer and seller do not pay fees or commissions. For instance, when an investor buys a new issue, no commission is due. If the stock is initially offered at $15 a share, the buyer's total cost is $15 per share.

NETWORK A *see* CONSOLIDATED TAPE.

NETWORK B *see* CONSOLIDATED TAPE.

NET WORKING CAPITAL CURRENT ASSETS minus CURRENT LIABILITIES. Usually simply called WORKING CAPITAL.

NET WORTH amount by which assets exceed liabilities. For a corporation, net worth is also known as *stockholders' equity* or NET ASSETS. For an individual, net worth is the total value of all possessions, such as a house, stocks, bonds, and other securities, minus all outstanding debts, such as mortgage and revolving-credit loans. In order to qualify for certain high-risk investments, brokerage houses require that an individual's net worth must be at or above a certain dollar level.

NET YIELD RATE OF RETURN on a security net of out-of-pocket costs associated with its purchase, such as commissions or markups. *See also* MARKDOWN.

NEW ACCOUNT REPORT document filled out by a broker that details vital facts about a new client's financial circumstances and investment objectives. The report may be updated if there are material changes in a client's financial position. Based on the report, a client may or may not be deemed eligible for certain types of risky investments, such as commodity trading or highly leveraged LIMITED PARTNERSHIP deals. *See also* KNOW YOUR CUSTOMER.

NEW HIGH/NEW LOW stock prices that have hit the highest or lowest prices in the last year. Next to each stock's listing in a newspaper will be an indication of a new high with a letter "u" or a new low with the letter "d." Newspapers publish the total number of new highs and new lows each day on the New York and American Stock Exchanges and on the NASDAQ Stock Market. Technical analysts pay great attention to the trend of new highs and new lows. If the number of new highs is expanding, that is considered a bullish indicator. If the number of new lows is rising, that is considered bearish. Many analysts also track the ratio of new highs to new lows as a reflection of the general direction of the stock market.

NEW ISSUE stock or bond being offered to the public for the first time, the distribution of which is covered by Securities and Exchange Commission (SEC) rules. New issues may be initial public offerings by previously private companies or additional stock or bond issues by companies already public and often listed on the exchanges. New PUBLIC OFFERINGS must be registered with the SEC. PRIVATE PLACEMENTS avoid SEC registration if a LETTER OF INTENT establishes that the securities are purchased for investment and not for resale to the public. *See also* HOT ISSUE; LETTER SECURITY; UNDERWRITE.

NEW LISTING security that has just begun to trade on a stock or bond exchange. A new listing on the New York or American Stock Exchange must meet all LISTING REQUIREMENTS, and may either be an INITIAL PUBLIC OFFERING or a company whose shares have previously traded on the NASDAQ STOCK MARKET. New listings on the New York and American Stock Exchanges or a non-U.S. market carry the letter "n" next to their listing in newspaper tables for one year from the date they started trading on the exchange.

NEW MONEY amount of additional long-term financing provided by a new issue or issues in excess of the amount of a maturing issue or by issues that are being refunded.

NEW MONEY PREFERRED PREFERRED STOCK issued after October 1, 1942, when the tax exclusion for corporate investors receiving preferred stock dividends was raised from 60% to 85%, to equal the exclusion on common stock dividends. The change benefited financial institutions, such as insurance companies, which are limited in the amount of common stocks they can hold, typically 5% of assets. New money preferreds offer an opportunity to gain tax advantages over bond investments, which have fully taxable interest. The corporate tax exclusion on dividends is currently 70%.

NEW YORK COTTON EXCHANGE (NYCE) oldest commodity exchange in New York, founded in 1870 by a group of cotton brokers and merchants. The exchange trades futures and options on cotton, frozen concentrated orange juice and potatoes, as well as an array of interest rate, currency and index futures and options through two subsidiaries. NYCE and the COFFEE, SUGAR & COCOA EXCHANGE merged in 1998, with each exchange retaining its identity and derivative products but operating under a newly-created holding company, the Board of Trade of the City of New York. The FINEX division was created in 1985 as the exchange's financial futures and options division; FINEX Europe, a trading floor in Dublin, Ireland, was established in 1994 to trade FINEX products during European business hours. In December 1993, NYCE acquired the NEW YORK FUTURES EXCHANGE (NYFE) from the NEW YORK STOCK EXCHANGE, as a wholly-owned subsidiary. The exchange collaborates with Cantor Fitzgerald Co. on an electronic futures exchange, combining NYCE's supervision and clearing expertise and Cantor Fitzgerald's execution and brokerage services. NYCE trading hours: 9:45 A.M. to 2:15 P.M., Monday to Friday. *See also* SECURITIES AND COMMODITIES EXCHANGES.

NEW YORK CURB EXCHANGE *see* AMERICAN STOCK EXCHANGE.

NEW YORK FUTURES EXCHANGE (NYFE) wholly-owned subsidiary of the NEW YORK COTTON EXCHANGE, acquired from the NEW YORK STOCK EXCHANGE (NYSE) in December 1993. NYFE trades futures and futures options on the NYSE Composite Index, based on its approximately 2,000 common stocks; the CRB/Bridge Index, based on the Commodity Research Bureau/Bridge Index of 21 commodity components; and the PSE (Pacific Stock Exchange) Technology Index, representing 100 listed and over-the-counter stocks from 15 different technology industries. NYSE Large Composite Index futures has a value of the NYSE Index times $1,000, double the regular NYSE Composite Index future. Trading hours: Monday to Friday, 9:15 A.M. to 4:15 P.M. *See also* SECURITIES AND COMMODITIES EXCHANGES.

NEW YORK MERCANTILE EXCHANGE (NYMEX) world's largest physical commodity futures exchange, following its 1994 merger with COMEX (Commodity Exchange). The exchange operates as two divisions since the merger. The exchange and the INTERNATIONAL PETROLEUM EXCHANGE (IPE) cooperate in an advanced electronic trading system designed to serve as a standard for the oil, natural gas, electricity and coal industries, based on IPE's Energy Trading System (ETS). The NYMEX division trades light, sweet crude oil, heating oil, New York Harbor unleaded gasoline, natural gas, electricity and platinum futures and options; sour crude, Gulf Coast unleaded gasoline, propane and palladium futures; and crack spread options (intercommodity spreads) for heating oil-crude oil and New York Harbor unleaded gasoline-crude oil. The COMEX division trades futures and options in aluminum, coal, copper, gold, silver and the FTSE Eurotop 100 Index, and five-day gold, five-day copper, and five-day silver options. Trading is by open outcry, and is conducted on the ACCESS after hours electronic trading system: Monday through Thursday, 4 P.M. to 8 A.M., and Sunday, 7 P.M. to 8 A.M. for copper, gold, and silver futures; and Monday to Thursday, 4 P.M. to 8 A.M. and Sunday from 7 P.M. to 8 A.M., trading crude oil, heating oil, New York Harbor gasoline, propane, sour crude, natural gas and electricity futures. NYMEX division trading hours are Monday through Friday, from 8:10 A.M. to 3:30 P.M. COMEX division hours are Monday through Friday, from 8:10 A.M. to 3 P.M. (FTSE Eurotop trades from 5:30 A.M. to 11:30 A.M.). *See also* SECURITIES AND COMMODITIES EXCHANGES.

NEW YORK STOCK EXCHANGE (NYSE) founded in 1792, it is the oldest and largest stock exchange in the U.S., located at 11 Wall Street in New York City; also known as the *Big Board* and *The Exchange*. NYSE is an unincorporated association governed by a board of directors which is headed by a full-time paid chairman and is composed of 24 individuals representing the public and the exchange membership in about equal proportion. Staff groups handle specialized functions, such as legal issues, government relations, and economic research; certain operational functions are handled by affiliated corporations, such as Depository Trust Company, National Securities Clearing Corporation (NSCC), and Securities Industry Automation Corporation (SIAC). Total voting membership is currently fixed at 1,366 "seats," which are owned by individuals, usually partners or officers of securities firms. The number of firms represented is over 400, more than 30 of which are specialists responsible for the maintenance of an orderly market in the securities they handle. Most members execute orders for the public, although a small number—called registered competitive market makers—deal exclusively for their own accounts. More than 3,000 companies are listed on the NYSE, representing large firms meeting the exchange's stringent LISTING REQUIREMENTS. STOCKS, BONDS, WARRANTS, OPTIONS, and RIGHTS are traded on the floor of the exchange at 17 figure eight-shaped installations, called trading posts.

Currently, NYSE-listed shares make up more than half of the total dollar volume in shares traded on all U.S. markets. Trading hours: 9:30 A.M. to 4:00 P.M., Monday through Friday. *See also* SECURITIES AND COMMODIITIES EXCHANGES.

NEW YORK STOCK EXCHANGE INDEX *see* STOCK INDEXES AND AVERAGES.

NEW ZEALAND FUTURES AND OPTIONS EXCHANGE electronic screen-trading exchange. A wholly owned subsidiary of the SYDNEY FUTURES EXCHANGE, the New Zealand Futures and Options Exchange allows SFE members access to the exchange's markets through SFE's Sycom trading system. The Forty Index Futures (FIF) contract is based on the NZSE 40 Capital Index; options are traded on the futures. Futures are traded on New Zealand Electricity; options are traded on equities. Futures and options are traded on the NZSE-10 Index, 90-day bank bills, New Zealand 3-year, and 10-year government stock.

NEW ZEALAND STOCK EXCHANGE automated, screen-based national trading system, based in Wellington. The principal index is the NZSE-40 Index of the 40 largest and most liquid stocks, weighted by total market capitalization. The NZSE-30 Selection Index includes the 30 stocks in the NZSE-40 with the largest float capital. Trading hours: 9:30 A.M. to 3:30 P.M., Monday through Friday, with a pre-opening session from 8:30 A.M. to 9:30 A.M. Clearing is through an automated broker-to-broker accounting system. Settlement is for cash on demand, unless otherwise stipulated. Maximum delivery time for a contract is five business days from the trade date.

NICHE particular specialty in which a firm has garnered a large market share. Often, the market will be small enough so that the firm will not attract very much competition. For example, a company that makes a line of specialty chemicals for use by only the petroleum industry is said to have a niche in the chemical industry. Stock analysts frequently favor such companies, since their profit margins can often be wider than those of firms facing more competition.

NICS acronym for *newly industrialized countries,* which are countries that have rapidly developing industrial economies. Some examples of NICS are Hong Kong, Singapore, Malaysia, South Korea, Mexico, Argentina, and Chile. NICS typically have instituted free-market policies which encourage exports to traditional Western industrialized countries and seek investment from Western corporations. Most NICS have increasingly been reducing trade barriers to imports from Western firms.

NIFTY FIFTY 50 stocks most favored by institutions. The membership of this group is constantly changing, although companies that continue to produce consistent earnings growth over a long time tend to remain institutional favorites. Nifty Fifty stocks also tend to have higher than market average price/earnings ratios, since their growth prospects are well recognized by institutional investors. The Nifty Fifty stocks were particularly famous in the bull markets of the 1960s and early 1970s, when many of the price/earnings ratios soared to 50 or more. *See also* PRICE/EARNINGS RATIO.

NIKKEI INDEX *See* NIKKEI STOCK AVERAGE.

NIKKEI STOCK AVERAGE index of 225 leading stocks traded on the Tokyo Stock Exchange. Called the Nikkei Dow Jones Stock Average until it was renamed in May 1985, it is similar to the Dow Jones Industrial Average because it is composed of representative BLUE CHIP companies (termed *first-section* companies in Japan) and is a PRICE-WEIGHTED INDEX. That means that the movement of each stock, in yen or dollars respectively, is weighed equally regardless of its market capitalization. The Nikkei Stock Average, informally called the Nikkei Index and often still referred to as the Nikkei Dow, is published by the *Nihon Keizai Shimbun (Japan Economic Journal)* and is the most widely quoted Japanese stock index.

Also widely quoted is the Tokyo Stock Price Index (Topix) of all issues listed in the First Section.

NINE-BOND RULE New York Stock Exchange (NYSE) requirement that orders for nine bonds or less be sent to the floor for one hour to seek a market. Since bond trading tends to be inactive on the NYSE (because of large institutional holdings and because many of the listed bond trades are handled OVER THE COUNTER), Rule 396 is designed to obtain the most favorable price for small investors. Customers may request that the rule be waived, but the broker-dealer in such cases must then act only as a BROKER and not as a PRINCIPAL (dealer for his own account).

19c3 STOCK stock listed on a national securities exchange, such as the New York Stock Exchange or the American Stock Exchange, after April 26, 1979, and thus exempt from Securities and Exchange Commission rule 19c3 prohibiting exchange members from engaging in OFF-BOARD trading.

NO-ACTION LETTER letter requested from the Securities and Exchange Commission wherein the Commission agrees to take neither civil nor criminal action with respect to the specific activity and circumstances. LIMITED PARTNERSHIPS designed as TAX SHELTERS, which are frequently venturing in uncharted legal territory, often seek no-action letters to clear novel marketing or financing techniques.

NO-BRAINER term used to describe a market the direction of which has become obvious, and therefore requires little or no analysis. This means that most of the stocks will go up in a strong bull market and fall in a bear market, so that it does not matter very much which stock investors buy or sell.

NOB SPREAD acronym for *notes over bonds* spread. Traders buying or selling a NOB spread are trying to profit from changes in the relationship between yields in Treasury notes, which are intermediate-term instruments maturing in 2 to 10 years, and Treasury bonds, which are long-term instruments maturing in 15 or more years. Most people trade the NOB Spread by buying or selling futures contracts on Treasury notes and Treasury bonds. *See also* MOB SPREAD.

NO-FAULT concept used in divorce law and automobile insurance whereby the parties involved are not required to prove blame in an action. The concept recognizes irreconcilable differences as a basis for divorce. In automobile insurance, the accident victim collects directly from his or her own insurance company for medical and hospital expenses, regardless of who was at fault. No-fault statutes vary widely among states that have them. No-fault automobile insurance typically contains provisions aimed at discouraging frivolous lawsuits.

NOISE stock-market activity caused by PROGRAM TRADES and other phenomena not reflective of general sentiment.

NO-LOAD FUND MUTUAL FUND offered by an open-end investment company that imposes no sales charge (load) on its shareholders. Investors buy shares in no-load funds directly from the fund companies, rather than through a BROKER, as is done in load funds. Many no-load fund families (*see* FAMILY OF FUNDS) allow switching of assets between stock, bond, and money market funds. The listing of the price of a no-load fund in a newspaper is accompanied with the designation NL. The net asset value, market price, and offer prices of this type of fund are exactly the same, since there is no sales charge. *See also* LOAD FUND.

NO-LOAD STOCK shares available for DIRECT PURCHASE from the issuing companies, thus avoiding brokers and sales commissions. Such shares are typically offered as a part of a company's DIVIDEND REINVESTMENT PLAN to encourage long-term investment. Prices are based on an average of recent market prices and may not be as low as the current market price. Broker commissions are payable if and when the shares are sold.

NOMINAL DOLLARS dollars unadjusted for inflation. For example, economists will refer to a product that cost 100 nominal dollars several years ago, and now costs $150. However, adjusted for inflation, the product's current price may be much higher or lower. Most financial statements are reported in nominal dollars.

NOMINAL EXERCISE PRICE EXERCISE PRICE (strike price) of a GOVERNMENT NATIONAL MORTGAGE ASSOCIATION (GNMA or Ginnie Mae) option contract, obtained by multiplying the unpaid principal balance on a Ginnie Mae certificate by the ADJUSTED EXERCISE PRICE. For example, if the unpaid principal balance is $96,000 and the adjusted exercise price is 58, the nominal exercise price is $55,680.

NOMINAL INCOME income unadjusted for changes in the PURCHAS-ING POWER OF THE DOLLAR. GENERALLY ACCEPTED ACCOUNTING PRINCI-PLES (GAAP) require certain large, publicly held companies to provide supplementary information adjusting income from continuing opera-tions for changing prices. FINANCIAL ACCOUNTING STANDARDS BOARD (FASB) Statement Number 89 removed the requirement to present general purchasing power and current cost/constant dollar supplement statements, however.

NOMINAL INTEREST RATE *see* NOMINAL YIELD.

NOMINAL QUOTATION bid and offer prices given by a market maker for the purpose of valuation, not as an invitation to trade. Securities industry rules require that nominal quotations be specifically identi-fied as such; usually this is done by prefixing the quote with the let-ters FYI (FOR YOUR INFORMATION) or FVO (for valuation only).

NOMINAL RATE OF INTEREST rate of interest unadjusted for infla-tion. The actual interest rate charged by a bank on a loan is in nominal dollars. This is in contrast to interest rates that have been adjusted for either past or projected inflation, called REAL INTEREST RATES.

NOMINAL YIELD annual dollar amount of income received from a fixed-income security divided by the PAR VALUE of the security and stated as a percentage. Thus a bond that pays $90 a year and has a par value of $1000 has a nominal yield of 9%, called its *coupon rate.* Similarly, a preferred stock that pays a $9 annual dividend and has a par value of $100 has a nominal yield of 9%. Only when a stock or bond is bought exactly at par value is the nominal yield equal to the actual yield. Since market prices of fixed-income securities go down when market interest rates go up and vice versa, the actual yield, which is determined by the market price and coupon rate (nominal yield), will be higher when the purchase price is below par value and lower when the purchase price is above par value. *See also* RATE OF RETURN.

NOMINEE person or firm, such as a bank official or brokerage house, into whose name securities or other properties are transferred by agreement. Securities held in STREET NAME, for example, are registered in the name of a BROKER (nominee) to facilitate transactions, although the customer remains the true owner.

NONACCREDITED INVESTOR investor who does not meet the net worth requirements of SEC Regulation D. Under Rules 505 and 506 of Regulation D, an investment can be offered to a maximum of 35 nonaccredited investors. Such investors tend to be wealthy and sophis-ticated, and therefore the SEC feels they need less investor protection than smaller, less sophisticated investors.

NONCALLABLE preferred stock or bond that cannot be redeemed at the option of the issuer. A bond may offer CALL PROTECTION for a par-ticular length of time, such as ten years. After that, the issuer may redeem the bond if it chooses and can justify doing so. U.S. government bond obligations are not callable until close to maturity. Provisions for noncallability are spelled out in detail in a bond's INDENTURE agreement or in the prospectus issued at the time a new preferred stock is floated. Bond yields are often quoted to the first date at which the bonds could be called. *See also* YIELD TO CALL.

NONCLEARING MEMBER member firm of the New York Stock Exchange or another organized exchange that does not have the operational facilities for clearing transactions and thus pays a fee to have the services performed by another member firm, called a *clearing member.* The clearing process involves comparison and verification of information between the buying and selling brokers and then the physical delivery of certificates in exchange for payment, called the *settlement.*

NONCOMPETITIVE BID method of buying Treasury bills without having to meet the high minimum purchase requirements of the regular DUTCH AUCTION; also called *noncompetitive tender.* The process of bidding for Treasury bills is split into two parts: competitive and noncompetitive bids.

COMPETITIVE BIDS are entered by large government securities dealers and brokers, who buy millions of dollars worth of bills. They offer the best price they can for the securities, and the highest bids are accepted by the Treasury in what is called the Dutch auction.

Noncompetitive bids are submitted by smaller investors through a Federal Reserve Bank, the Bureau of Federal Debt, or certain commercial banks. These bids will be executed at the average of the prices paid in all the competitive bids accepted by the Treasury. The minimum noncompetitive bid for a Treasury bill is $10,000. *See also* TREASURY DIRECT.

NONCONTESTABILITY CLAUSE provision found in insurance contracts stipulating that policyholders cannot be denied coverage after a specific period of time, usually two years, even if the policyholder provided inaccurate or even fraudulent information in his or her insurance application. In order to contest the policy, the insurer must find out about the incorrect information before the clause goes into effect. *See* INCONTESTABILITY CLAUSE.

NONCONTRIBUTORY PENSION PLAN pension plan that is totally funded by the employer, and to which employees are not expected to contribute. Most DEFINED BENEFIT PENSION PLANS are noncontributory. In contrast, DEFINED CONTRIBUTION PENSION PLANS offer employees the choice to contribute to a plan such as a 401(k) or 403(b).

NONCUMULATIVE term describing a preferred stock issue in which unpaid dividends do not accrue. Such issues contrast with CUMULATIVE PREFERRED issues, where unpaid dividends accumulate and must be paid before dividends on common shares. Most preferred issues are cumulative. On a noncumulative preferred, omitted dividends will, as a rule, never be paid. Some older railroad preferred stocks are of this type.

NONCURRENT ASSET asset not expected to be converted into cash, sold, or exchanged within the normal operating cycle of the firm, usually one year. Examples of noncurrent assets include FIXED ASSETS, such as real estate, machinery, and other equipment; LEASEHOLD IMPROVEMENTS; INTANGIBLE ASSETS, such as goodwill, patents, and trademarks; notes receivable after one year; other investments; miscellaneous assets not meeting the definition of a CURRENT ASSET. Prepaid expenses (also called DEFERRED CHARGES or *deferred expenses),* which include such items as rent paid in advance, prepaid insurance premiums, and subscriptions, are usually considered current assets by accountants. Credit analysts, however, prefer to classify these expenses as noncurrent assets, since prepayments do not represent asset strength and protection in the way that other current assets do, with their convertibility into cash during the normal operating cycle and their liquidation value should operations be terminated.

NONCURRENT LIABILITY LIABILITY due after one year.

NONDISCRETIONARY TRUST TRUST where the trustee has no power to determine the amount of distributions to the beneficiary. Contrast with DISCRETIONARY TRUST.

NONFINANCIAL ASSETS assets that are physical, such as REAL ESTATE and PERSONAL PROPERTY.

NON-INTEREST-BEARING NOTE note that makes no periodic interest payments. Instead, the note is sold at a discount and matures at face value. Also called a ZERO-COUPON BOND.

NONMEMBER FIRM brokerage firm that is not a member of an organized exchange. Such firms execute their trades either through member firms, on regional exchanges, or in the THIRD MARKET. *See* MEMBER FIRM; REGIONAL STOCK EXCHANGES.

NONPARTICIPATING LIFE INSURANCE POLICY life insurance policy that does not pay dividends. Policyholders thus do not participate in the interest, dividends, and capital gains earned by the insurer on premiums paid. In contrast, PARTICIPATING INSURANCE POLICIES pay dividends to policyholders from earnings on investments.

NONPARTICIPATING PREFERRED STOCK *see* PARTICIPATING PREFERRED STOCK.

NONPERFORMING ASSET ASSET not effectual in the production of income. In banking, commercial loans 90 days past due and consumer loans 180 days past due are classified as nonperforming.

NONPRODUCTIVE LOAN type of commercial bank loan that increases the amount of spending power in the economy but does not lead directly to increased output; for example, a loan to finance a LEVERAGED BUYOUT.

The Federal Reserve has on occasion acted to curtail such lending as one of its early steps in implementing monetary restraint.

NONPUBLIC INFORMATION information about a company, either positive or negative, that will have a material effect on the stock price when it is released to the public. Insiders, such as corporate officers and members of the board of directors, are not allowed to trade on material nonpublic information until it has been released to the public, since they would have an unfair advantage over unsuspecting investors. Some examples of important nonpublic information are an imminent takeover announcement, a soon-to-be-released earnings report that is more favorable than most analysts expect, or the sudden resignation of a key corporate official. *See also* DISCLOSURE; INSIDER.

NONPURPOSE LOAN loan for which securities are pledged as collateral but which is not used to purchase or carry securities. Under Federal Reserve Board REGULATION U, a borrower using securities as collateral must sign an affidavit called a PURPOSE STATEMENT, indicating the use to which the loan is to be put. Regulation U limits the amount of credit a bank may extend for purchasing and carrying margin securities, where the credit is secured directly or indirectly by stock.

NONQUALIFYING ANNUITY annuity purchased outside of an IRS-approved pension plan. The contributions to such an annuity are made with after-tax dollars. Just as with a QUALIFYING ANNUITY, however, the earnings from the nonqualifying annuity can accumulate tax deferred until withdrawn. Assets may be placed in either a FIXED ANNUITY, a VARIABLE ANNUITY, or a HYBRID ANNUITY.

NONQUALIFYING STOCK OPTION employee stock option not meeting the Internal Revenue Service criteria for QUALIFYING STOCK OPTIONS (INCENTIVE STOCK OPTIONS) and therefore triggering a tax upon EXERCISE. (The issuing employer, however, can deduct the nonqualifying option during the period when it is exercised, whereas it would not have a deduction when a qualifying option is exercised. A STOCK OPTION is a right issued by a corporation to an individual, normally an executive employee, to buy a given amount of shares at a stated price within a specified period of time. Gains realized on the exercise of nonqualifying options are treated as ordinary income in the tax year in which the options are exercised. Qualifying stock options, in contrast, are taxed neither at the time of granting or the time of exercise; only when the underlying stock is sold and a CAPITAL GAIN realized, does a tax event occur.

NONRATED bonds that have not been rated by one or more of the major rating agencies such as STANDARD & POOR'S, MOODY'S INVESTORS SERVICE or FITCH INVESTORS SERVICE. Issues are usually nonrated because they are too small to justify the expense of getting a rating. Nonrated bonds are not necessarily better or worse than rated bonds, though many institutions cannot buy them because they need to hold bonds with an investment-grade rating.

NONRECOURSE LOAN type of financial arrangement used by limited partners in a DIRECT PARTICIPATION PROGRAM, whereby the limited partners finance a portion of their participation with a loan secured by their ownership in the underlying venture. They benefit from the LEVERAGE provided by the loan. In case of default, the lender has no recourse to the assets of the partnership beyond those held by the limited partners who borrowed the money.

NONRECURRING CHARGE one-time expense or WRITE-OFF appearing in a company's financial statement; also called *extraordinary charge*. Nonrecurring charges would include, for example, a major fire or theft, the write-off of a division, and the effect of a change in accounting procedure.

NONREFUNDABLE provision in a bond INDENTURE that either prohibits or sets limits on the issuer's retiring the bonds with the proceeds of a subsequent issue, called REFUNDING. Such a provision often does not rule out refunding altogether but protects bondholders from REDEMPTION until a specified date. Other such provisions may preclude refunding unless new bonds can be issued at a specified lower rate. *See also* CALL PROTECTION.

NONVOTING STOCK corporate securities that do not empower a holder to vote on corporate resolutions or the election of directors. Such stock is sometimes issued in connection with a takeover attempt, when management creates nonvoting shares to dilute the target firm's equity and thereby discourage the merger attempt. Except in very special circumstances, the New York Stock Exchange does not list nonvoting stock. Preferred stock is normally nonvoting stock. *See also* VOTING STOCK; VOTING TRUST CERTIFICATE.

NO-PAR-VALUE STOCK stock with no set (par) value specified in the corporate charter or on the stock certificate; also called *no-par stock*. Companies issuing no-par value shares may carry whatever they receive for them either as part of the CAPITAL STOCK account or as part of the CAPITAL SURPLUS (paid-in capital) account, or both. Whatever amount is carried as capital stock has an implicit value, represented by the number of outstanding shares divided into the dollar amount of capital stock.

The main attraction of no-par stock to issuing corporations, historically, had to do with the fact that many states imposed taxes based on PAR VALUE, while other states, like Delaware, encouraged incorporations with no-par-value stock.

For the investor, there are two reservations: (1) that unwise or inept directors may reduce the value of outstanding shares by accepting bargain basement prices on new issues (shareholders are protected, to some extent, from this by PREEMPTIVE RIGHT—the right to purchase enough of a new issue to protect their power and equity) and (2) that too great an amount of shareholder contributions may be channeled into the capital surplus account, which is restricted by the law of many states from being a source of dividend payments. *See* ILLEGAL DIVIDEND.

Still, no-par stock, along with low-par stock, remains an appealing alternative, from the issuer's standpoint, to par-value shares because of investor confusion of par value and real value.

Most stock issued today is either no-par or low-par value.

NORMAL INVESTMENT PRACTICE history of investment in a customer account with a member of the National Association of Securities Dealers as defined in their rules of fair practice. It is used to test the bona fide PUBLIC OFFERINGS requirement that applies to the allocation of a HOT ISSUE. If the buying customer has a history of purchasing similar amounts in normal circumstances, the sale qualifies as a bona fide public offering and is not in violation of the Rules of Fair Practice. A record of buying only hot issues is not acceptable as normal investment practice. *See also* NASD FORM FR-1.

NORMALIZED EARNINGS earnings, either in the past or the future, that are adjusted for cyclical ups and downs in the economy. Earnings are normalized by analysts by generating a moving average over several years including up and down cycles. Analysts refer to normalized earnings when explaining whether a company's current profits are above or below its long-term trend.

NORMAL MARKET SIZE (NMS) share classification system that in 1991 replaced the alpha, beta, gamma, delta, system brought in with BIG BANG on the INTERNATIONAL STOCK EXCHANGE OF THE U.K. AND THE REPUBLIC OF IRELAND (ISE). The earlier system had unintentionally become a measure of corporate status, strength, and viability. The new system has 12 categories based on the size of the transactions that are normal for each security. The system fixes the size of transactions in which market makers are obligated to deal.

NORMAL RETIREMENT point at which a pension plan participant can retire and immediately receive unreduced benefits. Pension plans can specify age and length-of-service requirements that employees must meet to be eligible for retirement.

NORMAL TRADING UNIT standard minimum size of a trading unit for a particular security; also called a ROUND LOT. For instance, stocks have a normal trading unit of 100 shares, although inactive stocks trade in 10-share round lots. Any securities trade for less than a round lot is called an ODD LOT trade.

NOTE written promise to pay a specified amount to a certain entity on demand or on a specified date. See *also* MUNICIPAL NOTE; PROMISSORY NOTE; TREASURIES.

NOT-FOR-PROFIT type of incorporated organization in which no stockholder or trustee shares in profits or losses and which usually exists to accomplish some charitable, humanitarian, or educational purpose; also called *nonprofit.* Such groups are exempt from corporate income taxes but are subject to other taxes on income-producing property or enterprises. Donations to these groups are usually tax deductible for the donor. Some examples are hospitals, colleges and universities, foundations, and such familiar groups as the Red Cross and Girl Scouts.

NOT HELD instruction (abbreviated NH) on a market order to buy or sell securities, indicating that the customer has given the FLOOR BROKER time and price discretion in executing the best possible trade but will not hold the broker responsible if the best deal is not obtained. Such orders, which are usually for large blocks of securities, were originally designed for placement with specialists, who could hold an order back if they felt prices were going to rise. The Securities and Exchange Commission no longer allows specialists to handle NH orders, leaving floor brokers without any clear alternative except to persuade the customer to change the order to a LIMIT ORDER. The broker can then turn the order over to a SPECIALIST, who could sell pieces of the block to floor traders or buy it for his own account. *See* SPECIALIST BLOCK PURCHASE AND SALE. An older variation of NH is DRT, meaning disregard tape.

NOTICE OF SALE advertisement placed by an issuer of municipal securities announcing its intentions to sell a new issue and inviting underwriters to submit COMPETITIVE BIDS.

NOT RATED indication used by securities rating services (such as STANDARD & POOR'S, MOODY'S INVESTORS SERVICE, or FITCH INVESTORS SERVICE) and mercantile agencies (such as Dun & Bradstreet) to show that a security or a company has not been rated. It has neither negative nor positive implications. The abbreviation NR is used.

NOT-SUFFICIENT-FUNDS CHECK a bank check written against an inadequate balance. Also called *insufficient-funds check* and, informally, a *bounced check.*

NOUVEAU MARCHE equity market unit of the PARIS BOURSE dedicated to innovative, high-growth companies. Nouveau Marche, in turn, is linked to other European markets in EURO.NM, which is modeled on the NASDAQ market in the U.S.

NOVATION
1. agreement to replace one party to a contract with a new party. The novation transfers both rights and duties and requires the consent of both the original and the new party.
2. replacement of an older debt or obligation with a newer one.

NOW ACCOUNT *see* NEGOTIABLE ORDER OF WITHDRAWAL.

NUMISMATIC COIN coin that is valued based on its rarity, age, quantity originally produced, and condition. These coins are bought and sold as individual items within the coin collecting community. Most numismatic coins are legal tender coins that were produced in limited quantities to give them scarcity value. They are historic coins which also can be rare. The current price of gold is a minor factor when dealing with numismatic coins. Premiums are traditionally far higher than those of BULLION COINS, and values fluctuate to a much wider extent. For example, a $5 gold piece may contain $60 worth of gold and may sell for as much as $700. The minimum amount recovered from numismatic coin investments is always either its face value or its metal content. Most coins, however, sell substantially above these amounts. Since the markup over bullion value can vary widely from one dealer to another, investors need to shop around diligently to avoid paying exhorbitant markups.

O

OBLIGATION legal responsibility, as for a DEBT.

OBLIGATION BOND type of mortgage bond in which the face value is greater than the value of the underlying property. The difference compensates the lender for costs exceeding the mortgage value.

OBLIGOR one who has an obligation, such as an issuer of bonds, a borrower of money from a bank or another source, or a credit customer of a business supplier or retailer. The obligor *(obligator, debtor)* is legally bound to pay a debt, including interest, when due.

ODD LOT securities trade made for less than the NORMAL TRADING UNIT (termed a ROUND LOT). In stock trading, any purchase or sale of less than 100 shares is considered an odd lot, although inactive stocks generally trade in round lots of 10 shares. An investor buying or selling an odd lot pays a higher commission rate than someone making a round-lot trade. This odd-lot differential varies among brokers but for stocks is often ⅛ of a point (12½¢) per share. For instance, someone buying 100 shares of XYZ at $70 would pay $70 a share plus commission. At the same time, someone buying only 50 shares of XYZ would pay $70⅛ a share plus commission. *See also* ODD-LOT DEALER; ODD-LOT SHORT-SALE RATIO; ODD-LOT THEORY.

ODD-LOT DEALER originally a dealer who bought round lots of stock and resold it in odd lots to retail brokers who, in turn, accommodated their smaller customers at the regular commission rate plus an extra charge, called the odd-lot differential. The assembling of round lots from odd lots is now a service provided free by New York Stock Exchange specialists to member brokers, and odd-lot transactions can be executed through most brokers serving the retail public. Brokers handling odd lots do, however, receive extra compensation; it varies with the broker, but ⅛ of a point (12½¢) per share in addition to a regular commission is typical. *See also* ODD-LOT.

ODD-LOT SHORT-SALE RATIO ratio obtained by dividing ODD LOT short sales by total odd-lot sales, using New York Stock Exchange (NYSE) statistics; also called the *odd-lot selling indicator.* Historically, odd-lot investors—those who buy and sell in less than 100-share round lots—react to market highs and lows; when the market reaches a low point, odd-lot short sales reach a high point, and vice versa. The odd-lot ratio has followed the opposite pattern of the NYSE MEMBER SHORT SALE RATIO. *See also* ODD-LOT THEORY.

ODD-LOT THEORY historical theory that the ODD LOT investor—the small personal investor who trades in less than 100-share quantities—is usually guilty of bad timing and that profits can be made by acting contrary to odd-lot trading patterns. Heavy odd-lot buying in a rising market is interpreted by proponents of this theory as a sign of technical weakness and the signal of a market reversal. Conversely, an increase of odd-lot selling in a declining market is seen as a sign of technical strength and a signal to buy. In fact, analyses of odd-lot trading over the years fail to bear out the theory with any real degree of consistency, and it has fallen into disfavor in recent years. It is also a fact that odd-lot customers generally, who tend to buy market leaders, have fared rather well in the upward market that has prevailed over the last fifty years or so. *See also* ODD-LOT SHORT-SALE RATIO.

OEX pronounced as three letters, Wall Street shorthand for the Standard & Poor's 100 stock index, which comprises stocks for which options are traded on the CHICAGO BOARD OPTIONS EXCHANGE (CBOE). OEX index options are traded on the CHICAGO BOARD OF TRADE (CBOT), and futures are traded on the CHICAGO MERCANTILE EXCHANGE (CME). *See also* STOCK INDICES AND AVERAGES.

OFF-BALANCE-SHEET FINANCING financing that does not add debt on a balance sheet and thus does not affect borrowing capacity as it would be determined by financial ratios. The most common example would be a lease structured as an OPERATING LEASE rather than a CAPITAL LEASE and where management's intent is, in fact, to acquire an asset and corresponding liability without reflecting either on its balance sheet. Other examples include the sale of receivables with recourse, TAKE-OR-PAY CONTRACTS, and bank financial instruments such as guarantees, letters of credit, and loan commitments. GENERALLY ACCEPTED ACCOUNTING PRINCIPLES (GAAP) require that information be provided in financial statements about off-balance-sheet financing involving credit, market, and liquidity risk.

OFF-BOARD off the exchange (the New York Stock Exchange is known as the Big Board, hence the term). The term is used either for a trade that is executed OVER THE COUNTER or for a transaction entailing listed securities that is not completed on a national exchange. Over-the-counter trading is handled by telephone, with competitive bidding carried on constantly by market makers in a particular stock. The other kind of off-board trade occurs when a block of stock is exchanged between customers of a brokerage firm, or between a customer and the firm itself if the brokerage house wants to buy or sell securities from its own inventory. *See also* THIRD MARKET.

OFFER price at which someone who owns a security offers to sell it; also known as the ASKED PRICE. This price is listed in newspapers for stocks traded OVER THE COUNTER. The bid price—the price at which someone is prepared to buy—is also shown. The bid price is always lower than the offer price. *See also* OFFERING PRICE.

OFFERING *see* PUBLIC OFFERING.

OFFERING CIRCULAR *see* PROSPECTUS.

OFFERING DATE date on which a distribution of stocks or bonds will first be available for sale to the public. *See also* DATED DATE; PUBLIC OFFERING.

OFFERING PRICE price per share at which a new or secondary distribution of securities is offered for sale to the public; also called PUBLIC OFFERING PRICE. For instance, if a new issue of XYZ stock is priced at $40 a share, the offering price is $40.

When mutual fund shares are made available to the public, they are sold at NET ASSET VALUE, also called the *offering price* or the ASKED PRICE, plus a sales charge, if any. In a NO-LOAD FUND, the offering price is the same as the net asset value. In a LOAD FUND, the sales charge is added to the net asset value, to arrive at the offering price. *See also* OFFER.

OFFERING SCALE prices at which different maturities of a SERIAL BOND issue are offered to the public by an underwriter. The offering scale may also be expressed in terms of YIELD TO MATURITY.

OFFER WANTED (OW) notice by a potential buyer of a security that he or she is looking for an offer by a potential seller of the security. The abbreviation OW is frequently seen in the PINK SHEETS (listing of stocks) and YELLOW SHEETS (listing of corporate bonds) published by the NATIONAL QUOTATION BUREAU for securities traded by OVER THE COUNTER dealers. *See also* BID WANTED.

OFF-FLOOR ORDER order to buy or sell a security that originates off the floor of an exchange. These are customer orders originating with brokers, as distinguished from orders of floor members trading for their own accounts (ON-FLOOR ORDERS). Exchange rules require that off-floor orders be executed before orders initiated on the floor.

OFFICE OF MANAGEMENT AND BUDGET (OMB) at the federal level, an agency within the Office of the President responsible for (1) preparing and presenting to Congress the president's budget; (2) working with the Council of Economic Advisers and the Treasury Department in developing a fiscal program; (3) reviewing the administrative policies and performance of government agencies; and (4) advising the president on legislative matters.

OFFICE OF THRIFT SUPERVISION (OTS) agency of the U.S. Treasury Department created by the FINANCIAL INSTITUTIONS REFORM, RECOVERY AND ENFORCEMENT ACT OF 1989 (FIRREA), the bailout bill enacted to assist depositors that became law on August 9, 1989. The OTS replaced the disbanded FEDERAL HOME LOAN BANK BOARD and assumed responsibility for the nation's savings and loan industry. The legislation empowered OTS to institute new regulations, charter new federal savings and loan associations and federal savings banks, and supervise all savings institutions and their holding companies insured by the SAVINGS ASSOCIATION INSURANCE FUND (SAIF). *See also* BAILOUT BOND.

OFFICIAL NOTICE OF SALE notice published by a municipality inviting investment bankers to submit competitive bids for an upcoming bond issue. The notice provides the name of a municipal official from whom further details can be obtained and states certain basic information about the issue, such as its par value and important conditions. The *Bond Buyer* regularly carries such notices.

OFFICIAL STATEMENT *see* LEGAL OPINION.

OFFSET

Accounting: (1) amount equaling or counterbalancing another amount on the opposite side of the same ledger or the ledger of another account. *See also* ABSORBED. (2) amount that cancels or reduces a claim.

Banking: (1) bank's legal right to seize deposit funds to cover a loan in default—called *right of offset.* (2) number stored on a bank card that, when related to the code number remembered by the cardholder, represents the depositor's identification number, called *PAN-PIN pair.*

Securities, commodities, options: (1) closing transaction involving the purchase or sale of an OPTION having the same features as one already held. (2) HEDGE, such as the SHORT SALE of a stock to protect a capital gain or the purchase of a future to protect a commodity price, or a STRADDLE representing the purchase of offsetting put and call options on a security.

OFFSHORE term used in the United States for any financial organization with a headquarters outside the country. A MUTUAL FUND with a legal domicile in the Bahamas or the Cayman Islands, for instance, is called an *offshore fund.* To be sold in the United States, such funds must adhere to all pertinent federal and state regulations. Many banks have offshore subsidiaries that engage in activities that are either heavily regulated or taxed or not allowed under U.S. law.

OIL AND GAS LIMITED PARTNERSHIP partnership consisting of one or more limited partners and one or more general partners that is structured to find, extract, and market commercial quantities of oil and natural gas. The limited partners, who assume no liability beyond the funds they contribute, buy units in the partnership, typically for at least $5000 a unit, from a broker registered to sell that partnership. All the limited partners' money then goes to the GENERAL PARTNER, the partner with unlimited liability, who either searches for oil and gas (an exploratory or wildcat well), drills for oil and gas in a proven oil field (a DEVELOPMENTAL DRILLING PROGRAM), or pumps petroleum and gas from an existing well (a COMPLETION PROGRAM). The riskier the chance of finding oil and gas, the higher the potential reward or loss to the limited partner. Conservative investors who mainly want to collect income from the sale of proven oil and gas reserves are safest with a developmental or completion program.

Subject to PASSIVE income rules, limited partners also receive tax breaks, such as depreciation deductions for equipment used for drilling and oil depletion allowances for the value of oil extracted from the fields. If the partnership borrows money for increased drilling, limited partners also can get deductions for the interest cost of the loans. *See also* EXPLORATORY DRILLING PROGRAM; INCOME LIMITED PARTNERSHIP; INTANGIBLE COSTS; LIMITED PARTNERSHIP; WILDCAT DRILLING.

OIL AND GAS LOTTERY program run by the Bureau of Land Management at the U.S. Department of the Interior that permits anyone filing an application to be selected for the right to drill for oil and gas on selected parcels of federal land. Both large oil companies and small speculators enter this lottery. An individual winning the drawing for a particularly desirable plot of land may sublet the property to an oil company, which will pay him or her royalties if the land yields commercial quantities of oil and gas.

OIL PATCH states in America that produce and refine oil and gas. This includes Texas, Oklahoma, Louisiana, California, and Alaska. Economists refer to oil patch states when assessing the strength or weakness of a region of the country tied to movements in oil prices.

OLIGOPOLY market situation in which a small number of selling firms control the market supply of a particular good or service and are therefore able to control the market price. An oligopoly can be *perfect*—where all firms produce an identical good or service (cement)—or *imperfect*—where each firm's product has a different identity but is essentially similar to the others (cigarettes). Because each firm in an oligopoly knows its share of the total market for the product or service it produces, and because any change in price or change in market share by one firm is reflected in the sales of the others, there tends to be a high degree of interdependence among firms; each firm must make its price and output decisions with regard to the responses of the other firms in the oligopoly, so that oligopoly prices, once established, are rigid. This encourages nonprice competition, through advertising, packaging, and service—a generally nonproductive form of resource allocation. Two examples of oligopoly in the United States are airlines serving the same routes and tobacco companies. *See also* OLIGOPSONY.

OLIGOPSONY market situation in which a few large buyers control the purchasing power and therefore the output and market price of a good or service; the buy-side counterpart of OLIGOPOLY. Oligopsony prices tend to be lower than the prices in a freely competitive market, just as oligopoly prices tend to be higher. For example, the large tobacco companies purchase all the output of a large number of small tobacco growers and therefore are able to control tobacco prices.

OMITTED DIVIDEND dividend that was scheduled to be declared by a corporation, but instead was not voted for the time being by the board of directors. Dividends are sometimes omitted when a company has run into financial difficulty and its board decides it is more important to conserve cash than to pay a dividend to shareholders. The announcement of an omitted dividend will typically cause the company's stock price to drop, particularly if the announcement is a surprise.

OM STOCKHOLM AB screen-based derivatives market of Sweden, trading a wide variety of interest rate and bond futures. The exchange trades futures and options on the OMX Equity Index. It offers a clearing service for interbank futures trading on notional bonds, Treasury bills and mortgage bonds. OMLX, the London Securities and Derivatives Exchange, is a wholly-owned subsidiary of OM Stockholm, and the two exchanges have a trading and clearing link. Under an existing cooperation agreement between SOM of Finland and OM Stockholm, SOM products also trade in Stockholm at the OMLX. OM's products, in turn, trade in Finland. Trading hours: 9 A.M. to 5 P.M.

ON ACCOUNT
In general: in partial payment of an obligation.
Finance: on credit terms. The term applies to a relationship between a seller and a buyer wherein payment is expected sometime after delivery and the obligation is not documented by a NOTE. Synonymous with *open account*.

ON A SCALE *see* SCALE ORDER.

ON-BALANCE VOLUME TECHNICAL ANALYSIS method that attempts to pinpoint when a stock, bond, or commodity is being accumulated by many buyers or is being distributed by many sellers. The on-balance volume line is superimposed on the stock price line on a chart, and it is considered significant when the two lines cross. The chart indicates a buy signal when accumulation is detected and a sell signal when distribution is spotted. The on-balance method can be used to diagnose an entire market or an individual stock, bond, or commodity.

ONE-CANCELS-THE-OTHER ORDER *see* ALTERNATIVE ORDER.

ONE DECISION STOCK stock with sufficient quality and growth potential to be suitable for a BUY AND HOLD STRATEGY.

ONE-SHARE-ONE VOTE RULE the principle that public companies should not reduce shareholder voting rights. Originally, the New York Stock Exchange had a one-share, one-vote requirement for its listed companies. In 1988, the SEC adopted Rule 19c-4, which prohibited companies listed on a national securities exchange or quoted on the National Association of Securities Dealers Automated Quotation System (NASDAQ) from disenfranchising existing shareholders through, for example, issuances of super voting stock. The rule, however, was struck down by the Court of Appeals in *Business Roundtable v. SEC* in 1990. In December 1994, the SEC approved rules proposed by the New York Stock Exchange, American Stock Exchange, and National Association of Securities Dealers that establish a uniform voting standard. This new standard prohibits companies listed on the NYSE, the AMEX, or the NASDAQ system from taking any corporate action or issuing any stock that has the effect of disparately reducing or restricting the voting rights of existing common stock shareholders.

ON-FLOOR ORDER security order originating with a member on the floor of an exchange when dealing for his or her own account. The designation separates such orders from those for customers' accounts (OFF-FLOOR ORDERS), which are generally given precedence by exchange rules.

ON MARGIN *see* MARGIN.

ON THE CLOSE ORDER order to buy or sell a specified number of shares in a particular stock as close as possible to the closing price of the day. Brokers accepting on the close orders do not guarantee that the trade will be executed at the final closing price, or even that the trade can be completed at all. On an order ticket, on the close orders are abbreviated as "OTC" orders. *See also* AT THE CLOSE ORDER; MARKET-ON-CLOSE ORDER.

ON THE OPENING ORDER order to buy or sell a specified number of shares in a particular stock at the price of the first trade of the day. If the trader cannot buy or sell shares at that price, the order is immediately cancelled.

ON THE SIDELINES investors who refrain from investing because of market uncertainty are said to be on the sidelines. The analogy is to a football game, in which spectators on the sidelines do not actively participate in the game. Investors on the sidelines normally keep their money in short-term instruments such as money market mutual funds, which can be tapped instantly if the investor sees a good opportunity to reenter the stock or bond markets. Market commentators frequently say that trading activity was light "because investors stayed on the sidelines."

OPD ticker tape symbol designating (1) the first transaction of the day in a security after a DELAYED OPENING or (2) the opening transaction in a security whose price has changed significantly from the previous day's close—usually 2 or more points on stocks selling at $20 or higher, 1 or more points on stocks selling at less than $20.

OPEN
Securities:
  1. status of an order to buy or sell securities that has still not been executed. A GOOD-TILL-CANCELED ORDER that remains pending is an example of an open order.
  2. to establish an account with a broker.
  Banking: to establish an account or a LETTER OF CREDIT.
  Finance: unpaid balance.

See also OPEN-END LEASE; OPEN-END MANAGEMENT COMPANY; OPEN-END MORTGAGE; OPEN INTEREST; OPEN ORDER; OPEN REPO.

OPEN-END CREDIT revolving line of credit offered by banks, savings and loans, and other lenders to consumers. The line of credit is set with a particular limit, after which consumers can borrow using a credit card, check, or cash advance. Every time a purchase or cash advance is made, credit is extended on behalf of the consumer. Consumers may pay off the entire balance each month, thereby avoiding interest charges. Or they may pay a minimum amount, with interest accruing on the outstanding balance.

OPEN-END LEASE lease agreement providing for an additional payment after the property is returned to the lessor, to adjust for any change in the value of the property.

OPEN-END MANAGEMENT COMPANY INVESTMENT COMPANY that sells MUTUAL FUNDS to the public. The term arises from the fact that the firm continually creates new shares on demand, although an open-end fund may close itself to new investors when its management decides that it is too large. Mutual fund shareholders buy the shares at NET ASSET VALUE and can redeem them at any time at the prevailing market price, which may be higher or lower than the price at which the investor bought. The shareholder's funds are invested in stocks, bonds, or money market instruments, depending on the type of mutual fund company. The opposite of an open-end management company is a CLOSED-END MANAGEMENT COMPANY, which issues a limited number of shares, which are then traded on a stock exchange.

OPEN-END MORTGAGE
Real estate finance: MORTGAGE that allows the issuance of additional bonds having equal status with the original issue, but that protects the original bondholders with specific restrictions governing subsequent borrowing under the original mortgage. For example, the terms of the original INDENTURE might permit additional mortgage-bond financing up to 75% of the value of the property acquired, but only if total fixed charges on all debt, including the proposed new bonds, have been earned a stated number of times over the previous 5 years. The open-end mortgage is a more practical and acceptable (to the mortgage holder) version of the *open mortgage,* which allows a corporation to issue unlimited amounts of bonds under the original first mortgage, with no protection to the original bondholders. An even more conservative version is the *limited open-end mortgage,* which usually contains the same restrictions as the open-end, but places a limit on the amount of first mortgage bonds that can be issued, and typically provides that proceeds from new bond issues be used to retire outstanding bonds with the same or prior security.
Trust banking: corporate trust indenture that permits the trustee to authenticate and deliver bonds from time to time in addition to the original issue. *See also* AUTHENTICATION.

OPEN-END (MUTUAL) FUND *see* OPEN-END MANAGEMENT COMPANY.

OPENING

1. price at which a security or commodity starts a trading day. Investors who want to buy or sell as soon as the market opens will put in an order at the opening price.

2. short time frame of market opportunity. For instance, if interest rates have been rising for months, and for a few days or weeks they fall, a corporation that has wanted to FLOAT bonds at lower interest rates might seize the moment to issue the bonds. This short time frame would be called an *opening in the market* or a *window of opportunity. See also* WINDOW.

OPEN INTEREST total number of contracts in a commodity or options market that are still open; that is, they have not been exercised, closed out, or allowed to expire. The term also applies to a particular commodity or, in the case of options, to the number of contracts outstanding on a particular underlying security. The level of open interest is reported daily in newspaper commodity and options pages.

OPEN-MARKET COMMITTEE *see* FEDERAL OPEN MARKET COMMITTEE (FOMC).

OPEN-MARKET OPERATIONS activities by which the Securities Department of the Federal Reserve Bank of New York—popularly called the DESK—carries out instructions of the FEDERAL OPEN MARKET COMMITTEE designed to regulate the money supply. Such operations involve the purchase and sale of government securities, which effectively expands or contracts funds in the banking system. This, in turn, alters bank reserves, causing a MULTIPLIER effect on the supply of credit and, therefore, on economic activity generally. Open-market operations represent one of three basic ways the Federal Reserve implements MONETARY POLICY, the others being changes in the member bank RESERVE REQUIREMENTS and raising or lowering the DISCOUNT RATE charged to banks borrowing from the Fed to maintain reserves.

OPEN-MARKET RATES interest rates on various debt instruments bought and sold in the open market that are directly responsive to supply and demand. Such open, market rates are distinguished from the DISCOUNT RATE, set by the FEDERAL RESERVE BOARD as a deliberate measure to influence other rates, and from bank commercial loan rates, which are directly influenced by Federal Reserve policy. The rates on short-term instruments like COMMERCIAL PAPER and BANKER'S ACCEPTANCES are examples of open-market rates, as are yields on interest-bearing securities of all types traded in the SECONDARY MARKET.

OPEN ON THE PRINT BLOCK POSITIONER'S term for a BLOCK trade that has been completed with an institutional client and "printed" on the consolidated tape, but that leaves the block positioner open—that is, with a risk position to be covered. This usually happens when the block positioner is on the sell side of the transaction and sells SHORT what he lacks in inventory to complete the order.

OPEN ORDER buy or sell order for securities that has not yet been executed or canceled; a GOOD-TILL-CANCELED ORDER.

OPEN OUTCRY method of trading on a commodity exchange. The term derives from the fact that traders must shout out their buy or sell offers. When a trader shouts he wants to sell at a particular price and someone else shouts he wants to buy at that price, the two traders have made a contract that will be recorded.

OPEN REPO REPURCHASE AGREEMENT in which the repurchase date is unspecified and the agreement can be terminated by either party at any time. The agreement continues on a day-to-day basis with interest rate adjustments as the market changes.

OPERATING INCOME *see* OPERATING PROFIT (OR LOSS).

OPERATING IN THE RED operating at a loss. *See* OPERATING PROFIT (OR LOSS).

OPERATING LEASE type of LEASE, normally involving equipment, whereby the contract is written for considerably less than the life of the equipment and the lessor handles all maintenance and servicing; also called *service lease*. Operating leases are the opposite of capital leases, where the lessee acquires essentially all the economic benefits and risks of ownership. Common examples of equipment financed with operating leases are office copiers, computers, automobiles, and trucks. Most operating leases are cancelable, meaning the lessee can return the equipment if it becomes obsolete or is no longer needed.

OPERATING LEVERAGE *see* LEVERAGE.

OPERATING PROFIT MARGIN *see* NET PROFIT MARGIN.

OPERATING PROFIT (OR LOSS) the difference between the revenues of a business and the related costs and expenses, excluding income derived from sources other than its regular activities and before income deductions; synonymous with *net operating profit (or loss), operating income (or loss),* and *net operating income (or loss).* Income deductions are a class of items comprising the final section of a company's income statement, which, although necessarily incurred in the course of business and customarily charged before arriving at net income, are more in the nature of costs imposed from without than costs subject to the control of everyday operations. They include interest; amortized discount and expense on bonds; income taxes; losses from sales of plants, divisions, major items of property; prior-year adjustments; charges to contingency reserves; bonuses and other periodic profit distributions to officers and employees: write-offs of intangibles: adjustments arising from major changes in accounting methods, such as inventory valuation and other material and nonrecurrent items.

OPERATING RATE percentage of production capacity in use by a particular company, an industry, or the entire economy. While in theory a business can operate at 100% of its productive capacity, in practice the maximum output is less than that because machines need to be repaired, employees take vacations, etc. The operating rate is expressed as a percentage of the ideal 100% production output. For example, a company may be producing at an 85% operating rate, meaning its output is 85% of the maximum that could be produced with its existing resources. If a company has a low operating rate of under 50%, it usually is suffering meager profits or losses, though it has large potential for profit growth. A company operating at 80% of capacity or more is usually highly profitable, though it has less opportunity for improvement.

The Federal Reserve calculates the operating rate of U.S. industry on a monthly basis when its releases figures for industrial production. An operating rate of 85% or higher is generally considered to be full capacity by economists, who become concerned about inflationary pressures caused by production bottlenecks. An operating rate of less than 80% shows considerable slack in the economy, with few inflationary pressures.

OPERATING RATIO any of a group of ratios that measure a firm's operating efficiency and effectiveness by relating various income and expense figures from the profit and loss statement to each other and to balance sheet figures. Among the ratios used are sales to cost of goods sold, operating expenses to operating income, net profits to gross income, net income to net worth. Such ratios are most revealing when compared with those of prior periods and with industry averages.

OPERATIONS DEPARTMENT BACK OFFICE of a brokerage firm where all clerical functions having to do with clearance, settlement, and execution of trades are handled. This department keeps customer records and handles the day-to-day monitoring of margin positions.

OPINION *see* ACCOUNTANT'S OPINION.

OPINION SHOPPING dubious practice of changing outside auditors until one is found that will give an unqualified ACCOUNTANT'S OPINION.

OPM
1. other people's money; Wall Street slang for the use of borrowed funds by individuals or companies to increase the return on invested capital. *See also* FINANCIAL LEVERAGE.
2. options pricing model. *See* BLACK-SCHOLES OPTION PRICING MODEL.

OPORTO DERIVATIVES EXCHANGE (BOLSA DE DERIVADOS DO OPORTO) Portuguese exchange opened in June 1996 and similar in operation to the Spanish MEFF. The exchange trades futures on the

10-year government bond, Portuguese Stock Index, and 3-month interbank deposit rate LISBOR (Lisbon Interbank Offered Rate). Trading hours: Monday through Friday, 9:45 A.M. to 4:45 P.M.

OPPORTUNITY COST

In general: highest price or rate of return an alternative course of action would provide.

Corporate finance: concept widely used in business planning; for example, in evaluating a CAPITAL INVESTMENT project, a company must measure the projected return against the return it would earn on the highest yielding alternative investment involving similar risk. *See also* COST OF CAPITAL.

Securities investments: cost of forgoing a safe return on an investment in hopes of making a larger profit. For instance, an investor might buy a stock that shows great promise but yields only 2%, even though a higher safe return is available in a money market fund yielding 5%. The 3% yield difference is called the opportunity cost.

OPTIMUM CAPACITY level of output of manufacturing operations that produces the lowest cost per unit. For example, a tire factory may produce tires at $30 apiece if it turns out 10,000 tires a month, but the tires can be made for $20 apiece if the plant operates at its optimum capacity of 100,000 tires a month. *See also* MARGINAL COST.

OPTION

In general: right to buy or sell property that is granted in exchange for an agreed upon sum. If the right is not exercised after a specified period, the option expires and the option buyer forfeits the money. *See also* EXERCISE.

Securities: securities transaction agreement tied to stocks, commodities, or stock indexes. Options are traded on many exchanges.

1. a CALL OPTION gives its buyer the right to buy 100 shares of the underlying security at a fixed price before a specified date in the future—usually three, six, or nine months. For this right, the call option buyer pays the call option seller, called the writer, a fee called a PREMIUM, which is forfeited if the buyer does not exercise the option before the agreed-upon date. A call buyer therefore speculates that the price of the underlying shares will rise within the specified time period. For example, a call option on 100 shares of XYZ stock may grant its buyer the right to buy those shares at $100 apiece anytime in the next three months. To buy that option, the buyer may have to pay a premium of $2 a share, or $200. If at the time of the option contract XYZ is selling for $95 a share, the option buyer will profit if XYZ's stock price rises. If XYZ shoots up to $120 a share in two months, for example, the option buyer can EXERCISE his or her option to buy 100 shares of the stock at $100 and then sell the shares for $120 each, keeping the difference as profit (minus the $2 premium per share). On the other hand, if XYZ drops below $95 and stays there for three months, at the end of that time

the call option will expire and the call buyer will receive no return on the $2 a share investment premium of $200.

2. the opposite of a call option is a PUT OPTION, which gives its buyer the right to sell a specified number of shares of a stock at a particular price within a specified time period. Put buyers expect the price of the underlying stock to fall. Someone who thinks XYZ's stock price will fall might buy a three-month XYZ put for 100 shares at $100 apiece and pay a premium of $2. If XYZ falls to $80 a share, the put buyer can then exercise his or her right to sell 100 XYZ shares at $100. The buyer will first purchase 100 shares at $80 each and then sell them to the put option seller (writer) at $100 each, thereby making a profit of $18 a share (the $20 a share profit minus the $2 a share cost of the option premium).

In practice, most call and put options are rarely exercised. Instead, investors buy and sell options before expiration, trading on the rise and fall of premium prices. Because an option buyer must put up only a small amount of money (the premium) to control a large amount of stock, options trading provides a great deal of LEVERAGE and can prove immensely profitable. Options traders can write either covered options, in which they own the underlying security, or far riskier naked options, for which they do not own the underlying security. Often, options traders lose many premiums on unsuccessful trades before they make a very profitable trade. More sophisticated traders combine various call and put options in SPREAD and STRADDLE positions. Their profits or losses result from the narrowing or widening of spreads between option prices.

An *incentive stock option* is granted to corporate executives if the company achieves certain financial goals, such as a level of sales or profits. The executive is granted the option of buying company stock at a below-market price and selling the stock in the market for a profit. *See also* CALL; COVERED OPTION; DEEP IN (OUT OF) THE MONEY; IN THE MONEY; LEAPS; NAKED OPTION; OPTION WRITER; OUT OF THE MONEY.

OPTION ACCOUNT account at a brokerage firm that is approved to contain option positions or trades. Since certain option strategies require margin, an option account may be a margin account or a cash account. There are several prerequisites. The client must be given a copy of "Characteristics and Risks of Standardized Options Contracts," known as the Options Disclosure Documents, before the account can be approved. The client must complete an OPTION AGREE-MENT in order to open the account. The client must show that he is suitable for options transactions, both in financial resources and investing experience, before the brokerage firm will approve the account for options trading.

OPTION AGREEMENT form filled out by a brokerage firm's customer when opening an option account. It details financial information about the customer, who agrees to follow the rules and regulations of options trading. This agreement, also called the *option information form,* assures the broker that the customer's financial resources are adequate to withstand any losses that may occur from options trading. The customer must receive a prospectus from the OPTIONS CLEARING CORPORATION before he or she can begin trading.

OPTION CYCLE cycle of months in which options contracts expire. These cycles are used for options on stocks and indices, as well as options on commodities, currencies, and debt instruments. The three most common cycles are: January, April, July, October (JAJO); February, May, August, November (FMAN); and March, June, September, December (MJSD). In addition to these expiration months, options on individual stocks and indices generally also expire in the current month and subsequent month. As an example, an option in the February cycle trading during May would have May, June and August expiration months listed at a minimum. Because of option cycles, there are four days a year—in March, June, September, and December, when TRIPLE WITCHING DAY takes place, as several options contracts expire on the same day.

OPTIONAL DIVIDEND dividend that can be paid either in cash or in stock. The shareholder entitled to the dividend makes the choice.

OPTIONAL PAYMENT BOND bond whose principal and/or interest are payable, at the option of the holder, in one or more foreign currencies as well as in domestic currency.

OPTION HOLDER someone who has bought a call or put OPTION but has not yet exercised or sold it. A call option holder wants the price of the underlying security to rise; a put option holder wants the price of the underlying security to fall.

OPTION MARGIN MARGIN REQUIREMENT applicable to OPTIONS, as set forth in REGULATION T and in the internal policies of individual brokers. Requirements vary with the type of option and the extent to which it is IN-THE-MONEY, but are strictest in the case of NAKED OPTIONS and narrow-based INDEX OPTIONS. There, Regulation T requires the option premium plus 20% of the underlying value as the maximum and the premium plus 10% of the underlying value as the minimum. Merrill Lynch, for example, would also require a minimum of $10,000 per account and $1,000 per position.

OPTION MUTUAL FUND MUTUAL FUND that either buys or sells options in order to increase the value of fund shares. OPTION mutual funds may be either conservative or aggressive. For instance, a conservative fund may buy stocks and increase shareholders' income through the PREMIUM earned by selling put and call options on the stocks in the fund's portfolio. This kind of fund would be called an *option income fund.* At the opposite extreme, an aggressive *option growth fund* may buy puts and calls in stocks that the fund manager thinks are about to fall or rise sharply; if the fund manager is right, large profits can be earned through EXERCISE of the options. The LEVERAGE that options provide makes it possible to multiply the return on invested funds many times over.

OPTION PREMIUM amount per share paid by an OPTION buyer to an option seller for the right to buy (call) or sell (put) the underlying security at a particular price within a specified period. Option premium prices are quoted in increments of eighths or sixteenths of 1% and are printed in the options tables of daily newspapers. A PREMIUM of $5 per share means an option buyer would pay $500 for an option on 100 shares. *See also* CALL OPTION; PUT OPTION.

OPTION PRICE market price at which an option contract is trading at any particular time. The price of an option on a stock reflects the fact that it covers 100 shares of a stock. So, for example, an option that is quoted at $7 would cost $700, because it would be an option for 100 shares of stock at a $7 cost per share covered. The option price is determined by many factors, including its INTRINSIC VALUE, time to expiration, volatility of the underlying stock, interest rates, dividends, and marketplace adjustments for supply and demand. Options on indices, debt instruments, currencies, and commodities also have prices determined by many of the same forces. Options prices are published daily in the business pages of many newspapers.

OPTIONS CLEARING CORPORATION (OCC) the largest clearing organization in the world for financial derivative instruments. OCC issues, guarantees, and clears options on underlying financial assets including common stocks, foreign exchange, stock indices, U.S. Treasury securities and interest rate composites. As the issuer and guarantor of every options contract executed on every securities options exchange in the U.S., OCC serves as the counterparty for all transactions. OCC's ability to meet its obligations arising from its options contracts earned it an AAA rating by STANDARD & POOR'S CORPORATION. OCC is the only securities clearinghouse in the world to receive this accreditation. Its options disclosure document, "Characteristics and Risks of Standardized Options," is required reading for all investors prior to trading options. OCC is owned by the four U.S. exchanges that trade options. *See also* OPTION.

OPTION SERIES options of the same class (puts or calls with the same underlying security) that also have the same EXERCISE PRICE and maturity month. For instance, all XYZ October 80 calls are a series, as are all ABC July 100 puts. *See also* OPTION.

OPTION SPREAD buying and selling of options within the same CLASS at the same time. The investor who uses the OPTION spread strategy hopes to profit from the widening or narrowing of the SPREAD between the various options. Option spreads can be designed to be profitable in either up or down markets.

Some examples:

(1) entering into two options at the same EXERCISE PRICE, but with different maturity dates. For instance, an investor could buy an XYZ April 60 call and sell an XYZ July 60 call.

(2) entering into two options at different STRIKE PRICES with the same expiration month. For example, an investor could buy an XYZ April 60 call and sell an XYZ April 70 call.

(3) entering into two options at different strike prices with different expiration months. For instance, an investor could buy an XYZ April 60 call and sell an XYZ July 70 call.

OPTION WRITER person or financial institution that sells put and call options. A writer of a PUT OPTION contracts to buy 100 shares of stock from the put option buyer by a certain date for a fixed price. For example, an option writer who sells XYZ April 50 put agrees to buy XYZ stock from the put buyer at $50 a share any time until the contract expires in April.

A writer of a CALL OPTION, on the other hand, guarantees to sell the call option buyer the underlying stock at a particular price before a certain date. For instance, a writer of an XYZ April 50 call agrees to sell stock at $50 a share to the call buyer any time before April.

In exchange for granting this right, the option writer receives a payment called an OPTION PREMIUM. For holders of large portfolios of the premiums from stocks, option writing therefore is a source of additional income.

ORAL CONTRACT contract between two parties that has been spoken, but not agreed to in writing or signed by both parties. Oral contracts are usually legally enforceable, though not in the case of real estate.

OR BETTER indication, abbreviated OB on the ORDER TICKET of a LIMIT ORDER to buy or sell securities, that the broker should transact the order at a price better than the specified LIMIT PRICE if a better price can be obtained.

ORDER

Investments: instruction to a broker or dealer to buy or sell securities or commodities. Securities orders fall into four basic categories: MARKET ORDER, LIMIT ORDER, time order, and STOP ORDER.

Law: direction from a court of jurisdiction, or a regulation.

Negotiable instruments: payee's request to the maker, as on a check stating, "Pay to the order of (when presented by) John Doe."

Trade: request to buy, sell, deliver, or receive goods or services which commits the issuer of the order to the terms specified.

ORDER IMBALANCE large number of buy or sell orders for a stock, causing an unusually wide spread between bid and offer prices. Stock exchanges frequently halt trading of a stock with a significant order imbalance until more buyers or sellers appear and an orderly market can be reestablished. A significant order imbalance on the buying side can occur when there is an announcement of an impending takeover of the company, better-than-expected earnings, or other unexpected positive news. A significant order imbalance on the selling side can occur when a takeover offer has fallen through, a key executive has left the company, earnings came in far worse than expected, or there is other unexpected negative news.

ORDER ROOM department in a brokerage firm that receives all orders to buy or sell securities. ORDER TICKETS are processed through the order room.

ORDER SPLITTING practice prohibited by rules of the National Association of Securities Dealers (NASD) whereby brokers might split orders in order to qualify them as small orders for purposes of automatic execution by the SMALL ORDER EXECUTION SYSTEM (SOES).

ORDER TICKET form completed by a registered representative (ACCOUNT EXECUTIVE) of a brokerage firm, upon receiving order instructions from a customer. It shows whether the order is to buy or to sell, the number of units, the name of the security, the kind of order (ORDER MARKET, LIMIT ORDER or STOP ORDER) and the customer's name or code number. After execution of the order on the exchange floor or in the firm's trading department (if over the counter), the price is written and circled on the order ticket, and the completing broker is indicated by number. The order ticket must be retained for a certain period in compliance with federal law.

ORDINARY INCOME income from the normal activities of an individual or business, as distinguished from CAPITAL GAINS from the sale of assets. Prior to the TAX REFORM ACT OF 1986, the long-term CAPITAL GAINS TAX was lower than that on ordinary income. The 1986 Act eliminated the preferential capital gains rate, but it kept the separate statutory language to allow for future increases in ordinary income rates. In 1991, capital gains rates were limited to 28%, and in the TAXPAYER RELIEF ACT OF 1997, capital gains tax rates were cut to 20%.

ORDINARY INTEREST simple interest based on a 360-day year rather than on a 365-day year (the latter is called *exact interest*). The difference between the two bases when calculating daily interest on large sums of money can be substantial. The ratio of ordinary interest to exact interest is 1.0139.

ORGANIZATION CHART chart showing the interrelationships of positions within an organization in terms of authority and responsibility. There are basically three patterns of organization: *line organization,* in which a single manager has final authority over a group of foremen or middle management supervisors; *functional organization,* in which a general manager supervises a number of managers identified by function; and *line and staff organization,* which is a combination of line and functional organization, with specialists in particular functions holding staff positions where they advise line officers concerned with actual production.

ORGANIZED SECURITIES EXCHANGE STOCK EXCHANGE as distinguished from an OVER-THE-COUNTER MARKET. *See also* SECURITIES AND COMMODITIES EXCHANGES.

ORIGINAL COST
1. in accounting, all costs associated with the acquisition of an asset.
2. in public utilities accounting, the acquisition cost incurred by the entity that first devotes a property to public use; normally, the utility company's cost for the property. It is used to establish the rate to be charged customers in order to provide the utility company with a FAIR RATE OF RETURN on capital.

ORIGINAL ISSUE DISCOUNT (OID) discount from PAR VALUE at the time a bond or other debt instrument, such as a STRIP, is issued. (Although the par value of bonds is normally $1000, $100 is used when traders quote prices.) A bond may be issued at $50 ($500) per bond instead of $100 ($1000), for example. The bond will mature at $100 (1000), however, so that an investor has a built-in gain if the bond is held until maturity. The most extreme version of an original issue discount is a ZERO-COUPON BOND, which is originally sold at far below par value and pays no interest until it matures. The REVENUE RECONCILIATION ACT OF 1993 extended OID rules to include stripped preferred stock.

The tax treatment of original issue discount bonds is complex. The Internal Revenue Service assumes a certain rate of appreciation of the bond every year until maturity. No capital gain or loss will be incurred if the bond is sold for that estimated amount. But if the bond is sold for more than the assumed amount, a CAPITAL GAINS TAX or a tax at the ORDINARY INCOME rate is due.

SAVINGS BONDS are exempt from OID rules.

ORIGINAL MATURITY interval between the issue date and the maturity date of a bond, as distinguished from CURRENT MATURITY, which is the time difference between the present time and the maturity date. For example, in 2001 a bond issued in 1999 to mature in 2014 would have an original maturity of 15 years and a current maturity of 13 years.

ORIGINATOR
1. bank, savings and loan, or mortgage banker that initially made the mortgage loan comprising part of a pool of mortgages.
2. investment banking firm that worked with the issuer of a new securities offering from the early planning stages and that usually is appointed manager of the underwriting SYNDICATE; more formally called the *originating investment banker.*
3. in banking terminology, the initiator of money transfer instructions.

ORPHAN STOCK stock that has been neglected by research analysts. Since the company's story is rarely followed and the stock infrequently recommended, it is considered an orphan by investors. Orphan stocks may not attract much attention because they are too small, or because they have disappointed investors in the past. Because they are followed by so few investors, orphan stocks tend to trade at low price/earnings ratios. However, if the company assembles a solid record of rising profitability, it can be discovered again by research analysts, boosting the stock price and price/earnings ratio significantly. Investors who buy the stock when it is still a neglected orphan can thereby earn high returns. Also called a *wallflower.*

OSLO STOCK EXCHANGE founded in 1819 as a foreign exchange market, it later evolved as a commodity exchange; securities were launched in 1881. The stock exchanges in Bergen and Trondheim, Norway, are branches of the OSE. The OSE trades stocks, bonds, and stock options, and is considered the options market of Norway. Energy-related companies dominate the listings. The OSE General Price Index is made up of nearly 50 stocks. All trading is conducted electronically, and trades are settled three days from the transaction date. Pre-trading hours for stocks and options begins at 9:30 A.M., with continuous trading from 10 A.M. to 5 P.M., Monday through Friday.

OTC *see* OVER THE COUNTER.

OTC BULLETIN BOARD electronic listing of bid and asked quotations of over-the-counter stocks not meeting the minimum-net worth and other requirements of the NASDAQ stock-listing system. The new system, which was developed by the National Association of Securities Dealers (NASD) and approved by the Securities and Exchange Commission in 1990, provides continuously updated data on domestic stocks and twice-daily updates on foreign stocks. It was designed to facilitate trading and provide greater surveillance of stocks traditionally reported on once daily in the PINK SHEETS published by NATIONAL QUOTATION BUREAU.

OTC MARGIN STOCK shares of certain large firms traded OVER THE COUNTER that qualify as margin securities under REGULATION T of the Federal Reserve Board. Such stock must meet rigid criteria, and the list of eligible OTC shares is under constant review by the Fed. *See also* MARGIN SECURITY.

OTHER INCOME heading on a profit and loss statement for income from activities not in the normal course of business: sometimes called *other revenue.* Examples: interest on customers' notes, dividends and interest from investments, profit from the disposal of assets other than inventory, gain on foreign exchange, miscellaneous rent income. *See also* EXTRAORDINARY ITEM.

OTHER PEOPLE'S MONEY *see* OPM.

OUT-OF-FAVOR INDUSTRY OR STOCK industry or stock that is currently unpopular with investors. For example, the investing public may be disenchanted with an industry's poor earnings outlook. If interest rates were rising, interest-sensitive stocks such as banks and savings and loans would be out of favor because rising rates might harm these firms' profits. CONTRARIAN investors—those who consciously do the opposite of most other investors—tend to buy out-of-favor stocks because they can be bought cheaply. When the earnings of these stocks pick up, contrarians typically sell the stocks. Out-of-favor stocks tend to have a low PRICE/EARNINGS RATIO.

OUT OF LINE term describing a stock that is too high or too low in price in comparison with similar-quality stocks. A comparison of this sort is usually based on the PRICE/EARNINGS RATIO (PE), which measures how much investors are willing to pay for a firm's earnings prospects. If most computer industry stocks had PEs of 15, for instance, and XYZ Computers had a PE of only 10, analysts would say that XYZ's price is out of line with the rest of the industry.

OUT OF THE MONEY term used to describe an OPTION whose STRIKE PRICE for a stock is either higher than the current market value, in the case of a CALL, or lower, in the case of a PUT. For example, an XYZ December 60 CALL option would be out of the money when XYZ stock was selling for $55 a share. Similarly, an XYZ December 60 PUT OPTION would be out of the money when XYZ stock was selling for $65 a share.

Someone buying an out-of-the-money option hopes that the option will move IN THE MONEY, or at least in that direction. The buyer of the above XYZ call would want the stock to climb above $60 a share, whereas the put buyer would like the stock to drop below $60 a share.

OUTSIDE DIRECTOR member of a company's BOARD OF DIRECTORS who is not an employee of the company. Such directors are considered important because they are presumed to bring unbiased opinions to major corporate decisions and also can contribute diverse experience to the decision-making process. A retailing company may have outside directors with experience in finance and manufacturing, for instance. To avoid conflict of interest, outside directors never serve on the boards of two directly competing corporations. Directors receive fees from the company in return for their service, usually a set amount for each board meeting they attend.

OUTSTANDING
1. unpaid; used of ACCOUNTS RECEIVABLE and debt obligations of all types.
2. not yet presented for payment, as a check or draft.
3. stock held by shareholders, shown on corporate balance sheets under the heading of CAPITAL STOCK issued and outstanding.

OUT THE WINDOW term describing the rapid way a very successful NEW ISSUE of securities is marketed to investors. An issue that goes out the window is also called a BLOWOUT. *See also* HOT ISSUE.

OVER-AGE-55 HOME SALE EXEMPTION federal tax code regulation permitting an individual over the age of 55 a one-time exclusion up to $125,000 in capital gains on the sale of a home. The individual must have lived in the home as the primary residence for three of the past five years in order to qualify. The exclusion is allowed even if the proceeds from the home sale are not reinvested in another property. For example, if a 56-year-old person who bought a house for $100,000 sells the house for $300,000, he can choose to exclude $125,000 of the $200,000 gain and pay CAPITAL GAINS TAX on the remaining $75,000 profit. Congress enacted this rule to prevent older people from having to pay capital gains taxes on housing appreciation that was caused mainly by inflation. This exemption was superceded by a provision in the TAXPAYER RELIEF ACT OF 1997 allowing homeowners of any age who lived in their principal residence for at least two of the past five years to avoid capital gains taxes up to $500,000 for married couples filing jointly, and $250,000 for singles, when selling their home. Sellers do not have to reinvest the proceeds in another home.

OVERALL MARKET PRICE COVERAGE total assets less intangibles divided by the total of (1) the MARKET VALUE of the security issue in question and (2) the BOOK VALUE of liabilities and issues having a prior claim. The answer indicates the extent to which the market value of a particular CLASS of securities is covered in the event of a company's liquidation.

OVERBOOKED *see* OVERSUBSCRIBED.

OVERBOUGHT description of a security or a market that has recently experienced an unexpectedly sharp price rise and is therefore vulnerable to a price drop (called a CORRECTION by technical analysts). When a stock has been overbought, there are fewer buyers left to drive the price up further. *See also* MOMENTUM INDICATORS; OVERSOLD.

OVERDRAFT extension of credit by a lending institution. An overdraft check for which there are not sufficient funds (NSF) available may be rejected (bounced) by the bank. A bounced-check charge will be assessed on the check-writer's account. Alternatively, the bank customer may set up an overdraft loan account, which will cover NSF checks. While the customer's check will clear, the account will be charged overdraft check fees or interest on the outstanding balance of the loan starting immediately.

OVERHANG sizable block of securities or commodities contracts that, if released on the market, would put downward pressure on prices. Examples of overhang include shares held in a dealer's inventory, a large institutional holding, a secondary distribution still in registration, and a large commodity position about to be liquidated. Overhang inhibits buying activity that would otherwise translate into upward price movement.

OVERHEAD
1. costs of a business that are not directly associated with the production or sale of goods or services. Also called INDIRECT COSTS AND EXPENSES, *burden* and, in Great Britain, *on costs.*
2. sometimes used in a more limited sense, as in manufacturing or factory overhead.
   See also DIRECT OVERHEAD.

OVERHEATING term describing an economy that is expanding so rapidly that economists fear a rise in INFLATION. In an overheated economy, too much money is chasing too few goods, leading to price rises, and the productive capacity of a nation is usually nearing its limit. The remedies in the United States are usually a tightening of the money supply by the Federal Reserve and curbs in federal government spending. *See also* MONETARY POLICY; OPTIMUM CAPACITY.

OVERISSUE shares of CAPITAL STOCK issued in excess of those authorized. Preventing overissue is the function of a corporation's REGISTRAR (usually a bank acting as agent), which works closely with the TRANSFER AGENT in canceling and reissuing certificates presented for transfer and in issuing new shares.

OVERLAPPING DEBT municipal accounting term referring to a municipality's share of the debt of its political subdivisions or the special districts sharing its geographical area. It is usually determined by the ratio of ASSESSED VALUATION of taxable property lying within the corporate limits of the municipality to the assessed valuation of each overlapping district. Overlapping debt is often greater than the direct debt of a municipality, and both must be taken into account in determining the debt burden carried by taxable real estate within a municipality when evaluating MUNICIPAL BOND investments.

OVERNIGHT POSITION broker-dealer's LONG POSITION or SHORT POSITION in a security at the end of a trading day.

OVERNIGHT REPO overnight REPURCHASE AGREEMENT; an arrangement whereby securities dealers and banks finance their inventories of Treasury bills, notes, and bonds. The dealer or bank sells securities to an investor with a temporary surplus of cash, agreeing to buy them back the next day. Such transactions are settled in immediately available FEDERAL FUNDS, usually at a rate below the federal funds rate (the rate charged by banks lending funds to each other).

OVERSHOOT to exceed a target figure, such as an economic goal or an earnings projection.

OVERSOLD description of a stock or market that has experienced an unexpectedly sharp price decline and is therefore due, according to some proponents of TECHNICAL ANALYSIS, for an imminent price rise.

If all those who wanted to sell a stock have done so, there are no sellers left, and so the price will rise. *See also* MOMENTUM INDICATORS; OVERBOUGHT.

OVERSUBSCRIBED underwriting term describing a new stock issue for which there are more buyers than available shares. An oversubscribed, or *overbooked,* issue often will jump in price as soon as its shares go on the market, since the buyers who could not get shares will want to buy once the stock starts trading. In some cases, an issuer will increase the number of shares available if the issue is oversubscribed. *See also* GREEN SHOE; HOT ISSUE.

OVER THE COUNTER (OTC)
1. security that is not listed and traded on an organized exchange.
2. market in which securities transactions are conducted through a telephone and computer network connecting dealers in stocks and bonds, rather than on the floor of an exchange.

Over-the-counter stocks are traditionally those of smaller companies that do not meet the LISTING REQUIREMENTS of the New York Stock Exchange or the American Stock Exchange. In recent years, however, many companies that qualify for listing have chosen to remain with over-the-counter trading, because they feel that the system of multiple trading by many dealers is preferable to the centralized trading approach of the New York Stock Exchange, where all trading in a stock has to go through the exchange SPECIALIST in that stock. The rules of over-the-counter stock trading are written and enforced largely by the NATIONAL ASSOCIATION OF SECURITIES DEALERS (NASD), a self-regulatory group. Prices of over-the-counter stocks are published in daily newspapers, with the NATIONAL MARKET SYSTEM stocks listed separately from the rest of the over-the-counter market. Other over-the-counter markets include those for government and municipal bonds. *See also* NASDAQ.

OVERTRADING
Finance: practice of a firm that expands sales beyond levels that can be financed with normal WORKING CAPITAL. Continued overtrading leads to delinquent ACCOUNTS PAYABLE and ultimately to default on borrowings.
New issue underwriting: practice whereby a member of an underwriting group induces a brokerage client to buy a portion of a new issue by purchasing other securities from the client at a premium. The underwriter breaks even on the deal because the premium is offset by the UNDERWRITING SPREAD.
Securities: excessive buying and selling by a broker in a DISCRETIONARY ACCOUNT. *See also* CHURNING.

OVERVALUED description of a stock whose current price is not justified by the earnings outlook or the PRICE/EARNINGS RATIO. It is therefore expected that the stock will drop in price. Overvaluation may result from an emotional buying spurt, which inflates the market price of the stock, or from a deterioration of the company's financial strength. The opposite of overvalued is UNDERVALUED. *See also* FULLY VALUED.

OVERWITHHOLDING situation in which a taxpayer has too much federal, state, or local income tax withheld from salary. Because they have overwithheld, these taxpayers will usually be due income tax refunds after they file their tax returns by April 15. Overwithholding is not desirable for the taxpayer, because it is, in effect, granting the government an interest-free loan. To reduce overwithholding, a taxpayer must file a new W-4 form with his or her employer, increasing the number of dependents claimed, which will reduce the amount of tax withheld. *See also* UNDERWITHHOLDING.

OVERWRITING speculative practice by an OPTION WRITER who believes a security to be overpriced or underpriced and sells CALL OPTIONS or PUT OPTIONS on the security in quantity, assuming they will not be exercised. *See also* OPTION.

OWNER'S EQUITY PAID-IN CAPITAL, donated capital, and RETAINED EARNINGS less the LIABILITIES of a corporation.

P

PAC BOND acronym for *planned amortization class bond,* PAC is a TRANCHE class offered by some COLLATERIZED MORTGAGE OBLIGATIONS (CMOs), which is unlike other CMO classes in that (1) it has a sinking fund schedule that is observed as long as the prepayments on underlying mortgages remain within a broad range of speeds and (2) its ability to make principal payments is not subordinated to other classes. PAC bonds thus offer certainty of cash flow except in extreme prepayment situations, and because of this they trade at a premium to comparable traditional CMOs. *See also* TAC BONDS.

PACIFIC EXCHANGE (PCX) regional exchange founded in 1882, operating a trading floor in San Francisco. The Pacific Exchange changed its name from the Pacific Stock Exchange in 1997. In the following year, the PCX consolidated with the CHICAGO BOARD OPTIONS EXCHANGE (CBOE), combining the two exchange's product lines and operating under the CBOE name. In 1995, it joined the NATIONAL MARKET EXCHANGES—Boston, Chicago and Philadelphia—to establish a uniform definition and standard for measuring price improvement in the NATIONAL MARKET SYSTEM. The exchange trades more than 2,700 stocks, bonds, and warrants, including almost all of the most active issues on the NEW YORK STOCK EXCHANGE and AMERICAN STOCK EXCHANGE. PCX also trades every Asian security listed on the NYSE and Amex. More than 700 equity and index options are traded by open outcry. PCX also offers contracts in LEAPS, which are extended term options contracts. The Pacific Exchange is an originating market for small, emerging companies before they reach sufficient size to list in New York; once they achieve this eligibility, they continue listing on the Pacific. Technology companies comprise a large part of its equity listings. The PSE Technology 100 Index is a benchmark for the technology sector, measuring the performance of 100 stocks in 15 technology industries. Other index options offered include the Morgan Stanley Emerging Growth Index and the Wilshire Small Cap Index. PCX formed a partnership with Dow Jones & Co. to list options on its global indices, beginning with the Dow Jones Taiwan Stock Index. The only U.S. exchange on the Pacific Rim, the PCX enjoys formal relationships with exchanges in Hong Kong, Kuala Lumpur, the Philippines, Shaghai, Taiwan, Seoul and Bangkok. In 1998, the PCX was the first U.S. exchange to inaugurate the OptiMark Trading System, a sophisticated electronic system for automatic order formulation, matching, and execution for equities and equity options. Nearly 95% of all equity trades are processed electronically through the P/COAST system. POETS, the exchange's options trading system, generates more than 85% of the exchange's option quotes. The Automated Credit Exchange trades emissions credits for air pollution on the Internet. Trading hours: Monday to Friday, 6:30 A.M. to 4:00 P.M. EST.

PACKAGE MORTGAGE mortgage on both a house and durable personal property in the house, such as appliances and furniture. The borrower therefore repays one mortgage loan instead of having to carry two loans. In construction lending, interim and takeout loans made by the same investor.

PAC-MAN STRATEGY technique used by a corporation that is the target of a takeover bid to defeat the acquirer's wishes. The TARGET COMPANY defends itself by threatening to take over the acquirer and begins buying its common shares. For instance, if company A moves to take over company B against the wishes of the management of company B, company B will begin buying shares in company A in order to thwart A's takeover attempt. The Pac-Man strategy is named after a popular video game of the early 1980s, in which each character that does not swallow its opponents is itself consumed. *See also* TAKEOVER; TENDER OFFER.

PAID-IN CAPITAL capital received from investors in exchange for stock, as distinguished from capital generated from earnings or donated. The paid-in capital account includes CAPITAL STOCK and contributions of stockholders credited to accounts other than capital stock, such as an excess over PAR value received from the sale or exchange of capital stock. It would also include surplus resulting from RECAPITALIZATION. Paid-in capital is sometimes classified more specifically as *additional paid-in capital, paid-in surplus,* or *capital surplus.* Such accounts are distinguished from RETAINED EARNINGS or its older variation, EARNED SURPLUS. *See also* DONATED STOCK.

PAID-IN SURPLUS *see* PAID-IN CAPITAL.

PAID UP a situation in which all payments due have been made. For example, if all premiums on a life insurance policy have been paid, it is known as a PAID-UP POLICY.

PAID-UP POLICY life insurance policy in which all premiums have been paid. Some policies require premium payments for a limited number of years, and if all premium payments have been made over those years, the policy is considered paid in full and requires no more premium payments. Such a policy remains in force until the insured person dies or cancels the policy.

PAINTING THE TAPE
1. illegal practice by manipulators who buy and sell a particular security among themselves to create artificial trading activity, causing a succession of trades to be reported on the CONSOLIDATED TAPE and luring unwary investors to the "action." After causing movement in the market price of the security, the manipulators hope to sell at a profit.
2. consecutive or frequent trading in a particular security, resulting in its repeated appearances on the ticker tape. Such activity is usually attributable to special investor interest in the security.

PAIRED SHARES common stocks of two companies under the same management that are sold as a unit, usually appearing as a single certificate printed front and back. Also called *Siamese shares* or *stapled stock.*

P & I abbreviations for *principal* and *interest* on bonds or mortgage-backed securities. A traditional debt instrument such as a bond makes periodic interest payments and returns bondholders' principal when the bond matures. But in many cases, the principal payment and each of the interest payments are separated from each other by brokerage firms and sold in pieces. When accomplished with Treasury bonds, each of the individual interest payments and the final principal payment is sold as a "stripped" zero-coupon bond known as a STRIP. In the case of a mortgage-backed security, each of the interest payments and principal repayments from mortgagees is packaged into a COLLATERALIZED MORTGAGE OBLIGATION. A security composed of only interest payments is known as an *interest-only* or *IO* security. A security composed of just principal repayments is known as a *principal-only* or PO security. Both IOs and POs are forms of DERIVATIVE SECURITIES.

P & L *see* PROFIT AND LOSS STATEMENT.

PANIC BUYING OR SELLING flurry of buying or selling accompanied by high volume done in anticipation of sharply rising or falling prices. A sudden news event will trigger panic buying or selling, leaving investors little time to evaluate the fundamentals of individual stocks or bonds. Panic buying may be caused by an unexpected cut in interest rates or outcome of a political election. Short sellers may also be forced into panic buying if stock prices start to rise quickly, and they have to cover their short positions to prevent further losses. Panic selling may be set off by an international crisis such as a war or currency devaluation, the assassination of a head of state, or other unforeseen event. If stock prices start to fall sharply, investors may start to panic sell because they fear prices will fall much farther. *See also* CIRCUIT BREAKERS.

PAPER shorthand for *short-term commercial paper,* which is an unsecured note issued by a corporation. The term is also more loosely used to refer to all debt issued by a company, as in "ABC has $100 million in short and long-term paper outstanding."

PAPER DEALER brokerage firm that buys COMMERCIAL PAPER at one rate of interest, usually discounted, and resells it at a lower rate to banks and other investors, making a profit on the difference.

PAPER PROFIT OR LOSS unrealized CAPITAL GAIN or CAPITAL LOSS in an investment or PORTFOLIO. Paper profits and losses are calculated by comparing the current market prices of all stocks, bonds, mutual funds, and commodities in a portfolio to the prices at which those assets were originally bought. These profits or losses become realized only when the securities are sold.

PAPER TRADING *see* MOCK TRADING.

PAR equal to the nominal or FACE VALUE of a security. A bond selling at par, for instance, is worth the same dollar amount it was issued for or at which it will be redeemed at maturity—typically, $1000 per bond.

    With COMMON STOCK, par value is set by the company issuing the stock. At one time, par value represented the original investment behind each share of stock in goods, cash, and services, but today this is rarely the case. Instead, it is an assigned amount (such as $1 a share) used to compute the dollar accounting value of the common shares on a company's balance sheet. Par value has no relation to MARKET VALUE, which is determined by such considerations as NET ASSET VALUE, YIELD, and investors' expectations of future earnings. Some companies issue NO-PAR VALUE STOCK. *See also* STATED VALUE.

    Par value has more importance for bonds and PREFERRED STOCK. The interest paid on bonds is based on a percentage of a bond's par value—a 10% bond pays 10% of the bond's par value annually. Preferred dividends are normally stated as a percentage of the par value of the preferred stock issue.

PAR BOND bond that is selling at PAR, the amount equal to its nominal value or FACE VALUE. A corporate bond redeemable at maturity for $1000 is a par bond when it trades on the market for $1000.

PARENT COMPANY company that owns or controls subsidiaries through the ownership of voting stock. A parent company is usually an operating company in its own right; where it has no business of its own, the term HOLDING COMPANY is often preferred.

PARETO'S LAW theory that the pattern of income distribution is constant, historically and geographically, regardless of taxation or welfare policies; also called *law of the trivial many and the critical few* or *80-20 law*. Thus, if 80% of a nation's income will benefit only 20% of the population, the only way to improve the economic lot of the poor is to increase overall output and income levels.

    Other applications of the law include the idea that in most business activities a small percentage of the work force produces the major portion of output or that 20% of the customers account for 80% of the dollar volume of sales. The law is attributed to Vilfredo Pareto, an Italian-Swiss engineer and economist (1848–1923).

    Pareto is also credited with the concept called *Paretian optimum* (or *optimality*) that resources are optimally distributed when an individual cannot move into a better position without putting someone else into a worse position.

PARIS BOURSE national stock market of France, formed in 1991 when the computerized trading system in Paris was extended to the regional exchanges. It includes four markets: the official list of cash-settled securities; the second market of medium-sized companies; the Hors-Cote market of small companies that is subject to limited disclosure requirements; and NOUVEAU MARCHE, a stock market launched in

February 1996, dedicated to innovative, high-growth companies and linked to EURO.NM. Through the Super CAC electronic system, member firms enter orders during an 8:30 A.M. to 10 A.M. pre-opening period. Trading is then continued from 10 A.M. to 5 P.M. Clearing and settlement is done through RELIT, a computerized system based on the simultaneous exchange of securities and cash on the same day, and on the standard time frame for trade comparisons and settlement. Automatic delivery and payment occur three days after a trade. The CAC 40 INDEX is the underlying index for derivative products traded on the MONEP, a subsidiary of the Paris Bourse. The SBF 250 Index is made up of 250 stocks that serve as an indicator of the wider French economy. Structured by sector, the SBF 250 replaced the CAC 240 and the INSEE Weekly Index. The SBF 120 Index is made up of the top 120 stocks based on liquidity and capitalization, and is a benchmark for indexed funds. The Mid-CAC is based on mid-cap securities listed on the Paris Bourse.

PARITY *see* CONVERSION PARITY.

PARITY PRICE price for a commodity or service that is pegged to another price or to a composite average of prices based on a selected prior period. As the two sets of prices vary, they are reflected in an index number on a scale of 100. For example, U.S. farm prices are pegged to prices based on the purchasing power of farmers in the period from 1910 to 1914. If the parity ratio is below 100, reflecting a reduction in purchasing power to the extent indicated, the government compensates the farmer by paying a certain percentage of parity, either in the form of a direct cash payment, in the purchase of surplus crops, or in a NONRECOURSE LOAN.

The concept of parity is also widely applied in industrial wage contracts as a means of preserving the real value of wages.

PARKING placing assets in a safe investment while other investment alternatives are under consideration. For instance, an investor will park the proceeds of a stock or bond sale in an interest-bearing money market fund while considering what other stocks or bonds to purchase. Term also refers to an illegal practice whereby ownership of stock is concealed, and DISCLOSURE requirements circumvented, by holding stock in the name of a conspiring party.

PARTIAL DELIVERY term used when a broker does not deliver the full amount of a security or commodity called for by a contract. If 10,000 shares were to be delivered, for example, and only 7000 shares are transferred, it is called a partial delivery.

PARTICIPATING DIVIDEND dividend paid from PARTICIPATING PREFERRED STOCK.

PARTICIPATING LIFE INSURANCE POLICIES life insurance that pays dividends to policyholders. The policyholders participate in the success or failure of the company's underwriting and investment performance by having their dividends rise or fall. The fewer claims the company experiences and the better its investment performance, the higher the dividends. Policyholders have many choices in what they can do with the dividends. They can have them paid in cash, in which case the income is taxable in the year received; they can use them to reduce policy premiums; they can buy more paid-up insurance, either cash value or term; or they can put them in an account with the insurance company that earns interest. The opposite of a participating policy is a NONPARTICIPATING LIFE INSURANCE POLICY.

PARTICIPATING PREFERRED STOCK PREFERRED STOCK that, in addition to paying a stipulated dividend, gives the holder the right to participate with the common stockholder in additional distributions of earnings under specified conditions. One example would be an arrangement whereby preferred shareholders are paid $5 per share, then common shareholders are paid $5 per share, and then preferred and common shareholders share equally in further dividends up to $1 per share in any one year.

Participating preferred issues are rare. They are used when special measures are necessary to attract investors. Most preferred stock is *nonparticipating preferred stock,* paying only the stipulated dividends.

PARTICIPATION CERTIFICATE certificate representing an interest in a POOL of funds or in other instruments, such as a MORTGAGE POOL. The following quasi-governmental agencies issue and/or guarantee such certificates (also called PASS-THROUGH SECURITIES): FEDERAL HOME LOAN MORTGAGE CORPORATION, FEDERAL NATIONAL MORTGAGE ASSOCIATION, GOVERNMENT NATIONAL MORTGAGE ASSOCIATION, SALLIE MAE.

PARTICIPATION LOAN

Commercial lending: loan made by more than one lender and serviced (administered) by one of the participants, called the *lead bank* or *lead lender.* Participation loans make it possible for large borrowers to obtain bank financing when the amount involved exceeds the legal lending limit of an individual bank (approximately 10% of a bank's capital).

Real estate: mortgage loan, made by a lead lender, in which other lenders own an interest.

PARTNERSHIP contract between two or more people in a joint business who agree to pool their funds and talent and share in the profits and losses of the enterprise. Those who are responsible for the day-to-day management of the partnership's activities, whose individual acts are binding on the other partners, and who are personally liable for the partnership's total liabilities are called *general partners.* Those who contribute only money and are not involved in management decisions are called *limited partners;* their liability is limited to their investment.

Partnerships are a common form of organization for service professions such as accounting and law. Each accountant or lawyer made a partner earns a percentage of the firm's profits.

Limited partnerships are also sold to investors by brokerage firms, financial planners, and other registered representatives. These partnerships may be either public (meaning that a large number of investors will participate and the partnership's plans must be filed with the Securities and Exchange Commission) or private (meaning that only a limited number of investors may participate and the plan need not be filed with the SEC). Both public and private limited partnerships invest in real estate, oil and gas, research and development, and equipment leasing. Some of these partnerships are oriented towards offering tax advantages and capital gains to limited partners, while others are designed to provide mostly income and some capital gains.

See also GENERAL PARTNER; LIMITED PARTNERSHIP; OIL AND GAS LIMITED PARTNERSHIP; PRIVATE LIMITED PARTNERSHIP; PUBLIC LIMITED PARTNERSHIP.

PARTNERSHIP AGREEMENT written agreement among partners specifying the conduct of the partnership, including the division of earnings, procedures for dividing up assets if the partnership is dissolved, and steps to be followed when a partner becomes disabled or dies. Investors in LIMITED PARTNERSHIPS also receive partnership agreements, detailing their rights and responsibilities.

PAR VALUE *see* PAR.

PAR VALUE OF CURRENCY ratio of one nation's currency unit to that of another country, as defined by the official exchange rates between the two countries; also called *par of exchange* or *par exchange rate.* Since 1971, exchange rates have been allowed to float; that is, instead of official rates of exchange, currency values are being determined by the forces of supply and demand in combination with the buying and selling by countries of their own currencies in order to stabilize the market value, a form of PEGGING.

PASSBOOK book issued by a bank to record deposits, withdrawals, and interest earned in a savings account, usually known as a passbook savings account. The passbook lists the depositor's name and account number as well as all transactions. Passbook savings accounts, though usually offering low yields, are safe because deposits in them are insured up to $100,000 by the Federal Deposit Insurance Corporation. There are many alternatives to passbooks today, including ATM machines, telephone banking services, and unlimited transfers.

PASSED DIVIDEND *see* OMITTED DIVIDEND; CUMULATIVE PREFERRED.

PASSIVE income or loss from activities in which a taxpayer does not materially participate, such as LIMITED PARTNERSHIPS, as distinguished from (1) income from wages and active trade or business or

(2) *investment (or portfolio) income,* such as dividends and interest. Starting with the TAX REFORM ACT OF 1986, and after modification by the REVENUE RECONCILIATION ACT OF 1993, losses and credits from passive activities are deductible only against income and tax from passive activities, although one passive activity can offset another and unused passive losses can be carried forward until the earlier of (1) your realization of passive income to offset such losses; or (2) your sale of your entire interest in the activity, at which time suspended losses from that activity can be used without limitation. Under the 1986 Act, real estate rental activities were considered passive regardless of material participation. The 1993 Act liberalized that provision for tax years after 1993 by making an exception for professionals spending at least half their time or at least 750 hours involved in real property trade or services or for anyone, apparently including a landlord, meeting the same tests of material participation. Regular corporations (as opposed to S corporations) are exempt from passive activity rules unless they are closely held.

PASSIVE ACTIVITY LOSS (PAL) loss produced by PASSIVE investment activities. *See also* PASSIVE INCOME GENERATOR (PIG).

PASSIVE BOND BOND that yields no interest. Such bonds arise out of reorganizations or are used in NOT-FOR-PROFIT fund raising.

PASSIVE INCOME GENERATOR (PIG) investment whose main attraction is PASSIVE income. The most common example is an income-oriented real estate LIMITED PARTNERSHIP, especially an UNLEVERAGED PROGRAM. Since Tax Reform PASSIVE ACTIVITY LOSSES (PALs) are deductible to the limit of passive activity income, so an investor with excess PALs might buy a PIG as a source of tax-sheltered income.

PASSIVE INVESTING
1. putting money in an investment deemed *passive* by the Internal Revenue Service, such as a LIMITED PARTNERSHIP.
2. investing in a MUTUAL FUND that replicates a market index, such as the STANDARD & POOR'S INDEX, thus assuring investment performance no worse (or better) than the market as a whole. An INDEX FUND charges a much lower MANAGEMENT FEE than an ordinary mutual fund.

PASS THE BOOK system to transfer responsibility for a brokerage firm's trading account from one office to another around the world as trading ends in one place and begins in another. For example, a firm may start the day with the "book" of the firm's securities inventory controlled in London. As the London market closes, the book will be passed to New York, then Los Angeles, then Tokyo, then Singapore, and back to London. Passing the book is necessary because markets are now traded 24 hours a day. Customers wanting to trade at any time will often be referred to the office handling the book at that time.

PASS-THROUGH SECURITY security, representing pooled debt obligations repackaged as shares, that passes income from debtors through the intermediary to investors. The most common type of pass-through is a MORTGAGE-BACKED CERTIFICATE, usually government-guaranteed, where homeowners' principal and interest payments pass from the originating bank or savings and loan through a government agency or investment bank to investors, net of service charges. Pass-throughs representing other types of assets, such as auto loan paper or student loans, are also widely marketed. *See also* CERTIFICATE OF AUTOMOBILE RECEIVABLES (CARS); COLLATERALIZED MORTGAGE OBLIGATION; REMIC.

PATENT exclusive right to use a process or produce or sell a particular product for a designated period of time. In the United States the Patent and Trademarks Office issues design patents good for 14 years and plant and utility patents good for 17 years.

PATTERN technical chart formation made by price movements of stocks, bonds, commodities, or mutual funds. Analysts use patterns to predict future price movements. Some examples of patterns include ASCENDING TOPS; DOUBLE BOTTOM; FLAG; HEAD AND SHOULDERS; RISING BOTTOMS; SAUCER; and TRIANGLE. *See also* TECHNICAL ANALYSIS.

PAWNBROKER individual or employee of a pawn shop who lends money at a high rate of interest to a borrower leaving COLLATERAL such as jewelry, furs, appliances, or other valuable items. If the loan is repaid, the borrower gets the collateral back. If the loan is not repaid, the pawnbroker keeps the collateral, and in many cases, sells it to the public. Borrowers who turn to pawnbrokers and pawn shops typically do not have access to credit from banks or other financial institutions because they are in poor financial condition.

PAY-AS-YOU-GO BASIS INCOME TAX payment option, whereby an employer deducts and remits to the Internal Revenue Service a portion of an employee's monthly salary. Also refers generally to any service that is paid for as it is used.

PAYBACK PERIOD in capital budgeting; the length of time needed to recoup the cost of a CAPITAL INVESTMENT. The payback period is the ratio of the initial investment (cash outlay) to the annual cash inflows for the recovery period. The major shortcoming of the payback period method is that it does not take into account cash flows after the payback period and is therefore not a measure of the profitability of an investment project. For this reason, analysts generally prefer the DISCOUNTED CASH FLOW methods of capital budgeting—namely, the INTERNAL RATE OF RETURN and the NET PRESENT VALUE methods.

PAYDOWN
Bonds: refunding by a company of an outstanding bond issue through a smaller new bond issue, usually to cut interest costs. For instance, a company that issued $100 million of 12% bonds a few years ago will

pay down (refund) that debt with a new $80 million issue with an 8% yield. The amount of the net deduction is called the paydown.

Lending: repayment of principal short of full payment. *See also* ON ACCOUNT.

PAYEE person receiving payment through a check, bill, money order, promissory note, credit card, cash, or other payment method.

PAYER person making a payment to a PAYEE through a check, bill, money order, promissory note, cash, credit card, or other form of payment.

PAYING AGENT agent, usually a bank, that receives funds from an issuer of bonds or stock and in turn pays principal and interest to bondholders and dividends to stockholders, usually charging a fee for the service. Sometimes called *disbursing agent.*

PAYMENT DATE date on which a declared stock dividend or a bond interest payment is scheduled to be paid.

PAYMENT IN KIND payment for goods and services made in the form of other goods and services, not cash or other forms of money. Usually, payment in kind is made when the payee returns with the same kind of good or service. For example, if someone's tire blows out, the payee will buy another tire to replace the first one. In the securities world, PAYMENT-IN-KIND SECURITIES pay bondholders in more bonds instead of cash interest. Payment in kind is different from BARTER because the payer gets the same goods and services in return, not other goods or services of equivalent value, as is the case in barter.

PAYMENT-IN-KIND SECURITIES *see* PIK (PAYMENT-IN-KIND) SECURITIES.

PAYOUT RATIO percentage of a firm's profits that is paid out to shareholders in the form of dividends. Young, fast-growing companies reinvest most of their earnings in their business and usually do not pay dividends. Regulated electric, gas, and telephone utility companies have historically paid out larger proportions of their highly dependable earnings in dividends than have other industrial corporations. Since these utilities are limited to a specified return on assets and are thus not able to generate from internal operations the cash flow needed for expansion, they pay large dividends to keep their stock attractive to investors desiring yield and are able to finance growth through new securities offerings. *See also* RETENTION RATE.

PAYROLL WITHHOLDING *see* WITHHOLDING (under Taxes: 1).

PAY-TO-PLAY practice in the municipal bond underwriting business in which underwriters feel compelled to contribute to the political campaigns of elected officials who decide which underwriters are awarded the municipality's business. Rules curtailing the practice were promulgated by the MUNICIPAL SECURITIES RULEMAKING BOARD (MSRB), though underwriters still seek to gain influence with elected officials through other means.

PAY UP

   1. situation when an investor who wants to buy a stock at a particular price hesitates and the stock begins to rise. Instead of letting the stock go, he "pays up" to buy the shares at the higher prevailing price.

   2. when an investor buys shares in a high quality company at what is felt to be a high price. Such an investor will say "I realize that I am paying up for this stock, but it is worth it because it is such a fine company."

PBR abbreviation for price to BOOK VALUE ratio, which is the market value of a company's stock divided by its TANGIBLE NET WORTH. This ratio is especially significant to securities analysts where real estate not used in operations is a significant portion of assets, such as in the case of a typical Japanese company.

PC commonly used abbreviation for PARTICIPATION CERTIFICATE and, in brokerage parlance, for *plus commissions* (which are added to purchases and subtracted from sales).

PEACE DIVIDEND term used to describe the reallocation of spending from military purposes to peacetime priorities. After the end of World War II and at the end of the Cold War, government officials spoke of the peace dividend which could be spent on housing, education, social initiatives, deficit reduction, and other programs instead of on maintaining the military establishment.

PEGGING stabilizing the price of a security, commodity, or currency by intervening in a market. For example, until 1971 governments pegged the price of gold at certain levels to stabilize their currencies and would therefore buy it when the price dropped and sell when the price rose. Since 1971, a FLOATING EXCHANGE RATE system has prevailed, in which countries use pegging—the buying or selling of their own currencies—simply to offset fluctuations in the exchange rate. The U.S. government uses pegging in another way to support the prices of agricultural commodities, *see* PARITY PRICE.

   In floating new stock issues, the managing underwriter is authorized to try to peg the market price and stabilize the market in the issuer's stock by buying shares in the open market. With this one exception, securities price pegging is illegal and is regulated by the Securities and Exchange Commission. *See also* STABILIZATION.

PENALTY CLAUSE clause found in contracts, borrowing agreements, and savings instruments providing for penalties in the event a contract is not kept, a loan payment is late, or a withdrawal is made prematurely. *See also* PREPAYMENT PENALTY.

PENNANT technical chart pattern resembling a pointed flag, with the point facing to the right. Unlike a FLAG pattern, in which rallies and peaks occur in a uniform range, it is formed as the rallies and peaks that give it its shape become less pronounced. A pennant is also characterized by diminishing trade volume. With these differences, this pattern has essentially the same significance as a flag; that is, prices will rise or fall sharply once the pattern is complete.

PENNANT

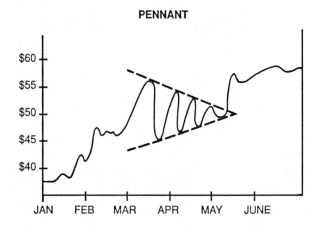

PENNY STOCK stock that typically sells for less than $1 a share, although it may rise to as much as $10 a share after the initial PUBLIC OFFERING, usually because of heavy promotion. Penny stocks are issued by companies with a short or erratic history of revenues and earnings, and therefore such stocks are more VOLATILE than those of large, well-established firms traded on the New York or American stock exchanges. Many brokerage houses therefore have special precautionary rules about trading in these stocks and the SECURITIES AND EXCHANGE COMMISSION (SEC) requires that brokers implement SUITABILITY RULES in writing and obtain written consent from investors.

All penny stocks are traded OVER-THE-COUNTER, many of them in the local markets of Denver, Vancouver, or Salt Lake City. These markets have had a history of boom and bust, with a speculative fervor for oil, gas, and gold-mining stocks in the Denver penny stock market in the late 1970s turning to bust by the early 1980s.

PENNY STOCK RULE *see* SECURITIES AND EXCHANGE COMMISSION RULES.

PENSION BENEFIT GUARANTY CORPORATION (PBGC) federal corporation established in 1974 under the EMPLOYEE RETIREMENT INCOME

SECURITY ACT (ERISA) to guarantee basic pension benefits in covered plans by administering terminated plans and placing liens on corporate assets for certain unfunded pension liabilities. To be covered, a plan must promise clearly defined benefits to more than 25 employees. PBGC collects insurance premiums from pension plans to fund its operations.

When PBGC terminates a pension plan, it pays benefits to pensioners according to the provisions of the plan up to PBGC maximum guarantees. This includes early retirement, disability, and survivor benefits. Under the single employer program, the PBGC limit is adjusted annually based on changes in Social Security contributions and benefit bases. For plans with a 1998 termination date, the maximum annual guarantee is $34,568 for a single life annuity beginning at age 65. The PBGC also conducts a "Pension Search" program which locates people who are owed benefits from terminated fully funded, PBGC-insured defined benefit plans. The agency also offers an "Early Warning" program to target underfunded plans posing the greatest risk of pension fund termination. *See also* PENSION FUND, RETIREMENT PROTECTION ACT OF 1994.

PENSION FUND fund set up by a corporation, labor union, governmental entity, or other organization to pay the pension benefits of retired workers. Pension funds invest billions of dollars annually in the stock and bond markets, and are therefore a major factor in the supply-demand balance of the markets. Earnings on the investment portfolios of pension funds are TAX DEFERRED. Fund managers make actuarial assumptions about how much they will be required to pay out to pensioners and then try to ensure that the RATE OF RETURN on their portfolios equals or exceeds that anticipated payout need. *See also* APPROVED LIST; EMPLOYEE RETIREMENT INCOME SECURITY ACT (ERISA); PRUDENT-MAN RULE; VESTING.

PENSION PARACHUTE pension agreement that specifies that in the event of a hostile takeover attempt, any excess assets in a company pension plan can be used for the benefit of pension plan participants, such as increasing pension payments. This prevents the raiding firm or individual from using the pension assets to finance the takeover, and therefore acts as an additional deterrent to help the firm ward off the acquisition. A pension parachute is a form of POISON PILL.

PENSION PLAN provides replacement for salary when a person is no longer working. In the case of a DEFINED BENEFIT PENSION PLAN, the employer or union contributes to the plan, which pays a predetermined benefit for the rest of the employee's life based on length of service and salary. Payments may be made either directly or through an annuity. Pension payments are taxable income to recipients in the year received. The employer or union has fiduciary responsibility to invest the pension funds in stocks, bonds, real estate, and other assets; earn a satisfactory rate of return; and make payments to retired workers. Pension funds holding trillions of dollars are one of the largest investment forces in the stock, bond, and real estate markets. If the employer defaults, pension plan payments are usually guaranteed by the PENSION BENEFIT GUARANTY CORPORATION (PBGC).

In the case of a DEFINED CONTRIBUTION PENSION PLAN, such as a 401(k) or 403(b) plan, employees choose whether or not to contribute to the plan offered by the employer, who may or may not match employee contributions. Pension benefits are determined by the amount of assets built up by the employee during his or her years of contributions. Self-employed individuals can also set up pension plans such as KEOGH PLANS. An INDIVIDUAL RETIREMENT ACCOUNT (IRA) is a form of pension plan. *See also* VESTING.

PENSION REVERSION procedure initiated by a company with an over-funded DEFINED BENEFIT PENSION PLAN to terminate the plan and reclaim the surplus assets for itself. Pension beneficiaries continue to receive their benefits because the company replaces the pension plan with a life insurance company-sponsored fixed annuity plan. In some cases, the company will offer current employees a DEFINED CONTRIBUTION PENSION PLAN to replace the terminated defined benefit plan. Employees are usually not pleased when their company carries out a pension reversion plan for two reasons: By replacing the pension plan backed by the company with a fixed annuity backed by an insurance company, pensioners are no longer covered by the guarantee of the Pension Benefit Guaranty Corporation; and pensioners lose the prospect for increased pension benefits that they might have enjoyed under the company's pension plan if it had achieved superior investment performance.

PENULTIMATE PROFIT PROSPECT (PPP) second lowest-priced of the ten highest-yielding stocks in the Dow Jones Industrial Average, identified (by co-author's of *Beating the Dow,* Michael B. O'Higgins and John Downes) as the single Dow stock with the greatest probability of outperforming the average as a whole.

PEOPLE PILL defensive tactic to ward off a hostile TAKEOVER. Management threatens that, in the event of a successful takeover, the entire management team will resign at once, leaving the company without experienced leadership. This is a version of the POISON PILL defense.

PER CAPITA in Latin translation, *per head.* In other words, *per person.*

PER CAPITA DEBT total bonded debt of a municipality, divided by its population. A more refined version, called *net per capita debt,* divides the total bonded debt less applicable sinking funds by the total population. The result of either ratio, compared with ratios of prior periods, reveals trends in a municipality's debt burden, which bond analysts evaluate, bearing in mind that, historically, defaults in times of recession have generally followed overexpansion of debts in prior booms.

PERCENTAGE-OF-COMPLETION   CAPITALIZED   COST METHOD *see* COMPLETED CONTRACT METHOD.

PERCENTAGE ORDER order to a securities broker to buy or sell a specified number of shares of a stock after a fixed number of these shares have been traded. It can be a LIMIT ORDER or a MARKET ORDER and usually applies to one trading day.

PERCS acronym for *preferred equity—redemption cumulative stock.* A form of preferred stock that allows common shareholders to exchange common stock for preferred shares, thereby retaining a high dividend rate. PERCS usually have little appreciation potential, however.

PERFECT COMPETITION market condition wherein no buyer or seller has the power to alter the market price of a good or service. Characteristics of a perfectly competitive market are a large number of buyers and sellers, a homogeneous (similar) good or service, an equal awareness of prices and volume, an absence of discrimination in buying and selling, total mobility of productive resources, and complete freedom of entry. Perfect competition exists only as a theoretical ideal. Also called *pure competition.*

PERFECT HEDGE *see* HEDGE/HEDGING.

PERFORMANCE BOND surety bond given by one party to another, protecting the second party against loss in the event the terms of a contract are not fulfilled. The surety company is primarily liable with the principal (the contractor) for nonperformance. For example, a homeowner having a new kitchen put in may request a performance bond from the home improvement contractor so that the homeowner would receive cash compensation if the kitchen was not done satisfactorily within the agreed upon time.

PERFORMANCE FEE *see* INCENTIVE FEE.

PERFORMANCE FUND MUTUAL FUND designed for growth of capital. A performance fund invests in high-growth companies that do not pay dividends or that pay small dividends. Investors in such funds are willing to take higher-than-average risks in order to earn higher-than-average returns on their invested capital. *See also* GROWTH STOCK; PERFORMANCE STOCK.

PERFORMANCE STOCK high-growth stock that an investor feels will significantly rise in value. Also known as GROWTH STOCK, such a security tends to pay either a small dividend or no dividend at all. Companies whose stocks are in this category tend to retain earnings rather than pay dividends in order to finance their rapid growth. *See also* PERFORMANCE FUND.

PERIODIC PAYMENT PLAN plan to accumulate capital in a mutual fund by making regular investments on a monthly or quarterly basis. The plan has a set pay-in period, which may be 10 or 20 years, and a mechanism to withdraw funds from the plan after that time. Participants in periodic payment plans enjoy the advantages of DOLLAR COST AVERAGING and the diversification among stocks or bonds that is available through a mutual fund. Some plans also include completion insurance, which assures that all scheduled contributions to the plan will continue so that full benefits can be passed on to beneficiaries in the event the participant dies or is incapacitated.

PERIODIC PURCHASE DEFERRED CONTRACT ANNUITY contract for which fixed-amount payments, called *premiums,* are paid either monthly or quarterly and that does not begin paying out until a time elected by the holder (the *annuitant*). In some cases, premium payments may continue after payments from the annuity have begun. A periodic purchase deferred contract can be either fixed or variable. *See also* FIXED ANNUITY; VARIABLE ANNUITY.

PERIOD-CERTAIN ANNUITY annuity that guarantees payments to an ANNUITANT for a particular period of time. For example, a 10-year period-certain annuity will make annuity payments for 10 years and no more. If the annuitant dies before the 10 years have expired, the payments will continue to the policy's beneficiaries for the remaining term. The monthly payment rate for a period-certain annuity is generally higher than the rate for a LIFE ANNUITY because the insurance company knows its maximum liability in advance.

PERIOD OF DIGESTION time period after the release of a NEW ISSUE of stocks or bonds during which the trading price of the security is established in the marketplace. Particularly when an INITIAL PUBLIC OFFERING is released, the period of digestion may entail considerable VOLATILITY, as investors try to ascertain an appropriate price level for it.

PERLS acronym for *principal exchange-rate-linked securities.* Debt instrument that is denominated in U.S. dollars and pays interest in U.S. dollars, but with principal repayment linked to the performance of the U.S. dollar versus a foreign currency. For example, a PERLS offering by the STUDENT LOAN MARKETING ASSOCIATION (Sallie Mae), underwritten by Morgan Stanley Dean Witter, links the principal repayment to the exchange rate of the Australian dollar versus the U.S. dollar. If the Australian dollar gains value against the U.S. dollar when the bond matures, redemption will be at a premium to par value. If the Australian dollar is weaker, redemption will be at a discount.

PERMANENT FINANCING
 Corporate finance: long-term financing by means of either debt (bonds or long-term notes) or equity (common or preferred stock).
 Real estate: long-term mortgage loan or bond issue, usually with a 15-, 20-, or 30-year term, the proceeds of which are used to repay a CONSTRUCTION LOAN.

PERPENDICULAR SPREAD option strategy using options with similar expiration dates and different strike prices (the prices at which the options can be exercised). A perpendicular spread can be designed for either a bullish or a bearish outlook.

PERPETUAL BOND bond that has no maturity date, is not redeemable and pays a steady stream of interest indefinitely; also called *annuity bond.* The only notable perpetual bonds in existence are the consols first issued by the British Treasury to pay off smaller issues used to finance the Napoleonic Wars (1814). Some persons in the United States believe it would be more realistic to issue perpetual government bonds than constantly to refund portions of the national debt, as is the practice.

PERPETUAL INVENTORY inventory accounting system whereby book inventory is kept in continuous agreement with stock on hand; also called *continuous inventory.* A daily record is maintained of both the dollar amount and the physical quantity of inventory, and this is reconciled to actual physical counts at short intervals. Perpetual inventory contrasts with *periodic inventory.*

PERPETUAL WARRANT investment certificate giving the holder the right to buy a specified number of common shares of stock at a stipulated price with no expiration date. *See also* SUBSCRIPTION WARRANT.

PERQUISITE commonly known as a *perk.* A fringe benefit offered to an employee in addition to salary. Some examples of perquisites are reimbursement for educational expenses, legal services, vacation time, pension plans, life insurance coverage, company cars and aircraft, personal financial counseling, and employee assistance hotlines. In general, the higher an employee's position and the more valued he or she in a company, the more perks he or she receives.

PERSONAL ARTICLE FLOATER policy or an addition to a policy, used to cover personal valuables, such as jewelry and furs.

PERSONAL EXEMPTION amount of money a person can exclude from personal income in calculating federal and state income tax. Taxpayers can claim one exemption for every person in their household. The amount of the personal exemption is adjusted for inflation each year. In 1998, it was $2,650. Taxpayers also can claim additional exemptions for each dependent parent living with them, if the dependent is blind, or over age 65. Exemptions are phased out for certain high-income taxpayers. For a married couple filing jointly, exemptions begin to be phased out when adjusted gross income reaches $181,800 and are eliminated completely for those reporting more than $304,300 in income. For single people, phaseout starts at $121,200, and are eliminated for those reporting over $243,700. For heads of household, the phaseout begins at an income level of $151,500 and is complete at income over $274,000. For married couples filing separately, the phaseout begins at $90,900 and is complete at levels over $152,150.

PERSONAL INCOME income received by persons from all sources: from participation in production, from both government and business

TRANSFER PAYMENTS and from government interest (which is treated like a transfer payment). "Persons" refers to individuals, nonprofit institutions that primarily serve individuals, private noninsured welfare funds, and private trust funds. Personal income is calculated as the sum of wages and salary disbursements, other labor income, proprietors' income with inventory valuation and capital consumption adjustment, rental income of persons, with capital consumption adjustment, personal dividend income, personal interest income, and transfer payments to persons, less personal contribution to Social Security.

PERSONAL INFLATION RATE rate of price increases as it affects a specific individual or couple. For example, a young couple with children who are buying and furnishing a home probably will have a much higher personal inflation rate than an elderly couple with their home paid off and self-supporting children, because the young couple needs to buy many more things that are likely to rise in price than the elderly couple. The personal inflation rate is far more relevant for most people than the general inflation rate tracked by the Labor Department's CONSUMER PRICE INDEX.

PERSONAL PROPERTY tangible and intangible assets other than real estate.

PER STIRPES formula for distributing the assets of a person who dies intestate (without a will) according to the "family tree." Under such a distribution, the estate is allocated according to the number of children the deceased had, and distributed accordingly to those surviving the decedent. If any children predeceased the decedent, the share allocated to them would be equally divided among their children and so on.

PETRODOLLARS dollars paid to oil-producing countries and deposited in Western banks. When the price of oil skyrocketed in the 1970s, Middle Eastern oil producers built up huge surpluses of petrodollars that the banks lent to oil-importing countries around the world. By the mid-1980s and 1990s, these surpluses had shrunk because consumption increased while oil exporters spent a good deal of the money on development projects. The flow of petrodollars, therefore, is very important in understanding the current world economic situation. Also called *petrocurrency* or *oil money*.

PHANTOM INCOME LIMITED PARTNERSHIP income that arises from debt restructuring and creates taxability without generating cash flow. Phantom income typically occurs in a tax shelter created prior to the TAX REFORM ACT OF 1986 where real estate properties, having declined in market value, are refinanced; income arises from portions of the debt that are forgiven and recaptured.

PHANTOM STOCK PLAN executive incentive concept whereby an executive receives a bonus based on the market appreciation of the company's stock over a fixed period of time. The hypothetical (hence phantom) amount of shares involved in the case of a particular executive is proportionate to his or her salary level. The plan works on the same principle as a CALL OPTION (a right to purchase a fixed amount of stock at a set price by a particular date). Unlike a call option, however, the executive pays nothing for the option and therefore has nothing to lose.

PHILADELPHIA BOARD OF TRADE (PBOT) subsidiary of the PHILADELPHIA STOCK EXCHANGE which trades currency futures on the Australian dollar, British pound, Canadian dollar, Deutsche mark, EURO, French franc, Japanese yen and Swiss franc. Options are traded on the PSE's United Currency Options Market.

PHILADELPHIA STOCK EXCHANGE (PHLX) founded in 1790 as the first organized stock exchange in the U.S. PHLX trades equities, equity options, sector index options and currency options. In 1998, the exchange became a charter member of the NASD/AMEX family of companies, formed with the merger of the AMERICAN STOCK EXCHANGE, (AMEX) and the NASDAQ STOCK MARKET. The alignment combines the best technology of the two entities and provides for operation of the PHLX trading floor in Philadelphia for up to five years. Trading is conducted through floor brokers or PACE (Philadelphia Automated Communication and Execution System), the exchange's electronic retail-oriented delivery and execution system. After the market officially closes at 4 P.M., PHLX's Post Primary Session (PPS) offers trading from 4:00 P.M. to 4:15 P.M. to allow institutional traders the ability to complete unfilled trades. PHLX also offers the VWAP (Volume Weighted Average Price) Trading System, which allows institutions to match equity orders before and after the market is open in an automated and electronic manner.

PHLX trades over 700 equity options, LEAPS (Long-Term Equity AnticiPation Securities) and FLEX (Flexible Exchange) options. LEAPS are options contracts with expiration dates as long as three years in the future. FLEX options allow users to tailor equity and index options to meet hedging and investment needs by allowing them to specify expiration dates, strike prices, and exercise styles. These options trades are executed by AUTOM (the Automated Options Market), which enables brokerage firms to electronically transmit retail customer orders directly to the trading floor for execution.

The exchange also trades several sector index options, covering both broad and industry specific market sectors. Some of the broad-based sectors include the National OTC Sector, SuperCap Sector, US TOP 100 Index, and Value Line Composite Index. Some of the industry-specific sectors include airlines, banking, forest and paper products, gold/silver, oil services, phones, semiconductors and utilities. Trading hours are 9:30 A.M. to 4:15 P.M.

PHLX, a leader in the trading of foreign currency options, offers the United Currency Options Market (UCOM) in such currencies as the Australian dollar, British pound, Canadian dollar, Deustsche mark, European Currency Unit, French franc, Italian lira, Japanese yen, Mexican peso, Spanish peseta, Swiss franc and U.S. dollar. UCOM offers trading in 3-D options,which are cash settled in U.S. dollars, and are also available in Japanese yen and Deutsche marks. Trading hours are 2:30 A.M. to 2:30 P.M. Monday through Friday. *See also* SECURITIES AND COMMODITIES EXCHANGES.

PHILIPPINE STOCK EXCHANGE operates two trading floors, Manila and Makati; Manila is the larger. Trading hours are from 9:30 A.M. to 12 noon, Monday through Friday, with a 15-minute extension at closing prices, and a 10-minute break at 10:50 A.M. Settlement takes place on the fourth business day after a trade.

PHYSICAL COMMODITY actual commodity that is delivered to the contract buyer at the completion of a commodity contract in either the SPOT MARKET or the FUTURES MARKET. Some examples of physical commodities are corn, cotton, gold, oil, soybeans, and wheat. The quality specifications and quantity of the commodity to be delivered are specified by the exchange on which it is traded.

PHYSICAL INVENTORY *see* PHYSICAL VERIFICATION.

PHYSICAL VERIFICATION procedure by which an auditor actually inspects the assets of a firm, particularly inventory, to confirm their existence and value, rather than relying on written records. The auditor may use statistical sampling in the verification process.

PICKUP value gained in a bond swap. For example, bonds with identical coupon rates and maturities may have different market values, mainly because of a difference in quality, and thus in yields. The higher yield of the lower-quality bond received in such a swap compared with the yield of the higher-quality bond that was exchanged for it results in a net gain for the trader, called his or her pickup on the transaction.

PICKUP BOND bond that has a relatively high coupon (interest) rate and is close to the date at which it is callable—that is, can be paid off prior to maturity—by the issuer. If interest rates fall, the investor can look forward to picking up a redemption PREMIUM, since the bond will in all likelihood be called.

PICTURE Wall Street jargon used to request bid and asked prices and quantity information from a specialist or from a dealer regarding a particular security. For example, the question "What's the picture on XYZ?" might be answered, "58⅛ [best bid] to ¾ [best offer is 58¾], 1000 either way [there are both a buyer and a seller for 1000 shares]."

PIG *see* PASSIVE INCOME GENERATOR.

PIGGYBACKING illegal practice by a broker who buys or sells stocks or bonds in his personal account after a customer buys or sells the same security. The broker assumes that the customer is making the trade because of access to material, nonpublic information that will make the stock or bond rise or fall sharply. Trading following customer orders is a conflict of interest, and may be disciplined by the broker's firm or regulatory authorities if discovered.

PIGGYBACK REGISTRATION situation when a securities underwriter allows existing holdings of shares in a corporation to be sold in combination with an offering of new public shares. The prospectus in a piggyback registration will reveal the nature of such a public/private share offering and name the sellers of the private shares. See also public offering.

PIK (PAYMENT-IN-KIND) SECURITIES bonds or preferred stock that pay interest/dividends in the form of additional bonds or preferred. PIK securities have been used in takeover financing in lieu of cash and are highly speculative.

PINK SHEETS daily publication of the national quotation bureau that details the bid and asked prices of over the counter (OTC) stocks not carried in daily newspaper listings of NASDAQ STOCK MARKET. Brokerage firms subscribe to the pink sheets—named for their color—because the sheets not only give current prices but list market makers who trade each stock. Debt securities are listed separately on YELLOW SHEETS. *See also* OTC BULLETIN BOARD.

PIN NUMBER acronym for *personal identification number.* Customers use PIN numbers to identify themselves, such as when performing transactions with a debit card at an automatic teller machine.

PIPELINE term referring to the underwriting process that involves securities being proposed for public distribution. The phrase used is "in the pipeline." The entire underwriting process, including registration with the Securities and Exchange Commission, must be completed before a security can be offered for public sale. Underwriters attempt to have several securities issues waiting in the pipeline so that the issues can be sold as soon as market conditions become favorable. In the municipal bond market, the pipeline is called the "Thirty Day Visible Supply" in the *Bond Buyer* newspaper.

PIT location at a futures or options exchange in which trading takes place. Pits are usually shaped like rings, often with several levels of steps, so that a large number of traders can see and be seen by each other as they conduct business.

PITI acronym for *principal, interest, taxes and insurance,* the primary components of monthly mortgage payments. Many mortgage lenders, to ensure that property taxes and homeowner's insurance premiums are paid on schedule, require that borrowers include these amounts in their monthly payments. The funds are then placed in escrow until needed. When calculating how much a house will cost a borrower on a monthly basis, the payment is expressed for PITI.

PLACE to market new securities. The term applies to both public and private sales but is more often used with reference to direct sales to institutional investors, as in PRIVATE PLACEMENT. The terms FLOAT and *distribute* are preferred in the case of a PUBLIC OFFERING.

PLACEMENT RATIO ratio, compiled by the *Bond Buyer* as of the close of business every Thursday, indicating the percentage of the past week's new MUNICIPAL BOND offerings that have been bought from the underwriters. Only issues of $1 million or more are included.

PLANNED AMORTIZATION CLASS BONDS *see* PAC BONDS.

PLAN PARTICIPANTS employees or former employees of a company, members of an employee organization or beneficiaries who may become eligible to receive benefits from an employee benefit plan. Participants are legally entitled to certain information about the plan and the benefits, including a summary annual report and summary plan description.

PLAN SPONSOR entity that establishes and maintains a pension or insurance plan. This may be a corporation, labor union, government agency, or nonprofit organization. Plan sponsors must follow government guidelines in the establishment and administration of these plans, including informing plan participants about the financial health of the plan and the benefits available.

PLANT assets comprising land, buildings, machinery, natural resources, furniture and fixtures, and all other equipment permanently employed. Synonymous with FIXED ASSET.

   In a limited sense, the term is used to mean only buildings or only land and buildings: "property, plant, and equipment" and "plant and equipment."

PLAYING THE MARKET unprofessional buying and selling of stocks, as distinguished from SPECULATION. Both players and speculators are seeking capital gains, but while playing the market is more akin to gambling, speculating is done by professionals taking calculated risks.

PLAZA ACCORD agreement in August of 1985 in which the finance ministers of the Group of 5—the United States, Great Britain, France, Germany, and Japan—met at the Plaza Hotel in New York City to mount a concerted effort to reduce the value of the U.S. dollar against other major currencies. Though the dollar had already begun its decline months earlier, the Plaza Accord accelerated the move. The action was necessary because the dollar had become so strong that it was difficult for U.S. exporters to sell their products abroad, weakening the American economy.

PLC *see* PUBLIC LIABILITY COMPANY.

PLEDGING transferring property, such as securities or the CASH SURRENDER VALUE of life insurance, to a lender or creditor as COLLATERAL for an obligation. *Pledge* and *hypothecate* are synonymous, as they do not involve transfer of title. ASSIGN, although commonly used interchangeably with *pledge* and *hypothecate,* implies transfer of ownership or of the right to transfer ownership at a later date. *See also* HYPOTHECATION.

PLOW BACK to reinvest a company's earnings in the business rather than pay out those profits as dividends. Smaller, fast-growing companies usually plow back most or all earnings in their businesses, whereas more established firms pay out more of their profits as dividends.

PLUS

1. plus sign (+) that follows a price quotation on a Treasury note or bond, indicating that the price (normally quoted as a percentage of PAR value refined to 32ds) is refined to 64ths. Thus $95.16 + (95^{16}/_{32}+$ or $95^{32}/_{64}+)$ means $95^{33}/_{64}$.

2. plus sign after a transaction price in a listed security (for example, $39\frac{1}{2}+$), indicating that the trade was at a higher price than the previous REGULAR WAY transaction. *See also* PLUS TICK.

3. plus sign before the figure in the column labeled "Change" in the newspaper stock tables, meaning that the closing price of the stock was higher than the previous day's close by the amount stated in the "Change" column.

PLUS TICK expression used when a security has been traded at a higher price than the previous transaction in that security. A stock price listed as 28+ on the CONSOLIDATED TAPE has had a plus tick from $27^{15}/_{16}$ or below on previous trades. It is a Securities and Exchange Commission rule that short sales can be executed only on plus ticks or ZERO PLUS TICKS. Also called *uptick. See also* MINUS TICK; TICK; ZERO-MINUS TICK.

POINT

Bonds: percentage change of the face value of a bond expressed as a point. For example, a change of 1% is a move of one point. For a bond with a $1000 face value, each point is worth $10, and for a bond with a $5000 face value, each point is $50.

Bond yields are quoted in basis points: 100 basis points make up 1% of yield. *See* BASIS POINT.

Futures/options: measure of price change equal to one one-hundredth of one cent in most futures traded in decimal units. In grains, it is one quarter of one cent; in Treasury bonds, it is 1% of par. *See also* TICK.

Real estate and other commercial lending: upfront fee charged by a lender, separate from interest but designed to increase the overall yield to the lender. A point is 1% of the total principal amount of the loan. For example, on a $100,000 mortgage loan, a charge of 3 points would equal $3000. Since points are considered a form of prepaid mortgage interest, they are tax-deductible, usually over the term of the loan, but in some cases in a lump sum in the year they are paid.

Stocks: change of $1 in the market price of a stock. If a stock has risen 5 points, it has risen by $5 a share.

The movements of stock market averages, such as the Dow Jones Industrial Average, are also quoted in points. However, those points refer not to dollar amounts but to units of movement in the average, which is a composite of weighted dollar values. For example, a 20-point move in the Dow Jones Average from 8000 to 8020 does *not* mean the Dow now stands at $8020.

POINT AND FIGURE CHART graphic technique used in TECHNICAL ANALYSIS to follow the up or down momentum in the price moves of a security or sector. Point and figure charting disregards the element of time and is solely used to record changes in price. Every time a price move is upward, an X is put on the graph above the previous point. Every time the price moves down, an O is placed one square down. When direction changes, the next column is used. The resulting lines of Xs and Os will indicate whether the security or sector being charted has maintained an up or a down momentum over a particular time period.

POINT AND FIGURE CHART

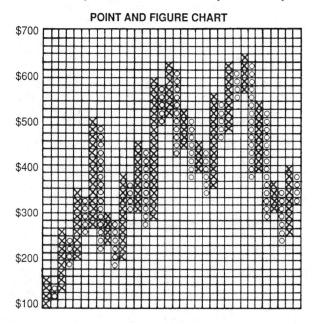

POISON PILL strategic move by a takeover-target company to make its stock less attractive to an acquirer. For instance, a firm may issue a new series of PREFERRED STOCK that gives shareholders the right to redeem it at a premium price after a TAKEOVER. Two variations: a *flip-in poison pill* allows all existing holders of target company shares except the acquirer to buy additional shares at a bargain price; a *flip-over poison pill* allows holders of common stock to buy (or holders of preferred stock to convert into) the acquirer's shares at a bargain price in the event of an unwelcome merger. Such measures raise the cost of an ACQUISITION, and cause DILUTION, hopefully deterring a takeover bid. A third type of poison pill, known as a PEOPLE PILL, is the threat that in the event of a successful takeover, the entire management team will resign at once, leaving the company without experienced leadership. *See also* PENSION PARACHUTE, POISON PUT, SUICIDE PILL.

POISON PUT provision in an INDENTURE giving bondholders the privilege of redemption at PAR if certain designated events occur, such as a hostile TAKEOVER, the purchase of a big block of shares, or an excessively large dividend payout. Poison puts, or *superpoison puts* as the more stringent variations are called, are popular antitakeover devices because they create an onerous cash obligation for the acquirer. They also protect the bondholder from the deterioration of credit quality and RATING that might result from a LEVERAGED BUYOUT that added to the issuer's debt. *See also* EVENT RISK.

POLICYHOLDER owner of an INSURANCE contract (policy). Term is commonly used synonymously with *insured,* although the two can be different parties and *insured* is the preferred designation for the person indemnified by the insurance company.

POLICYHOLDER LOAN BONDS packaged policyholder loans. Life insurance policyholders borrow against the CASH SURRENDER VALUE of their policies. The policyholder loan will be repaid either by the policyholder while alive or from the proceeds of the insurance policy if the policyholder dies before repayment. These loans are packaged by a broker/dealer that offers these asset-backed securities as policyholder loan bonds.

POLICY LIMIT limit of coverage provided by an insurance policy, known as a *maximum lifetime benefit.* For coverage of individuals, roughly two-thirds of existing policies have a limit of $1 million or more; 21% have no limit. Most employee plans are based on maximum lifetime coverage.

POLICY LOAN loan from an insurance company secured by the CASH SURRENDER VALUE of a life insurance policy. The amount available for such a loan depends on the number of years the policy has been in effect, the insured's age when the policy was issued, and the size of the death benefit. Such loans are often made at below-market interest rates to policyholders, although more recent policies usually only allow borrowing at rates that fluctuate in line with money market rates. If the loan is not repaid by the insured, the death benefit of the life insurance policy will be reduced by the amount of the loan plus accrued interest.

POOL
Capital budgeting: as used in the phrase "pool of financing," the concept that investment projects are financed out of a pool of funds rather

than out of bonds, preferred stock, and common stock individually. A weighted average cost of capital is thus used in analyses evaluating the return on investment projects. *See also* COST OF CAPITAL.

Industry: joining of companies to improve profits by reducing competition. Such poolings are generally outlawed in the United States by various ANTITRUST LAWS.

Insurance: association of insurers who share premiums and losses in order to spread risk and give small insurers an opportunity to compete with larger ones.

Investments:
1. combination of resources for a common purpose or benefit. For example, an INVESTMENT CLUB pools the funds of its members, giving them the opportunity to share in a PORTFOLIO offering greater diversification and the hope of a better return on their money than they could get individually. A *commodities pool* entrusts the funds of many investors to a trading professional **and** distributes profits and losses among participants in proportion to their interests.
2. group of investors joined together to use their combined power to manipulate security or commodity prices or to obtain control of a corporation. Such pools are outlawed by regulations governing securities and commodities trading.

 See also MORTGAGE POOL.

POOLING OF INTERESTS accounting method used in the combining or merging of companies following an acquisition, whereby the balance sheets (assets and liabilities) of the two companies are simply added together, item by item. This tax-free method contrasts with the PURCHASE ACQUISITION method, in which the buying company treats the acquired company as an investment and any PREMIUM paid over the FAIR MARKET VALUE of the assets is reflected on the buyer's balance sheet as GOODWILL. Because reported earnings are higher under the pooling of interests method, most companies prefer it to the purchase acquisition method, particularly when the amount of goodwill is sizable.

 The pooling of interests method can be elected only when the following conditions are met:
1. The two companies must have been autonomous for at least two years prior to the pooling and one must not have owned more than 10% of the stock of the other.
2. The combination must be consummated either in a single transaction or in accordance with a specific plan within one year after the plan is initiated; no contingent payments are permitted.
3. The acquiring company must issue its regular common stock in exchange for 90% or more of the common stock of the other company.
4. The surviving corporation must not later retire or reacquire common stock issued in the combination, must not enter into an arrangement for the benefit of former stockholders, and must not dispose of a significant portion of the assets of the combining companies for at least 2 years.

 See also MERGER.

PORCUPINE PROVISIONS *see* SHARK REPELLENTS.

PORTABILITY ability of employees to retain benefits from one employer to the next when switching jobs. The term is most frequently used in connection with pension and insurance coverage. Credits earned towards pension benefits in a DEFINED BENEFIT PENSION PLAN are rarely portable from one company to another. Conversely, accumulated assets in a DEFINED CONTRIBUTION PENSION PLAN may be transferable to the defined contribution plan of another employer through a rollover. Under the CONSOLIDATED OMNIBUS BUDGET RECONCILIATION ACT (COBRA), employees have the right to carry their group health insurance coverage with them to a new job for up to 18 months. An employee may wish to do so if the new employer's health plan is inferior to the previous employer's plan. Employees choosing to continue coverage with a previous employer's group plan under the COBRA provision pay the full premium, which is subject to change. Generally, this continued coverage costs considerably less than a policy at individual rates.

PORTFOLIO combined holding of more than one stock, bond, commodity, real estate investment, CASH EQUIVALENT, or other asset by an individual or institutional investor. The purpose of a portfolio is to reduce risk by diversification. *See also* PORTFOLIO BETA SCORE; PORTFOLIO THEORY.

PORTFOLIO BETA SCORE relative VOLATILITY of an individual securities portfolio, taken as a whole, as measured by the BETA coefficients of the securities making it up. Beta measures the volatility of a stock relative to the market as a whole, as represented by an index such as Standard & Poor's 500 Stock Index. A beta of 1 means the stock has about the same volatility as the market.

PORTFOLIO INCOME *see* INVESTMENT INCOME.

PORTFOLIO INSURANCE the use, by a PORTFOLIO MANAGER, of STOCK INDEX FUTURES to protect stock portfolios against market declines. Instead of selling actual stocks as they lose value, managers sell the index futures; if the drop continues, they repurchase the futures at a lower price, using the profit to offset losses in the stock portfolio. The inability of the markets on BLACK MONDAY to process such massive quantities of stock efficiently and the subsequent instituting of CIRCUIT BREAKERS all but eliminated portfolio insurance. *See also* PROGRAM TRADING.

PORTFOLIO MANAGER professional responsible for the securities PORTFOLIO of an individual or INSTITUTIONAL INVESTOR. Also called a *money manager* or, especially when personalized service is involved, an INVESTMENT COUNSEL. A portfolio manager may work for a mutual fund, pension fund, profit-sharing plan, bank trust department, or insurance company. In return for a fee, the manager has the fiduciary responsibility to manage the assets prudently and choose whether stocks, bonds, CASH EQUIVALENTS, real estate, or some other assets present the best opportunities for profit at any particular time. *See also* PORTFOLIO THEORY; PRUDENT-MAN RULE.

PORTFOLIO THEORY sophisticated investment decision approach that permits an investor to classify, estimate, and control both the kind and the amount of expected risk and return; also called *portfolio management theory* or *modern portfolio theory.* Essential to portfolio theory are its quantification of the relationship between risk and return and the assumption that investors must be compensated for assuming risk. Portfolio theory departs from traditional security analysis in shifting emphasis from analyzing the characteristics of individual investments to determining the statistical relationships among the individual securities that comprise the overall portfolio. The portfolio theory approach has four basic steps: *security valuation*—describing a universe of assets in terms of expected return and expected risk; *asset allocation decision*—determining how assets are to be distributed among classes of investment, such as stocks or bonds; *portfolio optimization*—reconciling risk and return in selecting the securities to be included, such as determining which portfolio of stocks offers the best return for a given level of expected risk; and *performance measurement*—dividing each stock's performance (risk) into market-related (systematic) and industry/security-related (residual) classifications.

POSITION

Banking: bank's net balance in a foreign currency.

Finance: firm's financial condition.

Investments:

1. investor's stake in a particular security or market. A LONG POSITION equals the number of shares *owned;* a SHORT POSITION equals the number of shares *owed* by a dealer or an individual. The dealer's long positions are called his *inventory of securities.*
2. Used as a verb, to take on a long or a short position in a stock.

POSITION BUILDING process of buying shares to accumulate a LONG POSITION or of selling shares to accumulate a SHORT POSITION. Large institutional investors who want to build a large position in a particular security do so over time to avoid pushing up the price of the security.

POSITION LIMIT

Commodities trading: number of contracts that can be acquired in a specific commodity before a speculator is classified as a "large trader." Large traders are subject to special oversight by the COMMODITY FUTURES TRADING COMMISSION (CFTC) and the exchanges and are limited as to the number of contracts they can add to their positions. The position limit varies with the type of commodity.

Options trading: maximum number of exchange-listed OPTION contracts that can be owned or controlled by an individual holder, or by a group of holders acting jointly, in the same underlying security. The current limit is 2000 contracts on the same side of the market (for example, long calls and short puts are one side of the market); the limit applies to all expiration dates.

POSITION TRADER commodities trader who takes a long-term approach—six months to a year or more—to the market. Usually possessing more than average experience, information, and capital, these traders ride through the ups and downs of price fluctuations until close to the delivery date, unless drastic adverse developments threaten. More like insurance underwriters than gamblers, they hope to achieve long-term profits from calculated risks as distinguished from pure speculation.

POSITIVE CARRY situation in which the cost of money borrowed to finance securities is lower than the yield on the securities. For example, if a fixed-income bond yielding 10% is purchased with a loan bearing 8% interest, the bond has positive carry. The opposite situation is called NEGATIVE CARRY.

POSITIVE YIELD CURVE situation in which interest rates are higher on long-term debt securities than on short-term debt securities of the same quality. For example, a positive yield curve exists when 20-year Treasury bonds yield 10% and 3-month Treasury bills yield 6%. Such a situation is common, since an investor who ties up his money for a longer time is taking more risk and is usually compensated by a higher yield. When short-term interest rates rise above long-term rates, there is a NEGATIVE YIELD CURVE, also called an INVERTED YIELD CURVE.

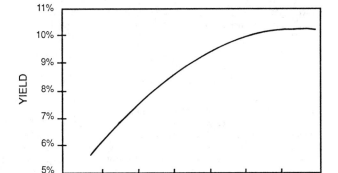

POSITIVE YIELD CURVE

POST

   Accounting: to transfer from a journal of original entry detailed financial data, in the chronological order in which it was generated, into a ledger book. Banks post checking account deposits and withdrawals in a ledger, then summarize these transactions on the monthly bank statement.

   Investments: horseshoe-shaped structure on the floor of the New York Stock Exchange where specialists trade specific securities. Video screens surround the post, displaying the bid and offer prices available for stocks traded at that location. Also called *trading post.*

POSTDATED CHECK check dated in the future. It is not negotiable until the date becomes current.

POSTING in bookkeeping terminology, the transfer of data from a journal to a ledger.

POSTPONING INCOME technique to delay receipt of income into a later year to reduce current tax liability. For example, if it seems likely that Congress or the state legislature may reduce income tax rates in the upcoming year, it may be advantageous to receive income in that year instead of in the current year when tax rates are higher. Salespeople can appeal to their managers to pay their commissions in the next year, and small business owners can send invoices after the first of the year so that they are paid in the next year. In addition to qualifying for a lower tax rate, the full tax on the income may be delayed until April 15 of the following year, unless the taxpayer receiving the income is required to file quarterly estimated tax payments.

POT securities underwriting term meaning the portion of a stock or bond issue returned to the MANAGING UNDERWRITER by the participating investment bankers to facilitate sales to INSTITUTIONAL INVESTORS. Institutions buying from the pot designate the firms to be credited with pot sales. *See also* RETENTION.

POT IS CLEAN MANAGING UNDERWRITER'S announcement to members of the underwriting group that the POT—the portion of the stock or bond issue withheld to facilitate institutional sales—has been sold.

POWER OF ATTORNEY

   In general: written document that authorizes a particular person to perform certain acts on behalf of the one signing the document. The document, which must be witnessed by a notary public or some other public officer, may bestow either *full power of attorney* or *limited power of attorney.* It becomes void upon the death of the signer.

   Investments: *full power of attorney* might, for instance, allow assets to be moved from one brokerage or bank account to another. A *limited power of attorney,* on the other hand, would only permit transactions within an existing account. A broker given a limited power of attorney, for instance, may buy and sell securities in an account but may not remove them. Such an account is called a DISCRETIONARY ACCOUNT. *See also* DISCRETIONARY ORDER; PROXY; STOCK POWER.

PREARRANGED TRADING questionable and probably fraudulent practice whereby commodities dealers arrange risk-free trades at predetermined prices, usually to gain tax advantages.

PREAUTHORIZED PAYMENT prearranged deductions from a bank account for the payment of a third party.

PRECEDENCE priority of one order over another on the floor of the exchanges, according to rules designed to protect the DOUBLE-AUCTION SYSTEM. The rules basically are that the highest bid and lowest offer have precedence over other bids and offers, that the first bid or first offer at a price has priority over other bids or offers at that price, and that the size of the order determines precedence thereafter, large orders having priority over smaller orders. Where two orders of equal size must compete for the same limited quantity after the first bid is filled, the impasse is resolved by a flip of the coin. *See also* MATCHED AND LOST. Exchange rules also require that public orders have precedence over trades for floor members' own accounts. *See also* OFF-FLOOR ORDER; ON-FLOOR ORDER.

PRECIOUS METALS gold, silver, platinum, and palladium. These metals are valued for their intrinsic value, backing world currencies, as well as their industrial applications. Fundamental issues of supply and demand are important factors in their prices, along with political and economic considerations, especially when producing countries are involved. Inflation fears will stimulate gold accumulation and higher prices, as will war and natural disaster, especially in major producing or consuming countries or regions. Precious metals are held by central banks and are considered a storehouse of value. While gold is often singled out, cultural factors assign different levels of significance to the metals. In the Far East, especially Japan, platinum traditionally is held in higher regard than gold, both in terms of physical metal and investment holdings, and for personal accumulation (e.g., jewelry and coins). Gold is favored in the West. In India and the Middle East, silver is highly prized, and the dowries of Indian women are replete with silver jewelry and coins. Investors can buy physical metal in bars, BULLION and NUMISMATIC COINS, and jewelry. There are numerous investment vehicles that do not involve physical delivery: futures and options contracts, mining company stocks, bonds, mutual funds, commodity indices, and commodity funds. The values of these investment vehicles are influenced by metal price volatility, with commodity funds and indices, and futures and options, more sensitive to daily price swings. Many metals analysts and advisors recommend that 5% to 15% of investor portfolios be held in some form of precious metals as a long-term hedge against inflation and political turmoil.

PRECOMPUTE in installment lending, methods of charging interest whereby the total amount of annual interest either is deducted from the face amount of the loan at the time the loan proceeds are disbursed or is added to the total amount to be repaid in equal installments. In both cases, the EFFECTIVE RATE to the borrower is higher than the stated annual rate used in the computation. "Truth in lending" laws require that the effective annual rate be expressed in SIMPLE INTEREST terms.

PREEMPTIVE RIGHT right giving existing stockholders the opportunity to purchase shares of a NEW ISSUE before it is offered to others. Its purpose is to protect shareholders from dilution of value and control when new shares are issued. Although 48 U.S. states have preemptive right statutes, most states also either permit corporations to pay stockholders to waive their preemptive rights or state in their statutes that the preemptive right is valid only if set forth in the corporate charter. As a result, preemptive rights are the exception rather than the rule. Where they do exist, the usual procedure is for each existing stockholder to receive, prior to a new issue, a SUBSCRIPTION WARRANT indicating how many new shares the holder is entitled to buy—normally, a proportion of the shares he or she already holds. Since the new shares would typically be priced below the market, a financial incentive exists to exercise the preemptive right. *See also* SUBSCRIPTION RIGHT.

PREFERENCE ITEM *see* TAX PREFERENCE ITEM.

PREFERENCE SHARES *see* PRIOR-PREFERRED STOCK.

PREFERRED DIVIDEND COVERAGE net income after interest and taxes (but before common stock dividends) divided by the dollar amount of preferred stock dividends. The result tells how many times over the preferred dividend requirement is covered by current earnings.

PREFERRED STOCK class of CAPITAL STOCK that pays dividends at a specified rate and that has preference over common stock in the payment of dividends and the liquidation of assets. Preferred stock does not ordinarily carry voting rights.

Most preferred stock is *cumulative;* if dividends are passed (not paid for any reason), they accumulate and must be paid before common dividends. A PASSED DIVIDEND on *noncumulative preferred* stock is generally gone forever. PARTICIPATING PREFERRED STOCK entitles its holders to share in profits above and beyond the declared dividend, along with common shareholders, as distinguished from *nonparticipating preferred,* which is limited to the stipulated dividend. *Adjustable-rate preferred* stock pays a dividend that is adjustable, usually quarterly, based on changes in the Treasury bill rate or other money market rates. *Convertible preferred stock* is exchangeable for a given number of common shares and thus tends to be more VOLATILE than *nonconvertible preferred,* which behaves more like a fixed-income bond. *See also* CONVERTIBLE; CUMULATIVE PREFERRED; PARTICIPATING PREFERRED; PIK (PAYMENT-IN-KIND) SECURITIES; PRIOR, PREFERRED STOCK.

PREFERRED STOCK RATIO PREFERRED STOCK at PAR value divided by total CAPITALIZATION; the result is the percentage of capitalization—bonds and net worth—represented by preferred stock.

PRELIMINARY PROSPECTUS first document released by an underwriter of a NEW ISSUE to prospective investors. The document offers financial details about the issue but does not contain all the information that will appear in the final or statutory prospectus, and parts of the document may be changed before the final prospectus is issued. Because portions of the cover page of the preliminary prospectus are printed in red ink, it is popularly called the *red herring.*

PREMIUM

In general: extra payment usually made as an incentive.

Bonds:
1. amount by which a bond sells above its face (PAR) value. For instance, a bond with a face value of $1000 would sell for a $100 premium when it cost $1100. The same meaning also applies to preferred stock. *See also* PREMIUM BOND; PREMIUM OVER BOND VALUE; PREMIUM OVER CONVERSION VALUE.
2. amount by which the REDEMPTION PRICE to the issuer exceeds the face value when a bond is called. *See also* CALL PREMIUM.

Insurance: fee paid to an insurance company for insurance protection. Also, the single or multiple payments made to build an ANNUITY fund.

Options: price a put or call buyer must pay to a put or call seller (writer) for an option contract. The premium is determined by market supply and demand forces. *See also* OPTION; PREMIUM INCOME.

Stocks:
1. charge occasionally paid by a short seller when stock is borrowed to make delivery on a SHORT SALE.
2. amount by which a stock's price exceeds that of other stocks to which it is comparable. For instance, securities analysts might say that XYZ Foods is selling at a 15% premium to other food company stocks—an indication that the stock is more highly valued by investors than its industry peers. It does not necessarily mean that the stock is overpriced, however. Indeed, it may indicate that the investment public has only begun to recognize the stock's market potential and that the price will continue to rise. Similarly, analysts might say that the food industry is selling for a 20% premium to Standard & Poor's 500 index, indicating the relative price strength of the industry group to the stock market as a whole.
3. in new issues, amount by which the trading price of the shares exceeds the OFFERING PRICE.
4. amount over market value paid in a *tender offer. See also* PREMIUM RAID.

PREMIUM BOND bond with a selling price above face or redemption value. A bond with a face value of $1000, for instance, would be called a premium bond if it sold for $1050. This price does not include any

ACCRUED INTEREST due when the bond is bought. When a premium bond is called before scheduled maturity, bondholders are usually paid more than face value, though the amount may be less than the bond is selling for at the time of the CALL.

PREMIUM INCOME income received by an investor who sells a PUT OPTION or a CALL OPTION. An investor collects premium income by writing a COVERED OPTION, if he or she owns the underlying stock, or a NAKED OPTION, if he or she does not own the stock. An investor who sells options to collect premium income hopes that the underlying stock will not rise very much (in the case of a call) or fall very much (in the case of a put).

PREMIUM OVER BOND VALUE upward difference between the market value of a CONVERTIBLE bond and the price at which a straight bond of the same company would sell in the same open market. A convertible bond, eventually convertible to common stock, will normally sell at a PREMIUM over its bond value because investors place a value on the conversion feature. The higher the market price of the issuer's stock is relative to the price at which the bond is convertible, the greater the premium will be, reflecting the investor's tendency to view it more as a stock than as a bond. When the stock price falls near or below the conversion price, investors then tend to view the convertible as a bond and the premium narrows or even disappears. Other factors affecting the prices of convertible bonds generally include lower transaction costs on the convertibles than would be incurred in buying the stock outright, an attraction that exerts some upward pressure on the premium; the demand from life insurance companies and other institutional investors that are limited by law as to the common stock investments they can have and that gain their equity participation through convertibles; the duration period of the option to convert—the longer it is, the more valuable the future and the higher the premium; high dividends on the issuer's common stock, a factor increasing demand for the common versus the convertible, and therefore a downward pressure. *See also* PREMIUM OVER CONVERSION VALUE.

PREMIUM OVER CONVERSION VALUE amount by which the MARKET PRICE of a CONVERTIBLE preferred stock or convertible bond exceeds the price at which it is convertible. Convertibles (CVs) usually sell at a PREMIUM for two basic reasons: (1) if the convertible is a bond, the bond value—defined as the price at which a straight bond of the same company would sell in the same open market—is the lowest value the CV will reach; it thus represents DOWNSIDE RISK protection, which is given a value in the marketplace, generally varying with the VOLATILITY of the common stock; (2) the conversion privilege is given a value by investors because they might find it profitable eventually to convert the securities.

At relatively high common-stock price levels, a convertible tends to sell for its common stock equivalent and the conversion value becomes negligible. This occurs because investors are viewing the security as a common stock, not as a bond, and because conversion would be preferable to redemption if the bond were called. On the other hand, when the market value of the convertible is close to its bond value, the conversion feature has little value and the security is valued more as a bond. It is here that the CONVERSION PREMIUM is highest. The conversion premium is also influenced to some extent by transaction costs, insurance company investment restrictions, the duration of the conversion OPTION, and the size of common dividends. *See also* PREMIUM OVER BOND VALUE.

PREMIUM RAID surprise attempt to acquire a position in a company's stock by offering holders an amount—or premium—over the market value of their shares. The term *raid* assumes that the motive is control and not simply investment. Attempts to acquire control are regulated by federal laws that require disclosure of the intentions of those seeking shares. *See also* TENDER OFFER; WILLIAMS ACT.

PRENUPTIAL CONTRACT agreement between a future husband and wife that details how the couple's financial affairs are to be handled both during the marriage and in the event of divorce. The agreement may cover insurance protection, ownership of housing and securities, and inheritance rights. Such contracts may not be accepted in a court of law.

PREPAID INTEREST asset account representing interest paid in advance. The interest is expensed, that is, charged to the borrower's profit and loss statement (P & L), as it is earned by the lender. Synonymous with UNEARNED INTEREST, which is the preferred term when DISCOUNT is involved.

PREPAYMENT

In general: paying a debt obligation before it comes due.

Accounting: expenditure for a future benefit, which is recorded in a BALANCE SHEET asset account called a DEFERRED CHARGE, then written off in the period when the benefit is enjoyed. For example, prepaid rent is first recorded as an asset, then charged to expense as the rent becomes due on a monthly basis.

Banking: paying a loan before maturity. Some loans (particularly mortgages) have a prepayment clause that allows prepayment at any time without penalty, while others charge a fee if a loan is paid off before due.

Installment credit: making payments before they are due. *See also* RULE OF THE 78s.

Securities: paying a seller for a security before the settlement date.

Taxes: prepaying taxes, for example, to have the benefit of deducting state and local taxes from one's federal income tax return in the current calendar year rather than in the next year.

PREPAYMENT PENALTY fee paid by a borrower to a bank when a loan or mortgage that does not have a prepayment clause is repaid before its scheduled maturity. Prepayment penalties are prohibited in many states, and by FANNIE MAE and FREDDIE MAC. Also called *prepayment fee.*

PREREFUNDING procedure, called a *pre-re* on Wall Street, in which a bond issuer floats a second bond in order to pay off the first bond at the first CALL date. The proceeds from the sale of the second bond are safely invested, usually in Treasury securities, that will mature at the first call date of the first bond issue. Those first bonds are said to be prerefunded after this operation has taken place. Bond issuers prerefund bonds during periods of lower interest rates in order to lower their interest costs. *See also* ADVANCE REFUNDING; REFUNDING; REFUNDING ESCROW DEPOSITS (REDS).

PRESALE ORDER order to purchase part of a new MUNICIPAL BOND issue that is accepted by an underwriting SYNDICATE MANAGER before an announcement of the price or COUPON rate and before the official PUBLIC OFFERING. Municipals are exempt from registration requirements and other rules of the Securities and Exchange Commission, which forbids preoffering sales of corporate bond issues. *See also* PRESOLD ISSUE.

PRESENT VALUE value today of a future payment, or stream of payments, discounted at some appropriate compound interest—or discount—rate. For example, the present value of $100 to be received 10 years from now is about $38.55, using a discount rate equal to 10% interest compounded annually.

The present value method, also called the DISCOUNTED CASH FLOW method, is widely used in corporate finance to measure the return on a CAPITAL INVESTMENT project. In security investments, the method is used to determine how much money should be invested today to result in a certain sum at a future time. Present value calculations are facilitated by present value tables, which are compound interest tables in reverse. Also called *time value of money.*

PRESIDENT highest-ranking officer in a corporation after the CHAIRMAN OF THE BOARD, unless the title CHIEF EXECUTIVE OFFICER (CEO) is used, in which case the president can outrank the chairman. The president is appointed by the BOARD OF DIRECTORS and usually reports directly to the board. In smaller companies the president is usually the CEO, having authority over all other officers in matters of day-to-day management and policy decision-making. In large corporations the CEO title is frequently held by the chairman of the board, leaving the president as CHIEF OPERATING OFFICER, responsible for personnel and administration on a daily basis.

PRESIDENTIAL ELECTION CYCLE THEORY hypothesis of investment advisers that major stock market moves can be predicted based on the four-year presidential election cycle. According to this theory, stocks decline soon after a president is elected, as the chief executive takes the harsh and unpopular steps necessary to bring inflation, government spending, and deficits under control. During the next two years or so, taxes may be raised and the economy may slip into a recession. About midway into the four-year cycle, stocks should start to rise in anticipation of the economic recovery that the incumbent president wants to be roaring at full steam by election day. The cycle then repeats itself with the election of a new president or the reelection of an incumbent.

PRESOLD ISSUE issue of MUNICIPAL BONDS or government bonds that is completely sold out before the price or yield is publicly announced. Corporate bond issues, which must be offered to the public with a Securities and Exchange Commission registration statement, cannot legally be presold. *See also* PRESALE ORDER.

PRETAX EARNINGS OR PROFITS NET INCOME (earnings or profits) before federal income taxes.

PRETAX RATE OF RETURN yield or capital gain on a particular security before taking into account an individual's tax situation. *See also* RATE OF RETURN.

PREVIOUS BALANCE METHOD method of charging credit card interest that uses the outstanding balance at the end of the previous month as the basis for the current month's interest computation. *See also* ADJUSTED BALANCE METHOD.

PRICE/BOOK RATIO ratio of a stock's price to its BOOK VALUE per share. This number is used by SECURITIES ANALYSTS and MONEY MANAGERS to judge whether a stock is undervalued or overvalued. A stock selling at a high price/book ratio, such as 3 or higher, may represent a popular GROWTH STOCK with minimal book value. A stock selling below its book value may attract value-oriented investors who think that the company's management may undertake steps, such as selling assets or restructuring the company, to unlock the hidden value on the company's BALANCE SHEET.

PRICE CHANGE net rise or fall of the price of a security at the close of a trading session, compared to the previous session's CLOSING PRICE. A stock that rose $2 in a day would have a + 2 after its final price in the newspaper stock listings. A stock that fell $2 would have a –2. The average of the price changes for groups of securities, in indicators such as the Dow Jones Industrial Average and Standard & Poor's 500 Stock Index, is calculated by taking into account all the price changes in the components of the average or index.

PRICE/EARNINGS RATIO (P/E) price of a stock divided by its earnings per share. The P/E ratio may either use the reported earnings from the latest year (called a *trailing P/E*) or employ an analyst's forecast of next year's earnings (called a *forward P/E*). The trailing P/E is listed along with a stock's price and trading activity in the daily newspapers. For instance, a stock selling for $20 a share that earned $1 last year has a trailing P/E of 20. If the same stock has projected earnings of $2 next year, it will have a forward P/E of 10.

The price/earnings ratio, also known as the *multiple*, gives investors an idea of how much they are paying for a company's earning power. The higher the P/E, the more investors are paying, and therefore the more earnings growth they are expecting. High P/E stocks—those with multiples over 20—are typically young, fast-growing companies. They are far riskier to trade than low P/E stocks, since it is easier to miss high-growth expectations than low-growth predictions. Low P/E stocks tend to be in low-growth or mature industries, in stock groups that have fallen out of favor, or in old, established, BLUE-CHIP companies with long records of earnings stability and regular dividends. In general, low P/E stocks have higher yields than high P/E stocks, which often pay no dividends at all.

PRICE GAP term used when a stock's price either jumps or plummets from its last trading range without overlapping that trading range. For instance, a stock might shoot up from a closing price of $20 a share, marking the high point of an $18–$20 trading range for that day, and begin trading in a $22–$24 range the next day on the news of a takeover bid. Or a company that reports lower than expected earnings might drop from the $18–$20 range to the $13–$15 range without ever trading at intervening prices. Price gaps are considered significant movements by technical analysts, who note them on charts, because such gaps are often indications of an OVERBOUGHT or OVERSOLD position.

PRICE INDEXES indices that track levels of prices and rates of inflation. The two most common price indexes published by the government are the CONSUMER PRICE INDEX (CPI) and the PRODUCER PRICE INDEX (PPI).

PRICE LEADERSHIP establishment of a price by a leading producer of a product that becomes the price adopted by other producers.

PRICE LIMIT *see* LIMIT PRICE.

PRICE RANGE high/low range in which a stock has traded over a particular period of time. In the daily newspaper, a stock's 52-week price range is given. In most companies' annual reports, a stock's price range is shown for the FISCAL YEAR.

PRICE/SALES RATIO ratio of a stock's price to its per-share sales. This ratio is used by financial analysts to gauge whether a stock's current market price is expensive or cheap. Some analysts maintain that investors consistently buying stocks with low price/sales ratios will outperform those buying stocks with low price/book value, price/cash flow, or PRICE/EARNINGS RATIOS. Advocates of P/S ratio analysis say it works because it relates the popularity of a company's stock to the size of its business. Since sales are more difficult to manipulate than earnings, P/S ratios are less subject to accounting gimmickry. Sales are typically less volatile than earnings or cash flow, so P/S ratios work particularly well on companies that stumble temporarily. When profits decline, a stock's price/earnings ratio may increase, but the impact on the P/S ratio is usually dominated by the stock's price. Value investors will use this fact to identify good values among stocks with high P/E but low P/S ratios. Price/sales ratios vary widely among different industries. For instance, the P/S ratio of a retailer is usually much lower than the ratio of a high-technology company.

PRICE SPREAD OPTIONS strategy in which an investor simultaneously buys and sells two options covering the same security, with the same expiration months, but with different exercise prices. For example, an investor might buy an XYZ May 100 call and sell an XYZ May 90 call.

PRICE SUPPORT government-set price floor designed to aid farmers or other producers of goods. For instance, the government sets a minimum price for sugar that it guarantees to sugar growers. If the market price drops below that level, the government makes up the difference. *See also* PARITY PRICE.

PRICE-WEIGHTED INDEX index in which component stocks are weighted by their price. Higher-priced stocks therefore have a greater percentage impact on the index than lower-priced stocks. In recent years, the trend of using price-weighted indexes has given way to the use of MARKET-VALUE WEIGHTED INDEXES.

PRICEY term used of an unrealistically low bid price or unrealistically high offer price. If a stock is trading at $15, a pricey bid might be $10 a share, and a pricey offer $20 a share.

PRIMARY DEALER one of the three dozen or so banks and investment dealers authorized to buy and sell government securities in direct dealings with the FEDERAL RESERVE BANK of New York in its execution of Fed OPEN MARKET OPERATIONS. Such dealers must be qualified in terms of reputation, capacity, and adequacy of staff and facilities.

PRIMARY DISTRIBUTION sale of a new issue of stocks or bonds, as distinguished from a SECONDARY DISTRIBUTION, which involves previously issued stock. All issuances of bonds are primary distributions. Also called *primary offering,* but not to be confused with *initial public offering,* which refers to a corporation's *first* distribution of stock to the public.

PRIMARY EARNINGS PER (COMMON) SHARE earnings available to common stock (which is usually net earnings after taxes and preferred dividends) divided by the number of common shares outstanding. This figure, called basic earnings per share after 1998, contrasts with earnings per share after DILUTION, which assumes warrants, rights, and options have been exercised and convertibles have been converted. *See also* CONVERTIBLE; EARNINGS PER SHARE; FULLY DILUTED EARNINGS PER (COMMON) SHARE; SUBSCRIPTION WARRANT.

PRIMARY MARKET market for new issues of securities, as distinguished from the SECONDARY MARKET, where previously issued securities are bought and sold. A market is primary if the proceeds of sales go to the issuer of the securities sold. The term also applies to government securities auctions and to opening option and futures contract sales.

PRIME
Banking: PRIME RATE.
Investments: acronym for Prescribed Right to Income and Maximum Equity. PRIME was a UNIT INVESTMENT TRUST, sponsored by the Americus Shareowner Service Corporation, which separated the income portion of a stock from its appreciation potential. The income-producing portion, called PRIME, and the appreciation potential, called SCORE (an acronym for Special Claim on Residual Equity) together made up a unit share investment trust, known by the acronym USIT. Both PRIME and SCORE were traded on the American Stock Exchange.

   The first version of this unit came into existence with American Telephone and Telegraph stock in late 1983, as AT&T was undergoing divestiture. PRIME units entitled their holders to the dividend income that a holder of one common share of the old AT&T would have gotten plus a proportionate share of the dividends of the seven regional operating companies split off from AT&T. PRIME holders also received all price APPRECIATION in the stock up to the equivalent of $75 a share. The trusts expired in 1988. SCORE holders received all appreciation over $75, but no dividend income.

   This form of unit trust allows investors who want income from a stock to maximize that income, and investors who want capital gains to have increased leverage in achieving those gains. *See also* CAPITAL GAIN.

PRIME PAPER highest quality COMMERCIAL PAPER, as rated by Moody's Investor's Service and other rating agencies. Prime paper is considered INVESTMENT GRADE, and therefore institutions with FIDUCIARY responsibility can invest in it. Moody's has three ratings of prime paper:
P-1: Highest quality
P-2: Higher quality
P-3: High quality
Commercial paper below P-3 is not considered prime paper.

PRIME RATE base rate that banks use in pricing commercial loans to their best and most creditworthy customers. The rate is determined by the Federal Reserve's decision to raise or lower prevailing interest rates for short-term borrowing. Though some banks charge their best customers more and some less than the official prime rate, the rate tends to become standard across the banking industry when a major bank moves its prime up or down. The rate is a key interest rate, since loans to less-creditworthy customers are often tied to the prime rate. For example, a BLUE CHIP company may borrow at a prime rate of 8%, but a less-well-established small business may borrow from the same bank at prime plus 2, or 10%. Many consumer loans, such as home equity, automobile, mortgage, and credit card loans, are tied to the prime rate. Although the major bank prime rate is the definitive "best rate" reference point, many banks, particularly those in outlying regions, have a two-tier system, whereby smaller companies of top credit standing may borrow at an even lower rate.

PRIME RATE FUND *mutual fund* that buys portions of corporate loans from banks and passes along interest, which is designed to approximate the PRIME RATE, to shareholders, net of load charges and management fees. Although the bank loans are senior obligations and fully collateralized, they are subject to DEFAULT, particularly in recessions. Prime rate funds thus pay 2–3% more than the yield on one-year CERTIFICATES OF DEPOSIT (CDs), and management fees tend to be higher than those of other mutual funds. Another possible disadvantage is limited liquidity; the only way investors can get out is to sell back their shares to the funds once each quarter.

PRINCIPAL
In General:
1. major party to a transaction, acting as either a buyer or a seller. A principal buys and sells for his or her own account and risk.
2. owner of a privately held business.

Banking and Finance:
1. face amount of a debt instrument or deposit on which interest is either owed or earned.
2. balance of a debt, separate from interest. *See also* PRINCIPAL AMOUNT.

Investments: basic amount invested, exclusive of earnings.

PRINCIPAL AMOUNT FACE VALUE of an obligation (such as a bond or a loan) that must be repaid at maturity, as separate from the INTEREST.

PRINCIPAL STOCKHOLDER stockholder who owns a significant number of shares in a corporation. Under Securities and Exchange Commission (SEC) rules, a principal stockholder owns 10% or more of the voting stock of a REGISTERED COMPANY. These stockholders are often on the board of directors and are considered insiders by SEC rules, so that they must report buying and selling transactions in the company's stock. *See also* AFFILIATED PERSON; CONTROL STOCK; INSIDER.

PRINCIPAL SUM
Finance: also used as a synonym for PRINCIPAL, in the sense of the obligation due under a debt instrument exclusive of interest.

Synonymous with CORPUS. *See also* TRUST.

Insurance: amount specified as payable to the beneficiary under a policy, such as the death benefit.

PRIORITY system used in an AUCTION MARKET, in which the first bid or offer price is executed before other bid and offer prices, even if subsequent orders are larger. Orders originating off the floor *(see* OFF-FLOOR ORDER*)* of an exchange also have priority over ON-FLOOR ORDERS. *See also* MATCHED AND LOST; PRECEDENCE.

PRIOR-LIEN BOND bond that has precedence over another bond of the same issuing company even though both classes of bonds are equally secured. Such bonds usually arise from REORGANIZATION. *See also* JUNIOR ISSUE.

PRIOR-PREFERRED STOCK PREFERRED STOCK that has a higher claim than other issues of preferred stock on dividends and assets in LIQUIDATION; also known as *preference shares.*

PRIVATE ACTIVITY BOND *see* PRIVATE PURPOSE BOND.

PRIVATE LETTER RULING Internal Revenue Service (IRS) response to a request for interpretation of the tax law with respect to a specific question or situation. Also called *letter ruling, revenue ruling.*

PRIVATE LIMITED PARTNERSHIP LIMITED PARTNERSHIP not registered with the Securities and Exchange Commission (SEC) and having a maximum of 35 limited partners. *See also* ACCREDITED INVESTOR.

PRIVATE MARKET VALUE (PMV) aggregate market value of a company if each of its parts operated independently and had its own stock price. Also called *breakup value* or *takeover value.* Analysts look for high PMV in relation to market value to identify bargains and potential TARGET COMPANIES. PMV differs from LIQUIDATING VALUE, which excludes GOING CONCERN VALUE, and BOOK VALUE, which is an accounting concept.

PRIVATE MORTGAGE INSURANCE (PMI) type of insurance available from lenders that insures against loss resulting from a default on a mortgage loan and can substitute for down payment money.

PRIVATE PLACEMENT sale of stocks, bonds, or other investments directly to an institutional investor like an insurance company. A PRIVATE LIMITED PARTNERSHIP is also considered a private placement. A private placement does not have to be registered with the Securities and Exchange Commission, as a PUBLIC OFFERING does, if the securities are purchased for investment as opposed to resale. *See also* LETTER SECURITY.

PRIVATE PURPOSE BOND category of MUNICIPAL BOND distinguished from PUBLIC PURPOSE BOND in the TAX REFORM ACT OF 1986 because 10% or more of the bond's benefit goes to private activities or

5% of the proceeds (or $5 million if less) are used for loans to parties other than governmental units. Private purpose obligations, which are also called *private activity bonds* or *nonessential function bonds,* are taxable unless their use is specifically exempted. Even tax-exempt *permitted private activity bonds,* if issued after August 7, 1986, are TAX PREFERENCE ITEMS, except those issued for 501(c)(3) organizations (hospitals, colleges, universities). Private purpose bonds specifically *prohibited* from tax-exemption effective August 15, 1986, include those for sports, trade, and convention facilities and large-issue (over $1 million) INDUSTRIAL DEVELOPMENT BONDS. Permitted issues, except those for 501(c)(3) organizations, airports, docks, wharves, and government-owned solid-waste disposal facilities, are subject to volume caps. *See also* TAXABLE MUNICIPAL BOND.

PRIVATIZATION process of converting a publicly operated enterprise into a privately owned and operated entity. For example, many cities and states contract with private companies to run their prison facilities instead of managing them with municipal personnel. Many countries around the world have privatized formerly state-run enterprises such as banks, airlines, steel companies, utilities, phone systems, and large manufacturers. A wave of privatization swept through Russia and Eastern Europe after the fall of Communism in the 1990s, and through some Latin American countries such as Peru, as new, democratic governments were established. When a company is privatized, shares formerly owned by the government, as well as management control, are sold to the public. The theory behind privatization is that these enterprises run far more efficiently and offer better service to customers when owned by stockholders instead of the government.

PROBATE judicial process whereby the will of a deceased person is presented to a court and an EXECUTOR or ADMINISTRATOR is appointed to carry out the will's instructions.

PROCEEDS
1. funds given to a borrower after all costs and fees are deducted.
2. money received by the seller of an asset after commissions are deducted—for example, the amount a stockholder receives from the sale of shares, less broker's commission. *See also* PROCEEDS SALE.

PROCEEDS SALE OVER THE COUNTER securities sale where the PROCEEDS are used to purchase another security. Under the FIVE PERCENT RULE of the NATIONAL ASSOCIATION OF SECURITIES DEALERS (NASD), such a trade is considered one transaction and the NASD member's total markup or commission is subject to the 5% guideline.

PRODUCER PRICE INDEX (PPI) measure of change in wholesale prices (formerly called the *wholesale price index),* as released monthly by the U.S. Bureau of Labor Statistics. The index is broken down into components by commodity, industry sector, and stage of processing. The PPI tracks prices of foods, metals, lumber, oil and gas, and many other commodities, but does not measure the price of services. Economists look at trends in the PPI as an accurate precursor to changes in the CPI, since upward or downward pressure on wholesale prices is usually passed through to consumer prices over time. The PPI, published by the Bureau of Labor Statistics in the Department of Labor, is based at 100 in 1982 and is released monthly. Economists also look at the PPI excluding the volatile food and energy components, which they call the "core" PPI. The consumer equivalent of this index is the CONSUMER PRICE INDEX.

PRODUCTION RATE coupon (interest) rate at which a PASS-THROUGH SECURITY guaranteed by the GOVERNMENT NATIONAL MORTGAGE ASSOCIATION (GNMA), popularly known as a Ginnie Mae, is issued. The rate is set a half percentage point under the prevailing Federal Housing Administration (FHA) rate, the maximum rate allowed on residential mortgages insured and guaranteed by the FHA and the Veterans Administration.

PRODUCTIVITY in labor and other areas of economics, the amount of output per unit of input, for example, the quantity of a product produced per hour of labor.

PROFIT
Finance: positive difference that results from selling products and services for more than the cost of producing these goods. *See also* NET PROFIT.
Investments: difference between the selling price and the purchase price of commodities or securities when the selling price is higher.

PROFIT AND LOSS STATEMENT (P & L) summary of the revenues, costs, and expenses of a company during an accounting period; also called INCOME STATEMENT, *operating statement, statement of profit and loss, income and expense statement.* Together with the BALANCE SHEET as of the end of the accounting period, it constitutes a company's financial statement. *See also* COST OF GOODS SOLD; NET INCOME; NET SALES.

PROFIT CENTER segment of a business organization that is responsible for producing profits on its own. A conglomerate with interests in hotels, food processing, and paper may consider each of these three businesses separate profit centers, for instance.

PROFIT FORECAST prediction of future levels of profitability by analysts following a company, as well as company officials. Investors base their buy and sell decisions on such earnings projections. Stock prices typically reflect analysts' profit expectations—companies expected to produce rapidly growing profits often have high price/earnings ratios. Conversely, projections of meager earnings result in lower P/E ratios. The company will often guide analysts so that their profit forecasts are not too high or too low, preventing unwelcome surprises. Analyst profit forecasts are tracked by the INSTITUTIONAL BROKERS ESTIMATE SYSTEM (I/B/E/S) and ZACKS ESTIMATE SYSTEM.

PROFIT MARGIN *see* MARGIN OF PROFIT.

PROFIT-SHARING PLAN agreement between a corporation and its employees that allows the employees to share in company profits. Annual contributions are made by the company, when it has profits, to a profit-sharing account for each employee, either in cash or in a deferred plan, which may be invested in stocks, bonds, or cash equivalents. The funds in a profit-sharing account generally accumulate tax deferred until the employee retires or leaves the company. Many plans allow employees to borrow against profit-sharing accounts for major expenditures such as purchasing a home or financing children's education. Because corporate profit-sharing plans have custody over billions of dollars, they are major institutional investors in the stock and bond markets.

PROFIT TAKING action by short-term securities or commodities traders to cash in on gains earned on a sharp market rise. Profit taking pushes down prices, but only temporarily; the term implies an upward market trend.

PRO FORMA Latin for "as a matter of form"; refers to a presentation of data, such as a BALANCE SHEET or INCOME STATEMENT, where certain amounts are hypothetical. For example, a pro forma balance sheet might show a debt issue that has been proposed but has not yet been consummated.

PROGRAM TRADING computer-driven buying *(buy program)* or selling *(sell program)* of baskets of 15 or more stocks by *index* ARBITRAGE specialists or institutional traders. "Program" refers to computer programs that constantly monitor stock, futures, and options markets, giving buy and sell signals when opportunities for arbitrage profits occur or when market conditions warrant portfolio accumulation or liquidation transactions. Program trading has been blamed for excessive volatility in the markets, especially on Black Monday in 1987, when PORTFOLIO INSURANCE—the since discredited use of index options and futures to hedge stock portfolios—was an important contributing factor.

PROGRESSIVE TAX income tax system in which those with higher incomes pay taxes at higher rates than those with lower incomes; also called *graduated tax.* The U.S. income tax system is based on the concept of progressivity. There are several tax brackets, based on the taxpayer's income, which determine the tax rate that applies to each taxpayer. *See also* FLAT TAX; REGRESSIVE TAX.

PROGRESS PAYMENTS

1. periodic payments to a supplier, contractor, or subcontractor for work satisfactorily performed to date. Such schedules are provided in contracts and can significantly reduce the amount of WORKING CAPITAL required by the performing party.

2. disbursements by lenders to contractors under construction loan arrangements. As construction progresses, bills and LIEN waivers are presented to the bank or savings and loan, which advances additional funds.

PROJECTION estimate of future performance made by economists, corporate planners, and credit and securities analysts. Economists use econometric models to project GROSS DOMESTIC PRODUCT (GDP), inflation, unemployment, and many other economic factors. Corporate financial planners project a company's operating results and CASH FLOW, using historical trends and making assumptions where necessary, in order to make budget decisions and to plan financing. Credit analysts use projections to forecast DEBT SERVICE ability. Securities analysts tend to focus their projections on earnings trends and cash flow per share in order to predict market values and dividend coverage. *See also* ECONOMETRICS.

PROJECT LINK econometric model linking all the economies in the world and forecasting the effects of changes in different economies on other economies. The project is identified with 1980 Nobel Memorial Prize in Economics winner Lawrence R. Klein. *See also* ECONOMETRICS.

PROJECT NOTE short-term debt issue of a municipal agency, usually a housing authority, to finance the construction of public housing. When the housing is finished, the notes are redeemed and the project is financed with long-term bonds. Both project notes and bonds usually pay tax-exempt interest to note- and bondholders, and both are also guaranteed by the U.S. Department of Housing and Urban Development.

PROMISSORY NOTE written promise committing the maker to pay the payee a specified sum of money either on demand or at a fixed or determinable future date, with or without interest. Instruments meeting these criteria are NEGOTIABLE. Often called, simply, a NOTE.

PROPERTY AND EQUIPMENT *see* FIXED ASSET.

PROPERTY INVENTORY personal finance term meaning a list of PERSONAL PROPERTY with cost and market values. A property inventory, which should be accompanied by photographs, is used to substantiate insurance claims and tax losses.

PROPERTY TAX tax assessed on property such as real estate. The tax is determined by several factors, including the use of the land (residential, commercial, or industrial), the assessed valuation of the property, and the tax rate, expressed in MILLS. Property taxes are usually assessed by county and local governments, school districts, and other special authorities such as for water and sewer service. Property taxes are usually deductible on federal income tax returns. If a mortgage lender requires that it pay all property taxes, borrowers must remit their property taxes as part of their monthly mortgage payments and the lender keeps the money in escrow until property taxes are due. *See also* AD VALOREM, PITI.

PROPORTIONAL REPRESENTATION method of stockholder voting, giving individual shareholders more power over the election of directors than they have under statutory voting, which, by allowing one vote per share per director, makes it possible for a majority shareholder to elect all the directors. The most familiar example of proportional representation is cumulative voting, under which a shareholder has as many votes as he has shares of stock, multiplied by the number of vacancies on the board, all of which can be cast for one director. This makes it possible for a minority shareholder or a group of small shareholders to gain at least some representation on the board. Another variety provides for the holders of specified classes of stock to elect a number of directors in certain circumstances. For example, if the corporation failed to pay preferred dividends, the preferred holders might then be given the power to elect a certain proportion of the board. Despite the advocacy of stockholders' rights activists, proportional representation has made little headway in American corporations.

PROPRIETORSHIP unincorporated business owned by a single person. The individual proprietor has the right to all the profits from the business and also has responsibility for all the firm's liabilities. Since proprietors are considered self-employed, they are eligible for Keogh accounts for their retirement funds. *See also* KEOGH PLAN.

PRO RATA Latin for "according to the rate"; a method of proportionate allocation. For example, a pro rata property tax rebate might be divided proportionately (prorated) among taxpayers based on their original assessments, so that each gets the same percentage.

PROSPECTUS formal written offer to sell securities that sets forth the plan for a proposed business enterprise or the facts concerning an existing one that an investor needs to make an informed decision. Prospectuses are also issued by MUTUAL FUNDS, describing the history, background of managers, fund objectives, a financial statement, and other essential data. A prospectus for a PUBLIC OFFERING must be filed with the Securities and Exchange Commission and given to prospective buyers of the offering. The prospectus contains financial information and a description of a company's business history, officers, operations, pending litigation (if any), and plans (including the use of the proceeds from the issue).

Before investors receive the final copy of the prospectus, called the *statutory prospectus,* they may receive a PRELIMINARY PROSPECTUS, commonly called a *red herring*. This document is not complete in all details, though most of the major facts of the offering are usually included. The final prospectus is also called the *offering circular*.

Offerings of limited partnerships are also accompanied by prospectuses. Real estate, oil and gas, equipment leasing, and other types of limited partnerships are described in detail, and pertinent financial information, the background of the general partners, and supporting legal opinions are also given.

PROTECTIONISM practice of protecting domestic goods and service industries from foreign competition with tariff and non-tariff barriers. Protectionism causes higher prices for consumers because domestic producers are not exposed to foreign competition, and can therefore keep prices high. But domestic exporters also may suffer, because foreign countries tend to retaliate against protectionism with tariffs and barriers of their own. Many economists say that the Depression of the 1930s was precipitated by the protectionist trade barriers erected by the United States under the Smoot-Hawley Act, which led to retaliation by many countries throughout the world. In more recent years, many protectionist trade barriers have fallen through the passage of GATT, the General Agreement on Tariffs and Trade, which went into effect in 1995, and the creation of the WORLD TRADE ORGANIZATION (WTO).

PROTECTIVE COVENANT *see* COVENANT.

PROVISION *see* ALLOWANCE.

PROVISION FOR INCOME TAXES item on a company's profit and loss statement (P & L) representing its estimated income tax liability for the year. Although taxes are actually paid according to a timetable determined by the Internal Revenue Service and a certain portion of the liability may be accrued, the provision gives an indication of the company's effective tax rate, which analysts compare to other companies as one measure of effective management and profitability. EARNINGS BEFORE TAXES is the net earnings figure before provision for income taxes.

PROXY
In general: person authorized to act or speak for another.
Business:
1. written POWER OF ATTORNEY given by shareholders of a corporation, authorizing a specific vote on their behalf at corporate meetings. Such proxies normally pertain to election of the BOARD OF DIRECTORS or to various resolutions submitted for shareholders' approval.
2. person authorized to vote on behalf of a stockholder of a corporation.

PROXY FIGHT technique used by an acquiring company to attempt to gain control of a TAKEOVER target. The acquirer tries to persuade the shareholders of the TARGET COMPANY that the present management of the firm should be ousted in favor of a slate of directors favorable to the acquirer. If the shareholders, through their PROXY votes, agree, the acquiring company can gain control of the company without paying a PREMIUM price for the firm.

PROXY STATEMENT information that the Securities and Exchange Commission requires must be provided to shareholders before they vote by proxy on company matters. The statement contains proposed members of the BOARD OF DIRECTORS, inside directors' salaries, and pertinent information regarding their bonus and option plans, as well as any resolutions of minority stockholders and of management.

PRUDENT-MAN RULE standard adopted by some U.S. states to guide those with responsibility for investing the money of others. Such fiduciaries (executors of wills, trustees, bank trust departments, and administrators of estates) must act as a prudent man or woman would be expected to act, with discretion and intelligence, to seek reasonable income, preserve capital, and, in general, avoid speculative investments. States not using the prudent-man system use the LEGAL LIST system, allowing fiduciaries to invest only in a restricted list of securities, called the *legal list.*

PUBLIC DEBT borrowings by governments to finance expenditures not covered by current tax revenues. *See also* AGENCY SECURITIES; MUNICIPAL BOND; TREASURIES.

PUBLIC HOUSING AUTHORITY BOND obligation of local public housing agencies, which is centrally marketed through competitive sealed-bid auctions conducted by the U.S. Department of Housing and Urban Development (HUD). These obligations are secured by an agreement between HUD and the local housing agency that provides that the federal government will loan the local authority a sufficient amount of money to pay PRINCIPAL and INTEREST to maturity.

   The proceeds of such bonds provide low-rent housing through new construction, rehabilitation of existing buildings, purchases from private builders or developers, and leasing from private owners. Under special provisions, low income families may also purchase such housing.

   The interest on such bonds is exempt from federal income taxes and may also be exempt from state and local income taxes.

PUBLIC LIMITED PARTNERSHIP real estate, oil and gas, equipment leasing, or other LIMITED PARTNERSHIP that is registered with the Securities and Exchange Commission and offered to the public through registered broker/dealers. Such partnerships may be oriented to producing income or capital gains, or, within PASSIVE income rules, to generating tax advantages for limited partners. The number of investors in such a partnership is limited only by the sponsor's desire to cap the funds raised. A public limited partnership, which does not have an active secondary market, is distinguished from a PRIVATE LIMITED PARTNERSHIP, which is limited to 35 limited partners plus ACCREDITED

INVESTORS, and a MASTER LIMITED PARTNERSHIP (MLP) that is publicly traded, often on the major stock exchanges.

PUBLIC, THE term for individual investors, as opposed to professional investors. Wall Street analysts like to deride the public for constantly buying at the top of a bull market and selling at the bottom of a bear market. The public participates in stock and bond markets both by buying individual securities and through intermediaries such as mutual funds and insurance companies. The term *public* is also used to describe a security that is available to be bought and sold by individual investors (as opposed to just large institutions or wealthy people, in which case the offering is a private one). Stocks that offer shares to the public are known as *publicly held*, in contrast to *privately held* concerns in which shares are owned by founders, employees, and a few large investors.

PUBLICLY HELD company with shares outstanding that are held by public investors. A company converts from a privately held firm to a publicly held one through an INITIAL PUBLIC OFFERING (IPO) of stock.

PUBLIC OFFERING
1. offering to the investment public, after registration requirements of the Securities and Exchange Commission (SEC) have been complied with, of new securities, usually by an investment banker or a syndicate made up of several investment bankers, at a public offering price agreed upon between the issuer and the investment bankers.

   Public offering is distinguished from PRIVATE PLACEMENT of new securities, which is subject to different SEC regulations. *See also* REGISTERED NEW ISSUE; UNDERWRITE.
2. SECONDARY DISTRIBUTION of previously issued stock. *See also* SECONDARY OFFERING.

PUBLIC OFFERING PRICE price at which a NEW ISSUE of securities is offered to the public by underwriters. *See also* OFFERING PRICE; UNDERWRITE.

PUBLIC OWNERSHIP
Government: government ownership and operation of a productive facility for the purpose of providing some good or service to citizens. The government supplies the capital, controls management, sets prices, and generally absorbs all risks and reaps all profits—similar to a private enterprise. When public ownership displaces private ownership in a particular instance, it is called NATIONALIZATION.
Investments: publicly traded portion of a corporation's stock.

PUBLIC PURPOSE BOND category of MUNICIPAL BOND, as defined in the TAX REFORM ACT OF 1986, which is exempt from federal income taxes as long as it provides no more than 10% benefit to private parties and no more than 5% of the proceeds or $5 million are used for loans to private parties; also called *public activity, traditional govern-*

ment purpose, and *essential purpose* bond. Public purpose bonds include purposes such as roads, libraries, and government buildings.

PUBLIC SYNDICATE *see* PURCHASE GROUP.

PUBLIC UTILITY HOLDING COMPANY ACT OF 1935 major landmark in legislation regulating the securities industry, which reorganized the financial structures of HOLDING COMPANIES in the gas and electric utility industries and regulated their debt and dividend policies. Prior to the Act, abuses by holding companies were rampant, including WATERED STOCK, top-heavy capital structures with excessive fixed-debt burdens, and manipulation of the securities markets. In summary:

1. It requires holding companies operating interstate and persons exercising a controlling influence on utilities and holding companies to register with the Securities and Exchange Commission (SEC) and to provide information on the organizational structure, finances, and means of control.
2. It provides for SEC control of the operation and performance of registered holding companies and SEC approval of all new securities offerings, resulting in such reforms as the elimination of NONVOTING STOCK, the prevention of the milking of subsidiaries, and the outlawing of the upstreaming of dividends (payment of dividends by operating companies to holding companies).
3. It provides for uniform accounting standards, periodic administrative and financial reports, and reports on holdings by officers and directors, and for the end of interlocking directorates with banks or investment bankers.
4. It began the elimination of complex organizational structures by allowing only one intermediate company between the top holding company and its operating companies (the GRANDFATHER CLAUSE).

PULLBACK reversal of an upward price trend when a stock or market rises in price for several trading sessions and then declines in price.

PULLING IN THEIR HORNS move to defensive strategies on the part of investors. If the stock or bond market has experienced a sharp rise, investors may want to lock in profits by selling part of their positions or instituting hedging techniques to guard against a downturn. If stock prices fall after a steep runup, commentators will frequently say that "investors are pulling in their horns" to describe the reason for the downturn.

PURCHASE ACQUISITION accounting method used in a business MERGER whereby the purchasing company treats the acquired company as an investment and adds the acquired company's assets to its own at their fair market value. Any premium paid over and above the FAIR MARKET VALUE of the acquired assets is reflected as GOODWILL on the buyer's BALANCE SHEET and must be written off against future earnings. Until 1993, goodwill amortization was not deductible for tax purposes, so the reduction of reported future earnings was a disadvantage of this method of merger accounting as compared with the alternative POOLING OF INTERESTS method. The purchase acquisition method is mandatory unless all the criteria for a pooling of interests combination are met.

PURCHASE FUND provision in some PREFERRED STOCK contracts and BOND indentures requiring the issuer to use its best efforts to purchase a specified number of shares or bonds annually at a price not to exceed par value. Unlike SINKING FUND provisions, which require that a certain number of bonds be retired annually, purchase funds require only that a tender offer be made; if no securities are tendered, none are retired. Purchase fund issues benefit the investor in a period of rising rates when the redemption price is higher than the market price and the proceeds can be put to work at a higher return.

PURCHASE GROUP group of investment bankers that, operating under the AGREEMENT AMONG UNDERWRITERS, agrees to purchase a NEW ISSUE of securities from the issuer for resale to the investment public; also called the UNDERWRITING GROUP or *syndicate*. The purchase group is distinguished from the SELLING GROUP, which is organized by the purchase group and includes the members of the purchase group along with other investment bankers. The selling group's function is DISTRIBUTION.

The agreement among underwriters, also called the *purchase group agreement,* is distinguished from the underwriting or purchase agreement, which is between the underwriting group and the issuer. *See also* UNDERWRITE.

PURCHASE GROUP AGREEMENT *see* PURCHASE GROUP.

PURCHASE LOAN in consumer credit, a loan made at a rate of interest to finance a purchase.

PURCHASE-MONEY MORTGAGE MORTGAGE given by a buyer in lieu of cash for the purchase of property. Such mortgages make it possible to sell property when mortgage money is unavailable or when the only buyers are unqualified to borrow from commercial sources.

PURCHASE ORDER written authorization to a vendor to deliver specified goods or services at a stipulated price. Once accepted by the supplier, the purchase order becomes a legally binding purchase CONTRACT.

PURCHASING POWER
Economics: value of money as measured by the goods and services it can buy. For example, the PURCHASING POWER OF THE DOLLAR can be determined by comparing an index of consumer prices for a given base year to the present.
Investment: amount of credit available to a client in a brokerage account for the purchase of additional securities. Purchasing power is determined by the dollar amount of securities that can be margined. For instance, a client with purchasing power of $20,000 in his or her account could buy securities worth $40,000 under the Federal

Reserve's currently effective 50% MARGIN REQUIREMENT. *See also* MARGIN SECURITY.

PURCHASING POWER OF THE DOLLAR measure of the amount of goods and services that a dollar can buy in a particular market, as compared with prior periods, assuming always an INFLATION or a DEFLATION factor and using an index of consumer prices. It might be reported, for instance, that one dollar in 1982 has 67 cents of purchasing power in the late 1990s because of the erosion caused by inflation. Deflation would increase the dollar's purchasing power.

PURE PLAY stock market jargon for a company that is virtually all devoted to one line of business. An investor who wants to invest in that line of business looks for such a pure play. For instance, Sears Roebuck may be considered a pure play in the retail business after spinning off its real estate and financial services businesses in the mid-1900s. Weyerhauser is a pure play in the forest products business. The opposite of a pure play is a widely diversified company, such as a CONGLOMERATE.

PURE MONOPOLY situation in which one firm controls the entire market for a product. This may occur because the firm has a patent on a product or a license from the government to be a monopoly. For example, an electric utility in a particular city may be a monopoly licensed by the city.

PURPOSE LOAN loan backed by securities and used to buy other securities under Federal Reserve Board MARGIN and credit regulations.

PURPOSE STATEMENT form filed by a borrower that details the purpose of a loan backed by securities. The borrower agrees not to use the loan proceeds to buy securities in violation of any Federal Reserve regulations. *See also* NONPURPOSE LOAN; REGULATION U.

PUT BOND bond that allows its holder to redeem the issue at specified intervals before maturity and receive full FACE VALUE. The bondholders may be allowed to put bonds back to the issuer either only once during the lifetime of the issue or far more frequently. In return for this privilege, a bond buyer sacrifices some yield when choosing a put bond over a fixed-rate bond, which cannot be redeemed before maturity.

PUT-CALL RATIO ratio of trading volume in put options to the trading volume in call options. The ratio provides a quantitative measure of the bullishness or bearishness of investors. A high volume of puts relative to calls indicates investors are bearish, whereas a high ratio of calls to puts shows bullishness. Many market technicians find the put-call ratio to be a good contrary indicator, meaning that when the ratio is high, a market bottom is near and when the ratio is low, a market top is imminent. This reading assumes that the majority of options investors are making the wrong move.

PUT GUARANTEE LETTER letter from a bank certifying that the person writing a put option on an underlying security or index instrument has sufficient funds on deposit at the bank to cover the exercise price of the put if needed. On a short put, the obligation is to pay the aggregate exercise price. There are two forms, as required under New York Stock Exchange Rule 431: the *market index option deposit letter* for index options, and the *equity/Treasury option deposit letter* for security options.

PUT OPTION

Bonds: bondholder's right to redeem a bond before maturity. *See also* PUT BOND.

Options: contract that grants the right to sell at a specified price a specific number of shares by a certain date. The put option buyer gains this right in return for payment of an OPTION PREMIUM. The put option seller grants this right in return for receiving this premium. For instance, a buyer of an XYZ May 70 put has the right to sell 100 shares of XYZ at $70 to the put seller at any time until the contract expires in May. A put option buyer hopes the stock will drop in price, while the put option seller (called a *writer)* hopes the stock will remain stable, rise, or drop by an amount less than his or her profit on the premium.

PUT TO SELLER phrase used when a PUT OPTION is exercised. The OPTION WRITER is obligated to buy the underlying shares at the agreed upon price. If an XYZ June 40 put were "put to seller," for instance, the writer would have to buy 100 shares of XYZ at $40 a share from the put holder even though the current market price of XYZ may be far less than $40 a share.

PYRAMIDING

In general: form of business expansion that makes extensive use of financial LEVERAGE to build complex corporate structures.

Fraud: scheme that builds on nonexistent values, often in geometric progression, such as a chain letter, now outlawed by mail fraud legislation. A famous example was the Ponzi scheme, perpetrated by Charles Ponzi in the late 1920s. Investors were paid "earnings" out of money received from new investors until the scheme collapsed.

Investments: using unrealized profits from one securities or commodities POSITION as COLLATERAL to buy further positions with funds borrowed from a broker. This use of leverage creates increased profits in a BULL MARKET, and causes MARGIN CALLS and large losses in a BEAR MARKET.

Marketing: legal marketing strategy whereby additional distributorships are sold side-by-side with consumer products in order to multiply market reach and maximize profits to the sales organization.

Q

Q-TIP TRUST qualified terminable interest property *trust,* which allows assets to be transferred between spouses. The grantor of a Q-tip trust directs income from the assets to his or her spouse for life but has the power to distribute the assets upon the death of the spouse. Such trusts qualify the grantor for the unlimited marital deduction if the spouse should die first.

A Q-tip trust is often used to provide for the welfare of a spouse while keeping the assets out of the estate of another (such as a future marriage partner) if the grantor dies first.

QUALIFICATION PERIOD period of time during which an insurance company will not reimburse a policyholder for a claim. The qualification period, which may be several weeks or months, gives the insurance company time to uncover fraud or deception in the policyholder's application for coverage. Such periods, which are stated in the insurance contract, are commonplace in health insurance plans.

QUALIFIED ENDORSEMENT endorsement (signature on the back of a check or other NEGOTIABLE INSTRUMENT transferring the amount to someone other than the one to whom it is payable) that contains wording designed to limit the endorser's liability. "Without recourse," the most frequently seen example, means that if the instrument is not honored, the endorser is not responsible. Where qualified endorsements are restrictive (such as "for deposit only") the term *restricted endorsement* is preferable.

QUALIFIED OPINION auditor's opinion accompanying financial statements that calls attention to limitations of the audit or exceptions the auditor takes to the statements. Typical reasons for qualified opinions: a pending lawsuit that, if lost, would materially affect the financial condition of the company; an indeterminable tax liability relating to an unusual transaction; inability to confirm a portion of the inventory because of inaccessible location. *See also* ACCOUNTANT'S OPINION.

QUALIFIED PLAN OR TRUST TAX-DEFERRED plan set up by an employer for employees under 1954 Internal Revenue Service rules. Such plans usually provide for employer contributions—for example, a profit-sharing or pension plan—and may also allow employee contributions. They build up savings, which are paid out at retirement or on termination of employment. The employees pay taxes only when they draw the money out. When employers make payments to such plans, they receive certain deductions and other tax benefits. *See also* 401 (K) PLAN; SALARY REDUCTION PLAN.

QUALIFYING ANNUITY ANNUITY that is purchased under, and forms the investment program for, a QUALIFIED PLAN OR TRUST, including pension and profit sharing plans, INDIVIDUAL RETIREMENT ACCOUNTS (IRAs), 403(b)s, and 457s. *See also* KEOGH PLAN.

QUALIFYING SHARE share of COMMON STOCK owned in order to qualify as a director of the issuing corporation.

QUALIFYING STOCK OPTION privilege granted to an employee of a corporation that permits the purchase, for a special price, of shares of its CAPITAL STOCK, under conditions sustained in the Internal Revenue Code. The law states (1) that the OPTION plan must be approved by the stockholders, (2) that the option is not transferable, (3) that the EXERCISE PRICE must not be less than the MARKET PRICE of the shares at the time the option is issued, and (4) that the grantee may not own stock having more than 10% of the company's voting power unless the option price equals 110% of the market price and the option is not exercisable more than 5 years after the grant. No income tax is payable by the employee either at the time of the grant or at the time the option is exercised. If the market price falls below the option price, another option with a lower exercise price can be issued. There is a $100,000 per employee limit on the value of stock covered by options that are exercisable in any one calendar year. *See also* INCENTIVE STOCK OPTION.

QUALIFYING UTILITY utility in which shareholders were, until the end of 1985, able to defer taxes by reinvesting up to $750 in dividends ($1500 for a couple filing jointly) in the company's stock. Taxes were due when the stock was sold. This plan was enacted by the Economic Recovery Tax Act of 1981 as a means of helping utilities raise investment capital cheaply. Most of the utilities qualifying for the plan were electric utilities.

QUALITATIVE ANALYSIS
In general: analysis that evaluates important factors that cannot be precisely measured.
Securities and credit analysis: analysis that is concerned with such questions as the experience, character, and general caliber of management; employee morale; and the status of labor relations rather than with the actual financial data about a company. *See also* QUANTITATIVE ANALYSIS.

QUALITY CONTROL process of assuring that products are made to consistently high standards of quality. Inspection of goods at various points in their manufacture by either a person or a machine is usually an important part of the quality control process.

QUALITY OF EARNINGS phrase describing a corporation's earnings that are attributable to increased sales and cost controls, as distinguished from artificial profits created by inflated values in inventories or other assets. In a period of high inflation, the quality of earnings tends to suffer, since a large portion of a firm's profits is generated by the rising value of inventories. In a lower inflation period, a company that achieves higher sales and maintains lower costs produces a higher quality of earnings—a factor often appreciated by investors, who are frequently willing to pay more for a higher quality of earnings.

QUANT person with mathematical and computer skills who provides numerical and analytical support services in the securities industry.

QUANTISE to denominate an asset or liability in a currency other than the one in which it usually trades.

QUANTITATIVE ANALYSIS analysis dealing with measurable factors as distinguished from such qualitative considerations as the character of management or the state of employee morale. In credit and securities analysis, examples of quantitative considerations are the value of assets; the cost of capital; the historical and projected patterns of sales, costs, and profitability and a wide range of considerations in the areas of economics; the money market; and the securities markets. Although quantitative and qualitative factors are distinguishable, they must be combined to arrive at sound business and financial judgments. *See also* QUALITATIVE ANALYSIS.

QUANTO OPTION option in one currency or interest rate that pays out in another. A quanto option can be used when an investor favors a foreign index, but is bearish on the outlook for that country's currency.

QUARTERLY
In general: every three months (one quarter of a year).
Securities: basis on which earnings reports to shareholders are made; also, usual time frame of dividend payments.

QUARTER STOCK stock with a par value of $25 per share.

QUASI-PUBLIC CORPORATION corporation that is operated privately and often has its stock traded publicly, but that also has some sort of public mandate and often has the government's backing behind its direct debt obligations. Some examples: COMSAT (Communications Satellite Corporation), which was sponsored by the U.S. Congress to foster the development of space; the FEDERAL NATIONAL MORTGAGE ASSOCIATION (Fannie Mae), which was founded to encourage growth in the secondary mortgage market; and the STUDENT LOAN MARKETING ASSOCIATION (Sallie Mae), which was started to encourage the growth of a secondary market for student loans.

QUICK ASSETS cash, marketable securities, and accounts receivable. *See also* QUICK RATIO.

QUICK RATIO cash, MARKETABLE SECURITIES, and ACCOUNTS RECEIVABLE divided by current liabilities. By excluding inventory, this key LIQUIDITY ratio focuses on the firm's more LIQUID ASSETS, and helps answer the question "If sales stopped, could this firm meet its current obligations with the readily convertible assets on hand?" Assuming there is nothing happening to slow or prevent collections, a quick ratio of 1 to 1 or better is usually satisfactory. Also called *acid-test ratio, quick asset ratio.*

QUID PRO QUO
In general: from the Latin, meaning "something for something." By mutual agreement, one party provides a good or service for which he or she gets another good or service in return.

Securities industry: arrangement by a firm using institutional research that it will execute all trades based on that research with the firm providing it, instead of directly paying for the research. This is known as paying in SOFT DOLLARS.

QUIET PERIOD period an ISSUER is "in registration" and subject to an SEC embargo on promotional publicity. It dates from the preunderwriting decision to 40 or 90 days after the EFFECTIVE DATE.

QUORUM minimum number of people who must be present at a meeting in order to make certain decisions go into effect. A quorum may be required at a board of directors, committee, shareholder, legislative, or other meeting for any decisions to have legal standing. A quorum may be achieved by providing a PROXY as well as appearance in person.

QUOTATION
Business: price estimate on a commercial project or transaction.

Investments: highest bid and lowest offer (asked) price currently available on a security or a commodity. An investor who asks for a quotation ("quote") on XYZ might be told "60 to 60½," meaning that the best bid price (the highest price any buyer wants to pay) is currently $60 a share and that the best offer (the lowest price any seller is willing to accept) is $60½ at that time. Such quotes assume ROUND-LOT transactions—for example, 100 shares for stocks.

QUOTATION BOARD electronically controlled board at a brokerage firm that displays current price quotations and other financial data such as dividends, price ranges of stocks, and current volume of trading.

QUOTED PRICE price at which the last sale and purchase of a particular security or commodity took place.

R

RACKETEER INFLUENCED AND CORRUPT ORGANIZATION ACT *see* RICO.

RADAR ALERT close monitoring of trading patterns in a company's stock by senior managers to uncover unusual buying activity that might signal a TAKEOVER attempt. *See also* SHARK WATCHER.

RAIDER individual or corporate investor who intends to take control of a company by buying a controlling interest in its stock and installing new management. Raiders who accumulate 5% or more of the outstanding shares in the TARGET COMPANY must report their purchases to the Securities and Exchange Commission, the exchange of listing, and the target itself. *See also* BEAR RAID; WILLIAMS ACT.

RAINMAKER individual who brings significant amounts of new business to a financial services organization. The rainmaker may bring in wealthy brokerage customers who generate a large dollar volume of commissions. Or he or she may be an investment banker who attracts corporate or municipal finance underwritings or merger and acquisition business. Because they are so important to the firm, rainmakers are usually given special PERQUISITES and bonus compensation.

RALLY marked rise in the price of a security, commodity future, or market after a period of decline or sideways movement.

R & D *see* RESEARCH AND DEVELOPMENT.

RANDOM WALK theory about the movement of stock and commodity futures prices hypothesizing that past prices are of no use in forecasting future price movements. According to the theory, stock prices reflect reactions to information coming to the market in random fashion, so they are no more predictable than the walking pattern of a drunken person. The random walk theory was first espoused in 1900 by the French mathematician Louis Bachelier and revived in the 1960s. It is hotly disputed by advocates of TECHNICAL ANALYSIS, who say that charts of past price movements enable them to predict future price movements.

RANGE high and low end of a security, commodity future, or market's price fluctuations over a period of time. Daily newspapers publish the 52-week high and low price range of stocks traded on the New York Stock Exchange, American Stock Exchange, and over-the-counter markets. Advocates of TECHNICAL ANALYSIS attach great importance to trading ranges because they consider it of great significance if a security breaks out of its trading range by going higher or lower. *See also* BREAKOUT.

RATE BASE value established for a utility by a regulatory body such as a Public Utility Commission on which the company is allowed to earn a particular rate of return. Generally the rate base includes the utility's operating costs but not the cost of constructing new facilities. Whether modernization costs should be included in the rate base, and thus passed on to customers, is a subject of continuing controversy. *See also* FAIR RATE OF RETURN.

RATE CAP *see* CAP.

RATE COVENANT provision in MUNICIPAL REVENUE BOND agreements or resolutions covering the rates, or methods of establishing rates, to be charged users of the facility being financed. The rate covenant usually promises that rates will be adjusted when necessary to cover the cost of repairs and maintenance while continuing to provide for the payment of bond interest and principal.

RATE OF EXCHANGE *see* EXCHANGE RATE; PAR VALUE OF CURRENCY.

RATE OF INFLATION *see* CONSUMER PRICE INDEX; INFLATION RATE; PRODUCER PRICE INDEX.

RATE OF RETURN
Fixed-income securities (bonds and preferred stock): CURRENT YIELD, that is, the coupon or contractual dividend rate divided by the purchase price. *See also* YIELD TO AVERAGE LIFE; YIELD TO CALL; YIELD TO MATURITY.
Common stock: (1) dividend yield, which is the annual dividend divided by the purchase price. (2) TOTAL RETURN rate, which is the dividend plus capital appreciation.
Corporate finance: RETURN ON EQUITY or RETURN ON INVESTED CAPITAL.
Capital budgeting: INTERNAL RATE OF RETURN.
    See also FAIR RATE OF RETURN; HORIZON ANALYSIS; MEAN RETURN; REAL INTEREST RATE; REQUIRED RATE OF RETURN; TOTAL RETURN; YIELD.

RATING
Credit and investments: evaluation of securities investment and credit risk by rating services such as Duff & Phelps/MCM, FITCH INVESTORS SERVICE INC., MOODY'S INVESTORS SERVICE, STANDARD & POOR'S CORPORATION, and VALUE LINE INVESTMENT SURVEY. *See also* CREDIT RATING; EVENT RISK; NOT RATED.
Insurance: using statistics, mortality tables, probability theory, experience, judgment, and mathematical analysis to establish the rates on which insurance premiums are based. There are three basic rating systems: *class rate,* applying to a homogeneous grouping of clients; *schedule system,* relating positive and negative factors in the case of a particular insured (for example, a smoker or nonsmoker in the case of a life policy) to a base figure; and *experience rating,* reflecting the historical loss experience of the particular insured. Also called *rate-making.*
    Insurance companies are also rated. *See* BEST'S RATING.

LEADING BOND RATING SERVICES	RATING SERVICE			
Explanation of corporate/ municipal bond ratings	*Duff & Phelps/MCM*	*Fitch*	*Moody's*	*Standard & Poor's*
Highest quality, "gilt edged" High quality Upper medium grade	AAA AA A	AAA AA A	Aaa Aa A	AAA AA A
Medium grade Predominantly speculative Speculative, low grade	BBB BB B	BBB BB B	Baa Ba B	BBB BB B
Poor to default Highest speculation Lowest quality, no interest	CCC	CCC CC C	Caa Ca C	CCC CC C
In default, in arrears, questionable value		⎧ DDD ⎨ DD ⎩ D		DDD DD D

Fitch and Standard & Poor's may use + or − to modify some ratings. Moody's uses the numerical modifiers 1 (highest), 2, and 3 in the range from Aa1 through Ca3.

RATIO ANALYSIS method of analysis, used in making credit and investment judgments, which utilizes the relationship of figures found in financial statements to determine values and evaluate risks and compares such ratios to those of prior periods and other companies to reveal trends and identify eccentricities. Ratio analysis is only one tool among many used by analysts. *See also* ACCOUNTS RECEIVABLE TURNOVER; ACID TEST RATIO; BOND RATIO; CAPITALIZATION RATIO; CAPITAL TURNOVER; CASH RATIO; COLLECTION PERIOD; COMMON STOCK RATIO; CURRENT RATIO; DEBT-TO-EQUITY RATIO; DIVIDEND PAYOUT RATIO; EARNINGS-PRICE RATIO; FIXED CHARGE COVERAGE; LEVERAGE; NET TANGIBLE ASSETS PER SHARE; OPERATING RATIO; PREFERRED STOCK RATIO; PRICE-EARNINGS RATIO; PROFIT MARGIN; QUICK RATIO; RETURN ON EQUITY; RETURN ON INVESTED CAPITAL; RETURN ON SALES.

RATIO WRITER OPTIONS writer who sells more CALL contracts than he has underlying shares. For example, an investor who writes (sells) 10 calls, 5 of them covered by 500 owned shares and the other 5 of them uncovered (or "naked"), has a 2 for 1 ratio write.

RAW LAND property in its natural state, prior to grading, construction, and subdividing. The property has no sewers, electricity, streets, buildings, water service, telephone service, or other amenities. Investors in raw land hope that the land's value will rise in the future if it is developed. While they wait, however, they must pay property taxes on the land's value.

RAW MATERIAL unfinished goods used in the manufacture of a product. For example, a steelmaker uses iron ore and other metals in producing steel. A publishing company uses paper and ink to create books, newspapers, and magazines. Raw materials are carried on a company's balance sheet as inventory in the current assets section.

REACHBACK ability of a LIMITED PARTNERSHIP or other tax shelter to offer deductions at the end of the year that reach back for the entire year. For instance, the investor who buys an OIL AND GAS LIMITED PARTNERSHIP in late December might be able to claim deductions for the entire year's drilling costs, depletion allowance, and interest expenses. Reachback on tax shelters was considered to be abusive by the Internal Revenue Service, and was substantially eliminated by 1984.

REACTION drop in securities prices after a sustained period of advancing prices, perhaps as the result of PROFIT TAKING or adverse developments. *See also* CORRECTION.

READING THE TAPE judging the performance of stocks by monitoring changes in price as they are displayed on the TICKER tape. An analyst reads the tape to determine whether a stock is acting strongly or weakly, and therefore is likely to go up or down. An investor reads the tape to determine whether a stock trade is going with or against the flow of market action. *See also* DON'T FIGHT THE TAPE.

REAGANOMICS economic program followed by the administration of President Ronald Reagan beginning in 1980. Reaganomics stressed lower taxes, higher defense spending, and curtailed spending for social services. After a reduction of growth in the money supply by the Federal Reserve Board combined with Reaganomics to produce a severe recession in 1981–82, the Reagan years were characterized by huge budget deficits, low interest and inflation rates, and continuous economic growth.

REAL ESTATE piece of land and all physical property related to it, including houses, fences, landscaping, and all rights to the air above and earth below the property. Assets not directly associated with the land are considered *personal property.*

REAL ESTATE AGENT licensed salesperson working for a licensed broker. The agent may hold an individual REAL ESTATE BROKER'S license.

REAL ESTATE APPRAISAL estimate of the value of property, usually required when a property is sold, financed, condemned, taxed, insured, or partitioned. An appraisal is not a determination of value. Three approaches are used. To produce an accurate resale price for a residence, appraisers compare the price of the property to the prices of similar nearby properties that have sold recently. For new construction and service properties such as churches and post offices, appraisers look at the reproduction or replacement cost of the improvements, less depreciation, plus the value of the land. For investment properties such as apartment buildings and shopping centers, an estimated value is based on the capitalization of net operating income from a property at an acceptable market rate.

REAL ESTATE BROKER person who arranges the purchase or sale of property for a buyer or seller in return for a commission. Brokers may help arrange financing of the purchase through contacts with banks, savings and loans, and mortgage bankers. Brokers must be licensed by the state to buy or sell real estate.

REAL ESTATE INVESTMENT TRUST (REIT) company, usually traded publicly, that manages a portfolio of real estate to earn profits for shareholders. Patterned after INVESTMENT COMPANIES, REITs make investments in a diverse array of real estate such as shopping centers, medical facilities, nursing homes, office buildings, apartment complexes, industrial warehouses, and hotels. Some REITs, called EQUITY REITS, take equity positions in real estate; shareholders receive income from the rents received and from the properties and receive capital gains as buildings are sold at a profit. Other REITs specialize in lending money to building developers; such MORTGAGE REITS pass interest income on to shareholders. Some REITs, called *hybrid REITs,* have a mix of equity and debt investments. To avoid taxation at the corporate level, 75% or more of the REIT's income must be from real property and 95% of its net earnings must be distributed to shareholders annually. Because REITs must distribute most of their earnings, they tend to pay high yields of 5% to 10% or more.

REAL ESTATE LIMITED PARTNERSHIP LIMITED PARTNERSHIP that invests in real estate. The partnership buys properties such as apartment or office buildings, shopping centers, industrial warehouses, and hotels and passes rental income through to limited partners. If the properties appreciate in value over time, they can be sold and the profit passed through to limited partners. A GENERAL PARTNER manages the partnership, deciding which properties to buy and sell and handling administrative duties, such as distributions to limited partners. In the early 1980s, many real estate partnerships were structured to reduce limited partners' tax liability, because operating losses, plus accelerated depreciation from real estate, could be used to offset other taxable income. But these deals were largely discontinued after the TAX REFORM ACT OF 1986 introduced the principle of PASSIVE LOSSES, meaning that investors could no longer use real estate partnership losses to offset their income from salaries and other investments. Since the mid-1980s, partnerships have been designed to produce high current income and long-term capital gains through appreciation in the underlying real estate, not tax benefits.

REAL ESTATE MORTGAGE INVESTMENT CONDUIT *see* REMIC.

REAL GAIN OR LOSS gain or loss adjusted for INFLATION. *See also* INFLATION ACCOUNTING.

REAL INCOME income of an individual, group, or country adjusted for changes in PURCHASING POWER caused by inflation. A price index is used to determine the difference between the purchasing power of a dollar in a base year and the purchasing power now. The resulting percentage factor, applied to total income, yields the value of that income in constant dollars, termed real income. For instance, if the cost of a market basket increases from $100 to $120 in ten years, reflecting a 20% decline in purchasing power, salaries must rise by 20% if real income is to be maintained.

REAL INTEREST RATE current interest rate minus inflation rate. The real interest rate may be calculated by comparing interest rates with present or, more frequently, with predicted inflation rates The real interest rate gives investors in bonds and other fixed-rate instruments a way to see whether their interest will allow them to keep up with or beat the erosion in dollar values caused by inflation. With a bond yielding 10% and inflation of 3%, for instance, the real interest rate of 7% would bring a return high enough to beat inflation. If inflation were at 15%, however, the investor would fall behind as prices rise.

REALIZED PROFIT (OR LOSS) profit or loss resulting from the sale or other disposal of a security. Capital gains taxes may be due when profits are realized: realized losses can be used to offset realized gains for tax purposes. Such profits and losses differ from a PAPER PROFIT OR LOSS, which (except for OPTION AND FUTURES CONTRACTS) has no tax consequences.

REAL PROPERTY land and all property attached to the land, such as houses, trees, fences, and all improvements.

REAL RATE OF RETURN RETURN on an investment adjusted for inflation.

REALTOR registered trade name that can be used only by members of state and local real estate boards affiliated with the National Association of Realtors (NAR). A realtor-associate is trained and licensed to help clients buy and sell real estate. Realtors must follow a strict code of ethics and receive ongoing training from the NAR. Any complaints about a particular realtor are dealt with at the local real estate board affiliated with the NAR.

REBATE
1. in lending, unearned interest refunded to a borrower if the loan is paid off before maturity.
2. in consumer marketing, payment made to a consumer after a purchase is completed, to induce purchase of a product. For instance, a customer who buys a television set for $500 may be entitled to a rebate of $50, which is received after sending a proof of purchase and a rebate form to the manufacturer. *See also* RULE OF THE 78s.

RECAPITALIZATION alteration of a corporation's CAPITAL STRUCTURE, such as an exchange of bonds for stock. BANKRUPTCY is a common reason for recapitalization; debentures might be exchanged for REORGANI-ZATION BONDS that pay interest only when earned. A healthy company might seek to save taxes by replacing preferred stock with bonds to gain interest deductibility. *See also* DEFEASANCE.

RECAPTURE

1. contract clause allowing one party to recover some degree of possession of an asset. In leases calling for a percentage of revenues, such as those for shopping centers, the recapture clause provides that the developer get a percentage of profits in addition to a fixed rent.

2. in the tax code, the reclamation by the government of tax benefits previously taken. For example, where a portion of the profit on the sale of a depreciable asset represented ACCELERATED DEPRECIATION or the INVESTMENT CREDIT, all or part of that gain would be "recaptured" and taxed as ORDINARY INCOME, with the balance subject to the favorable CAPITAL GAINS TAX. Recapture also has specialized applications in oil and other industries. Recapture assumed a new meaning under the 1986 Act whereby banks with assets of $500 million or more were required to take into income the balance of their RESERVE for BAD DEBTS. The Act called for recapture of income at the rate of 10%, 20%, 30%, and 40% for the years 1987 through 1990, respectively.

RECEIVABLES *see* ACCOUNTS RECEIVABLE.

RECEIVER court-appointed person who takes possession of, but not title to, the assets and affairs of a business or estate that is in a form of BANKRUPTCY called *receivership* or is enmeshed in a legal dispute. The receiver collects rents and other income and generally manages the affairs of the entity for the benefit of its owners and creditors until a disposition is made by the court.

RECEIVER'S CERTIFICATE debt instrument issued by a RECEIVER, who uses the proceeds to finance continued operations or otherwise to protect assets in receivership. The certificates constitute a LIEN on the property, ranking ahead of all other secured or unsecured liabilities in LIQUIDATION.

RECEIVE VERSUS PAYMENT instruction accompanying sell orders by institutions that only cash will be accepted in exchange for delivery of the securities at the time of settlement. Institutions are generally required by law to accept only cash. Also called *receive against payment.*

RECESSION downturn in economic activity, defined by many economists as at least two consecutive quarters of decline in a country's GROSS DOMESTIC PRODUCT.

RECLAMATION

Banking: restoration or correction of a NEGOTIABLE INSTRUMENT—or the amount thereof—that has been incorrectly recorded by the *clearing house.*

Finance: restoration of an unproductive asset to productivity, such as by using landfill to make a swamp developable.

Securities: right of either party to a securities transaction to recover losses caused by *bad delivery* or other irregularities in the settlement process.

RECORD DATE *see* DATE OF RECORD; EX-DIVIDEND DATE; PAYMENT DATE.

RECOURSE legal ability the purchaser of a financial asset may have to fall back on the original creditor if the current debtor defaults. For example, an account receivable sold with recourse enables the buyer of the receivable to make claim on the seller if the account doesn't pay.

RECOURSE LOAN
1. loan for which an endorser or guarantor is liable for payment in the event the borrower defaults.
2. loan made to a DIRECT PARTICIPATION PROGRAM or LIMITED PARTNER-SHIP whereby the lender, in addition to being secured by specific assets, has recourse against the general assets of the partnership. *See also* NONRECOURSE LOAN.

RECOVERY
Economics: period in a business cycle when economic activity picks up and the GROSS NATIONAL PRODUCT grows, leading into the expansion phase of the cycle.

Finance: (1) absorption of cost through the allocation of DEPRECIA-TION; (2) collection of an ACCOUNT RECEIVABLE that had been written off as a bad debt; (3) residual cost, or salvage value, of a fixed asset after all allowable depreciation.

Investment: period of rising prices in a securities or commodities market after a period of falling prices.

RECOVERY PERIOD
Economics: period of time in which the economy is emerging from a recession or depression. The recovery period is marked by rising sales and production, improved consumer confidence, and in many cases, rising interest rates.

Stocks: period of time in which a stock that has fallen sharply in price begins to rise again, thereby recovering some of its value.

Taxation: period over which property is subject to depreciation for tax purposes following the ACCELERATED COST RECOVERY SYSTEM (ACRS). Different classes of assets are assigned different periods in which costs can be recovered.

REDEEMABLE BOND *see* CALLABLE.

REDEMPTION repayment of a debt security or preferred stock issue, at or before maturity, at PAR or at a premium price.

Mutual fund shares are redeemed at NET ASSET VALUE when a shareholder's holdings are liquidated.

REDEMPTION DATE date on which a bond is scheduled to mature or be redeemed. If a bond is CALLED AWAY before scheduled maturity, the redemption date is the day that the bond will be taken back.

REDEMPTION FEES fees charged by a mutual fund on shareholders who sell fund shares within a short period of time. The time limit and size of the fee vary among funds, but the redemption fee usually is a relatively small percentage (1% or 2% of the amount withdrawn). Some mutual funds charge a small flat redemption fee of $5 or $10 to cover administrative charges. The intent of the redemption fee is to discourage rapid-fire shifts from one fund to another in an attempt to "time" swings in the stock or bond market. This fee often is confused with the contingent deferred sales charge, or BACK END SALES CHARGE, typically a feature of the broker-sold fund.

REDEMPTION PRICE *see* CALL PRICE.

RED HERRING *see* PRELIMINARY PROSPECTUS.

REDISCOUNT DISCOUNT short-term negotiable debt instruments, such as banker's ACCEPTANCES and COMMERCIAL PAPER, that have been *discounted* with a bank—in other words, exchanged for an amount of cash adjusted to reflect the current interest rate. The bank then discounts the paper a second time for its own benefit with another bank or with a Federal Reserve bank. Rediscounting was once the primary means by which banks borrowed additional reserves from the Fed. Today most banks do this by discounting their own notes secured by GOVERNMENT SECURITIES or other ELIGIBLE PAPER. But *rediscount rate* is still used as a synonym for DISCOUNT RATE, the rate charged by the Fed for all bank borrowings.

REDLINING discrimination in the pattern of granting loans, insurance coverage, or other financial benefits. Lenders or insurers who practice redlining "draw a red line" around a troubled area of a city and vow not to lend or insure property in that neighborhood because of poor economic conditions and high default rates. Insurance companies withdraw from an area because of high claims experience and widespread fraud. With mortgage and business loans and insurance hard to obtain, redlining therefore tends to accelerate the decline of such neighborhoods. Redlining is illegal because it discriminates against residents of an area on the basis of where they live. Congress has enacted legislation such as the Community Reinvestment Act, which forces banks to lend to underprivileged areas, to combat redlining.

REDS *see* REFUNDING ESCROW DEPOSITS.

REDUCTION-OPTION LOAN (ROL) hybrid between a fixed-rate and adjustable mortgage and a cheaper alternative to refinancing, whereby the borrower has the one-time option from the second through the fifth year to match the current mortgage rate, which then becomes fixed for the rest of the term. The reduction is usually permitted if rates drop more than 2% in any one year.

REFCORP *see* RESOLUTION FUNDING CORPORATION (REFCORP).

REFINANCING
Banking: extending the maturity date, or increasing the amount of existing debt, or both.
Bonds: REFUNDING; retiring existing bonded debt by issuing new securities to reduce the interest rate, or to extend the maturity date, or both.
Personal finance: revising a payment schedule, usually to reduce the monthly payments and often to modify interest charges.

REFLATION reversal of DEFLATION by deliberate government monetary action.

REFUND
Bonds: retirement of an existing bond issue through the sale of a new bond issue. When interest rates have fallen, issuers may want to exercise the CALL FEATURE of a bond and replace it with another debt instrument paying a lower interest rate. *See also* PREREFUNDING.
Commerce: return of merchandise for money. For example, a consumer who is not happy with a product has the right to return it for a refund of his money.
Taxes: *see* TAX REFUND.

REFUNDING
1. replacing an old debt with a new one, usually in order to lower the interest cost of the issuer. For instance, a corporation or municipality that has issued 10% bonds may want to refund them by issuing 7% bonds if interest rates have dropped. *See also* PREREFUNDING; REFINANCING.
2. in merchandising, returning money to the purchaser, e.g., to a consumer who has paid for an appliance and is not happy with it.

REFUNDING ESCROW DEPOSITS (REDS) financial instruments used to circumvent 1984 tax restrictions on tax-exempt PREREFUNDINGS for certain kinds of state or local projects, such as airports, solid-waste disposal facilities, wharves, and convention centers. The object of prerefundings was to lock in a lower current rate in anticipation of maturing higher-rate issues. REDs accomplish this by way of a forward purchase contract obligating investors to buy bonds at a predetermined rate when they are issued at a future date. The future date coincides with the first optional call date on existing high-rate bonds. In the interim, investors' money is invested in Treasury bonds bought in the secondary market. The Treasuries are held in escrow, in effect securing the investor's deposit and paying taxable annual income. The Treasuries mature around the call date on the existing bonds, providing the money to buy the new issue and redeem the old one. Also called *municipal forwards*.

REGIONAL BANK bank that specializes in collecting deposits and making loans in one region of the country, as distinguished from a MONEY CENTER BANK, which operates nationally and internationally.

REGIONAL MUTUAL FUND mutual fund that buys securities from just one region of the country. There are regional mutual funds specializing in the Southwest, Southeast, Northwest, Midwest and other regions. Investors may be interested in such funds because they provide a PURE PLAY on the economic growth in a particular region. People living in these regions may also want to invest in nearby companies because of their firsthand experience with such firms.

Regional mutual funds also specialize in different regions of the world. There are funds limited to investments in Latin America, Europe, Asia, and other regions. Regional funds, whether domestic or international, tend to be more volatile than funds with more geographically diversified holdings.

REGIONAL STOCK EXCHANGES organized national securities exchanges located outside of New York City and registered with the SECURITIES AND EXCHANGE COMMISSION. They include: the Boston, Cincinnati, Intermountain (Salt Lake City), Midwest (Chicago), Pacific (Los Angeles and San Francisco), Philadelphia (Philadelphia and Miami), and Spokane stock exchanges. These exchanges list both regional issues and many of the securities listed on the New York exchanges. Companies listed on the NEW YORK STOCK EXCHANGE and the AMERICAN STOCK EXCHANGE often are listed on regional exchanges to broaden the market for their securities. Using the INTERMARKET TRADING SYSTEM (ITS), a SPECIALIST on the floor of one of the New York or regional exchanges can see competing prices for the securities traded on video screens. Regional exchanges handle only a small percentage of the total volume of the New York exchanges, though most of the trading done on regional exchanges involves stocks listed on the New York exchanges. *See also* DUAL LISTING; GRADUATED SECURITY; SECURITIES AND COMMODITIES EXCHANGES.

REGISTERED BOND bond that is recorded in the name of the holder on the books of the issuer or the issuer's REGISTRAR and can be transferred to another owner only when ENDORSED by the registered owner. A bond registered for principal only, and not for interest, is called a *registered coupon bond.* One that is not registered is called a *bearer bond;* one issued with detachable coupons for presentation to the issuer or a paying agent when interest or principal payments are due is termed a COUPON BOND. Bearer bonds are NEGOTIABLE INSTRUMENTS payable to the holder and therefore do not legally require endorsement. Bearer bonds that may be changed to registered bonds are called *interchangeable bonds.*

REGISTERED CHECK check issued by a bank for a customer who places funds aside in a special register. The customer writes in his name and the name of the payee and the amount of money to be transferred. The bank, which collects a fee for the service, then puts on the bank's name and the amount of the check and gives the check a special number. The check has two stubs, one for the customer and one for the bank. The registered check is similar to a money order for someone who does not have a checking account at the bank.

REGISTERED COMPANY company that has filed a REGISTRATION STATEMENT with the Securities and Exchange Commission in connection with a PUBLIC OFFERING of securities and must therefore comply with SEC DISCLOSURE requirements.

REGISTERED COMPETITIVE MARKET MAKER

1. securities dealer registered with the NATIONAL ASSOCIATION OF SECURITIES DEALERS (NASD) as a market maker in a particular OVER-THE-COUNTER stock—that is, one who maintains firm bid and offer prices in the stock by standing ready to buy or sell round lots. Such dealers must announce their quotes through NASDAQ, which requires that there be at least two market makers in each stock listed in the system; the bid and asked quotes are compared to ensure that the quote is a *representative spread. See also* MAKE A MARKET.
2. REGISTERED COMPETITIVE TRADER on the New York Stock Exchange. Such traders are sometimes called market makers because, in addition to trading for their own accounts, they are expected to help correct an IMBALANCE OF ORDERS. *See also* REGISTERED EQUITY MARKET MAKER.

REGISTERED COMPETITIVE TRADER one of a group of New York Stock Exchange members who buy and sell for their own accounts. Because these members pay no commissions, they are able to profit on small changes in market prices and thus tend to trade actively in stocks doing a high volume. Like SPECIALISTS, registered competitive traders must abide by exchange rules, including a requirement that 75% of their trades be *stabilizing.* This means they cannot sell unless the last trading price on a stock was up, or buy unless the last trading price was down. Orders from the general public take precedence over those of registered competitive traders, which account for less than 1% of volume. Also called *floor trader* or *competitive trader.*

REGISTERED COUPON BOND *see* REGISTERED BOND.

REGISTERED EQUITY MARKET MAKER AMERICAN STOCK EXCHANGE member firm registered as a trader for its own account. Such firms are expected to make stabilizing purchases and sales when necessary to correct imbalances in particular securities. *See also* REGISTERED COMPETITIVE MARKET MAKER.

REGISTERED INVESTMENT ADVISER investment adviser registered with the Securities and Exchange Commission. An RIA must fill out a form detailing educational and professional experience and pay an annual fee to the SEC. The Registered Investment Adviser (RIA) designation carries no endorsement from the SEC, which regulates RIAs' activities. RIAs may pick stocks, bonds, mutual funds, partnerships or other SEC-registered investments for clients. They may be paid on a fee-only or fee-plus-commission basis. Usually, fees are based on a fixed percentage of assets under management.

REGISTERED INVESTMENT COMPANY investment company, such as an open-end or closed-end MUTUAL FUND, which files a registration statement with the Securities and Exchange Commission and meets all the other requirements of the INVESTMENT COMPANY ACT OF 1940.

REGISTERED OPTIONS TRADER specialist on the floor of the AMERICAN STOCK EXCHANGE who is responsible for maintaining a fair and orderly market in an assigned group of options.

REGISTERED REPRESENTATIVE employee of a stock exchange member broker/dealer who acts as an ACCOUNT EXECUTIVE for clients. As such, the registered representative gives advice on which securities to buy and sell, and he collects a percentage of the commission income he generates as compensation. To qualify as a registered representative, a person must acquire a background in the securities business and pass a series of tests, including the General Securities Examination and state securities tests. "Registered" means licensed by the Securities and Exchange Commission and by the New York Stock Exchange.

REGISTERED RETIREMENT SAVINGS PLAN (RRSP) tax-deductible and tax-sheltered retirement plan for individuals in Canada, similar in concept to the INDIVIDUAL RETIREMENT PLAN (IRA) in the United States.

REGISTERED SECONDARY OFFERING offering, usually through investment bankers, of a large block of securities that were previously issued to the public, using the abbreviated Form S-16 of the Securities and Exchange Commission. Such offerings are usually made by major stockholders of mature companies who may be *control persons* or institutions who originally acquired the securities in a private placement. Form S-16 relies heavily on previously filed SEC documents such as the S-1, the 10-K, and quarterly filings. Where listed securities are concerned, permission to sell large blocks off the exchange must be obtained from the appropriate exchange. *See also* LETTER SECURITY; SECONDARY DISTRIBUTION; SECONDARY OFFERING; SHELF REGISTRATION.

REGISTERED SECURITY
1. security whose owner's name is recorded on the books of the issuer or the issuer's agent, called a *registrar*—for example, a REGISTERED BOND as opposed to a *bearer bond,* the former being transferable only by endorsement, the latter payable to the holder.
2. securities issue registered with the Securities and Exchange Commission as a new issue or as a SECONDARY OFFERING. *See also* REGISTERED SECONDARY OFFERING; REGISTRATION.

REGISTRAR agency responsible for keeping track of the owners of bonds and the issuance of stock. The registrar, working with the TRANSFER AGENT, keeps current files of the owners of a bond issue and the stockholders in a corporation. The registrar also makes sure that no more than the authorized amount of stock is in circulation. For bonds, the registrar certifies that a bond is a corporation's genuine debt obligation.

REGISTRATION process set up by the Securities Exchange Acts of 1933 and 1934 whereby securities that are to be sold to the public are reviewed by the Securities and Exchange Commission. The REGISTRATION STATEMENT details pertinent financial and operational information about the company, its management, and the purpose of the offering. Incorrect or incomplete information will delay the offering.

REGISTRATION FEE charge made by the Securities and Exchange Commission and paid by the issuer of a security when a public offering is recorded with the SEC.

REGISTRATION STATEMENT document detailing the purpose of a proposed public offering of securities. The statement outlines financial details, a history of the company's operations and management, and other facts of importance to potential buyers. *See also* REGISTRATION.

REGRESSION ANALYSIS statistical technique used to establish the relationship of a dependent variable, such as the sales of a company, and one or more independent variables, such as family formations, GROSS DOMESTIC PRODUCT, per capita income, and other ECONOMIC INDICATORS. By measuring exactly how large and significant each independent variable has historically been in its relation to the dependent variable, the future value of the dependent variable can be predicted. Essentially, regression analysis attempts to measure the degree of correlation between the dependent and independent variables, thereby establishing the latter's predictive value. For example, a manufacturer of baby food might want to determine the relationship between sales and housing starts as part of a sales forecast. Using a technique called a scatter graph, it might plot on the X and Y axes the historical sales for ten years and the historical annual housing starts for the same period. A line connecting the average dots, called the regression line, would reveal the degree of correlation between the two factors by showing the amount of unexplained variation—represented by the dots falling outside the line. Thus, if the regression line connected all the dots, it would demonstrate a direct relationship between baby food sales and housing starts, meaning that one could be predicted on the basis of the other. The proportion of dots scattered outside the regression line would indicate, on the other hand, the degree to which the relationship was less direct, a high enough degree of unexplained variation meaning there was no meaningful relationship and that housing starts have no predictive value in terms of baby food sales. This proportion of unexplained variations is termed the *coefficient of determination,* and its square root the CORRELATION COEFFICIENT. The correlation coefficient is the ultimate yardstick of regression analysis: a correlation coefficient of 1 means the relationship is direct—baby food and housing starts move together; −1 means there is a negative relationship—

REGRESSION ANALYSIS
SCATTER GRAPH

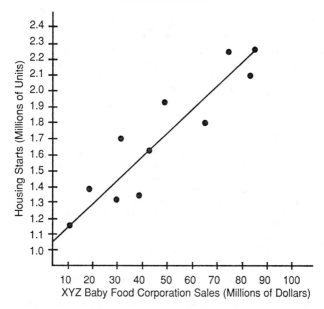

Housing Starts (Millions of Units) vs. XYZ Baby Food Corporation Sales (Millions of Dollars)

the more housing starts there are, the less baby food is sold; a coefficient of zero means there is no relationship between the two factors.

Regression analysis is also used in securities' markets analysis and in the risk-return analyses basic to PORTFOLIO THEORY.

REGRESSIVE TAX
1. system of taxation in which tax rates decline as the tax base rises. For example, a system that taxed values of $1000 to $5000 at 5%, $5000 to $10,000 at 4% and so on would be regressive. A regressive tax is the opposite of a PROGRESSIVE TAX.
2. tax system that results in a higher tax for the poor than for the rich, in terms of percentage of income. In this sense, a sales tax is regressive even though the same rate is applied to all sales, because people with lower incomes tend to spend most of their incomes on goods and services. Similarly, payroll taxes are regressive because they are borne largely by wage earners and not by higher income groups. Local property taxes also tend to be regressive because poorer people spend more of their incomes on housing costs, which are directly affected by property taxes. *See also* FLAT TAX.

REGULAR WAY DELIVERY (AND SETTLEMENT) completion of securities transaction at the office of the purchasing broker on (but not before) the third full business day following the date of the transaction, as required by the NEW YORK STOCK EXCHANGE. Government transactions are an exception; for them, regular way means delivery and settlement the next business day following a transaction.

REGULATED COMMODITIES all commodity futures and options contracts traded on organized U.S. futures exchanges. *See also* COMMODITY FUTURES TRADING COMMISSION.

REGULATED INVESTMENT COMPANY MUTUAL FUND or UNIT INVESTMENT TRUST eligible under *Regulation M* of the Internal Revenue Service to pass capital gains, dividends, and interest earned on fund investments directly to its shareholders to be taxed at the personal level. The process, designed to avoid double taxation, is called the *conduit theory*. To qualify as a regulated investment company, the fund must meet such requirements as 90% minimum distribution of interest and dividends received on investments less expenses and 90% distribution of capital gain net income. To avoid a 4% excise tax, however, a regulated investment company must pay out 98% of its net investment income and capital gains. Shareholders must pay taxes even if they reinvest their distributions.

REGULATION A
1. Securities and Exchange Commission provision for simplified REGISTRATION of small issues of securities. A Regulation A issue requires a shorter form of PROSPECTUS and carries lesser liability for officers and directors for false or misleading statements.
2. Federal Reserve Board statement of the means and conditions under which Federal Reserve banks make loans to member and other banks at what is called the DISCOUNT WINDOW. *See also* REDISCOUNT.

REGULATION D
1. FEDERAL RESERVE BOARD rule pertaining to the amount of reserves banks must maintain relative to deposits.
2. SECURITIES AND EXCHANGE COMMISSION (SEC) rules concerning PRIVATE PLACEMENTS and defining related concepts such as ACCREDITED INVESTOR.

REGULATION G Federal Reserve Board rule regulating lenders other than commercial banks, brokers or dealers who, in the ordinary course of business, extend credit to individuals to purchase or carry securities. Special provision is made for loans by corporations and credit unions to finance purchases under employee stock option and stock purchase plans.

REGULATION Q Federal Reserve Board ceiling on the rates that banks and other savings institutions can pay on savings and other time deposits. THE DEPOSITORY INSTITUTIONS DEREGULATION AND MONETARY CONTROL ACT OF 1980 provided for phasing out Regulation Q by 1986.

REGULATION T Federal Reserve Board regulation covering the extension of credit to customers by securities brokers, dealers, and members of the national securities exchanges. It establishes INITIAL MARGIN requirements and defines registered (eligible), unregistered (ineligible), and exempt securities. *See also* MARGIN REQUIREMENT; MARGIN SECURITIES.

REGULATION U Federal Reserve Board limit on the amount of credit a bank may extend a customer for purchasing and carrying MARGIN SECURITIES. *See also* NONPURPOSE LOAN.

REGULATION Z Federal Reserve Board regulation covering provisions of the CONSUMER CREDIT PROTECTION ACT OF 1968, known as the Truth in Lending Act.

REHYPOTHECATION pledging by brokers of securities in customers' MARGIN ACCOUNTS to banks as collateral for broker loans under a GENERAL LOAN AND COLLATERAL AGREEMENT. Broker loans cover the positions of brokers who have made margin loans to customers for margin purchases and SELLING SHORT. Margin loans are collateralized by the HYPOTHECATION of customers securities to the broker. Their rehypothecation is authorized when the customer originally signs a GENERAL ACCOUNT agreement.

REIMBURSEMENT paying someone back for out-of-pocket expenses. For example, a company reimburses employees for their out-of-pocket business-related expenses when employees file expense reports. Insurance companies reimburse policyholders for out-of-pocket expenses incurred paying medical bills (for health insurance) or for home repairs (homeowner's insurance).

REINSTATEMENT in INSURANCE, the restoration of coverage after a policy has lapsed because premium payments have not been made. Typically, life insurance can be reinstated within a three-year period if premiums are paid and subject to evidence of continued insurability.

REINSURANCE sharing of RISK among insurance companies. Part of the insurer's risk is assumed by other companies in return for a part of the premium fee paid by the insured. By spreading the risk, reinsurance allows an individual company to take on clients whose coverage would be too great a burden for one insurer to carry alone.

REINVESTMENT PRIVILEGE right of a shareholder to reinvest dividends in order to buy more shares in the company or MUTUAL FUND, usually at no additional sales charge.

REINVESTMENT RATE rate of return resulting from the reinvestment of the interest from a bond or other fixed-income security. The reinvestment rate on a ZERO-COUPON BOND is predictable and locked in, since no interest payments are ever made, and therefore all imputed interest is reinvested at the same rate. The reinvestment rate on coupon bonds is less predictable because it rises and falls with market interest rates.

REINVESTMENT RISK risk that rates will fall causing cash flows from an investment (dividends or interest), assuming reinvestment, to earn less than the original investment.

REIT *see* REAL ESTATE INVESTMENT TRUST.

REJECTION

   Banking: refusal to grant credit to an applicant because of inadequate financial strength, a poor credit history, or some other reason.

   Insurance: refusal to underwrite a risk, that is, to issue a policy.

   Securities: refusal of a broker or a broker's customer to accept the security presented to complete a trade. This usually occurs because the security lacks the necessary endorsements. or because of other exceptions to the rules for GOOD DELIVERY.

RELATIVE STRENGTH rate at which a stock falls relative to other stocks in a falling market or rises relative to other stocks in a rising market. Analysts reason that a stock that holds value on the downside will be a strong performer on the upside and vice versa. Comparative relative strength, as the concept is more accurately called, compares a security's price performance with that of a "base security," which is often a market index. The security price is divided by the base security's price to get the ratio between the two, which is called the comparative relative strength indicator. When the indicator is moving up, the security is outperforming the base security and vice versa.

   Comparative relative strength should not be confused with what technical analysts call the RELATIVE STRENGTH INDEX (RSI). The RSI is a MOMENTUM OSCILLATOR developed by J. Welles Wilder in the late 1970s and discussed in his book, *New Concepts in Technical Trading Systems.* The name relative strength index is somewhat misleading since it does not compare the relative strength of two securities, but rather the internal strength of a single security. The RSI measures the relative strength of the current price movement as increasing from 0 to 100. Although many variations are in use, Wilder favored the use of a 14-period measurement and set the significant levels of the indicator at 30 for oversold (signaling an imminent upturn) and 70 for overbought (signaling an imminent downturn). Thus the averages of up days and down days for 14-day periods would be plotted. If the security makes a new high but the RSI fails to surpass its previous high, this divergence is an indication of an impending reversal. When the RSI then turns down and falls below its most recent trough, it has completed a "failure swing" which confirms the impending reversal.

RELEASE CLAUSE provision in a MORTGAGE agreement allowing the freeing of pledged property after a proportionate amount of payment has been made.

REMAINDER remaining interest in a TRUST or ESTATE after expenses and after prior beneficiaries have been satisfied. *See also* CHARITABLE REMAINDER TRUST.

REMAINING MONTHLY BALANCE amount of debt remaining unpaid on a monthly statement. For example, a credit card customer may charge $300 worth of merchandise during a month, and pay $100, leaving a remaining monthly balance of $200, on which interest charges would accrue.

REMARGINING putting up additional cash or eligible securities to correct a deficiency in EQUITY deposited in a brokerage MARGIN ACCOUNT to meet MINIMUM MAINTENANCE REQUIREMENTS. Remargining usually is prompted by a MARGIN CALL.

REMIC acronym for *real estate mortgage investment conduit,* a pass-through vehicle created under the TAX REFORM ACT OF 1986 to issue multiclass mortgage-backed securities. REMICs may be organized as corporations, partnerships, or trusts, and those meeting qualifications are not subject to DOUBLE TAXATION. Interests in REMICs may be senior or junior, *regular* (debt instruments) or *residual* (equity interests). The practical meaning of REMICs has been that issuers have more flexibility than is afforded by the COLLATERALIZED MORTGAGE OBLIGATION (CMO) vehicle. Issuers can thus separate mortgage pools not only into different maturity classes but into different risk classes as well. Whereas CMOs normally have AAA bond ratings, REMICs represent a range of risk levels.

REMIT pay for purchased goods or services by cash, check, or electronic payment.

RENEWABLE TERM LIFE INSURANCE term life insurance policy offering the policyholder the option to renew for a specific period of time—frequently one year—for a particular length of time. Some term life policies stipulate a maximum age benefit. Some policies offer fixed premium rates for a certain number of years, usually ten, after which they are renewable at a higher premium rate. Other term policies are renewable every year, and charge escalating premium rates as the policyholder ages.

RENT payment from a tenant to a building owner for use of the specified property. For example, an apartment dweller must pay monthly rent to a landlord for the right to inhabit the apartment. A commercial tenant in an office or store must pay monthly rent to the building owner for the use of the commercial space.

RENT CONTROL state and local government regulation restricting the amount of rent landlords can charge their tenants. Rent control is used to regulate the quality of rental dwellings, with controls implemented only against those units that do not conform to building codes, as in New York City; or used across the board to deal with high rents resulting from a gross imbalance between housing supply and demand, as in Massachusetts and California. If a landlord violates rent control laws, the tenant may protest at the local housing authority charged with enforcing the law. While tenants may like rent control, landlords argue that it reduces their ability to earn a profit on their property, thereby discouraging them from investing any further to maintain or upgrade the property. In some cases, landlords argue that rent control encourages owners to abandon their property altogether since it will never be profitable to retain it.

REORGANIZATION financial restructuring of a firm in BANKRUPTCY. *See also* TRUSTEE IN BANKRUPTCY; VOTING TRUST CERTIFICATE.

REORGANIZATION BOND debt security issued by a company in REORGANIZATION proceedings. The bonds are generally issued to the company's creditors on a basis whereby interest is paid only if and when it is earned. *See also* ADJUSTMENT BOND; INCOME BOND.

REPATRIATION return of the financial assets of an organization or individual from a foreign country to the home country.

REPLACEMENT COST cost to replace an asset with another of similar utility at today's prices. Also called *current cost* and *replacement value. See also* BOOK VALUE, REPLACEMENT COST INSURANCE.

REPLACEMENT COST ACCOUNTING accounting method allowing additional DEPRECIATION on part of the difference between the original cost and current replacement cost of a depreciable asset.

REPLACEMENT COST INSURANCE property and casualty insurance that replaces damaged property. Replacement cost contents insurance pays the dollar amount needed to replace damaged personal property with items of like kind and quality, without deducting for depreciation. Replacement cost dwelling insurance pays the policyholder the cost of replacing the damaged property without deduction for depreciation, but limited by the maximum dollar amount indicated on the declarations page of the policy. *See also* REPLACEMENT COST.

REPURCHASE AGREEMENT (REPO; RP) agreement between a seller and a buyer, usually of U.S. government securities, whereby the seller agrees to repurchase the securities at an agreed upon price and, usually, at a stated time. Repos, also called RPs or buybacks, are widely used both as a money market investment vehicle and as an instrument of Federal Reserve MONETARY POLICY. Where a repurchase agreement is used as a short-term investment, a government securities dealer, usually a bank, borrows from an investor, typically a corporation with excess cash, to finance its inventory, using the securities as collateral. Such RPs may have a fixed maturity date or be OPEN REPOS, callable at any time. Rates are negotiated directly by the parties involved, but are generally lower than rates on collateralized loans made by New York banks. The attraction of repos to corporations, which also have the alternatives of COMMERCIAL PAPER, CERTIFICATES OF DEPOSIT, TREASURY BILLS and other short-term instruments, is the flexibility of maturities that makes them an ideal place to "park" funds on a very temporary basis. Dealers also arrange *reverse repurchase* *agreements,* whereby they agree to buy the securities and the investor agrees to repurchase them at a later date.

The FEDERAL RESERVE BANK also makes extensive use of repurchase agreements in its OPEN MARKET OPERATIONS as a method of fine tuning the MONEY SUPPLY. To temporarily expand the supply, the Fed arranges to buy securities from nonbank dealers who in turn deposit the proceeds in their commercial bank accounts thereby adding to reserves. Timed to coincide with whatever length of time the Fed needs to make the desired adjustment, usually 1 to 15 days, the dealer repurchases the securities. Such transactions are made at the Federal Reserve DISCOUNT RATE and accounts are credited in FEDERAL FUNDS. When it wishes to reduce the money supply temporarily, the Fed reverses the process. Using a procedure called the MATCHED SALE PUR-CHASE TRANSACTION, it sells securities to a nonbank dealer who either draws down bank balances directly or takes out a bank loan to make payment, thereby draining reserves.

In a third variation of the Repurchase agreement, banks and thrift institutions can raise temporary capital funds with a device called the *retail repurchase agreement.* Using pooled government securities to secure loans from individuals, they agree to repurchase the securities at a specified time at a price including interest. Despite its appearance of being a deposit secured by government securities, the investor has neither a special claim on the securities nor protection by the FED-ERAL DEPOSIT INSURANCE CORPORATION in the event the bank is forced to liquidate.

See also OVERNIGHT REPO.

REQUIRED RATE OF RETURN return required by investors before they will commit money to an investment at a given level of risk. Unless the expected return exceeds the required return, an investment is unacceptable. *See also* HURDLE RATE; INTERNAL RATE OF RETURN; MEAN RETURN.

REQUIRED RESERVE RATE factor used to determine the amount of reserves a bank must maintain on its deposits.

RESCHEDULED LOANS bank loans that, as an alternative to DEFAULT, were restructured, usually by lengthening the maturity to make it easier for the borrower to meet repayment terms.

RESCIND cancel a contract agreement. The Truth in Lending Act confers the RIGHT OF RESCISSION, which allows the signer of a contract to nullify it within three business days without penalty and have any deposits refunded. Contracts may also be rescinded in cases of fraud, failure to comply with legal procedures, or misrepresentation. For example, a contract signed by a child under legal age may be rescinded, since children do not have the right to take on contractual obligations.

RESCISSION *see* RIGHT OF RESCISSION.

RESEARCH AND DEVELOPMENT (R&D) scientific and marketing evolution of a new product or service. Once such a product has been created in a laboratory or other research setting, marketing specialists attempt to define the market for the product. Then, steps are taken to manufacture the product to meet the needs of the market. Research and development spending is often listed as a separate item in a company's financial statements. In industries such as high-technology and pharmaceuticals, R&D spending is quite high, since products are outdated or attract competition quickly. Investors looking for companies in such fast-changing fields check on R&D spending as a percentage of sales because they consider this an important indicator of the company's prospects. *See also* RESEARCH AND DEVELOPMENT LIMITED PARTNERSHIP.

RESEARCH AND DEVELOPMENT LIMITED PARTNERSHIP plan whose investors put up money to finance new product RESEARCH AND DEVELOPMENT. In return, the investors get a percentage of the product's profits, if any, together with such benefits as DEPRECIATION of equipment. R&D partnerships may be offered publicly or privately, usually through brokerage firms. Those that are offered to the public must be registered with the Securities and Exchange Commission. *See also* LIMITED PARTNERSHIP.

RESEARCH DEPARTMENT division within a brokerage firm, investment company, bank trust department, insurance company, or other institutional investing organization that analyzes markets and securities. Research departments include analysts who focus on particular securities, commodities, and whole industries as well as generalists who forecast movements of the markets as a whole, using both FUNDAMENTAL ANALYSIS and TECHNICAL ANALYSIS. An analyst whose advice is followed by many investors can have a major impact on the prices of individual securities.

RESERVE
1. segregation of RETAINED EARNINGS to provide for such payouts as dividends, contingencies, improvements, or retirement of preferred stock.
2. VALUATION RESERVE, also called ALLOWANCE, for DEPRECIATION, BAD DEBT losses, shrinkage of receivables because of discounts taken, and other provisions created by charges to the PROFIT AND LOSS STATEMENT.
3. hidden reserves, represented by understatements of BALANCE SHEET values.
4. deposit maintained by a commercial bank in a FEDERAL RESERVE BANK to meet the Fed's RESERVE REQUIREMENT.

RESERVE REQUIREMENT FEDERAL RESERVE SYSTEM rule mandating the financial assets that member banks must keep in the form of cash and other liquid assets as a percentage of DEMAND DEPOSITS and TIME DEPOSITS. This money must be in the bank's own vaults or on deposit with the nearest regional FEDERAL RESERVE BANK. Reserve requirements, set by the Fed's Board of Governors, are one of the key tools in deciding how much money banks can lend, thus setting the pace at which the nation's money supply and economy grow. The higher the reserve requirement, the tighter the money—and therefore the slower the economic growth. *See also* MONETARY POLICY; MONEY SUPPLY; MULTIPLIER.

RESET BONDS bonds issued with a provision that on specified dates the initial interest rate must be adjusted so that the bonds trade at their original value. Although reset provisions can work in an issuer's favor by lowering rates should market rates fall or credit quality improve, they were designed as a protective feature for investors to enhance the marketability of JUNK BOND issues. Should market rates rise or credit quality decline (causing prices to decline), the interest rate would be increased to bring the bond price to PAR or above. The burden of increased interest payments on a weak issuer could prompt DEFAULT.

RESIDENTIAL ENERGY CREDIT tax credit granted to homeowners prior to 1986 by the federal government for improving the energy efficiency of their homes. Installation of storm windows and doors, insulation, or new fuel-saving heating systems before the end of 1985 meant a maximum federal credit on expenditures of $300. Equipping a home with renewable energy devices such as solar panels or windmills meant a maximum federal credit of $4000. Many states offer incentives for installing such devices.

RESIDENTIAL MORTGAGE mortgage on a residential property. Interest on such mortgages is deductible for federal and state income tax purposes up to $1 million; for home equity loans, interest up to $100,000 is deductible.

RESIDENTIAL PROPERTY property zoned for single-family homes, townhouses, multifamily apartments, condominiums, and coops. Residential property falls under different zoning and taxation regulations than commercial property.

RESIDUAL SECURITY
1. SECURITY that has a potentially dilutive effect on earnings per common share. Warrants, rights, convertible bonds, and preferred stock are potentially dilutive because exercising or converting them into common stock would increase the number of common shares competing for the same earnings, and earnings per share would be reduced. *See also* DILUTION: FULLY DILUTED EARNINGS PER (COMMON) SHARE.
2. the term *residual* is also used informally to describe investments based on the excess cash flow generated by collateral pools. CMO REITs and the bottom tier of most COLLATERALIZED BOND OBLIGATIONS (CBOs) are examples of "residuals."

RESIDUAL VALUE
1. realizable value of a FIXED ASSET after costs associated with the sale.

2. amount remaining after all allowable DEPRECIATION charges have been subtracted from the original cost of a depreciable asset.
3. scrap value, which is the value to a junk dealer. Also called *salvage value.*

RESISTANCE LEVEL price ceiling at which technical analysts note persistent selling of a commodity or security. If XYZ's stock generally trades between a low of $50 and a high of $60 a share, $50 is called the SUPPORT LEVEL and $60 is called the resistance level. Technical analysts think it significant when the stock breaks through the resistance level because that means it usually will go on to new high prices. *See also* BREAKOUT; TECHNICAL ANALYSIS.

RESISTANCE LEVEL

RESOLUTION
1. in general, expression of desire or intent.
2. formal document representing an action of a corporation's BOARD OF DIRECTORS—perhaps a directive to management, such as in the declaration of a dividend, or a corporate expression of sentiment, such as acknowledging the services of a retiring officer. A *corporate resolution,* which defines the authority and powers of individual officers, is a document given to a bank.
3. legal order or contract by a government entity—called a *bond resolution*—authorizing a bond issue and spelling out the rights of bondholders and the obligations of the issuer.

RESOLUTION FUNDING CORPORATION (REFCORP) U.S. government agency created by Congress in 1989 to (1) issue BAILOUT BONDS and raise industry funds to finance activities of the RESOLUTION TRUST CORPORATION (RTC) and (2) merge or close sick institutions inherited from the disbanded FEDERAL SAVINGS AND LOAN INSURANCE CORPORATION (FSLIC). *See also* OFFICE OF THRIFT SUPERVISION (OTS).

RESOLUTION TRUST CORPORATION (RTC) U.S. government agency created by the 1989 bailout bill to merge or close savings and loan institutions becoming insolvent between 1989 and August 1992. The RTC was terminated in 1996 and its responsibilities were shifted to the SAVINGS ASSOCIATION INSURANCE FUND (SAIF), a unit of the FEDERAL DEPOSIT INSURANCE CORPORATION. The *Resolution Trust Corporation Oversight Board,* an arm of the executive branch, was charged with overseeing broad policy and the dispensing of funds to sick thrifts by RTC. *See also* OFFICE OF THRIFT SUPERVISION (OTS).

RESTRICTED ACCOUNT MARGIN ACCOUNT with a securities broker in which the EQUITY is less than the INITIAL MARGIN requirement set by the Federal Reserve Board's REGULATION T. A customer whose account is restricted may not make further purchases and must, in accordance with Regulation T's *retention requirement,* retain in the account a percentage of the proceeds of any sales so as to reduce the deficiency (debit balance). This retention requirement is currently set at 50%. *See also* MARGIN CALL.

RESTRICTED SURPLUS portion of RETAINED EARNINGS not legally available for the payment of dividends. Among the circumstances giving rise to such restriction: dividend arrearages in CUMULATIVE PREFERRED stock, a shortfall in the minimum WORKING CAPITAL ratio specified in an INDENTURE, or simply a vote by the BOARD OF DIRECTORS. Also called *restricted retained earnings.*

RESTRICTIVE COVENANT *see* COVENANT.

RESTRICTIVE ENDORSEMENT signature on the back of a check specifying the transfer of the amount of that check, under specific conditions. The most common type of restrictive endorsement is "for deposit only," meaning the check must be deposited in the payee's bank account and cannot be cashed.

RESTRUCTURING general term for major corporate changes aimed at greater efficiency and adaptation to changing markets. SPIN-OFFS, RECAPITALIZATIONS, STRATEGIC BUYOUTS, and major management realignments are all developments frequently associated with corporate restructurings. *See also* DOWNSIZING.

RESYNDICATION LIMITED PARTNERSHIP partnership in which existing properties are sold to new limited partners, who can gain tax advantages that had been exhausted by the old partnership. For instance, a partnership with government-subsidized housing may have given partners substantial tax benefits five years ago. Now the same housing development may be sold to a resyndication partnership, which will start the process of DEPRECIATION over again and claim additional tax benefits for its new limited partners. Resyndication partnerships are usually offered as PRIVATE PLACEMENTS through brokerage houses, although a few have been offered to the public.

RETAIL HOUSE brokerage firm that caters to retail investors instead of institutions. Such a firm may be a large national broker ca!led a WIRE HOUSE, with a large RESEARCH DEPARTMENT and a wide variety of products and services for individuals, or it may be a small BOUTIQUE serving an exclusive clientele with specialized research or investment services.

RETAIL INVESTOR investor who buys securities and commodities futures on his own behalf, not for an organization. Retail investors typically buy shares of stock or commodity positions in much smaller quantities than institutions such as mutual funds, bank trust departments, and pension funds and therefore are usually charged commissions higher than those paid by the institutions. In recent years, market activity has increasingly been dominated by INSTITUTIONAL INVESTORS.

RETAIL PRICE price charged to retail customers for goods and services. Retailers buy goods from wholesalers, and increase the price to cover their costs, plus a profit. Manufacturers list suggested retail prices for their products; retailers may adhere to these prices or offer discounts from them.

RETAINED EARNINGS net profits kept to accumulate in a business after dividends are paid. Also called *undistributed profits* or *earned surplus.* Retained earnings are distinguished from *contributed capital*—capital received in exchange for stock, which is reflected in CAPITAL STOCK or CAPITAL SURPLUS and DONATED STOCK or DONATED SURPLUS. STOCK DIVIDENDS—the distribution of additional shares of capital stock with no cash payment—reduce retained earnings and increase capital stock. Retained earnings plus the total of all the capital accounts represent the NET WORTH of a firm. *See also* ACCUMULATED PROFITS TAX; PAID-IN CAPITAL.

RETAINED EARNINGS STATEMENT reconciliation of the beginning and ending balances in the RETAINED EARNINGS account on a company's BALANCE SHEET. It breaks down changes affecting the account, such as profits or losses from operations, dividends declared, and any other items charged or credited to retained earnings. A retained earnings statement is required by GENERALLY ACCEPTED ACCOUNTING PRINCIPLES whenever comparative balance sheets and income statements are presented. It may appear in the balance sheet, in a combined PROFIT AND LOSS STATEMENT and retained earnings statement, or as a separate schedule. It may also be called *statement of changes in earned surplus* (or *retained income).*

RETENTION in securities underwriting, the number of units allocated to a participating investment banker (SYNDICATE member) minus the units held back by the syndicate manager for facilitating institutional sales and for allocation to firms in the selling group that are not also members of the syndicate. *See also* UNDERWRITE.

RETENTION RATE percentage of after-tax profits credited to RETAINED EARNINGS. It is the opposite of the DIVIDEND PAYOUT RATIO.

RETENTION REQUIREMENT *see* RESTRICTED ACCOUNT.

RETIREMENT
1. cancellation of stock or bonds that have been reacquired or redeemed. *See also* CALLABLE; REDEMPTION.
2. removal from service after a fixed asset has reached the end of its useful life or has been sold and appropriate adjustments have been made to the asset and depreciation accounts.
3. repayment of a debt obligation.
4. permanent withdrawal of an employee from gainful employment in accordance with an employer's policies concerning length of service, age, or disability. A retired employee may have rights to a pension or other retirement provisions offered by the employer. Such benefits may in some circumstances supplement payments from an INDIVIDUAL RETIREMENT ACCOUNT (IRA) or KEOGH PLAN.

RETIREMENT AGE age at which employees no longer work. Though there is no longer any mandatory retirement age, many institutions do impose a retirement age. The federal government has a retirement age of 70. Many corporations have a retirement age of 65, although this has become more flexible and is no longer standard. Employees reaching age 62 may start to receive Social Security benefits, though the minimum age for receiving full Social Security benefits starts at age 65 and gradually increases to age 67 starting in the year 2000.

RETIREMENT PROTECTION ACT OF 1994 legislation designed to protect the pension benefits of American workers and retirees by increasing funding of underfunded pension plans and strengthening the pension insurance program administered by the PENSION BENEFIT GUARANTY CORPORATION (PBGC). Reinforcing the special requirement known as the Deficit Reduction Contribution (DRC) to fund underfunded pension plans, the act required severely underfunded plans to have enough cash and marketable securities to cover current benefit payments. The law also increased PBGC premiums for pension plans posing the greatest liquidation risk. It also required employers whose plans are less than 90% funded to provide a notice to their employees in simple language on the plan's funding and the limits of PBGC guarantees. The act also created the "Pension Search Program" which locates people who are owed benefits from fully funded, PBGC-insured defined benefit plans that terminate. *See also* PENSION BENEFIT GUARANTY CORPORATION (PBGC).

RETURN
Finance and investment: profit on a securities or capital investment, usually expressed as an annual percentage rate. *See also* RATE OF

RETURN; RETURN ON EQUITY; RETURN ON INVESTED CAPITAL; RETURN ON SALES; TOTAL RETURN.

Retailing: exchange of previously sold merchandise for REFUND or CREDIT against future sales.

Taxes: form on which taxpayers submit information required by the government when they file with the INTERNAL REVENUE SERVICE. For example, Form 1040 is the tax return used by individual taxpayers.

Trade: physical return of merchandise for credit against an invoice.

RETURN OF CAPITAL distribution of cash resulting from DEPRECIATION tax savings, the sale of a CAPITAL ASSET or of securities in a portfolio, or any other transaction unrelated to RETAINED EARNINGS. Returns of capital are not directly taxable but may result in higher CAPITAL GAINS taxes later on if they reduce the acquisition cost base of the property involved. Also called *return of basis.*

RETURN ON COMMON EQUITY *see* RETURN ON EQUITY; RETURN ON INVESTED CAPITAL.

RETURN ON EQUITY amount, expressed as a percentage, earned on a company's common stock investment for a given period. It is calculated by dividing common stock equity (NET WORTH) at the beginning of the accounting period into NET INCOME for the period after preferred stock dividends but before common stock dividends. Return on equity tells common shareholders how effectually their money is being employed. Comparing percentages for current and prior periods reveals trends, and comparison with industry composites reveals how well a company is holding its own against its competitors.

RETURN ON INVESTED CAPITAL amount, expressed as a percentage, earned on a company's total capital—its common and preferred stock EQUITY plus its long-term FUNDED DEBT—calculated by dividing total capital into earnings before interest, taxes, and dividends. Return on invested capital, usually termed *return on investment,* or *ROI,* is a useful means of comparing companies, or corporate divisions, in terms of efficiency of management and viability of product lines.

RETURN ON SALES net pretax profits as a percentage of NET SALES— a useful measure of overall operational efficiency when compared with prior periods or with other companies in the same line of business. It is important to recognize, however, that return on sales varies widely from industry to industry. A supermarket chain with a 2% return on sales might be operating efficiently, for example, because it depends on high volume to generate an acceptable RETURN ON INVESTED CAPITAL. In contrast, a manufacturing enterprise is expected to average 4% to 5%, so a return on sales of 2% is likely to be considered highly inefficient.

REVALUATION change in the value of a country's currency relative to others that is based on the decision of authorities rather than on fluctuations in the market. Revaluation generally refers to an increase in the currency's value; DEVALUATION refers to a decrease. *See also* FLOATING EXCHANGE RATE; PAR VALUE OF CURRENCY.

REVENUE ANTICIPATION NOTE (RAN) short-term debt issue of a municipal entity that is to be repaid out of anticipated revenues such as sales taxes. When the taxes are collected, the RAN is paid off. Interest from the note is usually tax-free to RAN holders.

REVENUE BOND *see* MUNICIPAL REVENUE BOND.

REVENUE NEUTRAL guiding criterion in drafting the TAX REFORM ACT OF 1986 whereby provisions estimated to add revenue were offset by others estimated to reduce revenue, so that on paper the new bill would generate the same amount of revenue as the old tax laws. The concept, which has guided subsequent tax legislation, was theoretical rather than real, since estimates **are** subject to variation.

REVENUE RECONCILIATION ACT OF 1993 landmark legislation signed into law by President Clinton in August 1993 to reduce the federal budget deficit by curtailing spending and raising taxes. Among its major components:

Provisions Affecting Individuals

1. added a fourth tax bracket of 36% to the existing 15%, 28%, and 31% brackets. Single taxpayers earning over \$115,000 and married taxpayers filing jointly earning over \$140,000 pay at the 36% marginal rate.
2. added a 10% surtax on married couples filing jointly reporting more than \$250,000 in taxable income, or on married couples filing separately with taxable incomes of more than \$125,000, creating, in effect, a fifth tax bracket at 39.6%.
3. kept capital gains tax rate at 28% for assets held at least a year.
4. created special tax break for investing in small companies. Investors buying newly issued stock in a small company with less than \$50 million in gross assets who hold the stock for at least 5 years may exclude 50% of the profit from capital gains taxes. For each subsequent year the investor holds the stock, the tax rate declines 10% until there is no capital gains tax after 10 years.
5. gasoline taxes were increased from 14.1 cents to 18.4 cents a gallon.
6. taxes on Social Security benefits were raised. Couples with provisional income plus half their Social Security benefits totaling more than \$44,000 owe tax on up to 85% of their Social Security benefits. For singles, the equivalent level is \$34,000. Provisional income is defined as adjusted gross income, interest on tax-exempt bonds, and certain income from foreign sources. Previously, couples with taxable income over \$32,000 and singles with income over \$25,000 had to pay taxes on 50% of their Social Security benefits.
7. Medicare tax cap was eliminated. Before this Act, the Medicare tax of 1.45% on wages applied to the first \$135,000 of wages.
8. phaseout of personal exemptions, which had been temporary, was made permanent. Personal exemptions begin to phase out for

singles reporting adjusted gross incomes of $108,450. For married couples filing jointly, exemptions begin to phase out when adjusted gross income reaches $167,700. (These amounts are adjusted for inflation annually).

9. investment interest deductions were limited. Interest paid to finance the purchase of securities remain deductible from interest income earned from investments, but that interest can no longer be deducted against realized capital gains.

10. pension contributions were limited. The income limit for contributions to pension plans such as Keoghs and SEPs was lowered from $235,840 to $150,000.

11. earned income credit was expanded. For taxpayers with more than one child, a credit of up to 18.5% can be claimed for the first $7750 of income, up to a maximum of $1511. The credit rose to 36% in 1995 and 40% in 1996.

12. moving deductions were limited. Under the law, unreimbursed moving expenses for house-hunting, closing fees, broker's commissions, and food costs while living in temporary quarters are no longer deductible as they had been previously. In addition, moves must be 50 miles, up from 35 miles, from the previous home in order to qualify for tax benefits. Moving expenses were converted from an itemized deduction—available only to those who filed an itemized return—to an above-the-line deduction, similar to alimony.

13. estimated tax rules were changed. For married taxpayers filing jointly reporting more than $150,000 in taxable income, quarterly estimated taxes must be paid at 110% of the previous year's tax liability.

14. alternative minimum tax (AMT) rates were raised. The AMT tax rate on income exceeding $175,000 was raised from 24% to 28%.

15. estate tax rates were raised. The top rate on inheritance taxes was raised from 50% to 55% on estates worth more than $3 million.

16. luxury taxes were repealed. The 10% luxury tax on airplanes, boats, cars, furs, and jewelry was repealed on all items except cars selling for more than $32,000.

17. rules governing donations of appreciated property were made permanent. Temporary rules allowing donors to deduct the full value of appreciated property such as art, real estate, and securities were made permanent. Such donations were also removed from calculations towards the alternative minimum tax (AMT).

Provisions Affecting Business

18. corporate tax rates were increased from 34% to 35%, for companies with taxable income of at least $10 million.

19. deductions for executive salaries exceeding $1 million were limited.

20. meal and entertainment deductions were lowered from 80% to 50% for business-related meal and entertainment expenses.

21. deductions were increased for small business purchases of equipment up to $17,500 a year, up from $10,000 previously.

22. tax breaks were reinstated for real estate professionals. Certified real estate professionals, defined as those working at least 750

hours a year in a real-estate-related line of work such as sales or construction, are allowed to deduct losses on rental property against any form of income. Previously, such passive losses could only be offset against passive income.

23. commercial real estate depreciation was lengthened from 31 years to 39 years.
24. club dues for country clubs; airline lounges; and social, athletic, and health clubs were made nondeductible.
25. standard period for depreciating goodwill when acquiring a business was set at 15 years.
26. expenses for lobbying Congress were made nondeductible.
27. restrictions on deductions for traveling spouses were imposed. Expenses for spouses traveling on a business trip were made non-deductible, unless the spouse is an employee of the company paying for the trip and has a business reason for going.
28. empowerment zones were created. Businesses that invest and create jobs in authorized empowerment zones in particular depressed communities qualify for tax incentives and special grants.

REVENUE SHARING

Limited partnerships: percentage split between the general partner and limited partners of profits, losses, cash distributions, and other income or losses which result from the operation of a real estate, oil and gas, equipment leasing, or other partnership. *See also* LIMITED PARTNERSHIP.
Taxes: return of tax revenue to a unit of government by a larger unit, such as from a state to one of its municipalities. GENERAL REVENUE SHARING between the federal government and states, localities, and other subunits existed between 1972 and 1987.

REVERSAL change in direction in the stock or commodity futures markets, as charted by technical analysts. If the Dow Jones Industrial Average has been climbing steadily from 7400 to 7900, for instance, chartists would speak of a reversal if the average started a sustained fall back toward 7400. *See* chart on the next page.

REVERSE ANNUITY MORTGAGE (RAM) MORTGAGE instrument that allows an elderly person to live off the equity in a fully paid-for house. Such a homeowner would enter into a reverse annuity mortgage agreement with a financial institution such as a bank, which would guarantee a lifelong fixed monthly income in return for gradually giving up ownership of the house. The longer the payments continue, the less equity the elderly owner would retain. At the owner's death the bank gains title to the real estate, which it can sell at a profit. The law also permits such arrangements between relatives, so that, for instance, a son or daughter might enter into a reverse annuity mortgage transaction with his or her retiring parents, thus providing the parents with cash to invest in income-yielding securities and the son or daughter with the depreciation and other tax benefits of real estate ownership. *See also* ARM'S LENGTH TRANSACTION.

REVERSAL

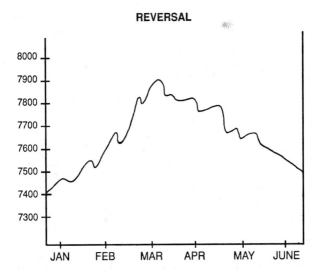

REVERSE A SWAP restore a bond portfolio to its former position following a swap of one bond for another to gain the advantage of a YIELD
SPREAD or a tax loss. The reversal may mean that the yield differential
has disappeared or that the investor, content with a short-term profit,
wishes to stay with the original bond for the advantages that may be
gained in the future. *See also* BOND SWAP.

REVERSE CONVERSION technique whereby brokerage firms earn
interest on their customers' stock holdings. A typical reverse conversion would work like this: A brokerage firm sells short the stocks it
holds in customers' margin accounts, then invests this money in short-
term money market instruments. To protect against a sharp rise in the
markets, the firm hedges its short position by buying CALL options and
selling PUT options. To unwind the reverse conversion, the firms buys
back the stocks, sells the call, and buys the put. *See also* MARGIN
ACCOUNT; OPTION.

REVERSE LEVERAGE situation, the opposite of FINANCIAL LEVER-
AGE, where the interest on money borrowed exceeds the return on
investment of the borrowed funds.

REVERSE LEVERAGED BUYOUT process of bringing back into
publicly traded status a company—or a division of a company—that
had been publicly traded and taken private. In the 1980s, many public
companies were taken private in LEVERAGED BUYOUTS by corporate
raiders who borrowed against the companies' assets to finance the deal.

When some or all of the debt incurred in the leveraged buyout was repaid, many of these companies were in sufficiently strong financial condition to go public again, enriching the private stockholders as well as the investment bankers who earned fees implementing these deals.

REVERSE MORTGAGE arrangement whereby a homeowner borrows against home equity and receives regular payments (tax-free) from the lender until the accumulated principal and interest reach the credit limit of equity; at that time, the lender either gets repayment in a lump sum or takes the house. Reverse mortgages are available privately and through the Federal Housing Administration (FHA). They are appropriate for cash-poor but house-rich older borrowers who want to stay in their homes and expect to live long enough to amortize high up-front fees but not so long that the lender winds up with the house. Lower income but greater security is provided by a variation, the REVERSE ANNUITY MORTGAGE (RAM).

REVERSE REPURCHASE AGREEMENT *see* REPURCHASE AGREEMENT.

REVERSE SPLIT procedure whereby a corporation reduces the number of shares outstanding. The total number of shares will have the same market value immediately after the reverse split as before it, but each share will be worth more. For example, if a firm with 10 million outstanding shares selling at $10 a share executes a reverse 1 for 10 split, the firm will end up with 1 million shares selling for $100 each. Such splits are usually initiated by companies wanting to raise the price of their outstanding shares because they think the price is too low to attract investors. Also called *split down. See also* SPLIT.

REVISIONARY TRUST IRREVOCABLE TRUST that becomes a REVOCABLE TRUST after a specified period, usually over 10 years or upon the death of the GRANTOR.

REVOCABLE TRUST agreement whereby income-producing property is deeded to heirs. The provisions of such a TRUST may be altered as many times as the GRANTOR pleases, or the entire trust agreement can be canceled, unlike irrevocable trusts. The grantor receives income from the assets, but the property passes directly to the beneficiaries at the grantor's death, without having to go through PROBATE court proceedings. Since the assets are still part of the grantor's estate, however, estate taxes must be paid on this transfer. This kind of trust differs from an IRREVOCABLE TRUST, which permanently transfers assets from the estate during the grantor's lifetime and therefore escapes estate taxes.

REVOLVING CREDIT
Commercial banking: contractual agreement between a bank and its customer, usually a company, whereby the bank agrees to make loans up to a specified maximum for a specified period, usually a year or more. As the borrower repays a portion of the loan, an amount equal to the repayment can be borrowed again under the terms of the agreement. In addition to interest borne by notes, the bank charges a fee for

the commitment to hold the funds available. A COMPENSATING BALANCE may be required in addition.

Consumer banking: loan account requiring monthly payments of less than the full amount due, and the balance carried forward is subject to a financial charge. Also, an arrangement whereby borrowings are permitted up to a specified limit and for a specified period, usually a year, with a fee charged for the commitment. Also called *open-end credit* or *revolving line of credit.*

REVOLVING LINE OF CREDIT *see* REVOLVING CREDIT.

RICH
1. term for a security whose price seems too high in light of its price history. For bonds, the term may also imply that the yield is too low.
2. term for rate of interest that seems too high in relation to the borrower's risk.
3. synonym for *wealthy.*

RICO acronym for *Racketeer Influenced and Corrupt Organization Act,* a federal law used to convict firms and individuals of INSIDER TRADING. Many critics have charged that the law was excessively enforced, and several indictments were dismissed for lack of evidence.

RIDER written form attached to an insurance policy that alters the policy's coverage, terms, or conditions. For example, after buying a diamond bracelet, a policyholder may want to add a rider to her homeowner's insurance policy to cover the jewelry. *See also* FLOATER.

RIEGLE-NEAL INTERSTATE BANKING AND BRANCHING EFFICIENCY ACT OF 1994 law allowing interstate banking in America. The legislation permitted banks to establish branches nationwide by eliminating all barriers to interstate banking at the state level. Before this legislation went into effect, banks had been required to set up separate subsidiaries in each state to conduct business and it was illegal for banks to accept deposits from customers out of their home states.

RIGGED MARKET situation in which the prices for a security are manipulated so as to lure unsuspecting buyers or sellers. *See also* MANIPULATION.

RIGHT *see* SUBSCRIPTION RIGHT.

RIGHT OF FIRST REFUSAL right of someone to be offered a right before it is offered to others. For example, a baseball team may have the right of first refusal on a ballplayer's contract, meaning that the club can make the first offer, or even match other offers, before the player plays for another team. A company may have the right of refusal to distribute or manufacture another company's product. A publishing company may have the right of refusal to publish a book proposed by one of its authors.

RIGHT OF REDEMPTION right to recover property transferred by a MORTGAGE or other LIEN by paying off the debt either before or after foreclosure. Also called *equity of redemption.*

RIGHT OF RESCISSION right granted by the federal CONSUMER CREDIT PROTECTION ACT OF 1968 to void a contract within three business days with full refund of any down payment and without penalty. The right is designed to protect consumers from high-pressure door-to-door sales tactics and hastily made credit commitments which involve their homes as COLLATERAL, such as loans secured by second mortgages.

RIGHT OF SURVIVORSHIP right entitling one owner of property held jointly to take title to it when the other owner dies. *See also* JOINT TENANTS WITH RIGHT OF SURVIVORSHIP; TENANTS IN COMMON.

RIGHTS OFFERING offering of COMMON STOCK to existing shareholders who hold rights that entitle them to buy newly issued shares at a discount from the price at which shares will later be offered to the public. Rights offerings are usually handled by INVESTMENT BANKERS under what is called a STANDBY COMMITMENT, whereby the investment bankers agree to purchase any shares not subscribed to by the holders of rights. *See also* PREEMPTIVE RIGHT; SUBSCRIPTION RIGHT.

RING location on the floor of an exchange where trades are executed. The circular arrangement where traders can make bid and offer prices is also called a *pit,* particularly when commodities are traded.

RISING BOTTOMS technical chart pattern showing a rising trend in the low prices of a security or commodity. As the range of prices is charted daily, the lows reveal an upward trend. Rising bottoms signify higher and higher basic SUPPORT LEVELS for a security or commodity. When combined with a series of ASCENDING TOPS, the pattern is one a follower of TECHNICAL ANALYSIS would call bullish. *See* chart on the next page.

RISK measurable possibility of losing or not gaining value. Risk is differentiated from uncertainty, which is not measurable. Among the commonly encountered types of risk are these:
Actuarial risk: risk an insurance underwriter covers in exchange for premiums, such as the risk of premature death.
Exchange risk: chance of loss on foreign currency exchange.
Inflation risk: chance that the value of assets or of income will be eroded as inflation shrinks the value of a country's currency.
Interest rate risk: possibility that a fixed-rate debt instrument will decline in value as a result of a rise in interest rates.
Inventory risk: possibility that price changes, obsolescence, or other factors will shrink the value of INVENTORY.
Liquidity risk: possibility that an investor will not be able to buy or sell a commodity or security quickly enough or in sufficient quantities because buying or selling opportunities are limited.

RISING BOTTOMS

Political risk: possibility of NATIONALIZATION or other unfavorable government action.

Repayment (credit) risk: chance that a borrower or trade debtor will not repay an obligation as promised.

Risk of principal: chance that invested capital will drop in value.

Underwriting risk: risk taken by an INVESTMENT BANKER that a new issue of securities purchased outright will not be bought by the public and/or that the market price will drop during the offering period.

RISK-ADJUSTED DISCOUNT RATE in PORTFOLIO THEORY and CAPITAL BUDGET analysis, the rate necessary to determine the PRESENT VALUE of an uncertain or risky stream of income; it is the risk-free rate (generally the return on short-term U.S. Treasury securities) plus a risk premium that is based on an analysis of the risk characteristics of the particular investment or project.

RISK ARBITRAGE ARBITRAGE involving risk, as in the simultaneous purchase of stock in a company being acquired and sale of stock in its proposed acquirer. Also called *takeover arbitrage*. Traders called *arbitrageurs* attempt to profit from TAKEOVERS by cashing in on the expected rise in the price of the target company's shares and drop in the price of the acquirer's shares. If the takeover plans fall through, the traders may be left with enormous losses. Risk arbitrage differs from riskless arbitrage, which entails locking in or profiting from the differences in the prices of two securities or commodities trading on different exchanges. *See also* RISKLESS TRANSACTION.

RISK AVERSE term referring to the assumption that, given the same return and different risk alternatives, a rational investor will seek the security offering the least risk—or, put another way, the higher the degree of risk, the greater the return that a rational investor will demand. *See also* CAPITAL ASSET PRICING MODEL; EFFICIENT PORTFOLIO; MEAN RETURN; PORTFOLIO THEORY.

RISK-BASED CAPITAL RATIO FIRREA-imposed requirement that banks maintain a minimum ratio of estimated total capital to estimated risk-weighted assets.

RISK CAPITAL *see* VENTURE CAPITAL.

RISK CATEGORY classification of risk elements used in analyzing MORTGAGES.

RISK-FREE RETURN YIELD on a risk-free investment. The 3-month Treasury bill is considered a riskless investment because it is a direct obligation of the U.S. government and its term is short enough to minimize the risks of inflation and market interest rate changes. The CAPITAL ASSET PRICING MODEL (CAPM) used in modern PORTFOLIO THEORY has the premise that the return on a security is equal to the risk-free return plus a RISK PREMIUM.

RISKLESS TRANSACTION
1. trade guaranteeing a profit to the trader that initiates it. An *arbitrageur* may lock in a profit by trading on the difference in prices for the same security or commodity in different markets. For instance, if gold were selling for $400 an ounce in New York and $398 in London, a trader who acts quickly could buy a contract in London and sell it in New York for a riskless profit.
2. concept used in evaluating whether dealer MARKUPS and MARKDOWNS in OVER THE COUNTER transactions with customers are reasonable or excessive. In what is known as the FIVE PERCENT RULE, the NATIONAL ASSOCIATION OF SECURITIES DEALERS (NASD) takes the position that markups (when the customer buys) and markdowns (when the customer sells) should not exceed 5%, the proper charge depending on the effort and risk of the dealer in completing a trade. The maximum would be considered excessive for a riskless transaction, in which a security has high marketability and the dealer does not simply act as a broker and take a commission but trades from or for inventory and charges a markup or markdown. Where a dealer satisfies a buy order by making a purchase in the open market for inventory, then sells the security to the customer, the trade is called a *simultaneous transaction*. To avoid NASD criticism, broker-dealers commonly disclose the markups and markdowns to customers in transactions where they act as dealers.

RISK PREMIUM in PORTFOLIO THEORY, the difference between the RISK-FREE RETURN and the TOTAL RETURN from a risky investment. In the CAPITAL ASSET PRICING MODEL (CAPM), the risk premium reflects market-related risk (SYSTEMATIC RISK) as measured by BETA. Other models also reflect specific risk as measured by ALPHA.

RISK-RETURN TRADE-OFF concept, basic in investment management, that RISK equals (varies with) RETURN; in other words, the higher the return the greater the risk and vice versa. In practice, it means that a speculative investment, such as stock in a newly formed company, can be expected to provide a higher potential return than a more conservative investment, such as BLUE CHIP or a BOND. Conversely, if you don't want the risk, don't expect the return. *See also* PORTFOLIO THEORY.

RISK TRANSFER shifting of risk, as with INSURANCE or the SECURITIZATION of debt.

ROAD SHOW presentation by an issuer of securities to potential buyers about the merits of the issue. Management of the company issuing stocks or bonds doing a road show travels around the country presenting financial information and an outlook for the company and answering the questions of analysts, fund managers, and other potential investors. Also known as a *dog and pony show.*

ROCKET SCIENTIST investment firm creator of innovative securities.

ROLL DOWN move from one OPTION position to another one having a lower EXERCISE PRICE. The term assumes that the position with the higher exercise price is closed out.

ROLL FORWARD move from one OPTION position to another with a later expiration date. The term assumes that the earlier position is closed out before the later one is established. If the new position involves a higher EXERCISE PRICE, it is called a *roll-up and forward;* if a lower exercise price, it is called a *roll-down and forward.* Also called *rolling over.*

ROLLING STOCK equipment that moves on wheels, used in the transportation industry. Examples include railroad cars and locomotives, tractor-trailers, and trucks.

ROLLOVER

    1. movement of funds from one investment to another. For instance, an INDIVIDUAL RETIREMENT ACCOUNT may be rolled over when a person retires into an ANNUITY or other form of pension plan payout system. Balances in regular IRAs can be rolled over into ROTH IRAs, although income taxes will be due on untaxed earnings in the regular IRA account. When a BOND or CERTIFICATE OF DEPOSIT matures, the funds may be rolled over into another bond or certificate of deposit. A stock may be sold and the proceeds rolled over into the same stock, establishing a different cost basis for the shareholder. *See also* THIRTY DAY WASH RULE.

2. term often used by banks when they allow a borrower to delay making a PRINCIPAL payment on a loan. Also, a country that has difficulty in meeting its debt payments may be granted a rollover by its creditors. With governments themselves, rollovers in the form of REFUNDINGS or REFINANCINGS are routine.

See also CERTIFICATE OF DEPOSIT ROLLOVER.

ROLL UP move from one OPTION position to another having a higher EXERCISE PRICE. The term assumes that the earlier position is closed out before the new position is established. *See also* MASTER LIMITED PARTNERSHIP.

ROTH IRA INDIVIDUAL RETIREMENT ACCOUNT created by the TAXPAYER RELIEF ACT OF 1997 permitting account holders to allow their capital to accumulate tax free under certain conditions. The Roth IRA is named after Delaware Senator William V. Roth Jr., who championed the idea of expanded IRAs. Individuals can invest up to $2,000 per year, and they can withdraw the principal and earnings totally tax free after age 59½, as long as the assets have remained in the IRA for at least 5 years after making the first contribution. If the account holder dies before they start withdrawing from a Roth, the proceeds go to their beneficiaries tax free. Unlike regular IRAs, participants do not have to take any distributions from a Roth IRA starting at age 70½, nor do they have to take any distributions at all during their lifetime. They can also continue to contribute after reaching age 70½.

Participants in Roth IRAs do not receive deductions for contributing to the account. However, the value of completely tax free withdrawals usually outweighs the tax break from upfront deductions. The Roth IRA also permits participants to withdraw assets without the usual 10% early withdrawal penalty if the proceeds are used to purchase a first home (withdrawals are limited to $10,000), for college expenses, or if the participant becomes disabled.

There are income limitations governing who can open Roth IRAs. Married couples with an adjusted gross income of $150,000 or less or singles with adjusted gross incomes of $95,000 or less can contribute the full $2,000. Contribution amounts are phased out for incomes between $150,000 and $160,000 for couples filing jointly and between $95,000 and $110,000 for singles. Those with income over these limits can not contribute to a Roth IRA.

Individuals with adjusted gross income of $100,000 or less can roll over existing and deductible IRA balances into a Roth without the usual 10% early distribution penalty, although regular income taxes are due on untaxed earnings in the account. For such ROLLOVERS completed before January 1, 1999, the resulting tax bill is spread over four years. After that, the rollover is fully taxable in the year it is completed. Figuring out whether or not it is advantageous to roll over assets from a regular IRA to a Roth IRA is a complex decision, and may require advice from a financial professional. *See* ROLLOVER.

ROUND LOT generally accepted unit of trading on a securities exchange. On the New York Stock Exchange, for example, a round lot is 100 shares for stock and $1000 or $5000 par value for bonds. In inactive stocks, the round lot is 10 shares. Increasingly, there seems to be recognition of a 500-share round lot for trading by institutions. Large denomination CERTIFICATES OF DEPOSIT trade on the OVER THE COUNTER market in units of $1 million. Investors who trade in round lots do not have to pay the DIFFERENTIAL charged on ODD LOT trades.

ROUND TRIP TRADE purchase and sale of a security or commodity within a short time. For example, a trader who continually is making short-term trades in a particular commodity is making round trip or *round turn* trades. Commissions for such a trader are likely to be quoted in terms of the total for a purchase and sale—$100 for the round trip, for instance. Excessive round trip trading is called CHURNING.

ROYALTY payment to the holder for the right to use property such as a patent, copyrighted material, or natural resources. For instance, inventors may be paid royalties when their inventions are produced and marketed. Authors may get royalties when books they have written are sold. Land owners leasing their property to an oil or mining company may receive royalties based on the amount of oil or minerals extracted from their land. Royalties are set in advance as a percentage of income arising from the commercialization of the owner's rights or property.

ROYALTY TRUST oil or gas company *spin-off* of oil reserves to a trust, which avoids DOUBLE TAXATION, eliminates the expense and risk of new drilling, and provides DEPLETION tax benefits to shareholders. In the mid-1980s, Mesa Royalty Trust, which pioneered the idea, led other trusts in converting to a MASTER LIMITED PARTNERSHIP form of organization, offering tax advantages along with greater flexibility and liquidity.

RUBBER CHECK check for which insufficient funds are available. It is called a rubber check because it bounces. *See also* OVERDRAFT.

RULE 405 New York Stock Exchange codification of an ethical concept recognized industry wide by those dealing with the investment public. These KNOW YOUR CUSTOMER rules recognize that what is suitable for one investor may be less appropriate for another and require investment people to obtain pertinent facts about a customer's other security holdings, financial condition, and objectives. *See also* SUITABILITY RULES.

RULE OF 72 formula for approximating the time it will take for a given amount of money to double at a given COMPOUND INTEREST rate. The formula is simply 72 divided by the interest rate. In six years $100 will double at a compound annual rate of 12%, thus: 72 divided by 12 equals 6.

RULE OF THE 78s method of computing REBATES of interest on installment loans. It uses the SUM-OF-THE-YEAR'S-DIGITS basis in determining the interest earned by the FINANCE COMPANY for each month of a year, assuming equal monthly payments, and gets its name from the fact that the sum of the digits 1 through 12 is 78. Thus interest is equal to $\frac{12}{78}$ths of the total annual interest in the first month, $\frac{11}{78}$ths in the second month, and so on.

RULE 144 *see* INVESTMENT LETTER; SECURITIES AND EXCHANGE COMMISSION RULES.

RULES OF FAIR PRACTICE set of rules established by the Board of Governors of the NATIONAL ASSOCIATION OF SECURITIES DEALERS (NASD), a self-regulatory organization comprising investment banking houses and firms dealing in the OVER THE COUNTER securities market. As summarized in the NASD bylaws, the rules are designed to foster just and equitable principles of trade and business; high standards of commercial honor and integrity among members; the prevention of fraud and manipulative practices; safeguards against unreasonable profits, commissions, and other charges; and collaboration with governmental and other agencies to protect investors and the public interest in accordance with Section 15A of the MALONEY ACT. *See also* FIVE PERCENT RULE; IMMEDIATE FAMILY; KNOW YOUR CUSTOMER; MARKDOWN; RISKLESS TRANSACTION.

RUMORTRAGE stock traders' term, combining rumor and ARBITRAGE, for buying and selling based on rumor of a TAKEOVER. *See also* DEAL STOCK; GARBATRAGE.

RUN
Banking: demand for their money by many depositors all at once. If large enough, a run on a bank can cause it to fail, as hundreds of banks did in the Great Depression of the 1930s. Such a run is caused by a breach of confidence in the bank, perhaps as a result of large loan losses or fraud.
Securities:
1. list of available securities, along with current bid and asked prices, which a market maker is currently trading. For bonds the run may include the par value as well as current quotes.
2. when a security's price rises quickly, analysts say it had a quick run up, possibly because of a positive earnings report.

RUNDOWN
In general: status report or summary.
Municipal bonds: summary of the amounts available and the prices on units in a SERIAL BOND that has not yet been completely sold to the public.

RUNNING AHEAD illegal practice of buying or selling a security for a broker's personal account before placing a similar order for a customer, also called FRONT RUNNING. For example, when a firm's analyst issues a positive report on a company, the firm's brokers may not buy the stock for their own accounts before they have told their clients the news. Some firms prohibit brokers from making such trades for a specific period, such as two full days from the time of the recommendation.

RUNOFF printing of an exchange's closing prices on a TICKER tape after the market has closed. The runoff may take a long time when trading has been very heavy and the tape has fallen far behind the action.

RUSSELL INDICES MARKET-CAPITALIZATION weighted U.S. equity indices published by Frank Russell Company of Tacoma, Washington. The Russell Indices are widely quoted on TV, radio and in newspapers, and are often used as benchmarks for institutional investors of mutual and pension funds. The *Russell 3000 Index*® measures the performance of the 3,000 largest U.S. companies based on market capitalization, which represents about 98% of the U.S. equity market. The stocks in the index have a market capitalization range of approximately $170 million to $200 billion, with an average of $2.8 billion. The *Russell 1000 Index*® represents the highest-ranking 1,000 stocks in the Russell 3000 Index, which represents about 90% of the total market capitalization of that index. The Russell 1000 Index has an average market capitalization of $7.6 billion; the median market capitalization is approximately $3 billion. The smallest company in the index has an average market capitalization of $1.1 billion. The *Russell 2000 Index*® consists of the 2,000 smallest companies in the Russell 3000 Index, about 10% of its total market capitalization. The average capitalization is approximately $467 million; the median market capitalization is $395 million. The largest company in the index has an approximate market capitalization of $1 billion. The Russell 2000 is a popular measure of the stock price performance of small companies.

The *Russell Top 200 Index*® measures the performance of the 200 largest companies (65% of total market capitalization) in the Russell 1000, with average market capitalization of $26.4 billion. The median capitalization is approximately $15.5 billion; the smallest company in the index has an average capitalization of $8.1 billion. The *Russell Midcap Index*® measures performance of the 800 smallest companies (35% of total capitalization) in the Russell 1000, with average market capitalization of approximately $2.9 billion, median capitalization of $15.5 billion and market capitalization of the largest company approximately $8 billion. The *Russell 2500 Index*® measures the performance of the 2,500 smallest companies in the Russell 3000 Index, or about 23% of its total capitalization. Average capitalization is approximately $733 million and median capitalization is $500 million. The largest company in the index is $2.9 billion.

Growth indices measure performance of the respective companies with higher PRICE/BOOK RATIOS and higher forecasted growth values. Value indices measure the performance of those companies with lower price/book ratios and lower forecasted growth values. *See also* STOCK INDICES AND AVERAGES.

RUSSIAN TRADING SYSTEM (RTS) electronic system operating in Russia since 1995, designed to emulate the NASDAQ system, on which the majority of Russian equities trading is conducted. The Russian securities market is principally an over-the-counter market in an informal dealer-to-dealer system. It is diverse: there are more than 60 officially registered stock and commodity exchanges. The Central Stock Exchange in Moscow and the St. Petersburg Stock Exchange specialize in securities trading.

RUST BELT geographical area of the United States, mainly in Pennsylvania, West Virginia, and the industrial Midwest, where iron and steel is produced and where there is a concentration of industries that manufacture products using iron and steel. Term is used broadly to mean traditional American manufacturing with its largely unmodernized plants and facilities.

S

SAFE HARBOR

1. financial or accounting step that avoids legal or tax consequences. Commonly used in reference to *safe harbor leasing,* as permitted by the ECONOMIC RECOVERY TAX ACT OF 1981 (ERTA). An unprofitable company unable to use the INVESTMENT CREDIT and ACCELERATED COST RECOVERY SYSTEM (ACRS) liberalized depreciation rules, could transfer those benefits to a profitable firm seeking to reduce its tax burden. Under such an arrangement, the profitable company would own an asset the unprofitable company would otherwise have purchased itself; the profitable company would then lease the asset to the unprofitable company, presumably passing on a portion of the tax benefits in the form of lower lease rental charges. Safe harbor leases were curtailed by provisions in the TAX EQUITY AND FISCAL RESPONSI-BILITY ACT OF 1982 (TEFRA).

2. provision in a law that excuses liability if the attempt to comply in good faith can be demonstrated. For example, safe harbor provisions would protect management from liability under Securities and Exchange Commission rules for financial PROJECTIONS made in good faith.

3. form of SHARK REPELLENT whereby a TARGET COMPANY acquires a business so onerously regulated it makes the target less attractive, giving it, in effect, a safe harbor.

SAFEKEEPING storage and protection of a customer's financial assets, valuables, or documents, provided as a service by an institution serving as AGENT and, where control is delegated by the customer, also as custodian. An individual, corporate, or institutional investor might rely on a bank or a brokerage firm to hold stock certificates or bonds, keep track of trades, and provide periodic statements of changes in position. Investors who provide for their own safekeeping usually use a *safe deposit box,* provided by financial institutions for a fee. *See also* SELL-ING SHORT AGAINST THE BOX; STREET NAME.

SAIF *see* SAVINGS ASSOCIATION INSURANCE FUND (SAIF).

SALARY regular wages received by an employee from an employer on a weekly, biweekly, or monthly basis. Many salaries also include such employee benefits as health and life insurance, savings plans, and Social Security. Salary income is taxable by the federal, state, and local government, where applicable, through payroll withholding.

SALARY FREEZE cessation of increases in salary throughout a company for a period of time. Companies going through a business downturn will freeze salaries in order to reduce expenses. When business improves, salary increases are frequently reinstated.

SALARY REDUCTION PLAN plan allowing employees to contribute pretax compensation to a qualified TAX DEFERRED retirement plan. Until the TAX REFORM ACT OF 1986, the term was synonymous with 401(k) PLAN, but the 1986 Act prohibited employees of state and local governments and tax-exempt organizations from establishing new 401(k) plans and added restrictions to existing government and tax-exempt unfunded deferred compensation arrangements and tax-sheltered annuity arrangements creating, in effect, a broadened definition of salary reduction plan. Current law permits employees of tax-exempt religious, charitable, or educational organizations and public schools to take nontaxable reductions to a limit of 20% of salary multiplied by years of service less tax-free contributions made in prior years by the employer to a tax-sheltered annuity or qualified plan. The reduction, however, may not exceed the lower of 25% of salary or $9500, except that employees with at least 15 years of service may defer up to $12,500. Such contributions purchase a nonforfeitable tax-sheltered annuity.

Federal government employees are allowed salary deductions up to the limits for 401(k) plans. State and local governments and tax-exempt organizations other than churches may set up *Section 457* plans allowing employees to defer annually the lesser of $7500 or one-third of compensation.

Irrevocable alternative or "catch-up" formulae are also available with limitations.

SALE
In general: any exchange of goods or services for money. *Contrast with* BARTER.
Finance: income received in exchange for goods and services recorded for a given accounting period, either on a cash basis (as received) or on an accrual basis (as earned). *See also* GROSS SALES.
Securities: in securities trading, a sale is executed when a buyer and a seller have agreed on a price for the security.

SALE AND LEASEBACK form of LEASE arrangement in which a company sells an asset to another party—usually an insurance or finance company, a leasing company, a limited partnership, or an institutional investor—in exchange for cash, then contracts to lease the asset for a specified term. Typically, the asset is sold for its MARKET VALUE, so the lessee has really acquired capital that would otherwise have been tied up in a long-term asset. Such arrangements frequently have tax benefits for the lessee, although there is normally little difference in the effect on income between the lease payments and the interest payments that would have existed had the asset been purchased with borrowed money. A company generally opts for the sale and leaseback arrangement as an alternative to straight financing when the rate it would have to pay a lender is higher than the cost of rental or when it wishes to show less debt on its BALANCE SHEET (called *off-balance-sheet financing*). *See also* CAPITAL LEASE.

SALES CHARGE fee paid to a brokerage house by a buyer of shares in a load MUTUAL FUND or a LIMITED PARTNERSHIP. Normally, the sales charge for a mutual fund starts at 4.5% to 5% of the capital invested and decreases as the size of the investment increases. The sales charge for a limited partnership can be even higher—as much as 10%. In return for the sales charge, investors are entitled to investment advice from the broker on which fund or partnership is best for them. A fund that carries no sales charge is called a NO-LOAD FUND. *See also* BACK-END LOAD; FRONT-END LOAD; LETTER OF INTENT; LOAD FUND; REDEMPTION FEES; 12B-1 MUTUAL FUND.

SALES LITERATURE
In general: written material designed to help sell a product or a service.
Investments: written material issued by a securities brokerage firm, mutual fund, underwriter, or other institution selling a product that explains the advantages of the investment product. Such literature must be truthful and must comply with disclosure regulations issued by the Securities and Exchange Commission and state securities agencies.

SALES LOAD *see* SALES CHARGE.

SALES TAX tax based on a percentage of the selling price of goods and services. State and local governments assess sales tax and decide what percentage to charge. The retail buyer pays the sales tax to the retailer, who passes it on to the sales tax collection agency of the government. For an item costing $1000 in a state with a 5% sales tax, the buyer pays $50 in sales tax, for a total of $1050. Sales taxes are not deductible on federal or state income tax returns.

SALLIE MAE *see* STUDENT LOAN MARKETING ASSOCIATION.

SALOMON BROTHERS WORLD EQUITY INDEX (SBWEI) a comprehensive top-down, float capitalization-weighted index that includes shares of approximately 6000 companies in 22 countries. It is one member of a family of Salomon Smith Barney performance indexes that measure domestic and international fixed income and equity markets. The index includes all companies with available market capitalization greater than $100 million. Each issue is weighted by the proportion of its available equity capital, its float, rather than by its total equity capital. The index is the successor to the Salomon-Russell Global Equity Index. Other SBWEI equity products include GDP and weighted indexes, and emerging market indexes.

SALVAGE VALUE *see* RESIDUAL VALUE.

SAME-DAY FUNDS SETTLEMENT (SDFS) method of settlement in good-the-same-day FEDERAL FUNDS used by the DEPOSITORY TRUST COMPANY for transactions in U.S. government securities, short-term municipal notes, medium-term commercial paper notes, COLLATERAL-IZED MORTGAGE OBLIGATIONS (CMOs), DUTCH AUCTION PREFERRED STOCK, and other instruments when both parties to the trade are properly collateralized.

SAME-DAY SUBSTITUTION offsetting changes in a MARGIN ACCOUNT in the course of one day, resulting in neither a MARGIN CALL nor a credit to the SPECIAL MISCELLANEOUS ACCOUNT. Examples: a purchase and a sale of equal value; a decline in the MARKET VALUE of some margin securities offset by an equal rise in the market value of others.

SAMURAI BONDS bonds denominated in yen issued by non-Japanese companies for sale mostly in Japan. The bonds are not subject to Japanese withholding taxes, and therefore offer advantages to Japanese buyers.

SANDWICH GENERATION middle-aged working people who feel squeezed by the financial pressures of supporting their aging parents, the costs of raising and educating their children, and the need to save for their own retirement.

SANTA CLAUS RALLY rise in stock prices in the week between Christmas and New Year's Day. Also called the *year-end rally*. Some analysts attribute this rally to the anticipation of the JANUARY EFFECT, when stock prices rise in the first few days of the year as pension funds add new money to their accounts.

SAO PAULO STOCK EXCHANGE *see* BOLSA DE VALORES DE SAO PAULO (BOVESPA).

S&P PHENOMENON tendency of stocks newly added to the STANDARD & POOR'S COMPOSITE INDEX to rise temporarily in price as S&P-related INDEX FUNDS adjust their portfolios, creating heavy buying activity.

SATURDAY NIGHT SPECIAL sudden attempt by one company to take over another by making a public TENDER OFFER. The term was coined in the 1960s after a rash of such surprise maneuvers, which were often announced over weekends. The WILLIAMS ACT of 1968 placed severe restrictions on tender offers and required disclosure of direct or indirect ownership of 5% or more of any class of EQUITY. It thus marked the end of what, in its traditional form, was known as the "creeping tender."

SAUCER technical chart pattern (see next page) signaling that the price of a security or a commodity has formed a bottom and is moving up. An inverse saucer shows a top in the security's price and signals a downturn. *See also* TECHNICAL ANALYSIS.

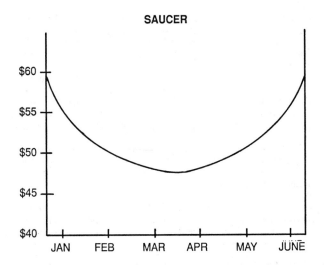

SAUCER

SAVING RATE ratio of personal saving to disposable personal income. Disposable personal income is personal income less personal tax and nontax payments. Personal saving is disposable personal income less personal outlays. The U.S. Commerce Department's Bureau of Economic Analysis and the Federal Reserve each publish estimates of the saving rate on a quarterly basis.

SAVINGS ACCOUNT deposit account at a commercial bank, savings bank, or savings and loan that pays interest, usually from a day-of-deposit to day-of-withdrawal basis. Financial institutions can pay whatever rate they like on savings accounts, but this rate tends to be in relation to the actions of the money center banks in repricing their PRIME RATE. Traditionally, savings accounts offered PASSBOOKS, but in recent years alternatives such as ATMs, monthly account statements and telephone banking services have been added to credit deposits and interest earned. Savings deposits are insured up to $100,000 per account if they are on deposit at banks insured by the FEDERAL DEPOSIT INSURANCE CORPORATION (FDIC) or a savings and loan insured by the SAVINGS ASSOCIATION INSURANCE FUND (SAIF).

SAVINGS AND LOAN ASSOCIATION depository financial institution, federally or state chartered, that obtains the bulk of its deposits from consumers and holds the majority of its assets as home mortgage loans. A few such specialized institutions were organized in the 19th century under state charters but with minimal regulation. Reacting to the crisis in the banking and home building industries precipitated by the Great

Depression, Congress in 1932 passed the Federal Home Loan Bank Act, establishing the FEDERAL HOME LOAN BANK SYSTEM to supplement the lending resources of state-chartered savings and loans (S&Ls). The Home Owners' Loan Act of 1933 created a system for the federal chartering of S&Ls under the supervision of the Federal Home Loan Bank Board. Deposits in federal S&Ls were insured with the formation of the Federal Savings and Loan Insurance Corporation in 1934.

A second wave of restructuring occurred in the 1980s. The DEPOSITORY INSTITUTIONS DEREGULATION AND MONETARY CONTROL ACT OF 1980 set a six-year timetable for the removal of interest rate ceilings, including the S&Ls' quarter-point rate advantage over the commercial bank limit on personal savings accounts. The act also allowed S&Ls limited entry into some markets previously open only to commercial banks (commercial lending, nonmortgage consumer lending, trust services) and, in addition, permitted MUTUAL ASSOCIATIONS to issue INVESTMENT CERTIFICATES. In actual effect, interest rate parity was achieved by the end of 1982.

The Garn-St Germain Depository Institutions Act of 1982 accelerated the pace of deregulation and gave the Federal Home Loan Bank Board wide latitude in shoring up the capital positions of S&Ls weakened by the impact of record-high interest rates on portfolios of old, fixed-rate mortgage loans. The 1982 act also encouraged the formation of stock savings and loans or the conversion of existing mutual (depositor-owned) associations to the stock form, which gave the associations another way to tap the capital markets and thereby to bolster their net worth.

In 1989, responding to a massive wave of insolvencies caused by mismanagement, corruption, and economic factors, Congress passed the FINANCIAL INSTITUTIONS REFORM, RECOVERY AND ENFORCEMENT ACT OF 1989 (FIRREA) that revamped the regulatory structure of the industry under a newly created agency, the OFFICE OF THRIFT SUPERVISION (OTS). Disbanding the FEDERAL SAVINGS AND LOAN INSURANCE CORPORATION (FSLIC), it created the SAVINGS ASSOCIATION INSURANCE FUND (SAIF) to provide deposit insurance under the administration of the FEDERAL DEPOSIT INSURANCE CORPORATION (FDIC). It also created the RESOLUTION TRUST CORPORATION (RTC) and RESOLUTION FUNDING CORPORATION (REFCORP) to deal with insolvent institutions and scheduled the consolidation of their activities with SAIF after 1996. The Federal Home Loan Bank Board was replaced by the FEDERAL HOUSING FINANCE BOARD (FHFB), which now oversees the Federal Home Loan Bank System. *See also* SAVINGS BANK.

SAVINGS ASSOCIATION INSURANCE FUND (SAIF) U.S. government entity created by Congress in 1989 as part of its SAVINGS AND LOAN ASSOCIATION bailout bill to replace the FEDERAL SAVINGS AND LOAN INSURANCE CORPORATION (FSLIC) as the provider of deposit insurance for thrift institutions. SAIF, pronounced to rhyme with *safe,* is administered by the FEDERAL DEPOSIT INSURANCE CORPORATION (FDIC) separately from its bank insurance program, which was renamed *Bank Insurance Fund (BIF)*. The new organization provides the same protection ($100,000 per depositor) as FSLIC. At the end of 1996, SAIF assumed responsibility for insolvent institutions from RESOLUTION TRUST CORPORATION (RTC). *See also* OFFICE OF THRIFT SUPERVISION (OTS).

SAVINGS BANK depository financial institution that primarily accepts consumer deposits and makes home mortgage loans. Historically, savings banks were of the mutual (depositor-owned) form and chartered in only 16 states; the majority of savings banks were located in the New England states, New York, and New Jersey. Prior to the passage of the Garn-St Germain Depository Institutions Act of 1982, state-chartered savings bank deposits were insured along with commercial bank deposits by the FEDERAL DEPOSIT INSURANCE CORPORATION (FDIC). The Garn-St Germain Act gave savings banks the options of a federal charter, mutual-to-stock conversion, supervision by the Federal Home Loan Bank Board, and insurance from the FEDERAL SAVINGS AND LOAN INSURANCE CORPORATION (FSLIC). In 1989, the Federal Home Loan Bank Board was replaced by the FEDERAL HOUSING FINANCE BOARD (FHFB), and the FSLIC by the newly created SAVINGS ASSOCIATION INSURANCE FUND (SAIF), a unit of the FDIC. *See also* MUTUAL SAVINGS BANK; SAVINGS AND LOAN ASSOCIATION.

SAVINGS BOND U.S. government bond issued in FACE VALUE denominations ranging from $50 to $10,000. From 1941 to 1979, the government issued SERIES E BONDS. Starting in 1980, Series EE and HH bonds were issued. Series EE bonds, issued at a discount of half their face value, range from $50 to $10,000; interest bearing Series HH bonds range from $500 to $10,000. Series EE bonds earn interest for 30 years; Series HH bonds earn interest for 20 years. Series EE bonds, if held for five years, pay 90% of the average yield on 5-year Treasury securities based on the previous six months. Series HH bonds, available only through an exchange of at least $500 in Series E or EE bonds, pay a fixed 4% rate in two semiannual payments. For many years, the government guaranteed a minimum yield on savings bonds. This yield decreased from 7.5% to 6% and then 4%. The guaranteed minimum feature was dropped in May 1995, and bonds issued on May 1, 1997 or later and held for less than five years are now subject to a 3-month interest penalty. For example, a bond cashed in after 18 months would receive 15 months' worth of interest. Savings bond yields are readjusted every six months, on May 1 and November 1.

The interest from savings bonds is exempt from state and local taxes, and no federal tax on EE bonds is due until redemption. Bondholders wanting to defer the tax liability on their maturing Series EE bonds can exchange them for Series HH bonds. Taxpayers meeting income qualifications can buy EE bonds to save for higher educational expenses and enjoy total or partial federal tax exemption. This applies to individuals with modified ADJUSTED GROSS INCOMES between $50,850 and $65,850 and married couples filing jointly with incomes

between $76,250 and $106,250. Income levels are adjusted for infla
tion annually. *See also* I-BONDS.

SAVINGS DEPOSITS interest-earning cash balances that can be withdrawn on demand, kept for the purpose of savings, in commercial
banks, savings banks, credit unions, and savings and loans. Passbook
savings, statement savings, and money market accounts are examples
of savings deposits.

SAVINGS ELEMENT cash value accumulated inside a life insurance
policy. A cash value policy has two components: a death benefit paid to
beneficiaries if the insured dies, and a savings element, which is the
amount of premium paid in excess of the cost of protection. This excess
is invested by the insurance company in stocks, bonds, real estate, and
other ventures and the returns build up tax-deferred inside the policy. A
policyholder can borrow against this cash value or take it out of the policy, at which point it becomes taxable income. Once a policyholder
reaches retirement age, he or she can ANNUITIZE the accumulated cash
value and receive a regular payment from the insurance company for
life. Insurance companies encourage people to buy policies with a sav
ings element because it provides a disciplined way to save.

SCALE
Labor: wage rate for specific types of employees. For example:
"Union scale for carpenters is $15.60 per hour."
Production economics: amount of production, as in "economy or dis-
economy of scale." *See also* MARGINAL COST.
Serial bonds: vital data for each of the scheduled maturities in a new
SERIAL BOND issue, including the number of bonds, the date they
mature, the COUPON rate, and the offering price.
    See also SCALE ORDER.

SCALE ORDER order for a specified number of shares that is to be executed in stages in order to average the price. Such an order might provide for the purchase of a total of 5000 shares to be executed in lots of
500 shares at each quarter-point interval as the market declines. Since
scale orders are clerically cumbersome, not all brokers will accept them.

SCALPER
In general: speculator who enters into quasi-legal or illegal transactions to turn a quick and sometimes unreasonable profit. For example,
a scalper buys tickets at regular prices for a major event and when the
event becomes a sellout, resells the tickets at the highest price possible.
Securities:
1. investment adviser who takes a position in a security before recommending it, then sells out after the price has risen as a result of the
recommendation. *See also* INVESTMENT ADVISERS ACT.
2. market maker who, in violation of the RULES OF FAIR PRACTICE of
the NATIONAL ASSOCIATION OF SECURITIES DEALERS, adds an excessive markup or takes an excessive MARKDOWN on a transaction. *See
also* FIVE PERCENT RULE.

    3. commodity trader who trades for small gains, usually establishing and liquidating a position within one day.

SCHEDULE C common reference to a section of the bylaws of the NATIONAL ASSOCIATION OF SECURITIES DEALERS (NASD) concerned with membership requirements and procedures.

SCHEDULE 13D form required under Section 13d of the SECURITIES ACT OF 1934 within ten business days of acquiring direct or BENEFICIAL OWNERSHIP of 5% or more of any class of equity securities in a PUBLICLY HELD corporation. In addition to filing with the Securities and Exchange Commission, the purchaser of such stock must also file the 13d with the stock exchange on which the shares are listed (if any) and with the company itself. Required information includes the way the shares were acquired, the purchaser's background, and future plans regarding the target company. The law is designed to protect against insidious TAKEOVER attempts and to keep the investing public aware of information that could affect the price of their stock. *See also* WILLIAMS ACT

SCORCHED-EARTH POLICY technique used by a company that has become the target of a TAKEOVER attempt to make itself unattractive to the acquirer. For example, it may agree to sell off the most attractive parts of its business, called the CROWN JEWELS, or it may schedule all debt to become due immediately after a MERGER. *See also* JONESTOWN DEFENSE; POISON PILL; SHARK REPELLENT.

SCORE acronym for *Special Claim on Residual Equity,* a certificate issued by the Americus Shareowner Service Corporation, a privately held company formed to market the product. A SCORE gave its holder the right to all the appreciation on an underlying security above a specified price, but none of the dividend income from the security. Its counterpart, called PRIME, passed all dividend income to its holders, who got the benefit of price appreciation up to the limit where SCORE began. PRIME and SCORE together formed a unit share investment trust (USIT), and both were listed on the American Stock Exchange. A buyer of a SCORE unit hoped that the underlying stock would rise steeply in value.

    The first USIT was formed with the shares of American Telephone and Telegraph. PRIME holders got all dividends and price appreciation in AT&T up to $75 a share; SCORE holders received all appreciation above $75. The trusts expired in 1988.

S CORPORATION *see* SUBCHAPTER S.

SCREEN (STOCKS) to look for stocks that meet certain predetermined investment and financial criteria. Often, stocks are screened using a computer and a data base containing financial statistics on thousands of companies. For instance, an investor may want to screen for all those companies that have a PRICE/EARNINGS RATIO of less than 10, an earnings growth rate of more than 15%, and a dividend yield of more than 4%.

SCRIP

In general: receipt, certificate, or other representation of value recognized by both payer and payee. Scrip is not currency, but may be convertible into currency.

Securities: temporary document that is issued by a corporation and that represents a fractional share of stock resulting from a SPLIT, exchange of stock, or SPIN-OFF. Scrip certificates may be aggregated or applied toward the purchase of full shares. Scrip dividends have historically been paid in lieu of cash dividends by companies short of cash.

SCRIPOPHILY practice of collecting stock and bond certificates for their scarcity value, rather than for their worth as securities. The certificate's price rises with the beauty of the illustration on it and the importance of the issuer in world finance and economic development. Many old certificates, such as those issued by railroads in the 19th century or by Standard Oil before it was broken up in the early 20th century, have risen greatly in value since their issue, even though the issuing companies no longer exist.

SDR *see* SPECIAL DRAWING RIGHTS.

SEASONALITY variations in business or economic activity that recur with regularity as the result of changes in climate, holidays, and vacations. The retail toy business, with its steep sales buildup between Thanksgiving and Christmas and pronounced dropoff thereafter, is an example of seasonality in a dramatic form, though nearly all businesses have some degree of seasonal variation. It is often necessary to make allowances for seasonality when interpreting or projecting financial or economic data, a process economists call *seasonal adjustment.*

SEASONED securities that have been trading in the secondary market for a lengthy period of time, and have established a track record of significant trading volume and price stability. Many investors prefer buying only seasoned issues instead of new securities that have not stood the test of time.

SEASONED ISSUE securities (usually from established companies) that have gained a reputation for quality with the investing public and enjoy LIQUIDITY in the SECONDARY MARKET.

SEAT figurative term for a membership on a securities or commodities exchange. Seats are bought and sold at prices set by supply and demand. A seat on the New York Stock Exchange, for example, traded for between $1 million and $2 million in the bull market of the late 1990s. *See also* ABC AGREEMENT; MEMBER FIRM.

SEC *see* SECURITIES AND EXCHANGE COMMISSION.

SEC FEE small (one cent per several hundred dollars) fee charged by the Securities and Exchange Commission (SEC) to sellers of EQUITY securities that are exchange traded.

SECONDARY DISTRIBUTION public sale of previously issued securities held by large investors, usually corporations, institutions, or other AFFILIATED PERSONS, as distinguished from a NEW ISSUE or PRIMARY DISTRIBUTION, where the seller is the issuing corporation. As with a primary offering, secondaries are usually handled by INVESTMENT BANKERS, acting alone or as a syndicate, who purchase the shares from the seller at an agreed price, then resell them, sometimes with the help of a SELLING GROUP, at a higher PUBLIC OFFERING PRICE, making their profit on the difference, called the SPREAD. Since the offering is registered with the Securities and Exchange Commission, the syndicate manager can legally stabilize—or peg—the market price by bidding for shares in the open market. Buyers of securities offered this way pay no commissions, since all costs are borne by the selling investor. If the securities involved are listed, the CONSOLIDATED TAPE will announce the offering during the trading day, although the offering is not made until after the market's close. Among the historically large secondary distributions were the Ford Foundation's offering of Ford Motor Company stock in 1956 (approximately $658 million) handled by 7 firms under a joint management agreement and the sale of Howard Hughes' TWA shares ($566 million) through Merrill Lynch, Pierce, Fenner & Smith in 1966.

A similar form of secondary distribution, called the SPECIAL OFFERING, is limited to members of the New York Stock Exchange and is completed in the course of the trading day. *See also* EXCHANGE DISTRIBUTION; REGISTERED SECONDARY OFFERING; SECURITIES AND EXCHANGE COMMISSION RULES 144 and 237.

SECONDARY MARKET
1. exchanges and over-the-counter markets where securities are bought and sold subsequent to original issuance, which took place in the PRIMARY MARKET. Proceeds of secondary market sales accrue to the selling dealers and investors, not to the companies that originally issued the securities.
2. market in which money-market instruments are traded among investors.

SECONDARY MORTGAGE MARKET buying, selling, and trading of existing mortgage loans and mortgage-backed securities. Original lenders are thus able to sell loans in their portfolios in order to build LIQUIDITY to support additional lending. Mortgages originated by lenders are purchased by government agencies (such as the FEDERAL HOME LOAN MORTGAGE CORPORATION and the FEDERAL NATIONAL MORTGAGE ASSOCIATION) and by investment bankers. These agencies and bankers, in turn, create pools of mortgages, which they repackage as mortgage-backed securities, called PASS-THROUGH SECURITIES or PARTICIPATION CERTIFICATES, which are then sold to investors. The secondary mortgage market thus encompasses all activity beyond the PRIMARY MARKET, which is between the homebuyers and the originating mortgage lender.

SECONDARY OFFERING *see* SECONDARY DISTRIBUTION.

SECONDARY STOCKS used in a general way to mean stocks having smaller MARKET CAPITALIZATION, less quality, and more risk than BLUE CHIP issues represented by the Dow Jones Industrial Average. Secondary stocks, which often behave differently than blue chips, are tracked by the Amex Market Value Index, the NASDAQ Composite Index, and broad indexes, such as the Standard & Poor's Index. Also called *second-tier stocks.*

SECOND MORTGAGE LENDING advancing funds to a borrower that are secured by real estate previously pledged in a FIRST MORTGAGE loan. In the case of DEFAULT, the first mortgage has priority of claim over the second.

A variation on the second mortgage is the *home equity loan,* in which the loan is secured by independent appraisal of the property value. A home equity loan may also be in the form of a line of credit, which may be drawn down on by using a check or even a credit card. *See also* HOMEOWNER'S EQUITY ACCOUNT; RIGHT OF RESCISSION.

SECOND-PREFERRED STOCK preferred stock issue that ranks below another preferred issue in terms of priority of claim on dividends and on assets in liquidation. Second-preferred shares are often issued with a CONVERTIBLE feature or with a warrant to make them more attractive to investors. *See also* JUNIOR SECURITY; PREFERRED STOCK; PRIOR-PREFERRED STOCK; SUBSCRIPTION WARRANT.

SECOND ROUND intermediate stage of VENTURE CAPITAL financing, coming after the SEED MONEY (or START-UP) and *first round* stages and before the MEZZANINE LEVEL, when the company has matured to the point where it might consider a LEVERAGED BUYOUT by management or an INITIAL PUBLIC OFFERING (IPO).

SECOND-TO-DIE INSURANCE insurance policy that pays a death benefit upon the death of the spouse who dies last. Such insurance typically is purchased by a couple wanting to pass a large estate on to their heirs. When the first spouse dies, the couple's assets are passed tax-free to the second spouse under the MARITAL DEDUCTION. When the second spouse dies, the remaining estate could be subject to large estate taxes. The proceeds from the second-to-die insurance are designed to pay the estate taxes, leaving the remaining estate for the heirs. Such insurance is appropriate only for those facing large estate tax liabilities. Because the policy is based on the joint life expectancy of both husband and wife, premiums typically cost less than those on traditional cash value policies on both lives insured separately. Also called *survivorship life insurance.*

SECTOR particular group of stocks, usually found in one industry. SECURITIES ANALYSTS often follow a particular sector of the stock market, such as airline or chemical stocks.

SECTOR FUND *see* SPECIALIZED MUTUAL FUND.

SECULAR long-term (10–50 years or more) as distinguished from seasonal or cyclical time frames.

SECURED BOND bond backed by the pledge of COLLATERAL, a MORTGAGE, or other LIEN. The exact nature of the security is spelled out in the INDENTURE. Secured bonds are distinguished from unsecured bonds, called DEBENTURES.

SECURED DEBT debt guaranteed by the pledge of assets or other COLLATERAL. *See also* ASSIGN; HYPOTHECATION.

SECURITIES ACT OF 1933 first law enacted by Congress to regulate the securities markets, approved May 26, 1933, as the Truth in Securities Act. It requires REGISTRATION of securities prior to public sale and adequate DISCLOSURE of pertinent financial and other data in a PROSPECTUS to permit informed analysis by potential investors. It also contains antifraud provisions prohibiting false representations and disclosures. Enforcement responsibilities were assigned to the SECURITIES AND EXCHANGE COMMISSION by the SECURITIES EXCHANGE ACT OF 1934. The 1933 act did not supplant BLUE SKY LAWS of the various states.

SECURITIES ACTS AMENDMENTS OF 1975 federal legislation enacted on June 4, 1975, to amend the SECURITIES EXCHANGE ACT OF 1934. The 1975 amendments directed the SECURITIES AND EXCHANGE COMMISSION to work with the industry toward establishing a NATIONAL MARKET SYSTEM together with a system for the nationwide clearance and settlement of securities transactions. Because of these provisions, the 1975 laws are sometimes called the *National Exchange Market System Act*. New regulations were also introduced to promote prompt and accurate securities handling, and clearing agencies were required to register with and report to the SEC. The 1975 amendments required TRANSFER AGENTS other than banks to register with the SEC and provided that authority with respect to bank transfer agents would be shared by the SEC and bank regulatory agencies. The Municipal Securities Rulemaking Board was created to regulate brokers, dealers, and banks dealing in municipal securities, with rules subject to SEC approval and enforcement shared by the NATIONAL ASSOCIATION OF SECURITIES DEALERS and bank regulatory agencies. The law also required the registration of broker-dealers in municipals, but preserved the exemption of issuers from REGISTRATION requirements. The amendments contained the prohibition of fixed commission rates, adopted earlier by the SEC in its Rule 19b-3.

SECURITIES ANALYST individual, usually employed by a stock brokerage house, bank, or investment institution, who performs investment research and examines the financial condition of a company or group of companies in an industry and in the context of the securities markets. Many analysts specialize in a single industry or SECTOR and make investment recommendations to buy, sell, or hold in that area. Among a corporation's financial indicators most closely followed by ANALYSTS are sales and earnings growth, CAPITAL STRUCTURE, stock price trend and PRICE/EARNINGS RATIO, DIVIDEND PAYOUTS, and RETURN ON INVESTED CAPITAL. Securities analysts promote corporate financial disclosure by sponsoring forums through local associations, the largest of which is the New York Society of Security Analysts, and through its national body, the Financial Analysts Federation. *See also* FORECAST-ING; FUNDAMENTAL ANALYSIS; QUALITATIVE ANALYSIS; QUANTITATIVE ANALYSIS; TECHNICAL ANALYSIS.

SECURITIES AND COMMODITIES EXCHANGES organized, national exchanges where securities, options, and futures contracts are traded by members for their own accounts and for the accounts of customers. In the U.S., the stock exchanges are registered with and regulated by the SECURITIES AND EXCHANGE COMMISSION (SEC); the commodities exchanges are registered with and regulated by the Commodity Futures Trading Commission (*see* REGULATED COMMODITIES); where options are traded on an exchange, such activity is regulated by the SEC.

STOCKS, BONDS, SUBSCRIPTION RIGHTS, SUBSCRIPTION WARRANTS, STOCK OPTIONS, INDEX OPTIONS, and other derivative products are traded on 9 STOCK EXCHANGES in the U.S. COMMODITY FUTURES, FUTURES OPTIONS, and FINANCIAL FUTURES are traded on 13 leading commodities exchanges.

Exchanges listing basic securities—stocks, bonds, rights, warrants, and options on individual stocks—are described under the entries for the NEW YORK STOCK EXCHANGE, AMERICAN STOCK EXCHANGE, NASDAQ STOCK MARKET, BOSTON STOCK EXCHANGE, and REGIONAL STOCK EXCHANGES. The exchanges listing futures and options contracts are:

American Stock Exchange (New York) *stock index options:* Airline Index, Amex Gold BUGS Index, Biotechnology Index, Computer Technology Index, de Jager Year 2000 Index, Disk Drive Index, Eurotop 100 Index, Hong Kong Option Index, Institutional Index, Inter@ctive Week Internet Index, Japan Index, Major Market Index, Mexico Index, Morgan Stanley Commodity Related Equity Index, Morgan Stanley Cyclical Index, Morgan Stanley Consumer Index, Morgan Stanley Healthcare Product Index, Morgan Stanley Healthcare Provider Index, Natural Gas Index, NatWest Energy Index, Networking Index, North American Telecommunications Index, Oil Index, Pharmaceutical Index, Pharmaceutical LEAPS Index, S&P MidCap 400 Index, Security Broker/Dealer Index, Tobacco Index.

Chicago Board of Trade (Chicago) *futures:* corn, oats, rough rice, soybeans, soybean oil, soybean meal, wheat, anhydrous ammonia, diammonium phosphate, corn yield insurance (Illinois, Indiana, Iowa, Nebraska, Ohio), silver (1,000 ounces, 5,000 ounces), gold (kilo, 100 ounces); CBOT Dow Jones Industrial Average Index, U.S. Treasury bonds,

Treasury notes (10-year, 5-year, 2-year), Long-Term Municipal Bond Index, 10-year Canadian government bond, German government bond, 30-day Fed funds, yield curve spread. *options:* wheat, corn, oats, soybeans, soybean oil, soybean meal, rough rice, silver (1,000 ounces), U.S. Treasury bonds, Treasury notes (10-year, 5-year, 2-year), Municipal Bond Index, Canadian government bond, Long-term Municipal Bond Index, Flexible U.S. Treasury bonds, Flexible Treasury options (10-year, 5-year, 2-year), German government bond, quarterly catastrophe insurance (national, Eastern, Northeastern, Southeastern, Midwestern, Texas and Florida), annual catastrophe insurance.

Chicago Board Options Exchange (Chicago) *equity options: equity LEAPS, FLEX equity options; index options:* Standard & Poor's 100 Index and LEAPS, Standard & Poor's 500 Index and LEAPS, Standard & Poor's long-dated options, S&P SmallCap 600 Index, S&P/BARRA Growth and Value Indexes, Dow Jones Industrial Average and LEAPS, Dow Jones Transportation Average and LEAPS, Dow Jones Utility Average and LEAPS, FLEX index options (S&P 500, Russell 2000 and NASDAQ-100 Indexes), CBOE Isreal Index, Latin 15 Index, CBOE Mexico Index and LEAPS, Morgan Stanley Multinational Company Index, NASDAQ-100 Index, Nikkei 300 Index and LEAPS, Russell 2000 Index and LEAPS, IPC options. *sector index options:* CBOE Automotive Index, CBOE Computer Software Index, CBOE Environmental Index, CBOE Gaming Index, CBOE Gold Index, CBOE Internet Index and LEAPS, CBOE Oil Index and LEAPS, CBOE REIT Index, CBOE Technology Index and LEAPS, GSTI Composite Index, GSTI (Computer) Hardware Index, GSTI Internet Index, GSTI Multimedia Networking Index, GSTI Semiconductor Index, GSTI (Computer) Services Index, GSTI (Computer) Software Index, S&P Banks Index, S&P Chemical Index, S&P Health Care Index, S&P Insurance Index, S&P Retail Index, S&P Transportation Index. *interest rate options and LEAPS:* 13-week U.S. Treasury bill, 5-year Treasury note, 10-year Treasury note, 30-year Treasury bond.

Chicago Mercantile Exchange (Chicago) *agricultural futures and options:* live cattle, feeder cattle, boneless beef, boneless beef trimmings, lean hogs, frozen pork bellies, fresh pork bellies, BFP (basic formula price) milk, old butter, new butter, cheddar cheese, random-length lumber, oriented strand board. *foreign currency futures and options:* Australian dollar, Brazilian real, British pound, Canadian dollar, Deutsche mark, French franc, Japanese yen, Mexican peso, New Zealand dollar, South African rand, Swiss franc. *cross-rate futures and options:* British pound/Deutsche mark, Deutsche mark/Japanese yen, Deutsche mark/Swiss franc, Deutsche mark/French franc. *foreign currency-denominated interest rate futures and options:* Euroyen, 3-month Euromark, 91-day Mexican Treasury bill, 28-day Mexican TIIE. *interest rate futures and options:* Eurodollar time deposit, 13-week U.S. Treasury bill, 1-year Treasury bill, 1-month LIBOR (London Interbank Offer Rate), Mexican Par Brady Bonds, Argentine FRB Bonds,

Brazilian C Bonds, Brazilian EI Bonds, Federal Funds rate (futures only). *stock index futures and options:* Standard & Poor's 500, E-Mini S&P 500 Stock Price Index, Standard & Poor's MidCap 400, Nikkei 225 Stock Average, Goldman Sachs Commodity Index, Russell 2000 Stock Price Index, Major Market Index, S&P 500/BARRA Growth Index, S&P 500 BARRA Value Index, NASDAQ 100 Index, IPC Stock Index, Dow Jones Taiwan Stock Index.

Coffee, Sugar and Cocoa Exchange (New York) *futures and options:* coffee, cocoa, sugar #11, butter, cheddar cheese, milk, BFP (basic formula price) milk, nonfat dry milk. *futures:* sugar #14, white sugar. *flexible options:* sugar #11.

Kansas City Board of Trade (Kansas City) *futures and options:* wheat, Mini Value Line Index, Western natural gas. *futures:* Value Line Index.

FINEX *index/interest rate futures and options:* U.S. dollar index, U.S. Treasury auction notes (5-year, 2-year). *cross-rate currency futures and options:* Deutsche mark/French franc, Deutsche mark/lira, Deutsche mark/yen, Deutsche mark/Swedish krona, Deutsche mark/Swiss franc, Deutsche mark/Spanish peseta, British pound/Deutsche mark, British pound/yen, British pound/Swiss franc, British pound/U.S. dollar. *U.S. dollar currency pairs futures:* Deutsche mark, yen, Swiss franc, Canadian dollar, Australian dollar, New Zealand dollar, South African rand, Malaysian ringgit, Indonesian rupiah, Singapore dollar, Thai baht.

Mid-America Commodity Exchange (Chicago) *futures and options:* corn, wheat, soybeans, soybean oil, NY gold, U.S. Treasury bond. *futures:* oats, soybean meal, cattle, hogs, NY silver, platinum, Australian dollar, British pound, Canadian dollar, Deutsche mark, Japanese yen, Swiss franc, Eurodollar, U.S. Treasury bills, U.S. Treasury notes (10-year, 5-year).

Minneapolis Grain Exchange (Minneapolis) *futures and options:* hard red spring wheat, soft white wheat, barley, white shrimp, black tiger shrimp. *futures:* American spring wheat.

New York Cotton Exchange (New York) *agricultural futures and options:* cotton, frozen concentrated orange juice, potatoes.

New York Futures Exchange (New York) *futures and options:* NYSE Composite Index, NYSE Large Composite Index, CRB/Bridge Index, PSE Technology Index.

New York Mercantile Exchange (New York) *NYMEX division: futures and options:* light, sweet crude oil, New York Harbor unleaded gasoline, heating oil, Henry Hub natural gas, Permian Basin natural gas, Alberta natural gas, Palo Verde and California/Oregon Border (COB) electricity, Eastern electricity, coal, platinum. *futures:* sour crude, Gulf Coast unleaded gasoline, propane, palladium. *COMEX division: futures and options:* copper, gold, silver, FTSE Eurotop 100 Index. *options:* 5-day copper, 5-day gold, 5-day silver.

Pacific Exchange (San Francisco and Los Angeles) *index options:* Morgan Stanley Emerging Growth Index, Wilshire Small Cap Index,

Dow Jones Taiwan Stock Index, PSE Technology 100 Index, LEAPS; FLEX options.

Philadelphia Stock Exchange (Philadelphia): *currency options:* Australian dollar, British pound, Canadian dollar, Deutsche mark, EURO, French franc, Italian lira, Japanese yen, Mexican peso, Spanish peseta, Swiss franc, U.S. dollar. *sector index options:* airline, KBW bank, forest and paper products, gold/silver, oil service, phone, semiconductor, utility, national over-the-counter, SuperCap, U.S. Top 100, Value Line Index, computer box maker.

SECURITIES AND EXCHANGE COMMISSION (SEC) federal agency created by the SECURITIES EXCHANGE ACT OF 1934 to administer that act and the SECURITIES ACT OF 1933, formerly carried out by the FEDERAL TRADE COMMISSION. The SEC is made up of five commissioners, appointed by the President of the United States on a rotating basis for five-year terms. The chairman is designated by the President and, to insure its independence, no more than three members of the commission may be of the same political party. The statutes administered by the SEC are designed to promote full public DISCLOSURE and protect the investing public against malpractice in the securities markets. All issues of securities offered in interstate commerce or through the mails must be registered with the SEC; all national securities exchanges and associations are under its supervision, as are INVESTMENT COMPANIES, investment counselors and advisers, OVER THE COUNTER brokers and dealers, and virtually all other individuals and firms operating in the investment field. In addition to the 1933 and 1934 securities acts, responsibilities of the SEC include the PUBLIC UTILITY HOLDING COMPANY ACT of 1935, the TRUST INDENTURE ACT of 1939, the INVESTMENT COMPANY ACT of 1940 and the INVESTMENT ADVISERS ACT of 1940. It also administers the SECURITIES ACTS AMENDMENTS OF 1975, which directed the SEC to facilitate the establishment of a NATIONAL MARKET SYSTEM and a nationwide system for clearance and settlement of transactions and established the Municipal Securities Rulemaking Board, a self-regulatory organization whose rules are subject to SEC approval. *See also* SECURITIES AND EXCHANGE COMMISSION RULES.

SECURITIES AND EXCHANGE COMMISSION RULES The following are some of the more commonly encountered rules of the SEC. The list highlights the most prominent features of the rules and is not intended as a legal interpretation. The rules are listed in numerical order.
Rule 3b-3: Definition of Short Sale defines short sale as one in which the seller does not own the SECURITY sold or which is consummated by delivery of a borrowed security; ownership is defined in terms of securities, CONVERTIBLES, OPTIONS, and SUBSCRIPTION WARRANTS.
Rule 10a-1: Short sales known as the SHORT SALE RULE, prohibits a short sale of securities below the price of the last regular trade and at that price unless it was higher than the last different price preceding it. In determining the price at which a short sale can be made after a security goes

EX-DIVIDEND, EX-RIGHTS, or ex- any other distribution, all sales prices prior to the ex- date may be reduced by the amount of the distribution.

Rule 10b-2: Solicitation of purchases on an exchange to facilitate distribution of securities prohibits parties concerned with a PRIMARY DISTRIBUTION or a SECONDARY DISTRIBUTION of a security from soliciting orders for the issue other than through the offering circular or formal PROSPECTUS.

Rule 10b-4: Short tendering of securities prohibits a SHORT TENDER—the sale of borrowed securities (as in SELLING SHORT) to a person making a TENDER OFFER.

Rule 10b-6: Prohibitions against trading by persons interested in a distribution rule that prohibits issuers, underwriters, broker-dealers, or others involved in a DISTRIBUTION of securities from buying the issue, or rights to it, during the distribution. The section permits transactions between the issuer and the underwriters and among the participating underwriters as required to carry out a distribution. The law extends to a repurchase by the issuer or to a purchase by participants in a new issue of CONVERTIBLE securities already on the market and convertible into the securities being offered.

Rule 10b-7: Stabilizing to effect a distribution provisions governing market STABILIZATION activities by issuers or underwriters in securities offerings.

Rule 10b-8: Distributions through rights prohibits market price MANIPULATION by interested parties in a RIGHTS OFFERING.

Rule 10b-10: Confirmation of transactions sets minimum information and disclosure requirements for the written confirmations of sales or purchases that broker-dealers send to clients, including disclosure of whether a firm is acting as AGENT (broker) or as PRINCIPAL (dealer).

Rule 10b-13: Other purchases during tender offer or exchange offer prohibits a person making a cash tender offer or an offer to exchange one EQUITY security for another from taking a position in the security being tendered or in a security CONVERTIBLE into the security being tendered until the tender offer or exchange offer expires.

Rule 10b-16: Credit terms in margin transactions terms and conditions concerning the interest charges on MARGIN loans to brokerage customers and the broker's disclosure responsibilities to borrowers.

Rule 11A: Floor trading regulations rules governing floor trading by exchange members, including those concerning PRIORITY and PRECEDENCE of transactions, transactions for the accounts of persons associated with members, HEDGE transactions, exchange bond trading, transactions by REGISTERED COMPETITIVE MARKET MAKERS and REGISTERED EQUITY MARKET MAKERS, and transactions between members.

Rule 12b-1: *see* 12b-1 MUTUAL FUND.

Rule 13d: Acquisition of beneficial interest disclosures required by any person who directly or indirectly acquires a beneficial interest of 5% or more of any class of a registered equity security. *See also* WILLIAMS ACT.

Rule 13e: Repurchase of shares by issuers prohibits purchase by an issuer of its own shares during a TENDER OFFER for its shares and regulates GOING PRIVATE transactions by issuers or their affiliates.

Rule 14a: Solicitation of proxies sets forth the information and documentation required with PROXY materials distributed to shareholders of a public corporation.

Rule 14d: Tender offers regulations and restrictions covering public TENDER OFFERS and related disclosure requirements. *See also* WILLIAMS ACT.

Rule 15c2-1: Hypothecation of customers' securities regulates a broker-dealer's SAFEKEEPING of customers securities in a MARGIN ACCOUNT, prohibiting the COMMINGLING of customers accounts without the consent of the respective customers and the commingling of customers' accounts with the securities of non-customers, and limiting broker borrowings secured by customers' collateral to the aggregate amount of customers' indebtedness. *See also* HYPOTHECATION.

Rule 15c3-1: Net capital requirements for brokers or dealers covers NET CAPITAL REQUIREMENTS relative to the aggregate indebtedness of brokers and dealers of different types.

Rule 15c3-2: Customers' free credit balances requires a broker-dealer to notify customers with credit balances in their accounts that such balances may be withdrawn on demand.

Rule 15c3-3: Customer-protection reserves and custody of securities regulates the handling of customers' fully paid securities and excess MARGIN securities (security value in excess of MARGIN REQUIREMENTS) with broker-dealers. Fully paid securities must be segregated, and the broker must make weekly deposits to a Special Reserve Bank Account for the Exclusive Benefit of Customers.

Rule 17f-1: Missing, lost, counterfeit, or stolen securities requires exchanges, broker-dealers, clearing agencies, banks and transfer agents to report promptly to both the SEC and the appropriate law enforcement agency any knowledge of missing, lost, counterfeit, or stolen securities and to check with the SEC whenever a security comes into their possession to make sure it has not been reported at large.

Rule 19b-3: Prohibiting fixing of rates of commission by exchanges prohibits fixed commissions on stock exchange transactions pursuant to the SECURITIES ACT AMENDMENTS OF 1975.

Rule 19c-3: Off-board trading by exchange members permits securities listed on an exchange after April 26, 1979, to be traded off the exchange by member firms, a step toward an experimental NATIONAL MARKET SYSTEM in compliance with the SECURITIES ACT AMENDMENTS OF 1975.

Rule 19c-4: One share, one vote prohibits U.S. exchanges and the NASD from listing or providing quotes for any issuer of stock with more voting power than other common shares of the same issuer.

Rule 144: Public sale of unregistered securities sets forth the conditions under which a holder of unregistered securities may make a public sale without filing a formal REGISTRATION STATEMENT. No LETTER SECURITY purchased through a PRIVATE PLACEMENT may be sold for at least two years after the date of purchase. Thereafter, during any three-month period, the following amounts may be sold: if listed securities, the greater of 1% of the amount outstanding or the average trading volume within the four preceding weeks; if unlisted, 1% of outstandings. Securities may be sold only in broker's transactions.

Rule 145: Securities acquired in recapitalization persons who acquire securities as a result of reclassification, MERGER, consolidation, or transfer of corporate assets may sell such securities without REGISTRATION under stipulated conditions.

Rule 156: Mutual fund sales literature forbids false and misleading sales materials promoting INVESTMENT COMPANY securities.

Rule 237: Public sale of unregistered securities expanding on Rule 144, provides that five years after full payment for the purchase of privately placed securities, the lesser of $50,000 of such securities or 1% of the securities outstanding in a particular CLASS may be sold within a one year period.

Rule 254: Registration of small issues provides for simplified registration of small issues ($1.5 million or less in the mid-1980s) including a short-form REGISTRATION STATEMENT and PROSPECTUS. *See also* REGULATION A.

Rule 415: Shelf registration permits corporations to file a REGISTRATION for securities they intend to issue in the future when market conditions are favorable. *See also* SHELF REGISTRATION.

Rule 419: Blank-check companies (companies that issue penny stock before operations have begun or before engaging in an acquisition or merger with an unspecified business entity) must put investors' funds in an escrow account for the benefit of the purchaser.

SECURITIES EXCHANGE ACT OF 1934 law governing the securities markets, enacted June 6, 1934. The act outlaws misrepresentation, MANIPULATION, and other abusive practices in the issuance of securities. It created the SECURITIES AND EXCHANGE COMMISSION (SEC) to enforce both the SECURITIES ACT OF 1933 and the Securities Exchange Act of 1934.

Principal requirements of the 1934 act are as follows:

1. REGISTRATION of all securities listed on stock exchanges, and periodic DISCLOSURES by issuers of financial status and changes in condition.
2. regular disclosures of holdings and transactions of "INSIDERS"—the officers and directors of a corporation and those who control at least 10% of equity securities.
3. solicitation of PROXIES enabling shareholders to vote for or against policy proposals.
4. registration with the SEC of stock exchanges and brokers and dealers to ensure their adherence to SEC rules through self-regulation.
5. surveillance by the SEC of trading practices on stock exchanges and over-the-counter markets to minimize the possibility of insolvency among brokers and dealers.

6. regulation of MARGIN REQUIREMENTS for securities purchased on credit; the FEDERAL RESERVE BOARD sets those requirements.

7. SEC subpoena power in investigations of possible violations and in enforcement actions.

The SECURITIES ACT AMENDMENTS OF 1975 ratified the system of free-market determination of brokers' commissions and gave the SEC authority to oversee development of a NATIONAL MARKET SYSTEM.

SECURITIES EXCHANGE OF THAILAND (SET) only stock market in Thailand, based in Bangkok. The *SET Index,* calculated by the exchange, and the *Bangkok Book Club Price Index,* compiled by the Book Club Finance and Securities Co. Ltd., include all corporate stocks and mutual funds and are the most widely watched. Trading is conducted through the ASSET automated electronic trading system Monday through Friday from 10 A.M. to 12:30 P.M., and 2 P.M. to 4 P.M. Trades are settled on the third business day after the trade date.

SECURITIES INDUSTRY ASSOCIATION (SIA) trade group that represents broker-dealers. The SIA lobbies for legislation affecting the brokerage industry. It also educates its members and the public about industry trends and keeps statistics on revenues and profits of brokers. The SIA represents only the segment of broker-dealers that sells taxable securities. Tax-exempt bond, government bond, and mortgage-backed security dealers are represented by the BOND MARKET ASSOCIATION.

SECURITIES INDUSTRY AUTOMATION CORPORATION (SIAC) organization established in 1972 to provide communications and computer systems and services for the New York Stock Exchange (NYSE) and the American Stock Exchange (AMEX). It is two-thirds owned by NYSE and one-third owned by AMEX.

SECURITIES INDUSTRY COMMITTEE ON ARBITRATION (SICA) private body that applies its arbitration code in cases of customer complaints against securities firms.

SECURITIES INVESTOR PROTECTION CORPORATION (SIPC) nonprofit corporation, established by Congress under the Securities Investor Protection Act of 1970, that insures the securities and cash in the customer accounts of member brokerage firms against the failure of those firms. All brokers and dealers registered with the Securities and Exchange Commission and with national stock exchanges are required to be members of SIPC. The Corporation acts similarly to the FEDERAL DEPOSIT INSURANCE CORPORATION (FDIC), which insures banks, and the SAVINGS ASSOCIATION INSURANCE FUND (SAIF), which insures savings and loans. When a brokerage firm fails, SIPC will first try to merge it into another brokerage firm. If this fails, SIPC will liquidate the firm's assets and pay off account holders up to an overall maximum of $500,000 per customer, with a limit of $100,000 on cash or cash equivalents. SIPC does not protect investors against market risks. *See also* SEPARATE CUSTOMER.

SECURITIES LOAN

1. loan of securities by one broker to another, usually to cover a customer's short sale. The lending broker is secured by the cash proceeds of the sale.

2. in a more general sense, loan collateralized by MARKETABLE SECURITIES. These would include all customer loans made to purchase or carry securities by broker-dealers under Federal Reserve Board REGULATION T margin rules, as well as by banks under REGULATION U and other lenders under REGULATION G. Loans made by banks to brokers to cover customers' positions are also collateralized by securities, but such loans are called *broker's loans* or *call loans. See also* HYPOTHECATION; LENDING AT A PREMIUM; LENDING AT A RATE; LENDING SECURITIES; REHYPOTHECATION; SELLING SHORT.

SECURITIES MARKETS general term for markets in which securities are traded, including both ORGANIZED SECURITIES EXCHANGES and OVER-THE-COUNTER (OTC) markets.

SECURITIZATION process of distributing risk by aggregating debt instruments in a pool, then issuing new securities backed by the pool. *See also* ASSET-BACKED SECURITIES.

SECURITY

Finance: collateral offered by a debtor to a lender to secure a loan called *collateral security.* For instance, the security behind a mortgage loan is the real estate being purchased with the proceeds of the loan. If the debt is not repaid, the lender may seize the security and resell it.

Personal security refers to one person or firm's GUARANTEE of another's primary obligation.

Investment: instrument that signifies an ownership position in a corporation (a stock), a creditor relationship with a corporation or governmental body (a bond), or rights to ownership such as those represented by an OPTION, SUBSCRIPTION RIGHT, and SUBSCRIPTION WARRANT.

SECURITY DEPOSIT money paid in advance to protect the provider of a product or service against damage or nonpayment by the buyer. For example, landlords require a security deposit of one month's rent when a tenant signs a lease, to cover the possibility that the tenant will move out without paying the last month's rent, or that the tenant will inflict substantial damage on the property while living there. In such a case, the money from the security deposit is used to cover repairs. Similarly, car leasing companies typically demand security deposits for the last month's lease payment to protect the leasing company against damage to the car or nonpayment of the lease. If all payments are made on time and there is no damage, security deposits must be returned to those who paid them.

SECURITY MARKET LINE relationship between the REQUIRED RATE OF RETURN on an investment and its SYSTEMATIC RISK.

SECURITY RATINGS evaluations of the credit and investment risk of securities issues by commercial RATING agencies.

SEED MONEY venture capitalist's first contribution toward the financing or capital requirements of a START-UP business. It frequently takes the form of a loan, often SUBORDINATED, or an investment in convertible bonds or preferred stock. Seed money provides the basis for additional capitalization to accommodate growth. *See also* MEZZANINE LEVEL; SECOND ROUND; VENTURE CAPITAL.

SEEK A MARKET to look for a buyer (if a seller) or a seller (if a buyer) of securities.

SEGMENT REPORTING *see* BUSINESS SEGMENT REPORTING.

SEGREGATION OF SECURITIES Securities and Exchange Commission rules (8c and 15c2-1) designed to protect customers' securities used by broker-dealers to secure broker loans. Specifically, broker-dealers may not (1) commingle the securities of different customers without the written consent of each customer, (2) commingle a customer's securities with those of any person other than a bona-fide customer, or (3) borrow more against customers' securities than the customers, in the aggregate, owe the broker-dealer against the same securities. *See also* COMMINGLING; HYPOTHECATION; REHYPOTHECATION; SECURITIES AND EXCHANGE COMMISSION RULE 15c2-1.

SELECTED DEALER AGREEMENT agreement governing the SELLING GROUP in a securities underwriting and distribution. *See also* UNDERWRITE.

SELECT TEN PORTFOLIO UNIT INVESTMENT TRUST offered at various times each year as a subcategory of the DEFINED ASSET FUNDS sponsored by a group of brokers including Merrill Lynch, Paine Webber, Morgan Stanley Dean Witter, Salomon Smith Barney, and Prudential Securities. The majority of the select ten trusts buy and hold for one year the ten stocks in the Dow Jones Industrial Average (DJIA) with the highest dividend yields. Stocks thus selected have usually outperformed the DJIA. Other select ten portfolios comprise the highest yielding stocks in the blue chip indices of foreign markets such as the United Kingdom, Hong Kong, and until 1998, Japan. *See also* DOGS OF THE DOW.

SELF-AMORTIZING MORTGAGE mortgage in which all principal is paid off in a specified period of time through periodic interest and principal payments. The most common self-amortizing mortgages are for 15 and 30 years. Lenders will provide a table to borrowers showing how much principal and interest is being paid off each month until the loan is retired.

SELF-DIRECTED IRA INDIVIDUAL RETIREMENT ACCOUNT (IRA) that can be actively managed by the account holder, who designates a CUSTODIAN to carry out investment instructions. The account is subject to the same conditions and early withdrawal limitations as a regular IRA. Investors who withdraw money from a qualified IRA plan have 60 days in which to roll over the funds to another plan before they become liable for tax penalties. Most corporate and U.S. government securities, stocks, mutual funds, and metals such as gold, silver, platinum, and palladium are eligible to be held by a self-directed IRA. *See also* ROTH IRA.

SELF-EMPLOYED INCOME net taxable income of a self-employed person, as reported on Schedule C of IRS Form 1040. Self-employment income may be generated by freelance work, royalties, consulting, or income from sole proprietorship businesses. Social Security taxes must be paid on self-employment income.

SELF-EMPLOYED RETIREMENT PLAN *see* KEOGH PLAN.

SELF-EMPLOYMENT TAX tax paid by self-employed people to Social Security, qualifying them for receiving Social Security benefits at retirement. The tax is filed on Schedule SE of IRS Form 1040, which indicates the type of business generating self-employment income, net earnings, and the amount of self-employment tax.

SELF-REGULATORY ORGANIZATION (SRO) principal means contemplated by the federal securities laws for the enforcement of fair, ethical, and efficient practices in the securities and commodities futures industries. It is these organizations that are being referred to when "industry rules" are mentioned, as distinguished from the regulatory agencies such as the Securities and Exchange Commission or the Federal Reserve Board. The SROs include all the national SECURITIES AND COMMODITIES EXCHANGES as well as the NATIONAL ASSOCIATION OP SECURITIES DEALERS (NASD), which represents all the firms operating in the over-the-counter market, and the *Municipal Securities Rulemaking Board,* created under the Securities Acts Amendments of 1975 to regulate brokers, dealers and banks dealing in municipal securities. Rules made by the MSRB are subject to approval by the SEC and are enforced by the NASD and bank regulatory agencies.

SELF-SUPPORTING DEBT bonds sold for a project that will produce sufficient revenues to retire the debt. Such debt is usually issued by municipalities building a public structure (for example, a bridge or tunnel) that will be producing revenue through tolls or other charges. The bonds are not supported by the taxing power of the municipality issuing them. *See also* REVENUE BOND.

SELF-TENDER *see* SHARE REPURCHASE PLAN.

SELLER FINANCING financing provided by the owner/seller of real estate, who takes back a secured note. The buyer may be unable to qualify for a mortgage from a lending institution, or interest rates may have risen so high that the buyer is unwilling to take on a market-rate loan. In order to sell their property, sellers offer to lend the buyer the money needed, often at a below-market interest rate. The buyer takes full title to the property when the loan is fully repaid. If the buyer defaults on the loan, the seller can repossess the property. Also called *creative financing*.

SELLER'S MARKET situation in which there is more demand for a security or product than there is available supply. As a result, the prices tend to be rising, and the sellers can set both the prices and the terms of sale. It contrasts with a buyer's market, characterized by excess supply, low prices, and terms suited to the buyer's desires.

SELLER'S OPTION securities transaction in which the seller, instead of making REGULAR WAY DELIVERY, is given the right to deliver the security to the purchaser on the date the seller's option expires or before, provided written notification of the seller's intention to deliver is given to the buyer one full business day prior to delivery. Seller's option deliveries are normally not made before 6 business days following the transaction or after 60 days.

SELLING CLIMAX sudden plunge in security prices as those who hold stocks or bonds panic and decide to dump their holdings all at once. Technical analysts see a climax as both a dramatic increase in volume and a sharp drop in prices on a chart. To these analysts, such a pattern usually means that a short-term rally will soon follow since there are few sellers left after the climax. Sometimes, a selling climax can signal the bottom of a BEAR MARKET, meaning that after the climax the market will start to rise.

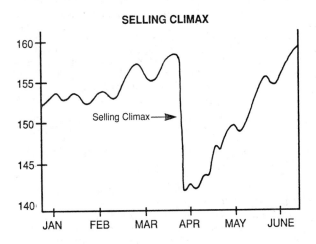

SELLING CLIMAX

SELLING CONCESSION discount at which securities in a NEW ISSUE offering (or a SECONDARY DISTRIBUTION) are allocated to the members of a SELLING GROUP by the underwriters. Since the selling group cannot sell to the public at a price higher than the PUBLIC OFFERING PRICE, its compensation comes out of the difference between the price paid to the issuer by the underwriters and the public offering price, called the SPREAD. The selling group's portion, called the CONCESSION, is normally one half or more of the gross spread, expressed as a discount off the public offering price. *See also* FLOTATION COST; UNDERWRITE; UNDERWRITING SPREAD.

SELLING DIVIDENDS questionable practice by sales personnel dealing in MUTUAL FUNDS whereby a customer is induced to buy shares in a fund in order to get the benefit of a dividend scheduled in the near future. Since the dividend is already part of the NET ASSET VALUE of the fund and therefore part of the share price, the customer derives no real benefit.

SELLING, GENERAL, AND ADMINISTRATIVE (SG&A) EXPENSES grouping of expenses reported on a company's PROFIT AND LOSS STATEMENT between COST OF GOODS SOLD and INCOME DEDUCTIONS. Included are such items as salespersons' salaries and commissions, advertising and promotion, travel and entertainment, office payroll and expenses, and executives' salaries. SG&A expenses do not include such items as interest or amortization of INTANGIBLE ASSETS, which would be listed as income deductions. *See also* OPERATING PROFIT (OR LOSS).

SELLING GROUP group of dealers appointed by the syndicate manager of an UNDERWRITING GROUP, as AGENT for the other underwriters, to market a new or secondary issue to the public; also called *selling syndicate.* The selling group typically includes members of the underwriting group but varies in size with the size of the issue, sometimes running into several hundred dealers. The selling group is governed by the selling group agreement, also called the SELECTED DEALER AGREEMENT. It sets forth the terms of the relationship, establishes the commission (or SELLING CONCESSION, as it is called), and provides for the termination of the group, usually in 30 days. The selling group may or may not be obligated to purchase unsold shares. *See also* UNDERWRITE.

SELLING OFF selling securities or commodities under pressure to avoid further declines in prices. Technical analysts call such action a *sell-off. See also* DUMPING.

SELLING ON THE GOOD NEWS practice of selling a stock soon after a positive news development is announced. Most investors, cheered by the news of a successful new product or higher earnings, buy a stock because they think it will go higher: this pushes up the price. Someone selling on this good news believes that the stock will have reached its top price once all those encouraged by the development have bought the stock. Therefore, it is better to sell at this point than to wait for more good news or to be holding the stock if the next announcement is disappointing. *Compare with* BUYING ON THE BAD NEWS.

SELLING SHORT sale of a security or commodity futures contract not owned by the seller; a technique used (1) to take advantage of an anticipated decline in the price or (2) to protect a profit in a LONG POSITION *(see* SELLING SHORT AGAINST THE BOX).

An investor borrows stock certificates for delivery at the time of short sale. If the seller can buy that stock later at a lower price, a profit results; if the price rises, however, a loss results.

A commodity sold short represents a promise to deliver the commodity at a set price on a future date. Most commodity short sales are COVERED before the DELIVERY DATE.

Example of a short sale involving stock: An investor, anticipating a decline in the price of XYZ stock, instructs his or her broker to sell short 100 XYZ when XYZ is trading at $50. The broker then loans the investor 100 shares of XYZ, using either its own inventory, shares in the MARGIN ACCOUNT of another customer, or shares borrowed from another broker. These shares are used to make settlement with the buying broker within five days of the short sale transaction, and the proceeds are used to secure the loan. The investor now has what is known as a SHORT POSITION—that is, he or she still does not own the 100 XYZ and, at some point, must buy the shares to repay the lending broker. If the market price of XYZ drops to $40, the investor can buy the shares for $4000, repay the lending broker, thus covering the short sale, and claim a profit of $1000, or $10 a share.

Short selling is regulated by REGULATION T of the Federal Reserve Board. *See also* LENDING AT A RATE; LENDING AT A PREMIUM; LOANED FLAT; MARGIN REQUIREMENT; SHORT SALE RULE.

SELLING SHORT AGAINST THE BOX SELLING SHORT stock actually owned by the seller but held in SAFEKEEPING, called the BOX in Wall Street jargon. The motive for the practice, which assumes that the securities needed to COVER are borrowed as with any short sale, may be simply inaccessibility of the box or that the seller does not wish to disclose ownership. The main motive is to protect a CAPITAL GAIN in the shares that are owned, while deferring a LONG-TERM GAIN into another tax year. This technique was curtailed as a way to defer taxes by the TAXPAYER RELIEF ACT OF 1997. Under the law, shorting against the box after June 8, 1997 is considered a "constructive sale," resulting in capital gains liability.

SELLING THE SPREAD spread where the sold option is trading at a higher premium than the purchased option. For example, purchasing a shorter term option and selling a longer term option (assuming both options have the same EXERCISE PRICE) would usually result in a net credit. *See* CALENDAR SPREAD. Another example would be purchasing a call with a higher exercise price and selling a call with a lower exercise price, assuming both options have the same expiration date. *See also* CREDIT SPREAD.

SELL-OFF massive selling of stocks or bonds after a steep decline in prices. Traders sell quickly in order to avoid further losses.

SELL ORDER order by an investor to a broker to sell a particular stock, bond, option, future, mutual fund, or other holding. There are several kinds of sell orders, including DAY ORDERS, GOOD-TILL-CANCELED ORDERS (GTC), LIMIT ORDERS, MARKET-ON-CLOSE ORDERS, MARKET ORDERS, ON THE CLOSE ORDERS, ON THE OPENING ORDERS, STOP-LIMIT ORDERS, STOP LOSS ORDERS, and STOP ORDERS.

SELL OUT
   1. liquidation of a MARGIN ACCOUNT by a broker after a MARGIN CALL has failed to produce additional equity to bring the margin to the required level. *See also* CLOSE A POSITION; MARGIN REQUIREMENT; MINIMUM MAINTENANCE.
   2. action by a broker when a customer fails to pay for securities purchased and the securities received from the selling broker are sold to cover the transaction. Term also applies to commodities futures transactions.
   3. expression used when all the securities in a NEW ISSUE underwriting have been distributed.

SELL PLUS sell order with instructions to execute only if the trading price in a security is higher than the last different preceding price. *See also* SHORT-SALE RULE.

SELL-STOP ORDER *see* STOP ORDER.

SELL THE BOOK order to a broker by the holder of a large quantity of shares of a security to sell all that can be ABSORBED at the current bid price. The term derives from the SPECIALIST'S BOOK—the record of all the buy and sell orders members have placed in the stock he or she handles. In this scenario, the buyers potentially include those in the specialist's book, the specialist for his or her own account, and the broker-dealer CROWD.

SENIOR DEBT loans or DEBT SECURITIES that have claim prior to junior obligations and EQUITY on a corporation's assets in the event of LIQUIDATION. Senior debt commonly includes funds borrowed from banks, insurance companies, or other financial institutions, as well as notes, bonds, or debentures not expressly defined as junior or subordinated.

SENIOR MORTGAGE BOND bond with the highest claim on the assets of the issuer in case of bankruptcy or liquidation. Senior mortgage bondholders are paid off in full before any payments are made to junior bondholders.

SENIOR REFUNDING replacement of securities maturing in 5 to 12 years with issues having original maturities of 15 years or longer. The objectives may be to reduce the bond issuer's interest costs, to consolidate several issues into one, or to extend the maturity date.

SENIOR SECURITY security that has claim prior to a junior obligation and EQUITY on a corporation's assets and earnings. Senior securities are repaid before JUNIOR SECURITIES in the event of LIQUIDATION. Debt, including notes, bonds, and debentures, is senior to stock; first mortgage bonds are senior to second mortgage bonds; and all mortgage bonds are senior to debentures, which are unsecured.

SENSITIVE MARKET market easily swayed by good or bad news.

SENSITIVITY ANALYSIS study measuring the effect of a change in a variable (such as sales) on the risk or profitability of an investment.

SENTIMENT INDICATORS measures of the bullish or bearish mood of investors. Many technical analysts look at these indicators as contrary indicators—that is, when most investors are bullish, the market is about to drop, and when most are bearish, the market is about to rise. Some financial newsletters measure swings in investor sentiment by tabulating the number of INVESTMENT ADVISORY SERVICES that are bullish or bearish.

SEP *see* SIMPLIFIED EMPLOYEE PENSION (SEP) PLAN.

SEPARATE CUSTOMER concept used by the SECURITIES INVESTOR PROTECTION CORPORATION (SIPC) in allocating insurance coverage. If there is a difference in the way investment accounts are owned, each account is viewed as a separate customer entitled to the maximum protection; thus two accounts, one in the name of John Jones and the other in the name of John Jones and his wife Mary Jones, would be treated as separate accounts and separate persons. On the other hand, a CASH ACCOUNT, a MARGIN ACCOUNT, and a special convertible bond account all owned by John Jones are not treated as separate customer accounts but as one.

SEPARATELY REPORTABLE SEGMENT *see* BUSINESS SEGMENT REPORTING.

SEPARATE TAX RETURNS tax returns filed by a married couple choosing the married, filing separately, status. Each person reports his or her own income, deductions, exemptions, and credits. Couples may choose to file separately instead of with a JOINT TAX RETURN for several reasons. A couple may choose to keep all of their financial affairs, including tax filing, separate. In some cases, a couple may find that the total amount of tax paid is less if they file separately than if they file jointly. This is usually the case when there is a wide disparity between the earnings of the husband and wife. However, because of the way the tax tables are designed, it is frequently more advantageous for a married couple to file a joint return than for them to file separate returns. *See also* FILING STATUS, HEAD OF HOUSEHOLD.

SERIAL BOND bond issue, usually of a municipality, with various MATURITY DATES scheduled at regular intervals until the entire issue is retired. Each bond certificate in the series has an indicated REDEMPTION DATE.

SERIAL REDEMPTION redemption of a SERIAL BOND.

SERIES E BOND savings bond issued by the U.S. government from 1941 to 1979. The bonds were then replaced by Series EE and Series HH bonds. Outstanding Series E bonds, which may be exchanged for Series HH bonds, continue to pay interest for between 30 and 40 years from their issue date. Those issued from 1941 to November 1965 accrue interest for 40 years; those issued from December 1965 and later, for 30 years. Their interest is exempt from state and local income and personal property taxes. *See also* SAVINGS BOND.

SERIES EE BOND *see* SAVINGS BOND.

SERIES HH BOND *see* SAVINGS BOND.

SERIES OF OPTION class of OPTION, either all CALL OPTIONS or all PUT OPTIONS, on the same underlying security, all of which have the same EXERCISE PRICE (strike price) and maturity date. For example, all XYZ May 50 calls would form a series of options.

SERIES 7 REGISTERED broker who has passed the General Securities Registered Representative Examination, commonly called the *Series 7,* and who is a REGISTERED REPRESENTATIVE. In addition to the Series 7, which is a six-hour multiple-choice test developed by the New York Stock Exchange (NYSE) and administered by the National Association of Securities Dealers (NASD), many states require that registered representatives pass a UNIFORM SECURITIES AGENT STATE LAW EXAMINATION.

SET-ASIDE percentage of a job set aside for bidding to minority contractors. In the securities business, many municipal and some corporate bond underwritings require that a certain percentage of the offering be handled by a minority-owned broker/ dealer underwriting firm. Other government and corporate contracts for products and services also stipulate that a certain percentage of the business must be handled by minority firms. Set-aside programs are designed to help minority firms become established more quickly than they might if they had to compete on an equal footing with entrenched competitors.

SETTLE
In general: to pay an obligation.
Estates: distribution of an estate's assets by an executor to beneficiaries after all legal procedures have been completed.
Law: (1) to resolve a legal dispute short of adjudication; (2) to arrange for disposition of property, such as between spouses or between parents and children, if there has been a dispute such as a divorce.
Securities: to complete a securities trade between brokers acting as AGENTS or between a broker and his customer. A trade is settled when the customer has paid the broker for securities bought or when the customer delivers securities that have been sold and the customer receives the proceeds from the sale. *See also* CONTINUOUS NET SETTLEMENT.

SETTLEMENT in general, a resolution of differences among various parties. For example, a labor dispute resulting in a strike may finally be settled by a new contract, or a conflict between a landlord and tenant may be settled in a housing court.

Securities: conclusion of a securities transaction in which a broker/dealer pays for securities bought for a customer or delivers securities sold and receives payment from the buyer's broker. REGULAR WAY DELIVERY AND SETTLEMENT is completed on the third full business day following the date of the transaction for stocks, called the SETTLEMENT DATE. Government bonds and options trades are settled the next business day. *See also* CONTINUOUS NET SETTLEMENT.

Futures/Options: the final price, established by exchange rule, for the prices prevailing during the closing period and upon which futures contracts are marked to market.

SETTLEMENT DATE date by which an executed order must be settled, either by a buyer paying for the securities with cash or by a seller delivering the securities and receiving the proceeds of the sale for them. In a REGULAR-WAY DELIVERY of stocks and bonds, the settlement date is three business days after the trade was executed. For listed options and government securities, settlement is required by the next business day. *See also* SELLER'S OPTION.

SETTLEMENT OPTIONS options available to beneficiaries when a person insured by a life insurance policy dies. The DEATH BENEFIT may be paid in one lump sum, in several installments over a fixed period of time, or in the form of an ANNUITY for the rest of the beneficiary's life, among other options.

SETTLOR person who creates an INTER VIVOS TRUST as distinguished from a TESTAMENTARY TRUST. Also called *donor, grantor,* or *trustor.*

SEVERALLY BUT NOT JOINTLY form of agreement used to establish the responsibility for selling a portion of the securities in an underwriting. UNDERWRITING GROUP members agree to buy a certain portion of an issue (severally) but do not agree to joint liability for shares not sold by other members of the syndicate. In a less common form of underwriting arrangement, called a *several and joint agreement,* syndicate members agree to sell not only the shares allocated to them, but also any shares not sold by the rest of the group. *See also* UNDERWRITE.

SEVERANCE PAY money paid to an employee who has been laid off by an employer. The money may be paid in the form of a LUMP SUM, as an ANNUITY, or in the form of paychecks for a specified period of time. The size of the termination benefit is based on the length of service and job level of the employee, union contracts, and other factors. Also called *termination benefit.*

SG&A EXPENSES *see* SELLING, GENERAL, AND ADMINISTRATIVE EXPENSES.

SHADOW CALENDAR backlog of securities issues in REGISTRATION with the Securities and Exchange Commission for which no OFFERING DATE has been set pending clearance.

SHAKEOUT change in market conditions that results in the elimination of marginally financed participants in an industry. For example, if the market for microcomputers suddenly becomes glutted because there is more supply than demand, a shakeout will result, meaning that companies will fall by the wayside. In the securities markets, a shakeout occurs when speculators are forced by market events to sell their positions, usually at a loss.

SHAM transaction conducted for the purpose of avoiding taxation. Once discovered by tax authorities, it will be considered null and void, and the parties to the transaction will have to pay the taxes due. Some limited partnerships have been ruled to be "sham transactions" in the past, causing limited partners to owe back taxes, penalties, and interest to the Internal Revenue Service.

SHANGHAI SECURITIES EXCHANGE (SHSE) established in November 1990 as a non-profit organization, regulated by the China Securities Regulatory Commission. B shares are restricted to foreign investors, and have the same rights and obligations as local A shares. Settlement is three days. Trading hours for B shares are 9:30 A.M. to 11:30 A.M. and 1 P.M. to 3 P.M., Monday through Friday.

SHARE
1. unit of equity ownership in a corporation. This ownership is represented by a stock certificate, which names the company and the shareowner. The number of shares a corporation is authorized to issue is detailed in its corporate charter. Corporations usually do not issue the full number of AUTHORIZED SHARES.
2. unit of ownership in a mutual fund. *See also* INVESTMENT COMPANY.
3. interest, normally represented by a certificate, in a general or LIMITED PARTNERSHIP.

SHARE BROKER DISCOUNT BROKER whose charges are based on the number of shares traded. The more shares in a trade, the lower the per-share cost will be. Trading with a share broker is usually advantageous for those trading at least 500 shares, or for those trading in high-priced shares, who would otherwise pay a percentage of the dollar amount. Those trading in small numbers of shares, or lower-priced ones, may pay lower commissions with a VALUE BROKER, the other kind of discount brokerage firm.

SHARED APPRECIATION MORTGAGE (SAM) mortgage in which the borrower receives a below-market rate of interest in return for agreeing to share part of the appreciation in the value of the underlying property with the lender in a specified number of years. If the borrower does not want to sell at that time, he or she must pay the lender its share of the appreciation in cash. If the borrower does not have that amount of cash on hand, the lender may force the borrower to sell the property to satisfy their claim.

SHARE DRAFT instrument similar to a bank check that is used by credit unions to withdraw from interest-bearing share draft accounts.

SHAREHOLDER
1. owner of one or more shares of STOCK in a corporation. A common shareholder is normally entitled to four basic rights of ownership: (1) claim on a share of the company's undivided assets in proportion to number of shares held; (2) proportionate voting power in the election of DIRECTORS and other business conducted at shareholder meetings or by PROXY; (3) DIVIDENDS when earned and declared by the BOARD OF DIRECTORS; and (4) PREEMPTIVE RIGHT to subscribe to additional stock offerings before they are available to the general public except when overruled by the ARTICLES OF INCORPORATION or in special circumstances, such as where stock is issued to effect a merger.
2. owner of one or more shares or units in a MUTUAL FUND. Mutual fund investors have voting rights similar to those of stock owners.
     Shareholders' rights can vary according to the articles of incorporation or BYLAWS of the particular company.
     See also PREFERRED STOCK.

SHAREHOLDER REPORT *see* STOCKHOLDER'S REPORT.

SHAREHOLDER'S EQUITY total ASSETS minus total LIABILITIES of a corporation. Also called *stockholder's equity,* EQUITY, and NET WORTH.

SHARE REPURCHASE PLAN program by which a corporation buys back its own shares in the open market. It is usually done when shares are UNDERVALUED. Since it reduces the number of shares outstanding and thus increases EARNINGS PER SHARE, it tends to elevate the market value of the remaining shares held by stockholders. *See also* GOING PRIVATE; TREASURY STOCK.

SHARES AUTHORIZED number of shares of stock provided for in the ARTICLES OF INCORPORATION of a company. This figure is ordinarily indicated in the capital accounts section of a company's BALANCE SHEET and is usually well in excess of the shares ISSUED AND OUTSTANDING. A corporation cannot legally issue more shares than authorized. The number of authorized shares can be changed only by amendment to the corporate charter, with the approval of the shareholders. The most common reason for increasing authorized shares in a public company is to accommodate a stock SPLIT.

SHARES OUTSTANDING *see* ISSUED AND OUTSTANDING.

SHARK REPELLENT measure undertaken by a corporation to discourage unwanted TAKEOVER attempts. Also called *porcupine provision.* For example:

(1) fair price provision requiring a bidder to pay the same price to all shareholders. This raises the stakes and discourages TENDER OFFERS designed to attract only those shareholders most eager to replace management.

(2) GOLDEN PARACHUTE contract with top executives that makes it prohibitively expensive to get rid of existing management.

(3) defensive merger, in which a TARGET COMPANY combines with another organization that would create antitrust or other regulatory problems if the original, unwanted takeover proposal was consummated. *See also* SAFE HARBOR.

(4) STAGGERED BOARD OF DIRECTORS, a way to make it more difficult for a corporate RAIDER to install a majority of directors sympathetic to his or her views.

(5) supermajority provision, which might increase from a simple majority to two-thirds or three-fourths the shareholder vote required to ratify a takeover by an outsider.

See also POISON PILL; SCORCHED-EARTH POLICY.

SHARK WATCHER firm specializing in the early detection of TAKEOVER activity. Such a firm, whose primary business is usually the solicitation of proxies for client corporations, monitors trading patterns in a client's stock and attempts to determine the identity of parties accumulating shares.

SHARPE RATIO average return, less the RISK-FREE RETURN, divided by the STANDARD DEVIATION of return. The ratio measures the relationship of reward to risk in an investment strategy. The higher the ratio, the safer the strategy.

SHELF REGISTRATION term used for SECURITIES AND EXCHANGE COMMISSION RULE 415 adopted in the 1980s, which allows a corporation to comply with REGISTRATION requirements up to two years prior to a PUBLIC OFFERING of securities. With the registration on the shelf, the corporation, by simply updating regularly filed annual, quarterly, and related reports to the SEC, can go to the market as conditions become favorable with a minimum of administrative preparation. The flexibility corporate issuers enjoy as the result of shelf registration translates into substantial savings of time and expense.

SHELL CORPORATION company that is incorporated but has no significant assets or operations. Such corporations may be formed to obtain financing prior to starting operations, in which case an investment in them is highly risky. The term is also used of corporations set up by fraudulent operators as fronts to conceal tax evasion schemes.

SHENZHEN STOCK EXCHANGE (SZSE) opened in July 1991 in the Shenzhen province of China. The exchange levies a fee on new listings, which is set aside in a fund used by exchange officials to even out price fluctuations; organization and structure are similar to the SHANGHAI SECURITIES EXCHANGE (SHSE).

SHERMAN ANTI-TRUST ACT OF 1890 *see* ANTITRUST LAWS.

SHOCK ABSORBERS *see* CIRCUIT BREAKERS.

SHOGUN SECURITY security issued and distributed exclusively in Japan by a non-Japanese company and denominated in a currency other than yen.

SHOP
1. area of a business location where production takes place, as distinguished from the office or warehouse areas.
2. factory work force of an employer, as in a "union shop."
3. office of a broker-dealer in securities.
4. the act of canvassing dealers for the most favorable price, as in shopping securities dealers for the best bid or offer.
5. a small retail establishment.

SHORT AGAINST THE BOX *see* SELLING SHORT AGAINST THE BOX.

SHORT BOND
1. bond with a short maturity; a somewhat subjective concept, but generally meaning two years or less. *See also* SHORT TERM.
2. bond repayable in one year or less and thus classified as a CURRENT LIABILITY in accordance with the accounting definition of SHORT-TERM DEBT.
3. SHORT COUPON bond.

SHORT COUPON
1. bond interest payment covering less than the conventional six-month period. A short coupon payment occurs when the original issue date is less than a half year from the first scheduled interest payment date. Depending on how short the coupon is, the ACCRUED INTEREST makes a difference in the value of the bond at the time of issue, which is reflected in the offering price.
2. bond with a relatively short maturity, usually two years or less. *See also* LONG COUPON.

SHORT COVERING actual purchase of securities by a short seller to replace those borrowed at the time of a short sale. *See also* LENDING SECURITIES; SELLING SHORT.

SHORTFALL amount by which a financial objective has not been met. For example, a municipality expecting $100 million in tax revenue will say there is a $10 million shortfall if it collects only $90 million. For individual investors, a shortfall is the amount by which investment objectives have not been reached. For instance, investors execting to earn 15% a year will have a 5% shortfall if they earn 10% a year.

SHORT HEDGE transaction that limits or eliminates the risk of declining value in a security or commodity without entailing ownership. Examples:

(1) SELLING SHORT AGAINST THE BOX leaves the owned securities untouched, possibly to gain in value, while protecting against a decline in value, since that would be offset by a profit on the short sale.

(2) purchasing a PUT OPTION to protect the value of a security that is owned limits loss to the cost of the option.

(3) buying a futures contract on raw materials at a specific price protects a manufacturer committed to sell a product at a certain price at a specified future time but who cannot buy the raw materials at the time of the commitment. Thus, if the price of the materials goes up, the manufacturer makes a profit on the contract; if the price goes down, he or she makes a profit on the product.

Compare with LONG HEDGE.

SHORT INTEREST total amount of shares of stock that have been sold short and have not yet been repurchased to close out SHORT POSITIONS. The short interest figure for the New York Stock Exchange, which is published monthly in newspapers, indicates how many investors think stock prices are about to fall. The Exchange reports all issues in which there are at least 5000 shares sold short, and in which the short interest position had changed by at least 2000 shares in the preceding month. The higher the short interest, the more people are expecting a downturn. Such short interest also represents potential buying pressure, however, since all short sales must eventually be covered by the purchase of shares. For this reason, a high short interest position is viewed as a bullish sign by many sophisticated market watchers. *See also* SELLING SHORT; SHORT INTEREST THEORY.

SHORT INTEREST THEORY theory that a large SHORT INTEREST in a stock presages a rise in the market price. It is based on the reasoning that even though short selling reflects a belief that prices will decline, the fact that short positions must eventually be covered is a source of upward price pressure. It is also called the CUSHION THEORY, since short sales can be viewed as a cushion of imminent buy orders. *See also* MEMBERS SHORT-SALE RATIO; ODD-LOT SHORT-SALE RATIO; SELLING SHORT; SPECIALIST'S SHORT-SALE RATIO.

SHORT POSITION

Commodities: contract in which a trader has agreed to sell a commodity at a future date for a specific price.

Stocks: stock shares that an individual has sold short (by delivery of borrowed certificates) and has not covered as of a particular date. *See also* COVER; SELLING SHORT.

SHORT SALE *see* SELLING SHORT.

SHORT-SALE RULE Securities and Exchange Commission rule requiring that short sales be made only in a rising market; also called PLUS TICK rule. A short sale can be transacted only under these conditions: (1) if the last sale was at a higher price than the sale preceding it (called an UPTICK or PLUS TICK); (2) if the last sale price is unchanged but higher than the last preceding different sale (called a ZERO-PLUS TICK). The short sale rule was designed to prevent abuses perpetuated by so-called pool operators, who would drive down the price of a stock by heavy short selling, then pick up the shares for a large profit.

SHORT-SHORT TEST Internal Revenue Service restriction on a regulated investment company limiting profits from short-term trading to 30% of gross income. Sometimes also called *short-3* test because the rule defines *short-term* as a holding period under three months. Excessive short-term trading could cause a mutual fund to lose its right not to pay taxes at the fund level. The short-short rule was repealed in the TAXPAYER RELIEF ACT OF 1997, freeing up managers of mutual funds to trade frequently without fear of losing their tax pass-through status.

SHORT SQUEEZE situation when prices of a stock or commodity futures contract start to move up sharply and many traders with short positions are forced to buy stocks or commodities in order to COVER their positions and prevent losses. This sudden surge of buying leads to even higher prices, further aggravating the losses of short sellers who have not covered their positions. *See also* SELLING SHORT.

SHORT TENDER using borrowed stock to respond to a TENDER OFFER. The practice is prohibited by SECURITIES AND EXCHANGE COMMISSION RULE 10b-4.

SHORT TERM

Accounting: assets expected to be converted into cash within the normal operating cycle (usually one year), or liabilities coming due in one year or less. *See also* CURRENT ASSETS; CURRENT LIABILITY.

Investment: investment with a maturity of one year or less. This includes bonds, although in differentiating between short-, medium-, and long-term bonds, short-term often is stretched to mean two years or less. *See also* SHORT-TERM BOND FUND; SHORT-TERM DEBT; SHORT-TERM GAIN (OR LOSS).

Taxes: HOLDING PERIOD of less than 12 months, used to differentiate SHORT-TERM GAIN OR LOSS from LONG-TERM GAIN or LOSS. *See also* CAPITAL GAINS TAX.

SHORT-TERM BOND FUND bond mutual fund investing in short-to-intermediate term bonds. Such bonds, maturing in 3 to 5 years, typically pay higher yields than the shortest maturity bonds of 1 year or less, which are held by ULTRA-SHORT-TERM BOND FUNDS. Short-term bond funds also usually pay higher yields than money market mutual funds, which buy short-term commercial paper maturing in 90 days or less. However, short-term bond funds usually yield less than long-term bond funds holding bonds maturing in 10 to 30 years. Short-term bond funds, while yielding less than long-term bond funds, are also considerably less volatile, meaning that their value falls less when interest rates rise and rises less when interest rates fall. Many short-term bond funds offer checkwriting privileges, making them a source of easy liquidity.

However, shareholders should remember than such checks will likely result in the realization of short- or long-term capital gains or losses.

SHORT-TERM DEBT all debt obligations coming due within one year; shown on a balance sheet as current liabilities. *See also* CURRENT LIABILITY.

SHORT-TERM GAIN (OR LOSS) for tax purposes, the profit or loss realized from the sale of securities or other capital assets held for less than 12 months. Short-term gains are taxable at ordinary income rates to the extent they are not reduced by offsetting capital losses. *See also* CAPITAL GAIN (OR LOSS).

SHORT-TERM INVESTMENT *see* SHORT-TERM.

SHOW STOPPER legal barrier erected to prevent a takeover attempt from becoming successful. For example, a target company may appeal to the state legislature to pass laws preventing the takeover. Or the company may embark on a SCORCHED-EARTH POLICY, making the company unappealing to the suitor. *See also* SHARK REPELLENT.

SHRINKAGE difference between the amount of inventory recorded in a firm's books and the actual amount of inventory on hand. Shrinkage may occur because of theft, deterioration, loss, clerical error, and other factors.

SIDE-BY-SIDE TRADING trading of a security and an OPTION on that security on the same exchange.

SIDEWAYS MARKET period in which prices trade within a narrow range, showing only small changes up or down. Also called HORIZONTAL PRICE MOVEMENT. *See also* FLAT MARKET.

SIGNATURE GUARANTEE written confirmation by a financial institution such as a bank or brokerage firm that a customer's signature is valid. The institution will compare a new signature from a customer with the signature on file. Transfer agents require signature guarantees when transferring stocks, bonds, mutual funds, or other securities from one party to another to ensure that the transactions are legitimate.

SIGNATURE LOAN unsecured loan requiring only the borrower's signature on a loan application. The lender agrees to make the loan because the borrower has good credit standing. Collateral is not required. Also known as a *good-faith loan* or *character loan.*

SIGNIFICANT INFLUENCE holding of a large enough equity stake in a corporation to require accounting for it in financial statements. Usually, a company that holds at least 20% of the voting stock in another company is considered a holder of significant influence. A company with such a large holding is likely represented on the board of directors of the other firm. The company owning such a stake has to declare its equity holdings, and all dividends received from the position, in its financial reports.

SIGNIFICANT ORDER order to buy or sell securities that is significant enough to affect the price of the security. Many institutional investors, such as mutual funds, will try to spread out their significant buying or selling of a particular security over several days or weeks so they do not adversely affect the price at which they buy or sell.

SIGNIFICANT ORDER IMBALANCE large number of buy or sell orders for a stock, causing an unusually wide spread between bid and offer prices. Stock exchanges frequently halt trading of a stock with a significant order imbalance until more buyers or sellers appear and an orderly market can be reestablished. A significant order imbalance on the buying side can occur when there is an announcement of an impending takeover of the company, better-than-expected earnings, or other unexpected positive news. A significant order imbalance on the selling side can occur when a takeover offer has fallen through, a key executive has left the company, earnings came in far worse than expected, or there is other unexpected negative news.

SILENT PARTNER
1. limited partner in a DIRECT PARTICIPATION PROGRAM, such as real estate and oil and gas limited partnerships, in which CASH FLOW and tax benefits are passed directly through to shareholders. Such partners are called silent because, unlike general partners, they have no direct role in management and no liability beyond their individual investment.
2. general partner in a business who has no role in management but represents a sharing of the investment and liability. Silent partners of this type are often found in family businesses, where the intent is to distribute tax liability.
     See also LIMITED PARTNERSHIP.

SILVER THURSDAY the day—March 27, 1980—when the extremely wealthy Hunt brothers of Texas failed to meet a MARGIN CALL by the brokerage firm of Bache Halsey Stuart Shields (which later became Prudential-Bache Securities) for $100 million in silver futures contracts. Their position was later covered and Bache survived, but the effects on the commodities markets and the financial markets in general were traumatic.

SIMPLE INTEREST interest calculation based only on the original principal amount. Simple interest contrasts with COMPOUND INTEREST, which is applied to principal plus accumulated interest. For example, $100 on deposit at 12% simple interest would yield $12 per year (12% of $100). The same $100 at 12% interest compounded annually would yield $12 interest only in the first year. The second year's interest would be 12% of the first year's accumulated interest and principal of $112, or $13.44. The third year's payment would be 12% of $125.44—the second year's principal plus interest—or $15.05. For computing interest on loans, simple interest is distinguished from various methods of calculating interest on a precomputed basis. *See also* PRECOMPUTE; CONSUMER CREDIT PROTECTION ACT OF 1968.

SIMPLE IRA form of SALARY REDUCTION PLAN that qualifying small employers may offer to their employees. Employers with no more than 100 employees earning $5,000 or more in a year who do not offer any other retirement plan can offer simple IRAs. Self-employed workers also are eligible to establish such accounts.

Workers offered a simple IRA may contribute up to $6,000 per year into the account. This $6,000 limit is adjusted for inflation by the IRS annually. Employee contributions are excluded from taxable pay on Form W-2 and are not subject to income tax withholding, although Social Security taxes are paid on those earnings. While the employer may pick the financial institution in which to deposit the simple IRA funds, employees have the right to transfer the funds to another financial institution of their choice without cost or penalty.

Employers must make either a matching contribution or a fixed "non-elective" contribution to their employees' accounts each year. If the employer chooses matching contributes, the employer must match the amount the employee contributes from a minimum of 1% to a maximum of 3%. There is no limit on the amount of compensation that can be matched, as long as the total amount of salary reduction in one year is no more than $6,000.

If the employer chooses to make a "non-elective" contribution instead, it must equal 2% of each employee's compensation per year. It must make the contribution for all employees, whether or not they contribute part of their pay to the plan. The maximum amount of compensation on which this 2% contribution can be made is $160,000, meaning a total contribution of $3,200 (2% of $160,000).

Distributions from simple IRAs follow the same rules as regular IRAs, with one exception. If premature distributions are taken before the employee reaches age 59½ and during the first two years after the employee starts participating in the plan, the penalty is 25%, not the usual 10%. After the first two years, the regular 10% penalty applies to pre-age 59½ withdrawals. Withdrawals taken after age 59½ are fully taxable at regular income tax rates, and mandatory withdrawals must begin at age 70½, according to IRS life expectancy tables.

Assets inside simple IRAs can be invested like any other IRAs, in stocks, bonds, mutual funds, bank deposits, annuities or precious metals.

The simple IRA replaced the Salary Reduction Simplified Employee Pension plan (known as SARSEP) in 1997. SARSEPs may be continued only by employers who established them before 1997. *See also* SIMPLIFIED EMPLOYEE PENSION (SEP) PLAN.

SIMPLE RATE OF RETURN rate of return that results from dividing the income and capital gains from an investment by the amount of capital invested. For example, if a $1000 investment produced $50 in income and $50 in capital appreciation in one year, the investment would have a 10% simple rate of return. This method of calculation does not factor in the effects of compounding.

SIMPLIFIED EMPLOYEE PENSION (SEP) PLAN pension plan in which both the employee and the employer contribute to an INDIVIDUAL RETIREMENT ACCOUNT (IRA). Under the TAX REFORM ACT OF 1986, employees (except those participating in SEPs of state or local governments) may elect to have employer contributions made to the SEP or paid to the employee in cash as with cash or deferred arrangements (401(k) PLANS). Elective contributions, which are excludable from earnings for income tax purposes but includable for employment tax (FICA and FUTA) purposes, are limited to 13.0435% of net wages up to a certain maximum, which was $160,000 in 1998. Employer contributions are limited to 15% of compensation, subject to the same limits. The total maximum contribution by employees and employers combined is $30,000 per year. SEPs are limited to small employers (25 or fewer employees) and at least 50% of employees must participate. Special provisions pertain to self-employed persons, the integration of SEP contributions and Social Security benefits and limitations on tax deferrals for highly compensated individuals.

SINGLE-COUNTRY MUTUAL FUNDS mutual funds investing in the securities of just one country. Such funds may be open-end, meaning they continue to create new shares as more money comes into the fund, or closed-end, meaning they issue a limited number of shares which then trade on the stock exchange at a premium or discount to net asset value. Single-country funds offer investors a PURE PLAY on the fortunes of securities in that country. This means that these funds typically are far more volatile than REGIONAL MUTUAL FUNDS holding securities in a wider region, or GLOBAL MUTUAL FUNDS investing in markets around the world. There are many single-country funds, including funds for Argentina, Australia, Canada, China, France, Germany, Israel, Japan, Korea, Mexico, Spain, Switzerland, and the United Kingdom.

SINGLE OPTION term used to distinguish a PUT OPTION or a CALL OPTION from a SPREAD or a STRADDLE, each of which involves two or more put or call options. *See also* OPTION.

SINGLE-PREMIUM DEFERRED ANNUITY (SPDA) tax-deferred investment similar to an INDIVIDUAL RETIREMENT ACCOUNT, without many of the IRA restrictions. An investor makes a lump-sum payment to an insurance company or mutual fund selling the annuity. That lump sum can be invested in either a fixed-return instrument like a CD or a variable-return portfolio that can be switched among stocks, bonds, and money-market accounts. Proceeds are taxed only when distributions are taken. In contrast to an IRA, there is no limit to the amount that may be invested in an SPDA. Like the IRA, the tax penalty for withdrawals before age 59½ is 10%.

SINGLE-PREMIUM LIFE INSURANCE WHOLE LIFE INSURANCE policy requiring one premium payment. Since this large, up-front payment begins accumulating cash value immediately, the policy holder will earn more than holders of policies paid up in installments. With its tax-free appreciation (assuming it remains in force); low or no net-cost; tax-free access to funds through POLICY LOANS; and tax-free proceeds to beneficiaries, this type of policy emerged as a popular TAX SHELTER under the TAX REFORM ACT OF 1986.

SINGLE-STATE MUNICIPAL BOND FUND MUTUAL FUND that invests entirely in tax-exempt obligations of governments and government agencies within a single state. Therefore, dividends paid on fund shares are not taxable to residents of that state when they file state tax returns although capital gains, if any, are taxable.

SINKER bond on which interest and principal payments are made from the proceeds of a SINKING FUND.

SINKING FUND money accumulated on a regular basis in a separate custodial account that is used to redeem debt securities or preferred stock issues. A bond indenture or preferred stock charter may specify that payments be made to a sinking fund, thus assuring investors that the issues are safer than bonds (or preferred stocks) for which the issuer must make payment all at once, without the benefit of a sinking fund. *See also* PURCHASE FUND.

SIZE
1. number of shares or bonds available for sale. A market maker will say, when asked for a quote, that a particular number of shares (the size) is available at a particular price.
2. term used when a large number of shares are for sale—a trader will say that "shares are available in size," for instance.

SKIP-PAYMENT PRIVILEGE
1. clause in some MORTGAGE contracts and installment loan agreements allowing borrowers to miss payments if ahead of schedule.
2. option offered some bank credit-card holders whereby they may defer the December payment on balances due.

SLD LAST SALE indication, meaning "sold last sale," that appears on the CONSOLIDATED TAPE when a greater than normal change occurs between transactions in a security. The designation, which appears after the STOCK SYMBOL, is normally used when the change is a point or more on lower-priced issues (below $20) or two points or more on higher-priced issues.

SLEEPER stock in which there is little investor interest but which has significant potential to gain in price once its attractions are recognized. Sleepers are most easily recognized in retrospect, after they have already moved up in price.

SLEEPING BEAUTY potential TAKEOVER target that has not yet been approached by an acquirer. Such a company usually has particularly attractive features, such as a large amount of cash, or undervalued real estate or other assets.

SLUMP short-term drop in performance. The economy may enter a slump when it goes into a RECESSION. An individual stock or mutual fund may be in a slump if its price falls over several weeks or months. A normally productive employee may go into a slump and be less productive if he or she is having financial or emotional difficulties. A slump is considered to be a temporary phenomenon, from which the economy, investment or employee will soon recover.

SMALL BUSINESS ADMINISTRATION (SBA) federal agency created in 1953 to provide financial assistance (through direct loans and loan guarantees) as well as management assistance to businesses that lack the access to CAPITAL MARKETS enjoyed by larger more creditworthy corporations. Further legislation authorized the SBA to contribute to the VENTURE CAPITAL requirements of START-UP companies by licensing and funding small business investment companies (SBICs), to maintain a loan fund for rehabilitation of property damaged by natural disasters (floods, hurricanes, etc.), and to provide loans, counseling and training for small businesses owned by minorities, the economically disadvantaged, and the disabled.

The SBA finances its activities through direct grants approved by Congress.

SMALL CAP shorthand for *small capitalization stocks* or mutual funds holding such stocks. Small cap stocks usually have a market capitalization (number of shares outstanding multiplied by the stock price) of $500 million or less. Those under $50 million in market cap are known as *microcap issues.* Small capitalization stocks represent companies that are less well established, but in many cases faster-growing than *mid-cap stocks* (from $500 million to $3 billion–$5 billion) or *large cap stocks* ($1 billion or more). (Ranges vary somewhat and may overlap, depending on the funds or indexer defining them.) Since they are less established, small cap stocks are usually more volatile than BLUE CHIPS.

SMALL FIRM EFFECT tendency of stocks of smaller firms, defined by MARKET CAPITALIZATION, to outperform larger firms. Theories to explain this phenomenon vary, but include the following: (1) smaller companies tend to have more growth potential; (2) small capitalization groupings include more companies in financial difficulty; when fortunes recover, price gains are dramatic and lift the return of the group as a whole; (3) small firms are generally neglected by analysts and hence by institutions; once discovered, they become appropriately valued, registering dramatic gains in the process. The term is also used to describe the tendency of lower priced stocks to rise or fall in greater percentage increments than higher priced shares, market capitalization, and other factors being equal. *See also* ANKLE BITER.

SMALL INVESTOR individual investor who buys small amounts of stock or bonds, often in ODD LOT quantities; also called the RETAIL INVESTOR. Although there are millions of small investors, their total holdings are dwarfed by the share ownership of large institutions such as mutual funds and insurance companies. Together with the proliferation of mutual funds, recent developments in the brokerage industry and its diversification along full-service lines have brought new programs specifically designed to make investing more convenient for small investors. Thus, much cash traditionally kept in savings banks has found its way into the stock and bond markets. *See also* ODD-LOT SHORT-SALE RATIO; ODD-LOT THEORY.

SMALL ORDER ENTRY (OR EXECUTION) SYSTEM *see* SOES.

SMART MONEY investors who make profitable investment moves at the right time, no matter what the investing environment. In a bull market, such investors buy the stocks that go up the most. In bear markets, they sell stocks short that fall the most. Smart money investors also have access to information about companies, either positive or negative, in advance of when the typical small investor learns of it. The term is also used in a more general sense to convey what sophisticated investors are doing now. Analysts will say "the smart money is buying cyclical stocks now because the economy is improving," for example.

SMOKESTACK INDUSTRIES basic manufacturing industries, such as autos, chemicals, steel, paper, and rubber, which typically have smokestacks on their plants. The fate of these industries, when viewed by Wall Street analysts, is closely tied to the ups and downs of the economy—they are therefore called CYCLICAL stocks. Many smokestack industries are located in what is known as the RUST BELT.

SNOWBALLING process by which the activation of STOP ORDERS in a declining or advancing market causes further downward or upward pressure on prices, thus triggering more stop orders and more price pressure, and so on.

SOCIALLY CONSCIOUS MUTUAL FUND mutual fund that is managed for capital appreciation while at the same time investing in securities of companies that do not conflict with certain social priorities. As a product of the social consciousness movements of the 60s and 70s, this type of mutual fund might not invest in companies that derive significant profits from defense contracts or whose activities cause environmental pollution, nor in companies with significant interests in countries with repressive or racist governments.

SOCIAL SECURITY benefits provided under the Social Security Act (1935), financed by the SOCIAL SECURITY TAX authorized by the FEDERAL INSURANCE CONTRIBUTORS ACT (FICA), and administered by the Social Security Administration. Term usually refers to retirement income benefits, but other benefits include SOCIAL SECURITY DISABILITY INCOME

INSURANCE; Aid to Families with Dependent Children (AFDC); the Food Stamp program; Unemployment Insurance; Medicare; Medicaid; Public Assistance for the Aged, Blind and Disabled; Veterans' Compensation and Pensions; Housing Subsidies and Public Housing; Nutritional Programs for Children; and Student Aid.

SOCIAL RESPONSIBILITY principle that businesses should actively contribute to the welfare of society and not only maximize profits. Most corporate annual reports will highlight what the company has done to further education, help minorities, give to the arts and social welfare agencies, and in general improve social conditions. The concept is also used by investors in picking companies that are fair to their employees, do not pollute or build weapons, and make beneficial products. *See also* SOCIALLY CONSCIOUS MUTUAL FUND.

SOCIAL SECURITY DISABILITY INCOME INSURANCE insurance financed by the SOCIAL SECURITY TAX that provides lost income to qualifying employees whose disabilities are expected to last at least one year. Benefits are payable until death.

SOCIAL SECURITY TAX federal tax created by the Social Security Act (1935) that is shared equally by employers and their employees, is levied on annual income up to a maximum level, and is invested in Social Security trust funds. Employees then qualify for retirement benefits based on years worked, amounts paid into the fund, and retirement age.

SOES acronym for the computerized *Small Order Entry (or Execution) System* used by NASDAQ, in which orders for under 1000 shares bypass brokers and are aggregated and executed against available firm quotes by market makers on the NASDAQ system. *See also* ORDER SPLITTING.

SOCIALISM political-economic doctrine that, unlike CAPITALISM, which is based on competition, seeks a cooperative society in which the means of production and distribution are owned by the government or collectively by the people.

SOFT CURRENCY funds of a country that are not acceptable in exchange for the hard currencies of other countries. Soft currencies, such as Russia's ruble, are fixed at unrealistic exchange rates and are not backed by gold, so that countries with hard currencies, like U.S. dollars or British pounds, are reluctant to convert assets into them. *See also* HARD MONEY (HARD CURRENCY).

SOFT DOLLARS means of paying brokerage firms for their services through commission revenue, rather than through direct payments, known as *hard-dollar fees.* For example, a mutual fund may offer to pay for the research of a brokerage firm by executing trades generated by that research through that brokerage firm. The broker might agree to this arrangement if the fund manager promises to spend at least $100,000 in commissions with the broker that year. Otherwise, the fund would have to pay a hard-dollar fee of $50,000 for the research. *Compare with* HARD DOLLARS.

SOFT LANDING term used to describe a rate of growth sufficient to avoid recession but slow enough to prevent high inflation and interest rates. When the economy is growing very strongly, the Federal Reserve typically tries to engineer a soft landing by raising interest rates to head off inflation. If the economy threatens to fall into a recession, the Fed may lower rates to stimulate growth.

SOFT MARKET market characterized by an excess of supply over demand. A soft market in securities is marked by inactive trading, wide bid-offer spreads, and pronounced price drops in response to minimal selling pressure. Also called *buyer's market.*

SOFTS term used to refer to tropical commodities—coffee, sugar, and cocoa—but in a broader sense could include grains, oilseeds, cotton, and orange juice. Metals, financial futures, and livestock generally are excluded from this category.

SOFT SPOT weakness in selected stocks or stock groups in the face of a generally strong and advancing market.

SOLD-OUT MARKET commodities market term meaning that futures contracts in a particular commodity or maturity range are largely unavailable because of contract liquidations and limited offerings.

SOLVENCY state of being able to meet maturing obligations as they come due. See *also* INSOLVENCY.

SOUR BOND bond in DEFAULT on its interest or principal payments. The issue will typically trade at a deep discount and have a low credit rating. Traders say that the bond has "gone sour" when it defaults.

SOURCES AND APPLICATIONS (or USES) OF FUNDS STATE-MENT financial statement section that analyzed changes affecting WORKING CAPITAL (or, optionally, cash) and that appeared as part of the annual reports of the publicly held companies prior to 1988. In that year, the Financial Accounting Standards Board (FASB) supplanted this statement with the STATEMENT OF CASH FLOWS, which analyzes all changes affecting cash in the categories of operations, investment, and financing.

SOUTH AFRICAN FUTURES EXCHANGE (SAFEX) trades futures and options on the Johannesburg Stock Exchange's All Share Index, All Gold Index, Financial Industrial Index and Industrial Index, as well as the KRUGGERAND, long-term bond, and short-term interest. Trading is electronic.

SOVEREIGN RISK risk that a foreign government will default on its loan or fail to honor other business commitments because of a change in national policy. A country asserting its prerogatives as an independent nation might prevent the REPATRIATION of a company or country's funds through limits on the flow of capital, tax impediments, or the nationalization of property. Sovereign risk became a factor in the growth of international debt that followed the oil price increases of the 1970s. Several developing countries that borrowed heavily from Western banks to finance trade deficits had difficulty later keeping to repayment schedules. Banks had to reschedule loans to such countries as Mexico and Argentina to keep them from defaulting. These loans ran the further risk of renunciation by political leaders, which also would have affected loans to private companies that had been guaranteed by previous governments. Beginning in the 1970s, banks and other multinational corporations developed sophisticated analytical tools to measure sovereign risk before committing to lend, invest, or begin operations in a given foreign country. Throughout periods of worldwide economic volatility, the United States has been able to attract foreign investment because of its perceived lack of sovereign risk. Also called *country risk* or *political risk.*

SPDR acronym for *Standard & Poor's Depositary Receipt,* traded on the American Stock Exchange under the ticker symbol "SPY." Called *spiders,* they are securities that represent ownership in a long-term UNIT INVESTMENT TRUST that holds a portfolio of common stocks designed to track the performance of the S&P 500 INDEX. A SPDR entitles a holder to receive proportionate quarterly cash distributions corresponding to the dividends that accrue to the S&P 500 stocks in the underlying portfolio, less trust expenses. Like a stock, SPDRs can be traded continuously throughout the trading day, or can be held for the long-term. In contrast, S&P 500 index mutual funds are priced only once, at the end of each trading day. Amex also trades MidCap SPDRs, which track the S&P MidCap 400 index. *See also* DIAMONDS.

SPECIAL ARBITRAGE ACCOUNT special MARGIN ACCOUNT with a broker reserved for transactions in which the customer's risk is hedged by an offsetting security transaction or position. The MARGIN REQUIREMENT on such a transaction is substantially less than in the case of stocks bought on credit and subject to price declines. *See also* HEDGE/HEDGING.

SPECIAL ASSESSMENT BOND municipal bond that is repaid from taxes imposed on those who benefit directly from the neighborhood-oriented public works project funded by the bond; also called *special assessment limited liability bond, special district bond, special purpose bond,* SPECIAL TAX BOND. For example, if a bond finances the construction of a sewer system, the homeowners and businesses hooked up to the sewer system pay a special levy that goes to repay the bonds. The interest from special assessment bonds is tax free to resident bondholders. These are not normally GENERAL OBLIGATION BONDS, and the FULL FAITH AND CREDIT of the municipality is not usually behind them. Where the full faith and credit does back such bonds, they are called general obligation special assessment bonds.

SPECIAL BID infrequently used method of purchasing a large block of stock on the New York Stock Exchange whereby a MEMBER FIRM, acting as a broker, matches the buy order of one client, usually an institution, with sell orders solicited from a number of other customers. It is the reverse of an EXCHANGE DISTRIBUTION. The member broker makes a fixed price offer, which is announced in advance on the CONSOLIDATED TAPE. The bid cannot be lower than the last sale or the current regular market bid. Sellers of the stock pay no commissions; the buying customer pays both the selling and buying commissions. The transaction is completed during regular trading hours.

SPECIAL BOND ACCOUNT special MARGIN ACCOUNT with a broker that is reserved for transactions in U.S. government bonds, municipals, and eligible listed and unlisted nonconvertible corporate bonds. The restrictions under which brokers may extend credit with margin securities of these types are generally more liberal than in the case of stocks.

SPECIAL CASH ACCOUNT same as CASH ACCOUNT.

SPECIAL DISTRICT BOND *see* SPECIAL ASSESSMENT BOND.

SPECIAL DRAWING RIGHTS (SDR) measure of a nation's reserve assets in the international monetary system; known informally as "paper gold." First issued by the INTERNATIONAL MONETARY FUND (IMF) in 1970, SDRs are designed to supplement the reserves of gold and convertible currencies (or hard currencies) used to maintain stability in the foreign exchange market. For example, if the U.S. Treasury sees that the British pound's value has fallen precipitously in relation to the dollar, it can use its store of SDRs to buy excess pounds on the foreign exchange market, thereby raising the value of the remaining supply of pounds.

This neutral unit of account was made necessary by the rapid growth in world trade during the 1960s. International monetary officials feared that the supply of the two principal reserve assets—gold and U.S. dollars—would fall short of demand, causing the value of the U.S. currency to rise disproportionately in relation to other reserve assets. (At the time SDRs were introduced, the price of gold was fixed at about $35 per ounce.)

The IMF allocates to each of its more than 140 member countries an amount of SDRs proportional to its predetermined quota in the fund, which in turn is based on its GROSS NATIONAL PRODUCT (GNP). Each member agrees to back its SDRs with the full faith and credit of its government, and to accept them in exchange for gold or convertible currencies.

Originally, the value of one SDR was fixed at one dollar and at the dollar equivalent of other key currencies on January 1, 1970. As world governments adopted the current system of FLOATING EXCHANGE RATES, the SDR's value fluctuated relative to the "basket" of major currencies. Increasing reliance on SDRs in settling international accounts coincided with a decline in the importance of gold as a reserve asset.

Because of its inherent equilibrium relative to any one currency, the SDR has been used to denominate or calculate the value of private contracts, international treaties, and securities on the EUROBOND market.

See also EUROPEAN CURRENCY UNIT (ECU).

SPECIALIST member of a stock exchange who maintains a fair and orderly market in one or more securities. A specialist or SPECIALIST UNIT performs two main functions: executing LIMIT ORDERS on behalf of other exchange members for a portion of the FLOOR BROKER'S commission, and buying or selling—sometimes SELLING SHORT—for the specialist's own account to counteract temporary imbalances in supply and demand and thus prevent wide swings in stock prices. The specialist is prohibited by exchange rules from buying for his own account when there is an unexecuted order for the same security at the same price in the SPECIALIST'S BOOK, the record kept of limit orders in each price category in the sequence in which they are received. Specialists must meet strict minimum capital requirements before receiving formal approval by the New York Stock Exchange. *See also* SPECIALIST BLOCK PURCHASE AND SALE; SPECIALIST'S SHORT SALE RATIO.

SPECIALIST BLOCK PURCHASE AND SALE transaction whereby a SPECIALIST on a stock exchange buys a large block of securities either to sell for his own account or to try and place with another block buyer and seller, such as a FLOOR TRADER. Exchange rules require that such transactions be executed only when the securities cannot be ABSORBED in the regular market. *See also* NOT HELD.

SPECIALIST'S BOOK record maintained by a SPECIALIST that includes the specialist's own inventory of securities, market orders to sell short, and LIMIT ORDERS and STOP ORDERS that other stock exchange members have placed with the specialist. The orders are listed in chronological sequence. For example, for a stock trading at 57 a broker might ask for 500 shares when the price falls to 55. If successful at placing this limit order, the specialist notifies the member broker who entered the request, and collects a commission. The specialist is prohibited from buying the stock for his own account at a price for which he has previously agreed to execute a limit order.

SPECIALIST'S SHORT-SALE RATIO ratio of the amount of stock sold short by specialists on the floor of the New York Stock Exchange to total short sales. The ratio signals whether specialists are more or less bearish (expecting prices to decline) on the outlook for stock prices than other NYSE members and the public. Since specialists must constantly be selling stock short in order to provide for an orderly market in the stocks they trade, their short sales cannot be entirely regarded as an indication of how they perceive trends. Still, their overall short sales activity reflects knowledge, and technical analysts watch the specialist's short-sale ratio carefully for a clue to imminent upturns or downturns in stock prices. Traditionally, when the ratio rises above 60%, it is considered a bearish signal. A drop below 45% is seen as bullish and below 35% is considered extremely bullish. *See also* ODD-LOT SHORT-SALE RATIO; SELLING SHORT; SPECIALIST.

SPECIALIST UNIT stock exchange SPECIALIST (individual, partnership, corporation, or group of two or three firms) authorized by an exchange to deal as PRINCIPAL and AGENT for other brokers in maintaining a stable market in one or more particular stocks. A specialist unit on the New York Stock Exchange is required to have enough capital to buy at least 5000 shares of the common stock of a company it handles and 1000 shares of the company's CONVERTIBLE preferred stock.

SPECIALIZED MUTUAL FUND mutual fund concentrating on one industry. By so doing, shareholders have a PURE PLAY on the fortunes of that industry, for better or worse. Some of the many industries with specialized mutual funds include banking, biotechnology, chemicals, energy, environmental services, natural resources, precious metals, technology, telecommunications, and utilities. These funds tend to be more volatile than funds holding a diversified portfolio of stocks in many industries. Also called *sector funds* or *specialty funds.*

SPECIAL MISCELLANEOUS ACCOUNT (SMA) memorandum account of the funds in excess of the MARGIN REQUIREMENT. Such excess funds may arise from the proceeds of sales, appreciation of market values, dividends, or cash or securities put up in response to a MARGIN CALL. An SMA is not under the jurisdiction of REGULATION T of the Federal Reserve Board, as is the INITIAL MARGIN requirement, but this does not mean the customer is free to withdraw balances from it. The account is maintained essentially so that the broker can gauge how far the customer might be from a margin call. Any withdrawals require the broker's permission.

SPECIAL OFFERING method of selling a large block of stock that is similar to a SECONDARY DISTRIBUTION but is limited to New York Stock Exchange members and takes place during normal trading hours. The selling member announces the impending sale on the CONSOLIDATED TAPE, indicating a fixed price, which is usually based on the last transaction price in the regular market. All costs and commissions are borne by the seller. The buyers are member firms that may be buying for customer accounts or for their own inventory. Such offerings must have approval from the Securities and Exchange Commission.

SPECIAL SITUATION
1. undervalued stock that should soon rise in value because of an imminent favorable turn of events. A special situation stock may be about to introduce a revolutionary new product or be undergoing a needed management change. Many securities analysts concentrate on looking for and analyzing special situation stocks.

2. stock that fluctuates widely in daily trading, often influencing market averages, because of a particular news development, such as the announcement of a TAKEOVER bid.

SPECIAL TAX BOND
1. MUNICIPAL REVENUE BOND that will be repaid through excise taxes on such purchases as gasoline, tobacco, and liquor. The bond is not backed by the ordinary taxing power of the municipality issuing it. The interest from these bonds is tax free to resident bondholders.
2. SPECIAL ASSESSMENT BOND.

SPECTAIL term for broker-dealer who is part retail broker but preponderantly dealer/speculator.

SPECULATION assumption of risk in anticipation of gain but recognizing a higher than average possibility of loss. Speculation is a necessary and productive activity. It can be profitable over the long term when engaged in by professionals, who often limit their losses through the use of various HEDGING techniques and devices, including OPTIONS trading, SELLING SHORT, STOP LOSS ORDERS, and transactions in FUTURES CONTRACTS. The term speculation implies that a business or investment risk can be analyzed and measured, and its distinction from the term INVESTMENT is one of degree of risk. It differs from gambling, which is based on random outcomes.

See also VENTURE CAPITAL.

SPECULATOR market participant who tries to profit from buying and selling futures and options contracts by anticipating future price movements. Speculators assume market price risk and add liquidity and capital to the futures markets. Speculators may purchase volatile stocks or mutual funds, and hold them for a short time in order to reap a profit. They may also sell stocks short and hope to cash in when the stock price drops quickly.

SPIDERS *see* SPDR.

SPIN-OFF form of corporate DIVESTITURE that results in a subsidiary or division becoming an independent company. In a traditional spin-off, shares in the new entity are distributed to the parent corporation's shareholders of record on a PRO RATA basis. Spin-offs can also be accomplished through a LEVERAGED BUYOUT by the subsidiary or division's management, or through an EMPLOYEE STOCK OWNERSHIP PLAN (ESOP).

SPINS acronym for *Standard & Poor's 500 Index Subordinated Notes,* as Salomon Brothers' product combining features of debt, equity, and options.

SPLIT increase in a corporation's number of outstanding shares of stock without any change in the shareholders' EQUITY or the aggregate MARKET VALUE at the time of the split. In a split, also called a *split up,* the share price declines. If a stock at $100 par value splits 2-for-1, the number of authorized shares doubles (for example, from 10 million to 20 million) and the price per share drops by half, to $50. A holder of 50 shares before the split now has 100 shares at the lower price. If the same stock splits 4-for-1, the number of shares quadruples to 40 million and the share price falls to $25. Dividends per share also fall proportionately. Directors of a corporation will authorize a split to make ownership more affordable to a broader base of investors. Where stock splits require an increase in AUTHORIZED SHARES and/or a change in PAR VALUE of the stock, shareholders must approve an amendment of the corporate charter.

See also REVERSE SPLIT.

SPLIT COMMISSION commission divided between the securities broker who executes a trade and another person who brought the trade to the broker, such as an investment counselor or financial planner. Split commissions between brokers are also common in real estate transactions.

SPLIT COUPON BOND debt instrument that begins as a zero-coupon bond and converts to an interest-paying bond at a specified date in the future. These bonds, issued by corporations and municipalities, are advantageous to issuers because they do not have to pay out cash interest for several years. They are attractive to investors, particularly in tax-sheltered accounts like IRAs and Keoghs, because they have locked in a reinvestment rate for several years, and then can receive cash interest. For example, a 55-year-old investor may want a split coupon bond because it will appreciate in value for 10 years, and then pay interest when he is retired and needs regular income. Also known as ZERO-COUPON CONVERTIBLE SECURITY.

SPLIT DOWN *see* REVERSE SPLIT.

SPLIT OFFERING new municipal bond issue, part of which is represented by SERIAL BONDS and part by term maturity bonds.

SPLIT ORDER large transaction in securities that, to avoid unsettling the market and causing fluctuations in the market price, is broken down into smaller portions to be executed over a period of time.

SPLIT RATING situation in which two major rating agencies, such as Standard & Poor's and Moody's Investors Service, assign a different rating to the same security.

SPLIT UP *see* SPLIT.

SPONSOR
   Limited partnerships: GENERAL PARTNER who organizes and sells a LIMITED PARTNERSHIP. Sponsors (also called *promoters)* rely on their reputation in past real estate, oil and gas, or other deals to attract limited partners to their new deals.
   Mutual funds: investment company that offers shares in its funds. Also called the *underwriter.*

Stocks: important investor—typically, an institution, mutual fund, or other big trader—whose favorable opinion of a particular security influences other investors and creates additional demand for the security. Institutional investors often want to make sure a stock has wide sponsorship before they invest in it, since this should ensure that the stock will not fall dramatically.

SPOT COMMODITY COMMODITY traded with the expectation that it will actually be delivered to the buyer, as contrasted to a FUTURES CONTRACT that will usually expire without any physical delivery taking place. Spot commodities are traded in the SPOT MARKET.

SPOT DELIVERY MONTH nearest month of those currently being traded in which a commodity could be delivered. In late January, therefore, the spot delivery month would be February for commodities with a February contract trade.

SPOT MARKET commodities market in which goods are sold for cash and delivered immediately. Trades that take place in FUTURES CONTRACTS expiring in the current month are also called *spot market trades.* The spot market tends to be conducted OVER-THE-COUNTER—that is, through telephone trading—rather than on the floor of an organized commodity exchange. Also called *actual market, cash market* or *physical market. See also* FUTURES MARKET.

SPOT PRICE current delivery price of a commodity traded in the SPOT MARKET. Also called *cash price.*

SPOUSAL IRA INDIVIDUAL RETIREMENT ACCOUNT that may be opened in the name of a nonworking spouse. The maximum annual IRA contribution for a married couple, only one of whom is employed, is $4000. The husband and wife can each contribute up to $2000, as long as their combined compensation is at least that much. Before 1997, the nonworking spouse could only contribute $250 to their IRA. The same rules apply ($2000 per person) when both spouses work. Contributions are deductible only if both husband and wife are not actively participating in a qualified retirement plan.

SPOUSAL REMAINDER TRUST means used prior to the TAX REFORM ACT OF 1986 to shift income to a person taxable at a lower rate. Income-producing property, such as securities, is transferred by the grantor to the trust for a specific time, typically five years. Trust income is distributed to the beneficiary (or to a minor's CUSTODIAL ACCOUNT) to be used for expenses such as a child's college education. The income is therefore taxed at the beneficiary's lower tax rate. When the trust term expires, the property passes irrevocably to the grantor's spouse. The TAX REFORM ACT OF 1986 provided that effective for trusts established or contributions to trusts made after March 1, 1986, income must be taxed at the grantor's tax rate if the beneficiary is under age 14 and the property can revert to the grantor or the grantor's spouse.

SPREAD

Commodities: in futures trading, the difference in price between delivery months in the same market, or between different or related contracts. *See also* MOB SPREAD; NOB SPREAD; TED SPREAD.

Fixed-income securities: (1) difference between yields on securities of the same quality but different maturities. For example, the spread between 6% short-term Treasury bills and 10% long-term Treasury bonds is 4 percentage points. (2) difference between yields on securities of the same maturity but different quality. For instance, the spread between a 10% long-term Treasury bond and a 14% long-term bond of a B-rated corporation is 4 percentage points, since an investor's risk of default is so much less with the Treasury bond. *See also* YIELD SPREAD.

Foreign exchange: spreading one currency versus another, or multiple spreads within various currencies. An example would be a long position in the U.S. dollar versus a short position in the Japanese yen or the Euro. An example of an intermonth spread would be a long March spot position in Swiss francs versus a short March position in the same currency. Spreads are frequently done in cash and futures markets. Interest rate differentials often have significant impact.

Options: position usually consisting of one long call and one short call option, or one long put and one short put option, with each option representing one "leg" of the spread. The two legs, if taken independently, would profit from opposite directional price movements. Spreads usually have lower cost and lower profit potential than an outright long option. They are entered into to reduce risk, or to profit from the change in the relative prices of the options. *See also* BEAR SPREAD; BULL SPREAD; BUTTERFLY SPREAD; CALENDAR SPREAD; CREDIT SPREAD; DEBIT SPREAD; DIAGONAL SPREAD; OPTION; PRICE SPREAD; SELLING THE SPREAD; VERTICAL SPREAD.

Stocks and bonds: (1) difference between the bid and offer price. If a stock is bid at $45 and offered at $46, the spread is $1. This spread narrows or widens according to supply and demand for the security being traded. *See also* BID-ASKED SPREAD; DEALER SPREAD. (2) difference between the high and low price of a particular security over a given period.

Underwriting: difference between the proceeds an issuer of a new security receives and the price paid by the public for the issue. This spread is taken by the underwriting syndicate as payment for its services. A security issued at $100 may entail a spread of $2 for the underwriter, so the issuer receives $98 from the offering. *See also* UNDERWRITING SPREAD.

SPREADING practice of buying and selling OPTION contracts of the same CLASS on the same underlying security in order to profit from moves in the price of that security. *See also* SPREAD.

SPREAD OPTION SPREAD position involving the purchase of an OPTION at one EXERCISE PRICE and the simultaneous sale of another option on the same underlying security at a different exercise price and/or expiration date. *See also* DIAGONAL SPREAD; HORIZONTAL SPREAD; VERTICAL SPREAD.

SPREAD ORDER OPTIONS market term for an order designating the SERIES of LISTED OPTIONS the customer wishes to buy and sell, together with the desired SPREAD—or difference in option premiums (prices)—shown as a net debit or net credit. The transaction is completed if the FLOOR BROKER can execute the order at the requested spread.

SPREAD POSITION status of an account in which a SPREAD has been executed.

SPREADSHEET ledger sheet on which a company's financial statements, such as BALANCE SHEETS, INCOME STATEMENTS, and sales reports, are laid out in columns and rows. Spreadsheets are used by securities and credit analysts in researching companies and industries. Since the advent of personal computers, spreadsheets have come into wide use, because software makes them easy to use. In an electronic spreadsheet on a computer, any time one number is changed, all the other numbers are automatically adjusted according to the relationships the computer operator sets up. For instance, in a spreadsheet of a sales report of a company's many divisions, the updating of a single division's sales figure will automatically change the total sales for the company, as well as the percentage of total sales that division produced.

SPRINKLING TRUST trust under which no beneficiary has a right to receive any trust income. Instead, the trustee is given discretion to divide, or "sprinkle," the trust's income as the trustee sees fit among a designated group of persons. Sprinkling trusts can be created both by LIVING TRUST agreements and by WILLS.

SPX ticker symbol for the Standard & Poor's 500 stock index options traded on the Chicago Board Options Exchange. The European-style index options contract is settled in cash, and can be exercised only on the last business day before expiration. The SPX is one of the most heavily traded of all index options contracts.

SQUEEZE
Finance: (1) tight money period, when loan money is scarce and interest rates are high, making borrowing difficult and expensive—also called a *credit crunch;* (2) any situation where increased costs cannot be passed on to customers in the form of higher prices.
Investments: situation when stocks or commodities futures start to move up in price, and investors who have sold short are forced to COVER their short positions in order to avoid large losses. When done by many short sellers, this action is called a SHORT SQUEEZE. *See also* SELLING SHORT; SHORT POSITION.

SRO *see* SELF-REGULATORY ORGANIZATION.

STABILIZATION

Currency: buying and selling of a country's own currency to protect its exchange value, also called PEGGING.

Economics: leveling out of the business cycle, unemployment, and prices through fiscal and monetary policies.

Market trading: action taken by REGISTERED COMPETITIVE TRADERS on the New York Stock Exchange in accordance with an exchange requirement that 75% of their trades be stabilizing—in other words, that their sell orders follow a PLUS TICK and their buy orders a MINUS TICK.

New issues underwriting: intervention in the market by a managing underwriter in order to keep the market price from falling below the PUBLIC OFFERING PRICE during the offering period. The underwriter places orders to buy at a specific price, an action called PEGGING that, in any other circumstance, is a violation of laws prohibiting MANIPU-LATION in the securities and commodities markets.

STAG speculator who makes it a practice to get in and out of stocks for a fast profit, rather than to hold securities for investment.

STAGFLATION term coined by economists in the 1970s to describe the previously unprecedented combination of slow economic growth and high unemployment (stagnation) with rising prices (inflation). The principal factor was the fourfold increase in oil prices imposed by the Organization of Petroleum Exporting Countries (OPEC) cartel in 1973–74, which raised price levels throughout the economy while further slowing economic growth. As is characteristic of stagflation, fiscal and monetary policies aimed at stimulating the economy and reducing unemployment only exacerbated the inflationary effects.

STAGGERED BOARD OF DIRECTORS board of directors of a company in which a portion of the directors are elected each year, instead of all at once. A board is often staggered in order to thwart unfriendly TAKEOVER attempts, since potential acquirers would have to wait a longer time before they could take control of a company's board through the normal voting procedure. Normally, all directors are elected at the annual meeting.

STAGGERING MATURITIES technique used to lower risk by a bond investor. Since long-term bonds are more volatile than short-term ones, an investor can HEDGE against interest rate movements by buying short-, medium- and long-term bonds. If interest rates decline, the long-term bonds will rise faster in value than the shorter-term bonds. If rates rise, however, the shorter-term bonds will hold their value better than the long-term debt obligations, which could fall precipitously.

STAGNATION

Economics: period of no or slow economic growth or of economic decline, in real (inflation-adjusted) terms. Economic growth of 3% or less per year—as was the case in the late 1970s, measured according to increases in the U.S. gross national product—generally is taken to constitute stagnation.

Securities: period of low volume and inactivetrading.

STAGS acronym for *Sterling Transferable Accruing Government Securities.* A British version of U.S. government STRIPS, STAGS are deep discount zero-coupon bonds backed by British Treasury securities. *See also* ZERO-COUPON SECURITY.

STANDARD & POOR'S CORPORATION subsidiary of The McGraw-Hill Companies that provides a broad range of investment services, including RATING corporate and municipal bonds, common stocks, preferred stocks, and COMMERCIAL PAPER; compiling the STANDARD & POOR'S 500 COMPOSITE INDEX, the Standard & Poor's MidCap 400 Index, the Standard & Poor's SmallCap 600 Index, and the Standard & Poor's 100 Index, among other indices; publishing a wide variety of statistical materials, investment advisory reports, and other financial information, including: *Bond Guide,* a summary of data on corporate and municipal bonds; *Earnings Guide,* earnings-per-share estimates on more than 5,500 publicly traded stocks; *Emerging & Special Situations,* information and analysis on the new issue market; *Stock Guide,* investment data on listed and unlisted common and preferred stocks and mutual funds; *Analyst's Handbook,* per-share data on the stocks and industry groups making up industrial, transportation, financial and utility groups; *Corporation Records,* six alphabetical volumes and a daily news volume of information on more than 12,000 publicly held companies; and *Stock Reports,* analytical reports on listed and unlisted companies. A subsidiary publishes the daily BLUE LIST of municipal and corporate bonds. Standard & Poor's also publishes *Standard & Poor's Register,* a national directory of companies and their officers, and *Securities Dealers of North America,* a directory of investment banking and brokerage firms in North America. *See also* STANDARD & POOR'S RATING; STOCK INDICES AND AVERAGES.

STANDARD & POOR'S 500 COMPOSITE INDEX broad-based measurement of changes in stock market conditions based on the average performance of 500 widely held common stocks; commonly known as the *Standard & Poor's 500* (or *S&P 500*). The selection of stocks, their relative weightings to reflect differences in the number of outstanding shares, and publication of the index itself are services of STANDARD & POOR'S CORPORATION, a financial advisory, securities rating, and publishing firm. The index tracks industrial, transportation, financial, and utility stocks; it is a large cap index. The composition of the 500 stocks is flexible and the number of issues in each sector varies over time. Standard & Poor's also publishes several other important indices including the *S&P MidCap 400,* the *S&P SmallCap 600,* and the *S&P 1500 Super Composite Index,* which totals the S&P 500, 400 and 600 indices. These three indices represent approximately 82% of the total market capitalization of stocks traded in the U.S. equity market. S&P also maintains over 90 individual industry indices. *See also* S&P PHENOMENON, STANDARD & POOR'S CORPORATION; STOCK INDICES AND AVERAGES.

STANDARD & POOR'S RATING classification of stocks and bonds according to risk issued by STANDARD & POOR'S CORPORATION. S&P's top four debt grades—called INVESTMENT GRADE AAA, AA, A, and BBB—indicate a minimal risk that a corporate or municipal bond issue will DEFAULT in its timely payment of interest and principal. Common stocks are ranked A+ through C on the basis of growth and stability, with a ranking of D signifying REORGANIZATION. *See also* EVENT RISK; LEGAL LIST; RATING.

STANDARD COST estimate, based on engineering and accounting studies, of what costs of production should be, assuming normal operating conditions. Standard costs differ from budgeted costs, which are forecasts based on expectations. Variances between standard costs and actual costs measure productive efficiency and are used in cost control.

STANDARD DEDUCTION individual taxpayer alternative to itemizing deductions. Current tax rules index the standard deduction to inflation, adjusting annually. They are:

	1998
Single Taxpayer	$4150
Head of Household	$6050
Married Filing Jointly	$6900
Married Filing Separately	$3450

STANDARD DEVIATION statistical measure of the degree to which an individual value in a probability distribution tends to vary from the mean of the distribution. It is widely applied in modern PORTFOLIO THEORY, for example, where the past performance of securities is used to determine the range of possible future performances and a probability is attached to each performance. The standard deviation of performance can then be calculated for each security and for the portfolio as a whole. The greater the degree of dispersion, the greater the risk. *See also* PORTFOLIO THEORY; REGRESSION ANALYSIS.

STANDARD INDUSTRIAL CLASSIFICATION (SIC) SYSTEM federally designed standard numbering system identifying companies by industry and providing other information. It is widely used by market researchers, securities analysts, and others. Computerized data bases frequently make use of this classification system.

STANDARD OF LIVING degree of prosperity in a nation, as measured by income levels, quality of housing and food, medical care, educational opportunities, transportation, communications, and other measures. The standard of living in different countries is frequently compared based on annual per capita income. On an individual level, the standard of living is a measure of the quality of life in such areas as housing, food, education, clothing, transportation, and employment opportunities.

STANDBY COMMITMENT

Securities: agreement between a corporation and an investment banking firm or group (the *standby underwriter)* whereby the latter contracts to purchase for resale, for a fee, any portion of a stock issue offered to current shareholders in a RIGHTS OFFERING that is not subscribed to during the two- to four-week standby period. A right, often issued to comply with laws guaranteeing the shareholder's PREEMPTIVE RIGHT, entitles its holder, either an existing shareholder or a person who has bought the right from a shareholder, to purchase a specified amount of shares before a PUBLIC OFFERING and usually at a price lower than the PUBLIC OFFERING PRICE.

The risk to the investment banker in a standby commitment is that the market price of shares will fall during the standby period. *See also* LAY OFF for a discussion of how standby underwriters protect themselves. *See also* FLOTATION COST; SUBSCRIPTION RIGHT; UNDERWRITE.

Lending: a bank commitment to loan money up to a specified amount for a specific period, to be used only in a certain contingency. The most common example would be a commitment to repay a construction lender in the event a permanent mortgage lender cannot be found. A COMMITMENT FEE is normally charged.

STANDBY UNDERWRITER *see* STANDBY COMMITMENT.

STANDSTILL AGREEMENT accord by a RAIDER to abstain from buying shares of a company for a specified period. *See also* GREENMAIL.

START-UP new business venture. In VENTURE CAPITAL parlance, start-up is the earliest stage at which a venture capital investor or investment pool will provide funds to an enterprise, usually on the basis of a business plan detailing the background of the management group along with market and financial PROJECTIONS. Investments or loans made at this stage are also called SEED MONEY.

STATE BANK bank organized under a charter granted by a regulatory authority in one of the 50 U.S. states, as distinguished from a NATIONAL BANK, which is federally chartered. The powers of a state-chartered commercial bank are generally consistent with those of national banks, since state laws tend to conform to federal initiatives and vice versa. State banks deposits are insured by the FEDERAL DEPOSIT INSURANCE CORPORATION. State banks have the option of joining the FEDERAL RESERVE SYSTEM, and even if they reject membership, they may purchase support services from the Fed, including check-processing and coin and currency services.

STATED INTEREST RATE

Banking: rate paid on savings instruments, such as PASSBOOK savings accounts and certificates of deposit. The stated interest rate does not take into account any compounding of interest.

Bonds: interest rate stated on a bond coupon. A bond with a 7% coupon has a 7% stated interest rate. This rate is applied to the face value of the bond, normally $1000, so that bondholders will receive 7% annually for every $1000 in face value of bonds they own.

STATED VALUE assigned value given to a corporation's stock for accounting purposes in lieu of par value. For example, the stated value may be set at $1 a share, so that if a company issued 10 million shares, the stated value of its stock would be $10 million. The stated value of the stock has no relation to its market price. It is, however, the amount per share that is credited to the CAPITAL STOCK account for each share outstanding and is therefore the legal capital of the corporation. Since state law generally prohibits a corporation from paying dividends or repurchasing shares when doing so would impair its legal capital, stated value does offer stockholders a measure of protection against loss of value.

STATEMENT
1. summary for customers of the transactions that occurred over the preceding month. A bank statement lists all deposits and withdrawals, as well as the running account balances. A brokerage statement shows all stock, bond, commodity futures, or options trades, interest and dividends received, margin debt outstanding, and other transactions, as well as a summary of the worth of the accounts at month end. A trade supplier provides a summary of open account transactions. *See also* ASSET MANAGEMENT ACCOUNT.
2. statement drawn up by businesses to show the status of their ASSETS and LIABILITIES and the results of their operations as of a certain date. *See also* FINANCIAL STATEMENT.

STATEMENT OF CASH FLOWS analysis of CASH FLOW included as part of the financial statements in annual reports of publicly held companies as set forth in Statement 95 of the FINANCIAL ACCOUNTING STANDARDS BOARD (FASB). The statement shows how changes in balance sheet and income accounts affected cash and cash equivalents and breaks the analysis down according to operating, investing, and financing activities. As an analytical tool, the statement of cash flows reveals healthy or unhealthy trends and makes it possible to predict future cash requirements. It also shows how actual cash flow measured up to estimates and permits comparisons with other companies.

STATEMENT OF CONDITION
Banking: sworn accounting of a bank's resources, liabilities, and capital accounts as of a certain date, submitted in response to periodic "calls" by bank regulatory authorities.
Finance: summary of the status of assets, liabilities, and equity of a person or a business organization as of a certain date. *See also* BALANCE SHEET.

STATEMENT OF INCOME *see* PROFIT AND LOSS STATEMENT.

STATEMENT OF OPERATIONS *see* PROFIT AND LOSS STATEMENT.

STATUTE OF LIMITATIONS statute describing the limitations on how many years can pass before someone gives up their right to sue for a wrongful action. For example, the INTERNAL REVENUE SERVICE has up to three years to assess back taxes from the time the return is filed, unless tax fraud is charged. Most states impose a statute of limitations of six years to challenge the violation of a written contract. Therefore, a suit claiming damages filed seven years after the alleged contract violation would be thrown out of court because the statute of limitations had run out.

STATUTORY INVESTMENT investment specifically authorized by state law for use by a trustee administering a trust under that state's jurisdiction.

STATUTORY MERGER legal combination of two or more corporations in which only one survives as a LEGAL ENTITY. It differs from *statutory consolidation,* in which all the companies in a combination cease to exist as legal entities and a new corporate entity is created. *See also* MERGER.

STATUTORY PROSPECTUS *see* PROSPECTUS.

STATUTORY VOTING one-share, one-vote rule that governs voting procedures in most corporations. Shareholders may cast one vote per share either for or against each nominee for the board of directors, but may not give more than one vote to one nominee. The result of statutory voting is that, in effect, those who control over 50% of the shares control the company by ensuring that the majority of the board will represent their interests. *Compare with* CUMULATIVE VOTING. *See also* PROPORTIONAL REPRESENTATION.

STAYING POWER ability of an investor to stay with (not sell) an investment that has fallen in value. For example, a commodity trader with staying power is able to meet margin calls as the commodities FUTURES CONTRACTS he has bought fall in price. He can afford to wait until the trade ultimately becomes profitable. In real estate, an investor with staying power is able to meet mortgage and maintenance payments on his or her properties and is therefore not harmed as interest rates rise or fall, or as the properties become temporarily difficult to sell.

STEP DOWN NOTE type of FLOATING RATE whose interest rate declines at specified times in the course of the loan.

STICKY DEAL new securities issue that the underwriter fears will be difficult to sell. Adverse market conditions, bad news about the issuing entity, or other factors may lead underwriters to say, "This will be a sticky deal at the price we have set." As a result, the price may be lowered or the offering withdrawn from the market.

STOCHASTICS INDEX computerized TECHNICAL ANALYSIS tool, or oscillator, that measures OVERBOUGHT and OVERSOLD conditions in a stock, using MOVING AVERAGES and RELATIVE STRENGTH techniques. In its simplest form, the stochastics index is expressed as a percentage of the difference between the low and high stock price during the stochastics period. For example, if the stochastics period is 14 days and the high in that period was 50 and the low 40, the difference would be 10. On the day it is calculated, the stochastics is the percentage of the difference that the current price represents. If the price at the time of calculation was 40, the stochastics reading would be zero. At a price of 50, the stochastics reading would be 100. At 45, the stochastics reading would be 50.

In practice, the stochastics index typically plots a five-day moving average of the stochastics. Lines drawn at the 25% and 75% levels on the graph represent overbought and oversold conditions. When the stochastics index falls below the 25% line, it generally indicates an oversold condition, and when the stochastics index goes above the 75% line it indicates an overbought condition. An upward reversal that breaks the 25% line is a positive BREAKOUT and a downward reversal that breaks the 75% line is a negative breakout, signaling new uptrends and downtrends respectively. *See also* MOMENTUM INDICATOR; MOVING AVERAGE CONVERGENCE/DIVERGENCE (MACD).

STOCK

1. ownership of a CORPORATION represented by shares that are a claim on the corporation's earnings and assets. COMMON STOCK usually entitles the shareholder to vote in the election of directors and other matters taken up at shareholder meetings or by proxy. PREFERRED STOCK generally does not confer voting rights but it has a prior claim on assets and earnings—dividends must be paid on preferred stock before any can be paid on common stock. A corporation can authorize additional classes of stock, each with its own set of contractual rights. *See also* ARTICLES OF INCORPORATION; AUTHORIZED SHARES; BLUE CHIP; BOOK VALUE; CAPITAL STOCK; CERTIFICATE; CLASS; CLASSIFIED STOCK; CLOSELY HELD; COMMON STOCK; COMMON STOCK EQUIVALENT; CONVERTIBLES; CONTROL STOCK; CORPORATION; CUMULATIVE PREFERRED; DIVIDEND; EARNINGS PER SHARE; EQUITY; FLOAT; FRACTIONAL SHARES; GOING PUBLIC; GROWTH STOCK; INACTIVE STOCK; INITIAL PUBLIC OFFERING; ISSUED AND OUTSTANDING; JOINT STOCK COMPANY; LETTER SECURITY; LISTED SECURITY; MARKET VALUE; NONVOTING STOCK; NO-PAR VALUE STOCK; OVER THE COUNTER; PAR VALUE; PARTICIPATING PREFERRED; PENNY STOCK; PREEMPTIVE RIGHT; PREFERENCE SHARES; PREFERRED STOCK; PRIOR PREFERRED STOCK; QUARTER STOCK; REGISTERED SECURITY; REGISTRAR; REVERSE SPLIT; SCRIP; SECURITY; SHARE; SHAREHOLDER; SPLIT; STATED VALUE; STOCK CERTIFICATE; STOCK DIVIDEND; STOCK EXCHANGE; STOCKHOLDER; STOCKHOLDER OF RECORD; STOCK MARKET; STOCK POWER; STOCK PURCHASE PLAN; STOCK SYMBOL; STOCK WATCHER; TRANSFER AGENT; TREASURY STOCK; VOTING STOCK; VOTING TRUST CERTIFICATE; WATERED STOCK.

   2. inventories of accumulated goods in manufacturing and retailing businesses.

   3. *see* ROLLING STOCK.

STOCK AHEAD situation in which two or more orders for a stock at a certain price arrive about the same time, and the exchange's PRIORITY rules take effect. New York Stock Exchange rules stipulate that the bid made first should be executed first or, if two bids came in at once, the bid for the larger number of shares receives priority. The bid that was not executed is then reported back to the broker, who informs the customer that the trade was not completed because there was stock ahead. *See also* MATCHED AND LOST.

STOCK BONUS PLAN plan established and maintained by an employer to provide benefits similar to those of a profit-sharing plan. Contributions by the employer, however, are not necessarily dependent on profits, and the benefits are distributed in shares of stock in the employer company. Stock bonus plans reward employee performance, and by giving employees a stake in the company they are used to help motivate them to perform at maximum efficiency.

STOCKBROKER *see* REGISTERED REPRESENTATIVE.

STOCK BUYBACK corporation's purchase of its own outstanding stock. A buyback may be financed by borrowings, sale of assets, or operating CASH FLOW. Its purpose is commonly to increase EARNINGS PER SHARE and thus the market price, often to discourage a TAKEOVER. When a buyback involves a PREMIUM paid to an acquirer in exchange for a promise to desist from takeover activity, the payment is called GREEN-MAIL. A buyback having a formula and schedule may also be called a SHARE REPURCHASE PLAN or SELF-TENDER. *See also* TREASURY STOCK.

STOCK CERTIFICATE documentation of a shareholder's ownership in a corporation. Stock certificates are engraved intricately on heavy paper to deter forgery. They indicate the number of shares owned by an individual, their PAR VALUE (if any), the CLASS of stock (for example, common or preferred), and attendant voting rights. To prevent theft, shareholders often store certificates in safe deposit boxes or take advantage of a broker's SAFEKEEPING service. Stock certificates become negotiable when endorsed.

STOCK DIVIDEND payment of a corporate dividend in the form of stock rather than cash. The stock dividend may be additional shares in the company, or it may be shares in a SUBSIDIARY being spun off to shareholders. The dividend is usually expressed as a percentage of the shares held by a shareholder. For instance, a shareholder with 100 shares would receive 5 shares as the result of a 5% stock dividend. From the corporate point of view, stock dividends conserve cash needed to operate the business. From the stockholder point of view, the advantage is that additional stock is not taxed until sold, unlike a cash dividend, which is declarable as income in the year it is received.

STOCK EXCHANGE organized marketplace in which stocks, COMMON STOCK EQUIVALENTS, and bonds are traded by members of the exchange, acting both as agents (brokers) and as principals (dealers or traders). Most exchanges have a physical location where brokers and dealers meet to execute orders from institutional and individual investors to buy and sell securities. Each exchange sets its own requirements for membership; the New York Stock Exchange has the most stringent requirements. *See also* AMERICAN STOCK EXCHANGE; LISTING REQUIREMENTS; NEW YORK STOCK EXCHANGE; REGIONAL STOCK EXCHANGES; SECURITIES AND COMMODITIES EXCHANGES.

THE STOCK EXCHANGE, MUMBAI (BSE) formerly known as the Bombay Stock Exchange, accounts for more than one-third of Indian trading volume, over 70% of listed capital and 90% of market capitalization. It is a voluntary, non-profit association of brokers. BSE is the largest of 23 stock exchanges in India. Market capitalization has decreased, however, since the establishment of the NATIONAL STOCK EXCHANGE (NSE) in 1994. BSE's on-line trading system, BOLT replaced open outcry. Settlement is in one week. Trading Hours: 10 A.M. to 2:30 P.M., Monday through Friday, and 11 A.M. to 3:30 P.M. on alternate Saturdays (exclusively for carry-over sessions).

STOCK EXCHANGE OF SINGAPORE (SES) only stock exchange in Singapore, trading through the Central Limit Order Book (CLOB) system, a fully computerized system. There is no trading floor. A direct link between SES and the NASDAQ Stock Market was established in 1988, with all prices quoted in U.S. currency. The *Straits Times Industrial Index* and the *SES Share Indices* are the most widely followed indicators of share performance. Trades are settled on a seven-day settlement. Trading hours are 9:00 A.M. to 12:30 P.M. and 2 P.M. to 5 P.M., Monday through Friday.

STOCK EXCHANGE OF THAILAND (SET) only stock market in Thailand, based in Bangkok. The SET Index includes all corporate securities and mutual funds. The SET 50 Index is composed of the 50 largest capitalized and most liquid stocks in the market. Both are calculated by the exchange. Trading is conducted through the asset automated electronic trading system Monday through Friday from 10 A.M. to 12:30 P.M., and 2 P.M. to 4:30 P.M. Trades are settled on the third business day after the trade date.

STOCKHOLDER individual or organization with an ownership position in a corporation; also called a SHAREHOLDER or *shareowner.* Stockholders must own at least one share, and their ownership is confirmed by either a stock certificate or a record by their broker, if shares are in the broker's custody.

STOCKHOLDER OF RECORD common or preferred stockholder whose name is registered on the books of a corporation as owning shares as of a particular date. Dividends and other distributions are made only to shareholders of record. Common stockholders are usually the only ones entitled to vote for candidates for the board of directors or on other matters requiring shareholder approval.

STOCKHOLDER'S EQUITY *see* OWNER'S EQUITY.

STOCKHOLDER'S REPORT company's ANNUAL REPORT and supplementary quarterly reports giving financial results and usually containing an ACCOUNTANT'S OPINION. Special stockholder's reports are sometimes issued covering major corporate developments. Also called *shareholder's report. See also* DISCLOSURE.

STOCKHOLM STOCK EXCHANGE only market in Sweden for official equity trading. The Stockholm Automatic Exchange (SAX) electronic trading system, introduced in 1989, includes all traded shares. A parallel system, called SOX, operates for fixed-interest securities. Clearing and settlement occur on the third business day following the trade. Trading is conducted Monday through Friday from 10 A.M. to 4 P.M.

STOCK INDICES AND AVERAGES indicators used to measure and report value changes in representative stock groupings. Strictly speaking, an AVERAGE is simply the ARITHMETIC MEAN of a group of prices, whereas an INDEX is an average expressed in relation to an earlier established BASE MARKET VALUE. (In practice, the distinction between indices and averages is not always clear; the AMEX Major Market Index is an average, for example.) Indices and averages may be broad based—comprised of many stocks representative of the overall market—or narrowly based, meaning they are composed of a smaller number of stocks reflecting a particular industry or market SECTOR. Selected indices and averages are also used as the underlying value of stock index futures, index options, or options on index futures; these derivative instruments enable investors to hedge a position against general market movement at relatively low cost. An extensive number and variety of indices and averages exist. Among the best known and most widely used are:

AMEX Composite Index (XAX): introduced in January 1997, it is a market capitalization-weighted, price appreciation index with a base level of 550 as of December 29, 1995. It replaces the AMEX Market Value Index (XAM), which had been in use since 1973, and was calculated on a total return basis to include reinvestment of dividends paid by AMEX companies. XAX reflects the aggregate market value of all of its components relative to their aggregate value on December 29, 1995. The index includes common stocks or AMERICAN DEPOSITARY RECEIPTS, AMEX-listed companies, REITs, master limited partnerships and closed-end investment funds. Each component's market value is determined by multiplying its price by the number of shares outstanding. The day-to-day price change in each issue is weighted by its market value at the start of the day as a percent of the total market value for all components. The level of the index is not altered by stock splits, stock dividends, trading halts, new listings, additional issuances, delistings or suspensions. Accompanying the AMEX Composite Index are five subindices that track the performance of companies in major industry sectors, and are measured against a base level of 100 as of December 29, 1995. These subindices are Technologies, Financial, Healthcare, Natural Resources and Industrials.

AMEX Major Market Index (XMI): AMERICAN STOCK EXCHANGE'S price-weighted (high-priced issues have more influence than low-priced issues) average of 20 BLUE CHIP industrial stocks listed on the NEW YORK STOCK EXCHANGE (NYSE), 17 of which are components of the DOW JONES INDUSTRIAL AVERAGE (DJIA). The index is designed to closely track the DJIA in measuring representative performance in the stocks of major industrial corporations. Futures on the XMI are traded on the CHICAGO BOARD OF TRADE. Options on the index are traded on Amex, and are traded under license on the Amsterdam Exchanges.

Dow Jones Global Industry Group and Economic Sector Indices: comprised of companies in the Dow Jones World Stock Index, classified on the basis of their business type, which then are sorted into more than 100 industry groups and nine broad economic sectors. The indices are computed to measure the movement of stock prices by industry groups and broad economic sectors on a global, regional, and national basis. These indices are tracked in real time. Country indices are calculated in each country's own currency, plus the U.S. dollar, British pound, German mark, and Japanese yen. The regional and world indices are calculated in these four global currencies, although all indices can be converted to any currency.

Dow Jones Global–U.S. Index: a broad-based, capitalization-weighted (price times the shares outstanding for each company) index (June 30, 1982 = 100) of more than 700 stocks traded on the NYSE, AMEX, and NASDAQ Stock Market, representing approximately 80% of the U.S. equity market. It is the U.S. portion of the Dow Jones World Stock Index.

Dow Jones Industrial Average (DJIA): price-weighted average of 30 actively traded BLUE CHIP stocks, primarily industrials like Alcoa, General Motors, and IBM but including American Express, Coca-Cola, McDonald's, J.P. Morgan, Walt Disney and other service-oriented firms. Prepared and published by Dow Jones & Co., it is the oldest and most widely quoted of all the market indicators. The components, which change from time to time, represent between 15% and 20% of the market value of NYSE stocks. The DJIA is calculated by adding the trading prices of the component stocks and using a divisor adjusted for STOCK DIVIDENDS and SPLITS, cash equivalent distributions equal to 10% or more of the closing prices of an issue, and substitutions and mergers. The average is quoted in points, not dollars. Futures are traded on the DJIA on the CHICAGO BOARD OF TRADE and index options on the DJIA are traded on the CHICAGO BOARD OPTIONS EXCHANGE. Other averages similarly prepared by Dow Jones & Co. are the *Dow Jones Transportation Average*— 20 stocks representative of the airline, trucking, railroad, and shipping businesses (*see also* DOW THEORY); and the *Dow Jones Utility Average* (DJUA)—15 geographically representative gas and electric utilities. Index options on the DJTA and DJUA are traded on the CHICAGO BOARD OPTIONS EXCHANGE. The combination of the Dow Industrials, Transportation, and Utility Averages encompasses 65 stocks and is known as the *Dow Jones Composite Average* or the *65 Stock Average.*

Dow Jones Stoxx Indices: four "pan-European" index products, calculated on a real-time basis. Dow Jones Stoxx includes 666 companies across Europe; Dow Jones Euro Stoxx is limited to 326 companies in countries participating in the European Monetary Union; Dow Jones Stoxx 50 includes shares of 50 European companies; and Dow Jones Euro Stoxx 50 is limited to 50 companies in countries that adopted the EURO. The Stoxx 50 indices include only a country's leading company in each key sector; pharmaceuticals, energy companies, banks, insurance and telecommunications companies dominate the Stoxx 50. The indices are traded on the SBF-Paris Bourse, Deutsche Borse AG, and Swiss Exchange; the three exchanges are partners with Dow Jones & Co. in these products.

Dow Jones World Stock Index: a broad-based, capitalization-weighted index (December 31, 1991 = 100) tracking approximately 3,000 companies in a growing list of countries and representing about 80% of the equity capital on stock markets around the globe.The index includes 34 countries in North America, Europe, and Asia/Pacific regions.

NASDAQ Composite Index: market value-weighted index that measures all domestic and non-U.S.-based securities—more than 5,400 companies—listed on the NASDAQ Stock Market. The index was introduced on February 5, 1971, with a base value of 100. The market value—the last-sale price multiplied by total shares outstanding—is calculated through the trading day, and is related to the total value of the index. Each security in the index is assigned to a NASDAQ subindex: Bank, Biotechnology, Computer, Industrial, Insurance, Other Finance, Transportation, Telecommunications. Values for the subindices began in February 1971, except for Biotechnology, Computer, and Telecommunications, which started November 1993.

NASDAQ-100 Index: a capitalization-weighted index, begun in January 1985, representing the largest and most active non-financial U.S. and foreign equities listed on the NASDAQ Stock Market. All securities in the index come from the top 125 eligible securities in terms of market value. Unless the security was in the top 100 during the previous year's ranking, larger eligible securities will replace issues ranked 101 to 125. To be eligible, a security must have a minimum average daily trading volume of 100,000 shares and be listed on NASDAQ for at least two years. Market value is determined annually on October 31. A foreign security must have a worldwide market value of at least $10 billion, a U.S. market value of at least $4 billion, and an average daily trading volume of at least 200,000 shares. Foreign securities must be eligible for listed-options trading. NASDAQ-100 futures and options on futures trade on the CHICAGO MERCANTILE EXCHANGE.

The NASDAQ-100 option is a European-style option, and can be exercised on its expiration date only.

New York Stock Exchange Composite Index: market value-weighted index which relates all NYSE stocks to an aggregate market value as of December 31, 1965, adjusted for capitalization changes. The base value of the index is $50 and point changes are expressed in dollars and cents. NYSE sub-indices include the *NYSE Finance, NYSE Industrials, NYSE Transportation*, and *NYSE Utilities* indices.

PSE Technology 100 Index: price-weighted, broad-based index representing 100 listed and over-the-counter stocks from 15 different industries on the PACIFIC EXCHANGE. The index measures the performance of the technology sector of the U.S. equities market, and is considered the industry benchmark. Options are traded on the PACIFIC EXCHANGE and the NEW YORK FUTURES EXCHANGE.

Russell Indices: market capitalization-weighted U.S. equity indices published by Frank Russell Company of Tacoma, Washington. The *Russell 3000 Index*® measures the performance of the 3,000 largest U.S. companies based on market capitalization, representing about 98% of the investable U.S. equities market. The highest-ranking 1,000 stocks in this index comprise the *Russell 1000 Index*®. The *Russell 2000 Index*® consists of the 2,000 smallest companies in the Russell 3000 Index. The *Russell Top 200 Index*® measures performance of the largest 200 companies in the Russell 1000, while the *Russell 2500 Index*® measures performance of the 2,500 smallest companies in the Russell 3000 Index. Growth indices on the Russell Indices measure performance of the respective companies with higher PRICE/BOOK RATIOS and higher forecasted growth values. Value indices on the Russell Indices measure performance of those companies with lower price/book ratios and lower forecasted growth values. *See also* RUSSELL INDICES.

Standard & Poor's 500 Composite Index: market value-weighted index showing the change in the aggregate market value of 500 stocks relative to the base period 1941-43. Mostly NYSE-listed companies with some AMEX and NASDAQ Stock Market stocks, it is comprised of 379 industrial stocks, 37 utilities, 74 financials, and 10 transportation issues representing about 74% of the market value of all issues traded on the NYSE. Index options are traded on the CHICAGO BOARD OPTIONS EXCHANGE and futures and options are traded on the CHICAGO MERCANTILE EXCHANGE. Other indices maintained by Standard & Poor's include the *Industrials, Utilities, 400 MidCap, 600 SmallCap* and *1500 Index.*

Standard & Poor's 100 Index (OEX): calculated on the same basis as the 500 Stock Index, is made up of stocks for which options are listed on the CHICAGO BOARD OPTIONS EXCHANGE. Its components are mainly NYSE industrials, with some transportation, utility, and financial stocks. Options on the S&P 100 Index are listed on the CHICAGO BOARD OPTIONS EXCHANGE.

Value Line Composite Average: equally weighted geometric average of approximately 1,700 NYSE, AMEX, and over-the-counter stocks tracked by the VALUE LINE INVESTMENT SURVEY. The index uses a base value of 100, established June 30, 1961; changes are expressed in index numbers rather than dollars and cents. Designed to reflect price changes of typical stocks (industrials, transportation, and utilities) without being price-weighted or market value-weighted, the index largely succeeds. Futures on the index are traded on the KANSAS CITY BOARD OF TRADE and futures options are traded on the PHILADELPHIA STOCK EXCHANGE.

Wilshire Indices: performance measurement indices created by Wilshire Associates Inc., of Santa Monica, California. The Wilshire 5000 Equity Index is the most widely followed and the broadest of all the averages and indices. It is market value-weighted and measures the performance of all U.S.-headquartered equity securities with readily available price data, or more than 7,000 security returns. Its capitalization is approximately 81% NYSE, 2% AMEX, and 17% NASDAQ Stock Market. Changes are measured against a base value established December 31, 1980. Other indices maintained by Wilshire include the *Wilshire 4500 Equity Index, Wilshire Small Cap Index*, four *Wilshire Asset Management Indexes* derived from the Wilshire 5000; six individual style indices and three *Real Estate Securities Indexes. Wilshire Small Cap Index* options are traded on the PACIFIC EXCHANGE, which helped develop the index.

Many indices and averages track the performance of stock markets around the world. The major indices include the: ALL ORDINARIES INDEX; AMSTERDAM EXCHANGES; ATHENS STOCK EXCHANGE; BOLSA DE COMMERCIO DE SANTIAGO; BOLSA DE VALORES DE SAO PAULO; BOLSA DE VALORES DO RIO DE JANIERO; CAC 40 INDEX; EAFE INDEX; EMERGING MARKET FREE (EMF) INDEX; HANG SENG INDEX; INTERNATIONAL MARKET INDEX; ITALIAN STOCK EXCHANGE; JOHANNESBURG STOCK EXCHANGE; KUALA LUMPUR STOCK EXCHANGE; LISBON STOCK EXCHANGE; LONDON STOCK EXCHANGE; MADRID STOCK EXCHANGE (BOLSO DE MADRID); MEXICAN STOCK EXCHANGE; MONTREAL EXCHANGE/BOURSE DE MONTREAL; MORGAN STANLEY CAPITAL INTERNATIONAL INDICES; NEW ZEALAND STOCK EXCHANGE; OSLO STOCK EXCHANGE; STOCK EXCHANGE OF SINGAPORE (SES); STOCK EXCHANGE OF THAILAND (SET); STOCKHOLM STOCK EXCHANGE; SWISS ELECTONIC BOURSE (EBS); TAIWAN STOCK EXCHANGE; TEL AVIV STOCK EXCHANGE; TOKYO STOCK EXCHANGE; TORONTO STOCK EXCHAGNE (TSE); VANCOUVER STOCK EXCHANGE; and VIENNA STOCK EXCHANGE.

See also BARRON'S CONFIDENCE INDEX; BOND BUYER'S INDEX; COMMODITY INDICES; ELVES; LIPPER MUTUAL FUND INDUSTRY AVERAGE; SECURITIES AND COMMODITIES EXCHANGES.

STOCK INDEX FUTURE security that combines features of traditional commodity futures trading with securities trading using composite stock indices. Investors can speculate on general market performance or buy an index future contract to hedge a LONG POSITION or SHORT POSITION against a decline in value. Settlement is in cash, since it is obviously impossible to deliver an index of stocks to a futures buyer. Among the most popular stock index futures traded are the Dow Jones Industrial Average on the CHICAGO BOARD OF TRADE, the NASDAQ 100 on the CHICAGO MERCANTILE

EXCHANGE, New York Stock Exchange Composite Index on the New York Futures Exchange (NYFE), the Standard & Poor's 500 Composite, Mini Index, the S&P Mini Index, and the S&P MidCap Index on the CHICAGO MERCANTILE EXCHANGE (CME), and the Value Line Composite Index on the KANSAS CITY BOARD OF TRADE (KCBT). It is also possible to buy options on stock index futures; the Dow Jones Industrials futures options trade on the Chicago Board of Trade and the Standard & Poor's 500 Stock Index futures options are traded on the Chicago Mercantile Exchange, for example. Unlike stock index futures or index options, however, futures options are not settled in cash; they are settled by delivery of the underlying stock index futures contracts. *See also* FUTURES CONTRACT, HEDGE/HEDGING; SECURITIES AND COMMODITIES EXCHANGES.

STOCK INSURANCE COMPANY insurance company that is owned by stockholders, as distinguished from a MUTUAL COMPANY that is owned by POLICYHOLDERS. Even in a stock company, however, policyholders interests are ahead of shareholder's dividends.

STOCK JOCKEY stockbroker who actively follows individual stocks and frequently buys and sells shares in his client's portfolios. If the broker does too much short-term trading in accounts over which he has discretion, he may be accused of CHURNING.

STOCK LIST function of the organized stock exchanges that is concerned with LISTING REQUIREMENTS and related investigations, the eligibility of unlisted companies for trading privileges, and the delisting of companies that have not complied with exchange regulations and listing requirements. The New York Stock Exchange department dealing with listing of securities is called the Department of Stock List.

STOCK MARKET general term referring to the organized trading of securities through the various exchanges and the OVER THE COUNTER market. The securities involved include COMMON STOCK, PREFERRED STOCK, BONDS, CONVERTIBLES, OPTIONS, rights, and warrants. The term may also encompass commodities when used in its most general sense, but more often than not the stock market and the commodities (or futures) market are distinguished. The query "How did the market do today?" is usually answered by a reference to the Dow Jones Industrial Average, comprised of stocks listed on the New York Stock Exchange. *See also* SECURITIES AND COMMODITIES EXCHANGES.

STOCK OPTION

1. right to purchase or sell a stock at a specified price within a stated period. OPTIONS are a popular investment medium, offering an opportunity to hedge positions in other securities, to speculate in stocks with relatively little investment, and to capitalize on changes in the MARKET VALUE of options contracts themselves through a variety of options strategies.

   See also CALL OPTION; PUT OPTION.

2. widely used form of employee incentive and compensation, usually for the executives of a corporation. The employee is given an OPTION to purchase its shares at a certain price (at or below the market price at the time the option is granted) for a specified period of years.

See also INCENTIVE STOCK OPTION; QUALIFIED STOCK OPTION.

STOCK POWER power of attorney form transferring ownership of a REGISTERED SECURITY from the owner to another party. A separate piece of paper from the CERTIFICATE, it is attached to the latter when the security is sold or pledged to a brokerage firm, bank, or other lender as loan COLLATERAL. Technically, the stock power gives the owner's permission to another party (the TRANSFER AGENT) to transfer ownership of the certificate to a third party. Also called *stock/bond power.*

STOCK PURCHASE PLAN organized program for employees of a company to buy shares of its stock. The plan could take the form of compensation if the employer matches employee stock purchases. In some companies, employees are offered the chance to buy stock in the company at a discount. Also, a corporation can offer to reinvest dividends in additional shares as a service to shareholders, or it can set up a program of regular additional share purchases for participating shareholders who authorize periodic, automatic payments from their wages for this purpose. *See also* AUTOMATIC INVESTMENT PROGRAM.

Another form of stock purchase plan is the EMPLOYEE STOCK OWNERSHIP PLAN (ESOP), whereby employees regularly accumulate shares and may ultimately assume control of the company.

STOCK RATING evaluation by rating agencies of common stocks, usually in terms of expected price performance or safety. Standard & Poor's and Value Line's respective quality and timeliness ratings are among the most widely consulted.

STOCK RECORD control, usually in the form of a ledger card or computer report, used by brokerage films to keep track of securities held in inventory and their precise location within the firm. Securities are recorded by name and owner.

STOCK RIGHT *see* SUBSCRIPTION RIGHT.

STOCK SPLIT *see* SPLIT.

STOCK SYMBOL letters used to identify listed companies on the securities exchanges on which they trade. These symbols, also called *trading symbols,* identify trades on the CONSOLIDATED TAPE and are used in other reports and documents whenever such shorthand is convenient. Some examples: ABT (Abbott Laboratories), AA (Aluminum Company of America), XON (Exxon), KO (Coca Cola). Stock symbols are not necessarily the same as abbreviations used to identify the same companies in the stock tables of newspapers. *See also* COMMITTEE ON UNIFORM SECURITIES IDENTIFICATION PROCEDURES (CUSIP).

STOCK-TRANSFER AGENT *see* TRANSFER AGENT.

STOCK WARRANT *see* SUBSCRIPTION WARRANT.

STOCK WATCHER (NYSE) computerized service that monitors all trading activity and movement in stocks listed on the New York Stock Exchange. The system is set up to identify any unusual activity due to rumors or MANIPULATION or other illegal practices. The stock watch department of the NYSE is prepared to conduct investigations and to take appropriate action, such as issuing clarifying information or turning questions of legality over to the Securities and Exchange Commission. *See also* SURVEILLANCE DEPARTMENT OF EXCHANGES.

STOP-LIMIT ORDER order to a securities broker with instructions to buy or sell at a specified price or better (called the *stop-limit price)* but only after a given *stop price* has been reached or passed. It is a combination of a STOP ORDER and a LIMIT ORDER. For example, the instruction to the broker might be "buy 100 XYZ 55 STOP 56 LIMIT" meaning that if the MARKET PRICE reaches $55, the broker enters a limit order to be executed at $56 or a better (lower) price. A stop-limit order avoids some of the risks of a stop order, which becomes a MARKET ORDER when the stop price is reached; like all price-limit orders, however, it carries the risk of missing the market altogether, since the specified limit price or better may never occur. The American Stock Exchange prohibits stop-limit orders unless the stop and limit prices are equal.

STOP LOSS
Insurance: promise by a reinsurance company that it will cover losses incurred by the company it reinsures over and above an agreed-upon amount.
Stocks: customer order to a broker that sets the sell price of a stock below the current MARKET PRICE. A stop-loss order therefore will protect profits that have already been made or prevent further losses if the stock drops.

STOP ORDER order to a securities broker to buy or sell at the MARKET PRICE once the security has traded at a specified price called the *stop price.* A stop order may be a DAY ORDER, a GOOD-TILL-CANCELED ORDER, or any other form of time-limit order. A stop order to buy, always at a stop price above the current market price, is usually designed to protect a profit or to limit a loss on a short sale *(see* SELLING SHORT). A stop order to sell, always at a price below the current market price, is usually designed to protect a profit or to limit a loss on a security already purchased at a higher price. The risk of stop orders is that they may be triggered by temporary market movements or that they may be executed at prices several points higher or lower than the stop price because of market orders placed ahead of them. Also called *stop-loss order. See also* GATHER IN THE STOPS; STOP LIMIT ORDER; STOP LOSS (stocks).

STOP-OUT PRICE lowest dollar price at which Treasury bills are sold at a particular auction. This price and the beginning auction price are averaged to establish the price at which smaller purchasers may purchase bills under the NONCOMPETITIVE BID system. *See also* BILL; DUTCH AUCTION.

STOP PAYMENT revocation of payment on a check after the check has been sent or delivered to the payee. So long as the check has not been cashed, the writer has up to six months in which to request a stop payment. The stop payment right does not carry over to electronic funds transfers.

STOPPED OUT term used when a customer's order is executed under a STOP ORDER at the price predetermined by the customer, called the *stop price.* For instance, if a customer has entered a stop-loss order to sell XYZ at $30 when the stock is selling at $33, and the stock then falls to $30, his or her position will be stopped out. A customer may also be stopped out if the order is executed at a guaranteed price offered by a SPECIALIST. *See also* GATHER IN THE STOPS; STOPPED STOCK.

STOPPED STOCK guarantee by a SPECIALIST that an order placed by a FLOOR BROKER will be executed at the best bid or offer price then in the SPECIALIST'S BOOK unless it can be executed at a better price within a specified period of time.

STOP PRICE *see* STOP ORDER.

STORY STOCK/BOND security with values or features so complex that a "story" is required to persuade investors of its merits. Story stocks are frequently from companies with some unique product or service that is difficult for competitors to copy. In a less formal sense, term is used by news organizations to mean stocks most actively traded.

STRADDLE strategy consisting of an equal number of PUT OPTIONS and CALL OPTIONS on the same underlying stock, stock index, or commodity future at the same STRIKE PRICE and maturity date. Each OPTION may be exercised separately, although the combination of options is usually bought and sold as a unit.

STRAIGHT-LINE DEPRECIATION method of depreciating a fixed asset whereby the asset's useful life is divided into the total cost less the estimated salvage value. The procedure is used to arrive at a uniform annual DEPRECIATION expense to be charged against income before figuring income taxes. Thus, if a new machine purchased for $1200 was estimated to have a useful life of ten years and a salvage value of $200, annual depreciation under the straight-line method would be $100, charged at $100 a year. This is the oldest and simplest method of depreciation and is used by many companies for financial reporting purposes, although faster depreciation of some assets with greater tax benefits in the early years is allowed under the MODIFIED ACCELERATED COST RECOVERY SYSTEM (MACRS).

STRAIGHT TERM INSURANCE POLICY term life insurance policy for a specific number of years in which the death benefit remains unchanged. A level premium policy will charge the same premium for a number of years, usually ten, and then increase. An annual renewable term policy will charge slightly higher premiums each year.

STRANGLE sale or purchase of a put option and a call option on the same underlying instrument, with the same expiration, but at strike prices equally OUT OF THE MONEY. A strangle costs less than a STRADDLE because both options are out of the money, but profits are made only if the underlying instrument moves dramatically.

STRAP OPTION contract combining one PUT OPTION and two CALL OPTIONS of the same SERIES, which can be bought at a lower total premium than that of the three options bought individually. The put has the same features as the calls—same underlying security, exercise price, and maturity. Also called *triple option. Compare with* STRIP.

STRATEGIC BUYOUT ACQUISITION based on analysis of the operational benefits of consolidation. Implicitly contrasts with the type of TAKEOVER based on "paper values" that characterized the "merger mania" of the 1980s—undervalued stock bought using JUNK BONDS ultimately repayable from the liquidation of acquired assets and activities. A strategic buyout focuses on how companies fit together and anticipates enhanced long-term earning power. *See also* SYNERGY.

STREET short for Wall Street, referring to the financial community in New York City and elsewhere. It is common to hear "The Street likes XYZ." This means there is a national consensus among securities analysts that XYZ's prospects are favorable. *See also* STREET NAME.

STREET NAME phrase describing securities held in the name of a broker or another nominee instead of a customer. Since the securities are in the broker's custody, transfer of the shares at the time of sale is easier than if the stock were registered in the customer's name and physical certificates had to be transferred.

STRIKE PRICE *see* EXERCISE PRICE.

STRIP
Bonds: brokerage-house practice of separating a bond into its CORPUS and COUPONS, which are then sold separately as ZERO-COUPON SECURITIES. The 1986 Tax Act permitted MUNICIPAL BOND strips. Some, such as Salomon Brothers' tax-exempt M-CATS, represent PREREFUNDINGS backed by U.S. Treasury securities held in escrow. Other strips include Treasuries stripped by brokers, such as TIGERS, and stripped mortgage-backed securities of government-sponsored issuers like Fannie Mae. A variation known by the acronym STRIPS (Separate Trading of Registered Interest and Principal of Securities) is a prestripped zero-coupon bond that is a direct obligation of the U.S. Treasury.
Options: OPTION contract consisting of two PUT OPTIONS and one CALL OPTION on the same underlying stock or stock index with the same strike and expiration date. *Compare with* STRAP.

Stocks: to buy stocks with the intention of collecting their dividends. Also called *dividend stripping. See also* DIVIDEND ROLLOVER PLAN.

STRIPPED BOND bond separated into its two components: periodic interest payments and principal repayment. Each of the interest payments and the principal repayment are stripped apart by a brokerage firm and sold individually as ZERO-COUPON SECURITIES. Investors therefore have a wide choice of maturities to pick from when shopping for a zero-coupon bond. When a U.S. government bond is stripped, it is often called a STRIP, which stands for *separate trading of registered interest and principal of securities.* Such bonds are also called CATS AND TIGRS.

STRONG DOLLAR dollar that can be exchanged for a large amount of a foreign currency. The dollar can gain strength in currency markets because the United States is considered a haven of political and economic stability, or because yields on American securities are attractive. A strong dollar is a blessing for American travelers going abroad, because they get more pounds, francs, marks, and yen and other currencies for their greenbacks. However, a strong dollar makes it difficult for American firms to export their goods to foreign countries because it raises the cost to foreigners of purchasing American products. In 1985, the dollar became so strong that the PLAZA ACCORD was signed to bring the dollar down. *See also* EXCHANGE RATE; WEAK DOLLAR.

STRUCTURED NOTE
1. derivative instrument based on the movement of an underlying index. For example, a structured note issued by a corporation may pay interest to noteholders based on the rise and fall of oil prices. This gives investors the opportunity to earn interest and profit from the change in price of a commodity at the same time.
2. complex debt instrument, usually a medium-term note, in which the issuer enters into one or more SWAP arrangements to change the cash flows it is required to make. A simple form utilizing interest-rate swaps might be, for example, a three-year FLOATING RATE NOTE paying the London Interbank Offered Rate (LIBOR) plus a premium semiannually. The issuer arranges a swap transaction whereby it agrees to pay a fixed semiannual rate for three years in exchange for the LIBOR. Since the floating rate payments (cash flows) offset each other, the issuer has synthetically created a fixed-rate note.

STRUCTURED SETTLEMENT agreement to pay a designated person a specified sum of money in periodic payments, usually for his or her lifetime, instead of in a single LUMP SUM payment. Structured settlements typically are used to pay court-ordered or privately-agreed upon damages to injured claimants or their survivors. Structured settlements are also used to pay lottery winners. In both cases, the settlement is funded with an ANNUITY.

STUB STOCK common stocks or instruments convertible to equity in a company that is overleveraged as the result of a BUYOUT or RECAPITAL-

IZATION and may have DEFICIT NET WORTH. Stub stock is highly speculative and highly volatile but, unlike JUNK BONDS, has unlimited potential for gain if the company succeeds in restoring financial balance.

STUDENT LOAN MARKETING ASSOCIATION (SLMA) publicly traded stock corporation that guarantees student loans traded in the SECONDARY MARKET. It was established by federal decree in 1972 to increase the availability of education loans to college and university students made under the federally sponsored Guaranteed Student Loan Program and the Health, Education Assistance Loan Program. Known as *Sallie Mae,* it purchases student loans from originating financial institutions and provides financing to state student loan agencies. It also sells short-and medium-term notes, some FLOATING RATE NOTES.

SUBCHAPTER M Internal Revenue Service regulation dealing with what is commonly called the *conduit theory,* in which qualifying investment companies and real estate investment trusts avoid double taxation by passing interest and dividend income and capital gains directly through, without taxation, to shareholders, who are taxed as individuals. *See also* REAL ESTATE INVESTMENT TRUST; REGULATED INVESTMENT COMPANY.

SUBCHAPTER S section of the Internal Revenue Code giving a corporation that has 35 or fewer shareholders and meets certain other requirements the option of being taxed as if it were a PARTNERSHIP. Thus a small corporation can distribute its income directly to shareholders and avoid the corporate income tax while enjoying the other advantages of the corporate form. These companies are known as *Subchapter S corporations, tax-option corporations,* or *small business corporations.*

SUBJECT Wall Street term referring to a bid and/or offer that is negotiable—that is, a QUOTATION that is not firm. For example, a broker looking to place a sizable order might call several dealers with the question, "Can you give me a *subject quote* on 20,000 shares of XYZ?"

SUBJECT QUOTE *see* SUBJECT.

SUBORDINATED junior in claim on assets to other debt, that is, repayable only after other debts with a higher claim have been satisfied. Some subordinated debt may have less claim on assets than other subordinated debt; a *junior subordinated debenture* ranks below a subordinated DEBENTURE, for example.

It is also possible for unsubordinated (senior) debt to become subordinated at the request of a lender by means of a subordination agreement. For example, if an officer of a small company has made loans to the company instead of making a permanent investment in it, a bank might request the officer's loan be subordinated to its own loan as long as the latter is outstanding. This is accomplished by the company officer's signing a subordination agreement. *See also* EFFECTIVE NET WORTH; JUNIOR SECURITY.

SUBORDINATION CLAUSE clause in a MORTGAGE loan agreement that permits a mortgage recorded at a subsequent date to have preference over the original mortgage.

SUBROGATION legal process by which an insurance company, after paying for a loss, seeks to recover the amount of the loss from another party who is legally liable for it.

SUBSCRIPTION agreement of intent to buy newly issued securities. *See also* NEW ISSUE; SUBSCRIPTION RIGHT; SUBSCRIPTION WARRANT.

SUBSCRIPTION AGREEMENT application submitted by an investor seeking to join a limited partnership. All prospective limited partners must be approved by the general partner before they are allowed to become limited partners.

SUBSCRIPTION PRICE price at which existing shareholders of a corporation are entitled to purchase common shares in a RIGHTS OFFERING or at which subscription warrants are exercisable. *See also* SUBSCRIPTION RIGHT; SUBSCRIPTION WARRANT.

SUBSCRIPTION PRIVILEGE right of existing shareholders of a corporation, or their transferees, to buy shares of a new issue of common stock before it is offered to the public. *See also* PREEMPTIVE RIGHT; SUBSCRIPTION RIGHT.

SUBSCRIPTION RATIO *see* SUBSCRIPTION RIGHT.

SUBSCRIPTION RIGHT privilege granted to existing shareholders of a corporation to subscribe to shares of a new issue of common stock before it is offered to the public; better known simply as a *right*. Such a right, which normally has a life of two to four weeks, is freely transferable and entitles the holder to buy the new common stock below the PUBLIC OFFERING PRICE. While in most cases one existing share entitles the stockholder to one right, the number of rights needed to buy a share of a new issue (called the *subscription ratio*) varies and is determined by a company in advance of an offering. To subscribe, the holder sends or delivers to the company or its agent the required number of rights plus the dollar price of the new shares.

Rights are sometimes granted to comply with state laws that guarantee the shareholders' PREEMPTIVE RIGHT—their right to maintain a proportionate share of ownership. It is common practice, however, for corporations to grant rights even when not required by law; protecting shareholders from the effects of DILUTION is seen simply as good business.

The actual certificate representing the subscription is technically called a SUBSCRIPTION WARRANT, giving rise to some confusion. The term *subscription warrant,* or simply *warrant,* is commonly understood in a related but different sense—as a separate entity with a longer life than a right—maybe 5, 10, or 20 years or even perpetual—

and with a SUBSCRIPTION PRICE higher at the time of issue than the MARKET VALUE of the common stock.

Subscription rights are offered to shareholders in what is called a RIGHTS OFFERING, usually handled by underwriters under a STANDBY COMMITMENT.

SUBSCRIPTION WARRANT type of security, usually issued together with a BOND or PREFERRED STOCK, that entitles the holder to buy a proportionate amount of common stock at a specified price, usually higher than the market price at the time of issuance, for a period of years or to perpetuity; better known simply as a *warrant*. In contrast, rights, which also represent the right to buy common shares, normally have a subscription price lower than the current market value of the common stock and a life of two to four weeks. A warrant is usually issued as a SWEETENER, to enhance the marketability of the accompanying fixed income securities. Warrants are freely transferable and are traded on the major exchanges. They are also called *stock-purchase warrants*. *See also* PERPETUAL WARRANT; SUBSCRIPTION RIGHT.

SUBSIDIARY company of which more than 50% of the voting shares are owned by another corporation, called the PARENT COMPANY. *See also* AFFILIATE.

SUBSTITUTION
Banking: replacement of COLLATERAL by other collateral.
Contracts: replacement of one party to a contract by another. *See also* NOVATION.
Economics: concept that, if one product or service can be replaced by another, their prices should be similar.
Law: replacement of one attorney by another in the exercise of stock powers relating to the purchase and sale of securities. *See also* STOCK POWER.
Securities:
1. exchange or SWAP of one security for another in a client's PORTFOLIO. Securities analysts often advise substituting a stock they currently favor for a stock in the same industry that they believe has less favorable prospects.
2. substitution of another security of equal value for a security acting as COLLATERAL for a MARGIN ACCOUNT. *See also* SAME-DAY-SUBSTITUTION.

SUICIDE PILL POISON PILL with potentially catastrophic implications for the company it is designed to protect. An example might be a poison pill providing for an exchange of stock for debt in the event of a *hostile takeover;* that would discourage an acquirer by making the TAKEOVER prohibitively expensive, but its implementation could put the TARGET COMPANY in danger of bankruptcy.

SUITABILITY RULES guidelines that those selling sophisticated and potentially risky financial products, such as limited partnerships or commodities futures contracts, must follow to ensure that investors have the financial means to assume the risks involved. Such rules are enforced through self-regulation administered by such organizations as the NATIONAL ASSOCIATION OF SECURITIES DEALERS, the SECURITIES AND COMMODITIES EXCHANGES, and other groups operating in the securities industry. Individual brokerage firms selling the products have their own guidelines and policies. They typically require the investor to have a certain level of NET WORTH and LIQUID ASSETS, so that he or she will not be irreparably harmed if the investment sours. A brokerage firm may be sued if it has allowed an unsuitable investor to buy an investment that goes sour. *See also* KNOW YOUR CUSTOMER.

SUM-OF-THE-YEARS'-DIGITS METHOD (SOYD) method of ACCELERATED DEPRECIATION that results in higher DEPRECIATION charges and greater tax savings in the earlier years of a FIXED ASSET'S useful life than the STRAIGHT-LINE DEPRECIATION method, where charges are uniform throughout. Sometimes called just *sum-of-digits method,* it allows depreciation based on an inverted scale of the total of digits for the years of useful life. Thus, for four years of life, the digits 4, 3, 2, and 1 are added to produce 10. The first year's rate becomes ⁴⁄₁₀ths of the depreciable cost of the asset (cost less salvage value), the second year's rate ³⁄₁₀ths, and so on. The effects of this method of accelerated depreciation are compared with the straight-line method in the following illustration, which assumes an asset with a total cost of $1000, a useful life of four years, and no salvage value:

YEAR	STRAIGHT LINE		SUM-OF-YEARS' DIGITS	
	Expense	Cumulative	Expense	Cumulative
1	$250	$250	$400	$400
2	$250	$500	$300	$700
3	$250	$750	$200	$900
4	$250	$1000	$100	$1000
	$1000		$1000	

See also MODIFIED ACCELERATED COST RECOVERY SYSTEM (MACRS).

SUNK COSTS costs already incurred in a project that cannot be changed by present or future actions. For example, if a company bought a piece of machinery five years ago, that amount of money has already been spent and cannot be recovered. It should also not affect the company's decision on whether or not to buy a new piece of machinery if the five-year old machinery has worn out.

SUNRISE INDUSTRIES figurative term for the emerging growth sectors that some believe will be the mainstays of the future economy, taking the place of declining *sunset industries.* Although the latter, including such mature industries as the automobile, steel, and other heavy manufacturing industries, will continue to be important, their lead role as employers of massive numbers of workers is expected to be superseded by the electronics and other computer-related high-technology, biotechnology, and genetic engineering sectors and by service industries.

SUNSET PROVISION condition in a law or regulation that specifies an expiration date unless reinstated by legislation. For examples a sunset provision in the TAX REFORM ACT OF 1986 prohibits tax-exempt single-family mortgage bonds after 1988.

SUNSHINE LAWS state or federal laws (also called *government in the sunshine laws)* that require most meetings of regulatory bodies to be held in public and most of their decisions and records to be disclosed. Many of these statutes were enacted in the 1970s because of concern about government abuses during the Watergate period. Most prominent is the federal Freedom of Information (FOI) Act, which makes it possible to obtain documents relating to most federal enforcement and rule-making agencies.

SUPER BOWL INDICATOR technical indicator that holds that if a team from the old American Football League pre-1970 wins the Super Bowl, the stock market will decline during the coming year. If a team from the old pre-1990 National Football League wins the Super Bowl, the stock market will end the coming year higher. The indicator has been a remarkably accurate predictor of stock market performance for many years.

SUPER DOT *see* DESIGNATED ORDER TURNAROUND (DOT).

SUPERMAJORITY AMENDMENT corporate AMENDMENT requiring that a substantial majority (usually 67% to 90%) of stockholders approve important transactions, such as mergers.

SUPER NOW ACCOUNT deregulated transaction account authorized for depository institutions in 1982. It paid interest higher than on a conventional NOW (NEGOTIABLE ORDER OF WITHDRAWAL) account but slightly lower than that on the MONEY MARKET DEPOSIT ACCOUNT (MMDA). With the deregulation of banking deposit accounts in 1986, however, banks are free to pay whatever rates they feel cost considerations and competitive conditions warrant. Although some banks continue to offer MMDA accounts which pay a slightly higher rate to compensate for the fact that checkwriting is limited to three checks a month, most banks now offer one transaction account with unlimited checkwriting.

SUPER SINKER BOND bond with long-term coupons (which might equal a 20-year-bond's yield) but with short maturity. Typically, super sinkers are HOUSING BONDS, which provide home financing. If homeowners move from their homes and prepay their mortgages, bondholders receive their principal back right away. Super sinkers may therefore have an actual life of as little as three to five years, even though their yield is about the same as bonds of much longer maturities. *See also* COUPON BOND.

SUPERVISORY ANALYST member firm research analyst who has passed a special New York Stock Exchange examination and is deemed qualified to approve publicly distributed research reports.

SUPPLEMENTAL AGREEMENT agreement that amends a previous agreement and contains additional conditions.

SUPPLEMENTAL SECURITY INCOME SOCIAL SECURITY program benefiting the blind, disabled, and indigent.

SUPPLY-SIDE ECONOMICS theory of economics contending that drastic reductions in tax rates will stimulate productive investment by corporations and wealthy individuals to the benefit of the entire society. Championed in the late 1970s by Professor Arthur Laffer *(see* LAFFER CURVE) and others, the theory held that MARGINAL TAX RATES had become so high (primarily as a result of big government) that major new private spending on plant, equipment, and other "engines of growth" was discouraged. Therefore, reducing the size of government, and hence its claim on earned income, would fuel economic expansion.

   Supporters of the supply-side theory claimed they were vindicated in the first years of the administration of President Ronald W. Reagan, when marginal tax rates were cut just prior to a sustained economic recovery. However, members of the opposing KEYNESIAN ECONOMICS school maintained that the recovery was a classic example of "demand-side" economics—growth was stimulated not by increasing the supply of goods, but by increasing consumer demand as disposable incomes rose. Also clashing with the supply-side theory were MONETARIST economists, who contended that the most effective way of regulating aggregate demand is for the Federal Reserve to control growth in the money supply. *See also* AGGREGATE SUPPLY.

SUPPORT LEVEL price level at which a security tends to stop falling because there is more demand than supply. Technical analysts identify support levels as prices at which a particular security or market has bottomed in the past. When a stock is falling towards its support level, these analysts say it is "testing its support," meaning that the stock should rebound as soon as it hits the support price. If the stock continues to drop through the support level, its outlook is considered very bearish. The opposite of a support level is a RESISTANCE LEVEL. *See* chart on next page.

SURCHARGE charge added to a charge, cost added to a cost, or tax added to a tax. *See also* SURTAX.

SURETY individual or corporation, usually an insurance company, that guarantees the performance or faith of another. Term is also used to mean *surety bond,* which is a bond that backs the performance of the person bonded, such as a contractor, or that pays an employer if a bonded employee commits theft.

SURRENDER VALUE *see* CASH SURRENDER VALUE.

SUPPORT LEVEL

Support Level

SURPLUS connotes either CAPITAL SURPLUS or EARNED SURPLUS. *See also* FEDERAL DEFICIT (SURPLUS); PAID-IN CAPITAL; RETAINED EARNINGS.

SURTAX tax applied to corporations or individuals who have earned a certain level of income. For example, the REVENUE RECONCILIATION ACT OF 1993 provided for a 10% surtax on adjusted gross incomes over $250,000.

SURVEILLANCE DEPARTMENT OF EXCHANGES division of a stock exchange that is constantly watching to detect unusual trading activity in stocks, which may be a tipoff to an illegal practice. These departments cooperate with the Securities and Exchange Commission in investigating misconduct. *See also* STOCK WATCHER.

SURVIVING SPOUSE spouse remaining alive when his or her spouse dies (in other words, the spouse who lives longer). In most states, the surviving spouse cannot be totally disinherited, but has a right to receive a share of the deceased spouse's estate, with the size of that share determined by state law.

SURVIVORSHIP ACCOUNT *see* JOINT TENANTS WITH RIGHT OF SURVIVORSHIP.

SURVIVORSHIP LIFE INSURANCE *see* SECOND-TO-DIE INSURANCE.

SUSPENDED TRADING temporary halt in trading in a particular security, in advance of a major news announcement or to correct an imbalance of orders to buy and sell. Using telephone alert procedures, listed companies with material developments to announce can give advance notice to the New York Stock Exchange Department of Stock List or the American Stock Exchange Securities Division. The exchanges can then determine if trading in the securities affected should be suspended temporarily to allow for orderly dissemination of the news to the public. Where advance notice is not possible, a *floor governor* may halt trading to stabilize the price of a security affected by a rumor or news development. Destabilizing developments might include a MERGER announcement, an unfavorable earnings report, or a major resource discovery. *See also* CIRCUIT BREAKER; DISCLOSURE; FORM 8-K; INVESTOR RELATIONS DEPARTMENT.

SUSPENSE ACCOUNT in accounting, an account used temporarily to carry receipts, disbursements, or discrepancies, pending their analysis and permanent classification.

SWAP traditionally, an exchange of one security for another to change the maturities of a bond PORTFOLIO or the quality of the issues in a stock or bond portfolio, or because investment objectives have shifted. Investors with bond portfolio losses often swap for other higher-yielding bonds to be able to increase the return on their portfolio and realize tax losses. Recent years have seen explosive growth in more complex *currency swaps,* used to link increasingly global capital markets, and in *interest-rate swaps,* used to reduce risk by synthetically matching the DURATION of assets and liabilities of financial institutions as interest rates got higher and more volatile. In a simple currency swap (swaps can be done with varying degrees of complexity), two parties sell each other a currency with a commitment to re-exchange the principal amount at the maturity of the deal. Originally done to get around the problems of exchange controls, currency swaps are widely used to tap new capital markets, in effect to borrow funds irrespective of whether the borrower requires funds within that market. The INTERNATIONAL BANK FOR RECONSTRUCTION AND DEVELOPMENT (WORLD BANK) has been an active participant in currency swaps with U.S. corporations.

An interest-rate swap is an arrangement whereby two parties (called counterparties) enter into an agreement to exchange periodic interest payments. The dollar amount the counterparties pay each other is an agreed-upon periodic interest rate multiplied by some predetermined dollar principal, called the *notational principal amount.* No principal (no notational amount) is exchanged between parties to the transaction; only interest is exchanged. In its most common and simplest variation, one party agrees to pay the other a fixed rate of interest in exchange for a floating rate. The benefit of interest-rate swaps, which can be used to synthetically extend or shorten the duration characteristics of an asset or liability, is that direct changes in the contractual characteristics of the assets or the liabilities become matters affecting only administrative, legal, and investment banking costs.

See also BOND SWAP; SUBSTITUTION.

SWAP ORDER *see* CONTINGENT ORDER.

SWAPTION option to enter an interest rate swap. A *payer swaption* gives its purchaser the right, but not the obligation, to enter into an interest-rate swap at a preset rate within a specific period of time. The swaption buyer pays a premium to the seller for this right. A *receiver swaption* gives the purchaser the right to receive fixed payments. The seller agrees to provide the specified swap if called upon, though it is possible for him to hedge that risk with other offsetting transactions.

SWEAT EQUITY equity created in a property by the hard work of the owner. For example, a small business may be built up more on the efforts of its founders than on the capital raised to finance it. Homeowners who renovate a house with their own labor create rising value with the sweat of their own brows, not the general increase in housing prices from inflation.

SWEETENER feature added to a securities offering to make it more attractive to purchasers. A bond may have the sweetener of convertibility into common stock added, for instance. *See also* KICKER.

SWISS ELECTRONIC BOURSE (EBS) formed in 1996, incorporating the former stock exchange trading floors in Zurich, Geneva, and Basel. The three exchanges operate simultaneously and are linked by computers, enabling orders to be executed on any of the three exchanges regardless of origin. Trading is by open outcry, although an electronic system is under development. The Swiss Performance Index, the official and most widely used index, is computed on 3-minute intervals using real-time prices at all three exchanges. There are three different market segments: the official market, official parallel market, and unofficial market. The official market is open from 10 A.M. to 1 P.M. and 2 P.M. to 4 P.M., while the official parallel market is open from 9:15 A.M. to 10 A.M., Monday through Friday. Trades are settled on the third business day after the trade.

SWISS OPTIONS AND FINANCIAL FUTURES EXCHANGE (SOFFEX) first fully electronic trading system in the world, with a completely integrated and automated clearing system. SOFFEX, the Swiss derivatives market, changed its name to EUREX ZURICH AG in keeping with the 1998 launch of EUREX, the joint German-Swiss electronic derivatives market. Contracts traded include: futures and options on the DAX Index (the German stock index) and the Swiss Market

Index (SMI); futures and future options on the DAX future, BOBL national government bonds (3.3 to 5 years), BUND naional government bonds (8.5 to 10 years), Swiss government bonds (Conf), Dow Jones STOXX 50 and Dow Jones Euro STOXX 50; futures on the one-month Euromark, three-month Euromark, Mid-Cap DAX and Jumbo Pfandbrief; stock options on German and Swiss blue chip equities; and U.S. dollar/Deutschemark options.

SWITCHING

Mutual funds: moving assets from one mutual fund to another, either within a FUND FAMILY or between different fund families. There is no charge for switching within a no-load family of mutual funds, which offer a variety of stock, bond, and money market funds. A sales charge might have to be paid when switching from one LOAD FUND to another. Customers of many discount brokerage firms can switch among fund families, sometimes at no fee and sometimes by paying a brokerage commission. Switching usually occurs at the shareholder's initiative, as a result of changes in market conditions or investment objectives. Some investment advisers and investment advisory newsletters recommend when to switch into or out of different mutual funds. *See also* NO-LOAD FUND.

Securities: selling stocks or bonds to replace them with other stocks and bonds with better prospects for gain or higher yields. *See also* SWAP.

SWITCH ORDER *see* CONTINGENT ORDER.

SYDNEY FUTURES EXCHANGE (SFE) Australia's derivatives market, trading through a combination of open outcry and Sycom, its electronic trading system for overnight trading. The exchange operates a link between Sycom and the NEW YORK MERCANTILE EXCHANGE'S ACCESS electronic trading system, allowing SFE members to trade NYMEX energy contracts. SFE also trades futures and futures options on wool and wheat. Financial futures and futures options are traded on Treasury bonds, bank bills, and the All Ordinaries Share Price Index; share futures are traded on some of the top Australian equities, including BHP and CRA. Trading hours are Monday to Friday, 9:50 A.M. to 4:30 P.M.

SYNDICATE *see* PURCHASE GROUP.

SYNDICATE MANAGER *see* MANAGING UNDERWRITER.

SYNERGY ideal sought in corporate mergers and acquisitions that the performance of a combined enterprise will exceed that of its previously separate parts. For example, a MERGER of two oil companies, one with a superior distribution network and the other with more reserves, would have synergy and would be expected to result in higher earnings per share than previously. *See also* STRATEGIC BUYOUT.

SYNTHETIC ASSET value that is artificially created by using other assets, such as securities, in combination. For example, the simultaneous purchase of a CALL OPTION and sale of a PUT OPTION on the same stock creates *synthetic stock* having the same value, in terms of CAPITAL GAIN potential, as the underlying stock itself.

SYNTHETIC SECURITIES *see* STRUCTURED NOTE; SYNTHETIC ASSET.

SYSTEMATIC INVESTMENT PLAN plan in which investors make regular payments into a stock, bond, mutual fund, or other investment. This may be accomplished through an AUTOMATIC INVESTMENT PROGRAM, such as a salary reduction plan with an employer, a dividend reinvestment plan with a company or mutual fund, or an automatic investment plan in which a mutual fund withdraws a set amount from a bank checking or savings account on a regular basis. By investing systematically, investors are benefiting from the advantages of DOLLAR-COST AVERAGING.

SYSTEMATIC WITHDRAWAL PLAN MUTUAL FUND option whereby the shareholder receives specified amounts at specified intervals.

SYSTEMATIC RISK that part of a security's risk that is common to all securities of the same general class (stocks and bonds) and thus cannot be eliminated by DIVERSIFICATION; also known as *market risk*. The measure of systematic risk in stocks is the BETA COEFFICIENT. *See also* PORTFOLIO BETA SCORE, PORTFOLIO THEORY.

T

TAC BONDS *see* TARGETED AMORTIZATION CLASS (TAC) BONDS.

TACTICAL ASSET ALLOCATION shifting percentages of portfolios among stocks, bonds, or cash, depending on the relative attractiveness of the respective markets. *See also* ASSET ALLOCATION.

TAFT-HARTLEY ACT federal law (in full, Labor Management Relations Act) enacted in 1947, which restored to management in unionized industries some of the bargaining power it had lost in prounion legislation prior to World War II. Taft-Hartley prohibited a union from
- refusing to bargain in good faith
- coercing employees to join a union
- imposing excessive or discriminatory dues and initiation fees
- forcing employers to hire union workers to perform unneeded or non-existent tasks (a practice known as *featherbedding)*
- striking to influence a bargaining unit's choice between two contesting unions (called a *jurisdictional strike)*
- engaging in secondary boycotts against businesses selling or handling nonunion goods
- engaging in sympathy strikes in support of other unions

Taft-Hartley also
- imposed disclosure requirements to regulate union business dealings and uncover fraud and racketeering
- prohibited unions from directly making contributions to candidates running for federal offices
- authorized the President of the United States to postpone strikes in industries deemed essential to national economic health or national security by declaring an 80-day "cooling-off period"
- permitted states to enact right-to-work laws, which outlaw compulsory unionization.

TAIL
Insurance: interval between receipt of premium income and payment of claims. For example, REINSURANCE companies have a long tail as compared to CASUALTY INSURANCE companies.

Treasury auctions: spread in price between the lowest COMPETITIVE BID accepted by the U.S. Treasury for bills, bonds, and notes and the average bid by all those offering to buy such Treasury securities. *See also* TREASURIES.

Underwriting: decimal places following the round-dollar amount of a bid by a potential UNDERWRITER in a COMPETITIVE BID underwriting. For instance, in a bid of $97.3347 for a particular bond issue, the tail is .3347.

TAILGATING unethical practice of a broker who, after a customer has placed an order to buy or sell a certain security, places an order for the same security for his or her own account. The broker hopes to profit either because of information the customer is known or presumed to have or because the customer's purchase is of sufficient size to put pressure on the security price.

TAIWAN STOCK EXCHANGE exchange of the Republic of China, located in Taipei. The *Taiwan Stock Exchange Capitalization Weighted Stock Index* is the oldest and most widely quoted of three leading indices, and is comparable to the STANDARD & POOR'S 500 INDEX in terms of its construction. Trading hours are Monday through Friday from 9 A.M. to noon, and Saturday from 9 A.M. to 11 A.M. Settlement by delivery of stock or cash payment must be made to the commissioning broker by the next business day.

TAKE
In general:
1. profit realized from a transaction.
2. gross receipts of a lottery or gambling enterprise.
3. open to bribery, as in *being on the take.*
Law: to seize possession of property. When a debtor defaults on a debt backed by COLLATERAL, that property is taken back by the creditor.
Securities: act of accepting an OFFER price in a transaction between brokers or dealers.

TAKE A BATH to suffer a large loss on a SPECULATION or investment, as in "I took a bath on my XYZ stock when the market dropped last week."

TAKE A FLIER to speculate, that is, to buy securities with the knowledge that the investment is highly risky.

TAKE A POSITION
1. to buy stock in a company with the intent of holding for the long term or, possibly, of taking control of the company. An acquirer who takes a position of 5% or more of a company's outstanding stock must file information with the Securities and Exchange Commission, the exchange the TARGET COMPANY is listed on, and the target company itself.
2. phrase used when a broker/dealer holds stocks or bonds in inventory. A position may be either long or short. *See also* LONG POSITION; SHORT POSITION.

TAKEDOWN
1. each participating INVESTMENT BANKER'S proportionate share of the securities to be distributed in a new or a secondary offering.
2. price at which the securities are allocated to members of the UNDERWRITING GROUP, particularly in municipal offerings.
  See also UNDERWRITE.

TAKE-HOME PAY amount of salary remaining after all deductions have been taken out. Some of the most common deductions are for federal, state, and local income tax withholding; Social Security tax withholding; health care premiums, flexible spending account contributions; and contributions to salary reduction or other retirement savings plans.

TAKE OFF to rise sharply. For example, when positive news about a company's earnings is released, traders say that the stock takes off. The term is also used referring to the overall movement of stock prices, as in "When the Federal Reserve lowered interest rates, the stock market took off."

TAKE-OR-PAY CONTRACT agreement between a buyer and a seller that obligates the buyer to pay a minimum amount of money for a product or a service, even if the product or service is not delivered. These contracts are most often used in the utility industry to back bonds to finance new power plants. A take-or-pay contract stipulates that the prospective purchaser of the power will take the power from the bond issuer or, if construction is not completed, will repay bondholders the amount of their investment. Take-or-pay contracts are a common way to protect bondholders. In a precedent-setting case in 1983, however, the Washington State Supreme Court voided take-or-pay contracts that many utilities had signed to support the building of the Washington Public Power Supply System (known as WHOOPS) nuclear plants. This action caused WHOOPS to default on some of its bonds, putting a cloud over the validity of the take-or-pay concept.

TAKEOUT
Real estate finance: long-term mortgage loan made to refinance a short-term construction loan (INTERIM LOAN). *See also* STANDBY COMMITMENT.
Securities: withdrawal of cash from a brokerage account, usually after a sale and purchase has resulted in a net CREDIT BALANCE.

TAKEOVER change in the controlling interest of a corporation. A takeover may be a friendly acquisition or an unfriendly bid that the TARGET COMPANY may fight with SHARK REPELLENT techniques. A hostile takeover (aiming to replace existing management) is usually attempted through a public TENDER OFFER. Other approaches might be unsolicited merger proposals to directors, accumulations of shares in the open market, or PROXY FIGHTS that seek to install new directors. *See also* ANY-AND-ALL BID; ARBITRAGEUR; ASSET STRIPPER; BEAR HUG; BLITZKREIG TENDER OFFER; BUST-UP TAKEOVER; CRAM-DOWN DEAL; CROWN JEWELS; DAWN RAID; DEAL STOCK; FAIR-PRICE AMENDMENT; GAP OPENING; GARBATRAGE; GODFATHER OFFER; GOLDEN PARACHUTE; GOOD-BYE KISS; GREENMAIL; GREY KNIGHT; HIGHLY CONFIDENT LETTER; HIGH-JACKING; HOSTILE TAKEOVER; IN PLAY; INSIDER TRADING; KILLER BEES; LADY MACBETH STRATEGY; LEVERAGED BUYOUT; LEVERAGED RECAPITAL-IZATION; LOCK-UP OPTION; MACARONI DEFENSE; MANAGEMENT BUYOUT;

MATERIALITY; MERGER; PAC-MAN STRATEGY; PEOPLE PILL; POISON PILL; POISON PUT; RADAR ALERT; RAIDER; RISK ARBITRAGE; REVERSE LEVER-AGED BUYOUT; RUMORTRAGE; SAFE HARBOR; SATURDAY NIGHT SPECIAL; SCHEDULE 13D; SCORCHED EARTH POLICY; SHARK WATCHER; SHOW STOP-PER; SLEEPING BEAUTY; STAGGERED BOARD OF DIRECTORS; STANDSTILL AGREEMENT; STOCK BUYBACK; STRATEGIC BUYOUT; SUICIDE PILL; SUPER-MAJORITY AMENDMENT; TAKEOVER TARGET; TWO-TIER BID; WAR CHEST; WHITE KNIGHT; WHITEMAIL; WHITE SQUIRE; WILLIAMS ACT.

TAKEOVER ARBITRAGE *see* RISK ARBITRAGE.

TAKEOVER TARGET company that is the object of a takeover offer, whether the offer is friendly or unfriendly. In a HOSTILE TAKEOVER attempt, management tries to use various defensive strategies to repel the acquirer. In a friendly takeover situation, management cooperates with the acquirer, negotiating the best possible price, and recommends that shareholders vote to accept the final offer. *See also* TAKEOVER.

TAKING DELIVERY
In general: accepting receipt of goods from a common carrier or other shipper, usually documented by signing a bill of lading or other form of receipt.
Commodities: accepting physical delivery of a commodity under a FUTURES CONTRACT or SPOT MARKET contract. Delivery requirements, such as the size of the contract and the necessary quality of the commodity, are established by the exchange on which the commodity is traded.
Securities: accepting receipt of stock or bond certificates that have recently been purchased or transferred from another account.

TANGIBLE ASSET any asset not meeting the definition of an INTANGI-BLE ASSET, which is a nonphysical right to something presumed to represent an advantage in the marketplace, such as a trademark or patent. Thus tangible assets are clearly those having physical existence, like cash, real estate, or machinery. Yet in accounting, assets such as ACCOUNTS RECEIVABLE are considered tangible, even though they are no more physical than a license or a lease, both of which are considered intangible. In summary: if an asset has physical form it is tangible; if it doesn't, consult a list of what accountants have decided are intangible assets.

TANGIBLE COST oil and gas drilling term meaning the cost of items that can be used over a period of time, such as casings, well fittings, land, and tankage, as distinguished from intangible costs such as drilling, testing, and geologist's expenses. In the most widely used LIMITED PARTNERSHIP sharing arrangements, tangible costs are borne by the GENERAL PARTNER (manager) while intangible costs are borne by the limited partners (investors), usually to be taken as tax deductions. In the event of a dry hole, however, all costs become intangibles. *See also* INTANGIBLE COST.

TANGIBLE NET WORTH total ASSETS less INTANGIBLE ASSETS and total LIABILITIES; also called *net tangible assets.* Intangible assets include non-material benefits such as goodwill, patents, copyrights, and trademarks.

TAPE
1. service that reports prices and size of transactions on major exchanges. Also called *composite tape* and *ticker tape* (because of the sound made by the machine that printed the tape before the process was computerized).
2. tape of Dow Jones and other news wires, usually called the BROAD TAPE.

   See also CONSOLIDATED TAPE.

TAPE IS LATE situation in which trading volume is so heavy that the consolidated tape is running more than a minute behind when the actual trades are taking place on the floor of the exchange. The tape will not run faster than 900 characters a minute because the human eye cannot take in information any faster. When trading volume is heavy and the tape is running late, some price digits will first be deleted, and then volume digits will be deleted.

TARGET COMPANY firm that has been chosen as attractive for TAKEOVER by a potential acquirer. The acquirer may buy up to 5% of the target's stock without public disclosure, but it must report all transactions and supply other information to the Securities and Exchange Commission, the exchange the target company is listed on, and the target company itself once 5% or more of the stock is acquired. *See also* TOEHOLD PURCHASE; SCHEDULE 13D; SLEEPING BEAUTY; TENDER OFFER; WILLIAMS ACT.

TARGETED AMORTIZATION CLASS (TAC) BONDS bonds offered as a tranche class of some COLLATERALIZED MORTGAGE OBLIGATIONS (CMOs). TACs are similar to PAC BONDS in that, unlike conventional CMO classes, they are based on a SINKING-FUND schedule. They differ from PAC bonds, however, in that whereas a PAC's amortization is guaranteed as long as prepayments on the underlying mortgages do not exceed certain limits, a TAC's schedule will be met at only one prepayment rate. At other prepayment rates, the TAC will experience either excesses or shortfalls. A TAC bond provides more cash flow stability than a regular CMO class but less than a PAC, and trades accordingly.

TARGET PRICE
Finance: price at which an acquirer aims to buy a company in a TAKEOVER.
Options: price of the underlying security after which a certain OPTION will become profitable to its buyer. For example, someone buying an XYZ 50 call for a PREMIUM of $200 could have a target price of 52, after which point the premium will be recouped and the CALL OPTION will result in a profit when exercised.

Stocks: price that an investor is hoping a stock he or she has just bought will rise to within a specified period of time. An investor may buy XYZ at $20, with a target price of $40 in one year's time, for instance.

TARIFF
1. federal tax on imports or exports usually imposed either to raise revenue (called a *revenue tariff*) or to protect domestic firms from import competition (called a *protective tariff*). A tariff may also be designed to correct an imbalance of payments. The money collected under tariffs is called DUTY or *customs duty.*
2. schedule of rates or charges, usually for freight.

TAXABLE ESTATE portion of an estate subject to the unified transfer tax of the federal government and to state taxes where applicable. The estate, not the recipients, is taxed on what remains after all expenses, contributions, transfers to a surviving spouse, debts, taxes, and losses. There is a federal EXCLUSION on property transferred by the person who died. According to the TAXPAYER RELIEF ACT OF 1997, the amount of assets that each person can exclude from federal estate taxes is $625,000 in 1998, rising to $1 million in 2006 and later years. This limit rises to $650,000 in 1999, $675,000 in 2000 and 2001, $700,000 in 2002 and 2003, $850,000 in 2004, $950,000 in 2005 and $1 million in 2006. The law created a special $1.3 million exclusion for qualifying farmers and small business owners starting January 1, 1998.

TAXABLE EVENT occurrence with tax consequences. For example, if a stock or mutual fund is sold at a profit, CAPITAL GAINS TAXES may be due. Withdrawal of assets from a tax-deferred retirement account like an IRA, KEOGH, or SALARY REDUCTION PLAN is a taxable event because some or all of the proceeds may be considered TAXABLE INCOME in the year withdrawn. Proper TAX PLANNING can help taxpayers time taxable events to maximum advantage.

TAXABLE INCOME amount of income (after all allowable deductions and adjustments to income) subject to tax. On an individual's federal income tax return, taxable income is ADJUSTED GROSS INCOME (the sum of wages, salaries, dividends, interest, capital gains, business income, etc., less allowable adjustments that, in part, include INDIVIDUAL RETIREMENT ACCOUNT contributions, alimony payments, unreimbursed business expenses and CAPITAL LOSSES up to $3000) less itemized or standard deductions and the total of personal exemptions. Once taxable income is known, the individual taxpayer finds the total income tax obligation for his or her TAX BRACKET by checking the Internal Revenue Service tax tables or by calculating the tax according to a rate schedule. TAX CREDITS reduce the tax liability dollar-for-dollar.

NET INCOME of a self-employed person (self-proprietorship) and distributions to members of a partnership are included in adjusted gross income, and hence taxable income, on an individual tax return.

Taxable income of an incorporated business, also called *net income before taxes,* consists of total revenues less cost of goods sold, selling and administrative expenses, interest, and extraordinary items.

TAXABLE MUNICIPAL BOND taxable debt obligation of a state or local government entity, an outgrowth of the TAX REFORM ACT OF 1986 (which restricted the issuance of traditional TAX-EXEMPT SECURITIES). Taxable MUNICIPAL BONDS are issued as PRIVATE PURPOSE BONDS to finance such prohibited projects as a sports stadium; as MUNICIPAL REVENUE BONDS where caps apply; or as PUBLIC PURPOSE BONDS where the 10% private use limitation has been exceeded.

TAX AND LOAN ACCOUNT account in a private-sector depository institution, held in the name of the district Federal Reserve Bank as fiscal agent of the United States, that serves as a repository for operating cash available to the U.S. Treasury. Withheld income taxes, employers' contributions to the Social Security fund, and payments for U.S. government securities routinely go into a tax and loan account.

TAX ANTICIPATION BILL (TAB) short-term obligation issued by the U.S. Treasury in competitive bidding at maturities ranging from 23 to 273 days. TABs typically come due within 5 to 7 days after the quarterly due dates for corporate tax payments, but corporations can tender them at PAR value on those tax deadlines in payment of taxes without forfeiting interest income. Since 1975, TABs have been supplemented by cash management bills, due in 30 days or less, and issued in minimum $10 million blocks. These instruments, which are timed to coincide with the maturity of existing issues, provide the Treasury with additional cash management flexibility while giving large investors a safe place to park temporary funds.

TAX ANTICIPATION NOTE (TAN) short-term obligation of a state or municipal government to finance current expenditures pending receipt of expected tax payments. TAN debt evens out the cash flow and is retired once corporate and individual tax revenues are received.

TAX AUDIT audit by the INTERNAL REVENUE SERVICE (IRS), or state or local tax collecting agency, to determine if a taxpayer paid the correct amount of tax. Returns will be chosen for audits if they have suspiciously high claims for deductions or credits, or if reported income is suspiciously low, or if computer matching of income uncovers discrepancies. Audits may be done on a relatively superficial level, or in great depth. If the auditor finds a tax deficiency, the taxpayer may have to pay back-taxes, as well as interest and penalties. The taxpayer does have the right of appeal through the IRS appeals process and, if warranted, to the U.S. Tax Court and even the U.S. Supreme Court.

TAX AVOIDANCE strategy to pay the least amount of tax possible through legal means. For example, taxpayers may buy tax-free municipal bonds; shelter gains inside tax-deferred IRA, KEOGH accounts, SALARY REDUCTION PLANS or tax free ROTH IRA accounts; shift assets to children who need not pay taxes on part of their income; make legitimate charitable contributions to generate tax deductions; and establish trusts to avoid ESTATE TAXES. Illegal strategies to avoid paying taxes are called TAX EVASION.

TAX BASE total amount of taxable property, assets, and income that can be taxed within a specific jurisdiction. A town's tax base is the assessed value of the homes and apartments (minus exempted property), income from businesses, and other sources of taxable activity. If a business moves out of the town, the tax base shrinks, shifting the tax burden onto remaining homeowners and businesses.

TAX BASIS

Finance: original cost of an ASSET, less accumulated DEPRECIATION, that goes into the calculation of a gain or loss for tax purposes. Thus, a property acquired for $100,000 that has been depreciated by $40,000 has a tax basis of $60,000 assuming no other adjustments; sale of that property for $120,000 results in a taxable CAPITAL GAIN of $60,000.

Investments: price at which a stock or bond was purchased, plus brokerage commission. The law requires that a PREMIUM paid on the purchase of an investment be amortized.

TAX BRACKET point on the income-tax rate schedules where TAXABLE INCOME falls; also called *marginal tax bracket*. It is expressed as a percentage applied to each additional dollar earned over the base amount for that bracket. Under a PROGRESSIVE TAX SYSTEM, increases in taxable income lead to higher marginal rates in the form of higher brackets. Under current tax law, there are five tax brackets for individuals: 15%, 28%, 31%, 36% and 39.6%. The final bracket is created by applying a 10% surtax on taxable income greater than $271,050. A DEDUCTION comes off the last marginal dollar earned; thus the 31% taxpayer would save $31 in taxes with each additional $100 of deductions until he worked his way back into the 28% bracket where each $100 deduction would save $28. (A deduction should not be confused with a tax credit.)

For corporations, there are four effective tax brackets. Firms with taxable income of $50,000 or less are subject to a 15% rate; incomes from $50,000 to $75,000 are taxed at 25%; and incomes from $75,000 and up are taxed at 35%.

TAX CREDIT direct, dollar-for-dollar reduction in tax liability, as distinguished from a tax DEDUCTION, which reduces taxes only by the percentage of a taxpayer's TAX BRACKET. (A taxpayer in the 31% tax bracket would get a 31 cent benefit from each $1.00 deduction, for example.) In the case of a tax credit, a taxpayer owing $10,000 in tax would owe $9,000 if he took advantage of a $1,000 tax credit. Under certain conditions, tax credits are allowed for low-income people over age 65, people with disabilities, income tax paid to a foreign country, child care expenses ($400 per child supported under age 17 in 1998 and $500 in 1999 and thereafter), costs of adopting a child (up to $6,000), rehabilitation of historic properties, conducting research and development, building low-income housing, and providing jobs for economically disadvantaged people. THE TAXPAYER RELIEF ACT OF 1997 also created the Hope Scholarship Credit, which can offset college tuition and related educational expenses for the first two years of post-secondary education, up to a maximum of $1,500. The Act also created the Lifetime Learning Credit, which applies to tuition costs for undergraduates, graduates, and those improving their skills through a training program. The credit is worth up to 20% of up to $5,000 of qualified expenses, or $1,000 starting June 30, 1998. Starting in the year 2002, this credit increases to a maximum of 20% of $10,000, or $2,000.

TAX DEDUCTIBLE expense that generates a tax deduction. For individuals, some tax deductible items include charitable contributions, mortgage interest, state, local and foreign taxes, casualty and theft losses, medical expenses and unreimbursed business expenses. In some cases, taxpayers must meet a minimum threshold before an expense is deductible. For example, unreimbursed medical expenses are deductible if they exceed 7.5% of ADJUSTED GROSS INCOME (AGI) in a tax year, and casualty and theft losses must exceed 10% of AGI before they are deductible. In order to deduct miscellaneous expenses, they must total at least 2% of adjusted gross income. If that threshold is reached, such expenses as professional dues and subscriptions, employer-required equipment or uniforms, unreimbursed business travel and entertainment expenses, investment and tax advice, moving expenses and some home office expenses are deductible. For businesses, the costs of doing business are generally tax deductible.

TAX DEDUCTION deductible expense that reduces taxable income for individuals or businesses. *See* TAX DEDUCTIBLE for examples of legal tax deductions.

TAX DEFERRED term describing an investment whose accumulated earnings are free from taxation until the investor takes possession of them. For example, the holder of an INDIVIDUAL RETIREMENT ACCOUNT postpones paying taxes on interest, dividends, or capital appreciation if he or she waits until after age 59½ to cash in those gains. Other examples of tax-deferred investment vehicles include KEOGH PLANS; ANNUITIES; VARIABLE LIFE INSURANCE, WHOLE LIFE INSURANCE, AND UNIVERSAL LIFE INSURANCE; STOCK PURCHASE or DIVIDEND REINVESTMENT PLANS; SIMPLE IRAS; SALARY REDUCTION PLANS and SERIES EE and SERIES HH U.S. SAVINGS BONDS.

TAX STATUS ELECTION selection of filing status. Individuals may choose single, married filing jointly, married filing separately, or head of household. Businesses may elect C corporation, S corporation, limited partnership, or sole proprietorship status, among others. Taxpayers may choose to figure their tax return under two filing status categories to find out which status is most advantageous.

TAX EQUITY AND FISCAL RESPONSIBILITY ACT OF 1982
(TEFRA) federal legislation to raise tax revenue, mainly through closing various loopholes and instituting tougher enforcement procedures. Among its major components:

1. penalties for noncompliance with tax laws were increased, and various steps were taken to facilitate the collection of taxes by the Internal Revenue Service (IRS).

2. ten percent of interest and dividends earned was required to be withheld from all bank and brokerage accounts and forwarded directly to the IRS. (This provision was later canceled by Congress after a major lobbying campaign to overturn it.)

3. TAX PREFERENCE ITEMS were added to the old add-on minimum tax to strengthen the ALTERNATIVE MINIMUM TAX.

4. the floor for medical expense deductions was raised from 3% to 5% of ADJUSTED GROSS INCOME (AGI).

5. casualty and theft losses were made deductible only if each loss exceeds $100 and the total excess losses exceed 10% of AGI.

6. deductions for original issue discount bonds were limited to the amount the issuer would deduct as interest if it issued bonds with a face amount equivalent to the actual proceeds and paying the market rate of interest. This amount must be reduced by the amount of the deductions for any actual interest.

7. more rapid rates for recovering costs under the ACCELERATED COST RECOVERY SYSTEM (ACRS), which had been scheduled to go into effect in 1985 and 1986, were repealed.

8. most of the rules providing for SAFE HARBOR leasing transactions authorized under ERTA were repealed.

9. excise taxes were raised to 3% on telephone use, to 16 cents a pack on cigarettes, and to 8% on airline tickets.

10. the Federal Unemployment Tax Act wage base and tax rate were increased.

11. numerous tax incentives for corporate mergers were reduced.

12. net extraction losses in foreign oil and gas operations in one country were allowed to offset net extraction income from such operations in other countries in the computation of oil and gas extraction taxes.

13. most bonds were required to be registered so that the government could ensure that bondholders are reporting interest.

14. As long as they are not prohibited by a Foreign Corrupt Practices Act, payments to foreign officials were authorized to be deducted as legitimate business expenses.

15. the basis of assets that generate tax INVESTMENT CREDITS was reduced by one-half the amount of the credit.

16. pension and profit-sharing qualified plans were curtailed with a series of new rules that restricted plan loans, required withholding on plan distributions, limited estate-tax exclusions on certain plan

distributions, and restricted "top-heavy" plans, those tilted to benefit mostly the top-earning employees of a company.

17. changes were made in the way life insurance companies were taxed.

TAX-EQUIVALENT YIELD pretax yield that a taxable bond would have to pay to equal the tax-free yield of a municipal bond in an investor's tax bracket. To figure out the tax-equivalent yield, an investor must subtract his or her marginal tax bracket from 100, which results in the *tax bracket reciprocal.* This figure must then be divided by the yield of the tax-free municipal bond. The result is the yield which a taxable bond would have to pay to give the investor the same dollars in his or her pocket after all taxes were paid. For example, an investor in the 31% tax bracket would first take 31 from 100, producing 69 (the tax bracket reciprocal). To evaluate a 7% tax-free bond, the investor would divide 7% by 69, resulting in a 10.1% yield. Therefore, the investor would have to find a taxable bond paying 10.1% to end up with the same after-tax return as the 7% tax-free bond is offering. In general, the higher tax rates become, the more attractive tax-free income becomes, because it allows investors to escape more taxes than if tax rates were lower. *See also* YIELD EQUIVALENCE.

TAX EVASION illegal practice of intentionally evading taxes. Taxpayers who evade their true tax liability may underreport income, overstate deductions and exemptions, or participate in fraudulent tax shelters. If the taxpayer is caught, tax evasion is subject to criminal penalties, as well as payment of back taxes with interest, and civil penalties. Tax evasion is different from TAX AVOIDANCE, which is the legal use of the tax code to reduce tax liability.

TAX-EXEMPT free from tax liability. This status is granted to most municipal bonds, which pay interest that is totally free from federal taxes. Municipal bond interest is also usually tax-exempt to bondholders who are residents of the issuing state. However, other states may impose taxes on interest earned from out-of-state bonds. Certain organizations, such as registered charities, religious organizations, educational institutions, and nonprofit groups, also hold tax-exempt status, meaning they are exempt from federal, state, or local government taxes. Earnings on assets held for at least five years inside a ROTH IRA also accumulate tax-free, as long as they are withdrawn after the account holder reaches age 59½.

TAX-EXEMPT MONEY MARKET FUND MONEY MARKET FUND invested in short-term municipal securities that are tax-exempt and that thus distributes income tax-free to shareholders. Such funds pay lower income than taxable funds and should be evaluated on an AFTER-TAX BASIS.

TAX-EXEMPT SECURITY obligation whose interest is exempt from taxation by federal, state, and/or local authorities. It is frequently called a MUNICIPAL BOND (or simply a *municipal),* even though it may have been issued by a state government or agency or by a county, town, or other political district or subdivision. The security is backed by the FULL FAITH AND CREDIT or by anticipated revenues of the issuing authority. Interest income from tax-exempt municipals is free from federal income taxation as well as from taxation in the jurisdiction where the securities have been issued. Thus, New York City obligations are TRIPLE TAX-EXEMPT to city residents whose income is taxed on the federal, state, and local levels. (A very few municipalities tax residents for their own otherwise tax-exempt issues.)

MUTUAL FUNDS that invest exclusively in tax-exempt securities confer the same tax advantages on their shareholders. However, while a fund's dividends would be entirely tax-exempt on a shareholder's federal tax return, they would be free from state income tax only in proportion to the amount of interest income derived from the taxpayer's home state, assuming no interstate reciprocity arrangements pertain.

The return to investors from a tax-exempt bond is less than that from a corporate bond, because the tax exemption provides extra compensation; the higher the TAX BRACKET of the investor, the more attractive the tax-free alternative becomes. Municipal bond yields vary according to local economic factors, the issuer's perceived ability to repay, and the security's quality RATING assigned by one of the bond-rating agencies. *See also* MORAL OBLIGATION BOND.

TAX-FREE EXCHANGE *see* 1031 TAX-FREE EXCHANGE.

TAX LIABILITY income, property, sales, or other taxes owed to a government entity. *See also* PROVISION FOR INCOME TAXES.

TAX HAVEN country offering outside businesses and individuals an environment with little or no taxation. Several Caribbean islands, such as the Cayman Islands, have attracted billions of dollars in bank deposits by creating a tax haven. Depositors and businesses not only lower the tax burdens in their home countries, but also are subject to less regulation and increased privacy for their financial affairs.

TAX LIEN statutory right obtained by a government to enforce a claim against the property of a person owing taxes until the debt is paid.

TAX LOSS CARRYBACK, CARRYFORWARD tax benefit that allows a company or individual to apply losses to reduce tax liability. A company may OFFSET the current year's capital or NET OPERATING LOSSES against profits in the three immediately preceding years, with the earliest year first. After the carryback, it may carry forward (also called a *carryover)* capital losses five years and net operating losses up to 15 years. By then it will presumably have regained financial health.

Individuals may carry over capital losses until they are used up for an unlimited number of years to offset capital gains. Unlike corporations, however, individuals generally cannot carry back losses to apply to prior years' tax returns. The 1986 tax act curbed tax-motivated BUYOUTS by limiting the use of NOLs where a loss corporation has had a 50% or more ownership change in a three-year period. A special set of complex rules pertains to carryback of losses for trading in commodity futures contracts.

The Revenue Reconciliation Act of 1993 introduced a provision requiring that short-term loss be first applied to reduce any long-term gain. Since previously the short-term loss would have been deductible against ordinary income up to $3000 per year, the provision effectively reduces the long-term gain available for the favorable long-term capital gains rate.

TAXPAYER RELIEF ACT OF 1997 landmark legislation signed into law by President Clinton in August 1997 as part of a larger act designed to balance the federal budget. Some of the major provisions of the law:

1. **Tax credits for children:** Parents or grandparents supporting children under the age of 17 are allowed to claim a TAX CREDIT of $400 per child in 1998 and $500 per child in 1999 and every year thereafter. The credit can be used in addition to the existing deduction for each dependent. This tax credit is phased out for families reporting an ADJUSTED GROSS INCOME of $110,000 on a joint return, $55,000 for those married filing separately, and $75,000 for a single filer. The credit is reduced by $50 for each $1,000 of the threshold, and it disappears altogether for couples with incomes of $119,000 or more and singles with incomes of $85,000 or higher. A tax credit of $5,000 was also added for taxpayers who adopt children, with up to $6,000 for adoptions of "special needs" children.

2. **Estate tax exclusion raised:** The amount of ASSETS that individuals can exclude from estate taxes was boosted from $600,000 to $1 million, and up to $1.3 million for small businessmen and farmers. The increase in the universal estate tax exclusion is phased in over a 9-year period, with the limit rising to $625,000 in 1998, $650,000 in 1999, $675,000 in 2000 and 2001, $700,000 in 2002 and 2003, $850,000 in 2004, $950,000 in 2005, and topping out at $1 million in 2006 and later years. However, the $1.3 million limit for farms and other small businesses went into effect fully on January 1, 1998. To qualify as a small business, an estate's business assets must represent at least 50% of its total assets. To preserve the tax break, heirs must also "materially participate" in running the business for at least five of the eight years within ten years of the owner's death. If heirs sell the business to nonfamily members within 10 years after the owner's death, they must pay some of the taxes from which they were originally exempt.

   In the Tax Act, three other estate tax limits were indexed to inflation, rounded to the next lowest multiple of $10,000:
   • the $1 million exemption from the generation-skipping transfer (GST) tax.

- the $750,000 maximum reduction in value on special use valuation of real property used in farming or a closely held business.
- the $1 million maximum value of a closely-held business eligible for a special 4% interest rate on estate tax installment payments.

3. **Gift tax limit indexed to inflation:** The $10,000 a year GIFT TAX limit was tied to the rate of inflation, and is adjustable in $1,000 increments starting on January 1, 1999.

4. **Lower capital gains tax rates:** The top tax rate on profits from the sale of assets like stocks, bonds, mutual funds and real estate was lowered from 28% to 20%. Before this law, those in the 15% and 28% income tax brackets paid the same tax rate on CAPITAL GAINS as on regular income. Only those in higher tax brackets benefited from the 28% capital gains tax rate cap. Under the 1997 law, those in the 28% bracket pay a maximum rate of 20%, while those in the 15% tax bracket pay a maximum of just 10% when they realize capital gains. The new rules apply to anyone selling assets after May 6, 1997, but do not apply to sales of hard assets like art, antiques, stamps, coins, gems and collectibles, for which the top capital gains tax rate remains 28%. These capital gains tax rates apply for ALTERNATIVE MINIMUM TAX (AMT) purposes as well as for regular federal taxes.

5. **New tax rate for property that received accelerated depreciation:** For those selling a business or investment real estate on which they took accelerated depreciation, the portion of the capital gain representing depreciation is eligible for a maximum tax rate of 25% if the asset is sold after May 6, 1997.

6. **Longer-term capital gains rates created:** For assets like stocks, bonds, and mutual funds purchased after January 1, 2000 and held for at least 5 years, the top capital gains rate was lowered to 18% for those in the 28% tax bracket or higher. The tax rate for holding assets for five years was lowered to 8% for those in the 15% tax bracket.

7. **Changed holding period for capital gains:** Previous law stated that assets had to be held for at least 12 months to qualify for long-term CAPITAL GAINS rates. Under the 1997 law, assets must be held for at least 18 months to qualify for the advantageous capital gains tax rates. Subsequently, the INTERNAL REVENUE SERVICE RESTRUCTURING AND REFORM ACT OF 1998, enacted into law in the summer of 1998, reduced the holding period back to 12 months.

8. **Expanded tax deductibility for individual retirement account contributions:** Under previous law, taxpayers could not fully deduct their contributions to INDIVIDUAL RETIREMENT ACCOUNTS if their adjusted gross income exceeded $40,000 on a joint tax return or $25,000 for a single tax return. The law raised those income caps to $50,000 for a joint return and $30,000 for a single, starting in 1998. The caps gradually climb over ten years (by 2007) to $80,000 for a couple and $50,000 for a single. Over those limits,

the deduction phases out for the next $10,000 in income. For singles, the deduction is phased out completely once income tops $40,000 in 1998, climbing to $60,000 in 2005. For married couples filing jointly, the deduction is phased out once income exceeds $60,000 in 1998, rising to $100,000 in 2007.

9. Introduction of the Roth IRA: A new kind of INDIVIDUAL RETIREMENT ACCOUNT was created called the ROTH IRA, which allows individuals to invest up to $2,000 in earnings a year, even after they reach age 70½. They can withdraw all the principal and earnings totally tax free after age 59½, as long as the assets have remained in the IRA for at least 5 years. Unlike regular IRAs, participants do not have to take distributions from a Roth IRA starting at age 70½. In fact, they do not have to take distributions at all in their lifetime if they prefer, allowing them to pass the assets in the Roth to their beneficiaries income-tax free. Contributions to Roth IRAs do not generate tax deductions.

Roth IRA rules also permit account holders to withdraw assets without the usual 10% early withdrawal penalty if they use the money for the purchase of a first home (withdrawals are limited to up to $10,000), for college expenses or if they become disabled.

Only married couples with adjusted gross incomes of $150,000 or less and singles with adjusted gross incomes of $95,000 or less can contribute the full amount to Roth IRAs. The amount they can contribute is phased out for incomes between $150,000 and $160,000 for married couples, and between $95,000 and $110,000 for singles. No contributions are allowed over those income limits.

For those with adjusted gross incomes of $100,000 or less, the law allows people to roll over existing deductible and nondeductible IRA balances into a Roth IRA without the normal 10% premature distribution penalty. When they do so, however, they must pay income tax on all previously untaxed contributions and earnings. For rollovers executed before January 1, 1999, the resulting tax bill is spread over 4 years. Starting in 1999, the rollover is fully taxable in the year it is completed.

10. "Cash-out" threshold for 401(k) plans raised: Under previous law, an employer could "cash out" any departing employee whose 401(k) balance was $3,500 or less. The employee could either take the money and pay taxes on it or roll it over into an IRA ROLLOVER ACCOUNT. The new tax law raised that limit to $5,000, meaning that more workers will be "cashed out" of their 401(k) plans than before.

11. More investments allowed in IRAs: Starting in 1998, IRA account holders can invest in metals such as gold, silver, platinum and palladium. Previously, such IRA investments were banned.

12. Repeal of the "short-short" rule: Under previous law, mutual funds lost their tax pass-through status if more than 30% of their gross income was generated from short-term investment gains under what was known as the "short-short" rule. As a result, fund managers were afraid to use trading strategies such as the use of options contracts, hedging, and short-selling that would generate short-term profits on holdings, even though the fund manager wanted to do so for investment reasons. The tax bill repealed the "short-short" rule, freeing up managers to trade frequently without fear of losing their tax pass-through status. *See also* SHORT-SHORT RULE.

13. **Eliminated "short against the box" as a tax delay technique:** A popular way for some investors to delay paying taxes was "SELL SHORT AGAINST THE BOX." In this technique, an investor who owns a particular stock would sell borrowed shares of the stock rather than shares already owned. This tactic is similar to selling because the investor no longer owns an economic interest in the stock, but previous tax law did not treat it as a sale. Under the 1997 law, shorting against the box after June 8, 1997 is considered a "constructive sale," and will result in a CAPITAL GAINS TAX liability. In effect, this law change means it no longer makes sense to use this technique to delay paying taxes.

14. **Simplifies reporting of taxes on foreign investments:** Starting with 1998 tax-year returns, investors with holdings in foreign stocks, bonds, or mutual funds no longer need to fill out the complicated IRS Form 116 to claim the foreign tax credit. This applies to single investors who pay up to $300 a year in foreign taxes and for married couples filing jointly up to $600 a year. The amount of foreign earned income that taxpayers can exclude from taxation increases from $72,000 in 1998 to $74,000 in 1999, $76,000 in 2000, $78,000 in 2001 and $80,000 in 2002 and later years.

15. **Repeal of excess accumulation and excess distributions tax:** In earlier legislation, Congress imposed a 15% "excess accumulation tax" on LUMP SUM payouts of more than $800,000 from pension plans and a 15% "excess distributions tax" on payouts from INDIVIDUAL RETIREMENT ACCOUNTS of more than $160,000. All of these taxes were repealed for distributions made after December 31, 1996.

16. **New capital gains rules for home sales:** Under previous law, homeowners could avoid CAPITAL GAINS TAXES on the sale of their home only if they bought another home within two years and reinvested the proceeds into a home of the same or greater value. Those over age 55 could escape capital gains tax when selling their homes up to $125,000 once in their lifetime. The 1997 tax law allows people to avoid all capital gains taxes on profits up to $500,000 for married couples filing jointly and up to $250,000 for those filing singly. The rule which benefits anyone selling their home after May 6, 1997, only applies to a person's primary residence, defined as a home occupied for at least two of the five years prior to the sale. Individuals can claim the $500,000 capital gains tax exemption every two years. The old $125,000 exemption for

those over 55 was superceded by the new law. In the past, someone with gains of more than $500,000 could avoid taxes by rolling the profits into a larger home. The 1997 law eliminates such a rollover. Capital gains taxes of up to 20% are due upon the sale of a home with profits over $500,000. One other twist affects real-estate investors who depreciate their property over time. When these investors sell the property, they must pay a maximum 25% capital gains tax for the part of their gain due to depreciation.

17. **Tax credits for college education:** The law created the "Hope Scholarship," a tax credit to help pay for the first two years of tuition and fees for students attending college or vocational school. The tax credit started at $1,500 in 1998 and rises to $2,000 in 2003. Starting on July 1, 1998, a yearly "Lifetime Learning Credit" of up to $1,000 for 20% of tuition and school fees up to $5,000 is available for third- and fourth-year college students, graduate students, and people returning to school to sharpen job skills. This credit rises to 20% of $10,000, or a maximum of $2,000, in 2002. These tax credits are available only to married couples filing jointly with adjusted gross incomes of $80,000 or less, or singles with $40,000 or less. The credit is phased out for couples with incomes of $100,000 and singles earning over $50,000.

18. **Deductible education-related interest:** Starting in 1998, up to $1,000 in interest on student loans is deductible for taxpayers repaying loans for their own or a dependent's college or vocational school expenses. The interest is deductible only for the first 60 months (5 years) that the loan is outstanding. The $1,000 cap increases by $500 annually until it reaches a maximum of $2,500 in 2001. Taxpayers can get this deduction even if they don't file an itemized return. This deductible interest is fully available to married taxpayers with $60,000 or less in income if filing jointly or $40,000 or less for singles. The deduction phases out for couples with incomes between $60,000 and $75,000 and for singles with incomes between $40,000 and $55,000, and is not available for those with incomes over those thresholds. Income levels will be adjusted for inflation starting in 2003.

19. **Tax-free employer-paid education:** Employees are entitled to receive up to $5,250 per year from their employers for undergraduate classes without having to declare that money as taxable income. This rule applies to classes not directly related to their job. The tax break remains in effect for courses beginning before June 1, 2000. Reimbursement for schooling that is job-related remains tax-free without limitation.

20. **Creation of Education IRA:** A new type of account, similar to an INDIVIDUAL RETIREMENT ACCOUNT, called the EDUCATION IRA, was created to allow parents to save up to $500 per year per child under age 18 to help pay educational expenses. The money invested does not generate a deduction when placed in the Education IRA, but the principal, income, and CAPITAL GAINS are

completely tax-free when withdrawn to pay for college expenses such as tuition, fees, books and room and board. *See also* EDUCATION IRA.

21. **Tax relief for children:** In the past, children earning more than $650 a year in wages could not use their standard deduction to shelter investment income from taxes. Beginning in 1998, children can use the standard deduction to shelter both their job earnings plus up to $250 in investment income.

22. **Bigger deductions for health insurance premiums for the self-employed:** Under previous law, only a portion of health insurance premiums paid by the self-employed were deductible, while all premiums paid by larger companies were deductible. This inequity was phased out by the law. In 1997, 40% of the premium paid by the self-employed were deductible. In 1998 and 1999, it rose to 45%. In 2000 and 2001, it rises to 50%. In 2002 it is 60%. From 2003 through 2005, the deduction rises to 80%. In 2006 it is 90%. From 2007 and future years, the deduction is 100%.

23. **Creation of the Medical Savings Account (MSA):** People with high-deductible health plans may participate in a Medical Savings Account. They can deduct MSA contributions even if they do not itemize deductions. MSAs are generally available for the self-employed and small employers with fewer than 50 workers.

24. **Social Security and Medicare taxes:** The maximum wages subject to Social Security tax (6.2%) was raised to $65,400. All wages are subject to the Medicare tax of 1.45%.

25. **Liberalization of the home office deduction:** For many years, the IRS rules and court decisions greatly restricted home office deductions. The 1997 tax law eased the rules and home office deductions are allowed starting in 1999 if the space used is essential to running or administering the business. No longer does the space have to be the only place where the taxpayer meets clients or conducts their work. However, taxpayers must use the home office space exclusively and regularly for business purposes.

26. **Higher exemption from filing quarterly estimated taxes:** Starting in 1998, the law exempts those expecting to pay less than $1,000 in taxes from having to make quarterly estimated tax payments. This doubles the previous limit of $500. In figuring estimated tax, however, taxpayers must include any expected employment taxes for household workers.

27. **Higher deduction for charitable use of your car:** The deduction for using an automobile to benefit a charity rose from 12 cents to 14 cents a mile, starting in 1998.

28. **Repeal of motorboat gas tax:** The 24.3 cent a gallon tax on diesel fuel for recreational motorboats was repealed.

29. **Paying taxes by credit card:** The bill authorized the Internal Revenue Service to accept payment of taxes by credit or debit card or electronic funds transfer, though the IRS is prohibited from paying fees to card issuers.

30. Higher cigarette taxes: The excise tax on cigarettes rises by 10 cents a pack to 34 cents in 2000 and by an additional 5 cents to 39 cents in 2002.

31. Higher airline ticket taxes: The excise tax on airline tickets rose from $6 to $12 on departures to international destinations, and a $12 per ticket fee was added on international arrivals. A $3 airport-to-airport segment tax was also added on all domestic flights. The airline ticket tax was gradually scaled back from 10% to 7.5%.

See also INTERNAL REVENUE SERVICE RESTRUCTURING AND REFORM ACT OF 1998.

TAX PLANNING strategy of minimizing tax liability for an individual or company by analyzing the tax implications of various options throughout a tax year. Tax planning involves choosing a FILING STATUS, figuring out the most advantageous time to realize capital gains and losses, knowing when to accelerate deductions and postpone income or vice versa, setting up a proper estate plan to reduce estate taxes, and other legitimate tax-saving moves.

TAX PREFERENCE ITEM item specified by the tax law that a taxpayer must include when calculating the ALTERNATIVE MINIMUM TAX (AMT). Preference items include: the (adjusted) excess of MODIFIED ACCELERATED COST RECOVERY SYSTEM (MACRS) deductions over alternative depreciation system (ADS) deductions (ADS is an alternative depreciation system with longer deduction periods) on real property placed into service before 1987; and tax-exempt interest on nonessential PRIVATE PURPOSE BONDS of municipalities issued after August 7, 1986.

Corporate preferences are generally the same as for individuals, but also include an adjustment for current earnings (ACE) aimed at profits reported to shareholders but not regularly taxed. The ACE adjustment is based on 75% of the difference between a corporation's alternative minimum taxable income (AMTI) for the tax year and its adjusted earnings and profits. The depreciation deduction for PERSONAL PROPERTY, a large part of AMTI, requires use of the 150% declining balance method. *See also* TAX EQUITY AND FISCAL RESPONSIBILITY ACT OF 1982, TAX REFORM ACT OF 1976, TAX REFORM ACT OF 1986.

TAX PREPARATION SERVICES businesses that specialize in preparing tax returns. Such services may range from national tax preparation chains such as H&R Block to local tax preparers, enrolled agents, CPA accountants, and tax lawyers. Services normally charge based on the complexity of the tax return and the amount of time needed to fill it out correctly. Many services can arrange to file a tax return with the Internal Revenue Service electronically, which can result in a faster TAX REFUND.

TAX RATE percentage of tax paid on a certain level of income. The U.S. uses a system of marginal tax rates, meaning that the rates rise with taxable income. The top rate is paid only on the portion of income over the threshold. Currently, the federal government imposes four tax rates—15%, 28%, 31%, and 36%. There is also a 10% surtax on married couples filing jointly or singles reporting taxable incomes of more than $271,050 or married couples filing separately with taxable incomes of more than $135,525. This creates an effective fifth tax rate of 39.6%.

TAX REFORM ACT OF 1976 federal legislation that tightened several provisions and benefits relating to taxation, beginning in the 1976 tax year. Among its major provisions:

1. extended the long-term CAPITAL GAINS holding period from six months to nine months in 1977 and to 12 months beginning in 1978.
2. instituted new rules on determining the TAX BASIS of inherited property.
3. set a new minimum capital gains tax on the sale of a house.
4. established, for homeowners over age 65, a once-in-a-lifetime exclusion of up to $35,000 in capital gains tax on the sale of a principal residence. (This amount was later raised by other tax bills, until it stood at $125,000 in the mid-1980s.)
5. increased the maximum net CAPITAL LOSS deduction from ordinary income on a personal income tax return to $3000 beginning in 1978.
6. extended the period of tax loss carryforward from five years to seven; gave companies the option of carrying losses forward without having first to carry them back; and prohibited acquiring corporations from taking advantage of an acquired firm's loss carryovers unless it gave the acquired firm's stockholders continuing ownership in the combined company.
7. limited deductions for home-office expenses to cases where homes are used as principal business locations, or for meeting with clients.
8. disallowed owners who rent their vacation homes from reporting losses, deducting maintenance costs or taking depreciation on those rentals unless the owners themselves used the homes less than two weeks per year, or less than 10% of total rental time.
9. instituted a deduction up to $3000 for "indirect" moving costs if a new job is more than 35 miles from a previous job.
10. established a child-care tax credit of up to $400 for one child and up to $800 for more than one child.
11. allowed a divorced parent, if contributing at least $1200 in child support, to claim a child as a dependent deduction.
12. instituted a spousal INDIVIDUAL RETIREMENT ACCOUNT, which allowed nonworking spouses to contribute up to $250.
13. disallowed losses on tax shelters financed through loans made without any obligation to pay, or where taxpayer's risk is limited by a form of guarantee, except for real estate investments.
14. treated the exercise of a STOCK OPTION as ordinary income rather than as a CAPITAL GAIN.

TAX REFORM ACT OF 1984 legislation enacted by Congress as part of the Deficit Reduction Act of 1984 to reduce the federal budget deficit. The following are highlights from the more than 100 provisions in the Act:

1. shortened the minimum holding period for assets to qualify for long-term capital gains treatment from one year to six months.
2. allowed contributions to be made to an INDIVIDUAL RETIREMENT ACCOUNT no later than April 15 after the tax year for which an IRA benefit is sought; previously the cut-off was the following October 15th.
3. allowed the Internal Revenue Service to tax the benefits of loans made on below-market, interest-free, or "gift" terms.
4. tightened INCOME AVERAGING requirements.
5. set a $150 per capita limit on the amount of INDUSTRIAL DEVELOPMENT BONDS that a state could issue in a year, and permitted interest to be tax-exempt only for certain "small issues."
6. retained the 15% minimum tax on corporate TAX PREFERENCE ITEMS as in the TAX REFORM ACT OF 1976, but increased from 15% to 20% the deduction allowed for a tax preference item.
7. restricted GOLDEN PARACHUTE payments to executives by eliminating the corporate tax deductibility of these payments and subjecting them to a nondeductible 20% excise tax.
8. required registration of TAX SHELTERS with the Internal Revenue Service and set penalties for failure to comply. Also set penalties for overvaluing assets used for depreciation in a tax shelter.
9. expanded rules in ERTA to cover additional types of stock and options transactions that make up TAX STRADDLES.
10. repealed the 30% withholding tax on interest, dividends, rents, and royalties paid to foreign investors by U.S. corporations and government agencies.
11. raised the liquor tax, reduced the cigarette tax, and extended the 3% telephone excise tax.
12. delayed to 1987 the scheduled decline in estate and gift taxes.
13. granted a specific tax exemption for many fringe benefits.
14. extended mortgage subsidy bonds through 1988.
15. required ALTERNATIVE MINIMUM TAX quarterly estimated payments.
16. changed the rules affecting taxation of life insurance companies.
17. disqualified from eligibility for long-term capital gains tax the appreciation of market discounts on newly issued ORIGINAL ISSUE DISCOUNT bonds.
18. real estate depreciation was lengthened from 15 to 18 years.
19. delayed implementation of new finance leasing rules until 1988.
20. restricted the sale of unused depreciation tax deductions by tax-exempt entities to companies that can use the deductions.
21. phased out the graduated corporate income tax on the first $100,000 of income for corporations with income over $1 million.
22. created Foreign Sales Corporations (FSCs) to provide American companies with tax deferral advantages to encourage exports.

23. limited tax breaks for luxury automobiles to a maximum writeoff of $16,000 in the first three years of ownership.
24. increased the earned income tax credit for lower-income taxpayers from 10% to a maximum of 11% of the first $5000 of income.
25. eliminated the tax on property transfers in a divorce.
26. increased the standard automobile mileage rate from 9 cents a mile to 12 cents a mile for expenses incurred in volunteer charity work.
27. tightened rules and increased penalties for those who try to inflate deductions by overvaluing property donated to charity.

TAX REFORM ACT OF 1986 landmark federal legislation enacted that made comprehensive changes in the system of U.S. taxation. Among the law's major provisions:

Provisions Affecting Individuals

1. lowered maximum marginal tax rates from 50% to 28% beginning in 1988 and reduced the number of basic TAX BRACKETS from 15 to 2—28% and 15%. Also instituted a 5% rate surcharge for high-income taxpayers.
2. eliminated the preferential tax treatment of CAPITAL GAINS. Starting in 1988, all gains realized on asset sales were taxed at ordinary income rates, no matter how long the asset was held.
3. increased the personal exemption to $1900 in 1987, $1950 in 1988, and $2000 in 1989. Phased out exemption for high-income taxpayers.
4. increased the STANDARD DEDUCTION, and indexed it to inflation starting in 1989.
5. repealed the deduction for two-earner married couples.
6. repealed income averaging for all taxpayers.
7. repealed the $100 ($200 for couples) dividend exclusion.
8. restricted the deductibility of IRA contributions.
9. mandated the phaseout of consumer interest deductibility by 1991.
10. allowed investment interest expense to be offset against investment income, dollar-for-dollar, without limitation.
11. limited unreimbursed medical expenses that could be deducted to amounts in excess of 7.5% of adjusted gross income.
12. limited the tax deductibility of interest on a first or second home mortgage to the purchase price of the house plus the cost of improvements and amounts used for medical or educational purposes.
13. repealed the deductibility of state and local sales taxes.
14. limited miscellaneous deductions to expenses exceeding 2% of adjusted gross income.
15. limited the deductibility of itemized charitable contributions.
16. strengthened the ALTERNATIVE MINIMUM TAX, and raised the rate to 21%.

17. tightened home office deductions.
18. lowered the deductibility of business entertainment and meal expenses from 100% to 80%.
19. eliminated the benefits of CLIFFORD TRUSTS and other income-shifting devices by taxing unearned income over $1000 on gifts to children under 14 years old at the grantor's tax rate.
20. repealed the tax credit for political contributions.
21. limited the use of losses from PASSIVE activity to offsetting income from passive activity.
22. lowered the top rehabilitation tax credit from 25% to 20%.
23. made all unemployment compensation benefits taxable.
24. repealed the deduction for attending investment seminars.
25. eased the rules for exercise of INCENTIVE STOCK OPTIONS.
26. imposed new limitations on SALARY REDUCTION PLANS and SIMPLIFIED EMPLOYEE PENSION (SEP) PLANS.

Provisions Affecting Business

27. lowered the top corporate tax rate to 34% from 46%, and lowered the number of corporate tax brackets from five to three.
28. applied the ALTERNATIVE MINIMUM TAX (AMT) to corporations, and set a 20% rate.
29. repealed the investment tax credit for property placed in service after 1985.
30. altered the method of calculating DEPRECIATION.
31. limited the deductibility of charges to BAD DEBT reserves to financial institutions with less than $500 million in assets.
32. extended the research and development tax credit, but lowered the rate from 25% to 20%.
33. eliminated the deductibility of interest that banks pay to finance tax-exempt securities holdings.
34. eliminated the deductibility of GREENMAIL payments by companies warding off hostile takeover attempts.
35. restricted COMPLETED CONTRACT METHOD accounting for tax purposes.
36. limited the ability of a company acquiring more than 50% of another firm to use NET OPERATING LOSSES to offset taxes.
37. reduced the corporate DIVIDEND EXCLUSION from 85% to 80%.
38. limited cash and installment method accounting for tax purposes.
39. restricted tax-exemption on MUNICIPAL BONDS to PUBLIC PURPOSE BONDS and specified PRIVATE PURPOSE BONDS. Imposed caps on the dollar amount of permitted private purpose bonds. Limited PRE-REFUNDING. Made interest on certain private purpose bonds subject to the AMT.
40. amended the rules for qualifying as a REAL ESTATE INVESTMENT TRUST and the taxation of REITs.
41. set up tax rules for real estate mortgage investment conduits (REMICs).
42. changed many rules relating to taxation of foreign operations of U.S. multinational companies.

43. liberalized the requirements for employee VESTING rules in a company's qualified pension plan, and changed other rules affecting employee benefit plans.
44. enhanced benefit of SUBCHAPTER S corporation status.

TAX REFORM ACT OF 1993 *see* REVENUE RECONCILIATION ACT OF 1993.

TAX REFUND refund of overpaid taxes from the government to the taxpayer. Refunds are due when the taxpayer has been OVERWITHHOLDING, or has overestimated income or underestimated deductions, exemptions, and credits. Though taxpayers may like the fact that they are getting a tax refund, in fact they are granting the government an interest-free loan for most of the year, which is not astute TAX PLANNING.

TAX SCHEDULES tax forms used in addition to the Form 1040 to report itemized deductions (Schedule A); dividend and interest income (Schedule B); profit or loss from business (Schedule C); capital gains and losses (Schedule D); supplemental income and loss (Schedule E); and Social Security Self-employment tax (Schedule SE).

TAX SELLING selling of securities, usually at year end, to realize losses in a PORTFOLIO, which can be used to OFFSET capital gains and thereby lower an investor's tax liability. *See also* LONG TERM GAIN; LONG TERM LOSS; SELLING SHORT AGAINST THE BOX; SHORT TERM GAIN OR LOSS; SWAP; THIRTY-DAY WASH RULE.

TAX SHIELD deductions that reduce tax liabilities. For example, mortgage interest, charitable contributions, unreimbursed business expenses, and medical expenses can be considered tax shields if a taxpayer qualifies for the deduction. The higher the marginal tax rate, the more the deduction is worth.

TAX SHELTER method used by investors to legally avoid or reduce tax liabilities. Legal shelters include those using DEPRECIATION of assets like real estate or equipment, or DEPLETION allowances for oil and gas exploration. LIMITED PARTNERSHIPS traditionally offered investors limited liability and tax benefits including "flow through" operating losses which offset income from other sources. The TAX REFORM ACT OF 1986 dealt a severe blow to such tax shelters by ruling that passive losses could only offset passive income, lengthening depreciation schedules, and extending AT RISK rules to include real estate investments. Vehicles that allow tax-deferred capital growth, such as INDIVIDUAL RETIREMENT ACCOUNTS (IRAs) and KEOGH PLANS (which also provide current tax deductions for qualified taxpayers), SALARY REDUCTION PLANS, SIMPLE IRAS, and LIFE INSURANCE, are also popular tax shelters as are tax-exempt MUNICIPAL BONDS. The ROTH IRA, created in the TAXPAYER RELIEF ACT OF1997, allows tax free accumulation of earnings on assets held in the account for at least five years.

TAX SOFTWARE software that helps taxpayers plan for and prepare their tax returns. Software such as TurboTax and TaxCut helps taxpayers analyze their tax situation and take actions to minimize tax liability. Different versions of tax software are appropriate for large and small businesses, partnerships, individuals, and estates. The software also comes in state-specific versions to aid in preparation and planning for state taxes. When integrated with a personal finance software package, a taxpayer does not have to reenter data, which can easily be exchanged from the personal finance side into the tax preparation side of the package.

TAX STRADDLE technique whereby OPTION or FUTURES CONTRACTS are used to eliminate economic risk while creating an advantageous tax position. In its most common use, an investor with a CAPITAL GAIN would take a position creating an offsetting "artificial" loss in the current tax year and postponing the gain until the next tax year. The ECONOMIC RECOVERY TAX ACT OF 1981 curtailed this practice by requiring traders to MARK TO THE MARKET at year-end and include unrealized gains in taxable income. The TAX REFORM ACT OF 1986 introduced a change whereby an exception for COVERED WRITERS of calls is denied if the taxpayer fails to hold the covered CALL OPTION for 30 days after the related stock is disposed of at a loss, if gain on the termination or disposition of the option is included in the next year.

TAX UMBRELLA tax loss carryforwards stemming from losses of a firm in past years, which shield profits earned in current and future years from taxes. *See also* TAX LOSS CARRYBACK, CARRYFORWARD.

TEAR SHEET sheet from one of a dozen loose-leaf books comprising Standard & Poor's Stock Reports, which provide essential background and financial data on several thousand companies. Brokers often tear and mail these sheets to customers (hence the name).

TEASER RATE introductory interest rate on an adjustable rate mortgage (ARM) designed to entice borrowers. The teaser rate may last for a few months, or as long as a year, before the rate returns to a market level. In a competitive mortgage market, some mortgage lenders may offer competing teaser rates to try to win over potential borrowers. In addition to the marketing rationale for teaser rates, lenders maintain that having a low initial rate makes it easier for homeowners to settle into a new home, with all the expenses entailed in moving in. Only portfolio lenders can offer teaser rates. Mortgage bankers cannot because they must comply with investor guidelines.

TECHNICAL ANALYSIS research into the demand and supply for securities, options, mutual funds, and commodities based on trading volume and price studies. Technical analysts use charts or computer programs to identify and project price trends in a market, security, fund, or futures contract. Most analysis is done for the short- or intermediate-term, but some technicians also predict long-term cycles based on charts and other data. Unlike FUNDAMENTAL ANALYSIS, technical analysis is not concerned with the financial position of a company. *See also* ADVANCE/DECLINE (A/D); ASCENDING TOPS; BREAKOUT; CORRECTION; DEAD CAT BOUNCE; DESCENDING TOPS; DIP; DOUBLE BOTTOM; ELVES; FALL OUT OF BED; FLAG; FLURRY; GAP; GAP OPENING; HEAD AND SHOULDERS; HORIZONTAL PRICE MOVEMENT; MOMENTUM INDICATORS; MOVING AVERAGE; MOVING AVERAGE CONVERGENCE/DIVERGENCE (MACD); NEW HIGH/NEW LOW; PENNANT; POINT AND FIGURE CHART; PUT-CALL RATIO; RELATIVE STRENGTH; RESISTANCE LEVEL; REVERSAL; RISING BOTTOMS; SAUCER; SELLING CLIMAX; STOCHASTICS INDEX; SUPPORT LEVEL; TRADING PATTERN; TRIANGLE; V FORMATION; VERTICAL LINE CHARTING; W FORMATION.

TECHNICAL RALLY short rise in securities or commodities futures prices within a general declining trend. Such a rally may result because investors are bargain-hunting or because analysts have noticed a particular SUPPORT LEVEL at which securities usually bounce up. Technical rallies do not last long, however, and soon after prices resume their declining pattern.

TECHNICAL SIGN short-term trend that technical analysts can identify as significant in the price movement of a security or a commodity. *See also* TECHNICAL ANALYSIS.

TED SPREAD difference between interest rates on U.S. Treasury bills and Eurodollars. The term *Ted* refers to *Treasuries over Eurodollars.* Many traders in the futures markets actively trade the Ted spread, speculating that the difference between U.S. Treasuries and Eurodollars will widen or narrow. The Ted spread also is used as an indicator of confidence in the U.S. government and the general level of fear or confidence in the markets for private financing. A narrow spread indicates confidence in financial markets in general and the U.S. Government in particular. When the spread is wide, confidence is diminished. *See also* FLIGHT TO QUALITY.

TEFRA *see* TAX EQUITY AND FISCAL RESPONSIBILITY ACT OF 1982.

TEL AVIV STOCK EXCHANGE only stock exchange in Israel. Trading hours for stocks, warrants, and convertible bonds are 10:30 A.M. to 3:30 P.M., Sunday through Thursday. Options are traded on the 25 companies with highest market value that are part of the *Maof Index.* All other derivatives and all shares are reflected in the *General Share Index.* Trades are settled on the day following the trade.

TELEPHONE SWITCHING process of shifting assets from one MUTUAL FUND or VARIABLE ANNUITY portfolio to another by telephone. Such a switch may be among the stock, bond, or money-market funds of a single FAMILY OF FUNDS, or it may be from a fund in one family to a fund in another. Transfers involving portfolios in annuity contracts do not trigger taxation of gains as do mutual fund switches.

TEMPORARY INVESTMENT investment designed to be held for a short period of time, typically a year or less. Some examples of temporary investments are money market mutual funds, money market deposit accounts, NOW checking accounts, Treasury bills, and short-term CDs. Investors shifting money into such investments may have sold stocks, bonds, or mutual funds, and are keeping their assets liquid while they decide which investments to buy next. They also may be fearful that securities prices are about to fall, and they want to keep their assets in temporary investments to sidestep such a downdraft. While their money is in temporary investments, it continues to earn interest at prevailing market interest rates. *See also* PARKING.

TENANCY AT WILL tenancy where a person holds or occupies real estate with the permission of the owner, for an unspecified term. A tenancy at will could occur when a lease is being negotiated, or under a valid oral lease or contract of sale. All the duties and obligations of a landlord-tenant relationship exist. Notice of termination is required by either party. The tenancy is not assignable.

TENANCY BY THE ENTIRETY (TBE) form of individual (versus corporate or partnership) co-ownership in which ownership passes automatically at the death of one co-owner to the surviving co-owner. The person with a TBE co-ownership interest lacks the power to freely dispose of that interest by WILL. In this respect, it is similar to JOINT TENANCY WITH RIGHT OF SURVIVORSHIP (JTWROS). Unlike JTWROS, however, the TBE ownership interests are limited to ownership by two persons who are husband and wife at the time the property is acquired. If the married couple then divorces, the form of ownership automatically changes to TENANCY IN COMMON (TIC). Generally, TBE ownership is limited to real estate, although about a dozen states permit TBE ownership of personal property.

TENANCY IN COMMON (TIC) ownership of real or personal property by two or more persons in which ownership at the death of one co-owner is part of the owner's disposable ESTATE, and does not pass to the co-owner(s). There is no limit to the number of persons who can acquire property as TIC, and those persons could be, but need not be, married to each other.

TENANT
Real Estate: (1) holder or possessor of real property; (2) lessee.
Securities: part owner of a security.
See also JOINT TENANTS WITH RIGHT OF SURVIVORSHIP; TENANCY IN COMMON.

TENBAGGER stock that grows in value by ten times. The term comes from baseball lingo, since a double is called a two-bagger because it earns the hitter the right to two bases, or bags. Similarly, a triple is a three-bagger and a home run a four-bagger. The term, as applied to investing, is also used in larger multiples, such as a twenty-bagger, for a stock that grows twenty-fold.

TENDER
  1. act of surrendering one's shares in a corporation in response to an offer to buy them at a set price. *See also* TENDER OFFER.

2. to submit a formal bid to buy a security, as in a U.S. Treasury bill auction. *See also* DUTCH AUCTION.

3. offer of money or goods in settlement of a prior debt or claim, as in the delivery of goods on the due date of a FUTURES CONTRACT.

4. agreed-upon medium for the settlement of financial transactions, such as U.S. currency, which is labeled "legal tender for all debts, public and private."

TENDER OFFER offer to buy shares of a corporation, usually at a PRE-MIUM above the shares' market price, for cash, securities, or both, often with the objective of taking control of the TARGET COMPANY. A tender offer may arise from friendly negotiations between the company and a corporate suitor or may be unsolicited and possibly unfriendly, resulting in countermeasures being taken by the target firm. The Securities and Exchange Commission requires any corporate suitor accumulating 5% or more of a target company to make disclosures to the SEC, the target company, and the relevant exchange. *See also* SCHEDULE 13D; TAKEOVER; TREASURY STOCK.

1040 EZ FORM simplified alternative to the 1040 FORM for taxpayers who (1) have single or "married filing jointly" status; (2) are under age 65; (3) are not blind; (4) claim no dependents; (5) have taxable income under $50,000; (6) have income only from salaries, wages, tips, taxable scholarship or fellowship grants, unemployment compensation and taxable interest income below $400; and (7) did not receive any advance EARNED INCOME CREDIT payments.

1040 FORM basic form issued by the INTERNAL REVENUE SERVICE for individual tax returns. *See also* TAX SCHEDULES.

10-K REPORT *see* FORM 10-K.

1099 annual statement sent to the Internal Revenue Service and to taxpayers by the payers of dividends (1099-DIV) and interest (1099-INT) and by issuers of taxable ORIGINAL ISSUE DISCOUNT securities (1099-OID).

TEN PERCENT GUIDELINE MUNICIPAL BOND analysts' guideline that funded debt over 10% of the ASSESSED VALUATION of taxable property in a municipality is excessive.

1031 TAX-FREE EXCHANGE "like-kind" exchange of business or investment property that is free of capital gain taxation under Section 1031 of the Internal Revenue Code. Properties held for rental income, for business purposes, as investment property, or as vacation homes may be exchanged for qualifying like-kind property (a piece of land and a building can be traded because both are real estate), provided certain conditions are met: (1) the seller must identify the replacement property within 45 days after escrow on the old property and (2) the seller must take title to the new property within the earlier of 180 days of the old property's close of escrow or the seller's tax deadline. To the extent *boot,* meaning cash or additional property, is part of the exchange, the transaction is taxable. *See also* POOLING OF INTERESTS.

TERM

1. period of time during which the conditions of a contract will be carried out. This may refer to the time in which loan payments must be made, or the time when interest payments will be made on a certificate of deposit or a bond. It also may refer to the length of time a life insurance policy is in force. *See also* TERM LIFE INSURANCE.

2. provision specifying the nature of an agreement or contract, as in *terms and conditions.*

3. period of time an official or board member is elected or appointed to serve. For example, Federal Reserve governors are appointed for 14-year terms.

TERM CERTIFICATE CERTIFICATE OF DEPOSIT with a longer-term maturity date. Such CDs can range in length from one year to ten years, though the most popular term certificates are those for one or two years. Certificate holders usually receive a fixed rate of interest, payable semiannually during the term, and are subject to costly EARLY WITHDRAWAL PENALTIES if the certificate is cashed in before the scheduled maturity.

TERMINATION BENEFIT *see* SEVERANCE PAY.

TERM LIFE INSURANCE form of life insurance, written for a specified period, that requires the policyholder to pay only for the cost of protection against death; that is, no cash value is built up as in WHOLE LIFE INSURANCE. Every time the policy is renewed, the premium is higher, since the insured is older and therefore statistically more likely to die. Term insurance is far cheaper than whole life, giving policyholders the alternative of using the savings to invest on their own.

TERM LOAN intermediate- to long-term (typically, two to ten years) secured credit granted to a company by a commercial bank, insurance company, or commercial finance company usually to finance capital equipment or provide working capital. The loan is amortized over a fixed period, sometimes ending with a BALLOON payment. Borrowers under term loan agreements are normally required to meet minimum WORKING CAPITAL and debt to net worth tests, to limit dividends, and to maintain continuity of management.

TEST

In general: examination to determine knowledge, competence, or qualifications.

Finance: criterion used to measure compliance with financial ratio requirements of indentures and other loan agreements (e.g., a current asset to current liability test or a debt to net worth test). *See also* QUICK RATIO.

Securities: term used in reference to a price movement that approaches a SUPPORT LEVEL or a RESISTANCE LEVEL established earlier by a commodity future, security, or market. A test is passed if the levels are not penetrated and is failed if prices go on to new lows or highs. Technical analysts say, for instance, that if the Dow Jones Industrials last formed a solid base at 7000, and prices have been falling from 7400, a period of testing is approaching. If prices rebound once the Dow hits 7000 and go up further, the test is passed. If prices continue to drop below 7000, however, the test is failed. *See also* TECHNICAL ANALYSIS.

TESTAMENT synonym for a WILL, a document that will dispose of property a person owns at his or her death. The testament is created by the TESTATOR or TESTATRIX, usually with the aid of an estate planning lawyer or will-writing software.

TESTAMENTARY TRUST trust created by a will, as distinguished from an INTER VIVOS TRUST created during the lifetime of the GRANTOR.

TESTATE having made and left a valid WILL; a person who dies with a will is said to die testate. A person who dies without a will is said to die INTESTATE.

TESTATOR/TESTATRIX a man/woman who has made and left a valid WILL at his/her death.

THEORETICAL VALUE (OF A RIGHT) mathematically determined MARKET VALUE of a SUBSCRIPTION RIGHT after the offering is announced but before the stock goes EX-RIGHTS. The formula includes the current market value of the common stock, the subscription price, and the number of rights required to purchase a share of stock:

theoretical value of a right

$$= \frac{\text{market value of common stock} - \text{subscription price per share}}{\text{number of rights needed to buy 1 share} + 1}$$

Thus, if the common stock market price is $50 per share, the subscription price is $45 per share, and the subscription ratio is 4 to 1, the value of one right would be $1:

$$\frac{50 - 45}{4 + 1} \quad = \quad \frac{5}{5} \quad = 1$$

THIN MARKET market in which there are few bids to buy and few offers to sell. A thin market may apply to an entire class of securities or commodities futures such as small OVER THE COUNTER stocks or the platinum market—or it may refer to a particular stock, whether exchange-listed or over-the-counter. Prices in thin markets are more volatile than in markets with great LIQUIDITY, since the few trades that take place can affect prices significantly. Institutional investors who buy and sell large blocks of stock tend to avoid thin markets, because it is difficult for them to get in or out of a POSITION without materially affecting the stock's price.

THIRD MARKET nonexchange-member broker/dealers and institutional investors trading OVER THE COUNTER in exchange-listed securities. The third market rose to importance in the 1950s when institutional investors began buying common stocks as an inflation hedge and fixed commission rates still prevailed on the exchanges. By trading large blocks with nonmember firms, they both saved commissions and avoided the unsettling effects on prices that large trades on the exchanges produced. After commission rates were deregulated in May 1975, a number of the firms active in the third market became member firms so they could deal with members as well as nonmembers. At the same time, member firms began increasingly to move large blocks of stock off the floor of the exchanges, in effect becoming participants in the third market. Before selling securities off the exchange to a nonmember, however, a member firm must satisfy all LIMIT ORDERS on the SPECIALIST'S BOOK at the same price or higher. *See also* OFF-FLOOR ORDER.

THIRD-PARTY CHECK
1. check negotiated through a bank, except one payable to the writer of the check (that is, a check written for cash). The *primary party* to a transaction is the bank on which a check is drawn. The *secondary party* is the drawer of the check against funds on deposit in the bank. The *third party* is the payee who endorses the check.
2. double-endorsed check. In this instance, the payee endorses the check by signing the back, then passes the check to a subsequent holder, who endorses it prior to cashing it. Recipients of checks with multiple endorsers are reluctant to accept them unless they can verify each endorser's signature.
3. payable-through drafts and other negotiable orders not directly serviced by the providing company. For example, a check written against a money market mutual fund is processed not by the mutual fund company but typically by a commercial bank that provides a "third-party" or "payable-through" service. Money orders, credit union share drafts, and checks drawn against a brokerage account are other examples of payable-through or third-party items.

THIRD WORLD name for the less developed countries of Africa, Asia, and Latin America.

THIRTY-DAY VISIBLE SUPPLY total dollar volume of new MUNICIPAL BONDS carrying maturities of 13 months or more that are scheduled to reach the market within 30 days. The figure is supplied on Thursdays in the *BOND BUYER*.

THIRTY-DAY WASH RULE Internal Revenue Service rule stating that losses on a sale of stock may not be used as losses for tax purposes (that is, used to OFFSET gains) if equivalent stock is purchased within 30 days before or 30 after the date of sale.

THREE STEPS AND A STUMBLE RULE rule holding that stock and bond prices will fall if the Federal Reserve raises the DISCOUNT RATE three times in a row. By raising interest rates, the Federal Reserve both raises the cost of borrowing for companies and makes alternative investments such as money market funds and CDs relatively more attractive than stocks and bonds. Many market historians have tracked this rule, and found it to be a good predictor of drops in stock and bond prices.

THRIFT INSTITUTION organization formed primarily as a depository for consumer savings, the most common varieties of which are the SAVINGS AND LOAN ASSOCIATION and the SAVINGS BANK. Traditionally, savings institutions have loaned most of their deposit funds in the residential mortgage market. Deregulation in the early 1980s expanded their range of depository services and allowed them to make commercial and consumer loans. Deregulation led to widespread abuse by savings and loans that used insured deposits to engage in speculative real estate lending. This resulted in the OFFICE OF THRIFT SUPERVISION (OTS), established in 1989 by the FINANCIAL INSTITUTIONS REFORM AND RECOVERY ACT (FIRREA), popularly known as the "bailout bill." CREDIT UNIONS are sometimes included in the thrift institution category, since their principal source of deposits is also personal savings, though they have traditionally made small consumer loans, not mortgage loans. *See also* DEPOSITORY INSTITUTIONS DEREGULATION AND MONETARY CONTROL ACT; MUTUAL ASSOCIATION; MUTUAL SAVINGS BANK.

TICK
1. upward or downward price movement in a security's trades. Technical analysts watch the tick of a stock's successive up or down moves to get a feel of the stock's trend. The term also applies to the overall market. In futures and options trading, a minimum change in price up or down.
2. market indicator representing the difference between the number of stocks whose last sale was on an up-tick and the number of stocks whose last sale was on a down-tick. A negative low tick, for example, would be a short-term technical signal of a weak market.

    See also CLOSING TICK; DOWNTICK; MINUS TICK; PLUS TICK; SHORT SALE RULE; TECHNICAL ANALYSIS; TRIN; UPTICK; ZERO-MINUS TICK; ZERO-PLUS TICK.

TICKER system that produces a running report of trading activity on the stock exchanges, called the TICKER TAPE. The name derives from machines that, in times past, printed information by punching holes in a paper tape, making an audible ticking sound as the tape was fed forth. Today's ticker tape is a computer screen and the term is used to refer both to the CONSOLIDATED TAPE, which shows the STOCK SYMBOL, latest price, and volume of trades on the exchanges, and to news ticker services. *See also* QUOTATION BOARD; TICKER TAPE.

TICKER SYMBOL letters that identify a security for trading purposes on the CONSOLIDATED TAPE, such as XON for Exxon Corporation. *See also* STOCK SYMBOL; TICKER TAPE.

TICKER TAPE device that relays the STOCK SYMBOL and the latest price and volume on securities as they are traded to investors around the world. Prior to the advent of computers, this machine had a loud printing device that made a ticking sound. Since 1975, the New York Stock Exchange and the American Stock Exchange have used a CONSOLIDATED TAPE that indicates the New York or REGIONAL STOCK EXCHANGE on which a trade originated. Other systems, known as news tickers, pass along the latest economic, financial and market news developments. See also TAPE. *See* illustration of consolidated tape, below.

TWX	MMM&P	IBM&T	XON&C
3S41⅝	83½	4S124¼	2S41

Sample section of the consolidated tape.

Trades in Time Warner, Minnesota Mining and Manufacturing, IBM, and Exxon are shown. Letters following the ampersands in the upper line indicate the marketplace in which the trade took place: P signifies the Pacific Exchange, T the THIRD MARKET, C the Chicago Stock Exchange; no indication means the New York Stock Exchange. Other codes not illustrated are X for Philadelphia Stock Exchange, B for Boston Stock Exchange, O for other markets, including INSTINET. In the lower line, where a number precedes the letter S, a multiple of 100 shares is indicated. Thus, 300 shares of Time Warner were transacted at a price of 41⅝ on the New York Stock Exchange; 100 shares of Minnesota Mining were traded on the Pacific Exchange at 83½, and so on.

TICKET short for ORDER TICKET.

TIER 1 AND TIER 2 in computing the capital adequacy of banks, Tier 1 refers to core capital, the sum of equity capital and disclosed reserves as adjusted, while Tier 2 refers to undisclosed reserves, revaluation reserves, general provisions and loan loss reserves, hybrid debt-equity instruments, and subordinated long-term debt.

TIGER acronym for Treasury Investors Growth Receipt, a form of ZERO-COUPON SECURITY first created by the brokerage firm of Merrill Lynch, Pierce, Fenner & Smith. TIGERS are U.S. government-backed bonds that have been stripped of their COUPONS. Both the CORPUS (principal) of the bonds and the individual coupons are sold separately at a deep discount from their face value. Investors receive FACE VALUE for the TIGERS when the bonds mature but do not receive periodic interest payments. Under Internal Revenue Service rules, however, TIGER holders owe income taxes on the imputed interest they would have earned had the bond been a FULL COUPON BOND. To avoid having to pay taxes without having the benefit of the income to pay them from, most investors put TIGERS in Individual Retirement or Keogh accounts, or in other TAX DEFERRED plans. Also called *TIGR*.

TIGHT MARKET market in general or market for a particular security marked by active trading and narrow bid-offer price spreads. In contrast, inactive trading and wide spreads characterize a *slack market. See also* SPREAD.

TIGHT MONEY economic condition in which credit is difficult to secure, usually as the result of Federal Reserve action to restrict the MONEY SUPPLY. The opposite is *easy money. See also* MONETARY POLICY.

TIME DEPOSIT savings account or CERTIFICATE OF DEPOSIT held in a financial institution for a fixed term or with the understanding that the depositor can withdraw only by giving notice. While a bank is authorized to require 30 days' notice of withdrawal from savings accounts, passbook accounts are generally regarded as readily available funds. Certificates of deposit, on the other hand, are issued for a specified term of 30 days or more, and provide penalties for early withdrawal. Financial institutions are free to negotiate any maturity term a customer might desire on a time deposit or certificate, as long as the term is at least 30 days, and to pay interest rates as high or low as the market will bear. *See also* DEPOSITORY INSTITUTIONS DEREGULATION AND MONETARY CONTROL ACT; REGULATION Q.

TIME DRAFT DRAFT payable at a specified or determinable time in the future, as distinguished from a *sight draft,* which is payable on presentation and delivery.

TIMES FIXED CHARGES *see* FIXED-CHARGE COVERAGE.

TIME SHARING
Computers: practice of renting time on a central computer through a smaller computer, frequently through modems and phone lines. The user can upload or download files, access electronic mail, use computer programs on the central computer, and perform other tasks, for a fee based on usage.
Real estate: practice of sharing a piece of real estate, such as a condominium, apartment, or house, with other owners. Typically, a buyer will purchase a particular block of time for a vacation, such as the second week of February, during which the buyer will have exclusive use of the property. In return, the buyer must pay his share of annual maintenance charges, whether he uses the property or not. One condominium may therefore be sold to 52 different parties, each for one week per year. Time share owners have the benefit of changing their weeks with other owners around the world through one of the worldwide exchange companies. Time shares should be viewed as a purchase of one's vacation, and not as a real estate investment.

TIMES INTEREST EARNED *see* FIXED-CHARGE COVERAGE.

TIME SPREAD OPTION strategy in which an investor buys and sells PUT OPTION and CALL OPTION contracts with the same EXERCISE PRICE but with different expiration dates. The purpose of this and other option strategies is to profit from the difference in OPTION PREMIUMS—the prices paid to buy the options. *See also* CALENDAR SPREAD; HORIZONTAL SPREAD; SPREAD.

TIME VALUE

In general: price put on the time an investor has to wait until an investment matures, as determined by calculating the PRESENT VALUE of the investment at maturity. *See also* YIELD TO MATURITY.

Options: that part of a stock option PREMIUM that reflects the time remaining on an option contract before expiration. The premium is composed of this time value and the INTRINSIC VALUE of the option.

Stocks: difference between the price at which a company is taken over and the price before the TAKEOVER occurs. For example, if XYZ Company is to be taken over at $30 a share in two months, XYZ shares might presently sell for $28.50. The $1.50 per share difference is the cost of the time value those owning XYZ must bear if they want to wait two months to get $30 a share. As the two months pass, the time value will shrink, until it disappears on the day of the takeover. The time that investors hold XYZ has a price because it could be used to invest in something else providing a higher return. *See also* OPPORTUNITY COST.

TIME-WEIGHTED RETURN portfolio accounting method that measures investment performance (income and price changes) as a percentage of capital "at work," effectively eliminating the effects of additions and withdrawals of capital and their timing that distort DOLLAR-WEIGHTED RETURN accounting. Since exact timing-weighting is impractical, the industry accepts an approximation that assumes all additions and withdrawals occur simultaneously at the midpoint of a reporting period. Performance thus equals the return on the value of assets at the beginning of the measuring period plus the return on the net amount of additions and withdrawals during the period divided in half. The periods, usually quarters, are then linked to produce a compound average TOTAL RETURN.

TIMING trying to pick the best time to make a decision. For example, MARKET TIMING involves the analysis of fundamental and technical data to decide when to buy or sell stocks, bonds, mutual funds or futures contracts. Timing is also important in making consumer decisions, such as when to make a major purchase. Consumers might want to time their purchase of real estate when prices and mortgage rates are especially attractive, or their purchase of a car when dealers are offering particularly good prices.

TIP

In general: payment over and above a formal cost or charge, ostensibly given in appreciation for extra service, to a waiter, bellhop, cabdriver, or other person engaged in service. Also called a *gratuity.*

Investments: information passed by one person to another as a basis for buy or sell action in a security. Such information is presumed to be of material value and not available to the general public. The Securities and Exchange Commission regulates the use of such information by so-called insiders, and court cases have established the liability of persons receiving and using or passing on such information (called tippees) in certain circumstances. *See also* INSIDER; INSIDE INFORMATION.

TITLE INSURANCE insurance policies, written by title insurance companies, protecting lenders against challenges to the title claim to a property. Title insurance protects a policyholder against loss from some occurrence that already has happened, such as a forged deed somewhere in the chain of title. If, for example, someone came along claiming that her parents formerly owned the house in question, and that, as beneficiary of her parents' estate, she now deserved to take possession of the property, the title insurance company would defend the present owner's title claim in court. Title insurance premiums are usually paid in one lump sum at the time the policy is issued, and the policy remains in force until the property is sold. Mortgage lenders normally require that borrowers obtain title insurance to protect the lenders' interest in the property. Property buyers also may purchase an owner's policy to protect their interest in the property.

TOEHOLD PURCHASE accumulation by an acquirer of less than 5% of the shares of a TARGET COMPANY. Once 5% is acquired, the acquirer is required to file with the Securities and Exchange Commission, the appropriate stock exchange, and the target company, explaining what is happening and what can be expected. *See also* SCHEDULE 13D; WILLIAMS ACT.

TOKYO COMMODITY EXCHANGE (TOCOM) trades futures on gold, silver, platinum, palladium, rubber, cotton yarn, and woolen yarn. Metal contracts are traded from 9 A.M. to 11 A.M. and 1 p.m. to 3:30 P.M.; rubber is traded from 9:45 A.M. to 3:30 P.M.; and yarns are traded from 8:50 A.M. to 3:10 P.M.

TOKYO INTERNATIONAL FINANCIAL FUTURES EXCHANGE screen-traded market for 3-month Euroyen futures and options, and futures on the 1-year Euroyen, 3-month Eurodollar and U.S. dollar/Japanese yen currency.

TOKYO STOCK EXCHANGE (TSE) largest of eight stock exchanges in Japan and one of the largest, most important, and most active stock markets in the world. TSE is a continuous auction market, similar to open outcry. It uses the Floor Order-Routing and Execution System (FORES), an electronic system, for trading the 150 most active domes-tic stocks. Less-active stocks are traded through the Computer-Assisted Order-Routing and Execution System (CORES). The *Tokyo Stock Price Index* (TOPIX) is a composite of all stocks on the first section of the exchange, supplemented by size groups that classify first section companies as small, medium, and large and by sub-indices for each of the 33 industry groups. The NIKKEI STOCK AVERAGE known as the Nikkei

225, and the Nikkei 500 are the principal indices and are calculated by a formula similar to the DOW JONES INDUSTRIAL AVERAGE (as simple averages of the component stock's prices). The Nikkei 300 on the Osaka Securities Exchange is weighted by market capitalization and includes 300 listed companies on the first section of the TSE. The majority of shares are settled on the third business day following the trade. Trading takes place Monday through Friday in two daily sessions: 9 A.M. to 11 A.M., and 12:30 P.M. to 3 P.M. The TSE derivatives market trades futures and options on the TOPIX, the Nikkei 225, Nikkei 300 and 10-year government bond, and futures on the 20-year government bond and U.S. Treasury bond.

TOKYO STOCK PRICE INDEX (TOPIX) *see* NIKKEI STOCK AVERAGE.

TOLL REVENUE BOND MUNICIPAL BOND supported by revenues from tolls paid by users of the public project built with the bond proceeds. Toll revenue bonds frequently are floated to build bridges, tunnels, and roads. *See also* REVENUE BOND.

TOMBSTONE advertisement placed in newspapers by investment bankers in a PUBLIC OFFERING of securities. It gives basic details about the issue and lists the UNDERWRITING GROUP members involved in the offering in alphabetically organized groupings according to the size of their participations. It is not "an offer to sell or a solicitation of an offer to buy," but rather it calls attention to the PROSPECTUS, sometimes called the *offering circular.* A tombstone may also be placed by an investment banking firm to announce its role in a PRIVATE PLACEMENT, corporate MERGER, or ACQUISITION; by a corporation to announce a major business or real estate deal; or by a firm in the financial community to announce a personnel development or a principal's death. *See also* MEZZANINE BRACKET.

TON bond traders' jargon for $100 million.

TOP-DOWN APPROACH TO INVESTING method in which an investor first looks at trends in the general economy, and next selects industries and then companies that should benefit from those trends. For example, an investor who thinks inflation will stay low might be attracted to the retailing industry, since consumers' spending power will be enhanced by low inflation. The investor then might look at Sears, Wal-Mart, Federated Department Stores, Dayton Hudson, and other retailers to see which company has the best earnings prospects in the near term. Or, an investor who thinks there will be rapid inflation may identify the mining industry as attractive, and then look at particular gold, copper, and other mining companies to see which would benefit most from a trend of rising prices. The opposite method is called the BOTTOM-UP APPROACH TO INVESTING.

TOPIX *see* NIKKEI STOCK AVERAGE.

TOPPING OUT term denoting a market or a security that is at the end of a period of rising prices and can now be expected to stay on a plateau or even to decline.

TORONTO FUTURES EXCHANGE wholly owned subsidiary of the TORONTO STOCK EXCHANGE (TSE), trading Toronto 35 Index and TSE 100 Index futures, TSE 100 Index and Toronto 35 Index options, and Toronto 35 Index Participation (TIPs) options. Options are traded on the TSE. Trading is by open outcry.

TORONTO STOCK EXCHANGE (TSE) largest stock exchange in Canada, listing some 1,200 company stocks and 33 options. The exchange uses both open outcry and the Computer Assisted Trading System (CATS). TSE is home to many resource-based companies in the mining, paper, timber, and other natural resource industries, but also trades manufacturing, biotechnology, and telecommunications equities. The *TSE Composite Index*, known as the TSE 300, is the most widely-quoted index tracking this marketplace. The *Toronto 35 Index*, composed of a cross-section of major Canadian stocks, is the base for derivative products such as the Toronto 35 Index option (TXO) and future (TXF). The *TSE 100 Index* is a performance benchmark for institutional investors, and is the base for the TSE 100 Index option and TSE 100 Index future contract. The *TSE 200 Index* is a small- to mid-cap index composed of 200 stocks in the TSE 300 that are not represented in the TSE 100. Toronto 35 Index Participation Units, or TIPs, and TIPs options, are proprietary products. Each TIPs unit represents an interest in a trust that holds BASKETS of stocks in the Toronto 35 Index. TIPs options are American exercise and physically settled, while TXO options are European exercise and cash settled. TSE Index 35 options, TSE Index 100 options, and TIPs products trade on the TSE. Trading hours are 9:30 A.M. to 4 P.M., Monday through Friday, with an extended afternoon session from 4:15 P.M. to 5 P.M. Settlement is the third day following the trade.

TOTAL CAPITALIZATION CAPITAL STRUCTURE of a company, including LONG-TERM DEBT and all forms of EQUITY.

TOTAL COST
   Accounting: (usually pl.) sum of FIXED COSTS, semivariable costs, and VARIABLE COSTS.
   Investments: contract price paid for a security plus the brokerage commission plus any ACCRUED INTEREST due the seller (if the security is a bond). The figure is not to be confused with the COST BASIS for the purpose of figuring the CAPITAL GAINS TAX, which may involve other factors such as amortization of bond premiums.

TOTAL DISABILITY injury or illness that is so serious that it prevents a worker from performing any functions for which he or she is educated and trained. Workers with total disability may qualify for

DISABILITY INCOME INSURANCE, either though a private employer's plan or through Social Security's disability insurance program. There is normally a waiting period before disability insurance payments begin, to determine if the disability is long-term. Waiting periods vary, from a month to several months, and are determined by the plan and premium structure of the employer.

TOTAL RETURN annual return on an investment including appreciation and dividends or interest. For bonds held to maturity, total return is YIELD TO MATURITY. For stocks, future appreciation is projected using the current PRICE/EARNINGS RATIO. In options trading, total return means dividends plus capital gains plus premium income.

TOTAL VOLUME total number of shares or contracts traded in a stock, bond, commodity future, or option on a particular day. For stocks and bonds, this is the aggregate of trades on national exchanges like the New York and American stock exchanges and on regional exchanges. For commodities futures and options, it represents the volume of trades executed around the world in one day. For over-the-counter securities, total volume is measured by the NASDAQ index.

TOUT to promote a particular security aggressively, usually done by a corporate spokesman, public relations firm, broker, or analyst with a vested interest in promoting the stock. Touting a stock is unethical if it misleads investors. *See also* INVESTMENT ADVISERS ACT; INVESTOR RELATIONS DEPARTMENT.

T-PLUS-THREE *see* DELIVERY DATE.

TRACKING STOCK category of common stock that pays a dividend based on the operating performance of a particular corporate segment. Tracking stock, which is sometimes informally called "designer stock," exists alongside the issuer's regular common shares, but, unlike the latter, usually has limited or no voting power and does not represent a legal claim on assets of the corporation. When identified with a letter, such as General Motors "H" shares, the stock is also called ALPHABET STOCK, but differs from CLASSIFIED STOCK.

TRADE
In general:
1. buying or selling of goods and services among companies, states, or countries, called *commerce.* The amount of goods and services imported minus the amount exported makes up a country's BALANCE OF TRADE. *See also* TARIFF; TRADE DEFICIT.
2. those in the business of selling products are called *members of the trade.* As such, they receive DISCOUNTS from the price the public has to pay.
3. group of manufacturers who compete in the same market. These companies form trade associations and publish trade journals.

4. commercial companies that do business with each other. For example, ACCOUNTS PAYABLE to suppliers are called *trade accounts payable;* the term TRADE CREDIT is used to describe accounts payable as a source of WORKING CAPITAL financing. Companies paying their bills promptly receive *trade discounts* when available.

5. synonymous with BARTER, the exchange of goods and services without the use of money.

Securities: to carry out a transaction of buying or selling a stock, a bond, or a commodity future contract. A trade is consummated when a buyer and seller agree on a price at which the trade will be executed. A TRADER frequently buys and sells for his or her own account securities for short-term profits, as contrasted with an investor who holds his positions in hopes of long-term gains.

TRADE BALANCE *see* BALANCE OF TRADE.

TRADE CREDIT open account arrangements with suppliers of goods and services, and a firm's record of payment with the suppliers. Trade liabilities comprise a company's ACCOUNTS PAYABLE. DUN & BRADSTREET is the largest compiler of trade credit information, rating commercial firms and supplying published reports. Trade credit data is also processed by MERCANTILE AGENCIES specializing in different industries.

Trade credit is an important external source of WORKING CAPITAL for a company, although such credit can be highly expensive. Terms of 2% 10 days, net 30 days (2% discount if paid in 10 days, the net [full] amount due in 30 days) translate into a 36% annual interest rate if not taken advantage of. On the other hand, the same terms translate into a borrowing rate of slightly over 15% if payment is made in 60 days instead of 30.

TRADE DATE day on which a security or a commodity future trade actually takes place. The SETTLEMENT DATE usually follows the trade date by five business days, but varies depending on the transaction and method of delivery used. *See also* DELAYED DELIVERY; DELIVERY DATE; REGULAR-WAY DELIVERY (AND SETTLEMENT); SELLER'S OPTION.

TRADE DEFICIT OR SURPLUS excess of imports over exports *(trade deficit)* or of exports over imports *(trade surplus),* resulting in a negative or positive BALANCE OF TRADE. The balance of trade is made up of transactions in merchandise and other movable goods and is only one factor comprising the larger *current account* (which includes services and tourism, transportation, and other *invisible items,* such as interest and profits earned abroad) in the overall BALANCE OF PAYMENTS. Factors influencing a country's balance of trade include the strength or weakness of its currency in relation to those of the countries with which it trades (a strong U.S. dollar, for example, makes goods produced in other countries relatively cheap for Americans), production advantages in key manufacturing areas (Japanese automobiles, for instance), or the domestic economy of a trading country where production may or may not be meeting demand.

TRADEMARK distinctive name, symbol, motto, or emblem that identifies a product, service, or firm. In the United States, trademark rights—the right to prevent competitors from using similar marks in selling or advertising—arise out of use; that is, registration is not essential to establish the legal existence of a mark. A trademark registered with the U.S. Patent and Trademark Office is good for 20 years, renewable as long as used. Products may be both patented and protected by trademark, the advantage being that when the patent runs out, exclusivity can be continued indefinitely with the trademark. A trademark is classified on a BALANCE SHEET as an INTANGIBLE ASSET.

   Although, like land, trademarks have an indefinite life and cannot technically be amortized, in practice accountants do amortize trademarks over their estimated life, not to exceed 40 years.

TRADER
   In general: anyone who buys and sells goods or services for profit; a DEALER or *merchant. See also* BARTER; TRADE.

   Investments:
   1. individual who buys and sells securities, such as STOCKS, BONDS, OPTIONS, or commodities, such as wheat, gold, or FOREIGN EXCHANGE, for his or her own account—that is, as a dealer or PRINCIPAL—rather than as a BROKER or AGENT.
   2. individual who buys and sells securities or commodities for his or her own account on a short-term basis in anticipation of quick profits; a *speculator. See also* DAY TRADE; COMPETITIVE TRADER; FLOOR TRADER; REGISTERED COMPETITIVE MARKET MAKER; REGISTERED COMPETITIVE TRADER; SPECULATION.

TRADING AUTHORIZATION document giving a brokerage firm employee acting as AGENT (BROKER) the POWER OF ATTORNEY in buy-sell transactions for a customer.

TRADING DIVIDENDS technique of buying and selling stocks in other firms by a corporation in order to maximize the number of DIVIDENDS it can collect. This action is advantageous, because 70% of the dividend income it receives from the stocks of other companies is not taxed, according to Internal Revenue Service regulations. *See also* DIVIDEND EXCLUSION.

TRADING HALT *see* SUSPENDED TRADING.

TRADING LIMIT *see* DAILY TRADING LIMIT; LIMIT UP, LIMIT DOWN.

TRADING PATTERN long-range direction of a security or commodity future price. This pattern is charted by drawing a line connecting the highest prices the security has reached and another line connecting the lowest prices the security has traded at over the same time frame. These two lines will be pointing either up or down, indicating the security's long-term trading pattern. *See also* TECHNICAL ANALYSIS, TRENDLINE.

TRADING PATTERN

TRADING POST physical location on a stock exchange floor where particular securities are bought and sold. It is here that the SPECIALIST in a particular security performs his market-making functions and that the CROWD (floor brokers with orders in that security) congregates. The New York Stock Exchange, for example, has 17 trading posts. *See also* FLOOR BROKER; FLOOR TRADER; MAKE A MARKET.

TRADING PROFIT profit earned based on short-term trades. For assets such as stocks, bonds, futures contracts, and mutual funds held under a year, such trading profits are taxed at regular income tax rates. In general commerce, *trading profit* refers to the difference between what a product is sold for by a retailer and what it costs to buy or produce at the wholesale or producer level.

TRADING RANGE

Commodities: trading limit set by a COMMODITIES futures exchange for a particular commodity. The price of a commodity future contract may not go higher or lower than that limit during one day's trading. *See also* LIMIT UP, LIMIT DOWN.

Securities: range between the highest and lowest prices at which a security or a market has traded. The trading range for XYZ Corporation might be $40 to $60 over the last two years, for example. If a security or a market seems to be stuck in a narrow price range, analysts say that it is a trading range market, which will eventually be followed by a significant up or down move. *See also* FLAG; PENNANT; TRIANGLE; WEDGE.

TRADING UNIT number of SHARES, BONDS, or other securities that is generally accepted for ordinary trading purposes on the exchanges, *See also* ODD LOT; ROUND LOT; UNIT OF TRADING.

TRADING VARIATION increments in which securities transaction prices are rounded. For example, stocks are rounded up or down to the nearest eighth of a point. Over the next several years, though, DECIMAL TRADING, in which stock prices are quoted in decimals, will gradually replace quotations in eighths. Options over $3 are also rounded to an eighth, but options under $3 are rounded to $\frac{1}{16}$. Corporate and municipal bonds are rounded to $\frac{1}{8}$, medium- and long-term government notes and bonds to $\frac{1}{32}$, and shorter-term government bonds to $\frac{1}{64}$. *See also* PLUS.

TRANCH CD *see* TRANCHES.

TRANCHES

1. risk maturity or other classes into which a multi-class security, such as a COLLATERALIZED MORTGAGE OBLIGATION (CMO) or a REMIC is split. For example, the typical CMO has A, B, C, and Z tranches, representing fast pay, medium pay, and slow pay bonds plus an issue (tranch) that bears no coupon but receives the cash flow from the collateral remaining after the other tranches are satisfied. More sophisticated CMO versions have multiple Z tranches and a Y tranch incorporating a sinking fund schedule.
2. in the United Kingdom, fixed-rate security issues are often pre-arranged by governments, local authorities, or corporations, then brought out in successive rounds, termed tranches. One thus speaks of new tranches of existing securities. A variation of the term, *tranchettes,* refers to small tranches of gilt-edged securities (government bonds) sold by the government to the Bank of England, which then sells them into the market at times it deems appropriate.
3. subunits of a large ($10–$30 million) Eurodollar certificate of deposit that are marketed to smaller investors in $10,000 denominations. Tranches are represented by separate certificates and have the same interest rate, issue date, interest payment date, and maturity of the original instrument, which is called a *tranch CD*.

TRANCHETTES *see* TRANCHES.

TRANSACTION
Accounting: event or condition recognized by an entry in the books of account.
Securities: execution of an order to buy or sell a security or commodity futures contract. After the buyer and seller have agreed on a price, the seller is obligated to deliver the security or commodity involved, and the buyer is obligated to accept it. *See also* TRADE.

TRANSACTION COSTS cost of buying or selling a security, which consists mainly of the *brokerage commission,* the dealer MARKDOWN or markup, or fee (as would be charged by a bank or broker-dealer to transact Treasuries, for example) but also includes direct taxes, such as the SEC FEE, any state-imposed TRANSFER TAXES, or other direct taxes.

TRANSFER exchange of ownership of property from one party to another. For example, a piece of real estate may be transferred from seller to buyer through the execution of a sales contract. Securities and mutual funds are typically transferred through a transfer agent, who electronically switches ownership of the securities. In banking, *transfer* refers to the movement of funds from one account to another, such as from a passbook account to a checking account.

TRANSFER AGENT agent, usually a commercial bank, appointed by a corporation, to maintain records of stock and bond owners, to cancel and issue certificates, and to resolve problems arising from lost, destroyed, or stolen certificates. (Preventing OVERISSUE of shares is the function of the REGISTRAR.) A corporation may also serve as its own transfer agent.

TRANSFER PAYMENTS money transferred to people from the government. Many payments under government benefit programs are considered transfer payments, including Social Security, disability payments, unemployment compensation, welfare, and veterans' benefits. A large portion of the federal government's yearly budget goes to make transfer payments.

TRANSFER PRICE price charged by individual entities in a multi-entity corporation on transactions among themselves; also termed *transfer cost.* This concept is used where each entity is managed as a PROFIT CENTER—that is, held responsible for its own RETURN ON INVESTED CAPITAL—and must therefore deal with the other internal parts of the corporation on an arm's-length (or market) basis. *See also* ARM'S LENGTH TRANSACTION.

TRANSFER TAX
1. combined federal tax on gifts and estates. *See* ESTATE TAX; GIFT TAX.
2. federal tax on the sale of all bonds (except obligations of the United States, foreign governments, states, and municipalities) and all stocks. The tax is paid by the seller at the time ownership is transferred and involves a few pennies per $100 of value.
3. tax levied by some state and local governments on the transfer of such documents as deeds to property, securities, or licenses. Such taxes are paid, usually with stamps, by the seller or donor and are determined by the location of the transfer agent. States with transfer taxes on stock transactions include New York, Florida, South Carolina, and Texas. New York bases its tax on selling price; the other states apply the tax to PAR value (giving NO-PAR-VALUE STOCK a value of $100). Bonds are not taxed at the state level.

TRANSMITTAL LETTER letter sent with a document, security, or shipment describing the contents and the purpose of the transaction.

TRAVEL AND ENTERTAINMENT ACCOUNT separate account set up by an employer to track and reimburse employees' travel and entertainment expenses. Many employers give special credit cards to employees so that all travel and entertainment expenses can be tracked separately from personal expenses. Employers need to track travel and entertainment expenses carefully if they are to claim the appropriate tax deductions for these business expenses.

TRAVEL AND ENTERTAINMENT EXPENSE expense for travel and entertainment that may qualify for a tax deduction. Under current tax law, employers may deduct 50% of legitimate travel and entertainment expenses. Expenses are deductible if they are directly related to business. For example, a business meal must include a discussion that produces a direct business benefit.

TRAVELER'S CHECK check issued by a financial institution such as American Express, Visa, or Mastercard that allows travelers to carry travel funds in a more convenient way than cash. The traveler buys the checks, often for a nominal fee, with cash, a credit card, or a regular check at a bank or travel service office and then signs each traveler's check. The check can then be used virtually anywhere in the world once it has been countersigned with the same signature. The advantage to the traveler is that the traveler's check cannot be used by someone else if it is lost or stolen, and can be replaced usually anywhere in the world. Traveler's checks are also issued in many foreign currencies, allowing a traveler to lock in at a particular exchange rate before the trip begins. Many issuers of traveler's checks offer a type of check that enables two travelers to share the same travel funds. American Express was the first issuer to introduce this form of check. Institutions issuing traveler's checks profit from the FLOAT, earning interest on the money from the time the customer buys the check to the time they use the check.

TREASURER company officer responsible for the receipt, custody, investment, and disbursement of funds, for borrowings, and, if it is a public company, for the maintenance of a market for its securities. Depending on the size of the organization, the treasurer may also function as the CONTROLLER, with accounting and audit responsibilities. The laws of many states require that a corporation have a treasurer. *See also* CHIEF FINANCIAL OFFICER (CFO).

TREASURIES NEGOTIABLE debt obligations of the U.S. government, secured by its FULL FAITH AND CREDIT and issued at various schedules and maturities. The income from Treasury securities is exempt from state and local, but not federal, taxes.
   1. *Treasury bills*—short-term securities with maturities of one year or less issued at a discount from FACE VALUE. Auctions of 91-day and 182-day BILLS take place weekly, and the yields are watched closely in the money markets for signs of interest rate trends. Many

floating-rate loans and variable-rate mortgages have interest rates tied to these bills. The Treasury also auctions 52-week bills once every four weeks. At times it also issues very short-term cash management bills, TAX ANTICIPATION BILLS, and treasury certificates of indebtedness. Treasury bills are issued in minimum denominations of $10,000, with $5000 increments above $10,000 (except for cash management bills, which are sold in minimum $10 million blocks). Individual investors who do not submit a COMPETITIVE BID are sold bills at the average price of the winning competitive bids. Treasury bills are the primary instrument used by the Federal Reserve in its regulation of MONEY SUPPLY through OPEN MARKET OPERATIONS. *See also* DUTCH AUCTION-REPURCHASE AGREEMENT.

2. *Treasury bonds*—long-term debt instruments with maturities of 10 years or longer issued in minimum denominations of $1000.

3. *Treasury notes*—intermediate securities with maturities of 1 to 10 years. Denominations range from $1000 to $1 million or more. The notes are sold by cash subscription, in exchange for outstanding or maturing government issues, or at auction.

TREASURY BILL *see* BILL; TREASURIES.

TREASURY BOND *see* TREASURIES.

TREASURY DIRECT system through which an individual investor can make a NONCOMPETITIVE BID on U.S. Treasury securities (TREASURIES), thus bypassing middlemen like banks or broker-dealers and avoiding their fees. The system works through FEDERAL RESERVE BANKS and branches, and the minimum purchase is $10,000.

TREASURY STOCK stock reacquired by the issuing company and available for RETIREMENT or resale. It is issued but not outstanding. It cannot be voted and it pays or accrues no dividends. It is not included in any of the ratios measuring values per common share. Among the reasons treasury stock is created are (1) to provide an alternative to paying taxable dividends, since the decreased amount of outstanding shares increases the per share value and often the market price; (2) to provide for the exercise of stock options and warrants and the conversion of convertible securities; (3) in countering a TENDER OFFER by a potential acquirer; (4) to alter the DEBT-TO-EQUITY RATIO by issuing bonds to finance the reacquisition of shares; (5) as a result of the STABILIZATION of the market price during a NEW ISSUE. Also called *reacquired stock* and *treasury shares. See also* ISSUED AND OUTSTANDING; UNISSUED STOCK.

TREND
In general: any general direction of movement. For example: "There is an upward (downward, level) trend in XYZ sales," or "There is a trend toward increased computerization of trading on Wall Street."
Securities: long-term price or trading volume movements either up, down, or sideways, which characterize a particular market, commodity or security. Also applies to interest rates and yields.

TRENDLINE line used by technical analysts to chart the past direction
of a security or commodity future in order to help predict future price
movements. The trendline is made by connecting the highest or lowest
prices to which a security or commodity has risen or fallen within a
particular time period. The angle of the resulting line will indicate if the
security or commodity is in a downtrend or uptrend. If the price rises
above a downward sloping trendline or drops below a rising uptrend
line, technical analysts say that a new direction may be emerging. *See*
chart on next page. *See also* TECHNICAL ANALYSIS; TRADING PATTERN.

TRENDLINE

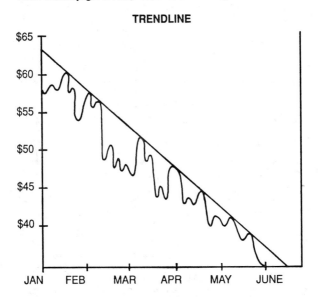

TRIANGLE technical chart pattern that has two base points and a top
point, formed by connecting a stock's price movements with a line. In
a typical triangle pattern, the apex points to the right, although in
reverse triangles the apex points to the left. In a typical triangle, there
are a series of two or more rallies and price drops where each suc-
ceeding peak is lower than the preceding peak, and each bottom is
higher than the preceding bottom. In a right-angled triangle, the sloping part of the formation often points in the direction of the breakout.
Technical analysts find it significant when a security's price breaks out
of the triangle formation, either up or down, because that usually
means the security's price will continue in that direction. *See also* PEN-
NANT; TECHNICAL ANALYSIS; WEDGE.

TRIANGLE

TRICKLE DOWN theory that economic growth can best be achieved by letting businesses flourish, since their prosperity will ultimately trickle down to middle- and lower-income people, who will benefit by increased economic activity. Proponents say that it produces more long-term growth than direct welfare grants to the middle- and lower-income sectors. *See also* SUPPLY-SIDE ECONOMICS.

TRIN measure of stock market strength that relates the ADVANCE-DECLINE ratio (the number of issues that advanced in price divided by the number of issues that declined in price) to the advance volume-decline volume ratio (the total number of shares that advanced divided by the total number of shares that declined). For example, if 800 stocks advanced and 750 issues declined while a total of 68 million shares advanced and 56 million shares declined, the trin would be calculated as follows:

$$\frac{\text{Advances }800 \div \text{Declines }750}{\text{Advance volume }68{,}000{,}000 \div \text{Decline volume }56{,}000{,}000} = \frac{1.067}{1.214}$$
$$= 0.88$$

A trin of under 1.00 is considered bullish while a trin over 1.00 is considered bearish. The above trin of 0.88 is thus a bullish sign. A trin based on closing figures is called a *closing trin. See also* CLOSING TICK.

TRIPLE NET LEASE lease requiring tenants to pay all ongoing maintenance expenses such as utilities, taxes, insurance, and upkeep of the property. There are many LIMITED PARTNERSHIPS investing in triple net lease real estate deals. In such a deal, the limited partnership owns the property and collects rent, but the tenants pay most of the operating expenses. This results in higher returns for limited partners with lower risks, because tenants bear any increased costs for utilities, insurance, or taxes.

TRIPLE TAX EXEMPT feature of MUNICIPAL BONDS in which interest is exempt from federal, state, and local taxation for residents of the states and localities that issue them. Such bonds are particularly attractive in states with high income tax rates. Many municipal bond funds buy only triple tax exempt bonds and market them to residents of the state and city of the issuer. *See also* SINGLE-STATE MUNICIPAL BOND FUND.

TRIPLE WITCHING DAY third Friday in March, June, September, and December when OPTIONS, INDEX OPTIONS, AND FUTURES CONTRACTS all expire simultaneously. At times there may be massive trades in index futures, options, and the underlying stocks by hedge strategists, arbitrageurs, and other investors, resulting in volatile markets on those days. In the past, all contracts expired in the same hour, but steps were taken so that contracts now expire at the open as well as the close of the day instead of all at once. Smaller-scale witching days occur in the other eight months, usually on the third Friday, when other options, index options, and futures contracts expire concurrently. *See also* DOUBLE WITCHING DAY.

TRUNCATION shortening of processing steps, in an effort to reduce paperwork and operating costs. For example, check truncation, or check SAFEKEEPING, where the bank holds the checks or microfilm records of them in a central file.

TRUST
Business: type of corporate combination that engaged in monopolies and restraint of trade and that operated freely until the ANTITRUST LAWS of the late 19th century and early 20th century. The name derived from the use of the voting trust, in which a small number of trustees vote a majority of the shares of a corporation. The voting trust survives as a means of facilitating the reorganization of firms in difficulty. *See also* INVESTMENT COMPANY; VOTING TRUST CERTIFICATE.
Law: FIDUCIARY relationship in which a person, called a *trustee,* holds title to property for the benefit of another person, called a BENEFICIARY. The agreement that establishes the trust, contains its provisions, and sets forth the powers of the trustee is called the *trust indenture.* The

person creating the trust is the *creator, settlor,* GRANTOR, or *donor;* the property itself is called the CORPUS, *trust res, trust fund,* or *trust estate,* which is distinguished from any income earned by it. If the trust is created while the donor is living, it is called a *living trust* or INTER VIVOS TRUST. A trust created by a will is called a TESTAMENTARY TRUST. The trustee is usually charged with investing trust property productively and, unless specifically limited, can sell, mortgage, or lease the property as he or she deems warranted. *See also* CHARITABLE REMAINDER TRUST; CLIFFORD TRUST; INVESTMENT TRUST; REVISIONARY TRUST; TRUST COMPANY; TRUSTEE IN BANKRUPTCY; TRUST INDENTURE ACT OF 1939.

TRUST COMPANY organization, usually combined with a commercial bank, which is engaged as a trustee, FIDUCIARY, or AGENT for individuals or businesses in the administration of TRUST funds, estates, custodial arrangements, stock transfer and registration, and other related services. Trust companies also engage in fiduciary investment management functions and estate planning. They are regulated by state law.

TRUSTEE *see* TRUST.

TRUSTEE IN BANKRUPTCY trustee appointed by a U.S. district court or by creditors to administer the affairs of a bankrupt company or individual. Under Chapter 7 of the U.S. BANKRUPTCY Code, the trustee has the responsibility for liquidating the property of the company and making distributions of liquidating dividends to creditors. Under the Chapter 11 provision, which provides for REORGANIZATION, a trustee may or may not be appointed. If one is, the trustee is responsible for seeing that a reorganization plan is filed and often assumes responsibility for the company.

TRUST FUND *see* TRUST.

TRUST INDENTURE ACT OF 1939 federal law requiring all corporate bonds and other debt securities to be issued under an INDENTURE agreement approved by the SECURITIES AND EXCHANGE COMMISSION (SEC) and providing for the appointment of a qualified trustee free of conflict of interest with the issuer. The Act provides that indentures contain protective clauses for bondholders, that bondholders receive semiannual financial reports, that periodic filings be made with the SEC showing compliance with indenture provisions, and that the issuer be liable for misleading statements. Securities exempted from regulation under the SECURITIES ACT OF 1933 are also exempted from the Trust Indenture Act, but some securities not requiring registration under the 1933 Act do fall under the provisions of the Trust Indenture Act, such as bonds issued in REORGANIZATION or RECAPITALIZATION.

TRUTH IN LENDING LAW legislation stipulating that lenders must disclose to borrowers the true cost of loans and make the interest rate and terms of the loan simple to understand. *See also* CONSUMER CREDIT PROTECTION ACT OF 1968; RIGHT OF RESCISSION.

TURKEY disappointing investment. The term may be used with reference to a business deal that went awry, or to the purchase of a stock or bond that dropped in value sharply, or to a new securities issue that did not sell well or had to be sold at a loss.

TURNAROUND favorable reversal in the fortunes of a company, a market, or the economy at large. Stock market investors speculating that a poorly performing company is about to show a marked improvement in earnings might profit handsomely from its turnaround.

TURNKEY any project constructed or manufactured by a company that ultimately turns it over in finished form to the company that will use it, so that all the user has to do is turn the key, so to speak, and the project is underway. The term is used of housing projects that, after construction, are turned over to property managers. There are also turnkey computer systems, for which the user needs no special computer knowledge and which can therefore be put right to work once they are installed.

TURNOVER
Finance:
1. number of times a given asset is replaced during an accounting period, usually a year. *See also* ACCOUNTS RECEIVABLE TURNOVER; INVENTORY TAKEOVER.
2. ratio of annual sales of a company to its NET WORTH, measuring the extent to which a company can grow without additional capital investment when compared over a period. *See also* CAPITAL TURNOVER.

Great Britain: annual sales volume.

Industrial relations: total employment divided by the number of employees replaced during a given period.

Securities: volume of shares traded as a percentage of total shares listed on an exchange during a period, usually either a day or a year. The same ratio is applied to individual securities and the portfolios of individual or institutional investors.

12b-1 MUTUAL FUND MUTUAL FUND that assesses shareholders for some of its promotion expenses. Adopted by the Securities and Exchange Commission in 1980, Rule 12b-1 provides mutual funds and their shareholders with an asset-based alternative method of covering sales and marketing expenses. At least half of the more than 10,000 mutual funds in existence today have a 12b-1 fee typically ranging from .25%, in the case of "no-load" funds that use it to cover advertising and marketing costs, to as high as 8.5%, the maximum "front-end load" allowed under National Association of Securities Dealers (NASD) rules, in cases where annual 12b-1 "spread loads" replaced traditional front-end loads. The predominant use of 12b-1 fees is in funds sold through brokers, insurance agents, and financial planners.

Changes to 12b-1 that became effective July 7, 1993, aim to limit fees paid by most fund investors to the 8.5% limit on front-end loads.

This is achieved by an annual limit and by a rolling cap placed on new sales. The annual limit is .85% of assets, with an additional .25% permitted as a service fee. The rolling cap on the total of all sales charges is 6.25% of new sales, plus interest, for funds that charge the service fee, and 7.25%, plus interest, for funds that do not. The new regulation also prohibits funds with front-end, deferred, and/or 12b-1 fees in excess of .25% from being called "no-load." *See also* NO-LOAD FUND.

TWENTY BOND INDEX index tracking the yields on 20 general obligation municipal bonds with 20-year maturities and an average rating equivalent to A1. The index, published weekly by *The Bond Buyer* in the newspaper's Friday edition, serves as a benchmark for the general level of municipal bond yields. *See also* BOND BUYER'S INDEX; ELEVEN BOND INDEX.

TWENTY-DAY PERIOD period required by the Securities and Exchange Commission (SEC) after filing of the REGISTRATION STATEMENT and PRELIMINARY PROSPECTUS in a NEW ISSUE or SECONDARY DISTRIBUTION during which they are reviewed and, if necessary, modified. The end of the twenty-day period—also called the COOLING-OFF PERIOD—marks the EFFECTIVE DATE when the issue may be offered to the public. The period may be extended by the SEC if more time is needed to respond to a DEFICIENCY LETTER.

TWENTY-FIVE PERCENT RULE MUNICIPAL BOND analyst's guideline that bonded debt over 25% of a municipality's annual budget is excessive.

TWENTY-PERCENT CUSHION RULE guideline used by analysts of MUNICIPAL REVENUE BONDS that estimated revenues from the financed facility should exceed the operating budget plus maintenance costs and DEBT SERVICE by a 20% margin or "cushion" to allow for unanticipated expenses or error in estimating revenues.

TWISTING unethical practice of convincing a customer to trade unnecessarily, thereby generating a commission for the broker or salesperson. Examples: A broker may induce a customer to sell one mutual fund with a sales charge in order to buy another fund, also with a sales charge, thereby generating a commission. A life insurance salesperson may persuade a policyholder to cancel his or her policy or allow it to lapse, in order to sell the insured a new policy, which would be more costly but which would produce sizable commissions for the salesperson. Also called CHURNING.

TWO-DOLLAR BROKER FLOOR BROKER who executes orders for other brokers too busy to do it themselves; a "broker's broker." Such brokers once were paid two dollars for a ROUND LOT trade, hence the name. Today they receive a negotiated commission rate varying with the dollar value of the transaction. *See also* INDEPENDENT BROKER.

200 PERCENT DECLINING BALANCE METHOD *see* DOUBLE DECLINING-BALANCE DEPRECIATION METHOD (DDB).

TWO-SIDED MARKET market in which both the BID AND ASKED sides are firm, such as that which a SPECIALIST and others who MAKE A MARKET are required to maintain. Both buyers and sellers are thus assured of their ability to complete transactions. Also called *two-way market*.

TWO-TIER BID TAKEOVER bid where the acquirer offers to pay more for the shares needed to gain control than for the remaining shares; contrasts with ANY-AND-ALL BID.

U

ULTRA-SHORT-TERM BOND FUND mutual fund buying bonds with maturities typically of one year or less. Such funds usually pay higher yields than money market mutual funds, but lower yields than SHORT-TERM BOND FUNDS. Their advantage to investors is that they offer more price stability than short-term bond funds, along with a yield that beats money funds. The NET ASSET VALUE of ultra-short-term bond funds does fluctuate, however, unlike the net asset value for money market mutual funds, which remains fixed at $1 a share. It is therefore possible to realize capital gains and losses with ultra-short-term bond funds.

ULTRA VIRES ACTIVITIES actions of a corporation that are not authorized by its charter and that may therefore lead to shareholder or third-party suits. *See also* ARTICLES OF INCORPORATION.

UMBRELLA PERSONAL LIABILITY POLICY liability insurance policy providing excess coverage beyond regular liability policies. For example, typical homeowner's policies offer $300,000 in liability coverage against lawsuits and other negligence claims. An umbrella policy may provide $1 million in liability coverage. An umbrella policy will begin to pay claims only after the underlying liability policy's coverage limits have been exceeded. People usually buy umbrella policies to protect themselves against the possibility of a large jury award in a lawsuit. An umbrella policy also protects in situations not covered by a standard liability policy found in homeowner's and automobile insurance, like slander and libel. An umbrella policy also links policies, raising the limits on underlying policies in a cost-effective manner.

UNAMORTIZED BOND DISCOUNT difference between the FACE VALUE (par value) of a bond and the proceeds received from the sale of the bond by the issuing company, less whatever portion has been amortized, that is, written off to expense as recorded periodically on the PROFIT AND LOSS STATEMENT. At the time of issue, a company has two alternatives: (1) it can immediately absorb as an expense the amount of discount plus costs related to the issue, such as legal, printing, REGISTRATION, and other similar expenses, or (2) it can decide to treat the total discount and expenses as a DEFERRED CHARGE, recorded as an ASSET to be written off over the life of the bonds or by any other schedule the company finds desirable. The amount still to be expensed at any point is the unamortized bond discount.

UNAMORTIZED PREMIUMS ON INVESTMENTS unexpensed portion of the amount by which the price paid for a security exceeded its PAR value (if a BOND or PREFERRED STOCK) or MARKET VALUE (if common stock). A PREMIUM paid in acquiring an investment is in the nature of an INTANGIBLE ASSET, and conservative accounting practice dictates it be written off to expense over an appropriate period. *See also* GOING-CONCERN VALUE.

UNCOLLECTED FUNDS portion of bank deposit made up of checks that have not yet been collected by the depository bank—that is, payment has not yet been acknowledged by the bank on which a check was drawn. A bank will usually not let a depositor draw on uncollected funds. *See also* FLOAT.

UNCOLLECTIBLE ACCOUNT customer account that cannot be collected because of the customer's unwillingness or inability to pay. A business normally writes off such a receivable as worthless after several attempts at collecting the funds.

UNCOVERED OPTION short option that is not fully collateralized. A short call position is uncovered if the writer does not have long stock to deliver or does not own another call on the same security with a lower or same strike price, and with a longer or same time of expiration. Also called NAKED OPTION. *See also* NAKED POSITION; COVERED OPTION; COVERED WRITER.

UNDERBANKED said of a NEW ISSUE underwriting when the originating INVESTMENT BANKER is having difficulty getting other firms to become members of the UNDERWRITING GROUP, or syndicate. *See also* UNDERWRITE.

UNDERBOOKED said of a NEW ISSUE of securities during the preoffering REGISTRATION period when brokers canvassing lists of prospective buyers report limited INDICATIONS OF INTEREST. The opposite of underbooked would be *fully circled. See also* CIRCLE.

UNDERCAPITALIZATION situation in which a business does not have enough capital to carry out its normal business functions. *See also* CAPITALIZATION; WORKING CAPITAL.

UNDERLYING DEBT MUNICIPAL BOND term referring to the debt of government entities within the jurisdiction of larger government entities and for which the larger entity has partial credit responsibility. For example, a township might share responsibility for the general obligations of a village within the township, the debt of the village being underlying debt from the township's standpoint. The term OVERLAPPING DEBT is also used to describe underlying debt, but overlapping debt can also exist with entities of equal rank where, for example, a school district crosses boundaries of two or more townships.

UNDERLYING FUTURES CONTRACT FUTURES CONTRACT that underlies an OPTION on that future. For example, the Chicago Board of Trade offers a U.S. Treasury bond futures option. The underlying future is the Treasury bond futures contract traded on the Board of Trade. If the option contract were exercised, delivery would be made in the underlying futures contract.

UNDERLYING SECURITY
Options: security that must be delivered if a PUT OPTION or CALL OPTION contract is exercised. Stock INDEX OPTIONS and STOCK INDEX FUTURES,

however, are settled in cash, since it is not possible to deliver an index of stocks.

Securities: common stock that underlies certain types of securities issued by corporations. This stock must be delivered if a SUBSCRIPTION WARRANT or SUBSCRIPTION RIGHT is exercised, if a CONVERTIBLE bond or PREFERRED STOCK is converted into common shares, or if an INCENTIVE STOCK OPTION is exercised.

UNDERMARGINED ACCOUNT MARGIN ACCOUNT that has fallen below MARGIN REQUIREMENTS or MINIMUM MAINTENANCE requirements. As a result, the broker must make a MARGIN CALL to the customer.

UNDERVALUED security selling below its LIQUIDATION value or the MARKET VALUE analysts believe it deserves. A company's stock may be undervalued because the industry is out of favor, because the company is not well known or has an erratic history of earnings, or for many other reasons. Fundamental analysts try to spot companies that are undervalued so their clients can buy before the stocks become FULLY VALUED. Undervalued companies are also frequently targets of TAKEOVER attempts, since acquirers can buy assets cheaply this way. *See also* FUNDAMENTAL ANALYSIS.

UNDERWATER OPTION OUT-OF-THE MONEY option. Being out of the money indicates the option has no intrinsic value; all of its value consists of time value. A call option is out of the money if its exercise price is higher than the current price of the underlying contract. A put option is out of the money if its exercise price is lower than the current price of the underlying contract.

UNDERWITHHOLDING situation in which taxpayers have too little federal, state, or local income tax withheld from their salaries. Because they have underwithheld, these taxpayers may owe income taxes when they file their tax returns. If the underwithholding is large enough, penalties and interest also may be due. To correct underwithholding, taxpayers must file a new W-4 form with their employers, decreasing the number of dependents claimed. *See also* OVERWITHHOLDING.

UNDERWRITE
Insurance: to assume risk in exchange for a PREMIUM.
Investments: to assume the risk of buying a NEW ISSUE of securities from the issuing corporation or government entity and reselling them to the public, either directly or through dealers. The UNDERWRITER makes a profit on the difference between the price paid to the issuer and the PUBLIC OFFERING PRICE, called the UNDERWRITING SPREAD.

Underwriting is the business of investment bankers, who usually form an UNDERWRITING GROUP (also called a PURCHASE GROUP or syndicate) to pool the risk and assure successful distribution of the issue. The syndicate operates under an AGREEMENT AMONG UNDERWRITERS, also termed a *syndicate contract* or PURCHASE GROUP contract.

The underwriting group appoints a MANAGING UNDERWRITER, also known as *lead underwriter, syndicate manager,* or simply *manager,* that is usually the *originating investment banker*—the firm that began working with the issuer months before to plan details of the issue and prepare the REGISTRATION materials to be filed with the SECURITIES AND EXCHANGE COMMISSION. The manager, acting as agent for the group, signs the UNDERWRITING AGREEMENT (or *purchase contract)* with the issuer. This agreement sets forth the terms and conditions of the arrangement and the responsibilities of both issuer and underwriter. During the offering period, it is the manager's responsibility to stabilize the MARKET PRICE of the issuer's shares by bidding in the open market, a process called PEGGING. The manager may also appoint a SELLING GROUP, comprised of dealers and the underwriters themselves, to assist in DISTRIBUTION of the issue.

Strictly speaking, *underwrite* is properly used only in a FIRM COMMITMENT underwriting, also known as a BOUGHT DEAL, where the securities are purchased outright from the issuer.

Other investment banking arrangements to which the term is sometimes loosely applied are BEST EFFORT, ALL OR NONE, and STANDBY COMMITMENTS; in each of these, the risk is shared between the issuer and the INVESTMENT BANKER.

The term is also sometimes used in connection with a REGISTERED SECONDARY OFFERING, which involves essentially the same process as a new issue, except that the proceeds go to the selling investor, not to the issuer. For these arrangements, the term *secondary offering* or SECONDARY DISTRIBUTION is preferable to *underwriting,* which is usually reserved for new, or primary, distributions.

There are two basic methods by which underwriters are chosen by issuers and underwriting spreads are determined: NEGOTIATED UNDERWRITINGS and COMPETITIVE BID underwritings. Generally, the negotiated method is used in corporate equity (stock) issues and most corporate debt (bond) issues, whereas the competitive bidding method is used by municipalities and public utilities. *See also* ALLOTMENT; BLOWOUT; FLOATING AN ISSUE; FLOTATION COST; HOT ISSUE; INITIAL PUBLIC OFFERING; PRESOLD ISSUE; PRIMARY MARKET; PUBLIC OFFERING; STANDBY UNDERWRITER.

UNDERWRITER
Insurance: company that assumes the cost risk of death, fire, theft, illness, etc., in exchange for payments, called *premiums.*
Securities: INVESTMENT BANKER who, singly or as a member of an UNDERWRITING GROUP or syndicate, agrees to purchase a NEW ISSUE of securities from an issuer and distribute it to investors, making a profit on the UNDERWRITING SPREAD. *See also* UNDERWRITE.

UNDERWRITING AGREEMENT agreement between a corporation issuing new securities to be offered to the public and the MANAGING UNDERWRITER as agent for the UNDERWRITING GROUP. Also termed the *purchase agreement* or *purchase contract,* it represents the underwriters' commitment to purchase the securities, and it details the PUBLIC OFFERING PRICE, the UNDERWRITING SPREAD (including all discounts and commissions), the net proceeds to the issuer, and the SETTLEMENT DATE.

The issuer agrees to pay all expenses incurred in preparing the issue for resale, including the costs of REGISTRATION with the SECURITIES AND EXCHANGE COMMISSION (SEC) and of the PROSPECTUS, and agrees to supply the managing underwriter with sufficient copies of both the PRELIMINARY PROSPECTUS (red herring) and the final, statutory prospectus. The issuer guarantees (1) to make all required SEC filings and to comply fully with the provisions of the SECURITIES ACT OF 1933; (2) to assume responsibility for the completeness, accuracy, and proper certification of all information in the registration statement and prospectus; (3) to disclose all pending litigation; (4) to use the proceeds for the purposes stated; (5) to comply with state securities laws; (6) to work to get listed on the exchange agreed upon; and (7) to indemnify the underwriters for liability arising out of omissions or misrepresentations for which the issuer had responsibility.

The underwriters agree to proceed with the offering as soon as the registration is cleared by the SEC or at a specified date thereafter. The underwriters are authorized to make sales to members of a SELLING GROUP.

The underwriting agreement is not to be confused with the AGREEMENT AMONG UNDERWRITERS. *See also* BEST EFFORT; FIRM COMMITMENT; STANDBY COMMITMENT; UNDERWRITE.

UNDERWRITING GROUP temporary association of investment bankers, organized by the originating INVESTMENT BANKER in a NEW ISSUE of securities. Operating under an AGREEMENT AMONG UNDERWRITERS, it agrees to purchase securities from the issuing corporation at an agreed-upon price and to resell them at a PUBLIC OFFERING PRICE, the difference representing the UNDERWRITING SPREAD. The purpose of the underwriting group is to spread the risk and assure successful distribution of the offering. Most underwriting groups operate under a *divided syndicate contract,* meaning that the liability of members is limited to their individual participations. Also called DISTRIBUTING SYNDICATE, PURCHASE GROUP, *investment banking group,* or *syndicate. See also* FIRM COMMITMENT; UNDERWRITE; UNDERWRITING AGREEMENT.

UNDERWRITING SPREAD difference between the amount paid to an issuer of securities in a PRIMARY DISTRIBUTION and the PUBLIC OFFERING PRICE. The amount of SPREAD varies widely, depending on the size of the issue, the financial strength of the issuer, the type of security involved (stock, bonds, rights), the status of the security (senior, junior, secured, unsecured), and the type of commitment made by the investment bankers. The range may be from a fraction of 1% for a bond issue of a big utility company to 25% for the INITIAL PUBLIC OFFERING of a small company. The division of the spread between the MANAGING UNDERWRITER, the SELLING GROUP, and the participating underwriters also varies, but in a two-point spread the manager might typically get 0.25%, the selling group 1%, and the underwriters 0.75%. It is usual, though, for the underwriters also to be members of the selling group, thus picking up 1.75% of the spread, and for the manager to be in all three categories, thus picking up the full 2%. *See also* COMPETITIVE BID; FLOTATION COST; GROSS SPREAD; NEGOTIATED UNDERWRITING; SELLING CONCESSION; UNDERWRITE.

UNDIGESTED SECURITIES newly issued stocks and bonds that remain undistributed because there is insufficient public demand at the OFFERING PRICE. *See also* UNDERWRITE.

UNDISTRIBUTED PROFITS (EARNINGS, NET INCOME) *see* RETAINED EARNINGS.

UNDIVIDED PROFITS account shown on a bank's BALANCE SHEET representing profits that have neither been paid out as DIVIDENDS nor transferred to the bank's SURPLUS account. Current earnings are credited to the undivided profits account and are then either paid out in dividends or retained to build up total EQUITY. As the account grows, round amounts may be periodically transferred to the surplus account.

UNEARNED DISCOUNT account on the books of a lending institution recognizing interest deducted in advance and which will be taken into income as earned over the life of the loan. In accordance with accounting principles, such interest is initially recorded as a LIABILITY. Then, as months pass and it is gradually "earned," it is recognized as income, thus increasing the lender's profit and decreasing the corresponding liability. *See also* UNEARNED INCOME.

UNEARNED INCOME (REVENUE)
Accounting: income received but not yet earned, such as rent received in advance or other advances from customers. Unearned income is usually classified as a CURRENT LIABILITY on a company's BALANCE SHEET, assuming that it will be credited to income within the normal accounting cycle. *See also* DEFERRED CHARGE.
Income taxes: income from sources other than wages, salaries, tips, and other employee compensation—for example, DIVIDENDS, INTEREST, rent.

UNEARNED INTEREST interest that has already been collected on a loan by a financial institution, but that cannot yet be counted as part of earnings because the principal of the loan has not been outstanding long enough. Also called DISCOUNT and UNEARNED DISCOUNT.

UNEMPLOYED OR UNEMPLOYMENT condition of being out of work involuntarily. The federal-state unemployment insurance system makes cash payments directly to laid-off workers. Most states now pay a maximum of 26 weeks; a few extend duration somewhat farther. In periods of very high unemployment in individual states, benefits are payable for as many as 13 additional weeks. These "extended benefits" are funded on a shared basis, approximately half from state funds and half from federal sources. In general, to collect unemployment benefits a person must have previously held a job and must be actively seeking employment. Unemployed people apply for and collect unemployment compensation from their state's Department of Labor. Except in states where there are small employee payments, the system is financed by a payroll tax on employers.

UNEMPLOYMENT RATE percentage of the civilian labor force actively looking for work but unable to find jobs. The rate is compiled by the U.S. Department of Labor, in cooperation with the Labor Departments in all the states, and released to the public on the first Friday of every month. The unemployment rate is affected by the number of people entering the workforce as well as the number of unemployed people. An important part of the Labor Department's report is "Payroll Employment," which covers data on hours, earnings, and employment for non-farm industries nationally, by state and for major metropolitan areas. The unemployment report is one of the most closely watched of all government reports, because it gives the clearest indication of the direction of the economy. A rising unemployment rate will be seen by analysts and the Federal Reserve as a sign of a weakening economy, which might call for an easing of monetary policy by the Fed. On the other hand, a drop in the unemployment rate shows that the economy is growing, which may spark fears of higher inflation on the part of the Fed, which may raise interest rates as a result.

UNENCUMBERED property free and clear of all liens (creditors' claims). When a homeowner pays off his mortgage, for example, the house becomes unencumbered property. Securities bought with cash instead of on MARGIN are unencumbered.

UNFUNDED PENSION PLAN pension plan that is funded by the employer out of current income as funds are required by retirees or beneficiaries. Also known as a *pay-as-you-go* pension plan, or a plan using the *current disbursement funding approach.* This contrasts with an ADVANCE FUNDED PENSION PLAN, under which the employer puts aside money on a regular basis into a separate fund that is invested in stocks, bonds, real estate, and other assets.

UNIFIED CREDIT federal TAX CREDIT that may be applied against the gift tax, the estate tax, and, under specified conditions, the generation-skipping transfer tax.

UNIFORM COMMERCIAL CODE (UCC) legal code adopted by most states that codifies various laws dealing with commercial transactions, primarily those involving the sale of goods, both tangible and intangible, and secured transactions. It was drafted by the National Conference of Commissioners of Uniform State Laws and covers bank deposits, bankruptcy, commercial letters of credit, commercial paper, warranties, and other commercial activities. Article 8 of the UCC applies to transactions in investment securities.

UNIFORM GIFTS TO MINORS ACT (UGMA) enacted to provide a simple way to transfer property to a minor without the complications of a formal trust, and without the restrictions applicable to the guardianship of a minor's property. In many states, gifts under the UGMA can be made both by lifetime gift and by the donor's WILL. Lifetime UGMA gifts qualify for the $10,000 annual GIFT TAX exclusion. Under the TAXPAYER RELIEF ACT OF 1997, the $10,000 limit on gifts free of the gift tax will be adjusted for inflation in $1,000 increments. An UGMA property is managed by a CUSTODIAN appointed by the donor. If the donor names him/herself as custodian and dies before the property is turned over to the minor, the value of the custodial property at the donor-custodian's death is included in the donor-custodian's taxable estate even though the property belongs to the minor from the instant the UGMA gift is made. The custodial property must be turned over to the minor when the minor attains the age specified in the UGMA law of the state in which the gift is made. In most states, the age is 18, but in some states it is 21. In New York State it is 18 unless the donor, at the time the UGMA gift is made, specifies age 21. All 50 states also enacted a UNIFORM TRANSFER TO MINORS ACT (UTMA), which in some case supplements the UGMA, and in others replaces it.

UNIFORM PRACTICE CODE rules of the NATIONAL ASSOCIATION OF SECURITIES DEALERS (NASD) concerned with standards and procedures for the operational handling of OVER THE COUNTER securities transactions, such as delivery, SETTLEMENT DATE, EX-DIVIDEND DATE, and other ex-dates (such as EX-RIGHTS and EX-WARRANTS), and providing for the arbitration of disputes through Uniform Practice committees.

UNIFORM SECURITIES AGENT STATE LAW EXAMINATION test required of prospective REGISTERED REPRESENTATIVES in many U.S. states. In addition to the examination requirements of states, all registered representatives, whether employees of member firms or OVER THE COUNTER brokers, must pass the General Securities Representative Examination (also known as the Series 7 Examination), administered by the National Association of Securities Dealers (NASD).

UNIFORM TRANSFERS TO MINORS ACT (UTMA) law adopted by all 50 states that is similar to the UNIFORM GIFTS TO MINORS ACT (UGMA) but different in that it extends the definition of GIFTS beyond cash and securities to include real estate, paintings, royalties, and patents. UTMA also prohibits the minor from taking control of the assets until age 21 (25 in California).

UNINSURED MOTORIST INSURANCE form of insurance that covers the policyholder and family members if injured by a hit-and-run motorist or driver who carries no liability insurance, assuming the driver is at fault. In most instances, reimbursements of costs of property damage and medical expenses resulting from the accident will be rewarded. The premiums for uninsured motorist coverage are usually rather modest, and are included as part of a regular auto insurance policy.

UNISSUED STOCK shares of a corporation's stock authorized in its charter but not issued. They are shown on the BALANCE SHEET along with shares ISSUED AND OUTSTANDING. Unissued stock may be issued by action of the board of directors, although shares needed for unexercised employee STOCK OPTIONS, rights, warrants, or convertible securities must not be issued while such obligations are outstanding. Unissued shares cannot pay dividends and cannot be voted. They are not to be confused with TREASURY STOCK, which is issued but not outstanding.

UNIT

In general: any division of quantity accepted as a standard of measurement or of exchange. For example, in the commodities markets, a unit of wheat is a bushel, a unit of coffee a pound, and a unit of shell eggs a dozen. The unit of U.S. currency is the dollar.

Banking: bank operating out of only one office, and with no branches, as required by states having unit banking laws.

Finance:

1. segment or subdivision (division or subsidiary, product line, or plant) of a company.
2. in sales or production, quantity rather than dollars. One might say, for example, "Unit volume declined but dollar volume increased after prices were raised."

Securities:

1. minimum amount of stocks, bonds, commodities, or other securities accepted for trading on an exchange. *See also* ODD LOT; ROUND LOT; UNIT OF TRADING.
2. group of specialists on a stock exchange, who maintain fair and orderly markets in particular securities. *See also* SPECIALIST; SPECIALIST UNIT.
3. more than one class of securities traded together; one common share and one SUBSCRIPTION WARRANT might sell as a unit, for example.
4. in primary and secondary distributions of securities, one share of stock or one bond.

UNITED STATES GOVERNMENT SECURITIES direct GOVERNMENT OBLIGATIONS—that is, debt issues of the U.S. government, such as Treasury bills, notes, and bonds and SERIES EE and SERIES HH SAVINGS BONDS as distinguished from government-sponsored AGENCY issues. *See also* GOVERNMENT SECURITIES; TREASURIES.

UNIT INVESTMENT TRUST (UIT) investment vehicle registered with the SECURITIES AND EXCHANGE COMMISSION under the INVESTMENT COMPANY ACT OF 1940, that purchases a fixed PORTFOLIO of securities, such as corporate, municipal or government bonds, mortgage-backed securities, COMMON STOCK, or PREFERRED STOCK. Units in the trust, which usually cost at least $1,000, are sold to investors by brokers for a sales charge that is typically 4% for traditional municipal bond trusts and 1%-2% for equity trusts, which feature reduced sales charges when the trusts are rolled over. The trust expires when bonds mature or, in the case of equity funds, at a specified future date. Unit holders receive an undivided interest in both the principal and the income portion of the portfolio in proportion to the amount of captial they invest.

Traditionally, the majority of UITs held municipal bonds. In the late 1990s, however, equity UITs became predominant. Among the most popular variations were those holding high-yield stocks in the DOW JONES INDUSTRIAL AVERAGE (DOGS OF THE DOW) or the Standard & Poor's 500 Index and their counterparts on foreign exchanges. A large proportion of equity trust money was invested in such DEFINED ASSET FUNDS offered by Merrill Lynch, Salomon Smith Barney Inc., Prudential Securities, Morgan Stanley Dean Witter and Paine Webber, as the Select 10 Portfolios based on the Dow, the S&P, and indices in Japan, Hong Kong, and the United Kingdom. *See also* DIAMONDS; SPDR; UNIT SHARE INVESTMENT TRUST (USIT).

UNIT OF TRADING normal number of shares, bonds, or commodities comprising the minimum unit of trading on an exchange. For stocks, this is usually 100 shares, although inactive shares trade in 10-share units. For corporate bonds on the NYSE, the unit for exchange trading is $1000 or $5000 par value. Commodities futures units vary widely, according to the COMMODITY involved. *See also* FUTURES CONTRACT; ODD LOT; ROUND LOT.

UNIT SHARE INVESTMENT TRUST (USIT) specialized form of UNIT INVESTMENT TRUST comprising one unit of PRIME and one unit of SCORE.

UNIVERSAL LIFE INSURANCE form of life insurance, first marketed in the early 1980s, that combines the low-cost protection of TERM LIFE INSURANCE with a savings portion, which is invested in a tax-deferred account earning money-market rates of interest. The policy is flexible; that is, as age and income change, a policyholder can increase or decrease premium payments and coverage, or shift a certain portion of premiums into the savings account, without additional sales charges or complications. A new form of the policy; called *universal variable life insurance,* combines the flexibility of universal life with the growth potential of variable life. *See also* VARIABLE LIFE INSURANCE; WHOLE LIFE INSURANCE.

UNIVERSE OF SECURITIES group of stocks sharing a common characteristic. For example, one analyst may define a universe of securities as those with $100 to $500 million in outstanding market capitalization. Another may define it as stocks in a particular industry, such as communications, paper, or airlines. A mutual fund will often define itself to investors as limiting itself to a particular universe of securities, allowing investors to know in advance which kinds of securities that fund will buy and hold.

UNLEVERAGED PROGRAM LIMITED PARTNERSHIP whose use of borrowed funds to finance the acquisition of properties is 50% or less of the purchase price. In contrast, a *leveraged program* borrows 50% or more. Investors seeking to maximize income tend to favor unleveraged partnerships, where interest expense and other deductions from income are at a minimum. Investors looking for TAX SHELTERS might favor leveraged programs despite the higher risk because of the greater amount of property acquired with the borrowed money and the greater amount of tax deductible interest but the longer depreciation periods required by tax legislation have substantially reduced the tax benefits from real estate.

UNLIMITED MARITAL DEDUCTION *see* MARITAL DEDUCTION.

UNLIMITED TAX BOND MUNICIPAL BOND secured by the pledge to levy taxes at an unlimited rate until the bond is repaid.

UNLISTED SECURITY security that is not listed on an organized exchange, such as the NEW YORK STOCK EXCHANGE, the AMERICAN STOCK EXCHANGE, or the REGIONAL STOCK EXCHANGES, and is traded in the OVER THE COUNTER market.

UNLISTED TRADING trading of securities not listed on an organized exchange but traded on that exchange as an accommodation to its members. An exchange wishing to trade unlisted securities must file an application with the SECURITIES AND EXCHANGE COMMISSION and make the necessary information available to the investing public. The New York Stock Exchange does not allow unlisted trading privileges, and the practice has declined at the American Stock Exchange and other organized exchanges.

UNLOADING
Finance: selling off large quantities of merchandise inventory at below-market prices either to raise cash quickly or to depress the market in a particular product.
Investments: selling securities or commodities when prices are declining to preclude further loss.
See also PUMP; PROFIT TAKING; SELLING OFF.

UNMARGINED ACCOUNT brokerage CASH ACCOUNT.

UNPAID DIVIDEND dividend that has been declared by a corporation but has still not been paid. A company may declare a dividend on July 1, for example, payable on August 1. During July, the declared dividend is called an unpaid dividend. *See also* EX-DIVIDEND.

UNQUALIFIED OPINION independent auditor's opinion that a company's financial statements are fairly presented, in all material respects, in conformity with generally accepted accounting principles. The justification for the expression of the auditor's opinion rests on the conformity of his or her audit with generally accepted auditing standards and on his or her feelings. Materiality and audit risk underly the application of auditing standards. *See also* ACCOUNTANT'S OPINION; ADVERSE OPINION; QUALIFIED OPINION.

UNREALIZED PROFIT (OR LOSS) profit or loss that has not become actual. It becomes a REALIZED PROFIT (OR LOSS) when the security or commodity future contract in which there is a gain or loss is actually sold. Also called a *paper profit or loss.*

UNREGISTERED STOCK *see* LETTER SECURITY.

UNSECURED DEBT obligation not backed by the pledge of specific COLLATERAL.

UNSECURED LOAN loan without COLLATERAL.

UNWIND A TRADE to reverse a securities transaction through an off-setting transaction. *See also* OFFSET.

UPGRADING increase in the quality rating of a security. An analyst may upgrade a company's bond or stock rating if its finances improve, profitability is enhanced, and its debt level is reduced. For municipal bond issues, upgrading will occur if tax revenues increase and expenses are reduced. The upgrading of a stock or bond issue may in itself raise the price of the security because investors will feel more confident in the financial soundness of the issuer. The credit rating of issuers is constantly being evaluated, which may lead to further upgradings, or, if conditions deteriorate, downgradings. The term *upgrading* is also applied to an entire portfolio of securities. For example, a mutual fund manager who wants to improve the quality of his bond holdings will say that he is in the process of upgrading his portfolio.

UPSET PRICE term used in auctions that represents the minimum price at which a seller of property will entertain bids.

UPSIDE POTENTIAL amount of upward price movement an investor or an analyst expects of a particular stock, bond, or commodity. This opinion may result from either FUNDAMENTAL ANALYSIS or TECHNICAL ANALYSIS.

UPSTAIRS MARKET transaction completed within the broker-dealer's firm and without using the stock exchange. Securities and Exchange Commission and stock exchange rules exist to ensure that such trades do not occur at prices less favorable to the customer than those prevailing in the general market. *See also* OFF BOARD.

UPSWING upward movement in the price of a security or commodity after a period of falling prices. Analysts will say "that stock has bottomed out and now has started an upswing which should carry it to new highs." The term is also used to refer to the general condition of the economy. An economy that is recovering from a prolonged downturn or recession is said to be in an upswing.

UPTICK transaction executed at a price higher than the preceding transaction in that security; also called PLUS TICK. A plus sign is displayed throughout the day next to the last price of each stock that showed a higher price than the preceding transaction in that stock at the TRADING POST of the SPECIALIST on the floor of the New York Stock Exchange. Short sales may only be executed on upticks or ZERO-PLUS TICKS. *See* also MINUS TICK; SELLING SHORT; TICK.

UPTICK RULE Securities and Exchange Commission rule that selling short may only be done on an UPTICK. In 1990, interpretation of the rule was extended to cover PROGRAM TRADING.

UPTREND upward direction in the price of a stock, bond, or commodity future contract or overall market. *See also* TRENDLINE.

USEFUL LIFE estimated period of time during which an asset subject to DEPRECIATION is judged to be productive in a business. Also called *depreciable life.* The MODIFIED ACCELERATED COST RECOVERY SYSTEM (MACRS) established useful lives for different property classes. *See also* RESIDUAL VALUE.

USES OF FUNDS *see* SOURCES AND APPLICATIONS (OR USES) OF FUNDS STATEMENT.

U.S. SAVINGS BOND *see* SAVINGS BOND.

USURY LAWS state laws limiting excessive interest rates on loans.

UTILITY power company that owns or operates facilities used for the generation, transmission, or distribution of electric energy. Utilities provide electric, gas, and water to their customers. In the United States, utilities are regulated at the state and federal level. State public service and public utility commissions regulate retail rates. The Federal Energy Regulatory Commission (FERC) regulates wholesale rates, the sale, resale, and interstate commerce for approximately 200 investor-owned utilities. On a percentage and revenue basis, however, the states regulate most of the trade. Rates for the sale of power and its transmission to retail customers, as well as approval for the construction of new plants, are regulated at the state level. The electric utility industry came under government regulation in the 1920s because it was a virtual MONOPOLY, vertically integrated, producing energy and transmitting it to customers. The industry has evolved to include public power agencies and electricity cooperatives. DEREGULATION of the natural gas industry in recent years has served to open that market to more competition, although transmission pipelines still come under FERC jurisdiction. The electric utility industry is also undertaking a similar deregulation process.

Utility stocks usually offer above-average dividend yields to investors, but less capital appreciation potential than growth stocks. Utility stocks are also very sensitive to the direction of interest rates. Rising interest rates tend to harm the value of utility shares because higher rates provide a more attractive alternative to investors. In addition, utilities tend to be heavy borrowers, so higher interest rates add to their borrowing costs. Conversely, falling interest rates tend to buoy the value of utility stocks because utility dividends look more attractive and because the companies' borrowing costs will be reduced.

UTILITY REVENUE BOND MUNICIPAL BOND issued to finance the construction of electric generating plants, gas, water and sewer systems, among other types of public utility services. These bonds are repaid from the revenues the project produces once it is operating. Such bonds usually have a reserve fund that contains an amount equal to one year's DEBT SERVICE, which protects bondholders in case there is a temporary cash shortage or revenues are less than anticipated. *See also* REVENUE BOND.

V

VALUABLES *see* HIGH-TICKET ITEMS.

VALUATION placing a value or worth on an asset. Stock analysts determine the value of a company's stock based on the outlook for earnings and the market value of assets on the balance sheet. Stock valuation is normally expressed in terms of price/earnings (P/E) ratios. A company with a high P/E is said to have a high valuation, and a low P/E stock has a low valuation. Other assets, such as real estate and bonds, are given valuations by analysts who recommend whether the asset is worth buying or selling at the current price. Estates also go through the valuation process after someone has died.

VALUATION RESERVE reserve or allowance, created by a charge to expenses (and therefore, in effect, taken out of profits) in order to provide for changes in the value of a company's assets. Accumulated DEPRECIATION, allowance for BAD DEBTS, and UNAMORTIZED BOND DISCOUNT are three familiar examples of valuation reserves. Also called *valuation account.*

VALUE-ADDED TAX (VAT) consumption tax levied on the value added to a product at each stage of its manufacturing cycle as well as at the time of purchase by the ultimate consumer. The value-added tax is a fixture in European countries and a major source of revenue for the EUROPEAN UNION (EU). Advocates of a value-added tax for the U.S. contend that it would be the most efficient method of raising revenue and that the size of its receipts would permit a reduction in income tax rates. Opponents argue that in its pure form it would be the equivalent of a national sales tax and therefore unfair and regressive, putting the greatest burden on those who can least afford it. As an example, for each part that goes into the assembling of an automobile, the auto manufacturer would pay a value-added tax to the supplier, probably a percentage of the purchase price, as is the case with a sales tax. When the finished car is sold, the consumer pays a value-added tax on the cost of the finished product less the material and supply costs that were taxed at earlier stages. This avoids double taxation and thus differs from a flat sales tax based on the total cost of purchase.

VALUE BROKER DISCOUNT BROKER whose rates are based on a percentage of the dollar value of each transaction. It is usually advantageous to place orders through a value broker for trades of low-priced shares or small numbers of shares, since commissions will be relatively smaller than if a shareholder used a SHARE BROKER, another type of discount broker, who charges according to the number and the price of the shares traded.

VALUE CHANGE change in a stock price adjusted for the number of outstanding shares of that stock, so that a group of stocks adjusted this way are equally weighted. A unit of movement of the group—called an INDEX—is thus representative of the average performance.

VALUE DATE

Banking: official date when money is transferred, that is, becomes good funds to the depositor. The value date differs from the *entry date* when items are received from the depositor, since the items must then be forwarded to the paying bank or otherwise collected. The term is used mainly with reference to foreign accounts, either maintained in a domestic bank or maintained by a domestic bank in foreign banks. *See also* FLOAT.

Eurodollar and foreign currency transactions: synonymous with SETTLEMENT DATE or DELIVERY DATE, which on spot transactions involving North American currencies (U.S. dollar, Canadian dollar, and Mexican peso) is one business day and on spot transactions involving other currencies, two business days. In the forward exchange market, value date is the maturity date of the contract plus one business day for North American currencies, two business days for other currencies. *See also* FORWARD EXCHANGE TRANSACTION; SPOT MARKET.

VALUE LINE INVESTMENT SURVEY investment advisory service that ranks about 1,700 stocks for "timeliness" and safety. Using a computerized model based on earnings momentum, Value Line projects which stocks will have the best or worst relative price performance over the next 6 to 12 months. In addition, each stock is assigned a risk rating, which identifies the VOLATILITY of a stock's price behavior relative to the market average. The service also ranks all major industry groups for timeliness. Value Line's ranking system for both timeliness and safety of an individual stock is as follows:

     1—highest rank
     2—above average rank
     3—average rank
     4—below average rank
     5—lowest rank

The weekly writeups of companies that Value Line subscribers receive include detailed financial information about a company, as well as such data as corporate INSIDER buying and selling decisions and the percentage of a company's shares held by institutions.

Value Line offers several specialized financial surveys. The *Value Line Convertibles Survey* is a subscription service that evaluates convertible securities. The *Value Line Mutual Fund Survey* offers details on fund holdings and performance and ranks funds on expected returns. Value Line also sponsors its own family of mutual funds. Value Line also produces several stock indices and averages, the most important of which is the *Value Line Composite Average,* which tracks the stocks followed by the *Value Line Investment Survey.*

VA MORTGAGE *see* VETERANS ADMINISTRATION (VA) MORTGAGE.

VANCOUVER STOCK EXCHANGE (VSE) securities and options exchange in Vancouver, British Columbia, Canada, specializing since 1907 in venture capital companies. VSE's securities market trades stocks, rights, warrants and units, while its options market focuses on equity and gold options. Mining stocks account for most of the trading, with junior mining companies making up the largest single group. Natural resource companies have raised billions of dollars on the exchange. The number of technology, entertainment, real estate and financial services companies listed on the exchange is increasing. Traditionally between 10% and 20% of the financings originate in the U.S., with 20% to 25% from Europe and Asia. The *VSE Composite Index* is capital-weighted and is a composite of three sub-indices: Commercial/Industrial, Resource, and Venture. In 1990, with the introduction of Vancouver Computerized Trading (VCT), VSE became the first North American exchange to convert from open outcry to a completely automated trading system. VISTA, an evening trading session that corresponds with the start of the business day in the Asia Pacific region, was introduced in 1996. Computerized clearing is conducted through the West Canada Clearing Corp. Settlement is on the third business day following a trade. Trading hours are 9 A.M. to 5 P.M., Monday through Friday.

VARIABLE ANNUITY life insurance ANNUITY contract whose value fluctuates with that of an underlying securities PORTFOLIO or other INDEX of performance. The variable annuity contrasts with a conventional or FIXED ANNUITY, whose rate of return is constant and therefore vulnerable to the effects of inflation. Income on a variable annuity may be taken periodically, beginning immediately or at any future time. The annuity may be a single-premium or multiple-premium contract. The return to investors may be in the form of a periodic payment that varies with the MARKET VALUE of the portfolio or a fixed minimum payment with add-ons based on the rate of portfolio appreciation. *See also* SINGLE PREMIUM DEFERRED ANNUITY.

VARIABLE COST cost that changes directly with the amount of production—for example, direct material or direct labor needed to complete a product. *See also* FIXED COST.

VARIABLE INTEREST RATE interest rate on a loan that rises and falls based on the movement of an underlying index of interest rates. For example, many credit cards charge variable interest rates, based on a specific spread over the prime rate. Most home equity loans charge variable rates tied to the prime rate. Also called *adjustable interest rate.*

VARIABLE LIFE INSURANCE innovation in LIFE INSURANCE that allows policyholders to invest the cash value of the policy in stock, bond, or money market portfolios. Investors can elect to move from one portfolio to another or rely on the company's professional money managers to make such decisions for them. As in WHOLE LIFE INSURANCE, the annual premium is fixed, but part of it is earmarked for the investment PORTFOLIO. The policyholder bears the risk of securities investments, meaning that cash values and death benefits will rise if the underlying investments do well, and fall if the investments drop in value. Some insurance companies guarantee a minimum death benefit for an extra premium. When portfolio investments rise substantially, policyholders can use a portion of the increased cash value to buy additional insurance coverage. Policyholders can borrow against the accumulated cash value or cash in the policy. As in an INDIVIDUAL RETIREMENT ACCOUNT, earnings from variable life policies are tax deferred until distributed. Income is then taxed only to the extent it exceeds the total premiums paid into the policy. Death benefits are not taxed as individual income but as taxable estate income, which carries an exclusion of $625,000. This ESTATE TAX exclusion is scheduled to rise to $1 million in 2006, according to the TAXPAYER RELIEF ACT OF 1997.

Variable life insurance is different from UNIVERSAL LIFE INSURANCE. Universal life allows policyholders to increase or decrease premiums and change the death benefit. It also accrues interest at market-related rates on premiums over and above insurance charges and expenses.

VARIABLE RATE CERTIFICATE a CERTIFICATE OF DEPOSIT (CD) whose rate of interest is periodically adjusted in relation to some benchmark, such as the prime rate or a stock index.

VARIABLE-RATE DEMAND NOTE note representing borrowings (usually from a commercial bank) that is payable on demand and that bears interest tied to a money market rate, usually the bank PRIME RATE. The rate on the note is adjusted upward or downward each time the base rate changes.

VARIABLE RATE MORTGAGE (VRM) *see* ADJUSTABLE RATE MORTGAGE (ARM).

VARIABLE RATE PREFERRED STOCK *see* ADJUSTABLE RATE PREFERRED STOCK (ARP).

VARIANCE
Accounting: difference between actual cost and STANDARD COST in the categories of direct material, direct labor, and DIRECT OVERHEAD. A positive variation (when the actual cost is lower than the standard or anticipated cost) would translate into a higher profit unless offset by negative variances elsewhere.

Finance: (1) difference between corresponding items on a comparative BALANCE SHEET and PROFIT AND LOSS STATEMENT. (2) difference between actual experience and budgeted or projected experience in any financial category. For example, if sales were projected to be $2 million for a period and were actually $2.5 million, there would be a positive variance of $500,000 or 25%.

Real estate: allowed exception to zoning rules. If a particular neighborhood were zoned for residential use only, a person wanting to open a store would need to be granted a variance from the zoning board in order to proceed.

Statistics: measure of the dispersion of a distribution. It is the sum of the squares of the deviation from the mean. *See also* STANDARD DEVIATION.

VELDA SUE acronym for *Venture Enhancement & Loan Development Administration for Smaller Undercapitalized Enterprises,* a federal agency that buys small business loans made by banks, pools them, then issues securities that are bought as investments by large institutions.

VELOCITY rate of spending, or turnover of money—in other words, how many times a dollar is spent in a given period of time. The more money turns over, the faster velocity is said to be. The concept of "income velocity of money" was first explained by the economist Irving Fisher in the 1920s as bearing a direct relationship to GROSS DOMESTIC PRODUCT (GDP). Velocity usually is measured as the ratio of GDP to the money supply. Velocity affects the amount of economic activity generated by a given money supply, which includes bank deposits and cash in circulation. Velocity is a factor in the Federal Reserve Board's management of MONETARY POLICY, because an increase in velocity may obviate the need for a stimulative increase in the money supply. Conversely, a decline in velocity might reflect dampened economic growth, even if the money supply holds steady. *See also* FISCAL POLICY.

VENDOR
1. supplier of goods or services of a commercial nature; may be a manufacturer, importer, or wholesale distributor. For example, one component of the Index of LEADING INDICATORS is vendor performance, meaning the rate at which suppliers of goods are making delivery to their commercial customers.
2. retailer of merchandise, especially one without an established place of business, as in *sidewalk vendor.*

VENTURE CAPITAL important source of financing for START-UP companies or others embarking on new or TURNAROUND ventures that entail some investment risk but offer the potential for above average future profits; also called *risk capital.* Sources of venture capital include wealthy individual investors; subsidiaries of banks and other corporations organized as small business investment companies (SBICs); groups of investment banks and other financing sources who pool investments in venture capital funds or VENTURE CAPITAL LIMITED PARTNERSHIPS. The SMALL BUSINESS ADMINISTRATION (SBA) promotes venture capital programs through the licensing and financing of SBICs. Venture capital financing supplements other personal or external funds that an ENTREPRENEUR is able to tap, or takes the place of loans of other funds that conventional financial institutions are unable or unwilling to risk. Some venture capital sources invest only at a certain stage of entrepreneurship, such as the start-up or SEED MONEY stage, the *first round* or SECOND ROUND phases that follow, or at the MEZZANINE LEVEL immediately preceding an INITIAL PUBLIC OFFERING. In return for taking an investment risk, venture capitalists are usually rewarded with some combination of PROFITS, PREFERRED STOCK, ROYALTIES on sales, and capital appreciation of common shares.

VENTURE CAPITAL LIMITED PARTNERSHIP investment vehicle organized by a brokerage firm or entrepreneurial company to raise capital for START-UP companies or those in the early processes of developing products and services. The partnership will usually take shares of stock in the company in return for capital supplied. Limited partners receive income from profits the company may earn. If the company is successful and goes public, limited partners' profits could be realized from the sale of formerly private stock to the public. This type of partnership differs from a RESEARCH AND DEVELOPMENT LIMITED PARTNERSHIP in that R&D deals receive revenue only from the particular products they UNDERWRITE, whereas a venture capital partnership participates in the profits of the company, no matter what product or service is sold. *See also* ENTREPRENEUR; LIMITED PARTNERSHIP.

VERTICAL LINE CHARTING form of technical charting on which the high, low, and closing prices of a stock or a market are shown on one vertical line with the closing price indicated by a short horizontal mark. Each vertical line represents another day, and the chart shows

VERTICAL LINE CHARTING

the trend of a stock or a market over a period of days, weeks, months, or years. Technical analysts discern from these charts whether a stock or a market is continually closing at the high or low end of its trading range during a day. This is useful in understanding whether the market's action is strong or weak, and therefore whether prices will advance or decline in the near future. *See also* TECHNICAL ANALYSIS.

VERTICAL MERGER merger between a company that supplies goods and services and a company that buys those goods and services. For example, if a publishing company buys a paper producer, it is considered a vertical merger because the publisher buys large amounts of paper. In some cases, vertical mergers may be challenged by the government if they are found to violate ANTITRUST LAWS. *See also* MERGER.

VERTICAL SPREAD OPTION strategy that involves purchasing an option at one STRIKE PRICE while simultaneously selling another option of the same class at the next higher or lower strike price. Both options have the same expiration date. For example, a vertical spread is created by buying an XYZ May 30 call and selling an XYZ May 40 call. The investor who buys a vertical spread hopes to profit as the difference between the option premium on the two option positions widens or narrows. Also called a PRICE SPREAD. *See also* OPTION PREMIUM.

VESTED INTEREST in law, an interest in something that is certain to occur as opposed to being dependent on an event that might not happen. In general usage, an involvement having the element of personal gain. *See also* VESTING.

VESTING right an employee gradually acquires by length of service at a company to receive employer-contributed benefits, such as payments from a PENSION FUND, PROFIT-SHARING PLAN, or other QUALIFIED PLAN OR TRUST. Under the TAX REFORM ACT OF 1986, employees must be vested 100% after five years of service or at 20% a year starting in the third year and becoming 100% vested after seven years.

VETERANS ADMINISTRATION (VA) independent agency under the president that operates various programs for veterans and their families, including hospital services and guarantees of home mortgage loans made by financial institutions at rates set by the VA.

VETERANS ADMINISTRATION (VA) MORTGAGE home mortgage loan granted by a lending institution to qualified veterans of the U.S. armed forces or to their surviving spouses and guaranteed by the VA. The guarantee reduces risk to the lender for all or part of the purchase price on conventional homes, mobile homes, and condominiums. Because of this federal guarantee, banks and thrift institutions can afford to provide 30-year VA mortgages on favorable terms with a relatively low down payment even during periods of TIGHT MONEY. Interest rates on VA mortgages, formerly fixed by the Department of

Housing and Urban Development together with those on Federal Housing Administration (FHA) mortgages, are now set by the VA.

VA mortgages comprise an important part of the mortgage pools packaged and sold as securities by such quasi-governmental organizations as the FEDERAL HOME MORTGAGE CORPORATION (Freddie Mac) and the GOVERNMENT NATIONAL MORTGAGE ASSOCIATION (Ginnie Mae).

V FORMATION technical chart pattern that forms a V. The V pattern indicates that the stock, bond, or commodity being charted has bottomed out and is now in a bullish (rising) trend. An upside-down (inverse) V is considered bearish (indicative of a falling market). *See also* BOTTOM; TECHNICAL ANALYSIS.

V FORMATION

VIENNA STOCK EXCHANGE (VSX) founded in 1771 as a state institution to provide a market for state-issued bonds, it is one of the world's oldest exchanges. VSX represents approximately 50% of Austrian stock transactions, with the balance traded over-the-counter. The *WBI Index* is made up of all domestic shares listed on the official market, while the *Austrian Traded Index* (ATX) measures the most liquid stocks and is favored by institutional investors who use it as a benchmark for their equity positions. All trading is conducted electronically through EQOS (Electronic Quote and Order-Driven System). Trades are settled three days after execution. Trading is conducted from 9:30 A.M. to 1:30 P.M., Monday through Friday. Futures and options are traded on the Osterreichische Termin-und Optionenborse (OTOB). Products include ATX futures, Austrian government bond futures, American-style stock options, and European-style ATX options.

VISIBLE SUPPLY dollar volume of municipal bonds scheduled to be issued over the coming month. Municipal bond investors, analysts, traders, and investment bankers watch the visible supply to determine whether the coming month might provide a good opportunity to buy bonds, sell bonds, or float a new bond issue. A large amount of new issues might depress bond prices and make it difficult to float a new issue. Conversely, a small amount of new issues may help bond prices and make it easier to float a new issue. The visible supply, also known as the calendar or the *30-day visible supply*, is compiled by *The Bond Buyer.*

VOID deprived of legal force or effect, as a CONTRACT.

VOIDABLE contract that can be annulled by either party after it is signed because fraud, incompetence, or another illegality exists or because a RIGHT OF RESCISSION applies.

VOLATILE tending to rapid and extreme fluctuations. The term is used to describe the size and frequency of the fluctuations in the price of a particular stock, bond, or commodity. A stock may be volatile because the outlook for the company is particularly uncertain, because there are only a few shares outstanding (*see also* THIN MARKET), or because of various other reasons. Where the reasons for the variation have to do with the particular security as distinguished from market conditions, return is measured by a concept called ALPHA. A stock with an alpha factor of 1.25 is projected to rise in price by 25% in a year on the strength of its inherent values such as growth in earnings per share and regardless of the performance of the market as a whole. Market-related volatility, also called SYSTEMATIC RISK, is measured by BETA. *See also* DURATION.

VOLATILITY characteristic of a security, commodity, or market to rise or fall sharply in price within a short-term period. A measure of the relative volatility of a stock to the overall market is its BETA. *See also* VOLATILE.

VOLUME total number of stock shares, bonds, or commodities futures contracts traded in a particular period. Volume figures are reported daily by exchanges, both for individual issues trading and for the total amount of trading executed on the exchange. Technical analysts place great emphasis on the amount of volume that occurs in the trading of a security or a commodity futures contract. A sharp rise in volume is believed to signify future sharp rises or falls in price, because it reflects increased investor interest in a security, commodity, or market. *See also* TECHNICAL ANALYSIS; TURNOVER.

VOLUME DELETED note appearing on the CONSOLIDATED TAPE, usually when the tape is running behind by two minutes or more because of heavy trading, that only the STOCK SYMBOL and the trading price will be displayed for transactions of less than 5000 shares.

VOLUME DISCOUNT any reduction in price based on the purchase of a large quantity.

VOLUNTARY ACCUMULATION PLAN plan subscribed to by a MUTUAL FUND shareholder to accumulate shares in that fund on a regular basis over time. The amount of money to be put into the fund and the intervals at which it is to be invested are at the discretion of the shareholder. A plan that invests a set amount on a regular schedule is called a dollar cost averaging plan or CONSTANT DOLLAR PLAN.

VOLUNTARY BANKRUPTCY legal proceeding that follows a petition of BANKRUPTCY filed by a debtor in the appropriate U.S. district court under the Bankruptcy Act. Petitions for voluntary bankruptcy can be filed by any insolvent business or individual except a building and loan association or a municipal, railroad, insurance, or banking corporation.

VOLUNTARY LIQUIDATION LIQUIDATION approved by a company's shareholders, as opposed to involuntary liquidation under Chapter 7 BANKRUPTCY. In the United Kingdom, a distinction is made between creditors' voluntary liquidation (or winding-up), which requires insolvency, and members' voluntary liquidation (or winding-up), which requires a declaration of solvency. *See also* VOLUNTARY BANKRUPTCY.

VOLUNTARY PLAN short for *voluntary deductible employee contribution plan,* a type of pension plan where the employee elects to have contributions (which, depending on the plan, may be before- or after-tax) deducted from each paycheck.

VOTING RIGHT right attending the ownership of most common stock to vote in person or by PROXY on corporate resolutions and the election of directors. *See also* NONVOTING STOCK.

VOTING STOCK shares in a corporation that entitle the shareholder to voting and PROXY rights. When a shareholder deposits such stock with a CUSTODIAN that acts as a voting TRUST, the shareholder retains rights to earnings and dividends but delegates voting rights to the trustee. *See also* COMMON STOCK; PROPORTIONAL REPRESENTATION; VOTING TRUST CERTIFICATE.

VOTING TRUST CERTIFICATE transferable certificate of beneficial interest in a *voting trust,* a limited-life trust set up to center control of a corporation in the hands of a few individuals, called *voting trustees.* The certificates, which are issued by the voting trust to stockholders in exchange for their common stock, represent all the rights of common stock except voting rights. The common stock is then registered on the books of the corporation in the names of the trustees. The usual purpose for such an arrangement is to facilitate REORGANIZATION of a corporation in financial difficulty by preventing interference with management. Voting trust certificates are limited to the five-year life of a TRUST but can be extended with the mutual consent of the holders and trustees.

VULTURE FUND type of LIMITED PARTNERSHIP that invests in depressed property, usually real estate, aiming to profit when prices rebound.

W

WAGE ASSIGNMENT loan agreement provision, prohibited in some states, that authorizes the lender to deduct payments from an employee's wages in the event of DEFAULT.

WAGE GARNISHMENT *see* GARNISHMENT.

WAGE-PUSH INFLATION inflationary spiral caused by rapid increases in wages. *See also* COST-PUSH INFLATION; DEMAND-PULL INFLATION; INFLATION.

WAITING PERIOD period of time before something goes into effect. In securities, there is a waiting period between the filing of registration statements and the time when securities may be offered for sale to the public. This waiting period may be extended if the Securities and Exchange Commission requires revisions to the registration statement. In DISABILITY INCOME INSURANCE, there is a waiting period of several months from the time the disability occurs to the time when disability benefits are paid. For insurance claims, the waiting period is also known as the *elimination period.*

WAIVER OF PREMIUM clause in an insurance policy providing that all policy premiums will be waived if the policyholder becomes seriously ill or disabled, either permanently or temporarily, and therefore is unable to pay the premiums. Some policies include a waiver-of-premium clause automatically, while in other cases it is an optional feature that must be paid with additional premiums. During the waiver period, all policy benefits remain in force.

WALLFLOWER *see* ORPHAN STOCK.

WALLPAPER worthless securities. The implication of the term is that certificates of stocks and bonds that have gone bankrupt or defaulted have no other use than as wallpaper. However, there may be value in the worthless certificates themselves by collectors of such certificates, who prize rare or historically significant certificates. The practice of collecting such certificates is known as SCRIPOPHILY.

WALL STREET
1. common name for the financial district at the lower end of Manhattan in New York City, where the New York and American Stock Exchanges and numerous brokerage firms are headquartered. The New York Stock Exchange is actually located at the corner of Wall and Broad Streets.
2. investment community, such as in "Wall Street really likes the prospects for that company" or "Wall Street law firm," meaning a firm specializing in securities law and mergers. Also referred to as "the Street."

WANTED FOR CASH TICKER tape announcement that a bidder will pay cash the same day for a specified block of securities. Cash trades are executed for delivery and settlement at the time the transaction is made.

WAR BABIES jargon for the stocks and bonds of corporations engaged primarily as defense contractors. Also called *war brides*.

WAR CHEST fund of liquid assets (cash) set aside by a corporation to pay for a takeover or to defend against a takeover. Traders will say that a company has a war chest that it plans to use to take over another company. Or traders might say that a particular company will be difficult to take over because it has a large war chest that it can use to defend itself by buying back its stock, making an acquisition of its own, paying for legal fees to mount defenses, or taking other defensive measures. *See also* TAKEOVER.

WAREHOUSE RECEIPT document listing goods or commodities kept for SAFEKEEPING in a warehouse. The receipt can be used to transfer ownership of that commodity, instead of having to deliver the physical commodity. Warehouse receipts are used with many commodities, particularly precious metals like gold, silver, and platinum, which must be safeguarded against theft.

WARRANT *see* SUBSCRIPTION WARRANT.

WARRANTY contract between the seller and the buyer of a product specifying the conditions under which the seller will make repairs or remedy other problems that may arise, at no additional cost to the buyer. The warranty document describes how long the warranty remains in effect, and which specific repairs will be performed at no extra charge. Warranties usually cover workmanship or the failure of the product if used normally, but not negligence on the part of the user if the product is used in ways for which it was not designed. Warranties are commonly issued for automobiles, appliances, electronic gear, and most other products. In some cases, manufacturers will offer extended warranties for several years beyond the original warranty period, at an extra charge. Consumers should consult federal and state laws for more extensive applications or interpretations of warranties.

WASH SALE purchase and sale of a security either simultaneously or within a short period of time. It may be done by a single investor or (where MANIPULATION is involved) by two or more parties conspiring to create artificial market activity in order to profit from a rise in the security's price. Wash sales taking place within 30 days of the underlying purchase do not qualify as tax losses under Internal Revenue Service rules.

Under the TAX REFORM ACT OF 1984, wash sale rules were extended to all taxpayers except those trading in securities in the normal course of business, such as securities dealers. Prior to the 1984

Act, noncorporate taxpayers engaged in a trade or business were exempt from wash sale rules. The Act also extended the wash sale prohibition to closing short sales of substantially identical securities, or to instances where short sales are made within 30 days of closing. *See also* THIRTY-DAY WASH RULE.

WASTING ASSET

1. fixed asset, other than land, that has a limited useful life and is therefore subject to DEPRECIATION.
2. natural resource that diminishes in value because of extractions of oil, ores, or gas, or the removal of timber, or similar depletion and that is therefore subject to AMORTIZATION.
3. security with a value that expires at a particular time in the future. An OPTION contract, for instance, is a wasting asset, because the chances of a favorable move in the underlying stock diminish as the contract approaches expiration, thus reducing the value of the option.

WATCH LIST list of securities singled out for special surveillance by a brokerage firm or an exchange or other self-regulatory organization to spot irregularities. Firms on the watch list may be TAKEOVER candidates, companies about to issue new securities, or others that seem to have attracted an unusually heavy volume of trading activity. *See also* STOCK WATCHER; SURVEILLANCE DEPARTMENT OF EXCHANGES.

WATERED STOCK stock representing ownership of OVERVALUED assets, a condition of overcapitalized corporations, whose total worth is less than their invested capital. The condition may result from inflated accounting values, gifts of stock, operating losses, or excessive stock dividends. Among the negative features of watered stock from the shareholder's standpoint are inability to recoup full investment in LIQUIDATION, inadequate return on investment, possible liability exceeding the PAR value of shares, low MARKET VALUE because of poor dividends and possible adverse publicity, reduced ability of the firm to issue new stock or debt securities to capitalize on growth opportunity, and loss of competitive position because of the need to raise prices to provide a return acceptable to investors. To remedy the situation, a company must either increase its assets without increasing its OUTSTANDING shares or reduce outstanding shares without reducing assets. The alternatives are to increase RETAINED EARNINGS or to adjust the accounting values of assets or of stock.

WEAK DOLLAR dollar that has fallen in value against foreign currencies. This means that those holding dollars will get fewer pounds, yen, marks, francs, or other currencies in exchange for their dollars. A weak dollar makes it easier for U.S. companies to export their goods to other countries because foreigners' buying power is enhanced. The dollar may weaken because of loose U.S. monetary policy (creating too many dollars) and lack of confidence in the U.S. government, large trade and budget deficits, unattractive interest rates on dollar-denominated investments compared to investments denominated in other currencies, or other reasons.

WEAK MARKET market characterized by a preponderance of sellers over buyers and a general declining trend in prices.

WEBS (WORLD EQUITY BENCHMARK SHARES) shares traded on the AMERICAN STOCK EXCHANGE (ASE) enabling investors to gain exposure to selected international equity markets. Introduced in March 1996, WEBS are issued in a number of country-specific Index Series by WEBS Index Fund, Inc., a registered investment company. The fund's objective is to track the price and yield performance of the underlying countries' stock markets, as defined by the securities contained in the Morgan Stanley Capital International (MSCI) Index. Currently 17 countries trade WEBS: Australia, Austria, Belgium, Canada, France, Germany, Hong Kong, Italy, Japan, Malaysia, Mexico, Netherlands, Singapore, Spain, Sweden, Switzerland and the United Kingdom.

Unlike index open-ended mutual funds, WEBS trade continuously on the secondary market at AMEX like any other publicly-traded stock. Mutual funds do not trade in the secondary market and are priced only at the end of each trading day. There are also no LOADS to buy or sell WEBS, though normal brokerage commissions do apply as they would on the purchase or sale of any individual stock. WEBS charge management fees, but they are lower than those charged by actively-managed mutual funds because, as index funds, WEBS involve very little investment, research, or trading decisions. WEBS prices reflect the reinvestment of net dividends, and the fund distributes CASH DIVIDENDS and CAPITAL GAINS DISTRIBUTIONS once a year.

Unlike closed-end mutual funds, WEBS do not trade at large discounts or premiums to their NET ASSET VALUE (NAV), because, unlike closed-end shares, of which only a limited number are issued investors can create or redeem WEBS every day. The NAV of WEBS fluctuate based on changes in the market value of the underlying portfolio securities and in the exchange rates between the relevant country's currency and the U.S. Dollar, and the income and expenses of each WEBS Index fund.

WEBS offer investors wanting to invest internationally several advantages. They allow exposure to an entire country's market in one trade which is executed in U.S. dollars on the ASE. This frees investors from the difficult process of stock selection and other complexities involved in direct foreign stock ownership.

WEDGE technical chart pattern similar to but varying slightly from a TRIANGLE. Two converging lines connect a series of peaks and troughs to form a wedge. These converging lines move in the same direction, unlike a triangle, in which one rises while the other falls or one rises or falls while the other line stays horizontal. Falling wedges usually occur as temporary interruptions of upward price rallies, rising wedges as interruptions of a falling price trend. *See also* TECHNICAL ANALYSIS.

WEDGE

WEIGHTED AVERAGE MATURITY also called *average life* or *weighted average life* and used in mortgage-backed PASS-THROUGH SECURITIES meaning the weighted-average time to the return of a dollar of principal. It is arrived at by multiplying each portion of principal received by the time at which it is received, and then summing and dividing by the total amount of principal. Fabozzi's *Handbook of Fixed Income Securities* uses this example: Consider a simple annual-pay, four-year bond with a face value of $100 and principal payments of $40 the first year, $30 the second year, $20 the third year, and $10 the fourth year. The average life would be calculated as: Average life = .4 × 1 year + .3 × 2 years + .2 × 3 years + .1 × 4 years = 2 years. An alternative measure of investment life is DURATION.

W FORMATION technical chart pattern of the price of a stock, bond, or commodity that shows the price has hit a SUPPORT LEVEL two times and is moving up; also called a *double bottom*.

A reverse W is just the opposite; the price has hit a resistance level and is headed down. This is called a DOUBLE TOP.

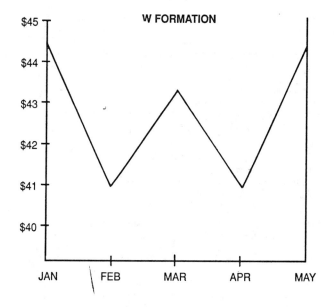

W FORMATION

JAN   FEB   MAR   APR   MAY

W-4 FORM tax form prepared by an employee for an employer indicating the employee's exemptions and Social Security number and enabling the employer to determine the amount of taxes to be withheld.

WHEN DISTRIBUTED transactions conditional on the SECONDARY DISTRIBUTION of shares ISSUED AND OUTSTANDING but CLOSELY HELD, as those of a wholly owned subsidiary, for example. *See also* WHEN ISSUED.

WHEN ISSUED short form of "when, as, and if issued." Term refers to a transaction made conditionally because a security, although authorized, has not yet been issued. NEW ISSUES of stocks and bonds, stocks that have SPLIT, and Treasury securities are all traded on a when issued basis. In a newspaper listing, a "WI" is placed next to the price of such a security. *See also* WHEN DISTRIBUTED.

WHIPSAWED caught in VOLATILE price movements while making losing trades as prices rise and fall. A trader is whipsawed if he or she buys just before prices fall and sells just before prices rise. A variation of this term is also used in TECHNICAL ANALYSIS referring to misleading signals, called *whipsaws* or *chatter,* in the chart trends of markets or particular securities.

WHISPER NUMBER unofficial earnings estimates made by security analysts. If an analyst is more optimistic about a company's earnings prospects than his official profit estimate reveals, he may speak of a "whisper number" to his clients that is higher than his published numbers. The opposite can be true on the downside. Investors and the media sometimes start to count on "whisper numbers" when earnings are announced. While a company may report profits in line with official estimates, those companies that do not meet their "whisper numbers," disappoint investors, which drives stock prices down.

WHISPER STOCK   stock that is rumored to be a takeover target. Speculators, arbitrageurs, and other investors may buy shares in the company hoping that the "whispers" they have heard are true, allowing them to reap huge profits when the takeover is officially announced. Whisper stocks may trade in heavier-than-usual volume once the rumors about the takeover spread widely. Investing in whisper stocks is risky, however, because the takeover rumors may prove to be inaccurate.

WHISTLE BLOWER employee or other person with inside knowledge of wrongdoing inside a company or government agency. The employee is supposed to be protected from retribution by the employer by several federal laws protecting whistle blowers, though whistle blowers frequently are punished for revealing wrongdoing by their employer. Several employees who disclosed illegal billing practices by defense contractors were demoted or fired, for example. In securities, under the Insider Trading and Securities Fraud Enforcement Act of 1988, whistle blowers who provide the SEC with information about illegal insider trading or other illegal activity that leads to a conviction may qualify for bounties.

WHITE COLLAR WORKER office worker in professional, managerial, or administrative position. Such workers typically wear shirts with white collars. Those working in factories or doing manual labor typically wear blue collars, and are therefore called *blue-collar workers.*

WHITE KNIGHT friendly acquirer sought by the target of an unfriendly TAKEOVER.

WHITEMAIL anti-TAKEOVER device whereby a vulnerable company sells a large amount of stock to a friendly party at below-market prices. This puts a potential raider in a position where it must buy a sizable amount of stock at inflated prices to get control and thus helps perpetuate existing management.

WHITE SHEETS list of prices published by the NATIONAL QUOTATION BUREAU for market makers in OVER-THE-COUNTER stocks traded in Chicago, Los Angeles, and San Francisco.

WHITE-SHOE FIRM anachronistic characterization of certain broker-dealers as venerable, "upper-crust" and "above" such practices as participating in hostile takeovers. Derives from tne '50s culture of Ivy League colleges, where white buck shoes were *de rigueur* in elite fraternities and clubs.

WHITE SQUIRE WHITE KNIGHT who buys less than a majority interest.

WHITE'S RATING White's Tax-Exempt Bond Rating Service's classification of municipal securities, which is based on market factors rather than credit considerations and which attempts to determine appropriate yields. *See also* MUNICIPAL BOND.

WHOLE LIFE INSURANCE form of life insurance policy that offers protection in case the insured dies and also builds up cash value. The policy stays in force for the lifetime of the insured, unless the policy is canceled or lapses. The policyholder usually pays a level PREMIUM for whole life, which does not rise as the person grows older (as in the case of TERM INSURANCE). The earnings on the cash value in the policy accumulate tax-deferred, and can be borrowed against in the form of a POLICY LOAN. The death benefit is reduced by the amount of the loan, plus interest, if the loan is not repaid.

Traditionally, life insurance companies invest insurance premiums conservatively in bonds, stocks, and real estate in order to generate increases in cash value for policyholders. Policyholders have no input into the investment decision-making process in a whole life insurance policy. Other forms of cash value policies, such as UNIVERSAL LIFE INSURANCE and VARIABLE LIFE INSURANCE give policyholders more options, such as stock, bond, and money market accounts, to choose from in investing their premiums. Whole life insurance is also known as *ordinary life, permanent life, or straight life insurance. See also* ADEQUACY OF COVERAGE; ANNUAL EXCLUSION; CASH VALUE INSURANCE; CONTINGENT BENEFICIARY; CONVERTIBILITY; DEATH BENEFIT; EXPERIENCE RATING; FINANCIAL NEEDS APPROACH; FIXED PREMIUM; FULLY PAID POLICY; GUARANTEED INSURABILITY; HIDDEN LOAD; INCOME EXCLUSION RULE; INSURABILITY; INSURABLE INTEREST; INSURANCE AGENT; INSURANCE CLAIM; INSURANCE DIVIDEND; INSURANCE POLICY; INSURANCE PREMIUM; INSURANCE SETTLEMENT; INSURED; LAPSE; LIFE INSURANCE; LIFE INSURANCE POLICY; LIVING BENEFITS; LUMP SUM; MORTALITY RISK; NONCONTESTABILITY CLAUSE; NONPARTICIPATING LIFE INSURANCE POLICY; PAID UP; PAID UP POLICY; PARTICIPATING DIVIDENDS; PARTICIPATING INSURANCE; SAVINGS ELEMENT; SECOND-TO-DIE INSURANCE; SETTLEMENT OPTIONS; SINGLE-PREMIUM LIFE INSURANCE; SURRENDER VALUE.

WHOLE LOAN SECONDARY MORTGAGE MARKET term that distinguishes an investment representing an original residential mortgage loan (whole loan) from a loan representing a participation with one or more lenders or a PASS-THROUGH SECURITY representing a pool of mortgages.

WHOLESALE PRICE INDEX *see* PRODUCER PRICE INDEX.

WHOLESALER
In general: middleman or DISTRIBUTOR who sells mainly to retailers, JOBBERS, other merchants, and industrial, commercial, and institutional users as distinguished from consumers. *See also* VENDOR.
Securities:
1. INVESTMENT BANKER acting as an UNDERWRITER in a NEW ISSUE or as a distributor in a secondary offering of securities. *See also* SECONDARY DISTRIBUTION.
2. broker-dealer who trades with other broker-dealers, rather than with the retail investor, and receives discounts and selling commissions.
3. SPONSOR of a MUTUAL FUND.

WHOLLY OWNED SUBSIDIARY SUBSIDIARY whose common stock is virtually 100%-owned by the PARENT COMPANY.

WHOOPS nickname for the Washington Public Power Supply System. In the late 1970s and early 80s, WHOOPS raised billions of dollars through MUNICIPAL BOND offerings to finance construction of five nuclear plants in the state of Washington. Because of cost overruns, bad management, and numerous delays, two of the plants were canceled, and it was doubtful that two others would ever be completed. WHOOPS defaulted on the payments to bondholders on the two canceled plants after the Washington Supreme Court ruled that the TAKE-OR-PAY CONTRACTS with the many utilities in the Northwest that had backed the bonds were invalid. This was the largest municipal bond default in history.

WIDE OPENING abnormally large SPREAD between the BID AND ASKED prices of a security at the OPENING of a trading session.

WIDGET symbolic American gadget, used wherever a hypothetical product is needed to illustrate a manufacturing or selling concept.

WIDOW-AND-ORPHAN STOCK stock that pays high dividends and is very safe. It usually has a low BETA COEFFICIENT and is involved in a noncyclical business. For years American Telephone and Telegraph was considered a widow-and-orphan stock, but it lost that status after the breakup of the Bell System in 1984. High-quality electric utility stocks are still considered widow-and-orphan stocks by and large.

WILDCAT DRILLING exploring for oil or gas in an unproven area. A wildcat OIL AND GAS LIMITED PARTNERSHIP is structured so that investors take high risks but can reap substantial rewards if oil or gas is found in commercial quantities.

WILL document, also called a *testament,* that, when signed and witnessed, gives legal effect to the wishes of a person, called a *testator,* with respect to disposal of property upon death.

WILLIAMS ACT federal legislation enacted in 1968 that imposes requirements with respect to public TENDER OFFERS. It was inspired by a wave of unannounced TAKEOVERS in the 1960s, which caught managers unawares and confronted stockholders with decisions they were ill prepared to make, The Williams Act and amendments now comprise Sections 13(d) and 14(d) of the SECURITIES EXCHANGE ACT OF 1934. The law requires the bidder opening a tender to file with both the SECURITIES AND EXCHANGE COMMISSION and the TARGET COMPANY a statement detailing the terms of the offer, the bidder's background, the cash source, and his or her plans for the company if there is a takeover. The same information is required within 10 days from any person or company acquiring 5% or more of another company. The law mandates a minimum offering period of 20 days and gives tendering shareholders 15 days to change their minds. If only a limited number of shares are accepted, they must be prorated among the tendering stockholders. *See also* SATURDAY NIGHT SPECIAL.

WILSHIRE INDICES performance measurement indices created by Wilshire Associates, Inc. of Santa Monica, California. The Wilshire 5000 Equity Index is the most widely followed index; it is published in national daily newspapers and is carried by the *Associated Press*. It measures the performance of all U.S.-headquartered equity securities with readily available price data; more than 7,000 capitalization-weighted security returns are used to adjust the index. The Wilshire 5000 base is its December 31, 1980 capitalization of $1,404.596; its capitalization is approximately 81% New York Stock Exchange (NYSE), 2% American Stock Exchange (AMEX), and 17% National Association of Dealers Automated Quotations (NASDAQ). Equity issues include common stocks, REITs, and master limited partnerships. Additions to the index are made monthly, after the month-end close. Initial public offerings (IPOs) are generally added at the end of the month. The Wilshire 4500 Equity Index is the Wilshire 5000 less the STANDARD & POOR'S 500 COMPOSITE INDEX; current capitalization is about 60% NYSE , 3% AMEX, and 37% NASDAQ. The Wilshire Small Cap Index consists of 250 companies with an average market capitalization of $933 million, and is designed to meet the need for derivative trading instruments reflecting the true character of the small cap market. Wilshire Small Cap Index options are traded on the PACIFIC EXCHANGE (PCX), which helped develop the index. Four Wilshire asset management indices are derived from the Wilshire 5000; six individual style indices (such as growth and value) and three real estate securities indices. *See also* STOCK INDICES AND AVERAGES.

WINDFALL PROFIT profit that occurs suddenly as a result of an event not controlled by the person or company profiting from the event. For example, oil companies profited in the 1970s from an explosion in the price of oil brought about by the Arab oil embargo and the price increases demanded by the Organization of Petroleum Exporting Countries. *See also* WINDFALL PROFITS TAX.

WINDFALL PROFITS TAX tax on profits that result from a sudden windfall to a particular company or industry. In 1980, federal legislation was passed that levied such a tax on oil companies because of the profits they earned as a result of the sharp increase in oil prices in the 1970s. Since then, the tax has not been reenacted.

WINDOW
1. limited time during which an opportunity should be seized, or it will be lost. For example, a period when new stock issues are welcomed by the public only lasts for a few months, or maybe as long as a year—that time is called the *window of opportunity.*
2. DISCOUNT WINDOW of a Federal Reserve bank.
3. cashier department of a brokerage firm, where delivery and settlement of securities transactions takes place.

WINDOW DRESSING
1. trading activity near the end of a quarter or fiscal year that is designed to dress up a PORTFOLIO to be presented to clients or shareholders. For example, a fund manager may sell losing positions in his portfolio so he can display only positions that have gained in value.
2. accounting gimmickry designed to make a FINANCIAL STATEMENT show a more favorable condition than actually exists—for example by omitting certain expenses, by concealing liabilities, by delaying WRITE-OFFS, by anticipating sales, or by other such actions, which may or may not be fraudulent.

WINNEPEG COMMODITY EXCHANGE Canada's only agricultural futures and options exchange, opened in 1887 as the Winnipeg Grain and Produce Exchange. It trades futures and options on canola and flaxseed, as well as Western domestic feed grades of barley and wheat, and feed pea futures. Trading is conducted Monday through Friday, from 9:30 A.M. to 1:15 P.M. for futures, and 9:30 A.M. to 1:20 P.M. for options.

WIRE HOUSE national or international brokerage firm whose branch offices are linked by a communications system that permits the rapid dissemination of prices, information, and research relating to financial markets and individual securities. Although smaller retail and regional brokers currently have access to similar data, the designation of a firm as a wire house dates back to the time when only the largest organizations had access to high-speed communications. Therefore, *wire house* still is used to refer to the biggest brokerage houses.

WIRE ROOM operating department of a brokerage firm that receives customers' orders from the REGISTERED REPRESENTATIVE and transmits the vital data to the exchange floor, where a FLOOR TICKET is prepared, or to the firm's trading department for execution. The wire room also receives notices of executed trades and relays them to the appropriate registered representatives. Also called *order department, order room,* or *wire and order.*

WITCHING HOUR *see* TRIPLE WITCHING HOUR.

WITHDRAWAL PLAN program available through most open-end MUTUAL FUND companies in which shareholders can receive fixed payments of income or CAPITAL GAINS (or both) on a regular basis, usually monthly or quarterly.

WITHHOLDING

Securities: violation of the RULES OF FAIR PRACTICE of the NATIONAL ASSOCIATION OF SECURITIES DEALERS whereby a participant in a PUBLIC OFFERING fails to make a bona fide public offering at the PUBLIC OFFERING PRICE—for example, by withholding shares for his or her own account or selling shares to a family member, an employee of the dealer firm, or another broker-dealer—in order to profit from the higher market price of a HOT ISSUE. *See also* IMMEDIATE FAMILY; INVESTMENT HISTORY.

Taxes:
1. deduction from salary payments and other compensation to provide for an individual's tax liability. Federal income taxes and Social Security contributions are withheld from paychecks and are deposited in a Treasury TAX AND LOAN ACCOUNT with a bank. The yearly amount of withholding is reported on an income statement (form W-2), which must be submitted with the federal, state, and local tax returns. Liability not provided for by withholding must be paid in four ESTIMATED TAX payments.
2. withholding by corporations and financial institutions of a flat 10% of interest and dividend payments due securities holders, as required under the TAX EQUITY AND FISCAL RESPONSIBILITY ACT OF 1982. The purpose was to levy a tax on people whose earnings escaped tracking by the Internal Revenue Service. The 10% withholding requirement was repealed in 1983. As a compromise, "backup withholding" was instituted, whereby, using Social Security numbers, payments can be reported to the IRS and matched against the actual income reported.
3. withholdings from pension and annuity distributions, sick pay, tips, and sizeable gambling winnings, as stipulated by law.
4. 30% withholding requirement on income from U.S. securities owned by foreigners—repealed by the TAX REFORM ACT OF 1984.

WORKERS COMPENSATION INSURANCE INSURANCE that pays benefits on behalf of an insured employer to employees or their families in the case of injury, disability, or death resulting from occupational hazards.

WORKING CAPITAL funds invested in a company's cash, ACCOUNTS RECEIVABLE, INVENTORY, and other CURRENT ASSETS *(gross working capital);* usually refers to *net working capital*—that is, current assets minus CURRENT LIABILITIES. Working capital finances the CASH CONVERSION CYCLE of a business—the time required to convert raw materials into finished goods, finished goods into sales, and accounts receivable into cash. These factors vary with the type of industry and the scale of production, which varies in turn with seasonality and with sales expansion and contraction. Internal sources of working capital include RETAINED EARNINGS, savings achieved through operating efficiencies and the allocation of CASH FLOW from sources like DEPRECIATION or deferred taxes to working capital. External sources include bank and other short-term borrowings, TRADE CREDIT, and term debt and EQUITY FINANCING not channeled into long-term assets. *See also* CURRENT RATIO; NET CURRENT ASSETS.

WORKING CONTROL effective control of a corporation by a shareholder or shareholders with less than 51% voting interest. Working control by a minority holder, or by two or more minority holders working in concert, is possible when share ownership of a firm is otherwise widely dispersed. *See also* MINORITY INTEREST.

WORKING INTEREST direct participation with unlimited liability, as distinguished from passive LIMITED PARTNERSHIP shares. The TAX REFORM ACT OF 1986 let investors with working interests in drilling ventures, such as GENERAL PARTNERS, offset losses against all types of income.

WORK-IN-PROCESS *see* INVENTORY.

WORKOUT situation, such as a bad loan or troubled firm, where remedial measures are being taken.

WORKSHEET computerized page allowing the user to manipulate many columns and rows of numbers. The worksheet can contain formulas so that if one number is changed, the entire worksheet is automatically updated, based on those formulas. Analysts, investors, and accountants track a company's financial statements, balance sheets, and other data on worksheets.

WORLD BANK *see* INTERNATIONAL BANK FOR RECONSTRUCTION AND DEVELOPMENT.

WORLD TRADE ORGANIZATION (WTO) independent multilateral agency administering world trade agreements. WTO, headquartered in Geneva, Switzerland, resulted from the Uruguay round of GENERAL AGREEMENT ON TRADE AND TARIFFS (GATT) concluded in 1995. WTO's tasks include fostering trade relations among its members, resolving disputes, and serving as a forum for future multilateral trade negotiations.

WRAP ACCOUNT investment consulting relationship in which a client's funds are placed with one or more money managers, and all administrative and management fees, along with commissions, are wrapped into one comprehensive fee, which is paid quarterly. The wrap fee varies, but usually ranges from 1% to 3% of the value of the assets in the account. Wrap accounts usually require a minimum initial investment of anywhere from $25,000 to $10 million for individual accounts. The term *wrap* has been expanded to involve mutual fund asset allocation programs. Technically, these are not wrap programs because they are not "all inclusive." Transaction commissions in these programs on mutual funds are still a variable and they are pooled accounts as distinguished from individual accounts. From the customer's point of view, a wrap account provides access to top investment managers. The broker overseeing the account is paid an ongoing fee to monitor the performance of the money managers. Although brokers may switch assets to other managers within the program if one manager consistently starts to underperform, most sponsors of wrap programs suggest a three- to five-year time horizon to reach investment goals.

WRAPAROUND ANNUITY ANNUITY contract allowing an annuitant discretion in the choice of underlying investments. Wraparound refers to the protection the annuity vehicle provides through its TAX-DEFERRED status, which becomes precarious when the annuity vehicle is being used as a technical way to avoid tax payment. The tax courts have ruled against tax deferment where money can be allocated by an annuity owner to a portfolio managed by an annuitant and where the annuitant can switch among funds of the sponsoring insurance company that are also marketed independently of annuities. On the other hand, the IRS has upheld tax deferral where an individual could not buy such funds without also buying the annuity. In any event, the insurer must legally own the annuity money.

WRAPAROUND MORTGAGE second mortgage that increases a borrower's indebtedness while leaving the original mortgage contract in force. The wraparound mortgage becomes the JUNIOR MORTGAGE and is held by the lending institution as security for the total mortgage debt. The borrower makes payments on both loans to the wraparound lender, who in turn makes scheduled installment payments on the original *senior mortgage.* It is a convenient way for a property owner to obtain additional credit without having first to pay off an existing mortgage.

WRINKLE novel feature that may attract a buyer for a new product or a security. For example, ZERO COUPON SECURITIES were a new wrinkle when they were introduced but soon thereafter became quite commonplace.

WRITE-OFF charging an ASSET amount to expense or loss. The effect of a write-off is to reduce or eliminate the value of the asset and reduce profits. Write-offs are systematically taken in accordance with allowable tax DEPRECIATION of a FIXED ASSET, and with the AMORTIZATION of certain other assets, such as an INTANGIBLE ASSET and a capitalized cost (like premiums paid on investments). Write-offs are also taken when assets are, for whatever reason, deemed worthless, the most common example being uncollectible ACCOUNTS RECEIVABLE. Where such write-offs can be anticipated and therefore estimated, the usual practice has been to charge income regularly in amounts needed to maintain a RESERVE, the actual losses then being charged to the reserve. The TAX REFORM ACT OF 1986 required that BAD DEBT write-offs be charged directly to income by taxpayers other than small banks and thrift institutions. *See also* EXTRAORDINARY ITEM: NONRECURRING CHARGE.

WRITE OUT procedure followed when a SPECIALIST on an exchange makes a trade involving his own inventory, on one hand, and an order he is holding for a FLOOR BROKER, on the other. Exchange rules require a two-part transaction: the broker first completes a trade with the specialist, who then completes the transaction by a separate trade with the customer. The write out involves no charge other than the normal broker's commission.

WRITER
  1. person who sells PUT OPTION and CALL OPTION contracts, and therefore collects PREMIUM INCOME. The writer of a put option is obligated to buy (and the writer of a call option is obligated to sell) the UNDERLYING SECURITY at a predetermined price by a particular date if the OPTION is exercised. *See also* COVERED CALL; NAKED OPTION; WRITING NAKED.
  2. insurance UNDERWRITER.

WRITE UP/WRITE DOWN upward or downward adjustment of the accounting value of an asset according to GENERALLY ACCEPTED ACCOUNTING PRINCIPLES GAAP. *See also* WRITE-OFF.

WRITING CASH-SECURED PUTS OPTION strategy that a trader who wants to sell PUT OPTIONS uses to avoid having to use a MARGIN ACCOUNT. Rather than depositing MARGIN with a broker, a put WRITER can deposit cash equal to the option EXERCISE PRICE. With this strategy, the put option writer is not subject to additional margin requirements in the event of changes in the underlying stock's price. The put writer can also be earning money by investing the PREMIUM he or she receives in MONEY MARKET instruments.

WRITING NAKED strategy used by an OPTION seller in which the trader does not own the UNDERLYING SECURITY. This strategy can lead to large profits if the stock moves in the hoped-for direction, but it can lead to large losses if the stock moves in the other direction, since the trader will have to go into the marketplace to buy the stock in order to deliver it to the option buyer. *See also* NAKED OPTION.

WRITING PUTS TO ACQUIRE STOCK strategy used by an OPTION writer (seller) who believes a stock is going to decline and that its purchase at a given price would represent a good investment. By writing a PUT OPTION exercisable at that price, the writer cannot lose. If the stock, contrary to his expectation, goes up, the option will not be exercised and he is at least ahead the amount of the PREMIUM he received. If, as expected, the stock goes down and the option is exercised, he has bought the stock at what he had earlier decided was a good buy, and he has the premium income in addition.

WRITTEN-DOWN VALUE BOOK VALUE of an asset after DEPRECIATION or other AMORTIZATION; also called *net book value*. For example, if the original cost of a piece of equipment was $1000 and accumulated depreciation charges totaled $400, the written-down value would be $600. *See also* INTANGIBLE ASSET.

WT abbreviation for *warrant. See also* SUBSCRIPTION WARRANT.

W-2 FORM tax form prepared by an employer for an employee to enclose with the 1040 FORM, summarizing wages earned for the year, federal and state taxes withheld, and SOCIAL SECURITY tax information.

X Y Z

X or XD symbol used in newspapers to signify that a stock is trading EX-DIVIDEND, that is, without dividend. The symbol X is also used in bond tables to signify without interest.

XR symbol used in newspapers to signify that a stock is trading EX-RIGHTS, that is, without rights attached. *See also* SUBSCRIPTION RIGHT.

XW symbol used in newspapers to signify that a stock is trading EX-WARRANTS, that is, without warrants attached. *See also* SUBSCRIPTION WARRANT.

YANKEE BOND MARKET dollar-denominated bonds issued in the U.S. by foreign banks and corporations. The bonds are issued in the U.S. when market conditions there are more favorable than on the EUROBOND market or in domestic markets overseas. Similarly, Yankee CERTIFICATES OF DEPOSIT are negotiable CDs issued in the U.S. by branches and agencies of foreign banks.

YEAR-END BONUS bonus payment given to employees at the end of a year, based on the employee's performance and the performance of the company. Most securities firms operate on a bonus system, providing employees with huge bonuses in highly profitable years and little or no bonuses in lean years. Many salespeople also operate on a year-end bonus system, in which they receive bonuses if they met or exceeded certain sales goals during the year.

YEAR-END DIVIDEND an additional or special DIVIDEND declared based on a company's profits during the fiscal year.

YEAR-TO-DATE (YTD) period from the beginning of the calendar year (or FISCAL YEAR (FY) if so indicated) to the reporting date. For example third-quarterly results of a company would be reported for the quarter alone and for the year-to-date, which would be nine months.

YELLOW SHEETS daily publication of the NATIONAL QUOTATION BUREAU that details the BID AND ASKED prices and firms that MAKE A MARKET in CORPORATE BONDS traded in the OVER THE COUNTER (OTC) market. Much of this information is not available in the daily OTC newspaper listings. The sheets are named for their color. OTC equity issues are covered separately on PINK SHEETS and regional OTC issues of both classes are listed on white sheets.

YEN BOND in general terms, any bond issue denominated in Japanese yen. International bankers using the term are usually referring to yen-denominated bonds issued or held outside Japan.

YIELD

In general: RETURN on an investor's CAPITAL INVESTMENT. A piece of real estate may yield a certain return, or a business deal may offer a particular yield. *See also* RETURN ON INVESTED CAPITAL.

Agriculture: agricultural output in terms of quantity of a crop

Bonds:

1. COUPON rate of interest divided by the purchase price, called CURRENT YIELD. For example, a bond selling for $1000 with a 10% coupon offers a 10% current yield. If that same bond were selling for $500, however, it would offer a 20% yield to an investor who bought it for $500. (As a bond's price falls, its yield rises and vice versa.)

2. rate of return on a bond, taking into account the total of annual interest payments, the purchase price, the redemption value, and the amount of time remaining until maturity; called *maturity yield* or YIELD TO MATURITY. *See also* DURATION; YIELD TO AVERAGE LIFE; YIELD TO CALL.

Lending: total money earned on a loan—that is, the ANNUAL PERCENTAGE RATE of interest multiplied by the term of the loan.

Stocks: percentage rate of return paid on a common or preferred stock in dividends. For example, a stock that sells for $20 and pays an annual dividend of $2 per share has a yield, also called a *dividend yield,* of 10%.

Taxes: amount of revenue received by a governmental entity as a result of a tax.

YIELD ADVANTAGE extra amount of return an investor will earn if he or she purchases a CONVERTIBLE security instead of the common stock of the same issuing corporation. If an XYZ Corporation convertible yields 10% and an XYZ common share yields 5%, the yield advantage is 5%. *See also* YIELD SPREAD.

YIELD BURNING MUNICIPAL BOND financing practice whereby underwriters in ADVANCE REFUNDINGS (PREREFUNDING) slap excessive MARKUPS on U.S. Treasury bonds bought and held in escrow to compensate investors during the time between issuance of the new bonds and repayment of the old ones. Since bond prices and yields move in opposite directions, when underwriters mark up the bonds, they "burn down" the yield, violating federal tax rules and costing the government tax revenues. Under IRS regulations, municipalities, not the underwriters, incur the tax liability. The SEC, which was conducting a wideranging probe of alleged yield-burning abuses by Wall Street firms in the late 1990s, favors making the underwriters responsible, not the municipalities.

YIELD CURVE graph showing the term structure of interest rates by plotting the yields of all bonds of the same quality with maturities ranging from the shortest to the longest available. The resulting curve shows if short-term interest rates are higher or lower than long-term rates. If short-term rates are lower, it is called a POSITIVE YIELD CURVE. If short-term rates are higher, it is called a NEGATIVE (or INVERTED) YIELD CURVE. If there is little difference between short-term and long-term rates, it is called a *flat yield* curve. For the most part, the yield curve is positive, since investors who are willing to tie up their money for a longer period of time usually are compensated for the extra risk they are taking by receiving a higher yield. The most common version of the yield curve graph plots Treasury securities, showing the range of yields from a three-month TREASURY BILL to a 20- or 30-year TREASURY BOND.

Fixed-income analysts study the yield curve carefully in order to make judgments about the direction of interest rates. *See also* DURATION.

YIELD EQUIVALENCE the rate of interest at which a tax-exempt bond and a taxable security of similar quality provide the same return. In the day of the 50% TAX BRACKET, for example, a tax-exempt bond paying 10% was the equivalent of a taxable corporate bond of 20%. To calculate the yield that must be provided by a taxable security to equal that of a tax-exempt bond for investors in different tax brackets, the tax exempt yield is divided by the reciprocal of the tax bracket (100 less 28%, for example) to arrive at the taxable yield. Thus, a person in the 28% tax bracket who wished to figure the taxable equivalent of a 10% tax free municipal bond would divide 10% by 72% (100 minus 28%) to get 13.9%—the yield a corporate taxable bond would have to provide to be equivalent, after taxes, to the 10% municipal bond. To convert a taxable yield to a tax-exempt yield, the formula is reversed—that is, the tax exempt yield is equal to the taxable yield multiplied by the reciprocal of the tax bracket.

YIELD SPREAD difference in YIELD between various issues of securities. In comparing bonds, it usually refers to issues of different credit quality since issues of the same maturity and quality would normally have the same yields, as with Treasury securities, for example. Yield spread also refers to the differential between dividend yield on stocks and the CURRENT YIELD on bonds. The comparison might be made, for example, between the STANDARD & POOR'S INDEX (of 500 stocks) dividend yield and the current yield of an index of corporate bonds. A significant difference in bond and stock yields, assuming similar quality, is known as a *yield gap*.

YIELD TO AVERAGE LIFE yield calculation used, in lieu of YIELD TO MATURITY or YIELD TO CALL, where bonds are retired systematically during the life of the issue, as in the case of a SINKING FUND with contractual requirements. Because the issuer will buy its own bonds on the open market to satisfy its sinking fund requirements if the bonds are trading below PAR, there is to that extent automatic price support for such bonds; they therefore tend to trade on a yield-to-average-life basis.

YIELD TO CALL yield on a bond assuming the bond will be redeemed by the issuer at the first CALL date specified in the INDENTURE agreement.

The same calculations are used to calculate yield to call as YIELD TO MATURITY except that the principal value at maturity is replaced by the first CALL PRICE and the maturity date is replaced by the first call date. Assuming the issuer will put the interest of the company before the interest of the investor and will call the bonds if it is favorable to do so, the lower of the yield to call and the yield to maturity can be viewed as the more realistic rate of return to the investor. *See also* DURATION.

YIELD TO MATURITY (YTM) concept used to determine the rate of return an investor will receive if a long-term, interest-bearing investment, such as a bond, is held to its MATURITY DATE. It takes into account purchase price, REDEMPTION value, time to maturity, COUPON yield, and the time between interest payments. Recognizing time value of money, it is the DISCOUNT RATE at which the PRESENT VALUE of all future payments would equal the present price of the bond, also known as INTERNAL RATE OF RETURN. It is implicitly assumed that coupons are reinvested at the YTM rate. YTM can be approximated using a bond value table (also called a bond yield table) or can be determined using a programmable calculator equipped for bond mathematics calculations. *See also* DURATION; HORIZON ANALYSIS; YIELD TO AVERAGE LIFE, YIELD TO CALL.

YO-YO STOCK stock that fluctuates in a VOLATILE manner, rising and falling quickly like a yo-yo.

ZACKS ESTIMATE SYSTEM service offer by Zacks Investment Research of Chicago compiling earnings estimates and brokerage buy/hold/sell recommendations from more than 200 Wall Street research firms, covering more than 4500 stocks. Zacks tracks the number of analysts following each stock, how many analysts have raised or lowered their estimates, and the high, low and average earnings estimate for each quarter and fiscal year. Zacks offers a multiple selection of data bases, of print reports, and software for institutional and individual investors. *See also* FIRST CALL, I/B/E/S INTERNATIONAL INC.

Z-BOND the fourth (Z) TRANCHE of bonds in the structure of a typical COLLATERALIZED MORTGAGE OBLIGATION (CMO). Combining features of ZERO-COUPON SECURITIES and mortgage PASS-THROUGH SECURITIES, Z bonds receive no coupon payments until the earlier A (fast-pay), B (medium-pay), and C (slow-pay) classes have been paid off. Z holders then receive all the remaining cash flow, although interest has been added to principal as cash was used to repay earlier tranches. Some CMOs have been issued with multiple Z and Y tranches, incorporating SINKING-FUND schedules.

ZERO-BASE BUDGETING (ZBB) method of setting budgets for corporations and government agencies that requires a justification of all expenditures, not only those that exceed the prior year's allocations. Thus all budget lines are said to begin at a zero base and are funded according to merit rather than according to the level approved for the preceding year, when circumstances probably differed.

ZERO-BRACKET AMOUNT until the TAX REFORM ACT OF 1986, the STANDARD DEDUCTION, that is, the income automatically not subject to federal income tax for taxpayers choosing not to itemize deductions. The zero-bracket amount was built into the tax tables and schedules used to compute tax. The 1986 Act replaced the zero-bracket amount with an increased standard deduction, which was subtracted from income before computing taxes rather than being part of the rate tables. Current (*see* REVENUE RECONCILIATION ACT OF 1993) law indexes the standard deduction to inflation and contains special provisions for the blind and elderly.

ZERO-COUPON CONVERTIBLE SECURITY

1. Zero-coupon BOND convertible into the common stock of the issuing company when the stock reaches a predetermined price. Introduced as Liquid Yield Option Notes (LYONS), these securities have a PUT OPTION that permits holders to redeem the bonds within three years after the initial offering. They tend to trade at a small PREMIUM OVER CONVERSION VALUE and provide a lower YIELD TO MATURITY than their nonconvertible counterparts.

2. Zero-coupon bond, usually a MUNICIPAL BOND, convertible into an interest bearing bond at some time before maturity. For example, a zero-coupon (tax-free) municipal bond would automatically accumulate and compound interest for its first 15 years at which time it would convert to a regular income-paying bond. Thus, an investor is able to lock in a current interest rate with a small initial investment. Varieties are marketed under the acronyms GAINS (Growth and Income Securities) and FIGS (Future Income and Growth Securities).

ZERO-COUPON SECURITY security that makes no periodic interest payments but instead is sold at a deep discount from its face value. The buyer of such a bond receives the rate of return by the gradual APPRECIATION of the security, which is redeemed at FACE VALUE on a specified maturity date. For tax purposes, the Internal Revenue Service maintains that the holder of a zero-coupon bond owes income tax on the interest that has accrued each year, even though the bondholder does not actually receive the cash until maturity. The IRS calls this interest *imputed interest.* Because of this interpretation, many financial advisers recommend that zero-coupon securities be used in INDIVIDUAL RETIREMENT ACCOUNTS or KEOGH ACCOUNTS, where they remain tax-sheltered.

There are many kinds of zero-coupon securities. The most commonly known is the zero-coupon bond, which either may be issued at a deep discount by a corporation or government entity or may be created by a brokerage firm when it strips the coupons off a bond and sells the CORPUS and the coupons separately. This technique is used frequently with Treasury bonds, and the zero-coupon issue is marketed under such names as CATS (CERTIFICATE OF ACCRUAL ON TREASURY SECURITIES), TIGER (Treasury Investors Growth Receipt) or STRIPS (separate trading of registered interest and principal of securities). Zero-coupon bonds are also issued by municipalities. Buying a municipal zero frees its purchaser of the worry about paying taxes on imputed interest, since the interest is tax-exempt. Zero-coupon certificates of deposit and zero mortgages also exist; they work on the same principle as zero-coupon bonds—the CD holder or mortgage holder receives face value at maturity, and no payments until then. Zero-coupon securities based on COLLATERALIZED MORTGAGE OBLIGATION bonds are called *Z-tranche bonds*. Some mutual funds buy exclusively zero-coupon securities, offering shareholders a diversified portfolio that will mature in a particular year.

Zero-coupon securities are frequently used to plan for a specific investment goal. For example, parents knowing their child will enter college in 10 years can buy a zero that will mature in 10 years, and thus be assured of having money available for tuition. People planning for retirement in 20 years can buy 20-year zeros, assuring them that they will get the money when they need it.

Because zero-coupon securities bear no interest, they are the most VOLATILE of all fixed-income securities. Since zero-coupon bondholders do not receive interest payments, zeros fall more dramatically than bonds paying out interest on a current basis when interest rates rise. However, when interest rates fall, zero-coupon securities rise more rapidly in value than full-coupon bonds, because the bonds have locked in a particular rate of reinvestment that becomes more attractive the further rates fall. The greater the number of years that a zero-coupon security has until maturity, the less an investor has to pay for it, and the more LEVERAGE is at work for him. For instance, a bond maturing in 5 years may double, but one maturing in 25 years may increase in value 10 times, depending on the interest rate of the bond. *See also* ACCRUAL BONDS; COUPON BOND; DEEP DISCOUNT BOND, SPLIT-COUPON BONDS; STAGS; STRIPPED BOND; ZERO-COUPON CONVERTIBLE SECURITY.

ZERO-MINUS TICK sale that takes place at the same price as the previous sale, but at a lower price than the last different price; also called a *zero downtick*. For instance, stock trades may be executed consecutively at prices of $52, $51, and $51. The final trade at $51 was made at a zero-minus tick, because it was made at the same price as the previous trade, but at a lower price than the last different price.

ZERO-PLUS TICK securities trade that takes place at the same price as the previous transaction but at a higher price than the last different price; also called *zero uptick*. For instance, with trades executed consecutively at $51, $52, and $52, the last trade at $52 was made at a zero-plus tick—the same price as the previous trade but a higher price than the last different price. Short sales must be executed only on zero-plus ticks or on PLUS TICKS. *See also* SHORT SALE RULE.

ZERO-SUM GAME situation in which the gains of the winners are matched by the losses of the losers. For example, futures and options trading are zero-sum games because for every investor holding a profitable contract, there is another investor on the other side of the trade who is losing money. The total amount of wealth held by all the traders in a zero-sum game remains the same, but the wealth is shifted from some traders to others.

ZOMBIES companies that continue to operate even though they are insolvent and bankrupt. For example, during the savings and loan industry bailout, many savings and loans that had lost millions of dollars in bad real estate loans continued to function, awaiting merger into another financial institution or closure by the RESOLUTION TRUST CORPORATION. Such companies, in addition to being called zombies, are called *brain dead* or *living dead*.

ZONING LAWS municipal ordinances that authorize the establishment of zoning boards to administer regulations concerning the use of property and buildings in designated areas.

ZURICH STOCK EXCHANGE *see* SWISS ELECTRONIC BOURSE (EBS).

ABBREVIATIONS AND ACRONYMS

A

A Includes Extra (or Extras) (in stock listings of newspapers)

AAII American Association of Individual Investors

AB Aktiebolag (Swedish stock company)

ABA American Bankers Association

ABA American Bar Association

ABLA American Business Law Association

ABS Automated Bond System

ABWA American Business Women's Association

ACE AMEX Commodities Exchange

ACRS Accelerated Cost Recovery System

A-D Advance-Decline Line

ADB Adjusted Debit Balance

ADR American Depositary Receipt

ADR Automatic Dividend Reinvestment

ADRS Asset Depreciation Range System

ADS American Depositary Shares

AE Account Executive

AFL-CIO American Federation of Labor-Congress of Industrial Organizations

AICPA American Institute of Certified Public Accountants

AID Agency for International Development

AIM American Institute for Management

AG Aktiengesellschaft (West German stock company)

AGI Adjusted Gross Income

AIP Automatic Investment Program

AMA American Management Association

AMA Asset Management Account

AMBAC American Municipal Bond Assurance Corporation

AMEX American Stock Exchange

AMPS Auction Market Preferred Stock

AMT Alternative Minimum Tax

AON All or None

APB Accounting Principles Board

APR Annual Percentage Rate

APS Auction Preferred Stock

ARB Airport Revenue Bond

Arb Arbitrageur

ARF American Retail Federation

ARM Adjustable Rate Mortgage

ARPS Adjustable Rate Preferred Stock

ART Annual Renewable Term (insurance)

ASAP As Soon as Possible

ASE American Stock Exchange

ASE Amsterdam Stock Exchange

ASPIRIN Australian Stock Price Riskless Indexed Notes

ASX Australia Stock Exchange

ATM Automatic Teller Machine

ATP Arbitrage Trading Program

B

B Annual Rate Plus Stock Dividend (in stock listings of newspapers)

BAC Business Advisory Council

BAN Bond Anticipation Note

BBB Better Business Bureau

BD Bank Draft

BD Bills Discontinued

B/D Broker-Dealer

BE Bill of Exchange

BEACON Boston Exchange Automated Communication Order-routing Network

BEARS Bond Enabling Annual Retirement Savings

BF Brought Forward

BFP Basic Formula Price (milk)
BIC Bank Investment Contract
BIF Bank Insurance Fund
BL Bill of Lading
BLS Bureau of Labor Statistics
BMA Bond Market Association
BO Branch Office
BO Buyer's Option
BOM Beginning of the Month
BOP Balance of Payments
BOT Balance of Trade
BOT Bought
BOT Board of Trustees
BOVESPA Bolsa de Valores de Sao Paulo
BPW Business and Professional Women's Foundation
BR Bills Receivable
BS Balance Sheet
BS Bill of Sale
BS Bureau of Standards
BSE Boston Stock Exchange
BSE Brussels Stock Exchange
BTCI Bankers Trust Commodity Index
BVRJ Bolsa de Valores de Rio de Janiero
BW Bid Wanted

C

C Liquidating Dividend (in stock listings of newspapers)
CA Capital Account
CA Chartered Accountant
CA Commercial Agent
CA Credit Account
CA Current Account
CACM Central American Common Market
CAD Cash against Documents
CAF Cost Assurance and Freight
C&F Cost and Freight
CAMPS Cumulative Auction Market Preferred Stocks
CAPM Capital Asset Pricing Model
CAPS Convertible Adjustable Preferred Stock

CARs Certificate for Automobile Receivables
CARDS Certificates for Amortizing Revolving Debts
CATS Certificate of Accrual on Treasury Securities
CATV Community Antenna Television
CBA Capital Builder Account
CBA Cost Benefit Analysis
CBD Cash Before Delivery
CBO Collateralized Bond Obligation
CBOE Chicago Board Options Exchange
CBT Chicago Board of Trade
CC Chamber of Commerce
CCH Commerce Clearing House
CD Certificate of Deposit
CD Commercial Dock
CDN Canadian Dealing Network
CEA Council of Economic Advisors
CEO Chief Executive Officer
CF Certificates (in bond listings of newspapers)
CF Carried Forward
CFA Chartered Financial Analyst
CFC Chartered Financial Counselor
CFC Consolidated Freight Classification
CFI Cost, Freight, and Insurance
CFO Chief Financial Officer
CFP Certified Financial Planner
CFTC Commodities Futures Trading Commission
CH Clearing House
CH Custom House
ChFC Chartered Financial Consultant
CHX Chicago Stock Exchange
Cía Compañía (Spanish company)
Cie Compagnie (French company)
CIF Corporate Income Fund
CIF Cost, Insurance, and Freight
CIPs Cash Index Participations

CLD Called (in stock listings of newspapers)
CLN Construction Loan Note
CLU Chartered Life Underwriter
CME Chicago Mercantile Exchange
CMO Collateralized Mortgage Obligation
CMV Current Market Value
CN Consignment Note
CN Credit Note
CNS Continuous Net Settlement
CO Cash Order
CO Certificate of Origin
Co. Company
COB Close of Business (with date)
COBRA Consolidated Omnibus Budget Reconciliation Act
COD Cash on Delivery
COD Collect on Delivery
CODA Cash or Deferred Arrangement
COFI Cost of Funds Index
COLA Cost-of-Living Adjustment
COLTS Continuously Offered Longer-Term Securities
COMEX Commodity Exchange (New York)
COMSAT Communications Satellite Corporation
CONNIE LEE College Construction Loan Insurance Association
COO Chief Operating Officer
CPA Certified Public Accountant
CPCI Chase Physical Commodity Index
CPD Commissioner of Public Debt
CPPF Cast Plus Fixed Fee
CPI Consumer Price Index
CPM Cost per Thousand
CPPC Cost plus a Percentage of Cost
CR Carrier's Risk
CR Class Rate
CR Company's Risk

CR Current Rate
CRB Commodity Research Bureau
CRT Charitable Remainder Trust
CSCE Coffee, Sugar and Coca Exchange
CSE Cincinnati Stock Exchange
CSE Copenhagen Stock Exchange
CSVLI Cash Surrender Value of Life Insurance
CUBS Calls Underwritten by Swanbrook
CUNA Credit Union National Association
CUSIP Committee on Uniform Securities Identification Procedures
CV Convertible Security (in bond and stock listings of newspapers)
CWO Cash with Order

D

DA Deposit Account
DA Documents against Acceptance
DAC Delivery against Cost
DAF Defined Asset Fund
D&B Dun and Bradstreet
DAPS Dutch Auction Preferred Stock
DBA Doing Business As
DC Deep Discount Issue (in bond listings of newspapers)
DCFM Discounted Cash Flow Method
DDB Double-Declining-Balance Depreciation Method
DENKS Dual-Employed, No Kids
DEWKS Dual Employed, With Kids
DF Damage Free
DIDC Depository Institutions Deregulatory Committee
DINKS Dual-Income, No Kids
DISC Domestic International Sales Corporation

DJIA Dow Jones Industrial Average
DJTA Dow Jones Transportation Average
DJUA Dow Jones Utility Average
DK Don't Know
DN Debit Note
DNI Do Not Increase
DNR Do Not Reduce
D/O Delivery Order
DOT Designated Order Turnaround
DP Documents against Payment
DPI Disposable Personal Income
DS Days After Sight
DTB Deutsche Terminbourse
DTC Depository Trust Company
DUNS Data Universal Numbering System (Dun's Number)
DVP Delivery Versus Payment

E

E Declared or Paid in the Preceding 12 Months (in stock listings of newspapers)
EAFE Europe and Australasia, Far East Equity Index
E&OE Errors and Omissions Excepted
EBIT Earnings Before Interest and Taxes
EBITA Earnings Before Interest, Taxes, Depreciation, and Amortization
EBS Swiss Electronic Bourse
EC European Community
ECB European Central Bank
ECM Emerging Company Marketplace
ECM European Common Market
ECOA Equal Credit Opportunity Act
ECT Estimated Completion Time
EDD Estimated Delivery Date
ECU European Currency Unit
EEC European Economic Community

EEOC Equal Employment Opportunity Commission
EMF INDEX Emerging Market Free Index
EMP End-of-Month Payment
EMS European Monetary System
ENMET Energy and Metals Index
EOA Effective On or About
EOD Every Other Day (advertising)
EOE European Options Exchange
EOM End of Month
EPR Earnings Price Ratio
EPS Earnings Per Share
ERISA Employee Retirement Income Security Act of 1974
ERM Exchange Rate Mechanism
ERTA Economic Recovery Tax Act of 1981
ESOP Employee Stock Ownership Plan
ESP Exchange Stock Portfolio
ETA Estimated Time of Arrival
ETD Estimated Time of Departure
ETLT Equal To or Less Than
ETM Escrowed to Maturity
ETS Energy Trading System (on the International Petroleum Exchange)
EU European Union
EXIMBANK Export-Import Bank

F

F Dealt in Flat (in bond listings in newspapers)
FA Free Alongside
FACT Factor Analysis Chart Technique
FAS Free Alongside
FASB Financial Accounting Standards Board
FAT Fixed Asset Transfer
FAX Facsimile
FB Freight Bill
FCA Fellow of the Institute of Chartered Accountants
FCBA Fair Credit Billing Act

FCC Federal Communications Commission

FCFAC Federal Credit Financial Assistance Corporation

FCRA Fair Credit Reporting Act

FCUA Federal Credit Union Administration

FDIC Federal Deposit Insurance Corporation

Fed Federal Reserve System

FET Federal Excise Tax

F&F Furniture and Fixtures

FFB Federal Financing Bank

FFCS Federal Farm Credit System

FGIC Financial Guaranty Insurance Corporation

FHA Farmers Home Administration

FHA Federal Housing Administration

FHFB Federal Housing Finance Board

FHLBB Federal Home Loan Bank Board

FHLMC Federal Home Loan Mortgage Corporation (Freddie Mac)

FIBOR Frankfurt Interbank Offered Rate

FICA Federal Insurance Contributions Act

FICB Federal Intermediate Credit Bank

FICO Financing Corporation

FIFO First In, First Out

FINEX Financial Derivatives Division of New York Cotton Exchange

FIRREA Financial Institutions Reform and Recovery Act

FIT Federal Income Tax

FITW Federal Income Tax Withholding

FLB Federal Land Bank

FLEX Flexible Exchange Options

FMAN February, May, August, November Cycle

FMC Federal Maritime Commission

FNMA Federal National Mortgage Association (Fannie Mae)

FOB Free on Board

FOC Free of Charge

FOCUS Financial and Operations Combined Uniform Single Report

FOI Freedom of Information Act

FOK Fill or Kill

FOMC Federal Open Market Committee

FOOTSIE Financial Times-SE 100 Index of U.K. Stocks

FOR Free on Rail (or Road)

FOT Free on Truck

FOX Finnish Options Index

FP Floating Policy

FP Fully Paid

FPM Fixed-Payment Mortgage

FRA Federal Reserve Act

FRB Federal Reserve Bank

FRB Federal Reserve Board

FRD Federal Reserve District

FREDDIE MAC Federal Home Loan Mortgage Corporation

FREIT Finite Life REIT.

FRS Federal Reserve System

FS Final Settlement

FSC Foreign Sales Corporation

FSLIC Federal Savings and Loan Insurance Corporation

FTC Federal Trade Commission

FTI Federal Tax Included

FUTA Federal Unemployment Tax Act

FVO For Valuation Only

FX Foreign Exchange

FY Fiscal Year

FYA For Your Attention

FYI For Your Information

G

G Dividends and Earnings In Canadian Dollars (in stock listings of newspapers)

GAAP Generally Accepted Accounting Principles

GAAS Generally Accepted Auditing Standards

GAI Guaranteed Annual Income

GAO General Accounting Office

GATT General Agreement on Tariffs and Trade

GDP Gross Domestic Product

GDR Global Depositary Receipt

G-8 Group of Eight Finance Ministers

GEM Growing Equity Mortgage

GIC Guaranteed Investment Contract

GINNIE MAE Government National Mortgage Association

GIT Guaranteed Income (or Investment) Contract

GM General Manager

GmbH Gesellschaft mit beschränkter Haftung (West German limited liability company)

GNMA Government National Mortgage Association

GNP Gross National Product

GO General Obligation Bond

GPM Graduated Payment Mortgage

GRIT Grantor Retained Income Trust

GSA General Services Administration

GSCI Goldman Sachs Commodity Index

GSE Government Sponsored Entity

GTC Good Till Canceled

GTM Good This Month

GTW Good This Week

GULP Group Universal Life Policy

H

H Declared or Paid After Stock Dividend or Split-Up (in stock listings of newspapers)

HEL Home Equity Loan

HEX Helsinki Stock and Derivatives Exchange

H/F Held For

HFR Hold For Release

HIBOR Hong Kong Interbank Offered Rate

HLT Highly Leveraged Transaction

HO Home Owner's Insurance Policy

HQ Headquarters

HR U.S. House of Representatives

HR U.S. House of Representatives Bill (with number)

HUD Department of Housing and Urban Development

I

I Paid This Year, Dividend Omitted, Deferred, or No Action Taken at Last Dividend Meeting (in stock listings of newspapers)

IAFP International Association for Financial Planning

I/B/E/S Institutional Broker's Estimate System

I-Bonds Inflation-indexed Savings Bonds

IBRD International Bank for Reconstruction and Development (World Bank)

ICC Interstate Commerce Commission

ICFP Institute of Certified Financial Planners

ICFTU International Confederation of Free Trade Unions

ICI Investable Commodity Index

ICI Investment Company Institute

ICMA Institute of Cost and Management Accountants

IDB Industrial Development Bond

IDEM Italian Derivatives Market

IET Interest Equalization Tax

IFC International Finance Corporation

ILA International Longshoremen's Association

ILGWU International Ladies' Garment Workers' Union

ILO International Labor Organization

IMF International Monetary Fund

IMM International Monetary Market of the Chicago Mercantile Exchange

Inc. Incorporated

INSTINET Institutional Networks Corporation

IO Interest Only

IOC Immediate-Or-Cancel Order

IOU I Owe You

IPE International Petroleum Exchange

IPO Initial Public Offering

IR Investor Relations

IRA Individual Retirement Account

IRB Industrial Revenue Bond

IRC Internal Revenue Code

IRR Internal Rate of Return

IRS Internal Revenue Service

ISBN International Standard Book Number

ISE International Stock Exchange of the U.K. and the Republic of Ireland

ISE Italian Stock Exchange

ISIS Intermarket Surveillance Information System

ISO Incentive Stock Option

ISRO International Securities Regulatory Organization

ISSN International Standard Serial Number

ITC Investment Tax Credit

ITS Intermarket Trading System

J

JA Joint Account

JAJO January, April, July, October Cycle

Jeep Graduated Payment Mortgage

JPMCI J.P. Morgan Commity Index

JSE Johannesburg Stock Exchange

JTWROS Joint Tenancy With Right of Survivorship

K

K Declared or Paid This Year on a Cumulative Issue with Dividends in Arrears (in stock listings of newspapers)

K Kilo- (prefix meaning multiplied by one thousand)

KCBT Kansas City Board Of Trade

KD Knocked Down (disassembled)

KIBOR Kuala Lumpur Interbank Offered Rate

KK Kabushiki-Kaisha (Japanese stock company)

KLOFFE Kuala Lumpur Options & Financial Futures Exchange Barhad

KLSE Kuala Lumpur Stock Exchange

KW Kilowatt

KWH Kilowatt-hour

KYC Know Your Customer Rule

L

L Listed (securities)

LBO Leveraged Buyout

L/C Letter Of Credit

LCL Less-Than-Carload Lot

LCM Least Common Multiple (mathematics)

LDC Less Developed Country

LEI Leading Conomic Indicators

LESOP Leveraged Employee Stock Ownership Plan

LEAPS Long-Term Equity AnticiPation Securities

LEI Leading Economic Indicators

LESOP Leveraged Employee Stock Ownership Plan

L/I Letter of Intent

LIBOR London Interbank Offered Rate

LIFFE London International Financial Futures and Options Exchange

LIFO Last In, First Out

LISBOR Lisbon Interbank Offered Rate

LME London Metal Exchange

LMRA Labor-Management Relations Act

LP Limited Partnership

LSE Lisbon Stock Exchange

LSE London Stock Exchange

Ltd Limited (British Corporation)

LTV Loan To Value

M

M Matured Bonds (in bond listings in newspapers)

M Milli- (prefix meaning divided by one thousand)

M Mega- (prefix meaning multiplied by one million)

M One Thousand (Roman Numeral)

MACD Moving Average Convergence/Divergence

MACRS Modified Accelerated Cost Recovery System

MATIF Marche a Terme International de France

M&L Matched And Lost

Max Maximum

MBA Master of Business Administration

MBIA Municipal Bond Insurance Association

MBO Management By Objective

MBS Mortgage-Backed Security

MC Marginal Credit

M-CATS Municipal Certificates of Accrual on Tax-exempt Securities.

MCE Malaysia Commodity Exchange

MD Months After Date

ME Montreal Exchange/ Bourse de Montreal

MFN Most Favored Nation (tariff regulations)

MGE Minneapolis Grain Exchange

MGM Milligram

MHR Member of the U.S. House of Representatives

MIBOR Madrid Interbank Offered Rate

MICEX Moscow Interbank Currency

MIF Mercato Italiano Futures Exchange

MIG-1 Moody's Investment Grade

MIMC Member of the Institute of Management Consultants

Min Minimum

MIS Management Information System

Misc Miscellaneous

MIT Market if Touched

MIT Municipal Investment Trust

MJSD March, June, September, December Cycle

MLP Master Limited Partnership

MLR Minimum Lending Rate

MM Millimeter (metric unit)

MMDA Money Market Deposit Account

MO Money Order

MOB Municipals Over Bonds

MOC Market-On-Close Order

MONEP Marche des Options Negociables de Paris

MPC Market Performance Committee

MSA Medical Savings Account

MSB Mutual Savings Bank

MSCI Morgan Stanley Capital International

MSE Madrid Stock Exchange (Bolsa de Madrid)

MSE Mexican Stock Exchange

MSRB Municipal Securities Rulemaking Board

MTN Medium-term Note
MTU Metric Units
MUD Municipal Utility District

N

N New Issue (in stock listings of newspapers)
NA National Association (National Bank)
NAFTA North American Free Trade Agreement
NAIC National Association of Investors Corporation
NAM National Association of Manufacturers
NAPA National Association of Purchasing Agents
NAPFA National Association of Personal Financial Advisors
NAPM National Association of Purchasing Management
NAR National Association of Realtors
NASA National Aeronautics and Space Administration
NASD National Association of Securities Dealers
NASDAQ National Association of Securities Dealers Automated Quotation
NATO North Atlantic Treaty Organization
NAV Net Asset Value
NBS National Bureau of Standards
NC No Charge
NCUA National Credit Union Administration
NCV No Commercial Value
ND Next Day Delivery (in stock listings of newspapers)
NEMS National Exchange Market System
NEO Nonequity Options
NFCC National Foundation for Consumer Credit
NH Not Held
NIC Net Interest Cost

NICS Newly Industrialized Countries
NIP Normal Investment Practice
NIT Negative Income Tax
NL No Load
NLRA National Labor Relations Act
NLRB National Labor Relations Board
NMAB National Market Advisory Board
NMB National Mediation Board
NMS National Market System
NMS Normal Market Size
NNP Net National Product
NOB Notes Over Bonds
NOL Net Operating Loss
NOW National Organization for Women
NOW Negotiable Order Of Withdrawal
NP No Protest (banking)
NP Notary Public
N/P Notes Payable
NPV Net Present Value
NPV No Par Value
NQB National Quotation Bureau
NQB No Qualified Bidders
NR Not Rated
NSBA National Small Business Association
NSCC National Securities Clearing Corporation
NSE National Stock Exchange (India)
NSF Not Sufficient Funds (banking)
NSTS National Securities Trading System
NTU Normal Trading Unit
NV Naamloze Vennootschap (Dutch corporation)
NYCE New York Cotton Exchange
NYCSCE New York Coffee, Sugar and Cocoa Exchange
NYFE New York Futures Exchange

NYMEX New York Mercantile Exchange

NYSE New York Stock Exchange

NYZE New Zealand Stock EXchange

NZFOE New Zealand Futures and Options Exchange

O

O Old (in options listing of newspapers)

OAPEC Organization of Arab Petroleum Exporting Countries

OB Or Better

OBV On-Balance Volume

OCC Option Clearing Corporation

OD Overdraft, overdrawn

ODE Oporto Derivatives Exchange (Bolsa de Derivados de Oporto) in Portugal

OECD Organization for Economic Cooperation and Development

OEX Standard & Poor's 100 Stock Index

OID Original Issue Discount

OMB Office of Management and Budget

OMLX London Securities and Derivatives Exchange

OPD Delayed Opening

OPEC Organization of Petroleum Exporting Countries

OPM Options Pricing Model

OPM Other People's Money

OSE Oslo Stock Exchange

O/T Overtime

OTC Over The Counter

OTS Office of Thrift Supervision

OW Offer Wanted

P

P Paid this Year (in stock listings of newspapers)

P Put (in options listings of newspapers)

PA Power of Attorney

PA Public Accountant

PA Purchasing Agent

PAC Planned Amortization Class

PAC Put and Call (options market)

PACE Philadelphia Automated Communication and Execution System

PAL Passive Activity Loss

PAYE Pay as You Earn

PBGC Pension Benefit Guaranty Corporation

PBOT Philadelphia Board of Trade

PBR Price-to-Book Value Ratio

PC Participation Certificates

PCX Pacific Exchange

PE Price Earnings Ratio (in stock listings of newspapers)

PEFC Private Export Funding Corporation

PER Price Earnings Ratio

PERCS Preferred Equity Redemption Cumulative Stock

PERLS Principal Exchange-Rate-Linked Securities

PFD Preferred Stock

PHLX Philadelphia Stock Exchange

P&I Principal and Interest

PIG Passive Income Generator

PIK Securities Payment-In-Kind Securities

PIN Personal Identification Number

PITI Principal, Interest, Taxes, and Insurance

P&L Profit and Loss Statement

PL Price List

PLC Public Liability Company

PLC (British) Public Limited Company

PMI Private Mortgage Insurance

PMV Private Market Value

PN Project Note

PN Promissory Note

PO Principal Only

POA Power of Attorney

POD Pay on Delivery

POE Port of Embarkation
POE Port of Entry
POR Pay on Return
PPI Producer Price Index
PPP Penultimate Profit Prospect
PPS Prior Preferred Stock
PR Public Relations
PRE-RE Pre-refunded Municipal Note
PRIME Prescribed Right to Income and Maximum Equity
Prop Proprietor
PSE Phillippine Stock Exchange
PSR Price/Sales Ratio
PUC Public Utilities Commission
PUHCA Public Utility Holding Company Act of 1935
PVR Profit/Volume Ratio

Q

QB Qualified Buyers
QC Quality Control
QI Quarterly Index
QT Questioned Trade
QTIP Qualified Terminable Interest Property Trust

R

R Declared or Paid in the Preceding 12 Months plus Stock Dividend (in stock listings of newspapers)
R Option Not Traded (in option listings in newspapers)
RAM Reverse Annuity Mortgage
RAN Revenue Anticipation Note
R&D Research and Development
RCIA Retail Credit Institute of America
RCMM Registered Competitive Market Maker
REA Rural Electrification Administration
REDs Refunding Escrow Deposits
REFCORP Resolution Funding Corporation
REIT Real Estate Investment Trust

RELP Real Estate Limited Partnership
REMIC Real Estate Mortgage Investment Conduit
Repo Repurchase Agreement
RIA Registered Investment Adviser
RICO Racketeer Influenced and Corrupt Organization Act
ROC Return on Capital
ROE Return on Equity
ROI Return on Investment (Return on Invested Capital)
ROL Reduction-Option Loan
ROP Registered Options Principal
ROS Return on Sales
RP Repurchase Agreement
RPA Retirement Protection Act of 1994
RRP Reverse Repurchase Agreement
RRSP Registered Retirement Savings Plan
RT Royalty Trust
RTC Resolution Trust Corporation
RTS Russian Trading System
RTW Right to Work

S

S No Option Offered (in option listings of newspapers)
S Signed (before signature on typed copy of a document, original of which was signed)
S Split or Stock Dividend (in stock listings of newspapers)
SA Sociedad Anónima (Spanish corporation)
SA Société Anonyme (French corporation)
SAA Special Arbitrage Account
SAB Special Assessment Bond
SAIF Savings Association Insurance Fund
SAFEX South African Futures Exchange
SALLIE MAE Student Loan Marketing Association

SAM Shared Appreciation Mortgage

S&L Savings and Loan

S&L Sale and Leaseback

S&P Standard & Poor's

SAX Stockholm Automatic Exchange

SB Savings Bond

SB U.S. Senate Bill (with number)

SB Short Bill

SBA Small Business Administration

SBIC Small Business Investment Corporation

SBLI Savings Bank Life Insurance

SBWEI Salomon Brothers World Equity Index

SCORE Special Claim on Residual Equity

SD Standard Deduction

SDB Special District Bond

SDBL Sight Draft, Bill of Lading Attached

SDRs Special Drawing Rights

SE Shareholders' Equity

SEAQ Stock Exchange Automated Quotations

SEC Securities and Exchange Commission

Sen Senator

SEP Simplified Employee Pension Plan

SES Stock Exchange of Singapore

SET Securities Exchange of Thailand

SET Stock Exchange of Thailand

SF Sinking Fund

SFE Sydney Futures Exchange

SG&A Selling, General and Administrative Expenses

SHSE Shanghai Securities Exchange

SIA Securities Industry Association

SIAC Securities Industry Automation Corporation

SIBE Spanish Stock Market Interconnection System

SIC Standard Industrial Classification

SICA Securities Industry Committee on Arbitration

SIMPLE IRA Savings Incentive Match Plan for Employees Individual Retirement Account

SIPC Securities Investor Protection Corporation

SL Sold

SLMA Student Loan Marketing Association (Sallie Mae)

SLO Stop-Limit Order, Stop-Loss Order

SMA Society of Management Accountants

SMA Special Miscellaneous Account

SN Stock Number

SOES Small Order Entry (or Execution) System

SOFFEX Swiss Options and Financial Futures Exchange

SOP Standard Operating Procedure

SOYD Sum of the Years' Digits Method

SpA Società per Azioni (Italian corporation)

SPDA Single Premium Deferred Annuity

SPDR Standard & Poor's Depository Receipt

SPLI Single Premium Life Insurance

SPQR Small Profits, Quick Returns

SPRI Société de Personnes a Responsabilité Limitée (Belgian corporation)

SPX Standard & Poor's 500 Stock Index

Sr Senior

SRO Self-Regulatory Organization

SRP Salary Reduction Plan

SRT Spousal Remainder Trust
SS Social Security
SSA Social Security Administration
SSE Stockholm Stock Exchange
STAGS Sterling Transferable Accruing Government Securities
STB Special Tax Bond
STRIPS Separate Trading of Registered Interest and Principal of Securities
SU Set Up (freight)
SZSE Shenzhen Stock Exchange

T

T- Treasury (as in T-bill, T-bond, T-note)
T&E Travel and Entertainment Expenses
TA Trade Acceptance
TA Transfer Agent
TAB Tax Anticipation Bill
TAC Targeted Amortization Class (TAC)
TAN Tax Anticipation Note
TASE Tel Aviv Stock Exchange
TBA To Be Announced
TBE Tenancy by the Entirety
TC Tax Court of the United States
TD Time Deposit
TED Spread Treasury Bills versus Eurodollar Futures
TEFRA Tax Equity and Fiscal Responsibility Act of 1982
TFE Toronto Futures Exchange
TIC Tenancy in Common
TIFFE Tokyo International Financial Futures Exchange
TIGER Treasury Investors Growth Receipt
TIP To Insure Promptness
TL Trade-Last
TM Trademark
TOCOM Tokyo Commodity Exchange
TOPIX Tokyo Stock Price Index
TRA Taxpayer Relief Act of 1997

TSE Taiwan Stock Exchange
TSE Toronto Stock Exchange
TT Testamentary Trust
TVA Tennessee Valley Authority

U

UAW United Automobile Workers
UCC Uniform Commercial Code
UCOM United Currency Options Market
UGMA Uniform Gifts To Minors Act
UIT Unit Investment Trust
UL Underwriters' Laboratories
ULC Underwriter's Laboratories of Canada
ULI Underwriter's Laboratories, Inc.
UMW United Mine Workers
UN United Nations
UPC Uniform Practice Code
US United States (of America)
USA United States of America
USBS United States Bureau of Standards
USC United States Code
USCC United States Chamber of Commerce
USIT Unit Share Investment Trust
USJCC United States Junior Chamber of Commerce (JAYCEES)
USS United States Senate
USS United States Ship
UTMA Uniform Transfer to Minors Act
UW Underwriter

V

VA Veterans Administration
VAT Value Added Tax
VD Volume Deleted
Veep Vice President
VELDA SUE Venture Enhancement & Loan Development Administration for Smaller Undercapitalized Enterprises

VI In bankruptcy or receivership; being reorganized under the Bankruptcy Act; securities assumed by such companies (in bond and stock listings of newspapers)

VIP Very Important Person

VL Value Line Investment Survey

VOL Volume

VP Vice President

VRM Variable Rate Mortgage

VSE Vancouver Stock Exchange

VSE Vienna Stock Exchange

VTC Voting Trust Certificate

W

WAM Weighted Average Maturity

WB Waybill

WCA Workmen's Compensation Act

WCE Winnipeg Commodity Exchange

WD When Distributed (in stock listings of newspapers)

WEBS World Equity Benchmark Shares

WHOOPS Washington Public Power Supply System

WI When Issued (in stock listings of newspapers)

WR Warehouse Receipt

WSJ Wall Street Journal

WT Warrant (in stock listings of newspapers)

W/Tax Withholding Tax

WTO World Trade Organization

WW With Warrants (in bond and stock listings of newspapers)

X

X Ex-Interest (in bond listings of newspapers)

XAM AMEX Market Value Index

XD Ex-Dividend (in stock listings of newspapers)

X-Dis Ex-Distribution (in stock listings of newspapers)

XMI AMEX Major Market Index

XR Ex-Rights (in stock listings of newspapers)

XW Ex-Warrants (in bond and stock listings of newspapers)

Y

Y Ex-Dividend and Sales in Full (in stock listings of newspapers)

YLD Yield (in stock listings of newspapers)

YTB Yield to Broker

YTC Yield to Call

YTD Year to Date

YTM Yield to Maturity

Z

Z Zero

ZBA Zero Bracket Amount

ZBB Zero-Based Budgeting

ZR Zero Coupon Issue (Security) (in bond listings of newspapers)